AVIATION TRENDS IN THE NEW MILLENNIUM

This book is dedicated to the memory of the late Trevor Pyman, who introduced me to air law at Monash University

AVIATION TRENDS IN THE NEW MILLENNIUM

RUWANTISSA I.R. ABEYRATNE

Ashgate

Aldershot • Burlington USA • Singapore • Sydney

Published by
Ashgate Publishing Limited
Gower House
Croft Road
Aldershot
Hants GU11 3HR
England

Ashgate Publishing Company
131 Main Street
Burlington, VT 05401-5600
USA

Ashgate website: http://www.ashgate.com

British Library Cataloguing in Publication Data
Abeyratne, R. I. R. (Ruwantissa Indranath Ramya), 1951–
Aviation trends in the new millennium
1. Airlines 2. Aeronautics, Commercial – Law and legislation
I.Title
387.7

Library of Congress Cataloging-in-Publication Data
Abeyratne, R. I. R. (Ruwantissa Indranath Ramya), 1951–
Aviation trends in the new millennium / Ruwantissa Abeyratne.
p. cm.
Includes index.
ISBN 0-7546-1299-6
1. Aeronautics, Commercial—Law and legislation. 2. Liability for aircraft accidents. I. Title.

K4095.A23 2000
341.7'567—dc21

00-042044

ISBN 0 7546 1299 6

Typeset by Manton Typesetters, Louth, Lincolnshire, UK.
Printed and bound in Great Britain by MPG Books Ltd, Bodmin, Cornwall.

Contents

Foreword

It gives me much pleasure to write a Foreword to the latest work of Dr Ruwantissa Abeyratne, a scholar who has made a significant contribution to the literature on international aviation law. This work of Abeyratne looks far into the future and addresses numerous questions which may seem futuristic or inconsequential now, but are certain to be of growing importance as tourism increases and airline passenger traffic reaches unprecedented levels.

At an individual level, he analyses in depth such questions as mental injury, unruly passengers, the spread of tuberculosis in aircraft cabins and the impact of turbulence on passengers. At a global level, he makes a survey of the aviation industry in different regions, and has valuable insights to offer on the vast range of problems peculiar to each region which need attention. The book thus traverses the whole fascinating field of aviation law, from micro to macro level, offering the reader a valuable synthesis of the principles applicable.

Many of the subjects treated, especially those relating to injuries, require a mastery of the principles of domestic law, as well as of the relevant principles and conventions of international aviation law. Dr Abeyratne has examined both in depth, and integrated the applicable principles in a manner useful to all practitioners. This fast-developing area of international law may turn out to be an important source of claims and litigation domestically as well. Matters such as these will not infrequently come within the range of work of the average legal practitioner who has not, thus far, had occasion to pay more than passing attention to them. Indeed, aviation law furnishes an apt illustration of the way in which legal practice in the future will be transformed in a manner requiring a knowledge of domestic and international law. This book serves this need extremely well.

The book also grapples with sophisticated information-based problems of the future, such as problems of slot allocation and functioning of computer reservation systems on the Internet. It also moves into traditional areas of public international law, as when it addresses problems related to refugees and inadmissible passengers. The new Convention for the Unification of Certain Rules for International

Carriage by Air, signed on 28 May 1999 by the Contracting States of the International Civil Aviation Organization, was intended to make a fundamental change in private air carrier liability. It heralded the need for a fresh approach to this problem which is as old as the aviation industry itself. This book fills the need for a new approach to air carrier liability problems which is consonant with the requirements of the new regime instituted by the Convention.

Throughout the book there runs the principle that the survival of airlines is dependent on service and its improvement. The book underlines the fact that service, however good it may be in some departments, is quite inadequate other than in the context of quality aircraft. An improvement of service is not, however, necessarily restricted to a few mega-carriers. Smaller carriers can also offer comparable services. This book, through its insightful analysis of the problems of the industry, especially in its legal aspects, will be invaluable to all carriers in showing them how best they can bring their entire services into line with customer expectation and, in particular, with the latest requirements of the law.

This comprehensive survey of the field by an able scholar, whose specialization in air law has already earned him considerable attention, will be a leading contribution both to the literature on aviation law and to a better understanding of the manner in which the problems attendant on the airline industry can be addressed and overcome. It is a work of great value, not only to the international lawyer and the specialist in aviation law, but also to the domestic lawyer, and to all those who are involved in the aviation industry. It is also true to its title, in that it charts long-term trends in one of the most rapidly moving spheres of international activity.

I commend this volume and wish it the special success that it deserves.

C.G. Weeramantry
Judge and Vice President,
International Court of Justice,
The Hague

11 February 2000

Preface

On 28 May 1999, Contracting States of the International Civil Aviation Organization (ICAO) signed the new Convention for the Unification of Certain Rules for International Carriage by Air, which emerged from the International Conference on Air Law, held in Montreal from 10 to 28 May 1999. The new Montreal Convention, once it receives the 30th instrument of ratification, is intended to draw together the various scattered pieces of treaty which govern the regime of private air carrier liability. It was also the last major initiative of ICAO before the dawn of the year 2000. The Montreal Convention symbolizes the compelling need for the aviation community to focus on new issues and to refurbish old ones in an appropriate garb for the dawning millennium.

There are two types of mega trends affecting the aviation industry today: country mergers and airline mergers. Both these trends affect the airline industry profoundly. Of these, the unification of Europe is the largest single influence on international airlines. On 1 January 1993, 12 European countries commenced sharing their air traffic rights and strengthening their airlines' marketing potential. Ever since, there have been significant developments within Europe sufficient to change completely the face of the aviation industry in the region over a short span of seven years.

In the new millennium, individual airlines would be compelled to remain competitive, just to survive. They would need to flow with the tide of such commercial trends as privatization, the use of information technology, removing infrastructure constraints and governmental restraints and, most importantly, changing travel patterns. These trends have given rise to the new phenomenon in the global aviation scene that survival (if not success) of airlines is now dependent not on pricing but on service. This new phenomenon calls for the airline product to be similar to one from the entertainment industry, bearing in mind that a passenger spends 70 per cent of his total travel time in the aircraft on long-distance flights. To counter strong alliances between countries and airlines, the smaller carriers (as well as the big ones) are now going in more for glamour and in-flight luxury to score on the 70 per cent in-flight time. Personal video screens for every seat, satellite-assisted telephone facilities and tele-conference services are some of the luxuries offered. Indeed, as David Shoenfeld, International Marketing Vice President of Federal Express said, 'if you view your services as flying between terminals, you miss the point'.

The view that 'marketing is determined from the view of the customer' is becoming more valid now than ever before. To survive, airlines have to build 'brand recognition'. In this context, the International Travel Market Research (INTRAMAR) study is one of the best indicators of the key strategic factors towards achieving passenger satisfaction. INTRAMAR usually measures for each airline a PAX/SAT (passenger satisfaction) index that correlates closely with the major indicators of airline performance. An INTRAMAR study, conducted on 44 of the world's most profitable and financially successful airlines, reveals that Singapore Airlines received an extremely high PAX/SAT index rating, coming second among all airlines of the world. The first was Swissair.

According to the INTRAMAR survey, there are 12 important factors influencing passenger choice: flight punctuality; excellence of in-flight service; superiority of aircraft; comfortable seats; clean cabins, seats and washrooms; good food and beverages; superior first class; superior business class; efficient reservations systems; pricing; good check-in service and attractive frequent flier programmes. At least seven of these factors are entirely dependent on the quality of the aircraft. The foremost important factor – punctuality – cannot, indeed, be achieved with aged aircraft. The matter becomes more crucial to a relatively small airline, running a small fleet of aircraft where, if one aircraft is grounded for reasons of repair or maintenance, the entire flight schedule of the airline will be in disarray, leading to delays down the line. Connecting services will be disrupted and passengers stranded. It is easy to envisage the effect this catastrophe would have on the airline's good name. No amount of superior in-flight service would atone for a six-hour delay where a connecting passenger has to sit inside an unknown airport terminal. It is therefore necessary for any airline to seriously consider removing one of its most burdensome infrastructural constraints – its ageing aircraft.

Another compelling reason for airlines to enter into commercial alliances, modernize their fleets and enter into other new trends such as franchising and leasing is that ageing aircraft do not conform to noise restrictions imposed by many countries and thus face being barred from certain airports. The noise issue has become a crucial environment issue in the world aviation community. At the 27th Session of the Assembly of the International Civil Aviation Organization (ICAO) held in Montreal in 1989, when the matter of possible noise restrictions on subsonic jet aircraft was taken up, the main concern of the Assembly was to achieve a balance between the desire to protect the environment around airports against unnecessary noise and the desire to avoid excessive costs associated with accelerated replacement of noisier aircraft, particularly where these aircraft were registered in countries which did not themselves intend to introduce noise-related operating instructions. In the sessional discussions, The Airport Associations Coordinating Council (AACC, now Airports Council International, ACI) noted that aircraft noise represented a major constraint upon the future viability and capacity of the aviation system. Unless concerted international action was taken, there would be a proliferation of various local legislation banning noisy aircraft from their airports – a measure that would have a devastating effect on air commerce. The International Air Transport Association (IATA) representing the airlines at the session noted that the airline industry recognized the need in many states to address political and other concerns relating to the environment and the fact that the noise climate in areas adjacent to airports is linked to the ability of airports to provide expanded travel facilities to meet the growing demand of air travel. The ICAO Assembly ultimately decided that further time was necessary for consultation and analysis with a view to reaching consensus, and deferred the issue to the 28th Session (Extraordinary) of the Assembly which was held in Montreal in October 1990.

At its 28th Session (Extraordinary), the ICAO Assembly, by its Resolution A28-3 determined to urge states not to commence phasing out noisy aircraft until 1 April 1995, and to spread out the phasing-in period over seven years from 1 April 1995, so that airlines would have time to renew their aircraft fleets or hush-kit them (silence the engines of aircraft) to conform to prescribed noise levels. ICAO further urged states not to restrict before the end of the phase-in period the operations of any aircraft less than 25 years of age from the date the aircraft was issued with its first certificate of airworthiness and to assist aircraft operators in their efforts to accelerate fleet modernization.

The standards of the international community on ageing aircraft are now clear. States have been given the right by the international civil aviation community to start phasing out aircraft from 1 April 1995, continuing until the year 2002. What this means is that airlines that have in their fleets ageing aircraft would have to commence modernizing their fleets soon. If they fail to modernize their fleet their ageing aircraft will not be admitted to countries which have phased them out by legislation. The need for modernizing ageing aircraft fleets has become more compelling than ever, and is amply reflected by the recommendations made by the Fourth Meeting of

ICAO's Committee on Aviation Environmental Protection (CAEP) which was held from 6 to 8 April 1998. CAEP has recommended the reduction by an average of about 16 per cent levels of nitrogen oxides (NO_x) that aircraft engines are currently allowed to emit under Annex 16 to the Chicago Convention. CAEP has also recommended that states implement ICAO's new Communications, Navigation, Surveillance and Air Traffic Management systems (CNS/ATM), thereby implicitly requiring aircraft to be equipped with the modern facilities on board to comply with the satellite navigation systems introduced by the CNS/ATM systems.

Another measure taken by CAEP at its Fourth Meeting which would have a serious impact upon airlines with ageing fleets, needing them to consider the modernization of their fleets, was CAEP's commitment to carry out more work in the future to establish new noise standards for jet aeroplanes that would be more stringent than the present Chapter 3 Standards in Annex 16 of the Convention on International Civil Aviation.

ICAO records that between 1989 and 1998 the reported number of commercial aircraft in service increased by about 60 per cent, from 11 253 to 18 139 aircraft. In 1998, 1463 jet aircraft were ordered, compared with 1309 in 1997, and 929 were delivered, compared with 674 aircraft in 1997. In 1998, the total scheduled traffic carried by airlines of the 185 Contracting States of ICAO amounted to a total of about 1462 million passengers and about 26 million tonnes of freight. These figures[1] are reflective of the rapidly increasing frequency of aircraft movements at airports, calling for drastic management of airport capacity. To cope with the demand, airlines are forming strategic alliances by utilizing such commercial tools as franchising, leasing and interchange of aircraft.

Competent airline managers now need to know that, in the foreseeable future, there will be a few mega-carriers operating in America, Europe, Asia and the Pacific Rim and that these carriers will probably be composites of strong strategic alliances between powerful airlines and powerful regional states. They will be well equipped to offer the quality of service and punctuality that the glamour of air travel requires. To compete with these carriers for a fair share of the market, a smaller airline would have to offer a comparable product. This book addresses some new issues that the aviation industry may find topical and applicable to modern aviation management in the new millennium.

RUWANTISSA ABEYRATNE

Note

1 The above figures were extracted from *The Annual Report of the Council* (1998) Montreal: ICAO, Doc. 9732, p.6.

PART I
COMMERCIAL ISSUES

1 Strategic Alliances of Airlines

Introduction

Today's commercial competition has transcended the past era, where dominant markets protected their established market shares. Most mega commercial activity was then the purview of governmental control under instrumentalities of state which were mostly cumbersome bureaucracies at best. Perhaps the best analogy is the biggest commercial market – the United States – which had, until recently, extensively regulated larger commercial activities pertaining to energy, transport and telecommunications.

Happily, over the past decade, commercial air carriers have broken the shackles of rigid regulation to form strategic alliances among themselves. These alliances have been formed in the realization that the performance of an airline can be affected by two factors: the average performance of all competitors in the airline industry, and whether the airline concerned is a superior or inferior performer in the industry. Michael Porter[1] encapsulates these two factors in the single premise that any business achieves superior profitability in its industry by attaining either higher prices or lower costs than rivals. Curiously, in the airline industry, it is the latter – lower costs – which has been the cornerstone of strategic alliances.

The reason for airlines banding together is to share an otherwise wasted market which is still regulated by bilateral governmental negotiations. This unfortunate state of affairs has been brought about by a lacuna in the Convention of International Civil Aviation[2] (Chicago Convention) which leaves the absolute prerogative of allowing air carriers to carry passengers, cargo and mail into and out of their territories to states.[3] This privilege has encouraged the protective instincts of states to ensure that their national carriers obtain optimum market share 'belonging' to them, based on a now antiquated belief that all passengers, cargo and mail destined for a particular state, or leaving that state, are the birthright of the national carrier of that state. This stifling phenomenon has encouraged airlines to think more strategically over the past two decades, resulting in the pursuit of improved operational effectiveness in their activities.

The seminal response of most strategic airlines to the interference of governments was to 'share' each other's resources, including air traffic rights, thus gaining access to what was disallowed under bilateral governmental agreement. Recently, airlines have become more aware than ever that they are becoming an increasingly capital-intensive industry and have a compelling need to reduce costs in order to survive. The end result has been an array of commercial arrangements between airlines, from statements of common interests to block space arrangements, code sharing and coordination of frequent flier programmes, to name just a few.[4]

This chapter will examine the semantics of strategic airline alliances and the manner in which such alliances overcome bureaucratic obstacles to gain access to open competition.

The Philosophy of Strategic Alliances

Arguably, the most spectacular strategic airline alliance so far is the 'Star' Alliance, which was launched in 1997 by Lufthansa, SAS, United Airlines, Thai Airways International and Air Canada. Brazilian carrier Varig joined later, and it was expected that Ansett Australia and Air New Zealand would join the alliance in 1999. Recently, Singapore Airlines signed a commercial agreement with SAS – one of the 'Star' Alliance members – which will bring Singapore Airlines inextricably close to the alliance itself.[5] It is evident that the carriers of North America, Europe and the Asia Pacific regions, which form the 'Star' Alliance, have skilfully manoeuvred their dominance of the regions they represent. The direction in which the alliance is heading, with the possible future membership of Japan's All Nippon Airways (ANA), is incontrovertibly to assert its presence in the burgeoning Asia Pacific market, in particular the Pacific Region.

The underlying philosophy of the airline alliances, typified by the 'Star' Alliance, is not so much an emphasis on the more effective use of resources such as labour, capital and national resources (which are inevitably important factors) but rather an overall reliance on the strategy of location, where the sharing of locations represented by the various airlines has enabled them to produce their goods and services in a consistent manner, thus achieving the status equivalent to a cartel, while still retaining their individual identities.

Airlines have developed both a corporate strategy and a competition strategy to cope with competition. Both these strategies are becoming increasingly complementary rather than being mutually exclusive, which they were at the inception of airline competition 50 years ago. As airlines began to compete with each other across the borders, they acquired the ability to locate themselves overseas, creating a compelling need for commercial airlines to be fully acquainted with locational strategy and competitive advantages of various locations. Very early in the game, giants such as PANAM and TWA began to realize that even the strongest company with an established position in the airline industry, unthreatened by competition from new entrants or smaller airlines, would start losing business if they faced a better or lower cost product. The threat of new entrants, the bargaining power of supplies and customers and the superior quality or low cost of substitute products were arguably the underlying reasons for established airlines to begin experiencing a downturn in the 1960s, which was exacerbated through the 1970s and 1980s. These threats could not be effectively circumvented or overcome by the established carriers, partly because of the sustained circumscription of market entry imposed by Article 6 of the Chicago Convention.

The genesis of airline alliances therefore was a contrived symbiosis or coexistence between the new entrants or new competitors – which had the clout of resources but not the dimensions of a larger carrier – and the larger carrier itself which had an established product to offer. Together, these two types of carriers could eradicate such obstacles as product differentiation (which was a distinct disadvantage to carriers which did not have an established brand), capital requirements (which again was a disadvantage faced by a smaller carrier), economies of scale (which forced a smaller carrier to compete on a large scale) and government policy (which affected both types of carriers, particularly the larger carrier which had the resources to operate air services but not the market access to a given region).

Another type of commercial alliance is the 'mega' alliance referred to earlier in analogy typified by the 'Star' Alliance. The precursor to this type of alliance could have been the modest 'pool agreement' between two carriers operating third and fourth freedom traffic; that is, traffic purely originating and ending in each other's territories. The pool agreement was written into a bilateral air services agreement between two states in order to ensure equal enjoyment of market share between their carriers in the route between their states' territories. This notion gave rise to an extension of the principle of pooling, which was to share locational traffic on a fifth freedom; that is, traffic which is picked up at intermediate points or points beyond on services between two states, and, more importantly, sixth freedom: traffic to which a carrier had no right but which it could operate under the air traffic rights of another carrier, through a commercial arrangement such as a code share agreement signed by and between the carriers.

Some Types of Strategic Alliances

Airline alliances, particularly code-sharing agreements, add destinations to a route network and offer more frequencies of service to customers. With such arrangements, an airline can add on flights using its code sharing partner's flight entitlement and operate to additional destinations without adding any resources. Of course, such an arrangement would create a duopoly, depriving customers of the benefit of competition, pricing and so on if the airlines concerned were in competition on a given route. Code sharing not only affects passenger traffic, but influences the consolidation of cargo carriage as well, as was seen in the Swissair–Delta Airlines cargo alliance across the Atlantic.[6]

In Europe, the 'open skies' concept, introduced by the European Union, as legislator, in 1977 was meant to open competition between European carriers in Europe in order to offer competitive airline services to customers. However, this has not had the desired effect, owing largely to airlines forming alliances under the umbrella of the open skies legislation. In particular, the four alliances headed by British Airways, Lufthansa, KLM and Swissair have vigorously entered into alliances with smaller carriers under franchising agreements in order to gain access to markets they have not obtained in their air services agreements.

There are approximately 1200 scheduled air carriers in the world. It is estimated that there are approximately 10 000 aircraft in the air at any given moment. Excluding China and the countries of the former Soviet Union, approximately 380 000 civil aircraft are registered in ICAO states. Of these, 45 000 are used by commercial operators.[7] Forecasts of the number of passengers carried on scheduled services in nine intercontinental route groups show the trans-Pacific and Europe–Asia markets as the fastest growing, at 8 per cent and 7.5 per cent per annum, respectively, for the forecast period through to the year 2003.[8] International scheduled passenger traffic is forecast to grow at an average rate of 6.5 per cent per annum compared with 4 per cent per annum for domestic traffic.[9] These rapidly evolving trends will no doubt be accommodated by equally rapidly developing technology and economic norms of the airline industry. Incontrovertibly, code sharing and computer reservation systems (CRS) are at the helm of this process.

Although, technically, code sharing and functions of computer reservations systems are two different activities of the air transport industry, they become inextricably linked to each other when two air carriers who share each other's codes may wish to have their shared flights displayed in each of their CRS. The placement of a code-shared flight in one CRS of a code-sharing partner differently from the system of the other would make no commercial sense either to the air carrier concerned or to the consumer. Thus multiple listings of the same flight may appear in CRS and airline schedules, often misleading the potential passenger, but certainly drawing an identifiable link between the two systems. Both activities, therefore, which have undergone a significant exponential growth over the past few years, warrant a close analysis in view of their inextricable link to each other and joint quest for commercial credibility and consistency. An inexorable implication of this symbiosis is the impact the two activities may bring to bear on the principles of the law of contract. This chapter will also discuss code sharing and CRS against the backdrop of contractual liability principles of air carriers and CRS users obtaining at international law and common law jurisdictions as they relate to the carriage by air of persons.

Code Sharing

Code sharing between two airlines is essentially two different airlines posing as one, sharing or rotating aircraft crew and responsibility.[10] It has been called a little more than a glorified inter-line agreement which occurs when one airline operates a flight but both its and another carrier's codes are used.[11] Thus, for example, a passenger who contracts with airline A to travel from Canada to Australia may find himself in the same aircraft with a passenger who contracted with airline B for the same journey.

The United States Department of Transportation (DoT) uses a somewhat technical definition for code sharing which it calls 'a common airline industry marketing practice where, by mutual agreement between cooperating carriers, at least one of the airline designator codes used on a flight is different from that of the airline operating the flight'.[12] The DoT then classifies code sharing under this definitive structure into two types: the first being the typical international airline operation where two or more airlines each use their own designator codes on the same aircraft operation; and, the second enunciating the domestic code shared flight where the code on the passenger's ticket is not that of the operator of the flight, but where the operator does not offer the service in his own name. DoT goes on to bifurcate international code sharing, where, in the first category, only one segment of the journey – which usually involves a connection – operates under two different codes, one used by an airline for its local traffic, and the other used by its partner for the entire journey, and in the second, the entire journey is advertised and displayed under the codes of the two airlines which share the flight concerned.[13]

The marketing benefits of code sharing have been identified as the ability of airlines to coordinate schedules, transfer baggage easily, maintain common marketing activity by the sharing of air carriers, use through fares, use single check-ins, share airport lounges, share frequent flier programmes, and agree upon exactly which airline is legally responsible for the passenger's whole journey by air. American Airlines, one of the early proponents and participants in the code-sharing concept, adds the safeguarding of traffic rights to this list, where it is claimed that a stronger carrier in the market could be forced to code share with a weaker national carrier, thus spreading commercial benefits on a given route among two carriers equitably.

One of the most scathing attacks on code sharing is that it seeks to create the illusion that inter-line connections between code-sharing partners are the equivalent of on-line connections, which is not so. It is claimed that this alleged illusion is successfully carried out because passengers prefer on-line to inter-line connections by a ratio of approximately four to one, fooling them to believing that a code-share is an on-line service. Robert Crandall, as Chairman, American Airlines, was of the view that allowing foreign carriers to deceive consumers into believing that a domestic code-shared service was really an extension of an international service of a foreign carrier effectively precluding genuine carriers from building strong, dependable on-line services.[14] Crandall also believed that code sharing was an anti-consumer marketing activity in that it causes multiple listings of the same flights in computer reservations systems and printed multi-airline schedules, thus debasing the quality of the information available to consumers.[15]

Code sharing really gathered momentum with the introduction of computer reservations systems. Major US airlines found it attractive to engage in code sharing in relation to CRS as it provided them with a better exposure on the CRS screen. Although a code-shared flight may not yet appear on a computer screen in its pristine form to be identified as such, code-shared flights now appear in CRS as on-line connections and are thus given priority over inter-line connections, giving them an overall higher profile in the CRS and making them more likely prospects for booking by a travel agent.[16] These code-shared flights which appear as 'connections with aircraft change' on the screen would enable such flights to appear at least four times on the same screen. Some countries therefore view code shared agreements as efficacious marketing tools and dissociate the concept entirely from the issue of traffic rights.

In January 1995, United States Secretary of State for Transportation, Fedrico Pena announced the International Aviation Policy Statement of the United States which primarily endorsed code sharing as a cost-efficient way for carriers to enter new markets and expand their systems.[17] Earlier, in December 1994, the US Department of Transport had released its report on international code sharing which it had commissioned from Gellman Research Associates (GRA).[18] Secretary of State Fedrico Pena referred to the study as follows:

> This study fully supports the department's international aviation policy statement. It demonstrates that the movement towards globalization and transnational alliances through code sharing and liberalized bilateral arrangements delivers benefits not only for United States consumers but for the United States airline industry as well.[19]

One of the issues that emerged from the study was that the critical factor in code sharing is not whether it is good or bad, but whether it has certain undesirable effects that need to be addressed by policy makers. Based on an econometric consumer choice model that was applied to certain code-sharing agreements, as against non-code shared flights, the study concludes that the negative impact on consumers as a result of potential deception is inconsequential as any impact of such misleading practices would be cushioned by existing DoT safety nets. The GRA study's findings were also consistent with the overall DoT perception that all international traffic will ultimately be restructured into long haul services linking intercontinental hubs, with intraregional spokes feeding traffic, leading to the proliferation of airlines and the expansion of code sharing.[20]

The study concluded that benefits to consumers, estimated at $37.4 million, were minuscule compared to approximately $10 billion that passengers spend each year on transatlantic tickets. Even if one were to assume, as the study suggests, that the number should be doubled, a gain of around $75 million was comparatively inconsequential. Another conclusion was that consumer benefits of code sharing were not so much quantifiable in fiscal terms but rather in terms of higher convenience, higher quality of airline service and time savings generated through the faster elapsed time offered by code-shared flights.

Computer Reservation Systems (CRS)

Airline computer reservation systems are one of the most rapidly developing industries today. This development is being driven in part by the enormous strides made by industrial technology. Traditionally, airlines have been at the helm of computer usage and their sustained use goes back 30 years. In the 1960s, the airlines inaugurated high speed real-time reservations systems, and today, these systems use some of the most sophisticated computer software in the world. CRS, which began as a simple means of placing an order for a seat on a plane, has now developed to add various new dimensions to the carriage of persons and goods from one point to another by air, such as hotel reservations, car rentals, authorization of credit facilities to customers and theatre reservations, all of which cumulatively make CRS an effective marketing tool.

Inevitably, from progress and development emerges the immutable fact that, while some may benefit from the whole process of development, others may feel left behind, even to the extent of being run out of business. One of the corollaries to the phenomenal growth and development of the CRS process is the plight of airlines and travel agents who do not have the ability to participate actively in sophisticated and widespread CRS programmes.

A travel agent usually gains access to a CRS through a terminal consisting of a keyboard and a visual display unit. The first step is usually to enter the key data – such as the departure and arrival points relating to an air journey. The system then responds by reflecting on the screen various flight options called upon by the system according to the requested data and time of travel and adjusted according to the priority criteria used in the reservations system concerned. Although CRS have the capacity to list all possible flight options between city pairs concerned, they usually display merely a small number of options, necessitating a 'search' for others. In view of pressures brought upon time and other resource constraints, the tendency is usually to settle for what is displayed on the screen. Needless to say, this process effectively precludes those options offered by airlines enjoying less priority than others from being made known to the prospective airline customer.[21]

The importance of code sharing in this process becomes all the more significant, since a flight jointly served by two airlines who share each other's codes would have the leverage of both those airlines in the CRS being displayed more prominently than a flight which is served by a single carrier. In other words, it is claimed that code sharing by airlines may *ipso facto* aggravate any imbalance that may already exist in the CRS in favour of those airlines which are prioritized in the systems for other commercial reasons. Barry Humphreys observes:

> The exclusion of an airline's services or the failure to show its correct fares or seat availability status can have a disastrous effect on its ability to compete effectively, and numerous cases have been documented to show that these are not merely hypothetical examples of anti-competitive behaviour.[22]

Notes

1 Michael E. Porter (1996), *On Competition*, Harvard Business Review Series: U.S.A., p.4.

2 Convention on International Civil Aviation, signed at Chicago on 7 December 1944, hereafter referred to in this chapter as the Chicago Convention. See ICAO, Doc. 7300/7, 7th edn, 1997.

3 Article 6 of the Chicago Convention provides: 'No scheduled international air service may be operated over or into the territory of a Contracting State, except with the special permission or other authorization of that State, or in accordance with the terms of such permission or authorization.'

4 See Russel Miller (1998), 'International Airline Alliances – A Review of Competition Law Aspects', *Air & Space Law*, XXIII(3), p.125.

5 *ITA Press*, 16–31 October 1998, p.4.

6 Robert Koenig (1998), 'Swissair, Delta Raise Trans Atlantic Cargo Status', *Journal of Commerce*, 2 June, 8A.

7 'Outlook for Air Transport to the Year 2003', *ICAO Circular 252-AT/103* (1995), ch. 2, 5.

8 Ibid., ch. 1, 2.

9 Ibid., ch. 5, 37.

10 'Code Sharing: If It's Tuesday, This Must be Aeroflot', *Airways*, January/February 1995, 19. See also 'Is Airline's Gain Consumer's Loss?', *The Avmark Aviation Economist*, II(8), October 1994, 13.

11 'Coded Warnings', *Airline Business*, January 1995, 26.

12 *The Avmark Aviation Economist*, October 1994, 16.

13 Ibid.

14 See Robert Crandall, 'Chicago's Legacy, Barriers to Multilateral Liberalization', *Viewpoint*, 2(1), 12. Crandall cites the example of the British Airways–US Air code sharing agreement which allegedly allows British Airways access to nearly six times as many world city-pair markets as are available to American Airlines. He further claims that, since British Airways now has the ability to gather passengers from almost anywhere in the United States and fly them across the Atlantic, and since it has created pseudo-hubs in the United States to connect with its real hub at London Heathrow, neither the British government not British Airways would have any incentive to let American Airlines or any other US carrier compete with British Airways for any substantial portion of the traffic flowing across Heathrow from countries around the world to and from the United States.

15 Ibid.

16 See Jan Ernest C. de Groot (1994), Code Sharing – U.S Policies and Lessons for Europe', *Air and Space Law*, XIX(2) April, 64.

17 'Coded Warnings', *Airline Business*, January 1995, 26.

18 The objectives of the study were to develop a methodology to assess the effects of code sharing on the level and distribution of traffic among carriers, with the capability to measure the effect of future code-sharing agreements; to examine the effects of code sharing on the costs and profitability of airlines; to assess the effects of code sharing on consumers of airline services; and to project the future use and impact of code sharing over the next 20 years.

19 'GRA Report Sanctifies DoT Policy', *The Avmark Aviation Economist*, December 1994, (2).

20 Ibid.

21 For a more detailed analysis of this problem, see Chris Lyle (1988), 'Computer Age Vulnerability in the International Airline Industry', *Journal of Air Law and Commerce*, 54, 161–178. See also Vladimir D. Zubkov (1987), 'The Development of Computer Reservation Systems: The ICAO Viewpoint', *ITA Magazine*, 42, March/April, 3–7.

22 Barry Humphreys (1989), 'Different Approaches to a Common Problem', *ITA Magazine*, 53, January/February, 9.

2 Aircraft Leasing

Introduction

Aircraft leasing became a strategic commercial manoeuvre of airlines only in the past 20 years. Of these, the first decade – the 1980s – saw a boom in commercial aviation and therefore a corresponding upsurge in aircraft manufacture, and the 1990s saw a downturn of this trend, contributed to in part by vacillations of the world economy which brought to bear regional economic crises such as the Asian slump in the late 1990s.

The downturn of the 1990s and the ensuing money market crisis has underscored the value of juggling the most expensive single asset of the aviation industry: the aircraft. Aircraft financiers are quick to offer flexible investment options to airlines to obviate the burden of outright purchase of aircraft. Apart from traditional loans, two of the most effective financial tools now available to the airline industry for the procurement of aircraft are finance leasing and operational leasing.[1] These leasing options are particularly beneficial to small airlines which are at high risk because of their limited asset bases.

Leasing of aircraft has effectively extended the operational life of aircraft to encompass second and third operators. The magnitude of this financial option is well borne out by the fact that at least 25 per cent of aircraft being used in the airline industry are leased.[2] Essentially, the three most basic benefits bestowed on the lessor and lessee by a lease are reduction and spreading of risk of the asset, attendant tax benefits and flexibility of operation. In terms of the nature of operation of a lease, the leasing process may take the form either of a wet lease – a lease where the air crew of the lessor is an integral part of the lease agreement – or of a dry lease, where the lessor transfers possession of the aircraft without crew.

Nature of Leasing

Very simplistically put, leasing is the transfer of possession without ownership. Legally speaking, however, the definition becomes somewhat longer, in that a lease at law is essentially a commercial arrangement whereby a lessor (or equipment owner) conveys to the lessee (or operator of the equipment) for valuable consideration in the form of rentals, over a period of time specified in the lease agreement, the right to use the equipment.[3] The lessee is legally obligated to return to the lessor the equipment he leases at the expiration of the term of the lease,[4] in reasonably good order, leaving a margin for wear and tear of normal usage.[5]

Donald Bunker, in his most informative treatise[6] on aerospace financing, cites the 1960s paradigm of IBM and XEROX leases which typifies the principles of the modern lease. Both companies utilized the lease of their equipment as a tool of marketing strategy which was calculated to maximize their profits over a standard sale, by amortizing the capital costs of the equipment and earning a profit over the sustenance of the lease period. Over and above this fundamental benefit, a lease effectively demarcates the market pricing between new and used equipment, thus allowing the resale market to flourish on its own by removing obsolete equipment from the marketplace. The blend of new and used equipment pricing policies balances an enterprise's cash flow and asset base while ensuring a more orderly growth of reported profits.[7] To the consumer, or operator, a lease offers maximum flexibility for selective use of a product, which, in lay terms, would be the equivalent of walking into a baker's shop and being able to buy a slice of pie to allay one's hunger, without having to buy the whole pie. In the context of aircraft leasing, this financial principle is of paramount importance, since leased aircraft can meet seasonal demand for additional capacity without the operator having to incur the capital outlay involved in the outright purchase of an aircraft. Additionally, leased aircraft can be selected to fit into routes and meet specific measurements and requirements of certain routes for which an operator obtains air traffic rights but does not own the equipment to enjoy the rights. This is particularly applicable in the case of smaller air carriers who have traffic rights to operate on certain routes but do not have the appropriate equipment for the purpose.

The registration of the airline is a paramount legal consideration which has to be addressed when an airline uses leased aircraft. The basic postulate of law which currently applies to the legal identity of aircraft lies in Article 17 of the Chicago Convention,[8] which states that aircraft have the nationality of the state in which they are registered. The Convention further provides that an aircraft cannot be validly registered in more than one state, but its registration may be changed from one state to another.[9] With regard to the registration or transfer of registration of aircraft, the Convention provides that such has to accord with the applicable national laws and regulations of the states concerned.[10]

The most fundamental characteristic of an aircraft at international law is its nationality. Both the Paris Convention of 1919[11] and the Chicago Convention provide that the nationality of an aircraft is governed by the state in which such aircraft is registered. The Tokyo Convention on Offences Committed on Board Aircraft (1963)[12] provides that the state of registration has jurisdiction over offences and acts committed on board.[13] Therefore it is reasonable to conclude that the national status of an aircraft would depend on the fact of its registration and to this extent is not dissimilar to the maritime law concept of nationality of ships. The most explicit pronouncement on nationality of vessels was given by the International Court of Justice in the famous *Nottebohm* case,[14] where the court held:

> The character thus recognized on the international level as pertaining to nationality is in no way inconsistent with the fact that international law leaves it to each State to lay down the rules governing the grant of its own nationality. The reason for this is that the diversity of demographic conditions has thus far made it impossible for any general agreement to be reached on the rules relating to nationality, although the latter by its very nature affects international relations. It has been considered that the best way of making such rules accord with the varying demographic conditions in different countries is to leave the fixing of such rules to the competence of each State. On the other hand, a State cannot claim that the rules it has thus laid down are entitled to recognition by another State unless it has acted in conformity with this general aim of making the legal bond of nationality accord with the individual's genuine connection with the State which assumes the defence of its citizens by means of protection as against other states.
>
> ... According to the practice of states, to arbitral and judicial decisions and to the opinions of writers, nationality is a legal bond having as its basis a social fact of attachment, a genuine connection of existence, interests and sentiments, together with the existence of reciprocal rights and duties. It may be said to constitute the juridical expression of the fact that the individual upon whom it is conferred, either directly by the law or as the result of an act of the authorities, is in fact more closely connected with the population of the State conferring nationality than with that of any other State. Conferred by a State, it only entitles that state to exercise protection vis-à-vis another State, if it constitutes a translation into juridical terms of the individual's connection with the State which has made him its national.[15]

In the particular instance of aircraft, the concept of registration and nationality has evolved with changing conditions of civil aeronautical activities relating to the development of airline contracts concerning the use of aircraft which brought in fiscal advantages to airlines. Specific contracts, such as leases, charters and interchange of aircraft, are now assisting air carriers to obviate the need to find money to buy new aircraft. More carriers are now entering into short-term lease agreements to keep their operations afloat and such dry or wet lease agreements necessitate a closer look at the requirements of registration and nationality as dictated to by the Chicago Convention.

In order to accord with commercial exigencies relating to lease and charters in the air transport industry, The International Civil Aviation Organization (ICAO)[16] has introduced Article 83 *bis* to the Chicago Convention, which provides inter alia that, when an aircraft registered in a contracting state is operated pursuant to a contract for the lease, charter or interchange of the aircraft by an operator who has his principal place of business or if he has no such place of business, his principal residence, in another state, the state of registry of the aircraft concerned may, by agreement with such state, transfer all or part of its duties as state of registry to such other state.[17] Technically, this means that a state may lease aircraft registered in another state, and, by mutual agreement, take over responsibilities of the state of registration in respect of that aircraft. Under these circumstances, it may be reasonable to assume that, in the event that an aircraft leased by a state performs functions of a military nature for the lessee state, such state could be considered the state of registration if an agreement to that effect had been put into effect between the lessor and lessee.

Article 83 *bis* of the Convention was timely, in that it was adopted at a time when trade barriers were being rapidly obviated and many industries were being globalized. Instances of as many as nine multinational partners in one industry are not uncommon in today's commercial world. In particular, commercial trends in the United States and United Kingdom show new emergent large airlines with the participation of more than one nationality.

Although the current bilateral regulatory structure calls for substantial ownership and effective control of airlines by nationals or companies of a designating state – which essentially means that for Country A to designate its airline to operate commercial flights the airline must be substantially owned and effectively controlled by nationals or companies of Country A – this requirement is increasingly becoming impracticable to fulfil in various instances. In recognition of one such circumstance, the ICAO Assembly, at its 24th Session, adopted Resolution A24-12 which recognized the political reality of regional groupings of states into composite economic entities, forming a community of interest. The Assembly recognized that such a community of interest, when applicable to groups of developing states, would require their airlines to be identified on a common basis with regard to their substantial ownership and effective control in the context of bilateral regulation of air traffic rights. Therefore the ICAO Assembly urged contracting states by its Resolution to accept the designation of airlines, and allow an airline substantially owned and effectively controlled by one or more developing state or states (or its or their nationals) belonging to a regional economic grouping to exercise the route rights and other air transport rights of any developing state or states within the same grouping under mutually acceptable terms.

There are other instances such as when airlines have multinational ownership (involving ownership of one airline by several states, such as in the instances of Gulf Air, Air Afrique, SAS and LIAT), have ownership registered in one country but are accepted as airlines of another (such as Britannia and Monarch, whose ownership rests in Canada and Switzerland, respectively but which operate air services as designated carriers of the United Kingdom), and are owned by legal persons whose businesses are not domiciled in the country in which the carrier has its place of business (such as Cathay Pacific Airlines).

The 'Third Package' of the European Union, which allows for airlines within the Union to be owned by nationals or companies of any member state, gives further credence to the compelling need to consider the element of designation of airlines outside the purview of the conventional philosophy of 'substantial ownership and effective control' as required by the current bilateral regulatory regime.

In view of the above developments, the dictates of aircraft financing require financiers to be aware of the multitude of possibilities of litigation for ownership and control of aircraft financed by them and also the legal implications of aircraft leasing in the modern context. Donald Bunker states:

> The concept of registration has now developed such that financiers of commercial aircraft for use internationally must be well aware of the effect that the country of registration could have on their rights. The relatively liquid world market in used aircraft makes aircraft financing quite attractive to many investors. However, most prudent financiers like to be assured of being able to obtain possession of their equipment, free and clear of a defaulting debtor's rights and deregistered by the operator's country so that an efficient realization of their security could be achieved.[18]

From the point of view of the airline which leases aircraft and sustains damage to the aircraft and to its passengers, the legal relationship between lessor and lessee of property would apply in common law jurisdictions. The lessor of the aircraft would usually be covered by his own insurance or by an indemnification agreement between the lessor and lessee. In a typical financial lease agreement of aircraft, the position of the lessor could be that of a lender at common law, and to that extent he would be protected from the mere presumption *ipso facto* that he is liable by virtue of his ownership of the aircraft. However, this is not strictly an inflexible rule and different jurisdictions may impose strict liability in certain situations.[19] There is also the possibility that rules of negligence may apply in certain jurisdictions where an injured party, the lessee, may seek redress from the lessor of the aircraft. Such claims are often prompted by the favourable financial circumstances that lessors are usually in.

The protection of the lessee in instances of damage is usually assured by the liability insurance obtained by the lessee. The lessee could also qualify the indemnity agreement he signs with the lessor that the lessee's liability would be valid and effectual only in instances when the lessor is not negligent or in default of his agreement. The lessee would therefore be protected against such acts as arbitrary seizure of property by the lessor. Other legal measures available to the lessee are his capacity and legal right to insert a clause in the lease agreement that the leased property is accepted by the lessee on condition of warranty as to the quality of the property, and his ability to obtain warranty direct from the manufacturer.

Legal Issues

The formation of a lease contract is like that in any other contract involving the offer of the offeror and acceptance by the offeree. However, unlike the contract of sale, when possession and ownership of the article in issue passes to the offeree, the lease contract passes only possession. In other words, the lessee obtains from the lease contract the rights to use and enjoy the property concerned but is precluded from having the right to alienate (or sell) it. Of course, the lessee is required, in exchange for the above rights, to pay the lessor a periodic rental.

Usually, as in any contractual agreement, the parties to the agreement have to place their signatures on the document of contract to conclude the deal and activate performance of the contract. There are exceptions to this rule, however, which may, albeit unusually, apply to an aircraft lease. An agreement would be enforceable without signature. In the 1988 Australian case of *Empirnall Holdings Pty Ltd* v. *Machon Paull Partners Pty Ltd*,[20] where a building contract required the signature of the client with the architects and the client refused to sign the contract form, the New South Wales Court of Appeal held that, since the project went through with the knowledge of the client and without his formal objection, the contract was valid. Analogically, if by practice or habit and repute a lease arrangement is sustained by the lessor and lessee, common law courts may presume that the offer by the lessor was accepted by the conduct of the lessee.

There is also the possibility of courts imputing to the parties their intent to implement a contractual agreement if the parties negotiate for some time and start to act as though a deal has been made. In the 1988 case of *Integrated Computer Services Pty Ltd.* v. *Digital Equipment Corporation (Australia) Pty Ltd*,[21] where the parties concerned negotiated for some time and slid into implementing the terms of their negotiation without a formal contractual document, the court said:

> Moreover, in an ongoing relationship, it is not always easy to point to the precise moment when the legal criteria of a contract have been fulfilled. Agreements concerning terms and conditions which might be too uncertain or too illusory to enforce at a particular time in the relationship may by reason of the parties' subsequent conduct become sufficiently specific to give rise to legal rights and duties. In a dynamic commercial relationship new terms will be added or will supersede older terms. It is necessary therefore to look at the whole relationship and not only at what was said and done when the relationship was first formed.

It may well be that a lessee airline may need an aircraft on lease urgently and therefore negotiate with the lessor on terms which, before they are enshrined in a contractual agreement, are put into practice to provide urgent air transport services. In such cases, the *Integrated Computer Services* case[22] may be seen as a persuasive judicial pronouncement. An extension to the principle of performance of a contract without formal agreement lies in the principle of estoppel where, even though a contract is not signed it is considered to be legally binding on the basis of the conduct of the parties whereby one party may be estopped from regarding the contract as voidable on the grounds of lack of formal documentation or signature. For the doctrine of estoppel to operate, the following criteria have to be satisfied: there must be a definite assurance or representation by words or conduct (which can include doing nothing); there must be reasonable detrimental reliance by the other party; and there must be unconscionable conduct by the party estopped.[23]

If the lease is put up for tender by the lessee, the tenderer or prospective lessor may make an offer, to be accepted by the lessee. In such an instance, courts no longer find the tendering process mutually exclusive from the contractual process in that the tendering process is called the 'pre-contractual' process which itself may be governed by common law principles of contract. The Canadian Supreme Court, in 1981, pronounced that there are two contractual processes which run parallel to each other: the tendering process and the contractual implementation process.[24] Therefore, according to this principle, one cannot argue that the tendering process or period covering tendering negotiations were not covered by enforceable obligations.

Frustration of a lease, or non-performance of the lease contract owing to intervening circumstances such as the outbreak of war, is indeed a realistic circumstance that has to be considered on the subject of aircraft lease. On the question as to what recourse either party has to a lease if, after the execution of a lease agreement for the lease of an aircraft the contract cannot be performed owing to the outbreak of war, both parties to the agreement may find the contract frustrated at least temporarily. In such an instance, the court invested with the case would inquire as to whether the lease could have been carried through on a long-term basis, and the 1945 *Cricklewood*[25] principle, established by the House of Lords – that a temporary event such as the outbreak of war would not strike at the root of a lease transaction if such transaction could have been executed in the long term – would apply. However, it has since been established in certain circumstances that the doctrine of frustration can affect a lease, particularly before the lessee takes possession of the leased property.[26]

The lessor usually opts for the law of his domicile as choice of law in the event of a dispute or adjudication, or even for the administration of the lease. Often the lessee negotiates this issue by suggesting another form, particularly if the lessee's choice does not adversely affect the lessor's rights. The lessee gains the right to 'quiet use and enjoyment' of the property through a fundamental covenant of aircraft lease, which essentially guarantees the lessee uninterrupted and untrammelled use of the leased aircraft. Margo[27] points out that in some instances a lessor may attempt to preserve for himself residual rights with regard to uninterrupted and untrammelled use, by hedging the absolute covenant. This hedging process could take place particularly in instances where the leased property comes with a lien or rights of a head lessor or financier.[28]

One of the critical factors of an aircraft lease, particularly from the perspective of the lessee, is the date of delivery of the aircraft. This is yet another area where lessees have to be cautious about exclusionary language in the lease transaction allowing a lessor to have unreasonable flexibility with regard to the delivery date. A security deposit of an advance of rental is usually requested by the lessor and this condition is usually incorporated in the memorandum of understanding or letter of interest which forms the base document of the lease transaction. The memorandum, which is the precursor to a formal agreement, usually covers the fundamental terms of the agreement and records the fact that the parties will, at a future date, enter into a formal lease agreement. Obviously, the lessee will exercise caution as to the terms of the contract, which could be heavily weighted in favour of the lessor in the usual instance of the letter of intent and formal agreement being drafted by the lessor's lawyers.

Maintenance of the leased aircraft is another issue which has to be addressed by the lessee with caution, particularly in the event of an operational lease. The lessor, in this instance, would insist on stringent maintenance terms, at least in accordance with the lessee's approved maintenance standards, prudent airline industry practice and pertinent manufacturer's manuals. The lessor is also usually cautious in avoiding the possibility of the lessee surrendering possession of the leased aircraft during the time of the lease to a third party for maintenance purposes.

The lessee usually has options such as subleasing, particularly when it becomes necessary to be consistent with the demand faced by the lessee for air transport, and pooling of aircraft components with other carriers. The interchange of aircraft components within the lessee's aircraft fleet is another option that the lessee may wish to negotiate.

Regulatory Issues

Leasing of aircraft has far-reaching consequences in the regulatory field in that several provisions of the Chicago Convention affect the commercial activity of leasing. As discussed earlier, Article 17 of the Convention provides that aircraft have the nationality of the state in which they are registered, which, prima facie, means that a leased aircraft would be considered as bearing the nationality of the state in which it is registered. There is no dual registration under the Convention as per Article 18. Furthermore, each contracting state is obligated by Article 12 to ensure that every aircraft entered in its register complies with the laws and regulations in force therein, wherever the aircraft may be at any given time. There are three other relevant provisions: Articles 30, 31 and 32(a) of the Convention which prescribe that the state of registry shall be responsible for the certification of aircraft's airworthiness, licensing of radios as well as the licensing of operating crew. Such certificates are required to be issued and validated according to the relevant Annexes to the Convention: Annex 1 (Personnel Licensing) and Annex 8 (Airworthiness of Aircraft). In addition, Annex 6 pertains to the operation of aircraft which devolves the responsibility of compliance with the rules of the annex on the state of the operator.

A later development in the annals of the Chicago Convention is the formal adoption by ICAO Contracting States of Article 83 *bis* on

20 June 1997 where the 98th instrument of ratification of the article was received by ICAO. Article 83 *bis*, which was approved by the ICAO Assembly on 6 October 1980 at its 23rd Assembly, essentially provides that, notwithstanding the abovementioned provisions of the Convention, when an aircraft registered in a contracting state is operated in pursuance of an agreement for the lease, charter or interchange of the aircraft or any similar arrangement by an operator who has his principal place or business, of if he has no principal place of business, his permanent residence, in another contracting state, the state of registry may, by agreement with such other states, transfer to it all or part of its functions and duties as state of registry and the state of registry shall be relieved of responsibility in respect of the functions and duties so transferred.[29]

According to guidelines of the ICAO Secretariat[30] on the application of Article 83 *bis*, states should not enter into a transfer agreement if the state of the operator concerned is not capable of adequately performing the duties and functions which are envisaged for transfer. The aircraft concerned should be clearly identified in the agreement by including reference to the aircraft type, registration and serial numbers. Any type of commercial arrangement for cross-border lease, charter or interchange of aircraft, or any similar arrangement, may give rise to a transfer agreement.

The ICAO Secretariat guidelines also provide that wet-leased aircraft may be subject to a transfer agreement between the state of registry (normally the state of the lessor) and the state of the lessee or sublessee, provided that they are operated under the air operator certificate (AOC) of the lessee or, in the case of a sublease, under the AOC of the sublessee. The issuance of an AOC, as required by Annex 6 for (international) commercial operations, is not a precondition for such a transfer agreement, whose object may be general aviation aircraft as well.

It is also recommended that the duration of the agreement on the transfer should not exceed the period covered by the corresponding commercial arrangement (for example, the lease). Accordingly, the period of validity of the transfer should be mentioned in the agreement, taking into consideration that the registration of the aircraft concerned will not be changed. The level of authority for signing transfer agreements should be equivalent to that required for administrative arrangements between aeronautical authorities.

The ICAO guidelines note that, pursuant to Article 83, as referred to in Article 83 *bis*, paragraph (b), the 'Rules for Registration with ICAO of Aeronautical Agreements and Arrangements' (Doc. 6685) apply to any agreement or arrangement relating to international civil aviation. Implementation of Article 83 *bis* can be made through agreements between civil aviation authorities, usually signed at the level of Director General, that is, which do not require diplomatic credentials for signature, nor do they require ratification.

Any transfer agreement signed between states parties to Article 83 *bis* will be binding upon the other states parties thereto, on condition that it has been formally registered with the Council of ICAO and made public in accordance with Article 83 of the Chicago Convention, or that any third state concerned has been officially advised by way of direct notification, normally by the state of the operator. Consequently, the state of registry shall be relieved of responsibility (and, where applicable, of liability) in respect of the functions and duties duly transferred to the state of the operator, and the latter shall comply with them in accordance with its own laws and regulations.

States are required to ensure that, as state of registry, their legislation enables them to divest themselves of the functions and duties which are the object of a transfer agreement. Furthermore, as state of the operator, states should ensure that their legislation will apply to foreign-registered aircraft subject to a transfer agreement. States which have ratified Article 83 *bis* should ensure that, in order to be consistent with the provisions of Article 33 of the Convention, their legislation recognizes the validity of certificates of airworthiness, as well as of radio licences and crew licences, issued or validated by the state of the operator in accordance with Article 83 *bis*.

Furthermore, states which ratify Article 83 *bis* should ensure that the information they have received concerning the existence of transfer agreements relating to aircraft operating to/from their territory is promptly relayed to the authorities involved in inspection. For the purpose of identifying the responsible states during the verification process, a certified true copy of the transfer agreement should be carried on board the aircraft at all times while the transfer agreement is in force.[31]

In the instance of an aircraft under an Article 83 *bis* agreement entering the airspace of contracting states which are not parties to the provision, or which are parties but have not been duly advised about a transfer agreement in accordance with this provision, the certificates and licences on board the aircraft should be issued or rendered valid by the state of registry as the latter would in this case remain fully responsible in regard to Articles 30, 31 and 32(a) of the Convention despite the transfer agreement with the state of the operator.

The European Civil Aviation Conference (ECAC) in July 1997, issued its policies and practices of states on aircraft leasing.[32] According to these policies, it is recommended that, before granting approval for a lease, authorities should obtain the following information:

- type of lease,
- names of the parties to the agreement,
- start date and duration of lease,
- number and type of aircraft, registration mark(s) and country of registration, and noise certificate(s) where appropriate,
- evidence of passenger and third party insurance,
- name of air carrier under whose AOC the aircraft will be operated and maintained,
- name of air carrier with commercial control of the aircraft.

ECAC has recommended that member states may also require additional information, for example concerning the reason for the lease and the planned operations, to the extent that such information is necessary to ensure compliance with their national rules and international obligations.

On the subject of transfer of functions and duties in a leasing situation, the ECAC recommendation is that, in the case of a dry lease, all or part of the functions and duties in respect of the leased aircraft under Articles 12, 30, 31 and 32(a) of the Chicago Convention should normally be transferred to the authorities of the lessee in accordance with Article 83 *bis*. For this purpose it is recommended that all member states ratify this Article as soon as possible to enable it to enter into force.

In the case of a wet lease the ECAC recommendations are as follows.

1 Before granting approval to an air carrier to lease in an aircraft, an aeronautical authority shall be satisfied, if necessary by means of an audit, that the lessor meets safety standards equivalent to those which its own airlines are required to meet under their AOC.
2 Furthermore, an air carrier shall only be permitted to wet lease in an aircraft of a type not included in its own AOC if the authority considers that this will not affect the maintenance of safety standards equivalent to those which the lessee is required to meet under its own AOC.
3 A lessor may not fulfil its obligations towards the lessee with capacity wet leased in from a third carrier unless this has been approved by the aeronautical authority of the lessee.
4 Approval for the use of wet-leased aircraft should not be given for an unlimited period of time.
5 The information listed in paragraph 2 of the ECAC regulation should also be obtained before approval is granted for short notice leases. However, alternative arrangements for the prior approval of such leases may be implemented by the appropriate

aeronautical authorities. Such alternative arrangements might include, for example, the establishment of a list of air carriers approved by its national aeronautical authorities from whom an air carrier may lease an aircraft at short notice to meet an unforeseen need for a short period.

6 The use of wet-leased aircraft should not be used as a means to circumvent applicable laws, regulations or international agreements.

7 Aeronautical authorities should respond promptly to requests from their counterparts in other member states for information about leases.

8 Consumers should be informed, as soon as practicable and in any event prior to boarding, of the actual operator if a flight is to be operated with a wet-leased aircraft.

9 Member states may also, for safety and/or economic reasons, and where this is compatible with national and international regulations, choose to ensure that air carriers are not excessively dependent on wet-leased aircraft registered in another state.

ECAC urges member states to cooperate in the provision of information concerning leases, in particular in connection with the ECAC Action Programme for the Safety Assessment of Foreign Aircraft (SAFA).

Technically, Article 83 *bis* is calculated to tighten and ensure the more efficient operation of aircraft in terms both of safety and of commercial expediency by attaching responsibility to the state of the operator since it is the state of the operator which is immediately concerned with the operation of the aircraft concerned, rather than the state of registry, which may be far away from the actual operational site. However, this transfer of functions and duties does not take effect automatically, but has to be given effect by bilateral accord between the state of registry and state of operation. The transfer shall only have effect upon states which ratify the protocol implementing Article 83 *bis*. The particular transfer of functions and duties must be registered with ICAO.

The words 'any similar arrangement' in Article 83 *bis* widens the scope of commercial activity envisaged from lease, charter or interchange to any other arrangement of a similar character.

Safety Issues

The basic postulate in determining the safety aspects of the use of leased aircraft in international air transport lies on the fact that responsibility for safety should devolve on clear and identified states parties in the context of the use of leased aircraft. The questions as to which state (state of registry or state of the operator) is responsible for ensuring compliance with applicable safety standards provided by the Chicago Convention and its annexes, and which operator (air carrier or company) is responsible for complying with the relevant international safety standards which have been incorporated into the applicable national laws and regulations, become compelling and relevant.

Although the Chicago Convention devolves responsibility of ensuring compliance with applicable safety standards primarily upon the state of registry of the aircraft, it also assigns responsibility to the state of the operator on certain aspects of a lease agreement. This bifurcation is to take into consideration contingencies where traffic rights are exchanged on a bilateral/regional basis, and national laws and regulations which may be applicable to the registration of aircraft, where, in most cases, operators which are designated or authorized by a state for international commercial service use aircraft registered in that state. In these circumstances, responsibilities with regard to safety on the part of both the state and the operator become eminently clear.

Whether it be a dry or wet lease, safety considerations are equally significant and important. In the case of a dry lease, where the leased aircraft is registered in the state designating or authorizing the lessee operator for international commercial services, essentially the same principles would apply from a safety standpoint as when that operator uses its own aircraft. Accordingly, when an airline takes on a dry lease of an aircraft from another airline domiciled in the same state and uses such aircraft for international air transport, there is no change in the state's safety oversight responsibility, although the responsibility for air carrier compliance rests with the lessee. Where an airline enters into a wet lease of an aircraft with another airline of the same state, the safety responsibilities remain at status quo ante, that is, with the lessee who operates the aircraft, but compliance of other responsibilities such as certification generally remain with the lessor.

Safety problems may also arise where a leased aircraft is registered in a state other than that of the operator who uses the leased aircraft in international commercial services. For this reason, approval of dry and wet leases should clearly stipulate the scope of responsibilities and liabilities of parties with respect to safety standards undertaken by each of them.

The issue of crew competence, or capability, which is a critical factor in aviation safety oversight, arises particularly in instances where a dry-leased aircraft is not registered in the state of the operator. It is noteworthy that, in this regard, Article 32(a) of the Chicago

Convention requires that the pilot of every aircraft and the other members of the operating crew of every aircraft engaged in international navigation shall be provided with certificates of competency and licences issued or rendered valid by the state in which the aircraft is registered. As discussed earlier, the application of Article 83 *bis* and ICAO Secretariat guidelines require an agreement between the two states which sets forth the specific responsibilities to be transferred and the particular aircraft to which they will apply.[33] Any transfer agreement signed between states parties to the protocol relating to Article 83 *bis* legally binds all other other states parties to the protocol, on condition that any such transfer agreement has been formally registered with the Council of ICAO and made public in accordance with Article 83 of the Chicago Convention. This principle would also apply in instances where any third state concerned has been officially advised by way of direct notification, normally by the state of the operator.

An incentive for states in considering whether or not to conclude an agreement under Article 83 *bis* lies in the assurance that the state to which safety responsibilities are to be transferred has the capability of fulfilling its safety oversight responsibilities with respect to the specific aircraft involved. Of a particularly persuasive stature in this regard is the fact that states parties to Article 83 *bis* can also use the results of audits carried out under the ICAO Safety Oversight Audit Programme which are available to states through summary reports.

Notes

1 A finance lease involves the substantial transfer of risks and rewards appurtenant to ownership, from lessor to lessee; and an operational lease keeps such risks and rewards within the lessor's scope of legal status. A finance lease is calculated to amortize the lessor's capital outlay and provide a profit at the end of the lease term with the lease payments received from the lessee. An operational lease does not amortize capital outlay at the end of the term and profits are derived usually after more than one lease term.

2 Maria Wagland (1999), 'A New Lease of Life', *Aerospace International*, March, 22.

3 *Beecham Foods Limited* v. *North Supplies (Edmonton) Ltd.* [1959] 1 WLR 643.

4 *Ballet* v. *Mingay* [1943] 1 KB 281.

5 *Lang* v. *Brown* (1898) 34 NBR 492.

6 Donald H. Bunker (1988), *The Law of Aerospace Finance in Canada*, Institute and Centre of Air and Space Law, McGill, p.22.

7 Ibid.

8 Convention on International Civil Aviation, signed at Chicago, 7 December 1944. See 15 U.N.T.S. 295, ICAO Doc. 7300/7 (7th edn, 1997).

9 Ibid., Article 18.

10 Ibid., Article 19.

11 Convention for the Regulation of Aerial Navigation, Paris 1919, Articles 5–10.

12 Convention on Offences and Certain Other Acts Committed on Board Aircraft, signed at Tokyo on 14 September 1963. See ICAO Doc. 8364.
13 Ibid., Article 3.
14 ICJ Reports (1955), 1.
15 Ibid., at 3.
16 The International Civil Aviation Organization is the specialized agency of the United Nations responsible for the regulation of international civil aviation. ICAO has 185 member states.
17 On 20 June 1997, the 98th instrument of ratification of Article 83 *bis* was received by ICAO, making the provision applicable to states of ratification.
18 Donald H. Bunker, *The Law of Aerospace Finance in Canada*, *supra*, n.6, p.157.
19 Ibid., p.288.
20 (1988) 14 NSWLR 523.
21 NSWCA, 23.12.88, p.16.
22 *Supra*, n.21.
23 See *Waltons Stores (Interstate) Ltd* v. *Maher* (1988) 164 CLR 387.
24 *The Queen in Right of Ontario* v. *Ron Engineering and Construction Eastern Ltd* (1981) 119 DLR (3d) 167. Courts may also construct a collateral contract containing terms negotiated at the tendering stage, if such terms are not included in the formal lease document. See *City and Westminster Properties Ltd.* v. *Mudd* [1958] 2All ER 733 (Ch).
25 *Cricklewood Property and Investment Trust Ltd.* v. *Leighton's Investment Trust Ltd* [1945] AL 221.
26 See *Rom Securities Ltd.* v. *Rogers (Holdings) Ltd* (1967) 205 Estates Gazette 427.
27 Rod Margo (1996), 'Aircraft Leasing: The Airline's Objectives', *Air and Space Law*, XXI (4/5), 167.
28 Ibid.
29 Article 83 *bis* admits of all or part of the duties and functions pertaining to Articles 12, 30, 31 and 32(a) of the Chicago Convention being transferred from the state of registry to the state of the operator. The duties and functions to be transferred must be mentioned specifically in the transfer agreement as, in the absence of such mention, they are deemed to remain with the state of registry.
30 See ICAO State Letter EC 2/82, LE 4/55-99/54, Attachment B.
31 It is also recommended that a certified true copy of the AOC under which the aircraft is operated, and in which it should be listed, be carried on board.
32 ECAC Recommendation on Leasing of Aircraft Recommendation ECAC/21-1.
33 Bermuda (UK) and Colombia signed on 18 December 1998 an agreement implementing Article 83 *bis*, which was the first one of this sort to be registered with ICAO (No. 4171 dated 1 February 1999).

3 Slot Allocation and Airport Congestion

Introduction

This chapter examines the problem of airport congestion and its aggravation by the issue of slot allocation for the arrival and departure of aircraft at international airports. Recent trends in the liberalization of market access by many commercial airlines have opened the skies to virtually unlimited flights between many countries. However, this liberalization is stultified by the lack of airport capacity to accommodate the many flights that are generated by demand for capacity. Accordingly, the allocation of slots for 'open skies' airlines remain dependent on the expansion and effective management of airport capacity.

The International Civil Aviation Organization has been addressing the issue of traffic peaks at international airports from 1973. In June 1975, the ICAO Council, at its 85th Session, acting upon its consideration of the subject at an earlier session in March 1974 of traffic peaks at airports from the standpoint of facilitation, which was initially brought up at its 8th Session of the ICAO Facilitation Division in March 1973, requested the Secretariat of ICAO to study the matter further.

Pursuant to the Council's request of 1975, the Secretary General of ICAO established a Study Group on Traffic Peaks at International Airports (TRAP Study Group), which held two sessions between October 1976 and August 1977. The group was charged with undertaking studies of the traffic peak situations (current or recent) at a limited number of international airports, the aim being to establish the facts and experience associated with those situations as fully as possible and thereby facilitate the formulation of guidance and other international action helpful in attacking such situations when they arise. The study group was also required to identify to the extent possible from the studies, as well as from other related experience and information available to the group, such elements as were sufficiently typical to enable it to formulate conclusions and guidance of general applicability, and to develop therefrom, recommendations as to: (a) specific guidance of general applicability that would be of assistance in combating peak problems, and (b) any other international action that the group believed ICAO might usefully consider taking in the matter.[1]

The airports selected for the study were Sydney, Copenhagen, Frankfurt, Cairo, Nairobi, New York/J.F. Kennedy, Toronto, Caracas/Maiguetia, Bordeaux, Marseilles, London/Heathrow, Prestwick, Hong Kong and Bombay. On the basis of results of the questionnaire sent by ICAO to the states concerned, the study group concluded that, at that time, the severity of passenger peaks (as measured by the average to peak hour ratios) was greatest at Bordeaux and Prestwick (with ratios below 5 per cent) followed by Marseilles, Bombay, Sydney, London/Heathrow (long haul, terminal 3) and Caracas/Marguetia (with ratios in the 10 per cent – 18 per cent range).[2] The group also found that, in the light of the responses from states received, the utilization of passenger facilities was, in general, substantially below that achieved for aircraft movement facilities, when taking the ratios of average-hour to peak-hour traffic as broad indicators of overall utilization at various airports.[3]

The factors significantly contributing to peaks were preference for travel at certain times of the day rather than certain times of the year and the influence of seasonal fares on the market, which, although creating peaks of their own, were considered beneficial from an overall perspective, in that they widened the spread of traffic throughout the year and thereby decelerated growth of the summer traffic peak.

The effect of wide-body aircraft, which were relatively new at that time, was a 'mixed bag' in that, while several airports considered that wide-body aircraft contributed significantly to peaks, it was evident that, in spite of the spatial problem created by these aircraft in the apron and terminal areas, the aircraft delayed runway saturation, thereby deferring the usually more costly development work associated with runway expansion.

The problems brought about by attendant commercial arrangements such as interlining and transiting of passengers were of a somewhat different dimension, in that the demand for increased terminal capacity, gate-lounge space and increase of baggage capacity with regard to baggage handling, directly brought to bear several complex facilitation problems at airports at peak times. These same problems would emerge from such practices as optimization of aircraft utilization and carrier competition.

Curfews imposed on aircraft, calculated to obviate peak problems, were found to be counterproductive in that they tended not only to result in a loss of revenue to activities and airports, but also to transfer aircraft to already busy airports, aggravating the peak problems experienced therein, while creating peak problems for not so busy airports at given times, which had to take in diverted aircraft from curfew-affected airports. Another factor which adversely affected airport congestion was found to be incompetent governmental controls at departure and arrival gates, which created facilitation problems at the terminals.

The study group was of the view that there were two ways in which to ameliorate the peak problem at airports: (a) seeking ways in which to accommodate the peaks, or (b) handling the problem by efficient management of traffic flow. The first measure was found to be proactive, when considering the service rendered to a rapidly evolving and developing air transport industry and the complex needs of a wider travelling public. The inevitable recommendations, therefore, from the study group related to the expansion of physical facilities at airports and aerodromes, more effective use of existing resources and more efficient application of handling procedures. Fundamental to accommodating peak trends, however, was the need at every airport for a cost–benefit analysis of peaks, wherein the costs increased additionally by accommodating peaks could be assessed against benefits brought about by the addition of capacity.

On the issue of management of traffic flows at airports, the group noted the usefulness of scheduling committees in the situation where amelioration of peaks needs to be sought through the management of traffic flow, and recommended that, where such situations existed, their establishment should be considered at least by the more important airports. The procedure seen as being most suitable would be for airport management to decide on the overall capacity to be allocated to commercial operators, and thereafter to leave the scheduling committee to allocate that capacity since, being composed of airlines concerned, it would be best informed as to their individual circumstances and requirements. The International Air Transport Association (IATA)'s support for the recommendation was qualified to the effect that the establishment of a scheduling committee should normally only be necessary when the costs involved in expanding facilities were completely unacceptable, or for the period during which such expansion was proceeding. The group noted that the airlines in particular, through IATA, had been active in the field of scheduling, but airports too were studying this subject in detail.

At many airports the national airline or, where there was more than one, the major national carrier, acted as spokesman of the scheduling committee and also served as the channel through which the administration makes known the constraints applying to airport capacity. In this regard the group pointed out that it was important that all airlines, scheduled and non-scheduled alike, be given the same opportunity for making their requirements known, and be afforded the same treatment subject to the basic stipulation that they make their tentative schedules known well in advance. This last requirement had often proved difficult for charter airlines to meet and they were consequently often obliged to accept more inconvenient arrival and departure slots than the scheduled carriers.

It was also the group's observation that airport regulations and government regulations sometimes endeavoured to control peak problems by ordering the transfer of certain categories of traffic (usually general aviation and charter flights) to other airports. The group understood, however, that little existed in the form of legally enforceable regulations, and concluded that the main reason why such directives tended not to be challenged was that it lay in the airlines' own interest to see an orderly administration of traffic capacity even at the cost of penalties to certain categories of traffic. The group considered it important that in such circumstances all government regulations in this area should be equitable and fairly administered, since they might otherwise have the effect of inducing retaliatory action from other states which felt their airlines had been unfairly treated.

According to the study, surcharges on traffic movements during peak hours were only levied at two airports. The surcharges had only been in existence for a relatively short period and the group judged that there was no conclusive evidence as to whether or not they had proved effective in reducing peaks. It was recognized that small-aircraft movements might be most discouraged by such charges, but the group also saw the same effect being achieved through a pricing policy that set minimum charges at a high level.

For peak surcharges to be effective, the group was of the view that surcharges would have to be incorporated into the fare structure in a manner whereby they could be passed on to the passengers using the airport at times when the surcharges applied, and even then a shift in travel away from peak hours could be expected only to the extent that demand was price-elastic. Incorporating surcharges in such a manner on a worldwide fare-construction basis would be difficult, but less so on a regional basis. Charter traffic, on the other hand, was recognized as a specific case where such charges could be directly passed on to the passenger. Turning to the broader aspects of the question of airport administrations employing their pricing policy to ameliorate peak problems, the group would emphasize that caution should be exercised in employing this tool, since airports more often than not are in a monopolistic position shielding them from the usual competitive forces that would enable the financial reasonableness and acceptability of changes in their pricing policy to be realistically assessed.

The effectiveness of airline pricing policy as a means of improving peak problems was something that the group found difficult to quantify in any precise terms. However, on the basis of the experience with airline pricing to date, it was recognized that offering significant reductions from base fares during off-peak hours or periods had resulted in a spreading of traffic, and this in itself had caused peaks to be generally less severe than otherwise would have been the case, since even new traffic resulting from normal growth was, in part, directed by such fares to off-peak hours or periods. The group noted that such fares had principally affected the weekly peak patterns, but there was also evidence of a change in the pattern within seasons.

The group also pointed to the feasibility of further educating the general public about airport capacity shortages and the problems that arise at peak times of travel, with a view to achieving a better spread of demand over time. British Airports Authority was engaged in an advertising campaign to this effect that had already been productive of encouraging results. Also relevant in this context was the success achieved by the efforts made in the German Federal Republic to spread travel by staggering vacation periods and school holidays in different areas of the country. As originally conceived, this plan had been seen as a means of improving the utilization of the highway system, but air transport had also benefited from its application.

Apart from the several means of improving peak problems just discussed, the group also suggested that it could be useful for airports to review carefully the various factors contributing to peaks, such as those that may prompt ideas as to the kind of remedial action that may be most effective in the particular circumstances of any given airport. Additionally, the group drew attention to the improvement of peak problems that may be secured through implementation of the Standards and Recommended Practices in Annex 9 (Facilitation) to the Chicago Convention.

The ECAC Study

In March 1993, the European Civil Aviation Conference (ECAC) considered a report pertaining to a study on Modulated Airport Charges Against Airport Congestion: An Economic Way of Regulation,[4] which focused exclusively on modulated charges as a deterrent to traffic peaks at airports. It reviewed some economic principles which were relevant to the analysis as to whether, inter alia, airport congestion on the airside could be minimized by the imposition of air navigation services charges and taxes. The conclusion of the study was that modulation of airport charges (passengers charges, landing and takeoff charges) could be an effective way of dealing with congestion-prone airport facilities. The report hastened to add that scheduling committees and other short-dated strategic regulatory systems were not to be impinged upon, but as a long-dated solution the imposition of changes was considered desirable.

Initiatives of ICAO

The 27th Session of the ICAO Assembly in 1989 adopted Resolution A27-11 (Airport and Airspace Congestion) which directed the Council, when developing Standards and Recommended Practices and Procedures for Air Navigation Services, to pay particular attention to their impact on airport and airspace capacity and to ensure effective coordination in order to avoid duplication of activities of other international organizations. At its 29th Session in 1994, the Assembly endorsed the Strategic Action Plan developed by ICAO which defined, inter alia, objectives[5] of ICAO concerning airport and airspace congestion and ways of achieving those objectives. ICAO objectives with respect to airside aspects of airport and airspace congestion were defined as

> to develop measures for overcoming airport and airspace congestion on a global basis with the following objectives:
>
> 1. identify tasks within the competence of ICAO which can contribute significantly to easing airport and airspace congestion;
> 2. study possible solutions for alleviating congestion problems;
> 3. develop the overall ICAO action plan with objectives defined in the short- medium- and long-term and assist States in its implementation; and
> 4. accelerate the development of systems and procedures for enhancing existing airport and airspace capacity and promote the development of additional capacity.

The Air Navigation Commission of ICAO, which undertook the task of formulating an action plan on airport and airspace congestion, concluded that factors such as the 'knock on' effect of airport curfews on scheduling international operations, particularly for long-haul flights were influenced by environmental restraints on airport arrival/departure flight paths, runway usage, airline hubbing and recognition of a new generation of quieter aircraft.[6] It was also concluded by the Commission that airport and airspace congestion was related to safety regulations and that, in the development of any technical or operational standards associated with enhancing capacity, due regard must be given to existing levels of safety. The Council of ICAO noted the report of the Air Navigation Commission and requested the Commission to keep the Council advised of further work conducted in the area of airport and airspace congestion.

There are compelling factors that any airport administration should take into account when planning for the injection of additional capacity. These are the responses of the international community in the form of Standards and Recommended Practices as promulgated by ICAO, in order that international civil aviation retains a certain consistency and uniformity in its global activity. For instance, ICAO has in use an *Airport Planning Manual*,[7] in two parts, setting out in detail all aspects of airport planning. ICAO has developed in this document a master planning process which involves plans, programmes and stringent policy that go to make a viable airport. The document serves as a basis for providing for the orderly and timely development of an airport adequate to meet the present and future air transport needs of an area or state.[8] The manual starts from the fact that early aviation history recognized the need for some public control of land in the vicinity of an airport[9] and divides this need to reflect airport needs, that is, obstacle limitation areas and future airport development and so on, and the need to ensure minimal interference with the environment and the public.[10] By this dual approach, ICAO has introduced a whole new area of thought into airport development. What was once a concern to merely provide easy facilities for the fluid movement of air traffic has now become in addition an ecological concern. By this process, airport development now falls into three main areas: (a) the development of airport capacity and facilities; (b) the balancing of airport development with necessary security measures, and (c) the balancing of airport development with ecology: that is, city planning, noise pollution avoidance and so on. The ICAO *Airport Planning Manual* ensures a balance between airport development and ecological considerations.

In its findings, ICAO points out that studies of air quality at certain large airports and nearby areas reflect the fact that cars, airport ground vehicles and other urban pollution sources account for most of the atmospheric pollution[11] and that airports may destroy the natural habitat and feeding grounds of wildlife and may eradicate or deplete certain flora important to the ecological balance of the area.[12] Another ICAO document[13] establishes that bird hazards may be avoided if in the process of planning an airport, migratory bird habits and bird migration routes are considered. The *Airport Planning Manual* also considers the necessity to avoid contamination of rivers and streams by airport waste disposal and drainage systems,[14] the avoidance of noise caused by aircraft to human habitation[15] and highway planning.[16] It even considers revenue generation where airport lands not used for air transport purposes may be used for agricultural[17] and recreational purposes.[18] Finally, the document calls for a detailed study of the impact of airport development on the environment in the form of an environmental impact statement.[19]

Ecological considerations of airport planning are considered in detail by ICAO in Annex 16 to the Chicago Convention. Annex 16, which has two volumes,[20] deals extensively with aircraft noise pollution in Volume I and with aircraft engine emissions in Volume II.[21] In these documents ICAO sets standards for noise evaluation measures for subsonic aircraft,[22] airworthiness requirements (noise) for supersonic aircraft[23] and the overall monitoring of noise,[24] aircraft smoke emissions,[25] gaseous emissions[26] and measurement techniques thereof.[27] The role of ICAO in the area of securing a harmonious balance between the gigantic strides made by aviation technology and the preservation of the environment has been one of responsibility. It is no mean task to pair off such interests as the economic development of international civil aviation, standard setting for meeting of challenges of the new decade and the next century and the problems of pollution caused by aircraft. In fact ICAO's endeavours at developing civil aviation in these areas go as far back as 1970, when a Special Committee on Aircraft Noise was created. This Committee published a report[28] with futuristic prognoses on noise reduction. Other landmarks in ICAO history reflecting positive action taken on aircraft noise pollution are the Resolution on Aircraft Noise in the Vicinity of Airports passed at the 16th Session of the ICAO Assembly in September 1968[29] and the two ICAO Resolutions[30] passed consequent to the Stockholm Declaration on the Human Environment.[31] The role of ICAO in airport planning has been succinctly identified by one author in the following words:

> The International Civil Aviation Organization has done admirable work in a short span of time in response to the challenge offered. It has made available a manual for airport planning, Annex 16 for the regulation of aircraft noise, and has suggested standards for the preservation of environments through the use of air pollution control measures.[32]

From the preceding paragraphs one could gather that, while the airport congestion problem is grave and statistics throughout the world show alarming trends, much has been done to alleviate the problem. Many nations have already commenced contrived planning and in some cases even the implementation of such plans to accommodate the exodus of air traffic of the next decade and the 21st century. ICAO in the regulatory field and IATA in the operational field have so far abundantly shown their concern and indeed taken concrete action to meet the future challenge. The question now is what more needs to be done in the future, if anything, and how should the problem be approached? This question will be addressed later in this chapter.

Airport Planning Laws

On an examination of the foregoing discussions on airport congestion no one could say that the problem has not been perceived so far; a fortiori, no one could even say that those responsible for the alleviation of the problem have not attempted to solve it. What now remains to be done is to examine the most proper manner in which to approach this problem in the coming decade and the 21st century. There is no doubt that the planners can take off from where we are at present. However, any future planning by individual states on the expansion of their airport programmes would have to be done with the primary consideration that, 'Looking to the immediate future, air transport will require new forms of international cooperation in technical and economic areas.'[33]

The cooperation referred to in technical and economic areas would have to be further expanded to include security and ecological factors in the technical field and all economic research in city planning and infrastructural development in the economic field. These studies would have to be done in the form of committed and in-depth country studies by individual states taking into consideration futuristic studies of a country's outlook and the financial outlay that the country would be prepared to make for an airport expansion programme. The outcome of these studies could then form legislation for the planning of airports in a state. Such legislation would present, for the first time, a cohesive and enforceable set of laws in that state that would meet the airport congestion problem.

Guidelines for Drafting Laws

Although the concept of airport planning laws can be summed up easily in one paragraph, as above, the three broad areas of ecology, security and infrastructural planning need a sustained approach of study before such are incorporated into laws. For a start, ICAO's *Airport Planning Manual* is geared to provide information and guidance to those responsible for airport planning,[34] where information on a comprehensive list of planning subjects such as sizes and types of projects,[35] task identification,[36] preparation of manpower and cost budgets,[37] selection of consultants[38] and standard contract provisions[39] are given. With these guidelines each state can start its planning process.

The first step to the planning process which would eventually lead to the drafting of legislation is to predict demand for each area and facet of the airport passenger and cargo terminal. Four basic steps have been suggested for this process: the analysis of handling passengers, baggage, goods and mail in the terminal; the identification of optimum capacity levels; the coordination of research in futuristic studies; and the laying of emphasis on areas that need more research in airport planning.[40] It is submitted that the last element, areas that need more research, serves as an appropriate culminating point of fact finding in airport planning. The appropriate end to the ultimate planning process would then be to identify actual demands in quantifiable terms in order that regulations and laws could be drafted to ensure adequate supply for the demands.

Once the economic studies are completed, the final outcome of the process (the drafting of the laws) could begin its phase. At its first phase, the legal draughtsman would have a preconceived set of ecological and security standards to fit into the overall economic picture. To fit ecological and security aspects into the overall economic plan that would make the final airport planning laws, certain factors would have to be made available to the legal draughtsman. Firstly, the planner should outline some critical facts that would be incorporated into the planning law together with substantiating facts and figures. These are the location of the area for the airport and its relation to the city and essential facilities, the location of facilities for the proposed airport or extension (such as fuel tanks, handling and supply access), aeronautical requirements, maintenance facilities and areas, passenger access and cargo areas, designing requirements of terminal buildings and noise mufflers in crucial areas.[41] These considerations would have to be specified in detail in order that the law may unequivocally set out the standards upon which an airport building or extension programme may be undertaken. Further, the requirements should be carefully blended to accord with minimum cost levels and maximum aesthetic standards, both of which require skilled economists, engineers and architects. These elements should then be incorporated into an overall airport system plan allowing for international and domestic air transport. Major issues that may be considered in the introduction of planning laws include the following:

- the relationship between airport and city (distance, access, communication links and so on);
- all personnel involved with airport operations would presumably live in close proximity to the planned airport;
- all air transport-related industry and trading would be centred in the airport region;
- all infrastructure, such as road transport, shopping, schools

and recreational facilities, would have to be provided for or planned for in order that the second and third points above are properly supported;
- daily airport activities must not interfere with the existence of people within the region of the airport.

In other words, ecological considerations should be considered closely with economic planning in order that environment planning and facility planning be interrelated.[42] At this stage the draughtsman of the planning law would have to be guided by environmental considerations that are specified by the planner. It is on this basis that the Swiss legislature has formally incorporated into their Ordinances ICAO Annex 16 standards[43] and the Singaporean government has banned the issue of permits for schools, hospitals and certain residential buildings in specified areas around the Changi Airport buildings.[44]

Secondly, matters of aviation security concerning overall air transport of a state as it affects the airport should be researched in detail. Although placed second in the planning process, this aspect of airport planning is by no means of less importance. Indeed, in the words of Dr Assad Kotaite, President of the ICAO Council:

> In the absence of any international enforcement machinery, it is only for the sovereign States to safeguard that security by strict adherence to the internationally agreed rules and international morality. The security of international civil aviation is not a local or regional problem. It is a global problem of worldwide dimension. Furthermore, the security of international aviation is indivisible on the global scale and any local or regional arrangements are only as strong as the weakest link in the entire international community on a worldwide basis.[45]

The airport planner should find an excellent guide in Annex 17 to the Chicago Convention which is geared to safeguard international civil aviation against acts of unlawful interference. Procedures on all aspects of aviation security are incorporated into this Annex and the overall airport plan could do well to include the recommendations therein for the consideration of the legislator.

Allocation of Slots

Slots are essentially times allocated to airlines to land and take off at international airports. Although airlines may claim that slots allocated to them over a sustained period of time are 'historic' slots and thereby claim proprietary interest over those slots, airlines by no means 'own' any slots in terms of being able to legally claim slots as a matter of course.

In September 1998, six unions representing 80 000 British airline workers vehemently objected to British Airways and American Airlines being 'paid' for the 267 slots they were giving up at London Heathrow airport as part of their transatlantic alliance. The six union aviation forum claimed that legally, since slots are allocated, they cannot be transacted for valuable consideration. Besides, the unions claimed, slot sales were bad for the air transport industry, and might lead to the rise of airport charges and fees and decrease of choice for the consumer. George Ryde, chairman of the forum, said: 'It would lead to a Heathrow largely monopolised by the more profitable wide-bodied aircraft, primarily serving long distance destinations, squeezing out short distance and feeder airlines, some of which could collapse.'[46] The sale of slots, although claimed by some as pro-competitive, in that it would attract fierce competition for the slots offered for sale, is considered by many as unduly oligopolistic and favouring only a few powerful air carriers of the world.

The contrary view to the claim that slots are 'allocated' and therefore not 'owned': that slots are assets just as are airports or breweries, has been put forward by interested parties in the European Union, contrary to the European Commission's fair trading laws which prohibit the sale of slots in Europe.[47]

Another lobby against the policies concerning the allocation of slots has come from the charter carriers who recently hit out at London Gatwick airport for giving slot allocation on a preferential basis to scheduled carriers. The basis of the complaint is that Gatwick Airport is primarily charter carrier oriented and the allocation of slots to preferred scheduled airlines would wipe the unscheduled airline industry from the Gatwick area.[48]

The allocation of slots, if applied strategically, could be an effective marketing tool. An example of this approach could be seen in the allocation of slots at Narita Airport in Tokyo in mid-1998, when Japan's three big airlines received extra weekly landing slots at the airport in the ratio of Japan Airlines 28, All Nippon Airways 44, and Japan Air systems 14, thus giving Japanese airlines 44 per cent of the total slots at Narita Airport. This measure, taken after seven years of historical allocation of slots, incontrovertibly provokes intense competition among the three airlines of Japan, thus admitting of more scope in scheduling and consumer interest.[49]

Speaking in terms of marketing strategy, a hub in Tokyo is what airlines dream of, and the awarding of slots to generate competition among similar carriers bodes well for the airport. Narita is further boosted in its strategic slot allocation by the fact that its second runway is to open in March 2001, adding up to 260 more take-offs and landings per day. Of course, the inevitable 'turf war' has already begun in Narita, where European carriers claim that they are being left out of the race for slots by the American carriers and Japanese carriers in Tokyo.[50] Conversely, Japanese carriers claim that Narita is already controlled by far too many foreign carriers.[51] One of the compromises suggested is the invocation of the 'use it or lose it' rule, whereby an airline would automatically lose a slot which it does not use over an allocated period.

The problem of ever common delays over European skies owing to airspace congestion contributed to by ground congestion has been tackled by the use of sophisticated equipment, such as the new surface movement guidance control system (SMGCS) which uses object-oriented technology (OOT) that works on a software application from pre-assembled blocks known as objects, to speed aircraft movements on the tarmac and optimize the use of runways.[52]

With regard to airport management, the dichotomy emerges between the rights of airports to manage the capacity they create, and slot congestion and unsatisfactory demand for slots that a non-market-based system created by airport autonomy may generate. Indeed, the answer may well rest with encouraging airport capacity growth, rather than managing existing limited capacity to fit in slot requirements. The latter may well stultify the growth of air transport. To this effect the International Chamber of Commerce (ICC) most strongly urged governments, through the ICC's Commission on Air Transport in 1992,[53] to make adequate and timely investments in airports as part of the aviation infrastructure. The ICC observed in its statement that failure to invest would result in serious airport and airspace congestion which would in turn damage international trading.

In 1991, at the Third Meeting of the European Civil Aviation Conference (ECAC) Working Group on Intra-European Air Transport Policy (Paris, 14–16 May), IATA addressed the issue of slot allocation in its working paper,[54] explaining that schedules were decided as 'slots allocated' at schedule coordination conferences, during which schedules are adjusted mainly through bilateral discussions between airlines and coordinators regarding alternatives offered, or between airlines to exchange slots offered or accepted. In this instance, IATA gave a balanced view of the advantages and shortcomings of this system and introduced various solutions which had been considered by the aviation community to improve slot allocation in keeping with demand. One solution IATA reported was to scrap the bilateral system which existed in favour of some kind of market mechanism. Another was to have government regulation of slot allocation. A third alternative was to maintain the present system, but modify procedures and priorities by law.

At the same meeting, the ECAC Secretariat queried the existing practice, particularly the justification for giving preference to historical slots ('grandfather rights') and 50 per cent of the remainder of slots to 'new entrants', the passive governmental role played in slot allocation and the possibility of using a slot pricing mechanism (for example, auctioning of slots between competing airlines).[55]

In May 1998, the Organization for Economic Cooperation and Development (OECD), in addressing the issue of competition policy and international airport services, observed that, where there is a vertical relationship between an airport and an airline, and the airport is price-regulated, the airline may have strong incentives to attempt to exclude other air carriers from access to the airport, which may need to be addressed through regulatory controls.[56] Be that as it may, regulatory concerns over slot allocation may also arise at a number of airports where there is no vertical relationship with airlines. A profit-maximizing airport has incentives to allocate slots and expand capacity efficiently. In this case there would be no regulatory concern over the allocation of slots. In particular, regulatory intervention would make more transparent the number of available slots and the use of those slots, in order to make it more difficult for incumbent airlines to prevent access by new airlines (on the basis of lack of capacity) and encourage, through administrative means, an allocation of slots which might have arisen if airports had appropriate incentives to price-discriminate efficiently between flights.

OECD also felt that, where there was adequate inter-airport competition, regulatory controls on airports should be removed so that airports faced appropriate economic incentives; where it was not possible to rely on inter-airport competition, vertical relationships between airports and airlines should be avoided. Also recommended by OECD was that regulation of airports should be improved so that airports faced efficient incentives in setting of charges and in rationing access to take-off and landing rights.

One of the most significant recommendations of the OECD study was that where, for whatever reason, it was not possible to establish efficient incentives on airports, the slot allocation process should be regulated. In this context, it was suggested that slots should be allocated using market processes, in both the primary and secondary markets, subject to established competition law.

Notes

1 Secretariat Study Group on Traffic Peaks at International Airports (1977), *Report of the Two Sessions* (Montreal, 25–9 October 1976 and 22–6 August 1977), Montreal: ICAO, p.1.

2 Ibid., p.9.

3 The average levels were 19 per cent and 35 per cent, for utilization of passenger facilities and aircraft movement facilities, respectively. (Ibid., p.10.)

4 EURPOL-1/SG, Information Paper No. 1, 16/3/93.
5 ICAO has adopted eight Strategic Objectives (A–H), Objective E of which lists nine sub-objectives. One of these is to respond on a timely basis to major challenges to the safe and efficient development and operation of civil aviation on the subject of airport and airspace congestion.
6 *ANC Action Report*, No. 282, 6 January 1993, p.2.
7 Doc. 9184-AN/902, Parts 1 and 2.
8 Ibid., Part 1, 2.9.1(a).
9 Ibid., Part 2, 1.3.1.
10 Ibid., 1.3.2.
11 Ibid., 2.1.3.
12 Ibid., 2.2.1.
13 *Airport Services Manual*, Doc. 9137, Part 3.
14 *Airport Planning Manual* (*supra*, n.7), Part 2, 2.4.1.
15 Ibid., 2.5.2.
16 Ibid., 4.3.1.
17 Ibid., 4.2.1.
18 Ibid., 4.4.1.
19 Ibid., 2.6.1.
20 Annex 16 to the Convention on International Civil Aviation, Environmental Protection, Vols I and II.
21 See also, generally, Frank A. Spencer (1980), *Transport Jet Aircraft Noise Abatement in Foreign Countries: Growth, Structure and Impact, Final Report, Vol. 1: Europe*, Geneva: Pyman, July, pp.26–41.
22 Annex 16 (*supra*, n.20), Vol. I, 2.2.1; Appendix 1, 3.2.1 and Appendix 2.
23 Ibid., ch. 4.
24 Ibid., Part III.
25 Ibid., Vol. II, 2.2.
26 Ibid., Appendix 3.
27 Ibid., Appendix 5.
28 Doc. 8993, Montreal, 15–26 November 1971.
29 Resolution 16-3. See Annex 16, Vol. I, 17/11/88, Foreword, V.
30 Resolutions A 18-11 and A 18-12, Doc. 8958, A 18-RES 18th Assembly Session, Vienna, 15 June–7 July 1971, 36–7.
31 See, generally, *Harvard International Law Journal*, 14(3), Summer 1973, 423.
32 S. Bhatt (1988), *Aviation, Environment and World Order*, New Delhi: Tandon, p.159.
33 Eugene Sochor (1984), 'From the DC 3 to Hypersonic Flight: ICAO in a Changing Environment', *Air Law*, 4, 35.
34 *Airport Planning Manual* (*supra*, n.7), Doc 9184-AN/902, Part 3.
35 Ibid., 1.3.1–1.3.5.
36 Ibid., 2.2.1.
37 Ibid., 2.4.
38 Ibid., 3.1.
39 Ibid., Appendix.
40 *Interavia Aerospace Review*, 4/1990, 305.
41 Alan H. Stratford (1986), 'Airports and the Environment', *Environmental Planning Law Journal*, 1, 84.
42 'Organization for Economic Co-operation and Development', *Airports and the Environment*, (1975) Paris: OECD, p.53.
43 Spencer, (*supra*, n.21), p.93.
44 Ibid., Vol. II August 1980, p.161.
45 Assad Kotaite (1985), 'ICAO Policy and Programmes in the Field of Aviation Security', *Annals of Air and Space Law*, Montreal: McGill, Vol. X, p.87.

46 'U.K. Unions Object to Slot Sale by BA, AMR', *Interavia Air Letter*, Thursday 3 September 1998, no. 14, 068, p.2. See also 'Slots Available, competitors wide position, American-BA Tell DOT', *Aviation Daily*, 30 September 1998, p.400.
47 See 'BA will sell slots despite objections', *Interavia Air Letter*, August 1998, no. 14, 060, p.2.
48 Another complaint has been received by corporate business jet operators against London Heathrow airport slot allocation policy, giving preference to scheduled and unscheduled carriers over them.
49 'Top Japan airlines get 86 more Narita slots', *Interavia Air Letter*, August 1998, no. 14, 051, p.3.
50 'Narita slots scramble', *Airline Business*, August 1998, p.28. See also 'Spoilt', *The Economist*, 4 April 1998, p.71
51 Ibid. See also 'DOT encounters plenty of takers for 22 U.S. slots at Japan Narita', *Travel Weekly*, 23 July 1998, p.44.
52 Geoff Naisn (1998), 'Keeping the runways cleared for more take-offs', *Financial Times*, 1 April 1998, p.3.
53 International Chamber of Commerce, Commission on Air Transport, 'Slot allocation', Doc. No. 310/391 Rev. 2 *bis*, 1992-07-10.
54 EURPOL-I/3-WP/4, 22/4/91.
55 See EURPOL-I/3-WP/2, 21/3/91, pp.2, 3 and 4.
56 OECD (1998), 'Competition Policy and International Airport Services', *DAFFE/CLP*, (98)3, 7 May.

4 Privatization of Airports

Introduction

Privatization of airports is yet another commercial tool which is sweeping the globe clear of modern challenges faced by the aviation industry. The almost uncontrollable growth in demand for air transport services has prompted countries across the world, from Australia to Zimbabwe, to consider seriously the selling of their airports or handing over their management to private entrepreneurs. It is distinctly possible that, in keeping with this trend, hundreds of airports may be sold over the next few years in order that airport infrastructures will be broad-based to accommodate the overall passenger growth of 5.7 per cent between 1999 and 2000,[1] and of 6 per cent thereafter, until the year 2005.[2]

Another reason which impels airports to go in for privatization and optimize their services is the impact of airline alliances on airport facilities. A good example is Miami International Airport, which has made changes to a capital improvement programme, adding $500 million to an already buffered $5.4 billion programme in order to accommodate the alignment of airlines under Oneworld, Star and North West–Continental alliances.[3]

Privatization involves a whole spectrum of economic activities which affect infrastructural services and could extend to such facilities as power generation and bank clearing services. Two of the main advantages of privatization are of course maximizing profit and improving efficiency of the services at airports.[4] Public enterprises, in sharp contrast, tend to focus on job creation, supporting national identity and pride and stimulating tourism, all of which could have a stultifying effect on profit making and efficiency. Be that as it may, public enterprise has largely lost its appeal, not only because of the cumbersome bureaucracy involved but also because of the evolution of globalization which has changed economic reality and made enterprises move towards markets and efficiency, away from being mere non-profit-making services and facilities.

The liberalization and globalization of markets were a necessary corollary to the shift in perception of world leaders from the evils of monopoly to the advantages and virtues of competition. This change in attitude was mainly due to the realization that with liberalization come more entrepreneurs and companies who in turn, with their market entry, make larger markets potentially available. Furthermore, with liberalization and globalization come better opportunities for entrepreneurs to enter markets, thus intensifying competition. The result is of course more quality service at more competitive prices. In the case of airports, this effect can immediately be seen in the typical reduction of consumer goods in some airport shops immediately after they are privatized.

In 1994, the World Bank reported that privatization provides countless examples of dramatic improvements in efficiency as a result of the alleged superiority of the private enterprise system and pointed out that, in developing countries in which utilities were largely run by instrumentalities of state, 40 per cent of power generating capacity was out of commission.[5] Harry P. Hatry contradicts the World Bank's thesis by stating: 'the major advantage of the privatization movement is not that the private sector can reduce costs or improve service to a great extent, but that consideration of privatization encourages public officials and public employees to innovate and to break down obstacles to improving public employee efficiency'.[6] Hatry continues with the argument (that privatization would not necessarily lower costs) by showing the inherent disadvantages of privatization as encouraging corruption, reducing quality of service and reducing access to service by disadvantaged citizens.[7] Concern has also been raised elsewhere with regard to disadvantages which may accompany privatization of airports with the possibility of private airport owners taking on projects or opening new businesses under the umbrella of airport activity which are not related to the core airport business.[8] There is also the apprehension that the sale of equity shares may lead new owners of airports to hasten towards quick profit making and a short term mentality that would effectively preclude the essential act of reinvesting profits for infrastructure development.[9] Another negative throwback of airport privatization could well be related to public accountability or lack thereof where privatization may lead to cutbacks in expansion programmes and a reluctance to invest in infrastructure expansion.

On balance, however, it could be argued a fortiori that the advantages of airport privatization outweigh the disadvantages. For instance, privatization usually results in improved operational efficiency and aggressive market-related business practice such as opening up new non-traditional capital sources calculated to contribute towards financing airport infrastructure and service development. Privatization remains a part of an overall strategy to replace the public sector culture with a private sector culture by more efficient use of resources and modernization of the economy concerned.[10]

Perhaps the most important feature of privatization is that it is essentially a political process involving a change in the role of the state with the sale of state or publicly owned property, or with transfer of management from state to private sources. This inevitably leads to issues of responsibility and legal liability. For instance, an airport previously publicly owned may not be under the same rules of legal liability as it would once privatized. This chapter addresses legal liability issues which necessarily follow privatization.

Legal Issues

The fundamental postulate which establishes a global legal basis for the provision of airports is contained in Article 28 of the Convention or International Civil Aviation,[11] which provides that each contracting state undertakes, as far as practicable, to provide in its territory, airports, radio services, meteorological services and other air navigational facilities to facilitate international air navigation in accordance with the standards and practices recommended or established from time to time, pursuant to the Convention. In addition, the Chicago Convention also stipulates inter alia that every aircraft which enters the territory of a state shall, if the regulations of that state so dictate, land at an airport designated by that state for purposes of customs and other examination.[12] Each contracting state to the Chicago Convention could also, subject to the provisions of the Convention, designate to an aircraft which passes through the airspace over the territory of the state and another state the route it may follow within the territory of the state concerned and the airports it may use within the territory of the state.[13]

An airport, whether publicly owned and operated or privately owned or operated, has to follow a prescribed policy with regard to the recovery of costs incurred in providing airport and air navigation services. This policy is enshrined in Article 15 of the Chicago Convention which requires that a state is obligated not to impose higher charges on aircraft of another state engaged in international operations than those paid by its national aircraft engaged in similar international operations. This charges policy is a universal one applying to any type of airport, whether public or private since the regulation of airports within the territory of a state is usually the responsibility of that state concerned.

The United Nations General Assembly, at its 93rd Plenary Session in December 1992, endorsed privatization in the context of economic restructuring, economic growth and sustainable development. By Assembly Resolution A 47/171, the General Assembly, while noting inter alia that many countries were attaching growing importance, in the context of their economic restructuring policies, to the privatization of enterprises, urged member states to support when requested the national efforts of states in implementing privatization. In 1993, the General Assembly followed up on its stance on privatization by adopting Resolution A 48/180 which inter alia requested the Secretary General to strengthen the activities of the United Nations system related to the promotion of entrepreneurship and to the implementation of privatization programmes.

On the specific issue of airport privatization, the Latin American Civil Aviation Commission (LACAC), at its Thirteenth Ordinary Assembly held in Chile in July 1998, adopted Recommendation A 13-4 which recognized inter alia that airport privatization was becoming more prevalent in the Latin American region and that the process of privatization involves a detailed analysis of different factors. Accordingly, the Assembly recommended that the LACAC member states consider the following issues in order to obtain the best results from the privatization process:

a Define the role of the state and the responsibilities it must fulfil in order to guarantee the rights of users, as well as airport security and operational safety, in accordance with international standards in force.
b Consider the convenience of maintaining public ownership of airports, granting concessions for suitable periods of time in keeping with investments made.
c Clearly establish the required infrastructure, whose costs the state and/or the users will be willing to recognize, avoiding surpluses or deficiencies which may be detrimental to them.
d Determine the services to be transferred to the private sector and those which will remain in the hands of the state, describing the standards to be used in defining the quality of the services provided.
e As much as possible, aim at establishing a competitive environment for providers of the various services, seeking mechanisms such as public tenders. Maximum allowable rates should be established for monopolistic services.
f Define the financing of the air transport sector, deciding whether higher-income airports should support economically the less profitable ones or those working at a loss, in order to maintain a self-financed airport network compatible with national civil aviation needs.
g The contract between the state and private airport service opera-

tors must be the result of an open public tender where the required conditions, evaluation formulae and criteria to be used to award the contract must be clearly established and made known to all interested parties, in an absolutely transparent way.

h Reserve the right to implement the relevant measures to follow up on, and maintain operational control over the concession contract.

i Pay special attention to the contract termination clause for its timely enforcement in case of non-compliance and recovery of the relevant value.

j The Civil Aviation Administrations should actively participate in all privatization processes.

The privatization process would usually involve a sustained consultation period between the parties, particularly involving the fundamental issue of the exact mode of privatization involved. Some of the options which may be considered are the creation of a new corporation whereby existing assets could be vested in the new entity and be floated publicly. Privatization could also be partial, involving just some assets of the enterprise. There may also be a full public share flotation of the enterprise or a management buy-out structure where a company could provide backing finance in order to take the airport concerned into the private sector. There could also be a joint venture arrangement in airport privatization where private sector and government could share their equity involvements.

At the implementation stage of the privatization process, a tremendous amount of information is usually exchanged, particularly between the owners of the enterprise and the investors. Such information should demonstrate the legal rights of the parties and stipulate the rights and liabilities that would remain as residual rights and obligations of the state. A privatization process, whether it be by concession or trade sale would also entail a complex series of negotiation and contractual wrangling. Competing companies would bid against each other for the enterprise being offered for privatization.

It is incontrovertible that the responsibility of the state is not extinguished merely because an airport is made subject to private ownership or private management control. In international air transport, the mere fact that the state has to provide airport services under Article 28 of the Chicago Convention and indeed designate airports within its territory for landing purposes as per Articles 10 and 68, imposes legal responsibility upon the state to be accountable at public international law for any liability incurred as a result of action on the part of airports within its territory.

The provisions of the Chicago Convention, which is an international treaty, are binding on contracting states to the Convention and therefore are principles of public international law. The International

Court of Justice (ICJ), in the *North Sea Continental Shelf* case,[14] held that legal principles that are incorporated in treaties become customary international law by virtue of Article 38 of the 1969 Vienna Convention on the Law of Treaties.[15] Article 38 recognizes that a rule set forth in a treaty would become binding upon a third state as a customary rule of international law if it is generally recognized by the states concerned as such. Article 28 of the Chicago Convention, which requires states to provide airports for purposes of air transport operations, therefore becomes a principle of customary international law, or *jus cogens*. Obligations arising from *jus cogens* are considered applicable *erga omnes*, which would mean that states using space technology owe a duty of care to the world at large in the provision of such technology. The ICJ, in the *Barcelona Traction* case, held:

> an essential distinction should be drawn between the obligations of a State towards the international community as a whole, and those arising *vis-à-vis* another State in the field of diplomatic protection. By their very nature, the former are the concerns of all States. In view of the importance of the rights involved, all States can be held to have a legal interest in their protection; they are obligations *erga omnes*.[16]

The International Law Commission has observed of the ICJ decision: 'in the Court's view, there are in fact a number, albeit limited, of international obligations which, by reason of their importance to the international community as a whole, are – unlike others – obligations in respect of which all States have legal interest'.[17] The views of the ICJ and the International Law Commission, which has supported the approach taken by the ICJ, give rise to two possible conclusions relating to *jus cogens* and its resultant obligations *erga omnes*: (a) obligations *erga omnes* affect all states and thus cannot be made inapplicable to a state or group of states by an exclusive clause in a treaty or other document reflecting legal obligations without the consent of the international community as a whole; (b) obligations *erga omnes* pre-empt other obligations which may be incompatible with them. Some examples of obligations *erga omnes* cited by the ICJ are prohibition of acts of aggression, genocide, slavery and discrimination.[18] It is indeed worthy of note that all these obligations are derivatives of norms which are *jus cogens* at international law.

International responsibility relates both to breaches of treaty provisions and to other breaches of legal duty. In the *Spanish Zone of Morocco Claims* case, Huber J observed: 'responsibility is the necessary corollary of a right. All rights of an international character involve international responsibility. If the obligation in question is not met, responsibility entails the duty to make reparation'.[19] It is also now recognized as a principle of international law that the breach of a duty involves an obligation to make reparation appropriately and adequately. This reparation is regarded as the indispensable complement of a failure to apply a convention and is applied as an inarticulate premise that need not be stated in the breached convention itself.[20] The ICJ affirmed this principle in 1949, in the *Corfu Channel* case,[21] by holding that Albania was responsible under international law to pay compensation to the United Kingdom for not warning that Albania had laid mines in Albanian waters which caused explosions, damaging ships belonging to the United Kingdom. Since the treaty law provisions of liability and the general principles of international law as discussed complement each other in endorsing the liability of states to compensate for damage caused by space objects, there is no contention as to whether, in the use of nuclear power sources in outer space, damage caused by the uses of space objects or use thereof would not go uncompensated. The rationale for the award of compensation is explicitly included in Article XII of the Liability Convention which requires that the person aggrieved or injured should be restored (by the award of compensation to him) to the condition in which he would have been if the damage had not occurred. Furthermore, under the principles of international law, moral damages based on pain, suffering and humiliation, as well as on other considerations, are considered recoverable.[22]

The sense of international responsibility that the United Nations ascribed to itself had reached a heady stage at this point, where the role of international law in international human conduct was perceived to be primary and above the authority of states. In its Report to the General Assembly, the International Law Commission recommended a draft provision which required: 'Every State has the duty to conduct its relations with *other* States in accordance with international law and with the principle that the sovereignty of each State is subject to the supremacy of international law.'[23] This principle, which forms a cornerstone of international conduct by states, provides the basis for strengthening international comity and regulating the conduct of states both internally – within their territories – and externally, towards other states. States are effectively precluded by this principle from pursuing their own interests untrammelled and with disregard to principles established by international law.

Liability of the state at common law is best exemplified by the legal process of the United Kingdom. At private law involving issues of state liability and responsibility, the perennial adage that 'the king can do no wrong' extended from immunity of the sovereign to cover actions of the central government and its servants when acting within the scope of their employment. This immunity was focused more on exemption from tortuous liability than on contractual liability and obviated the state's exposure to compensatory damages arising out of injury. There was, however, no bar to imposing personal liability of civil servants and, in 1765, the British government agreed to pay *ex gratia* damages awarded against one of its servants.[24] In the 1946 case of *Adams* v. *Naylor*,[25] the principle of *ex gratia* payment was rejected, giving way to the enactment in Britain of the Crown Proceedings Act of 1947, which allowed a plaintiff the right to take up a matter involving Crown liability direct in the courts of law. The Act did not apply to members of the armed forces, which essentially meant that, if an airport were to be manned by the armed forces, there would be no Crown liability for acts committed officially by the airport management concerned.

Private Liability

Liability towards Users

Irrespective of the responsibility of a state with regard to airports within its territories, which is founded both at customary international law and at private law for liability incurred by airports, a privately run airport may incur tortuous liability on a private basis, as the occupier of the premises. Legal liability of airports run by private entities would be liable to the various users of airports including air carriers and to non-users who may be outside the premises of the airport but be injured by the activities of the airport. A good example of the latter is damage caused by environmental pollution through noise within the vicinity of the airport.

In the instance of a privately managed airport where the entity charged with managing airport services is located within the airport premises, such an entity would be considered as a legal occupier for purposes of liability. The leading case which expands the definition of 'occupier' is the House of Lords decision in *Wheat* v. *E. Lacon & Co. Ltd.*,[26] where the defendants owned a public house of which R was their manager. R and his wife were allowed by agreement to live in the upper floor, access to which was by a door separate from the licensed premises. Mrs R was allowed to take paying guests on the upper floor. An accident was sustained by a paying guest on the staircase leading to the upper floor. It was held that the defendants were occupiers of the upper floor. Mr R was only a licensee of that part, and the defendants had enough residuary control to be treated as occupiers. In fact the defendants, Mr R and Mrs R were all occupiers.

The case recognizes three principles: that there may be two or more occupiers at one time;[27] that exclusive occupation is not required; and that the test is whether a person has some degree of control associated with and arising from his presence in and use of or activity in the premises. The following principles, enunciated by earlier decisions, that a concessionaire without a lease in a fairground is an occupier;[28] that a contractor converting a ship into a troopship in dry dock occupies the ship;[29] and that a local authority which has requisitioned a house[30] is an occupier (even in respect of those parts of the house in which it is allowing homeless persons to live)[31] are also valid.

Although the *Wheat* case contains a decision on the meaning of 'occupier' for the purposes of the Occupiers' Liability Act 1957 of the United Kingdom, the judgments following the case show that it applies to all cases, whether at common law or under that Act, or the Occupiers' Liability Act 1984 which now regulates occupiers' duties to trespassers, where it is necessary to determine the duty of care owed by occupiers to entrants.

The Occupiers' Liability Act, 1957 was enacted to give effect to the recommendations of the Law Reform Committee[32] and to eliminate the confusion that had clouded the common law rules on liability to entrants on premises. The rules enacted by sections 2 and 3 of the Act 'have effect, in place of the rules of the common law, to regulate the duty which an occupier of premises owes to his visitors in respect of dangers due to the state of the premises or to things done or omitted to be done on them'.[33]

At common law it was necessary to distinguish between invitees, licensees and other entrants on premises. The approximate distinction was that an invitee was requested to enter the premises in the interest of the occupier, whereas a licensee was merely permitted to enter. 'Visitors' for the purposes of the Act are those persons who were invitees or licensees at common law:

> The common duty of care of an occupier is a duty to take such care as in all the circumstances of the case is reasonable to see that the visitor will be reasonably safe in using the premises for the purposes for which he is invited or permitted by the occupier to be there.[34]

If the entrant does not use the premises for that purpose which entitles him to be there no duty is owed to him under the 1957 Act and any remedy which he might have would be regulated by the 1984 Act on the duty owed to trespassers.

Those entering as of right are not 'invited or permitted' by the occupier for any purpose. Section 2(6) of the Act nonetheless makes the common law duty extend to them by providing that 'persons who enter premises for any purpose in the exercise of a right conferred by law are to be treated as permitted by the occupier to be there for that purpose, whether they in fact have his permission or not'. Section 2(6) does not extend the category of visitors beyond the common law definition: it merely extends the circumstances when a visitor will be owed the common law duty of care by providing that visitors who enter for any purpose in the exercise of a right conferred by law are to be treated as permitted by the occupier to be there for that purpose.[35]

Whether the standard required by the common duty of care has been attained in a case involving liability of an airport authority is a question of fact and the important issues will be resolved by inference rather than on primary facts. The circumstances relevant would include the degree of care, and want of care, which would ordinarily be looked for in a visitor, on the following basis: (a) an occupier must expect children to be less careful than adults; and (b) an occupier may expect that a person, in the exercise of his calling, will appreciate and guard against any special risks ordinarily incident to it, so far as the occupier leaves him free to do so.[36] These principles reiterate existing rules of common law, and therefore support the view that in deciding the countless issues of fact which will arise in applying the 'common duty of care', it will be proper to consider cases decided before the Act as guides (but certainly no more than guides) in interpreting the duty where no unambiguous rule is laid down in the Act itself.

One of the most significant principles at common law on occupier's liability is the consideration of the child visitor. In deciding whether there is a danger, an occupier, such as an airport authority must especially consider the physical and mental powers of a child visitor on the basis that what is not a danger to an adult may be a danger to a child.[37] And this may be so because of the allurement or property of temptation, to a child, of some condition on the land.[38] In determining the standard of care owed to a child who is not accompanied by a guardian, it will be material to inquire whether, in the circumstances, the occupier could reasonably have expected the presence of the infant unaccompanied.[39]

At common law an occupier discharged his duty to a visitor by a warning sufficient to convey to the visitor full knowledge of the nature and extent of the danger. That rule is changed by section 2(4)(*a*) of the Act[40] which provides that, where damage is caused to a visitor by a danger[41] of which he had been warned by the occupier, the warning is not to be treated without more as absolving the occupier from liability, unless in all the circumstances it was enough to enable the visit or to be reasonably safe.

For example, the farmer who warns the veterinary surgeon whom he has summoned to the farm at night to attend a sick cow by saying, 'Be careful how you go down the yard or you may fall into a tank', or the railway company which warns of the dangerous roof over what is the sole approach to the ticket office, can no longer absolve themselves from liability by that warning alone. On the other hand, where a customer does not heed the warning of a shopkeeper not to go to the far end of the shop because there is a dangerous hole, it might presumably be held in all the circumstances that the common duty of care owed to him under the Act has been discharged. If the defendant does not know of the danger, he cannot rely on section 2(4)(*a*), although he may still have a defence under section 2(1).[42]

Assumption of Risk

The common duty of care does not impose on an occupier any obligation to a visitor in respect of risks willingly accepted as his by the visitor (the question whether a risk is so accepted should be decided on the same principles as in other cases in which one person owes a duty of care to another).[43] According to the ordinary principles of negligence, a defendant breaches no duty of care towards a plaintiff who has voluntarily assumed the risk.

At common law no duty of care was owed to a visitor who had full knowledge of the nature and extent of the danger.[44] Knowledge is not specifically mentioned as a relevant circumstance in determining whether the common duty of care has been discharged. But since the Act expressly provides that voluntary assumption of a risk discharges the duty of care, its silence about the effect of mere knowledge of the risk makes it clear that knowledge on the part of the visitor in itself no longer serves to discharge the duty of care. Yet the visitor's knowledge of the danger remains relevant in deciding whether in all the circumstances it was enough to enable him to be reasonably safe.[45]

Liability towards Neighbours

The risk created by dangers caused by the defective state of premises is not confined to entrants to those premises. Slates falling from roofs, crumbling walls and dangerous activities carried out on premises are just a few examples of risks as likely to endanger passers-by on the highway, or persons on adjoining premises, as to injure persons actually on the occupier's premises. The circumstances in which a duty of care is owed to such persons by the occupier of premises therefore warrant brief consideration.

An action in nuisance, derived from public nuisance, often lies at the instance of those injured on a highway as a result of harmful conditions on adjoining land. Because of this historical anomaly, in a large number of situations a plaintiff may now sue either in negligence or in nuisance (or, as often happens, in both) for personal injuries; and yet the law is the same whichever tort is relied on. In several House of Lords cases, it has been a matter of indifference whether the case was decided in negligence or in nuisance, both of which were pleaded.[46] Often it seems quite fortuitous which tort is relied on: if, for instance, some act of negligent omission stands out, the claim will often be negligence. The 1948 decision in *Holling* v. *Yorkshire Traction Co. Ltd.* is a typical example of this ambivalence.

> The defendants emitted so much steam and smoke on to the highway from their adjoining factory that the view was obscured and two vehicles collided, killing the plaintiff, who was on the highway. It was held to be negligence on the part of the defendants to fail to post a man at each end of the affected area. They were also held liable in nuisance.[47]

Accordingly, there is no room for doubt that the ordinary principles of negligence can be applied where highway users are injured because of harmful operations being carried out there.[48]

Occupiers are also under a general duty to take reasonable care to prevent dangers existing on their premises from damaging persons or property on adjoining premises.[49] This is so whether the danger arises from disrepair on the premises or from some natural or man-made hazard, for example fire caused by lightning striking a tree.[50] It has been held that, where adjoining properties have mutual rights of support, an occupier who negligently allows a property to fall into dereliction so as to damage the adjoining premises is liable in negligence as well as in nuisance.[51] There are two issues of particular difficulty affecting the duties of care owed inter se by occupiers of adjoining premises.

First, where a plaintiff tenant sues his landlord for damage resulting from the defective state of repair of premises retained by the landlord, the case law is somewhat ambivalent. The facts in *Cunard* v. *Antifyre Ltd.*[52] were that some defective roofing and guttering, which formed part of the premises retained by the defendant landlord, fell into a part of the premises let by him to the plaintiff tenant. As a result, his wife was injured and his goods were damaged. Damages in general negligence were awarded to both the tenant and his wife.

However, in *Cheater* v. *Cater*,[53] the Court of Appeal had held earlier that a landlord, who had let a field to a tenant at a time when there was a yew tree on the adjoining premises retained by the landlord, was not liable in negligence when the tenant's horse died through eating leaves from that tree which was then in the same state as at the date of the lease. The Court of Appeal in *Shirvell* v. *Hackwood Estates Co. Ltd.*,[54] a later case, questioned *Cunard* v. *Antifyre Ltd.* and held that a workman of a tenant could not recover in negligence from the landlord whose tree on adjoining land fell on him. In *Taylor* v. *Liverpool Corpn*, the plaintiff, the daughter of a tenant of one of the defendant landlords' flats, was injured by the fall of a chimney stack belonging to these flats into the yard adjoining the premises. The landlords had negligently maintained this chimney, which formed part of the building retained by them.[55]

Stable J found for the plaintiff in negligence, following *Cunard* v. *Antifyre Ltd.*, and distinguishing *Cheater* v. *Cater* on the ground that the tenant had there impliedly agreed to take the risk in respect of danger existing on the premises at that time. His Lordship treated the observations in *Shirvell* as *obiter* on the ground that no negligence had in any event occurred. The above notwithstanding, the principle in the *Cunard* case is more plausible than one which gives the landlord blanket immunity.

Conclusion

An airport should generally improve its efficiency levels upon privatization. This could only be optimized if the airport concerned receives a fresh start, preferably with a debt write-off and a clean slate for a balance sheet. There should also be potential for new capital injection and effective measures should be taken to offset the loss of government support which the airport would have had while under public control.

It is important to bear in mind that it can take a long time to make profits out of infrastructural improvements carried out as a result of airport privatization. This may discourage foreign investment in the privatization process of an airport. However, airports are essentially monopolies in their geographic regions and therefore could recover profits easily.

Legally, as was discussed, neither the state nor the airport can avoid liability on account of privatization. The state entails liability primarily at public international law and also at public law in general, and the airport incurs liability on a private basis in a private action that may be brought, under tort law principles or under contract law, as the case may be.

Notes

1 *The World of Civil Aviation 1998–2001*, ICAO Doc. 275, Table 5-6.
2 'Outlook for Air Transport to the Year 2005', ICAO Circular 270-AT/111, p.37. See also A32-WP/105, p.4.
3 James Ott (1999), 'Alliances Spawn a Web of Global Networks', *Aviation Week and Space Technology*, 23 August, p.53.
4 Adam M. Pilarski (1993), 'Columnist Bureaucrats and the Transition to the Market Economy', in Neil Garston (ed.), *Bureaucracy: Three Paradigms*, Boston: Kluwer Academic Publishing, p.207.

5 Adam M. Pilarski (1999), 'Airline Privatization: As a Response to Globalization', *The Handbook of Airline Economics*, 1st edn, in Darryl Jenkins (ed.), Washington, DC: *Aviation Weekly Group*, p. 204. See also Maxim Boycko, A. Shleifer and R. Vishney (1993), *A Theory of Privatization*, Boston: Howard University Press, p.1.
6 Harry P. Hatry (1999), *Privatization: The Provision of Public Services by the Private Sector*, Jefferson, NC: McFarland & Company Inc., p.263.
7 Ibid.
8 Airports Council International (1998), 'Update', *Airport Privatization*, no. 6, September, p.4.
9 Ibid., p.3.
10 See United Nations Conference on Trade and Development (1993), *Report of the Ad hoc Working Group on Comparative Experiences with Privatization on its Second Session*, Geneva, p.12.
11 Convention on International Civil Aviation, signed at Chicago on 7 December 1944, ICAO Doc. 7300/7, 7th edn 1997 (hereafter referred to as the Chicago Convention).
12 Ibid., Article 10.
13 Ibid., Article 68.
14 *I.C.J. Reports*, 1970, 32.
15 'Vienna Convention on the Law of Treaties', United Nations General Assembly Document *A/CONF.39/27*, 23 May 1969.
16 *Barcelona Traction, Light and Power Company Limited, I.C.J. Reports*, 1974, 269–70.
17 *Yearbook of International Law Commission*, 1976, vol. II, Part One, p.29.
18 *I.C.J. Reports*, 1970, 32.
19 *1925 RIAA, ii*, 641.
20 *In Re. Chorzow Factory (Jurisdiction)* case, (1927) PCIJ, Ser. A, no. 9, 21.
21 *I.C.J. Reports*, (1949), 23.
22 Carl Q. Christol (1991), *Space Law Past, Present and Future,* Deventer: Kluwer Law and Taxation Publishers, p.231.
23 *Report of the International Law Commission to the General Assembly on the Work of the 1st Session*, A/CN.4/13, 9 June 1949, p.21.
24 *Entick* v. *Carrington* (1765) 19 St. Tr 1030.
25 [1946] AC 543.
26 [1966] AC 552, [1966] 1 All ER 582, HL.
27 In *Fisher* v. *CHT Ltd. (No 2)* [1966] 1 All ER 88, CA, the owners of a club and the defendants who ran a restaurant in the club under licence from the club were both held to be occupiers. In *AMF International Ltd.* v. *Magnet Bowling Ltd.* [1968] 2 All ER 789, a contractor (as well as the owner) was an occupier of the whole building although part of the building was separated by a screen beyond which he went only to attend to heating and lighting. It is doubtful whether someone who has granted a right of way occupies that right of way: see *Holden* v. *White* [1982] QB 679, [1982] 2 All ER 328, CA. A highway authority which owns the land but has not adopted the highway is not an occupier of the highway. See *Holmes* v. *Norfolk County Council* (1981) 131 NLJ 401. A highway authority does not occupy a footpath on land owned by another although it has a statutory obligation to maintain it. See *Whiting* v. *Hillingdon London Borough Council* (1970) 68 LGR 437.
28 *Humphreys* v. *Dreamland (Margate) Ltd.* [1930] All ER Rep 327, HL.
29 *Hartwell* v. *Grayson Rollo and Clover Docks Ltd.* [1947] KB 901, CA. However, a contractor merely painting a house is not an occupier. See *Page* v. *Read* (1984) 134 NLJ 723.
30 *Hawkins* v. *Coulsdon and Purley UDC* [1954] 1 QB 319, [1954] 1 All ER 97,CA.
31 *Greene* v. *Chelsea Borough Council* [1954] 2 QB 127, [1954] 2 All ER 318, CA. See

also *Harris* v. *Birkenhead Corporation* [1976] 1 All ER 341, CA where a local authority, having acquired a house by compulsory purchase, occupies it even before its staff enter it.

32 Cmnd 9305.

33 Section 1.

34 Section 2(2) of the Occupiers' Liability Act, 1957.

35 *Greenhalgh* v. *British Railways Board* [1969] 2 QB 286, [1969] 2 All ER 114, CA, *per* Lord Denning MR, 292–3.

36 Section 2(3).

37 *Cooke* v. *Midland Great Western Rly of Ireland* [1909] AC 229 at 238 (*per* Lord Atkinson), HL; also *Gough* v. *National Coal Board* [1954] 1 QB 191, [1953] 2 All ER 1283, CA. The cases are legion but they all turn on their particular facts: for example, *Williams* v. *Cardiff Corporation* [1950] 1 KB 514 [1950] 1 All ER 250, CA (a grassy slope with broken glass at the foot is a trap for a four-year-old child). The principle stated in the text also applied at common law in the case of adults suffering from mental or physical handicap and, it is submitted, will continue to apply to them under the Act.

38 See *Glasgow Corporation* v. *Taylor* [1922] 1 AC 44, HL which concerned liability for brightly coloured poisoned berries in a park and within easy reach of the child. Their decision can be contrasted with D *(a minor)* v. *Department of Environment (NI)* [1992] 4 BNIL 117, where there was no liability when a six-year-old climbed a tree and fell out!

39 See *Phipps* v. *Rochester Corporation* [1955] 1 QB 450, [1955] 1 All ER 129, containing an excellent review by Devlin J of the rights of child visitors which was applied in *Simkiss* v. *Rhondda Borough Council* (1982) 81 LGR 460, CA.

40 *Roles* v. *Nathan* [1963] 2 All ER 908, CA.

41 Here it is valid to consider whether 'danger' means the peril or the thing which creates the peril.

42 *White* v. *Blackmore* [1972] 2 QB 651, [1972] 3 All ER 158, CA.

43 Section 2(5).

44 *London Graving Dock Co. Ltd.* v. *Horton* [1951] AC 737, [1951] 2 All ER 1, HL.

45 *Bunker* v. *Charles Brand & Son Ltd.* [1969] 2 QB 480, [1969] 2 All ER 59. See also *McMillan* v. *Lord Advocate* 1991 SLT 150n.

46 *Longhurst* v. *Metropolitan Water Board* [1948] 2 All ER 834, HL; *Caminer* v. *Northern and London Investment Trust Ltd.* [1951] AC 88, [1950] 2 All ER 486; *Bolton* v. *Stone* [1951] AC 850, [1951] All ER 1078, HL. Sometimes it is not clear on which tort a judgment is based. See Denning LJ in *Mint* v. *Good* [1951] 1 KB 517 at 526, [1950] 2 All ER 1159 at 1168, CA.

47 [1948] 2 All ER 662; cf. *Wheeler* v. *Morris* (1915) 84 LJKB 1435, CA.

48 For example, *Hilder* v. *Associated Portland Cement Manufacturers Ltd.* [1961] 3 All ER 709, [1961] 1 WLR 1434. In this case the defendant occupiers of a field allowed children to play football in the field and were held liable to a motorcyclist who, when driving along an adjoining highway, was knocked off his machine by a ball kicked by the children from the field.

49 *Hughes* v. *Percival* (1883) 8 App Cas 443, HL: the premises for the benefit of which the present rule applies are those in respect of which someone other than the defendant has a vested interest in possession. Also *Murphy* v. *Brentwood District Council* [1990] 2 All ER 908 and 926 (*per* Lord Bridge).

50 *Goldman* v. *Hargrave* [1907] 1 AC 645, [1966] 2 All ER 989, PC. Water normally percolates from the defendant's land to the plaintiff's, and the defendant pumps out the water from his land, and by so stopping the subterranean flow causes settlement damage to the plaintiff's land. The plaintiff has no remedy, because the defendant has no duty to adjoining occupiers in respect of percolating

water; *Langbrook Properties Ltd.* v. *Surrey County Council* [1969] 3 All ER 1424, [1970] 1 WLR 161.

51 *Bradburn* v. *Lindsay* [1983] 2 All ER 408.

52 [1933] 1 KB 551; the principle on which this case was based was approved *obiter* by Parcq J in *Bishop* v. *Consolidated London Properties Ltd.* (1933) 102 LJKB 257 at 262.

53 [1918] 1 KB 247, CA (not cited in *Cunard* v. *Antifyre Ltd.*).

54 [1938] 2 KB 577 at 594–5 (*per* Greer LJ), [1938] 2 All ER 1, CA.

55 [1939] 3 All ER 329.

5 The Display of Airline Computer Reservation Systems on the Internet

Introduction

The Internet is the network created by the interconnection of computers and computer networks worldwide. It is not a tangible or physical entity, but remains an amorphous and giant network which links together numerous smaller groupings of computer networks which are linked together.[1] Within this intangible spacial concept lies the entirety of the computer spectrum, commonly called 'cyberspace'. Cyberspace can be described as a global medium of communication which links people, corporations, institutions and governments throughout the world.[2]

Cyberspace has attracted numerous illegal acts by its very nature, of being intangible and elusive. Copyright infringement is by far the most prolific illegal activity in cyberspace, causing the loss of tens of billions of dollars' worth of revenue on the Internet.[3] This prolific trend of copyright infringement on the Internet may be attributable to the ease with which one could copy a work into a computer. Courts in common law jurisdictions are generally of the view that the copying of a work into a computer's random access memory (RAM) which may take place automatically when the work is transmitted from another computer, could ipso facto infringe the copyright owner's reproduction right. A fortiori, a third party who accesses such information without permission, even though he or she would not know that the information had been decoded by a person other than the owner of the information, would also be guilty of the copyright infringement.

Against this backdrop which offers the 'cyber offender' a fertile ground to manoeuvre, the airline product in the form of computer reservation systems (CRS) remains vulnerable to copyright infringement. This chapter will examine the legal implications of copyright infringement relating to CRS and the liability of the offender. There will also be an initial discussion on the evolution of CRS in the airline industry and the attendant regulatory regime which applies to CRS.

On 25 June 1996, the Council of the International Civil Aviation Organization (ICAO)[4] adopted a revised Code of Conduct for the Regulation and Operation of Computer Reservation Systems. The revised Code replaced its earlier version which the ICAO Council adopted in 1991[5] and took effect from 1 November 1996. The revised Code addresses current market practices and certain recommendations made on CRS at ICAO's World-wide Air Transport Conference held in 1994[6] which were that a revised ICAO CRS Code should:

1 take into account developments in national and regional regulation, as well as technological and commercial development since the adoption of the Code in 1991;
2 reflect transparency, accessibility and non-discriminatory application;
3 include elements which give particular attention to booking data and display criteria;
4 maintain particular focus on the participation of developing countries and address the retention of Article 10 of the present Code (Safeguards for Developing Countries); and
5 seek compatibility with the General Agreement on Trade in Services which includes coverage of computer reservation systems.

The revision of the Code was also encouraged by ICAO Assembly Resolution A31-13 of the 31st Session of the ICAO Assembly (Montreal, 1995) which recognizes inter alia that computer reservation systems provide substantial benefit both to the air transport industry and to air transport users and are also powerful marketing tools which play an important role in the effective use of market access. The Resolution inter alia requested the Council of ICAO to review the form and content of the ICAO CRS Code of Conduct of 1991 and urged states to cooperate at bilateral, regional and interregional levels to implement the Code.

The main revisions contained in the revised Code of 1996 relate to the extension of its application to non-scheduled air services (such as charter services) and information systems such as the Internet. The Code also inter alia further strengthens the protection of privacy of personal data, ensures that passengers are informed of code-shared and non-scheduled flights, establishes more criteria for financial mechanisms relating to the charging of fees for services rendered and prescribes more specific ways in which flight details can be displayed. The revised Code does not require formal notification by states of its ratification or adherence, but ICAO has requested that each state advise ICAO if it decides to adhere to the principles laid out in the Code.

One of the main thrusts of the ICAO Code is applied through Article 3, which extends its scope of application to computer information systems which provide displays of schedules, space availability and tariffs of air carriers, without the capability of making reservations. Therefore, in general terms, although the Code is designed to regulate the distribution of international passenger air service products through CRS, it is deemed to apply to computer systems such as the Internet in the area of computer information systems. Of course, the Code essentially and exclusively applies to computer reservation systems (systems of more than one airline) thus effectively precluding its applicability to the instance of a web site of an airline accessed through the Internet, which displays only that airline's flight schedule details.

Article 3 brings to bear the significance of legal implications that may follow the use of the Internet for tracking airline schedules and flight information. The legal consequences of transformer data flows and the competition that would follow the possibility of non-airline private companies and organizations placing airline schedules in their own web sites pose real challenges to legal reasoning. This chapter will address these issues in the light of international regulation of computer reservation systems.

Regulatory Implications

The ICAO Code

The 1996 ICAO Code of Conduct on CRS has the support of a Council Resolution which highlights the fact that the Code is the result of comments by states at the 1994 ICAO World-wide Air Transport Conference and urges all contracting states to follow the Code and notify the secretary general when they decide to do so.[7]

The Code is based on three basic postulates, transparency, accessibility and non-discrimination, with the fundamental aim of promoting and enforcing fair competition among airlines. Wherever possible, therefore, the Code adopts a common approach to encompass and accommodate the general thrust of national legislation and regulations, while assisting developing countries who may not have the infrastructure to conform strictly to all the provisions of the Code.

Article 4 of the Code requires states to ensure compliance with the provisions of the Code by air carriers, subscribers and system vendors (an entity that operates or markets a CRS). In this context, it is interesting to note that the Code is wide in application in defining a system vendor as any entity which operates or markets a CRS, bringing into its scope entities other than airlines which may market CRS. These system vendors are allowed by the Code to provide CRS services in the territories they conduct business in, on a non-discriminatory basis and consistent with any bilateral or multilateral agreements or arrangements to which relevant states are parties. The Code also requires states to treat all system vendors impartially regarding their CRS activities in their territories. One of the ways in which this impartiality is achieved by the Code is by prescribing the free flow of information within the national boundaries of states.

A system vendor is required by the Code to permit any air carrier who is prepared to pay the vendor's fees to participate in the CRS system run by the system vendor. Article 5 of the Code, which contains this requirement, clearly precludes any possibility of a system vendor selecting its own airlines for its reservation system. The provision further prohibits a system vendor from imposing conditions on airlines so that the system vendor can only use a certain proportion of the airlines' activities in the CRS or use aspects of the system which are not directly related to the process of distributing a carrier's air transport products through the CRS. The system vendor cannot disseminate among participating carriers the CRS services it offers, nor can he charge fees which are discriminatory. He cannot structure the CRS in a manner which leaves small air carriers at a disadvantage, or unreasonably structure it so as not to relate to the service provided. Article 5 further requires the system vendor inter alia not to manipulate the information provided by carriers in any way that would result in information being displayed inaccurately or with discrimination.

Article 6 of the Code effectively precludes a system vendor from discriminating among subscribers and, inter alia, from linking any commercial arrangements applying to the sale of air transport services of any carrier to the manner or form in which a subscriber may attempt to select air services through the system vendor's CRS. Article 7 strengthens this requirement by prescribing that the system vendor make available a principal display or displays of airline schedules with consistency in terms of the schedules of all participating air carriers and all city-pair markets. Moreover, the system vendor cannot be influenced, directly or indirectly, by the type of identity of the carrier or airport concerned when he places information on his CRS.

Article 7 also prescribes government criteria for the inclusion of information on CRS. These include the type of flights that a principal display should include and their order (non-stop flights to be reflected first, followed by other direct flights not involving change of aircraft, and so on) objectively.

An air carrier who provides the system vendor with information has to make sure that the information provided is accurate and does not misrepresent services. Article 8, which requires this standard, also ensures that air carriers cannot unreasonably refuse to participate in CRS available in their jurisdictions, or refuse to provide a system vendor with information on schedules or tariffs when such information is vital to a subscriber. The air carrier cannot restrict the system vendor to using a particular CRS for sales or services of the carrier, particularly in instances where the carrier has a financial interest in the CRS concerned or when such restrictions would adversely affect the fairness of the CRS transaction between the system vendor and the air carrier concerned by unfairly favouring the CRS.

According to Article 10 of the Code, a subscriber or travel agent who passes on information contained in CRS to a user has to abide by Article 7 of the Code. Furthermore, Article 10 provides that a subscriber may not manipulate information given by the CRS in order to misrepresent information to the air transport services user, or make fictitious and invalid reservations through a CRS. The subscriber is also required, inter alia, to be responsible for the accuracy of information entered into the CRS by the subscriber.

The ICAO Code has stringent standards on safeguarding the privacy of personal data, which are contained in Article 11. This provision calls for states to take appropriate steps to ensure that all concerned with CRS operations safeguard their privacy of personal data and not release such data without the consent of the passenger concerned.

In the context of the above discussion, it is incontrovertible that the ICAO CRS Code also applies to any entity which would provide information of two or more air carriers on the Internet World Wide Web. It is immaterial whether the browser is to make available the CRS information. However, the Code ensures that the entity who provides such information has to do so within certain parameters which would not transcend the irreducible minimum of transparency, accessibility and non-discrimination. The Code also implicitly permits an entity other than an airline to be a system vendor and provide CRS services to users, but does not address issues of competition which may ensue between the airlines who provide such services and other commercial entities whose principal business is not related to the provision of commercial air services but who provide CRS through a browser on the World Wide Web.

Another issue which the ICAO CRS Code does not address – and indeed one which is not within the scope or mandate of the Code – is the question of transborder data flows and rights and liabilities of the service provider or systems vendor and the service user in relation to access to information across national boundaries. This issue is largely one of private international law and should be addressed outside the purview of the international regulatory regime now applicable to CRS.

Other CRS Codes

In October 1993, the Ministers of the European Commission adopted a CRS Code developed by the European Civil Aviation Conference (ECAC) for application to the European states which are members of ECAC. The ECAC CRS Code, which is generally not incompatible with the ICAO Code introduced later (and which, unlike the ECAC Code, is deemed to apply worldwide) does not rigidly restrict itself to intra-European application except in the context of CRS and the sale or marketing of the air transport product within ECAC member states. In other words, Article 1 of the Code provides inter alia that system vendors need not necessarily be of European nationality. While Article 3 of the ECAC Code prohibits a system vendor from attaching any unreasonable conditions of contract to a participating carrier, the Code also explicitly provides in the same Article that a participating carrier need not be restricted to one CRS system in the matter of displaying its flight schedules in CRS systems.

The ECAC Code of 1993, which entered into force on 1 August 1994, replacing a Code which entered into force on 1 August 1989, identifies a system vendor as any entity and its affiliates which is or are responsible for the operation or marketing of CRS and provides in Article 5 that displays generated by a system vendor must be clear, non-discriminatory, and must not display inaccurate or misleading information as a result of the system vendor's or any other person's negligence. The provision also requires the system vendor to provide a principal display or displays for each individual transaction through its CRS and specifies that a consumer shall have the right to have, on request, a principal display limited to scheduled or non-scheduled services.

The United States' CRS rules, which were issued on 15 September 1992 are somewhat different in content from both the ICAO and ECAC CRS rules. Firstly, the US rules provide for the operation of a computer reservation system comprising information on schedules, fares and so on offered by only one carrier or its affiliates in the United States. The US Code recognizes a system owner (as against a system vendor) who is a carrier holding 5 per cent or more of the equity of a system, that has one or more affiliates that hold such an equity interest, or that together with affiliates holds such an interest. Therefore the US Code, *in limine,* rules out the involvement of entities other than airlines in the provision of CRS services within the United States. Furthermore, the Code allows one carrier to operate a

CRS service within the country. The overall principles of the Code, however, are not incompatible with those of the ICAO and ECAC Codes, in that the Code provides for fair and equal display of information without discrimination.

The US Code, in Part 255.9 (Carrier-owned Computer Reservation Systems) allows the use of third-party computer hardware or software in conjunction with CRS services, except in instances where such use would adversely affect the integrity of the CRS system. Furthermore, the same provision adds that no system may prohibit the use of a CRS terminal to access directly any other system or database by the system. It also calls for a system to make available to developers of third-party hardware and software the non-proprietary system architecture specifications and other non-proprietary technical information needed to enable such developers to create products which would be compatible with the system.

The above provision seemingly leaves it open for entities other than airlines to offer on CRS details of airline flight schedules through the owner airlines concerned. Of course, for these entities to make available to subscribers the facility of booking a seat on an airline, there has to be agreement between the airline and the entity concerned, but the entity may find it easier merely to offer information of airline flight schedules on a composite CRS without giving the user the ability to pre-book.

The General Agreement on Trade in Services and Related Instruments (GATS) of the General Agreement on Tariffs and Trade (GATT) which now falls under the purview of the World Trade Organization (WTO), also encompasses computer reservation systems of air carriers.[8] The Annex (of GATS) on Air Transport Service includes CRS within GATS and defines CRS as 'services provided by computerized systems that contain information about air carriers' schedules, availability, fares and fare rules, through which reservations can be made or tickets may be issued'. This definition too, does not necessarily exclude any computerized system offering details of flight information and fares of airlines, thereby leaving room for any entity other than owner airlines to participate in CRS over the World Wide Web.

The cornerstone of GATS – the most-favoured-nation treatment clause – applies to CRS under GATS by virtue of Article II of the Agreement which provides that each member (state) shall accord immediately and unconditionally to services and service supplies of any other member (state) treatment no less favourable than that it accords to like services and service suppliers of any other country. Although this principle establishes a cohesive system of commercial unity and equity among WTO member states, the most-favoured-nation principle is not sacrosanct and can be obviated by an exemption filed under the Annex on Article II Exemptions. In practicality, therefore, while the most-favoured-nation treatment ensures that all WTO member states are treated on the same basis (or not worse than the member who gets the best deal) in terms of the exchange of information under CRS, this treatment can be withdrawn by any member state from another, by filing an exemption under the Agreement itself. Such exemptions are reviewed by the Council for Trade in Services when they exceed five years, and no exemption is expected under the Annex to exceed a period of 10 years.

Article XIV of the GATS Agreement provides exceptions to the practices enshrined in the Agreement by providing that a member (state) may invoke the necessity to take measures on the grounds, inter alia, of public order or public morality and to protect human, animal and plant life or health.

The GATS Agreement has incorporated some positive measures which are calculated to assist trade in relation to CRS. Article IV encourages and assists the participation of developing countries by requiring the improvement of their access to distribution channels and information networks. The provision also calls for the strengthening of domestic services in developing countries and provides for the liberalization of market access in sectors and modes of supply of export interest.

There are also other provisions in the GATS Agreement which establish general principles which may apply to the provision of CRS by entities other than air carriers. The principles of transparency which are enshrined in Article III call upon members (states) to provide information and publish, where necessary, the details of implementation of the Agreement. Article III *bis* precludes members (states) from requiring of other members (states) confidential information which, when disclosed, would hinder or impede law enforcement or otherwise be contrary to public interest. The provision also applies the requirement of confidentiality to preserve the commercial interests of parties, whether public or private.

Some 20 years ago the commercial interests involved in the distribution of the airline product was autonomous and neutral. The travel agent who was located around the corner would provide information on the best connection and fare. The agent frequently obtained this information by thumbing through a compendium of schedules provided neutrally by airlines and put together by a publishing house. After the best connection is identified, the agent uses the ticket stock of the airline concerned (with which he is provided by the airline) and writes a ticket for the passenger.

Today, this same process is accomplished by 'displaying' the best connection on a computer screen and punching the necessary codes onto the keyboard of the computer to make or confirm a reservation.

Most airlines own the CRS which operate in these agents' offices and earn 40 per cent on average of the gross income on the provision of such automation facilities to the agent.

The automation revolution of the 1990s have reached a pitch at the present time, where organizations have realized the vast earning potential in diversifying their information networks to commercial activities other than their principal businesses. It is not unrealistic, therefore, to expect some of these large commercial entities to reach for the airline product, which is so dependent on information. As a result, some airlines at least have shown apprehension at losing control over the distribution of their product.

Legal Implications

The initial issue which emerges when the display of CRS on the Internet is considered is the fact that a CRS system would be legally considered 'computer software' which is developed for a specific project and 'sold' as packaged software to commercial entities operating their web site on the Internet. Strictly speaking, the word 'sold' cannot be used in this context since, legally, software is considered a species of intellectual property which would in turn be protected by the law of copyright. Therefore the operator or owners of such software as a CRS system would license the right of another entity to use the computer program in question.

Fundamentally, one has to determine who has what legal right to use the information contained in a CRS over the Internet. The starting point is when the initial database of the CRS owner initially connects to telecommunications distribution networks, which then deposit the information on the Internet after crossing national borders with no delay and no physical conveyance to work the transfer. These information transfers cannot be placed in the control of a single nation and bring to bear the inherent difficulties posed by the notion of 'tangibility'. This notion articulates the necessity for the application of copyright laws to a tangible medium of expression. Although in the incipient stage of copyright law enforcement, the notion of 'tangibility' was not applied to information existing in databases in electronic form, the U.S. Copyright Act of 1976 in Section 102(*a*) provided the basis for electronic information to be considered tangible by stipulating that any original works of authorship, if they are in a medium of expression from which they can be perceived, reproduced or otherwise communicated, either directly or with the aid of a machine or device, can be treated as tangible information for the purpose of copyright laws.

The seminal United States case of *Leon* v. *Pacific Telephone and Telegraph Co.*[9] established the principle of copyright infringement even in the instance where a person uses an original work of authorship to rearrange the contents of that work. The *Leon* decision is a relevant source to the area of copyright and CRS, since it concerned the use of an alphabetical telephone directory for a numerical telephone directory, where the defendant rearranged the original information compiled by the plaintiff into a directory which ran in numerical succession, according to telephone numbers.

Although the *Leon* decision influenced subsequent decisions[10] that copyright laws should protect the labours of the initial author and not the substance of information in particular, the case of *Triangle Publications* v. *Sports Eye Inc.*[11] reflects the fact that copyright laws do not exclude the protection of organization. In this instance the court held that copyright extended to the method or form of expressing the data.[12]

The 1977 case of *New York Times Co.* v. *Roxbury Data Interface*[13] introduced a new dimension when the court held that protection could be afforded to rearrange or recompile information based on the 'doctrine of fair use'. Under the doctrine, the court held that the defendant's copying of entries from the New York Times Index for its own index was not a copyright infringement. The court based its reasoning on the fact that the defendant had made 'slight' use of the plaintiff's index in building his own and, as such, the defendant's act constituted 'fair use' of the plaintiff's index.

It has been judicially recognized that copyright infringement may be direct or indirect. While direct copyright infringement may be enforced on the basis of the actual knowledge of the offender that he was infringing copyright in a given instance, there have been instances where knowledge may be imputed to the offender by the courts, on the basis that he ought to have known that the inclusion of material on the Internet would infringe copyright of an owner. In *Playboy Enterprises* v. *Frena*,[14] the defendant was a bulletin board operator who was sued for including 170 images of copyrighted photographs on his system. The defendant was totally unaware of the inclusion of the photographs in question on his web site. The court held: 'There is irrefutable evidence of direct copyright infringement in this case. It does not matter that defendant Frena may have been unaware of the copyright infringement. Intent to infringe is not needed to find copyright infringement.'[15] The *Frena* decision imposed a standard of strict liability on operators for copyright infringement caused or initiated by users of their bulletin boards.

A person guilty of contributory infringement of copyright is considered responsible for third party liability on the basis that he causes or materially contributes to the infringing conduct of another, by willingly and with knowledge inducing or causing to influence another to perform the act of infringement.[16]

As opposed to the theory of direct infringement, courts have allowed persons other than the initiator of a copyright infringement to be found liable. In the case of *Sony Corp. of Am.* v. *Universal City Studios*,[17] the Supreme Court described contributory infringement as 'merely a species of the broader problem of identifying the circumstances in which it is just to hold one individual accountable for the actions of another'.[18] Endorsement of strict liability for direct infringement followed in the case of *Sega Enterprises* v. *MAPHIA*,[19] where the court held that the defendant bulletin board operator had knowledge of the unauthorized copying involved and also actively participated in distributing copies over the Internet. Significantly, the court found for the plaintiff on both counts of direct and contributory infringement by the defendant on the basis that the defendant had not only been directly involved in the infringement, but had also facilitated and encouraged the copying.

A significant distinction from the *Sega* decision was made by the same court in the case of *Religious Technology Center* v. *Netcom On-line Communication Services Inc.*[20] where the court held that there is a difference between a person who initiates a process which leads to copyright infringement and a person who has to make copies incidentally and as a part of the process of operating a network.[21] The court further held that it would be inappropriate to impose liability on a service which acts more in the nature of a conduit, which, for instance, does not keep an archive of files for more than a short period of time. By the *Netcom* decision, the court has seemingly rejected the *Playboy* decision by acknowledging that to find a service guilty such as the one which was found guilty in the *Playboy* case would place an unreasonably broad construction on public distribution and display rights, which in turn would be able to find persons who do not have the ability to control the information which they release to the public.[22]

Other intellectual property rights protection which may affect the use of CRS on the Internet can be attenuated from patent law, the laws relating to trade secrets and the laws of unfair competition. Of these, perhaps the most relevant to CRS are the legal principles related to unfair competition,[23] which are intended to protect the fruits of one's labour from being misappropriated by another. Principles of unfair competition are usually contained in national laws and therefore are applied on a common law basis.

The second consideration in the area of CRS and its use over the Internet relates to trans-border data flow and proprietary rights in information. In other words, who is the owner of a CRS which is displayed over the Internet? Is information on airline schedules provided at the international level an intellectual asset which belongs to the whole of humanity and is it an international service provided to the world at large and therefore a marketing tool? The obvious answer to this seems to lie in the fact that trans-border data flow will have no value if there is no market value for the information provided. Consequently, a CRS system which appears on the Internet would obviously aim at accomplishing airline reservations and would therefore be a marketing tool. It could therefore be categorized as an international service and an asset which broadly belongs to the intellectual community.[24] However, one has to draw a line against piracy of information by unscrupulous entities. For this purpose, new rules have been considered necessary, particularly when the authors of a system are in various locations contributing information to a composite 'work product'.

In the event that an author's work is unjustly taken by an entity and displayed on the Internet, which is consequently accessed by the world at large, questions such as 'When or at what point is liability incurred by the entity?', 'When is a contract concluded? Is it at the point when the airline reservation is made across the boundaries of a state or country in which the CRS was put onto the Internet, or is it at the input of information stage?' become relevant. In 1980, two American professors addressed these questions and concluded:

> First, liability is incurred neither at input nor output, but within the computer network. Second, what protects the author or publisher is physical control of the text for there is no count of its reproduction once it is out of his hands. Third, a billing system operated by the network is necessary if fee collection is to be easy. Without that there is too much red tape in making arrangements for occasional access. Fourth, once the publisher's text has been read by someone else, evasion of royalty payments is quite easy because the reader can store the text in his computer and do whatever he wants with it. Computer copying is even easier than photocopying.[25]

These commentators also envisaged difficulty in controlling the display of information obtained through trans-border data flows and recognized that, each time a person accesses such information anywhere in the world, the information would be used and would be tantamount to being printed. Their conclusions, which are valid to the area of CRS on the Internet, were that a proper definition and delineation should be accomplished by the application of types of conduct leading to computer fraud, abuse, negligence and breach of contract. It was their view that mechanisms through which such grievances may be redressed would then logically follow.[26]

Notes

1 See *ACLU* v. *Reno*, 929 F. Supp. 824 at 830 (E.D. Pa. 1996).
2 Ibid., 831. The term 'cyberspace' was coined by William Gibson in his novel *Neuromancer*, (1984).
3 See Marc S. Friedman, (1995), 'Infojacking: Crimes on the Information Superhighway', *New Jersey Law Journal*, 140, 658.
4 The International Civil Aviation Organization is a specialized agency of the United Nations which is responsible for the regulation of international civil aviation worldwide. ICAO comprises a membership of 185 states.
5 See R.I.R. Abeyratne (1995), *Legal and Regulatory Issues of Computer Reservation Systems and Code Sharing Agreements in Air Transport*, Paris: Editions Frontier.
6 For a detailed discussion of the conference, see R.I.R. Abeyratne (1995), 'The World-wide Air Transport Conference and Air Traffic Rights – A Commentary', *European Transport Law*, XXX(2), 131–47.
7 Attachment A to State Letter E.C. 2/28-96/74. The State Letter communicated to contracting states the 1996 ICAO CRS Code of Conduct and the Council Resolution.
8 Other areas included in the Annex are aircraft repair and maintenance services and the selling and marketing of air transport services.
9 91 F. 2d 484 (9th Cir. 1937).
10 *National Business Lights* v. *Dun and Bradstreet Inc.*, 552 F. Supp 89 (N.D. 111. 1982); *Dow Jones & Company Inc.* v. *Board of Trade of the City of Chicago*, 546 F. Supp. 113 (S.D.N.Y. 1982).
11 415 F. Supp. 682 (E.D. Penn. 1976).
12 Ibid., 685–6.
13 434 F. Supp. 217 (D.N.J. 1977).
14 839 F. Supp. 1552 at 1554 (M.D. Fla. 1993).
15 Ibid., 1559.
16 See *Gershwin Publishing Corp.*v. *Columbia Artists Management Inc.*, 443 F. 2d 1159 at 1162 (2d Cir. 1971).
17 464 U.S. 417 at 434–5 (1984).
18 Ibid., 435.
19 857 F. Supp. 679 (N.D. Cal. 1994).
20 907 F. Supp. at 1365–6.
21 Ibid., 1368–9.
22 Ibid., 1370.
23 Patent law relates to mechanical devices and trade secrets relate to formulae or information which give the author a competitive edge over other competitors. Since CRS is a 'service' provided by airlines, it may not strictly conform to the definition of 'trade secret'.
24 See Ralph Lemoine (1979), 'Transborder Data Flows', *Information Systems Magazine*, Spring, p.30.
25 Stan Pool and Steven Solomon (1982), 'Intellectual Property and Transborder Data Flows', *Stanford Journal of International Law*, 16, 121.
26 Ibid., pp.123, 133, 137–8.

6 The Use of the Smart Card

Introduction

One of the most exciting developments in recent times related to air transport is the involvement of the aviation and tourism community in the 'smart card' – a plastic card the size of an average credit card – which would enable the air traveller to 'swipe' his way through customs and immigration control at the airport on the basis of spontaneous computer clearance. Once it is introduced effectively and efficiently on a large scale, automatic screening of travellers is expected to offer a major breakthrough in the facilitation of air transport. The 'smart card' is essentially linked to its holder, so that positive identification is achieved at the entry point by a computer-driven determination for consistency between the stored data in the card and the physical attributes of the holder of the card.

The consistency is achieved by the use of a biometric measuring device which scans and delivers in automated format for storage certain physical characteristics of a person. These characteristics are encoded in the 'smart card', which is used as the travel document, and can verify the identity of the holder of the card as the true owner of the card through a 'matching' process with his biometric data. At its most advanced stage of usage, the smart card and physical check can be used to determine the identity of the person electronically at departure and transmit the details through a system of electronic data interchange to his point of arrival, where the information already transmitted by the departure point can be compared for verification by the 'swiping' process on arrival.

The preferred, and perhaps easiest, method of electronic determination of a traveller's identity is the use of biometric technology which extrapolates and determines accurately the geometry of a person's hand and stores the information so obtained in the card which he 'swipes' at the control point. The identification process and subsequent clearance of the passenger only take seconds and require the simple process of the placement by him of his hand on a hand scanner, while at the same time 'swiping' or sending his card (travel document) through a reader. The gate at the immigration control would automatically open if the data stored in the card related to the image of the passenger's hand match the 'live' reading of the passenger's hand by the scanner.

There are already in use some systems of automated screening of passengers, notably the INSPASS system of the United States, which is of limited application at the present time and uses biometric technology to measure a person's hand geometry and compare it with the data stored in the card which he carries as his travel document. Australia, Canada, the United Kingdom, the Netherlands and Germany are others who are positively considering the introduction of the 'smart card'. It has been envisaged that a worldwide use of automated screening of travellers would greatly expedite the admission process of an air traveller, guarantee greater security, utilize available immigration and customs resources more effectively and efficiently, obviate the need to incur unnecessary expenditure involving inadmissible passengers and, most importantly, alleviate the airport congestion problem which looms ahead with the increased passenger traffic at airports in the years to come.

However efficient the automated screening of air travellers is, it is incontrovertible that such a process would have legal implications. For one, the screening process, which is strictly for the purposes of identification of the traveller, would have to be accomplished with the consent of the traveller, particularly in the context of the use of his hand geometry. A more serious implication would be the legalities involved in a technical flaw in the automation process which disallows a genuine passenger from entering a country. In such an instance the legal validity of the computer records which pertain to the data of the passenger, their admissibility in courts and the liability of the authorities concerned become relevant.

This chapter will examine some of the areas of law which have emerged in common law jurisdictions on the subject of electronic data interchange and legal liability which may analogically apply to the instance of inadmissible passengers who are so categorized as a result of their automatic screening.

Regulatory Provisions

Regulatory provisions pertaining to the custody and care of passengers are contained in Section E of Chapter 3 of Annex 9 to the Chicago Convention, which provides *in limine* that the public authorities concerned shall, without unreasonable delay, accept passengers and crew for examination as to their admissibility into the state.[1] There is also a provision of travel documents.[2] Furthermore, each contracting state is empowered to seize fraudulent, falsified or counterfeit travel documents of inadmissible persons. The same provision requires the state authorities who discover the inadmissible passenger to provide a photocopy of the forged travel document together with a covering letter to the carrier who brought in the inadmissible passenger to the removing country.[3] The operator is responsible for transporting the passenger back to his point of departure.[4]

In the event of a 'smart card' being used as a travel document, operators will not be obligated to ensure compliance with Annex 9. Instead, they would have to provide the operator with details of computer records and so on which evidence the fraud or irregular conduct of the inadmissible passenger. The difficulty posed by this eventuality would be that, in the event of a disgruntled or aggrieved inadmissible passenger deciding to seek adjudication in the courts of law, against the authorities concerned and/or against the operator, the courts would have to consider the validity and admissibility of the computer data presented as evidence in support of the claim.

Indeed, the anomaly is compounded by the fact that Standard 3.41 of Annex 9, which requires the removing state to issue a covering letter together with the photocopy of the fraudulent document, has a note which directs the reader to a suggested format of the covering letter. The covering letter, which appears in Appendix 9 to the Annex, is addressed to the appropriate authority of the original point of embarkation of the passenger to which he is carried back by the operator. The letter states inter alia that the fraudulent travel document, which will be required as evidence in the inadmissible passenger's prosecution in the removing state, has been impounded. The photocopy is issued presumably as an interim measure, until the original is returned after legal proceedings. The question is whether, in the case of an inadmissible passenger so determined through automated screening, if that passenger elects to institute action against the operator in the state of issue of the document for the automation irregularity which denied him access into the removing country, he would be left with only a photocopy of the card which carried his data as evidence before the court?

Therefore, in order to comply with Appendix 9 to the Annex in a meaningful way, the removing state may have to produce electronic data evidence to the inadmissible passenger as to why he was refused entry into the country.

Legal Issues

Case Law

The obligatory notion of the requirement for a removing state to produce computer evidence of an inadmissible passenger's deportation is judicially supported in the analogous decision of *American Banker Insurance Co.* v. *Caruth*[5] where the court held that failure to produce computer documents can result in the court ruling in the opponent's favour. In this instance, the Texas Court of Appeal awarded judgment against a complainant who failed to produce relevant computer files as requested within the time ordered by the court. The principle that the state is obligated to produce files containing electronically stored data is contained in the 1979 judgment of *Ball* v. *State of New York*,[6] where Moriarty J held that, if a claimant demanded the retrieval of computer information pertaining to his case, a state was legally obliged to produce that information to the court. That principle was endorsed by the 1993 decision of *First Technology Safety Systems Inc.* v. *Depinet*,[7] where it was held that a trial court has judicial discretion to grant an *ex parte* seizure order to preserve electronic evidence or to promote the interests of justice.

The information provided must be reasonably decipherable and usable. Above all, the person requesting the information as evidence should be able to access the data. In *Greyhound Computer Corp., Inc.* v. *IBM*[8] where the defendant provided computer data which were unreadable by the plaintiff, the court ordered the defendant to assist the plaintiff in accessing the information with materials and personnel.

Judicial support and the topical relevance of the requirement in Appendix 9 to Annex 9 and its adaptability to the 'smart card' concept is reflected in the 1995 decision of *National Union Electric Corporation* v. *Matsushita Electric Industries*,[9] where the court held: 'we now live in a society where much of the data which our society desires is stored in computer discs. This process will escalate in years to come; we suspect that by the year 2000 virtually all data will be stored in some form of computer memory'.[10] The court further held that the information stored in electronic form would be easier to search and manipulate, and, in this particular instance, requested the parties to litigation to provide electronic copies of evidence, even though the information was already available on paper. Therefore, by applying the *Matsushita* decision to Annex 9, one could validly argue that the requirement to produce a photocopy of the fraudulent document in Appendix 9 would still remain valid, but be construed as being applicable to electronic data retrieval and evidence as necessary.

A Paradigm Regime of Liability

The significance of automated passenger screening in air transport becomes relevant at law particularly in its ultimate state, where the passenger's physical attributes and travel card are checked both at the point of departure and at the point of arrival. This ensures that the biometric data of the passenger are transmitted from one point to another while the passenger is still airborne, to be verified on arrival. Although automated screening is an admittedly efficient identification process and an effective security measure, there has been no documented legal study which has specifically addressed issues of admissibility of evidence and liability in relation to the use of biometric identification by automated screening.

Perhaps the only analogy is the study conducted by the United Nations Commission on International Trade Law (UNCITRAL) in 1997 on electronic commerce. This study and principles formulated thereby may serve as a paradigm to biometric identification, particularly in the context of UNCITRAL's deliberations in March 1997 on digital signatures in electronic commerce. At its 30th Session, held in Vienna, 12–30 May 1997, the UNCITRAL General Assembly considered the Report of the Working Group on Electronic Commerce (New York, 18–28 February 1997)[11] which identified a digital signature that could be used to approve transnational commercial transactions conducted through electronic data interchange. The technique used was the transfer of an original signature to a numerical value, which is affixed to a data message and which, by using a known mathematical procedure, is associated with the originator's private cryptographic key and makes it possible uniquely to determine that this numerical value has been obtained with the originator's private cryptographic key.[12]

By using this principle analogically to a hand print which may be encrypted dimensionally to be stored by a computer and decrypted when necessary, one could also apply analogically the recommendations of UNCITRAL for approved authorities to inspect, monitor and use such electronic data interchange. They would then be liable to any person who acts in good faith in relying on such information for any loss due to defects or technical breakdowns of the software.[13] UNCITRAL has also suggested liability based on tortious principles of negligence which could be mitigated by the contributory negligence of the person aggrieved.[14]

Notes

1 Annex 9 to the Convention on International Civil Aviation, 10th edn, April 1997 (Facilitation), Standard 3.38.

2 Ibid., Standard 3.40.3.
3 Ibid., Standard 3.41.
4 Ibid.
5 786 S.W. 2d 427 Texas Ct. App. 1990.
6 421 N.Y.S. 2d 328 (Ct. Cl. 1979).
7 11.F. 3d 641 (6th Cir. 1993).
8 3. Computer Law Serv. Rep. 138 at 139 (D. Minn. 1971).
9 494 F. Supp. 1262.
10 Ibid., 1275.
11 A/CN.9/437, 12 March 1997.
12 Ibid., p. 10, Draft Article A.
13 Ibid., para. 51, Draft Article H, p.17.
14 Ibid.

7 The Exchange of Trade Secrets Relating to Information Technology

Introduction

The aviation industry is heavily permeated by information technology. Foremost among the areas which use computer software are the aircraft manufacturing industry and airline marketing divisions. There is no doubt that, among the software used in aviation, some may be considered by the owners of such information as trade secrets. This being the case, owners of information technology cannot avoid their employees, particularly those who are employed in the technological and scientific aspects of such information, acquiring intimate knowledge and know-how of the technology involved in such instances. It is possible, therefore, that such information may be leaked in certain circumstances by the employers concerned or any other person who may acquire knowledge of the technology through partnerships and other collaborative relationships with the owner of the technology. Employees, in particular, may become dangerous competitors for their employer once their employment ceases, thus becoming a potential threat to the latter in his endeavour to safeguard his information.

In the landmark 1987 case of *Ticketnet Corp* v. *Air Canada*,[1] which established the principle of sanctity of information in software, the Ontario High Court found that, if parties concerned envisioned a contractual relationship *in futuro* between them, their conduct should necessarily reflect a mutual duty of confidence in that one party must not reveal information technology gathered from the other party in the process of negotiations. In the *Air Canada* case, the plaintiff Ticketnet Corp was the originator of a concept in developing a software product which created a system of making reservations for theatrical and other entertainment. The defendant Air Canada, when approached by the plaintiff, expressed its intent to be associated with the projects. In the lengthy process of negotiations, much information relating to the information technology of the project was exchanged between the parties. Each party had made known to the other its intent to be in a contractual relationship with the other, whereby Ticketnet would retain ownership of the software while granting certain rights to Air Canada. Although the parties had never reached *consensus ad idem* and there was no binding contract between them, they had reached an understanding of collaboration involving information technology sharing. While negotiations were in progress, Ticketnet had disclosed information relating to the intended project to American Airlines, which can be regarded as a competitor and business rival of Air Canada. Air Canada pleaded in the Ontario High Court for an interlocutory injunction which would restrain Ticketnet from releasing information relating to the Air Canada–Ticketnet project to third parties. White J granted the injunction, on the basis that Air Canada could reasonably have expected that a contract would come into being and negotiations were in progress. His Honour therefore concluded that Ticketnet was under a duty at law not to divulge information relating to an ongoing contractual process until and unless that process came to an incontrovertible end.[2]

This chapter will examine the general principles of common law which apply to the exchange of trade secrets in the aviation industry, with particular emphasis on trade secrets related to information technology.

Legal Principles

The incidence of trade secrets being exchanged in the business world has reached such substantial proportions as to make it an inarticulate premise that competition from former employees is presumptive evidence of dishonesty. There is, of course, a thin line between the genuine skill acquired by a technical person through years of experience which he takes with him to a new employer and a specific detailed revelation by him of a subjective piece of information technology used by specified parties exclusively, such as in the Air Canada–Ticketnet relationship. In general terms, an aircraft manufacturer or airline marketing division cannot allege that a former employee has misused information gathered during his work with them if he legitimately uses the knowledge and skills gained in a general way for the execution of his work with his new employer. As was stated by Hoffman J in the British case of *Lock International Plc* v. *Beswick*,[3] courts are at a disadvantage when trying to determine a difference between genuine use of acquired skill and the release of trade secrets by a technical expert, and it may well turn out that what may appear to be information specific to one business enterprise is really a general practice used by many in the relevant field.[4]

However, if, as in the case of *Telex Corp* v. *IBM Corp*,[5] there is a manifest and overt attempt by an employer to extract detailed confidential and trade information from its employees who had brought such information from their work at a former employer, the courts would find it easy to distinguish such an instance as a conscious and knowing exchange of trade secrets.

Decided instances of common law are numerous,[6] where employees have terminated their employment with one employer in order to gain more lucrative employment elsewhere by using as a tool the intimate knowledge of their employers' information technology secrets in order to convince their new employer of their worth.

A salutary principle obtaining at common law with regard to the safeguard of trade secrets is the fiduciary relationship principle which *in limine* precludes a party in contractual relationship with another to form a contractual relationship with a business competitor of the latter, particularly if certain information of a confidential nature has been exchanged between the parties. It need not necessarily be that the confidential information may be used in the contract. For instance, if A enters into contract with aircraft manufacturer B for the provision of computer software to the latter, and in the process B reveals confidential information including B's system requirements to A, A cannot enter into a contract with aircraft manufacturer C for the reason that A is already privy to confidential information belonging to B which may be of use to C. The relationship between A and B has been judicially identified as a fiduciary one.[7] The 1988 British House of Lords decision in *A.G.* v. *Guardian Newspapers Ltd.*[8] has extended this principle to provide relief even where no fiduciary relationship exists between parties who enter into an arm's-length contract with each other, if one party believes that the other has been provided with what the former considers to be confidential information.

Courts have been mindful of the extremity of legal principles which protect or safeguard trade secrets at common law and which may sometimes genuinely restrain open competition and business opportunity. To this end, covenants in restraint of trade are considered prima facie illegal and therefore unenforceable and this principle can be rebutted only when a covenant is drawn up reasonably and is calculated to protect the intellectual property of an employer. Although in *Herbert Morris Ltd.* v. *Saxelby*[9] the House of Lords established the non competition rule as above, it has since been embellished to the extent that the rule cannot be construed as one restraining an employee from making genuine use of his knowledge, experience and skill or one being injurious to the public.[10]

On the reverse side of the coin lies a situation where an employee who developed an information software package for his former employer while he acted for him as an independent contractor may find his software package being used by the former employer after his departure. The fact that the person who developed the software package did so as an independent contractor imputes a copyright to him which the former employer cannot use unless otherwise agreed to between the parties. In the modern commercial context, where outsourcing is gaining ground as a business practice, it would not be uncommon to find aircraft manufacturers, airlines and travel agents contracting services of computer experts to develop software packages for their business. In such a situation the expert would function as an independent contractor and consequently might have more independence in the use of information technology developed by him during a previous contractual relationship.

In the 1991 United States decision of *MacLean Associates* v. *Wm. M. Mercer-Meidlinger-Hansen Inc.*,[11] the Court of Appeals held that, if work involved the development of information technology produced by a worker outside the scope of employment, such work would not belong to the employer. However, any work done within the employee's scope of employment would be 'work for hire' and come under the ownership of the employer. The court viewed with favour the earlier Supreme Court decision in *Community for Creative non-Violence* v. *Reid*,[12] which held that the Copyright Act of 1976 provides that copyright ownership is vested initially with the author of a work concerned – the author being the person who creates the work and therefore owns it. The court in the *Reid* case found that the Copyright Act made exception in instances of hire or employment where the employer or person for whom the work is prepared becomes the author ipso facto and is considered the owner of the work. The Court of Appeals in the *MacLean* case attenuated the basic principle of 'work for hire' as enunciated in the *Reid* case and added that factors such as the skill required in carrying out the work, the tools used, the location of the work and the duration of the relationship between the parties inter alia would be persuasive and determinative of authorship of the work concerned.

In the regulatory field, Article 6 of the World Intellectual Property Organization (WIPO) Copyright Treaty, adopted by the Diplomatic Conference on 20 December 1996, grants authors of literary and artistic works the exclusive right of authorizing or making available to the public the original copies of their works and further provides that such unfettered right does not derogate the right of parties to determine contractual terms that would affect such author's rights in the case of a valid contract at law. The WIPO Copyright Treaty, which is a special agreement between parties to the Berne Convention of

1971,[13] protects computer programs in Article 4 by providing that computer programs are protected within the meaning of Article 2 of the Berne Convention, which establishes copyright of authors of literary works and artistic material.

Copyright and Trade Secrets in Aviation

The first instance of a trade secret dispute in aviation commenced with the first ever flight by the Wright brothers in Kitty Hawk, North Carolina. The brothers discovered that the problem of lateral stability which was so important to flight could be solved by following the flight of buzzards. Watching the gliding birds, the Wright brothers mimicked the wing twisting of the birds by constructing a mechanism that warped the horizontal plane of an aeroplane's wings at either side in opposite directions. After patenting this mechanism as applying to any system that varied the lateral margins in opposite directions, the brothers applied it to their inaugural flight in 1903.

Ironically, at the same time as the Wright brothers were perfecting their mechanism, a young building apprentice by the name of Curtiss was working as a member of Alexander Graham Bell's team of experts conducting flying experiments. Curtiss developed 'wing flaps' in the nature of ailerons by using the Wright brothers' 'wing twist' method and applied for a patent that recognized the wing flap mechanism. By 1915, the wing flap method had obviated the Wrights' wing twist method and all planes were using it. The Wright brothers sued Curtiss for infringement of patent in 1909, on the grounds that their method also applied to wing flaps. They won the case.[14]

The *Wrights* v. *Curtiss* dispute was the genesis in the United States of the 'Cross Licencing' Agreement, where manufacturers of aircraft formed an association in 1917 which entitled each member to grant all its aircraft patents to all other members. However, the United States government in 1972 claimed that the 'Cross Licencing Agreement' hampered competition in research and development and succeeded in dismantling the Agreement in 1975 by common decree.

The *Wrights–Curtiss* case was preceded in 1879 by the seminal case of *Baker* v. *Selden*,[15] where the United States Supreme Court grappled with the question as to whether copyright protects an idea or concept. The answer was in the negative, and the Supreme Court concluded that copyright applied to the expression of an idea rather than the idea itself. The *Baker* decision, which concerned the ruled lines and headings of a ledger used by Selden which were allegedly used in the same form by Baker, forms a sound analogy to trade secrets in aviation, in the context of the principle that blank account books do not form the subject matter of copyright protection.[16] The blank account book in the *Baker* decision could well be a user interface for aircraft design or format for an airline computer reservation system.

Trade secrets in the field of aviation could well be regarded by courts of common law jurisdiction as those that can be used with flexibility and changed, unlike musical recordings and radio programmes, which have to be copied exactly as the original arrangement.[17] For example, a computer program's expression, which is accompanied by screen displays in the instance of computer reservations systems, could come under the protection of copyright since it can be duplicated by several different computing methods which may slightly alter the user interface.

Although the early decision in the *Baker* case held that blank layouts, if not accompanied by expression, cannot claim protection under copyright law, this principle seems to be questionable in the light of later decisions. The 1986 decision of *Broderbund Software Inc.* v. *Unison World Inc.*[18] held that display screens, even though they do not convey specific identifiable and unique expressions, are protectable under copyright laws. The court established that the structure, sequence and organization of a display screen is per se copyrightable together with the text and artwork of their displays. However, the later decision handed down in 1987 in the case of *Digital Communications Assocs* v. *Softclone Distributor Corporation*[19] held that copyright does not extend to screen displays, disputing the current practice at that time that screen displays were copyrightable. In the context of airline computer reservation systems, the *Softclone* decision would impose the need to bring under copyright the design and structural organization of a computer display screen of a particular CRS system.

Fortunately, the confusion caused by the polarization between the *Broderbund* decision and the *Softclone* decision seems to have been settled rationally by the United States Supreme Court decision in 1993 in *Apple Computer* v. *Microsoft and Hewlett-Packard*,[20] where the court held that, to establish a prima facie case of copyright infringement, the plaintiff must prove that the works at issue are substantially similar, if not identical, in both ideas and expression.[21] This broad principle would apply equally to aircraft manufacturing designs as well as to airline computer reservation systems and any other software designed for the aviation industry.

Under English law, although trade secrets are recognized as being vital to the sustenance of a business, stealing trade secrets does not mean that the person who commits the offence can be prosecuted for the offence of theft. The Data Protection Act of 1984, in section 5(2) provides, inter alia, that a person who has access to a data entry in a computer shall not obtain the data from any source not described in the data entry and use the data for any purpose other than the one specified in the entry. Nor shall he transfer the data directly or indirectly to a source other than one described in the entry.

In the 1996 case of *R. v. Brown*,[22] the defendant, a one-time police officer having access to data stored in the police national register on persons, divulged information thereof to his friend, a debt collector, for the latter's professional benefit. The purpose for which the defendant was given access to the data was for policing, and it was found by a jury that the defendant was guilty on two counts under section 5(2) of the Data Protection Act of 1984 and fined £500 on each count. On appeal, the Court of Appeal quashed the defendant's conviction on both counts, on the grounds that the word 'use' in Section 5(2) meant that the offender has to do something to the data once he accesses it in order for it to be construed that he 'used' the data. In the defendant's case, the Court of Appeal contended that the defendant had done nothing to the data once he had accessed it other than to give the information contained in the data to his friend.

In the House of Lords, which heard the appeal of the prosecution against the Court of Appeal's finding, Lord Goff of Chieveley disagreed with the construction placed on the word 'use' by the Court of Appeal, stating: 'I approach the matter as follows. I accept that, since the word "use" is not defined in the Act, it must be given its natural and ordinary meaning. Synonyms of the word "use" are to "make use of" or to "employ for a purpose".'[23] His Lordship applied the above interpretation in relation to 'data' accessed through a computer, conceding that data are actually information recorded in a computer-readable form which can be made use of by the mere act of reading it and relaying its contents to a third party who is not supposed to read the data.

Lord Griffiths, in concurring with Lord Goff of Chieveley, observed that, once information is made public through a computer system, the only protection that the data reflecting that information have is through legislation such as the Data Protection Act and that the purpose of the offence created by Section 5(2) was essentially to protect the value and integrity of the information.[24]

If the *Brown* decision were to be applied to the general common law principles obtaining in the area of trade secrets, one could conclude incontrovertibly that the mere 'use' of a trade secret or, in other words, a mere disclosure of data information displayed on a computer screen by one to another, would constitute the exchange of that trade secret.

Notes

1 (1987) 21 C.P.C. (2d) 38 (Ont. HC).

2 Ibid., 43.
3 [1989] 3 All ER 373.
4 Ibid., 383–4.
5 510 F. 2d 894 (10th Cir. 1975).
6 See *DCF Systems Ltd.* v. *Gelman* (1978) 41 C.P.R. (2d) 145 (Ont. H.C.); *Gemologists International Inc.* v. *GemScan International Inc.* (1986) 7 C.I.P.R. 225 (Ont. H.C.); *Geac Canada Ltd.* v. *Prologic Computer Corp*, B.C.S.C. 6 A.C.W.S. (3d) 320, 1987; *Godin* v. *Gary Abraham Consultants Inc* (1986) 2 Q.A.C. 317 (Que C.A.); *Marque d'Or Inc* v. *Clayman* (1988) 21 C.P.R. (3d) 490 (Que S.C.); *Software Solutions Associates* v. *Depou* (1989) 25 C.P.R. (3d) (N.B. Q.B.).
7 See *Computer Workshops Ltd.* v. *Banner Capitol Market Brokers Ltd.* (1988) 64 O.R. (2d) 266 Ont. H.C.
8 [1988] 3 All ER 545 (HL).
9 [1916] 1 A.C. 688 (HL).
10 *Quantum Management Services Ltd.* v. *Hann* (1989) 25 C.P.R. (3d) 218 (Ont. H.C.).
11 952 F. 2d 769.
12 490 U.S. 730 (1989).
13 Berne Convention for the Protection of Literary and Artistic Works, 24 July 1971. See United Nations Treaty Series, vol. 828, 1977, no. 11850, New York.
14 For the details, see George Bittlingmayer (1988), 'Property Rights, Progress and the Aircraft Patent Agreement', *The Journal of Law and Economics*, XXXI(1), April, 227–48.
15 101 U.S. 99 (1879).
16 The Baker rule has been incorporated in section 102(b) of the Copyright Act of 1976, 17 U.S.C. which states: 'In no case does copyright protection for an original work of authorship extend to any idea, procedure, process, system, method of operation, concept, principle or discovery, regardless of the form in which it is described, explained, illustrated or embodied in such work.'
17 Although in *Motown Record Corp* v. *George A. Hormel & Co.*, 657 F. Supp. 1236 (D.C. Cal 1987) the court held that a song or musical composition could be considered under copyright since the original music sheet of that composition would have been under copyright, this may not be logical reasoning, since a song would be duplicated only if the same musical notes were prepared under the same musical arrangement as in the original composition.
18 648 F. Supp 1127 (N.D. Cal. 1986).
19 659 F. Supp 449 (N.D. Ga. 1987).
20 821 F. Supp 616 (N.D. Cal. 1993).
21 Ibid., 628.
22 (1996) A.C. 543 (HL).
23 Ibid., 548.
24 Ibid., 556.

8 Trademarks of the Airline Industry

Introduction

Branding is a major management tool in modern commercial marketing. Needless to say, commercial airlines rely heavily upon their trademarks, from the airline logo displayed at the back of the aircraft and the livery of the aircraft to the dress worn by the glamorous stewardess. Furthermore, as in every other competitive business, airlines have their own catch phrases for advertising their product, which have been the cornerstone of their business development. Since all trademarks used by airlines are distinctive, they have an inherent legal right to consider them exclusive and to bring an action in a common law court if any person were to copy their trademark or to introduce similarity with intent to confuse the consumer into believing a link to exist between the original trademark holder and the person who borrows the idea.

The extent to which common law courts would enforce trademark rights is clearly demonstrated in the 1992 decision of *Two Pesos, Inc.* v. *Taco Cabana Inc.*,[1] where the United States Court of Appeals for the Fifth Circuit held that a trade dress which is inherently distinctive is capable of identifying products or services as coming from a specific source. Although this case involved an operator of a Mexican restaurant who sued an operator of a similar chain of restaurants for introducing a dress for the staff which was similar to the former's staff dress, a distinct analogy can be drawn between the *Two Pesos* case and one that would involve an airline and another business enterprise faced with the same problem.

This chapter will examine the common law principles applicable to an airline's protection of its trademarks in the context of the international nature of business operations of the airline industry.

Trademarks

A trademark is defined in the United States as 'Any word, name, symbol or device or any combination thereof, adopted and used by a manufacturer or merchant to identify its goods and distinguish them from those manufactured or sold by others.'[2] A trademark serves the initial purpose of identifying the source or origin of goods or services, whether or not that source is familiar to the potential customer. It also symbolizes goodwill by identifying a particular characteristic to potential customers, thereby accomplishing the most important task of commercial enterprise – offering a warranty of quality.

In general terms, a trademark by its very nature goes to the root of the philosophy behind intellectual property, which is that intellectual property, of which trademarks is a species, is the product of human thinking and therefore cannot be restricted to parochial visual parameters. For example, a trademark, to be illegally used by one, need not necessarily be an identical reproduction. All that a trademark needs to have is what is known as 'secondary meaning' or any characteristic which is unique. In this sense, even a particular blend of colour, such as gold and green, would entitle the original user to protection under trademark law. In the 1995 decision of *Qualitex Co.* v. *Jacobson Products Co. Ltd.*,[3] the United States Court of Appeals for the Ninth Circuit held that a mere colour combination, if it reflects secondary meaning, would be protected under trademark law in the United States. In the *Qualitex* case, the petitioner Qualitex Company had for years coloured the dry cleaning press pads it manufactures with a special shade of green–gold. After respondent Jacobson Products (a Qualitex rival) began to use a similar shade on its own press pads, Qualitex registered its colour as a trademark and added a trademark infringement count to the suit it had previously filed challenging Jacobson's use of the green–gold colour. Qualitex won in the District Court, but the Ninth Circuit set aside the judgment on the infringement claim because, in its view, the Langham Trademark Act of 1946 which applied to this case did not permit registration of colour alone as a trademark.

On further appeal, The United States Supreme Court held that colour alone can meet the basic legal requirements for use as a trademark as is demonstrated both by the language of the Act, which describes the universe of things that can qualify as a trademark in the broadest of terms, and by the underlying principles of trademark law, including the requirements that the mark 'identify and distinguish [the seller's] goods … from those manufactured or sold by others and to indicate [their] source', and that it not be functional.[4] The Supreme Court further held that the District Court's findings (accepted by the Ninth Circuit and here undisputed) showed

Qualitex's green–gold colour had met these requirements. The court further held that the colour acted as a symbol, as customers would identify the colour with Qualitex. Therefore it was the court's view that the colour had developed secondary meaning.

A person using a trademark which is not registered is legally entitled under common law to stop another from using a confusing trademark with intent to pass off his goods or services as those of the user of the original trademark. Such an act would come within the purview of the tort of passing off,[5] which in essence prevents unfair competition by which one sells one's goods or services as being those of another supplier. The plaintiff, or person who alleges the tort, has to show that the defendant, or person who faces the civil suit, created actual confusion with the use of his trademark. The plaintiff has also to prove that he had built sufficient reputation in the market-place and that a regular customer would have been sufficiently confused by the defendant's act into believing that the defendant's product was actually that of the plaintiff.

The above principle could not, however, derogate the fact that a long term non-user of a registered trademark would be in jeopardy of losing its link with the person who registered such trademark. In the case of *Perfumes Nautee, Ltd.* v. *American Int'l Industries*,[6] decided in 1992, the Trademark Trial and Appeal Board held that the user of a trademark 'Naughty' for a perfume had lost his rights to the trademark owing to his non-user for two years, causing abandonment of the trademark. A subsequent purchase of the trademark in question by another trader was held to be valid and effectual at law.

In certain instances, criminal liability is imposed upon a person who may deface or alter a trademark. This has now become a common offence with the advent of the computer. For example, a person who defaces a trademark placed on the Internet by an airline would be found criminally liable, as in the 1985 Canadian Case of *R.* v. *Locquet*,[7] where the accused was convicted under Sections 406 to 412 of the Canadian Criminal Code for falsifying a trademark on a computer program.

Airlines would find it relevant that the most fundamental principle in trademark law is that mere creation of a trademark does not create a right towards it. The famous *Exxon* case[8] of 1981 established the seminal principle that only use, or its surrogates, that is, public recognition that a trademark relates to a person, or an intention by that person to use such trademark creates a valid legal right. The *Exxon* case also held that it is not the creator of the trademark who obtains the right but the person who registers the trademark as its user.

Once a trademark is registered and it is clear to the world that the person who registers it is already using it or intends to use it, the most significant factor which would apply towards the protection of the trademark is its use by another or, as is seen more often in commercial practice, the act of passing off, which was referred to earlier on in this chapter. The legal entitlement to a trademark would enable a person, in such an instance, to challenge the practice by another, on proof of the following:

1 a reputation or goodwill accruing to the holder of the trademark through a business name, work or other trading symbol;
2 a misrepresentation by the person who is passing off his goods or services as the trademark holder, calculated to confuse the customers as to the true identity of his product and thereby linking his product with that represented by the genuine trademark;
3 the cause of actual or likely damage to the trademark holder; and
4 public policy which would support a remedy against the act of passing off.

In addition to the above, the following characteristics of registration and passing off enable one to compare the two areas.

1 Passing off usually requires a symbol both to be used and to have gained a market reputation before protection can be claimed. By contrast, an application to register a mark can be filed well before use. Use must still be proved before registration, but no market reputation need normally be shown to derive from the use.
2 Passing off will protect a symbol only in the locality of its reputation. By contrast, a registration is usually Canada-wide. It can also be used as the basis for corresponding applications for similar protection in most other countries in the world.
3 Passing off requires proof that a defendant misrepresented its products, service or business as, or connected with, the plaintiff's. It also requires proof of consequential injury to the claimant's relations with those who do business with it (that is, its 'goodwill'). A registration, by contrast, may protect the mark for the whole range of goods or services for which it is registered, without proof of damage. The registrant can also stop the use of different, but confusingly similar, marks for different businesses, even if the defendant prominently disclaims any connection between the two businesses.
4 Passing off requires the plaintiff to prove the existence and extent of its reputation each time an action is brought. By contrast, a registration is, until expunged, presumed valid for Canada for all the wares and services for which it is registered. Protection continues, though the mark is little used or known.
5 Passing off does not prevent a mark's image from being diluted

> or tarnished. A misrepresentation of trade source must first still be shown, although this concept is sometimes stretched to breaking point. By contrast, a registration (controversially) directly protects a mark from any depreciation of its goodwill, even without any misrepresentation.

The tort of passing off may be maintainable even if a trademark holder's licence to hold such trademark is inoperable or has expired.

International Perspectives

Inasmuch as domestic jurisdiction is significant for a discussion on the subject of trademarks, so is international adjudication, if an overall perspective on the legal issues dealing with trademarks is to be obtained. Furthermore, the issue of internationality in trademark cases concerning airlines would be particularly relevant in instances where substantive ownership and effective control of such airlines would be vested in a state.[9]

The issue of dispute resolution in a commercial activity is addressed as a primary concern in the drafting of legal instruments relating to that activity. Transactions involving trade-related intellectual property rights (TRIPS) form a much evolved commercial process which stands today as one of the most prolific financial activities of the commercial world. It comes within the purview of the General Agreement on Tariffs and Trade (GATT) and it therefore owes its genesis to the Marrakesh Declaration of 15 April 1994, which heralded the conclusion of the Uruguay Round of Multilateral Trade Negotiations and established the WTO.[10] Therefore, although TRIPS has its own dispute settlement provisions under its own agreement under the WTO umbrella, the TRIPS dispute settlement mechanism may well end up within the WTO dispute settlement arena and, therefore, it would be useful to examine the overall WTO dispute resolution principles in this regard.

The WTO Dispute Settlement Principles

The Marrakesh Agreement (hereafter sometimes referred to as the Agreement) ushered in a new era of global economic cooperation, reflecting the widespread desire to operate in a fairer and more open multilateral trading system for the benefit and welfare of its member states.[11] A critical issue that emerged from this legal instrument was the function of the WTO as a forum for negotiations among its members concerning their multilateral trade relations in matters which are dealt with under the agreements in the annexes to the Agreement.

The WTO may also provide a forum for further negotiations among its members concerning their multilateral trade relations, and a framework for the implementation of the results of such negotiations, as may be decided by the Ministerial Conference.[12] The WTO also administers the Understanding on Rules and Procedures Governing the Settlement of Disputes (hereafter referred to as the Dispute Settlement Understanding or DSU) in Annex 2 to the Agreement.[13] Annex 2 to the Agreement, which addresses issues on dispute settlement and contains an Understanding on Rules and Procedures Governing the Settlement of Disputes, underscores the philosophy of dispute settlement reflected in the Agreement as being to strengthen the multilateral system of trade relations that the WTO represents. Article 23 of Annex 2 provides that, when members seek the redress of a violation of obligations or other nullification or impairment of benefits under the covered agreements or an impediment to the attainment of any objective of the covered agreements, they shall have recourse to, and abide by, the rules and procedures of the Understanding. In such cases, members are required to abstain from making a determination to the effect that a violation has occurred, that benefits have been nullified or impaired or that the attainment of any objective of the covered agreements has been impeded, except through recourse to dispute settlement in accordance with the rules and procedures of the Understanding.[14] Members are also required to follow the procedures set forth in Article 21, which call for prompt compliance with recommendations of the dispute settlement body, with particular attention being given to developing country members with respect to measures which are subject to dispute settlement. This measure has been taken to determine the reasonable period of time for the member concerned to implement the recommendations and rulings,[15] and follow the procedures set forth in Article 22. Article 22 provides for international conditions for compensation and the suspension of concessions, in order to determine the level of suspension of concessions or other obligations and obtain authorization from the dispute resolution body before suspending concessions or other obligations in response to the failure of the member concerned to implement the recommendations and rulings within that reasonable period of time.

There is also provision in Annex 2 for particular consideration to be given to a least developed country member in the dispute resolution process under the WTO umbrella. Members are required in this regard to exercise due restraint in raising matters under the procedures of the Marrakesh Agreement when a least developed country member is involved in a dispute. If nullification or impairment is found to result from a measure taken by a least developed country member, complaining parties should exercise due restraint in asking for compensation or seeking authorization to suspend the application of concessions or other obligations pursuant to procedures prescribed by the Agreement.[16]

As already indicated, Annex 2 of the Agreement contains principles relating to the Understanding on Rules and Procedures Governing the Settlement of Disputes. These principles have attempted to rectify some of the perceived inadequacies of the GATT system which prevailed prior to the adoption of the Marrakesh Agreement. Some reasons for dissatisfaction with the GATT procedures for dispute settlement[17] have been identified in the past as the lack of automatic access to panels, delays in appointing them, lack of terms of reference of panels, slow and inexpedient consideration of the cases owing to the lack of strict adherence to time limits for procedural discipline, an inadequate panel selection process, and poor-quality panel reports. Furthermore, the practice of GATT has been to focus more on conciliation and negotiated settlements rather than the recognition and enforcement of obligations. Under this system, recommendations were made only in instances where the parties were unable to reach a mutually acceptable solution to their dispute. The much needed practical implementation of recommendations and rulings of the GATT dispute resolution system and the absence of recourse to the losing party were not addressed in the GATT system. The early system of GATT dispute resolution was accused of lacking legalistic procedures which were formulated through a cohesive system of rules and more precise decisions which were taken on the merits of the disputes. GATT's preference for negotiated settlements – which were accused of favouring member countries with political and economic leverage over less able nations – has also been criticized. Instead, an adjudicative system has been recommended as the most expedient and fair manner in which the settlement of disputes could be effected through GATT. Some of the suggestions that were made for improving the GATT system were development of a mechanism for early warning; notification to the Council of mutually agreed solutions where any GATT member could address and raise matters relating to such solutions; provisions for approaching the Council direct and gaining access thereto; mediation by the Director General of GATT in certain circumstances; the establishment of panels by the Council within specified and strict time limits; the establishment of a group of legal experts devoted exclusively to dispute settlement; the standardization of terms of reference of panels; the establishment of and insistence on time limits on the work of panels and the examination of the findings of the panels by the Council; expansion of the role of the legal staff of the GATT Secretariat in dispute settlement; and a better quality government participation in the settlement process. It was also felt that there was a compelling need for a special and more favourable treatment to be accorded to developing countries, such treatment to include specialized legal aid, training courses and post-consultation review by the Council. As discussed above, the last concern was addressed by the Uruguay Round and provision has been for more favourable treatment to be given to least developed countries.

It is now evident that the careful consideration given by the Uruguay Round of Negotiations to the compelling issue of dispute resolution in multilateral trade has resulted in the Understanding as reflected in Annex 2 of the Agreement being structured in such a detailed manner. The rules and procedures of the Understanding apply to disputes brought pursuant to the consultation and dispute settlement provisions of the agreements (referred to in the Understanding as 'covered agreements') of which trade in civil aircraft is one.[18] The rules and procedures of the Understanding also apply to consultations and the settlement of disputes between members concerning their rights and obligations under the provisions of the Marrakesh Agreement which established the WTO.

The Dispute Settlement Body (DSB) which is established under the Council for Trade in Services, which are in turn established under the General Council of the WTO, was established to administer the rules and procedures in the Annex and, except as otherwise provided in a covered agreement, the consultation and dispute settlement provisions of the covered agreements. Accordingly, the DSB has the authority to establish panels, adopt panel and Appellate Body reports, maintain surveillance of implementation of rulings and recommendations, and authorize suspension of concessions and other obligations under the covered agreements.[19] The DSB is required to inform the relevant WTO councils and committees of any developments in disputes related to provisions of the respective covered agreements.[20] Under Article 3 of the Annex, members affirm their adherence to the principles of the management of disputes heretofore applied under Articles XXII and XXIII of GATT 1947, and the rules and procedures as further elaborated and modified in the Annex.[21] This means that, effectively, trade in civil aircraft and services related thereto would be governed by the initial structural format of the 1947 rules as amended. Emphasis is placed on the prompt settlement of situations in which a member considers that any benefits accruing to it directly or indirectly under the covered agreements are being impaired by measures taken by another member. The effective functioning of the WTO and the maintenance of a proper balance between the rights and obligations of members have been identified as critical in the dispute settlement process, which is required to be expedient.[22] Recommendations or rulings made by the DSB are calculated to aim at achieving a satisfactory settlement of the matter in accordance with the rights and obligations under the Understanding and under the covered agreements.[23] The Annex also insists that all solutions to matters formally raised under the consultation and dispute settlement provisions of the covered agreements are consistent with those agreements and that they should not nullify or impair benefits accruing to any member under those agreements, nor impede the attainment of any objective of those agreements.[24] Before bringing a case before the DSB, a member has to exercise judgment as to whether action under the procedures of the Agreement would be fruitful. Therefore a solution which is mutually acceptable to the parties to a dispute and consistent with the covered agreements is clearly preferred. In the absence of a mutually agreed solution, the first objective to be achieved under the agreement would be to secure the withdrawal of the measures concerned if these are considered to be inconsistent with the provisions of any of the covered agreements.[25] The Understanding further prescribes that the provision of compensation should be resorted to only if the immediate withdrawal of the measure is impracticable, and as a temporary measure pending the withdrawal of the measure which is so inconsistent.[26] An infringement of the obligations assumed under a covered agreement is prima facie considered to constitute a case of nullification or impairment. In such cases there is normally a presumption that a breach of the rules has an adverse impact on other members of that covered agreement and, in such instances, the member against whom the charge is laid is required to rebut the charge.[27]

One of the fundamental principles of the Understanding is that requests for conciliation and the use of the dispute resolution procedures should not be intended or considered as contentious acts. If a dispute arises, all members are required to be involved in the procedures in good faith in an effort to resolve the dispute. Furthermore, complaints and counter-complaints in regard to distinct matters should not be linked.[28]

The Understanding is applied only with respect to new requests for consultations under the consultation provisions of the covered agreements made on or after the date of entry into force of the Agreement. Developing member countries are given the benefit of invoking certain provisions of the Agreement that are calculated to be to their benefit, in instances where complaints or charges are brought by developing member countries under the rules of the Agreement.[29] If a request for consultations is made pursuant to a covered agreement, the member to whom the request is made is required to reply to the request within 10 days after the date of its receipt and to enter into consultation in good faith within a period of no more than 30 days after the date of receipt of such request, with a view to reaching a satisfactory solution, unless otherwise mutually agreed upon.[30] Consultations are confidential and held without prejudice to the rights of any member in any further proceedings.[31]

As discussed earlier, the WTO dispute settlement structure encourages conciliation and mediation under procedures that are undertaken voluntarily if the parties to the dispute so agree.[32] Any party to a dispute may, at any time, request good offices, conciliation and mediation. They may begin at any time and be terminated at any time. Once procedures for good offices, conciliation or mediation are terminated, a complaining party may then proceed towards the establishment of a panel. At the request of the complaining party, a panel is established under the Agreement at the latest at the DSB meeting following that at which the request first appears as an item on the agenda of the DSB, unless of course, the DSB decides not to establish a panel at its meeting.[33] A panel is composed of well-qualified governmental and/or non-governmental individuals, including persons who have served on or presented a case to a panel, who have served as a representative of a member or of a contracting party to GATT 1947, or as a representative to the Council or committee of any covered agreement or its predecessor agreement, or in the Secretariat, who have taught or published on international trade law or policy, or served as a senior trade policy official or member,[34] and they are selected in such as way as to ensure the independence of the members and to give the panel a diverse selection of individuals with a wide spectrum of experience and exposure.[35] To this end, the WTO Secretariat maintains an indicative list of governmental and non-governmental individuals possessing the qualifications to assist in the selection of panellists as required.[36]

The function of panels is to assist the DSB in discharging its responsibilities under the Understanding and the covered agreements. Accordingly, a panel is required to make an objective assessment of the matter before it.[37] While the reports of the panels are not considered by the DSB until 20 days after the date they are circulated to members,[38] objections of members to these reports have to be filed with the DSB at least 10 days prior to the DSB meeting that would discuss such objections.[39] The parties to a dispute have a right to participate in DSB hearings concerning their dispute. The reports are adopted by the DSB within 60 days after their circulation by a panel unless otherwise decided.[40]

For the purpose of hearing appeals from the dispute resolution process of panels, a standing Appellate Body is established by the DSB. Such body is composed of seven people, for a four-year term, three of whom will hear any one case. The Appellate Body comprises people of recognized authority, with demonstrated expertise in law, international trade and the subject matter of the covered agreements generally. They are not affiliated to any government and their membership is generally indicative of that of the WTO.

Where a panel or the Appellate Body concludes that a measure is inconsistent with a covered agreement, such body will recommend to the member concerned to bring the measure into conformity with the Agreement. In addition, the panel or Appellate Body may suggest ways in which the member concerned could implement the recommendations.[41] The time frame for a decision of the DSB to be taken conclusively is set as nine months from the date of establishment of the panel by the DSB until the DSB considers the report of the panel or Appellate Body for adoption.[42] Prompt compliance with the rulings or recommendations of the DSB is mandatory. Any member who is so obligated shall convey his intention to comply with such ruling or recommendation to the DSB at a meeting of the DSB held within 30 days after the adoption of the report of the panel or Appellate Body affecting such member.[43] A reasonable period of time is granted to a member who is unable to comply with such rules or recommendations.[44]

The TRIPS Dispute Settlement System

TRIPS has certainly introduced a new dimension to legal issues that may arise as a result of the exercise of intellectual property rights. The TRIPS Agreement, which is formally called the WTO Agreement on Trade-Related Aspects of Intellectual Property Rights, is the only agreement under the WTO umbrella which requires member states of the WTO to incorporate into their domestic legislation substantive legal matters of a complex nature, both for domestic and imported goods and services. The TRIPS Agreement makes copious cross-references to treaties other than the WTO and stipulates minimum standards applicable for the enforcement of the provisions of the Agreement. The Agreement also prescribes that any state may seek settlement of an allegation of inadequate implementation of the TRIPS Agreement by another state, by bringing its case before the WTO Dispute Settlement Body.

The TRIPS dispute settlement system operates on a codependent basis, by anchoring itself to the WTO Dispute Settlement Understanding.[45] While Article 64 of the TRIPS Agreement settles the issue of dispute settlement, Article 68 stipulates that the TRIPs Council shall provide assistance as requested by WTO members on dispute settlement, to the WTO Secretariat, Director General and its Secretariat with respect to dispute settlement panels and their compositor. The TRIPS Council has the authority, under this provision, to recommend experts to the panel as required.

The World Intellectual Property Organization (WIPO) which administers several multilateral conventions on intellectual property rights, has been included in the TRIPS Agreement to the extent that the Agreement carries several substantive provisions of WIPO treaties.[46] This notwithstanding, the WIPO Secretariat does not receive an automatic mandate to sit in on TRIPS adjudication panels, although it may render an interpretation of a state's observation or position on a dispute settlement issue relating to WIPO rules.

The TRIPS Agreement essentially carries rights for the acquiring and maintaining of intellectual property rights, guaranteeing them in the process. It also offers relief by way of prescribing effective means of enforcing such rights. However, the Agreement does not contain a guarantee of market access for goods developed through the intellectual property rights process, thereby raising a doubt as to whether the TRIPS Agreement could entertain complaints against violation of TRIPS under its Article 64.3.

Articles 20 and 21, on the use of trademarks, explicitly protects the rights holder of a trademark in furthering his rights under his trademark and therefore can be considered to be among the rare TRIPS provisions which may offer relief in dispute settlement.

Notes

1 505 U.S. 763 (1992). See also *Laureyssens* v. *Idea Group, Inc.*, 964 F. 2d 131 (1992). In the case of *George Basch Co., Inc.* v. *Blue Coral Inc.*, 968 F. 2d 1532 (1992) the United States Court of Appeals in the Second Circuit held that, in order to be awarded compensation, a plaintiff has a legal obligation to establish that the defendant engaged in wilful deception.

2 15 U.S.C. s. 1121. The North American Free Trade Agreement (NAFTA) definition encompasses 'any sign or any combination of signs … including personal names, designs, letters, numerals, colours and figurative elements' (NAFTA, 12 December 1992; also Ottawa: Supply and Services, 1993) at Article 1708(1). The case of *Pizza Pizza Ltd.* v. *Canada (Registrar of Trade Marks)* [1989] 3 F.C. 379 (C.A.) established that even a phone number could be a trademark.

3 Case No. 93-1577, argued on 9 January 1995 and decided on 25 March 1995. See also *Cooper Industries* v. *Channellock, Inc.*, 788 F. Supp 873 (1992). The Canadian case of *Smith, Kline & French Canada Ltd.* v. *Registrar of Trade Marks* (No. 2) [1987] 2 F.C. 633 (TD) is also a good analogy for a colour being established as a trademark. In this case the medical drug *Tagamet* was found to be identifiable by its pale green colour as its trademark.

4 *Inwood Laboratories, Inc.* v. *Ives Laboratories, Inc.*, 456 U.S. 844, at 850.

5 See *Enterprise Rent-A-Car Co.* v. *Singer* (1996), 66 C.P.R. (3d) 453 (F.C.T.D.). See also *Consumers Distributing Company Limited* v. *Seiko Time Canada Ltd.* [1984] 1 S.C.R. 583 [*Seiko*], where adequate notice posted to buyers at the point of sale regarding the differences in services offered with a product precluded a finding of passing off; and George S. Takach, 'Passing-Off, Trade Mark Protection and Parallel Imports After *Consumers Distributing* v. *Seiko*' (1985) *Canadian Bar Review*, 63, 645. The *Seiko* case may be of important precedential value to certain suppliers in the computer industry.

6 22 U.S. P.Q. 2d 1306 (TTAB 1992).

7 (1985) S.C.P.R. (3d) 173.

8 *Exxon Corp.* v. *Exxon Insurance Consultants International Limited* (1981) 119 (C.A.).

9 The Convention on International Civil Aviation provides that an aircraft shall bear the nationality of the state in which it is registered. See Convention on International Civil Aviation, signed on 7 December 1944, ICAO Doc. 7300/7, 7th edn, 1997, Article 17. Most bilateral air services agreements signed between states for the operation of air services between their territories still contain a provision that substantial ownership and effective control must be vested in the state, if such were to be considered that state's national airline for the purpose.

10 The WTO comprises a Ministerial Conference composed of representatives of all member countries and meets at least once every two years. The Ministerial Conference carries out the functions of the WTO and takes necessary action to this effect. There is also, within the WTO structure, a General Council composed of representatives of all member countries and this Council meets as deemed appropriate. As necessary, the General Council conducts the functions of the Ministerial Conference when the latter does not meet. It also carries out its functions as assigned by the Agreement. Furthermore, the General Council also discharges the responsibilities of the Dispute Settlement Body (DSB) under the Dispute Settlement Understanding (DSU). The Dispute Settlement Body may have its own chairman and shall establish such rules of procedure as it deems necessary for the fulfilment of those responsibilities. See Marrakesh Agreement, *infra*, n.11, Article IV 1,2 and 3.

11 Marrakesh Declaration of 15 April 1994, para. 2. The Marrakesh Agreement came into being with the Marrakesh Declaration and is therefore an integral part of the Marrakesh Declaration. See *The Results of the Uruguay Round of Multilateral Trade Negotiations, The Legal Texts*, Geneva: GATT Secretariat, 1994, for the text of the Declaration.

12 Marrakesh Declaration, Article III.2. The Ministerial Conference is composed of representatives of all members, which meets at least once every two years. The Conference carries out the functions of the WTO and takes action necessary to this effect. The Ministerial Conference also has the authority to take decisions on all matters under any multilateral trade agreements if so requested by a member, in accordance with the specific requirements for decision making in the Marrakesh Agreement and in the relevant multilateral trade agreement. See ibid., Article IV.1.

13 Ibid., Article III.3. Annex 2 to the Agreement will be discussed in some detail below.

14 Annex 2, Article 23(a).

15 Annex 2, Article 23(b).

16 Ibid., Article 24.1.

17 See K.R. Symonds and B.H. Hill (1988), *Law and Practice Under GATT*, W.J. Davey (1987), 'Dispute Settlement in GATT', *Fordham International Law Journal*, 11, 51; R.E. Hudec (1975), *The GATT Legal System and World Trade Diplomacy*; R.E. Hudec (1978), *Adjudication of International Trade Disputes*; R.E. Hudec (1980), 'GATT Dispute Settlement After Tokyo Round: An Unfinished Business', *Cornell International Law Journal*, 13, 145. See also J.C. Bliss (1987), 'GATT Dispute Settlement Reform in the Uruguay Round: Problems and Prospects', *Stanford Journal of International Law*, 31; E. McGovern (1986), *International Trade Regulation: GATT, the United States and The European Community*, Geneva: GATT; K Dam (1970), *The GATT: Law and International Economic Organization*, Geneva: GATT.

18 Marrakesh Declaration (*supra*, n.11), Appendix 1 to Annex 2.

19 Annex 2, Article 2.1.

20 Annex 2, Article 2.2.

21 Annex 2, Article 3.2.
22 Annex 2, Article 3.3.
23 Annex 2, Article 3.4.
24 Annex 2, Article 3.5.
25 Annex 2, Article 3.7.
26 Ibid.
27 Annex 2, Article 3.8.
28 Annex 2, Article 3.10.
29 Annex 2, Article 3.12.
30 Annex 2, Article 4.3.
31 Annex 2, Article 4.6.
32 Annex 2, Article 5.1.
33 Annex 2, Article 6.1.
34 Annex 2, Article 8.1.
35 Annex 2, Article 8.2.
36 Annex 2, Article 8.4.
37 Annex 2, Article 11.
38 Annex 2, Article 16.1.
39 Annex 2, Article 16.2.
40 Annex 2, Article 16.4.
41 Annex 2, Article 19.1.
42 Annex 2, Article 20.
43 Annex 2, Article 21.
44 Ibid.
45 See Article I, para. I of the WTO Dispute Settlement Understanding.
46 See TRIPS Agreement, Articles 1–5, 9, 10, 14–16, 22, 35 and 39.

9 Carriage of Inadmissible Passengers and Refugees

Introduction

At the 32nd Session of the Assembly of the International Civil Aviation Organization, held in Montreal from 22 September to 2 October 1998, the Assembly addressed a claim by the International Transport Workers' Federation (ITF), that states faced a genuine dilemma between their rights to protect their borders against passport fraud and other crimes and their obligations to protect rights of asylum seekers who were often unable to produce travel documents. The question arises whether a genuine refugee, fleeing for his life from a country which no longer offers him protection, is always in a position to collect the proper documentation to leave the country. The ITF claimed: 'It is well established that it is unreasonable to demand that refugees have proper documentation. These carrier liability laws have the effect of obstructing people genuinely at risk from arriving in a safe country and seeking protection as a refugee.'[1] ITF claimed that carrier liability laws, imposed by states in order to discourage the carriage by air of spurious claimants for refugee status in their territories, posed serious problems for the carrier who wished to avoid fines imposed by the authorities. One desperate measure cited by ITF as being adopted by carriers to circumvent this difficulty is the requirement imposed by carriers on their check-in staff to make decisions on the legality of passenger documentation.[2]

Through the paper on this subject submitted by ITF to the ICAO Assembly, ITF requested that the appropriate ICAO body consult the United Nations High Commissioner for Refugees on these matters and also reminded ICAO member states of their obligations under the 1951 Refugee Convention relating to the Status of Refugees and

Annex 9 to the Chicago Convention. The Assembly of ICAO agreed to refer these proposals to the ICAO Council with a view to possible consideration by the Facilitation Panel of ICAO, set up by the Organization to make recommendations to the ICAO Council on issues affecting the facilitation of air transport.

This chapter will examine the legal and regulatory regime applicable to inadmissible persons and refugees with a view to determining airline liability for their carriage, and state responsibility for accepting them into their territories.

Inadmissible Persons and Refugees

An inadmissible person is defined at air law as 'a person who is or will be refused admission to a State by its authorities'.[3] A refugee, on the other hand, is generally a person who has his origin in a country which no longer offers him protection. The Convention relating to the Status of Refugees signed at Geneva on 28 July 1951[4] provides, in Article 1, that the term 'refugee' shall apply inclusively, both in a pre-Second World War, and postwar sense to 14 categories of persons.[5] When viewed *ex facie*, the two definitions are seemingly mutually exclusive, in that a refugee is a person who ipso facto has a right under the 1951 Convention to be accepted into the country of asylum, whereas an inadmissible person is refused admission by a country perforce for non-conformance with that country's immigration regulations. Unfortunately, however, the distinction is blurred in instances where persons claiming to be refugees are not considered as such by the country concerned and are therefore categorized as inadmissible passengers. In many instances, the countries refusing admission to persons arriving by air and claiming refugee status are found to be justified in refusing admission to such persons who are found to be *mala fide*.

In the recent past, the international community has witnessed an exponential growth in the number of refugees (asylum seekers) arriving by air. When such persons fail to produce documents of identification satisfactory to the immigration authorities, they are classified as inadmissible persons and sent back on the carrier which brought them. Invariably, the carrier is required in addition to pay a fine (or 'administration fee' as it is sometimes referred to) to the country refusing admission to the person carried in.

Inadmissible Persons

The Chicago Convention of 1944,[6] in its Article 13, provides that the laws and regulations of a contracting state with regard to the admission to or departure from such state of passengers, crew or cargo of aircraft, in relation to their entry, clearance, immigration, passports, customs and quarantine, should be complied with by or on behalf of such passengers, crew or cargo, upon entrance into or departure from, or while within the territory of that state. This provision prima facie imposes a legal duty on the airline passenger concerned to comply with the legislation of the country he is attempting to enter, presumably by ensuring inter alia that he carries all necessary legal documentation to enter that country. The provision also carries the implied requirement that, if the passenger fails to comply with such laws, they should be complied with on behalf of the passenger. By this, Article 13 of the Chicago Convention, without explicitly stating that it is the airline's responsibility to ensure, on behalf of the passenger, compliance with laws of the country of arrival, imputes to the airline that responsibility. Of course, one can argue that, in the absence of explicit mention in the provision, the airline is not responsible for ensuring that a passenger is admissible in the country to which it carries that passenger, particularly since the Chicago Convention is a treaty establishing the obligation of states towards each other. Therefore, logically, it may be arguable that, when Article 13 uses the words 'on behalf of', it may well be applicable to the duty devolving upon the authorities of the state in which the person embarked on his flight.

Annex 9 to the Chicago Convention, on facilitation of air transport, dedicates Section E of its Chapter 3 to inadmissible persons carried by air. The Annex provides that the operator (airline) which carries a passenger to a country shall be responsible for the custody and care of passengers and crew until they are accepted for examination for the purposes of immigration,[7] which that country is obligated to do without unreasonable delay.[8] The authorities take responsibility for such passengers and crew once they are so accepted for examination, until a determination is made whether they are admissible to the country or not.[9] A person found inadmissible is required to be handed over by the authorities who find him so inadmissible to the operator (airline) who brought him in.[10] The airline is then responsible for taking the person back to his country of origin (where he commenced his flight) or to any other place which accepts him.[11]

The Annex casts a burden on a state in which a person has stayed for a period of time (not merely in transit) prior to his landing in another state which finds him inadmissible, to accept such person for examination, subject to the fact that, by doing so, the state which accepts the person for examination does not jeopardize his life or freedom.[12] Perhaps the most relevant provision of Annex 9 to the question at issue is Standard 3.40.1, which stipulates: 'Contracting States shall not fine operators in the event that passengers are found inadmissible unless there is evidence to suggest that the carrier was negligent in taking precautions to the end that passengers complied with the documentary requirements for entry into the receiving State.' There is also the provision that contracting states and operators shall cooperate, where practicable, in establishing the validity and authenticity of passports and visas,[13] with a recommendation that, where operators cooperate with the control authorities to the satisfaction of those authorities, contracting states should mitigate fines and penalties that might otherwise be applicable to the operators for inadmissible passengers carried to those states.[14]

A strict interpretation of regulatory provisions on air carrier liability for the carriage of inadmissible persons seems to suggest that there is no prima facie presumption of guilt on the airline. On the contrary, Article 13 of the Chicago Convention, which is strictly an international treaty containing provisions setting out legal obligations between states, provides that applicable laws have to be complied with by the passenger, *or on behalf of the passenger* (my emphasis), which may be interpreted as saying that state authorities, such as customs and immigration or consular authorities, would have a greater burden of ensuring compliance with Article 13 than the airlines.

A fortiori, Annex 9, by Standard 3.40.1, explicitly requires that, in the absence of evidence of the carrier's negligence, the carrier shall not be fined. Although the linkage between the Convention and Annex is at times doubted, in view of the Statement in Article 54(l) in the Convention that the annexes to the Convention are so named for convenience, nonetheless it is an incontrovertible fact that Annex 9 derives its authority from the Convention and therefore is an integral part of it. Standard 3.40.1, which has been developed by the Council of ICAO with the approval of ICAO member states, is therefore international in scope and not diminished in its legal authority, but rather acts as an explanatory note to Article 13 of the Convention.[15]

The security and integrity of the passport,[16] which is usually recognized as the fundamental legal document of travel between countries, becomes a critical issue in the determination of liability. The passport carries details of a person's identity, country of citizenship and entitlement to travel privileges. Above all, and in the context of inadmissible passengers, the passport would serve as assurance to the country in which a person is found inadmissible that he can return to the country which issued the passport.

Unless otherwise specified, a passport remains the property of the state of issue, and therefore misuse or destruction of a passport becomes an infringement of law against that state. Conversely, a grave responsibility devolves upon states to ensure that their property is secure from such misuse or fraud – particularly the commonest known abuse or fraud in the nature of forgery. The use of forged or counterfeit passports, the use of valid passports by imposters and the misuse of valid passports by their rightful owners in the perpetration of an offence are some of the common ways in which passport fraud is perpetrated today.[17]

At its 32nd Session, held in Montreal between 22 September and 2 October 1998, the ICAO Assembly adopted a resolution which requests the Council of ICAO to study specific actions and measures for enhancing the effectiveness of controls on passport fraud, including the possible preparation of necessary Standards and Recommended Practices (SARPs) and guidance material, to be implemented by contracting states in the interests of maintaining the integrity and security of passports and other travel documents. The resolution also calls upon all contracting states to intensify their efforts to safeguard the security and integrity of their passports, to protect their passports against passport fraud, and to assist one another in these matters.[18]

The United Nations General Assembly, at its 85th Plenary Meeting in December 1993, adopted a resolution[19] concerning the prevention of smuggling of aliens, wherein the General Assembly condemned the practice of smuggling aliens in violation of national and international law, and, inter alia, requested states that had not done so to make special efforts to prevent their airports, means of ground transport and air carriers from being used by smugglers of aliens. The resolution also requested the relevant specialized agencies (ICAO being mentioned as one) to consider ways and means, within their respective spheres of competence, to enhance international cooperation to combat the smuggling of aliens.

In a subsequent (1997) resolution,[20] the United Nations General Assembly, at its 51st session, inter alia, recognized that international criminal groups often convinced individuals to migrate illegally by various means for enormous profits and that socioeconomic factors influenced the problem of the smuggling of aliens and also contributed to the complexity of current international migration. The Assembly requested states to cooperate bilaterally and on a multilateral basis to prevent the use of fraudulent documents and reaffirmed the need to fully observe international and national law in dealing with the smuggling of aliens, including the provision of humane treatment and strict observance of all human rights of migrants.

Judicial Decisions

The pre-eminent responsibility of the passenger to ensure he holds valid travel documents was upheld and recognized by a US court in 1991, which held that the provisions of tariffs filed by an air carrier with the Department of Transportation (DoT) constituted a binding contract between the air carrier and the passenger, even if the passenger was unaware of the tariff provisions.[21] An earlier case[22] had set the precedent that the tariff provisions were seminal in establishing the contractual nexus between the airline and the passenger.

In the 1995 case of *Diaz Aguasviva* v. *Iberia Lineas Aereas de Espana*,[23] a federal Puerto Rican trial court asserted that filing of applicable tariff provisions by the airline with the DoT effectively precluded any possibility of the passenger imposing contractual liability on the part of the carrier for failing to advise a passenger of the requirement to carry appropriate travel documents. The court held:

> The passenger shall comply with all laws, regulations, orders, demands or travel requirements of the countries to be flown from, into or over ... the carrier shall not be liable for any aid or information given by any agent or employer of the carrier in connection with obtaining the necessary documents ... or for the consequences to any passenger resulting from his failure to obtain such documents.[24]

The tariff provisions were held, however, to be applicable to establishing the liability of the passenger for the carriage of proper documentation with him, and not to obviate the airline's tortious liability with regard to claims of false arrest, false imprisonment, defamation, assault and negligence based on alleged failure on the part of the carrier to assist the passenger.

In 1995, the United States Court of Appeals for the Second Circuit affirmed that air carriers are not responsible for the detention costs of excludable aliens who arrive in the United States on the basis that they are in transit to another country and apply for asylum upon arrival. In the case of *Linea Area Nacional de Chile, S.A.* v. *Meissner*,[25] some passengers on board a flight transiting through the United States requested political asylum and the Immigration and Naturalization Services (INS) of the United States ordered the airline to assume physical and financial responsibility for the passengers pending the determination of their applications. The INS acted on longstanding practice, where the carrier usually is required to assume responsibility for inadmissible passengers. The passengers, who held valid documentation to their ultimate destination, had thereupon been accommodated by the carrier in a hotel with a 24-hour armed guard. The passengers' lodging, food and medical services were all paid for by the carrier.

The court awarded full compensation for the carrier, on the basis that the passengers were 'excludable aliens' who had fraudulently misrepresented material facts to the carrier. The court in this instance professed that the absence of negligence on the part of the carrier, and the attendant burden of detaining excludable aliens on the part of INS, clearly established that it was not the responsibility of the carrier to pay pecuniary charges for inadmissible passengers which was the real responsibility of the immigration authorities. The court, however, distinguished excludable aliens from stowaways, whose presence in an aircraft would impute to the carrier knowledge of such presence, on the basis of negligence to discover such passengers and eject them from the flight prior to take-off.[26] In such an instance where the airline ought to have known of the stowaway, a penalty is imposed by INS, as a penal sanction rather than as coverage for administration costs involved in the application for asylum made by the stowaway. The courts have held:

> This penalty is clearly designed as a sanction for carriers who fail to detain or deport a stowaway and has nothing to do with the cost of detention of stowaways who are properly detained pending a hearing ... As a result, the availability of this fine does not relieve the airline of its statutory responsibility ... to bear the full maintenance costs associated with the detention of excluded stowaways.[27]

American courts have also held that information given to immigration authorities by the captain of an aircraft upon landing, about a passenger of his flight if such information is bona fide, cannot give rise to liability of the airline where the passenger is arrested and detained by the authorities. In *Curley* v. *American Airlines Inc.*,[28] the captain informed his ground crew that a passenger on board his flight was suspected of having smoked marijuana in the aircraft lavatory during descent. When the aircraft landed at its destination – Puerto Vallarta, Mexico – the ground crew informed the Mexican customs authorities who detained the passenger and strip-searched him. The passenger alleged that, during the process of the search, he was threatened, his body was touched by loaded firearms, he was verbally humiliated, his teeth and gums were scraped and various other humiliating and demeaning tests were performed on him.

The court, in determining the alleged liability of the airline, found that the action of the captain, whether or not it disseminated false information, did not entail the liability of the airline.

> In the case at bar, the captain's passing on to ground personnel accurate or inaccurate information concerning a passenger's smoking liability certainly has no relation to any rates or routes nor does it refer to services normally expected of flight personnel. It seems to come squarely within the exception ... which affects airline services in 'too tenuous, remote or peripheral a manner to have any pre-emptive effect'.[29]

In addition to the above instances of adjudication, there have been several instances of litigation in the United States and the United

Kingdom, specifically on the subject of whether airlines which bring in inadmissible persons to their territories are legally liable. These cases have indeed set the policy on the subject in these jurisdictions.

In the United States, there has been a spate of adjudication in the past decade, which commenced with the fundamental question as to whether airlines were legally bound to keep in their custody, at their expense, stowaways and transit passengers, whom the airlines concerned carried into the United States and who sought asylum therein, until they were sent back. In the 1992 case of *Air Transport Association* v. *Reno*,[30] all domestic airlines challenged this requirement, which was imposed by the INS of the United States. Although initial judgment was awarded to the INS, the airlines triumphed in getting the rule set aside in 1994.[31] This decision, called the *Lan-Chile* decision, also held that monies collected under the 1986 User Fee Statute should be allocated inter alia to the Attorney General in order that she defrays the costs incurred by her office in the pre-inspection, inspection, detention and deportation of aliens.[32] The court also held that the 1986 law stipulated in a compelling manner that the air carrier bringing in aliens who were subsequently judged by the INS as not eligible to enter the country was responsible for such persons only so long as it was necessary to ensure 'such immediate and continuous transit through, and departure from, the United States'.[33] The court consequently ordered that the INS reimburse *Lan-Chile*, with interest, for the cost of the detention.[34]

On the subject of stowaways, where the *cursus curiae*[35] had already established that airlines cannot be reimbursed for costs incurred in the detention of stowaways by the airline, the *Lan-Chile* court differed from the established principle and held with the airline that it was entitled to equitable relief (and not monetary relief per se), which had hitherto been refused by the the courts on their interpretation of the applicable rules and regulations. The *Lan-Chile* court, in interpreting the word 'entitlement' contained in the User Fee Act, held that such entitlement should be the carrier's for expenses incurred by the carrier in detaining the stowaways in their custody while the authorities processed their asylum claims.[36] This reasoning was found to be acceptable to several other courts whose decisions followed immediately.[37]

The position taken by the US authorities in respect of asylum seekers who destroy their travel documents during the course of the journey before they come into the place in which they seek asylum has been to generally require reasonable diligence on the part of the carrier concerned, while strictly eschewing the application of strict liability on the airline.[38]

The United Kingdom, like the United States, Canada, Australia and Germany, has enacted legislation[39] which admits of imposing fines on a carrier which brings inadmissible persons to the country. In 1993, this law was extended to impose fines on an air carrier for bringing in persons without transit visas where they were required. It is worthy of note that the UK law sits somewhat alone in requiring stringent checks on passengers, in the face of more liberal approaches in the European Union (EU) which has established a single market in goods, capital and labour, and the liberal movement of labour within the European Economic Area, between the European Union and the European Free Trade Agreement (EFTA) member states, a practice which has been allowed since 1994. In addition, the zone of free movement established by the Schengen states admits of the free movement of persons and goods between the Schengen states.[40]

Also the Immigration (Carriers' Liability) Act of 1987 (the Act) does not acknowledge the rights of refugees fleeing from persecution, although it is claimed that the United Kingdom has obligations at international law in this regard.[41] However, the British immigration authorities have made very positive progress towards assisting airlines in their checking procedures in order for the airlines to avoid fines being imposed upon them for carrying spurious persons with falsified or no documents into the United Kingdom.

British courts have held that the Act is consistent with established norms of public international law which does not address and never intended to address persons who have not arrived in the United Kingdom, even if they have already left the country from which they hope to flee, and even if it were to result in such persons being compelled by a third country to return to the country from which they fled.[42]

It is interesting to note that the position in Germany with respect to the liability of the carrier on this subject would be made clear some time in 1999 or 2000, when the Federal Supreme Court is expected to rule whether airports in Germany should be reimbursed by airlines with costs incurred in the detention of inadmissible passengers brought by them into Germany.[43]

Refugees

At its 30th Plenary Meeting on 12 February 1946, the United Nations General Assembly adopted Resolution A/8(1),[44] which recognized that the problem of refugees and displaced persons of all categories was one of immediate urgency. The resolution went on to mark a clear distinction between genuine refugees and displaced persons, on the one hand, and war criminals, quislings and criminals, and others, who may claim to be refugees. Recognizing that the problem of refugees and displaced persons was an international one, the General Assembly recommended to the Economic and Social Council

(ECOSOC) of the United Nations that the Council recognize the principle that no refugees or displaced persons who have finally and definitely, in complete freedom, and after receiving full knowledge and facts, including adequate information from the governments of their countries of origin, expressed valid objections to returning to their countries of origin, shall be compelled to return to their country of origin. By this pronouncement Resolution A/8(1) became the first ever official international recognition that a genuine refugee could not be compelled to return to his country of origin.

Resolution A/8(1) also called upon the ECOSOC to establish a special committee for the purpose of carrying out promptly the preparation of a report on the subject of refugees and displaced persons for submission to the General Assembly.[45] In accordance with the recommendations of the special committee, the General Assembly, at its second session held in the latter part of 1946, established the International Refugee Organization (IRO) to succeed the existing international organizations[46] engaged in assisting and repatriating refugees, displaced persons and prisoners-of-war, of whom there were, initially, some 21 million scattered throughout Europe. The tasks of the IRO were mainly the protection and resettlement of 1 620 000 persons who were reluctant to return to their homelands either because they had lost all ties there or because of a well-founded fear of persecution.

The IRO was intended as a temporary specialized agency of the United Nations whose primary objective was to seek solutions to the problems of refugees and displaced persons still living in camps, mostly in Austria, Germany and Italy. Like the United Nations Relief and Rehabilitation Administration (UNRRA), it was essentially a field agency conducting its own assistance activities with the help and support of local authorities and voluntary agencies. However, it quickly became clear that the refugee problem was not a temporary phenomenon and that some further organized international effort would have to be made. The member states of the IRO[47] considered it appropriate that the responsibility for refugees should be taken over by the United Nations itself. Their main considerations were that the time had come for all member states of the United Nations to share the expenditure involved in aid to refugees, and that, since conditions had improved in many reception countries, the United Nations was in a better position to provide refugees with the necessary assistance.

In 1949, when the United Nations decided to assume more direct responsibility for international action in favour of refugees, upon the demise of the IRO, two possibilities were open to the Assembly: either to entrust this task to a department of the United Nations Secretariat, or to establish, within the administrative and financial framework of the United Nations, an ad hoc body capable of acting independently. On the proposal of the Secretary-General, the latter formula was adopted. In adopting it, the General Assembly felt that it was preferable for the future body to remain as far as possible outside the political considerations with which the United Nations Secretariat had to deal. It also felt that a United Nations High Commissioner for Refugees would have the independence, authority and prestige required to enable him to intervene with governments, especially in the task of ensuring the international protection of refugees.

The Office of the United Nations High Commissioner for Refugees (UNHCR) was set up on 1 January 1951 for a period of three years in accordance with General Assembly resolutions 319(IV) of 3 December 1949 and 428(V) of 14 December 1950. The Office was established as a subsidiary organ of the General Assembly, under Article 22 of the Charter, on a basis similar to that of other programmes of the United Nations, such as UNICEF and UNDP. It soon became clear that refugee problems required the continued attention of the United Nations; thus the General Assembly decided to prolong UNHCR's mandate for a period of five years, renewable, beginning on 1 January 1954. At its 42nd session, the Assembly adopted resolution 42/108 by which the Office was continued for a further five-year period from 1 January 1989 to 31 December 1993.

Under paragraph 13 of UNHCR's Statute, the High Commissioner is elected by the General Assembly on the nomination of the Secretary-General. Under the terms of Chapter I of the Statute, the High Commissioner acts under the authority of the General Assembly and follows policy directives given to him by the Assembly and ECOSOC. He also reports to the Executive Committee of the High Commissioner's Programme. Paragraph 2 of the Statute declares: 'The work of the High Commissioner shall be of an entirely non-political character; it shall be humanitarian and social and shall relate, as a rule, to groups and categories of refugees.' Its universal nature is reflected in the fact that UNHCR is called on to protect refugees whoever[48] and wherever they may be. In order to fulfil his or her worldwide responsibilities, the High Commissioner is represented by some 90 representatives, including nine regional representatives, accredited to over 120 countries.

Persons of concern to UNHCR are those defined as refugees under the Statute annexed to General Assembly Resolution 428(V) of 14 December 1950, as well as persons whom UNHCR may be called upon to assist, mainly through the provision of material assistance, pursuant to resolutions adopted by the General Assembly and ECOSOC. Under the terms of paragraphs 6 and 7 of the Statute, a refugee falling within the mandate of UNHCR is defined as:

> Any person who, owing to well-founded fear of being persecuted for reasons of race, religion, nationality, or political opinion, is outside the country of his nationality and is unable or, owing to such fear or for reasons other than personal convenience, is unwilling to avail himself of the protection of that country; or who, not having a nationality and being outside the country of his former habitual residence, is unable or, owing to such fear or for reasons other than personal convenience, is unwilling to return to it.

The emergence of new and large-scale problems of refugees, notably outside Europe, led governments to adopt a more flexible interpretation of the criteria to be applied by UNHCR, especially with regard to uprooted persons qualifying for material assistance. Resolutions adopted by the General Assembly and ECOSOC[49] have requested the High Commissioner to assist specific groups of refugees and displaced persons of a particular origin or located in a particular area. UNHCR has thus provided emergency relief and other forms of material assistance to uprooted persons for whom individual determination of refugee status would be impracticable on account of such factors as the size of the group, its rapid rate of influx and the urgency of its needs.

Some of the above-mentioned resolutions also call upon the High Commissioner to concern himself with displaced persons, often within the framework of United Nations humanitarian endeavours for which his Office may have particular expertise. He may participate in such endeavours with other United Nations agencies, as required, at the invitation of the Secretary-General or the General Assembly. UNHCR can be authorized to act on behalf of persons who are displaced as a result of man-made disasters and who are in a situation analogous to that of refugees. In other instances, UNHCR is called upon to assist persons displaced within their own country. This is the case, for example, when assistance to reintegrate into their countries of origin is provided to refugees who return home. Such measures may be equally necessary for internally displaced persons returning to their homes after independence or the cessation of hostilities.

The protection of refugees and the seeking of durable solutions to their problems are the two main functions of UNHCR. This is reflected in the wording of the first sentence of paragraph 1 of the Statute which states:

> The United Nations High Commissioner for Refugees acting under the authority of the General Assembly shall assume the function of providing international protection, under the auspices of the United Nations, to refugees who fall within the scope of the present Statute and of seeking permanent solutions for the problem of refugees.

In discharging the first function, UNHCR seeks to promote the adoption of international standards for the treatment of refugees and the effective implementation of these standards in such fields as employment, education, residence, freedom of movement and safeguard against being returned to a country where a refugee may have reason to fear persecution. In discharging its second function, UNHCR seeks to facilitate the voluntary repatriation of refugees, or, where this is not feasible, to assist governments of countries of asylum to enable the refugees to become self-supporting as rapidly as possible. UNHCR has a major role in coordinating aid to refugees. Except in special circumstances, its material assistance activities are conducted through national or local authorities of the country concerned, other organizations of the United Nations system, non-governmental organizations or private technical agencies.

The legal basis for the protection function carried out by UNHCR is contained in paragraph 1 of the Statute. In the exercise of this function, UNHCR seeks in particular

- to promote accessions to the basic international instruments relating to refugees and to ensure that the standards defined in these instruments are effectively implemented through the adoption of legislative and/or administrative measures at national level;
- to ensure that refugees are treated in accordance with recognized international standards and receive an appropriate legal status and, in their country of durable asylum, are placed as far as possible on the same footing as nationals of that country in so far as economic and social rights are concerned so that their local integration may be facilitated;
- to promote the granting of asylum to refugees and to ensure that refugees are not forcibly returned to a country where they have reason to fear persecution (*non-refoulement*);
- to ensure that applications for asylum by persons claiming to be refugees are examined within the framework of appropriate procedures and that, while their requests are being examined, asylum seekers are protected against forcible return to a country where they have reason to fear persecution;
- to promote a wider knowledge and understanding at the universal and regional levels of the recognized international principles for the treatment of refugees;
- to help refugees to cease being refugees either through voluntary repatriation to their countries of origin or, if this is not feasible, through the eventual acquisition of the nationality of their country of residence.

In a number of situations, the personal security of refugees and asylum seekers has been seriously threatened or infringed through physical violence, acts of piracy or abusive detention. Efforts to ensure that refugees are safeguarded against action of this kind have assumed increasing importance for UNHCR.

A further important aspect of UNHCR's protection function consists of efforts to promote the reunification of separated refugee families. The reunification of the family members of refugees, who may still be in the country of origin or who are in a country of asylum and who wish to join the head of the family in a resettlement country, is clearly in keeping with the purely humanitarian and social character of UNHCR's activities. It has been the subject of numerous recommendations by the Executive Committee of the High Commissioner's Programme and was already highlighted in section IV.B. of the Final Act of the United Nations Conference of Plenipotentiaries on the Status of Refugees and Stateless Persons, adopted in July 1951.[50]

The protection function of UNHCR is derived from the Statute of the High Commissioner's office. However, international legal instruments are also of basic importance for the effective protection of refugees. The most important of these is the United Nations Convention relating to the Status of Refugees of 1951 as supplemented by the 1967 United Nations Refugee Protocol of 1967.[51] These instruments provide a general and universally applicable definition of the term 'refugee' and lay down minimum standards for the treatment of refugees. The Convention regulates in a detailed manner the status of refugees, thereby providing contracting states with a uniform basis for the treatment of persons or groups of persons eligible for protection. The Convention also establishes a formal link between UNHCR and the national authority responsible for the protection of refugees by requesting the contracting states, under article 35, to cooperate with UNHCR in the exercise of its functions. By 1 January 1989, 105 states were party to the 1951 Convention and/or the 1967 Protocol.[52]

Of the numerous other international legal instruments that are directly or indirectly concerned with refugees, special mention should be made of the Convention Governing the Specific Aspects of Refugee Problems in Africa adopted by the Organization of African Unity (OAU) in 1969 to which most African states are now party.[53] This Convention by its Article II-2 emphasizes, inter alia, the fact that the granting of asylum to refugees is a peaceful and humanitarian act and should not be regarded as unfriendly by any member state. A similar provision may be found in the United Nations Declaration on Territorial Asylum.[54]

In order to be fully effective, it is important that the standards defined in the international instruments established for the benefit of refugees be reflected in legislative and/or administrative measures adopted at the national level. In the exercise of international protection, UNHCR therefore seeks to promote the adoption of such national implementing measures. The standards defined in the international instruments and the legislative and/or administrative measures adopted for their implementation have more recently come to be designated 'refugee law'.

One of the core principles of refugee law, and indeed guiding principles of the UNHCR, is that people seeking economic security do not fall under UNHCR's mandate. The greatest danger or threat to Europe, in its endeavour to give genuine refugees asylum, is the proliferation of requests from people who are not really refugees. Governments who are faced with such requests are apprehensive of reprisals from the press, public sympathy, public opinion or the energetic efforts of non governmental organizations towards considering a refusal for asylum a human rights issue.

Underlying the criterion for the grant of political asylum – which is the prevention of physical harm which may befall a claimant if he is deported to his country of origin – is the fact that states assess stringently the element of persecution which is faced by the claimant in his home country. In the 1985 case of *Herandez-Ortiz* v. *United States*,[55] the court held that persecution: 'On account of political opinion ... includes persecution not only on political opinions that the alien actually holds, but also on account of opinions that the persecutor falsely attributes to the alien.'[56] The US courts have also ruled that it is not necessary for the grant of asylum that the seeker be politically opposed to the government in his country or be perceived to be so opposed; the mere association with a family politically opposed to such government could form a basis for a clear possibility of persecution on the basis of implied political opinion.[57]

The deportee is usually given the right to select the country to which he will be deported. In the 1990 case of *Doherty* v. *United States Immigration and Naturalization Services*,[58] the US court of Appeals, at its second circuit, recognized that American law grants a deportee the right to select the country to which he will be deported subject to the right of the Attorney General to reject such selection if it were found to be detrimental to the interests of the United States. In such an instance, the airline concerned would be required to seek the directives of the US government prior to entertaining requests for seat reservation on behalf of the deportee.

It is arguable that, in the United States, if an airline brings into its territory a person with a criminal record, who may be considered inadmissible ipso facto, the airline may not be found negligent if the person proved to be a genuine refugee who faced persecution in his home country. In the case of *Beltran-Zavada* v. *United States Immigration and Naturalization Services*,[59] the Court of Appeals, at its ninth circuit, held that an alien, the target of persecution by death squads in his country, is eligible for asylum relief, whatever his criminal actions which were unconnected with his political position may be.

Usually, airlines do not know beforehand that they are carrying refugees. Consequently, they become aware after the fact, and are sometimes requested to pay administrative charges or fines by the immigration authorities, particularly if the claimants for refugee status carried by the airline are considered mere inadmissible passengers. If, however, an airline were to be aware that its passengers intend to claim refugee status on arrival (or even one passenger among the complement), there is no known legal provision at public international law that compels airlines to undergo punitive sanction. On the other hand, the 1951 Refugee Convention makes it impossible for contracting states to turn back genuine refugees or charge them administrative fees for processing their claims.

Airlines could also benefit from the decision in the 1992 Canadian case of *Veeravagu* v. *Canada*,[60] where the Federal Court of Appeal held that an individual, to apply for refugee status, need not be part of a social group giving rise to refugee status under the 1951 Convention. This decision removes from the airline the burden of being perceived as prudent only if it brings in a person who belongs to a whole social group that is persecuted in his home country.

The British case of *R.* v. *Secretary of State ex parte Stanislaus Arul Rubandraj*[61] offers the common law principle that the United Kingdom can refuse a person on arrival, even though he claims refugee status and seeks political asylum, on the basis that he can be deported to a 'safe country'. The decision in the case also recognized that there is no rule of law or practice for one country to send an applicant back to another country merely because he has spent more time in the latter country.

The Australian Migration Act 1958 contains the requirement in paragraph 6A(1)(c) that an application for refugee status and determination made thereupon by the Department of Immigration and Ethnic Affairs are reviewable in a court of law. However, in the 1987 case of *Gunaleela* v. *Minister of Immigration and Ethnic Affairs*,[62] the Federal Court of Australia held that, under the Migration Act, aliens who arrive at an airport without an entry permit are deemed not to have entered Australia and therefore decisions *sua sponte* denying them refugee status are not reviewable under paragraph 6A(1)(c). The court also held that, in exercising his wide discretion, a decision maker need not consider in an application for an entry permit of an individual who has not entered Australia that the applicant seeks permanent resident status as a refugee.

The significance of the *Gunaleela* decision to an airline carrying a passenger without an entry permit to a country which requires such is that such a passenger, even if he claims asylum, would be deemed not to have entered that particular country and would therefore remain the responsibility and in the custody of the carrier until he is transported either to a safe country or to his country of origin. In this particular instance, although Australia had signed the 1951 Refugee Convention, it had not become part of Australian municipal law at the time the case was heard. Therefore Australia was not bound by the Convention provision which required that no contracting state should deport a person who claims refugee status without examining such claim first.

Notes

1 A32-WP/54, EC/7, 2/6/98, pp.1–2.
2 Ibid., p.1.
3 See Annex 9 (Facilitation) to the Convention on International Civil Aviation, 10th edn, April 1997, Chapter I – Definitions and Applicability.
4 The Convention was adopted by the United Nations Conference of Plenipotentiaries on the Status of Refugees and Stateless Persons, held at Geneva from 2 to 25 July 1951. The Conference was convened pursuant to Resolution 429(v) adopted by the General Assembly of the United Nations on 14 September 1950. For the text of the Resolution, see Official Records of the General Assembly, Fifth Session, Supplement No. 20 (A/1775), p.48.
5 See Convention Relating to the Status of Refugees, done at Geneva on 28 July 1951. Definitions of 'Refugee', *Collection of International Instruments Concerning Refugees*, Geneva: UNHCR: 1979, p.45.
6 Convention on International Civil Aviation, signed at Chicago on 7 December 1944. For full text, see ICAO Doc. 7300/6, 7th edn, 1997.
7 Annex 9 (*supra*, n.3), Chapter 3, Section E, 3.38.1.
8 Ibid., 3.38.
9 Ibid., 3.38.2.
10 Ibid., 3.39.
11 Ibid.
12 Ibid., 3.39.1.
13 Ibid., 3.40.3.
14 Ibid., Recommended Practice, 3.40.2.
15 It is noteworthy that the ICAO Facilitation Panel which met in Montreal from 17 to 21 November 1997 has suggested two new Recommended Practices to Annex 9 which provides:

- the appropriate public authorities of Contracting States either singly or jointly should enter into co-operative arrangements such as memoranda of understanding with the airlines providing international services to and from that State, setting out guidelines for their mutual support and co-operation in countering the abuses associated with travel document fraud. Such arrangements should assign mutual responsibilities to the public authorities and to the airlines, in the ascertainment of the validity and authenticity of the travel documents of embarking passengers, and in the necessary steps to prevent the loss or destruction of documents by passengers en route to their destinations; and

- Contracting States are encouraged to make arrangements such as memoranda of understanding (MOUs) with other Contracting States with the intention of permitting the positioning of 'liaison officers' at airports or to establish other forms of international co-operation in order to assist airlines to establish the validity and authenticity of the passports and visas of embarking passengers.

  See Facilitation Panel Report, First Meeting, Montreal, 17–21 November 1997, 1–4.

16 For a more detailed discussion of the legal nature of the passport, see R.I.R. Abeyratne (1992), 'The Development of the Machine Readable Passport and Visa and the Legal Rights of the Data Subject', *Annals of Air & Space Law*, XVII (Part II), pp.12–14.

17 In conformity with Article 22 of the Chicago Convention, which confirms the agreement of all contracting states to adopt all practicable measures to prevent unnecessary delays to aircraft, passenger and crews especially in the administration of laws relating to immigration, quarantine customs and clearance, ICAO is actively seized of the development of a machine-readable travel document which uses various devices to secure the passport, visa and other travel documents against fraud.

18 The full text of the Resolution is as follows:

International co-operation in protecting the security and integrity of passports

Whereas the passport is the basic official document which denotes a person's identity and citizenship and provides an assurance for the State of transit or destination that the bearer can return to the State which issued the passport;

Whereas international confidence in the security and integrity of the passport is of prime importance in the functioning of the international travel system;

Taking into account the resolution adopted by the United Nations General Assembly which requests that ICAO consider ways and means to enhance international co-operation to combat the smuggling of aliens, while emphasizing that such efforts should not undercut the protection provided by international law to refugees;

Taking into account the resolutions adopted by the United Nations General Assembly and the Economic and Social Council which request that Member States establish or improve procedures to permit the ready discovery of false travel documents, that States co-operate bilaterally and on a multilateral basis to prevent the use of fraudulent documents, and that States take measures to provide penalties for the production and distribution of false travel documents and the misuse of international commercial aviation; and

Whereas high level co-operation among States is required in order to strengthen resistance to passport fraud, including the forgery or counterfeiting of passports, the use of forged or counterfeit passports, the use of valid passports by imposters, the misuse of authentic passports by rightful holders in furtherance of the commission of an offence, the use of expired or revoked passports, and the use of fraudulently-obtained passports.

The Assembly:

1. *endorses* the actions taken by the Council through the Air Transport Committee to strengthen and approve specifications for machine readable passports as they relate to security of such documents;
2. *requests* the Council to study specific actions and measures for enhancing the effectiveness of controls on passport fraud, including the possible preparation of necessary SARPs and guidance material, to be implemented by Contracting States in the interests of maintaining the integrity and security of passports and other travel documents; and

3. *calls upon* all Contracting States to intensify their efforts to safeguard the security and integrity of their passports, to protect their passports against passport fraud, and to assist one another in these matters.

19 A/RES/48/102.
20 A/RES/51/60.
21 *Fontan-de-Maldonado* v. *Lineas Aereas Costarricenses.S.A.*, 936 F. 2d 630 (1st Cir. 1991).
22 *Trans World Airlines* v. *American Coupon Exchange Inc.*, 682 F. Supp. 1476, 1481 (C.D. Cal. 1990).
23 902 F. Supp. 315 (D.P.R. 1995).
24 Ibid., 319.
25 65 F. 3d 1034 (2nd Cir. 1995).
26 *Argenbright Security* v. *Ceskoslovenske Aeroline*, 849 F. Supp. 276 (S.D.N.Y. 1994).
27 Ibid., 281.
28 846 F. Supp. 280 (S.D.N.Y. 1994).
29 Ibid., 285.
30 80 F. 2d 477 (D.C. Cir. 1996).
31 *Linea Area Nactionale de-Chile Airlines* v. *Sale* (Lan-Chile) 865 F. Supp. 971.
32 Ibid., at 978.
33 Ibid., 973.
34 For a more detailed discussion of this case and immigration issues in the United States, see generally Constance O'Keefe (1997), 'Immigration Issues and Airlines: an Update', *Journal of Air Law and Commerce*, 63, 17–65.
35 *Dia Navigation Co.* v. *Reno*, 831 F. Supp. 360 (D.N.J. 1993); *Argenbright Security* v. *Ceskoslovenske Aeroline*, 849 F. Supp. 276 (S.D.N.Y. 1994).
36 See also *Katz* v. *Cisneros*, 164 3d 1204 (Fed. Cir. 1994), which the *Lan-Chile* court followed in this regard.
37 See in particular *Aerolineas Argentinas* v. *United States* 773 F. 3d 1564 (Fed. Cir. 1996); *Air Transport Association* v. *Reno*. 80 F. 3d 477 (D.C. Cir. 1996).
38 See Constance O'Keefe (*supra*, n.34), 43–53, for a detailed and *au fait* discussion of this subject.
39 The Immigration (Carriers' Liability) Act 1987 which was made ex post facto applicable to persons arriving in the United Kingdom from 4 March 1987.
40 See generally Frances Nicholson (1997), 'Implementation of the Immigration (Carriers' Liability) Act 1987: Privatising Immigration Functions at the Expense of International Obligations', *International and Comparative Law Quarterly*, 47, July, 586–634.
41 Ibid., 587. However, in 1996, the UK government made its position clear that at international law: 'its obligations extend to genuine refugees on our territory, but that it has no responsibility to encourage or assist asylum seekers around the world to come here. Such a committment is not part of our international obligation' (ibid., 614).
42 *R.* v. *Secretary of State for the Home Departrment ex. P. Robert Denzil Sritharan and Benet Mariyanayagam* (1993) Imm. A.R. 184–6.
43 Sven Hartung (1998), 'Asylum Seeking Persons Arriving at Frankfurt International Airport – Who Pays the Accommodation Costs?', *Zeitschrift fur Luft- und Weltraumrecht* (German Journal of Air and Space Law), 47, 307.
44 *United Nations Resolutions*, ed. Dusan J. Djanovich, Series I, Volume I, 1946, p.8.
45 Ibid.
46 That is, United Nations Relief and Rehabilitation Administration (UNRRA), the Intergovernmental Committee for Refugees (IGCR) and the Office of the League of Nations High Commissioner for Refugees.
47 Eighteen out of a total of 42 members of the United Nations at that time.

48 With the exception of persons who continue to receive humanitarian assistance from the United Nations Relief and Works Agency for Palestine Refugees in the Near East (UNRWA). UNRWA was established in 1949 and provides essential services for Palestine refugees living in Lebanon, the Syrian Arab Republic, Jordan and the Gaza Strip.
49 See United Nations Resolutions and Decisions relating to the Office of the United Nations High Commissioner for Refugees (HCR/INF/49).
50 See Convention and Protocol relating to the Status of Refugees, HCR/INF/29/Rev.4, p.9.
51 The importance of the protocol lies in the fact that it extends the scope *ratione personae* of the 1951 Convention by removing the dateline of 1 January 1951 contained in the definition of the term 'refugee' in article 1 A(2), thus making the Convention applicable to new groups of refugees, that is, persons who became refugees as a result of events that took place after 1 January 1951.
52 See Annex I, Convention relating to the Status of Refugees.
53 See Annex II, Convention relating to the Status of Refugees.
54 Adopted by the General Assembly on 14 December 1967 (Resolution 2312 (XXII). The Declaration deals with the granting or refusal of asylum and with the interest of the international community in the question of asylum.
55 777 F. 2d 509 (1985).
56 Ibid., 512.
57 *Ramirez-Rivas* v. *United States Immigration and Naturalization Service*, 910 F2d 864 (9th Cir. 1990).
58 908 F. 2d 1108 (2nd Cir. 1990).
59 912 F. 2d 1027 (9th Cir. 1990).
60 27 May 1992, Federal Court of Appeal, Vancouver Appeal No. A-630-89.
61 Ref: 11 March 1993, QBD co/630/93.
62 1989 2 C.L.R. 257.

10 The Fuel Tax and Emissions Trading as Market-based Options in Air Transport

Introduction

In 1997, the Antarctic ozone hole was one of the largest, and was no different from the holes of other years of the past decade. For nearly three months, the surface of the ozone hole remained constantly larger than a square area of 10 million km^2. In September and October it nearly doubled and reached its peak at around 24 million km^2.[1] Also, there was ozone depletion in the lower stratosphere, which added to the overall dimensions of the ozone hole, which extended in 1998 to the southernmost tip of South America.[2]

The contribution of aircraft engine emissions to the depletion of the ozone layer was initially identified as being through the oxides of nitrogen which are emitted by supersonic aircraft in flight. However, later on, it was discovered that sulphur in the fuel of any aircraft resulted in the emission of sulphur compounds into the air, which could affect the ozone layer adversely. The sulphuric process of aircraft engine emissions can be equated to the chemical process taking place in polar stratospheric clouds. The sulphur trioxide in the exhaust gases rapidly converts itself into sulphate particles, which in turn attach themselves to chlorinated substances in the atmosphere to form a powerful chemical combination which is capable of attacking the ozone layer.[3] The good news is that, usually, at a non-supersonic height of around 10 kilometres, these chemical compounds do not pose a significant threat to the ozone layer. Meteorological scientists claim that, on the other hand, at a height below 10 kilometres, such particles could contribute to global warming by acting as condensation nuclei for water vapour, thereby forming high-altitude cirrus clouds that effectively preclude the escaping of heat into space.[4]

Although the clear offender is the supersonic aircraft, large subsonic aircraft which fly at high altitudes on long-haul flights traversing the stratosphere can emit significant quantities of sulphur trioxide which may well compare with the emissions of the supersonic Concorde.[5] In 1995, a joint Swiss project called NOXAR, in which one of the participants – Swissair – dedicated a Boeing 737 aircraft for the project, was carried out where a large part of the northern hemisphere was covered by the jumbo covering the most frequented North Atlantic routes such as Zurich to New York, Washington, Boston, Toronto, Chicago and Atlanta and also routes covering the Far East to Bombay, Hong Kong, Beijing and Shanghai. The emissions of the jumbo jet were calibrated while it was in flight and revealed that the results of earlier studies conducted on the basis of particular measurements and calculations which showed concentrations of oxides of nitrogen (NO_x) between 0,2 and 0,3 ppb in the upper troposphere of the northern hemisphere were consistent with the findings of the NOXAR study. In addition, the NOXAR study revealed that there could be higher concentrations of gases over a short period of time. Both vertical interference of anthropogenic concentrations close to the ground with upper air layers and brief flights directly in the exhaust plume of aircraft flying immediately ahead were significant in this respect.[6]

On its own initiative, Airbus Industrie headed a European Union-backed project called MOZAIC (Measurement of Ozone by Airbus In-service Aircraft) which comprised testing long-term measurements of ozone and water. Three Airbus A-340 aircraft belonging to Lufthansa, Air France and Austrian Airlines were used as measuring platforms. The MOZAIC project was based on the fact that, at the time the study was carried out, airlines flew around 2000 billion passenger-seat kilometres a year, and, despite sporadic lulls in traffic, this figure would double by the year 2005. The inexorable assumption was that the growth in traffic would spur increased fuel consumption, gravely aggravating the already tainted reputation of aircraft, which produced eight times more pollution than cars and 22 times more pollution than electric trains per passenger mile.[7]

At the Symposium on Global Atmospheric Effects on Aviation, held in Virginia Beach, USA (15–19 April 1996), the three fundamental postulates affecting the interaction of aircraft with the atmosphere were succinctly set out.

1 Aircraft emissions occur predominantly in the upper troposphere and lower stratosphere. This is in contrast to surface-level pollution sources, which are subject to effective removal processes (for example, rainout). As a result, although there are local and regional impacts close to the surface arising from emissions around

airports, the primary concern here is with global impacts occurring at the higher altitudes.

2 The relevant chemical and dynamical processes at aviation cruise altitudes have proved difficult to understand. The processes involved are different from those near the surface. The chemical and meteorological timescales can vary widely. They can also be comparable to each other, yielding a scientific problem that requires a simultaneous understanding of both. The species of emissions occur in a wide range of densities, ranging from relatively dense plumes to trace global background levels.

3 The species of emissions emitted by aircraft are involved in various ways with multiple environmental issues, including stratospheric ozone-layer depletion, radiative forcing of climate change and changes in tropospheric chemical composition. For example, carbon dioxide is a direct component of global warming, while emitted particles can influence ozone depletion and cloud formation, both of which in turn influence the radiation balance.[8]

The Symposium recognized that effective measures which would assist in controlling aircraft emissions[9] would lie in modern technology, new operational procedures and the wider use of economic instruments calculated to compensate or manage pollution by aircraft engine emissions. This chapter will discuss the economic instruments that are being currently considered by the world aviation community in the form of market-based options, namely taxation on fuel related to aircraft engine emissions, and emissions trading. It will also discuss legal and regulatory issues associated with market-based options in aviation and environmental protection.

Taxation on Fuel Consumption Related to Emissions

Economic theory suggests that, if a tax were to be levied on environmental pollution, it should be a Pigouvian tax.[10] However, the validity and effectiveness of this theory has been eroded by the widespread levy of environmental taxes that differ from Pigouvian taxes, in that they are not levied on units of emission or damage but on other bases or none at all, and their uses are not related to environmental damage. This anomaly is further aggravated by the fact that the methodology, design and implementation of environmental taxes show significant divergence across national boundaries, creating a patchwork of national environmental taxes on a global fiscal quilt.

The main task of an environmental tax is to influence the damage caused by pollution to the environment by causing change in relative costs. These costs are factors which indicate environmental damage in a given instance, by enabling one to ascertain the point at which the marginal social cost involved in the use of environmental resources exceeds the marginal social benefit derived from the use of such resources. In this context the Pigouvian tax is by far the most efficient, although there are two other categories of taxes: those levied on the basis of production or consumption of goods which are directly or indirectly linked to environmental damage, and other taxes which contain provisions relating to environmental damage.

In the instance of the Pigouvian tax, its efficiency and effectiveness are dependent upon the fact that the tax itself hinges upon the unit of emission or damage. Conceptually, this methodology is analogous to a taxi fare which a passenger pays, which is based on distance travelled. The Pigouvian tax bases its levy on the marginal social cost at emission levels which are socially efficient. For instance, emission levels of an industry would become socially efficient at the point where the industry concerned breaks even between the marginal benefit accrued to the industry from the activity which causes environmental damage and the marginal cost to society. Essentially, therefore, the Pigouvian tax achieves the dual objectives of ensuring that the polluter pays for the social and private cost of his action, by raising the price to be paid for pollution.

One of the most beneficial aspects of the Pigouvian tax is that it is based on the price system which is calculated to reduce the cost of environmental policy. The pricing criterion of this particular tax ensures social efficiency, as against the ineptitude of a policy based on command and control. Another characteristic of expediency of the Pigouvian tax is that it enables industries to reduce pollution in a cost-effective manner. This is achieved when an industry adjusts its pollution abatement at the lowest cost and is further encouraged to lower to an irreducible minimum its cost abatement on the activities of that industry.

As for the environment tax which is linked indirectly to environmental damage by taxing production and the consumption of goods, as against the direct tax against emissions as in the Pigouvian tax, it encourages industries to manage their emission levels at a socially acceptable level. Although this tax tends to be equitable and efficacious in certain instances, such as in the case of carbon taxes which are linked to the minimization of global warming, in other instances, such as in fuel taxes which are intended to diffuse the problem of the general unclean state of the atmosphere, the tax becomes ambivalent and ineffective. Therefore the criterion of measurement of the relevance and effect of the indirect tax is its linkage to the environmental damage caused.

The attendant benefits of the Pigouvian tax over the indirect tax are that the former imposes lesser costs on industry than the latter by enabling industries to base their efficiency of production and reduction of pollution essentially on a specific pricing policy, and it remains a unit measure of pollution payment, as against an indirect tax such as a fuel tax, which is ambivalent.

The third category of environmental tax which has so far been identified, the non-environmental tax which has provisions relating to the environment, does not serve the objective of environmental pollution abatement well. The reason for this is that the mere inclusion of provisions relating to environmental pollution or damage may not necessarily encourage industry to carry out a concrete programme of environmental management. Such provisions may only succeed in raising costs of production and, inevitably, the increase of aggregate emissions.

Ex facie, environmental taxes in any form are perceived as regressive, for the reason that they raise prices of commodities which are largely used by consumers of a low income level. In addition, environmental taxes are difficult to craft and implement and, from an international perspective, it would be all the more difficult to design environmental taxes which would be country-specific on a global scale. However, the most difficult obstacle to efficient global environmental taxation is the adverse impact such a levy would have on various economic factors related to production, such as employment, market competition, economic output and equity.

The other consideration in environmental taxation – equity – brings to bear the complexity of the problem of legal implementation of an environmental tax. Although, in theory, it can be easily established that an environmental tax can be calculated on the basis of the marginal internal benefit and marginal social cost of a given source of pollution, whether such a levy could be legally implemented on a global scale is another question. Given the zealously guarded internal fiscal policies of nations and their internal economic factors, it would be a difficult task to seek global accord on an appropriate internationally applicable environmental tax.

Legal Aspects of the Environmental Tax

ICAO Policy

At its 15th Session in June/July 1965, the ICAO Assembly adopted Resolution A15-16 which explored the possibility of a new initiative in this field pursuant to which the Council undertook a comprehensive review of all aspects related to this subject matter and, at the

Fourth Meeting of its 59th Session, on 14 November 1966, decided to recast the Resolutions and the Recommendation, taking into account developments since 1951, while reaffirming at the same time their underlying principles. The Council further decided to publish them in the policy document (Doc. 8632-C/968) for action by contracting states and to provide certain explanatory material for guidance to states and international operators.

The 1966 Resolutions/Recommendation which appear in Doc. 8632 dealt with the following:

Section I: taxation of fuel, lubricants and other consumable technical supplies when an aircraft registered in one state arrives in or departs from a customs territory of another state;

Section II: taxation of fuel, lubricants and other consumable technical supplies when an aircraft registered in one state makes successive stops at two or more airports in one customs territory of another state;

Section III: taxation of the income and aircraft of international air transport enterprises;

Section IV: taxes related to the sale or use of international air transport.

The essence of the Resolution contained in Section I is that, when an aircraft registered in one state arrived in another, the fuel, lubricants and other consumable technical supplies contained in the tanks or other receptacles of the aircraft were exempt from customs duties. This exemption applied only if such substances were not off-loaded except when under customs control. In addition, when an aircraft left for another state or a customs territory of the same state, the substances enumerated above that the aircraft takes on board during the flight were deemed to be exempt from duties. These exemptions were to apply to scheduled, non-scheduled and private flights. This Resolution included, in addition to fuel and lubricants, consumable technical supplies such as de-icing fluid, hydraulic fluid and cooling fluid, which, in their usage, furnish a parallel with fuel and lubricants.

The Resolution contained in Section I was influenced by Article 2(1)(a) of the 1939 London Convention on the Exemption from Taxation for Liquid Fuel and Lubricants used in Air Traffic and admits of the fuel and lubricants contained in the tanks of aircraft being exempt from taxes only if such items were contained in an arriving aircraft and not subsequently unloaded. The ICAO Council also took note of Article 2(1)(b) which required exemption from taxes on fuel and lubricants loaded on aircraft which leave from one customs territory for another.

The Recommendation in Section II exempts from customs duties such substances as were described above that are taken on board aircraft when that aircraft is engaged in making successive stops at two or more international airports in a customs territory of a state on its way to another international airport of that state or even when the aircraft leaves the state for another.

In the realization that further revision was necessary, the Assembly, at its 26th Session in September/October 1986, adopted Resolution A26-15 which instructed the Council to review compliance with these Resolutions and the Recommendation and to consider the need for new practical measures to reaffirm and strengthen the principles underlying its policies in this field. After consultation with states, the Council reported the results of its review to the 29th Session of the Assembly in September 1992, which agreed with the Council's approach to the revision of the 1966 Resolutions and Recommendation. The revision maintains the previous format but, in view of the evidence of increased acceptance by states of the policy therein, upgrades the Recommendation in Section II to a Resolution (making it correspond to the other three Resolutions in Sections I, II and III of Doc. 8632). It also incorporates certain enhancements to the first three sections described above and a more substantive revision of the last section dealing with taxes related to the sale or use of international air transport and makes the Resolutions contained in Sections I and II applicable both to local and national taxes in instances where states may impose both categories. The revised document also gives a wider definition of taxes and charges, as they relate to ICAO's policies. These changes take into account the realities of the current situation in civil aviation, while reaffirming the underlying principles of ICAO's policies in this field.

The 29th Session of the Assembly also reinforced the importance of this policy statement by adopting Resolution A29-18, which calls upon states to follow the Resolutions of the Council as contained in this document.

Aviation fuel costs represent 10–25 per cent of variable costs of an average airline. A small airline may have to bear even as much as 40 per cent of its operating costs on the purchase of fuel. The volatile fluctuation of the world fuel market, and the rapidly changing economic conditions, would bear upon the fortune of an international carrier. Any taxes imposed upon aviation fuels, however small, would have a significant impact on aviation fuel costs, and therefore on an airline's budgetary and cash flow management. For this reason, there is growing concern over the question of taxation of aviation fuels and attempts have been made in the past, as indeed, will be pursued in the future, by IATA to negotiate reductions in fuel facility charges and taxes.

International airlines and other air transport enterprises face taxation conventionally in two broad areas, which may be termed 'consumption' taxes and 'revenue' taxes. The first category comprises taxes related to consumption by air transport enterprises and airlines. These are property taxes on aircraft engaged in international air transport and taxes on fuel and ground equipment and spare parts and aircraft equipment. The latter group envelopes income tax (whether it be based on gross receipts or any other evaluation), based primarily on the sale or use of international transport by air, business taxes, municipal taxes, employee taxes, capital gains taxes and so on. There is a third category which has been entitled by some 'nuisance' tax, that is, head taxes such as the passenger facility charge (PFC), airport taxes, security taxes and so on. The 'nuisance' tax is generally absorbed by the passenger or client of the airline or air transport enterprise and is therefore not a direct tax imposed on the air transport industry.

A crucial element in defining a tax is the ultimate purpose and destination of the revenue concerned. Thus a tax may be described as a levy to raise revenue for the national or local treasury which will be used for general or specific public (that is, non-aviation) purposes. Clearly, if the Resolution in Section IV were to be read with this concept of a tax in mind, there would be fewer problems with the prohibition on all forms of taxation on the sale or use of international transport by air because all taxes or charges that are directly *or indirectly* intended to finance the cost of aviation facilities would be considered acceptable and not falling within the scope of Section IV.

A tax is a 'pecuniary contribution made by persons liable, for the support of government'.[11] Courts have adjudicated that a tax is 'a pecuniary burden laid upon individuals or property to support the government and is a payment exacted by legislative authority'. It has also been identified as 'annual compensation paid to government for annual protection and for current support of government'. An early American decision identified a tax as follows:

> A ratable portion of the produce of the property and labor of the individual citizens, taken by the nation, in the exercise of its sovereign rights, for the support of government, for the administration of the laws, and as the means for continuing in operation the various legitimate functions of the State.[12]

According to these definitions, a tax is a very general imposition, often described as a 'once and for all' payment. Therefore a tax could not be named as a specific tax, such as 'aviation fuel tax' or 'aircraft equipment tax'. The fact that a tax was levied 'for the support of the government' makes its general nature more explicit.

In the 1956 case of *Heirs* v. *Mitchel*,[13] the court held that a tax was:

> An enforced contribution of money or other property, assessed in accordance with some reasonable rule or apportionment by authority of some sovereign State on persons or property within its jurisdiction for the purpose of defraying the public expenses. Therefore, a tax came to be known as a 'contribution' and was regarded in a general sense to be any contribution imposed by government upon individuals, for the use and service of the State, whether under the name of toll, tribute, tallage, gable, impost, duty, custom, excise, subsidy, supply, aid or *any other name*. (Original emphasis)

The legal definition of a tax is that it is an enforced contribution by the public or a section thereof, introduced by legislative decree, for the purposes of defraying public expenses. Judicially, a tax has been identified as a 'contribution', among other synonyms, including, quite disturbingly, with 'any other word'.[14] Experts in taxation maintain that the 'efficiency' test in taxation calls for devising tax levies which cause minimal reduction in, or disruption of, overall productivity of a society. It is in this perspective that the overall context of taxation in the field of international air transport should be viewed.

In many instances 'taxes' imposed on international air transport have been labelled iniquitous.[15] It is strongly claimed that a tax which is 'a compulsory contribution levied upon persons, property or business for the support of government: any assessment'[16] is an onerous demand upon anyone's person or resources and when imposed upon international air transport justifies its definition as a verb: 'to subject to a severe strain'.[17] While it is accepted that taxation must be for a public purpose,[18] the amount of the tax charged must be compatible with principles of commerce and should be proportionate to the cost of the specific facility or services used rather than the cost of overall governmental services in general. The formula must admit of the tax being directly proportionate to the cost of the service or facility used.

Imposition of an International Tax

General principles An international tax on the environment, if introduced, would fall within the realm of international economic law – or law relating to economic relations between states. Under this genus would be the species of international law of taxation (ILT). International economic law, and its generic specimen taxation law, are both in turn governed by the overriding rubric of public international law, which, according to the Statute of the International Court of Justice, is governed by international treaties, international custom, the general principles of law as recognized by civilized nations, and judicial decisions and teachings of respected jurists.[19] An international tax on environmental protection would, therefore, have to be introduced under a multilateral treaty between nations.

In order for states to accept the reality of an international tax on environmental pollution, they would have to be convinced of the legal principles and their underlying duties and obligations with regard to international accord. Secondly, states would have to embark upon a sustained examination of the emergent trend in international relations: that the international community is responsible for its citizens, wherever they may be. In other words, the legal cliché, that the citizens of a state are subject only to national laws of their state, would have to give way to the realization that the entire international community now has an obligation towards its citizens, whatever country they may belong to. This by no means implies that a state legislature no longer has jurisdiction over the citizens of that state. It merely means that the state and the international community have to act as a whole when legislating, and that a state has to recognize and take into account the international implications of its laws.

While it has been recognized that states' own definition of taxes may vary, depending on their internal fiscal and legislative arrangements, the ICAO Council considered that it would be helpful to include in Section IV reference to the elements which are essential for defining a tax for the purposes of this Resolution. For example, if the revenue concerned is to be paid into the national or local treasury but is subsequently dedicated to the civil aviation budget or is used to fund aviation related facilities and services then it would not be categorized as a tax in this context. The commentary could then highlight the desirability for states to clearly identify in the relevant national document the ultimate purpose and destination of any new 'tax' or 'charge' under whatever name it is levied and, where possible, use the terminology or designation for the levy concerned which is consistent with the guidance as to what constitutes a tax in the ICAO document.

Definition of Charge

A 'charge' has reference to impositions for improvements which are specially beneficial to particular individuals or property, and which are imposed in proportion to the benefits supposed to be conferred. Charges are special and local impositions upon property in the immediate vicinity of municipal improvements and are laid with reference to the special benefit which the property is expected to have derived therefrom.

A charge levied upon the products of a particular industry is expected to be utilized in the improvement of that industry, while a tax is generally imposed in the national interest and is directed accordingly towards the national treasury. In concept, the former is not objectionable, since it is calculated to benefit a particular industry for which the charge is collected, while the latter, it is claimed, should be borne by states as part of their national responsibility. However, this clear demarcation has often been shrouded in anomalous terminology resulting in a passenger service charge being identified as a tax imposed for the national benefit.

In a broader sense, taxes, as they have been judicially defined, could be considered as including assessments and charges, but, practically, a tax is a public burden imposed generally on the inhabitants of a state or upon a division thereof for governmental purposes, without reference to particular or peculiar benefits to particular individuals or property. The main criticism of a tax is that it is a compulsory contribution levied upon persons ... for the support of government[20] and therefore is a heavy demand upon one's person or resources.

With respect to 'charges', the Council, when reviewing the agenda for the 1991 Conference on Airport and Route Facility Management (CARFM) had made particular reference to the growing concern being expressed over the proliferation of charges on air traffic. CARFM itself was informed of over 680 different taxes, charges and fees imposed around the world by 184 states, some 70 of whom require them to be remitted to other than aviation authorities (for example, Ministry of Finance, Treasury, tax offices or Ministries of Tourism, Immigration and Works). The Conference was also informed of IATA's belief that taxes, charges or fees should not be imposed for functions which are the responsibility of states and should not discriminate against international air transport in relation to other modes of transport; any tax, charge or fee should be imposed only for services which are of direct benefit to international air transport and should not be used for general revenue purposes.

CARFM particularly noted the charges recently introduced by a few states to recover the cost of functions they need to carry out to process air traffic entering or leaving their territory to ensure that they meet the requirements, rules and regulations the state has established for its protection and that of its citizens (for example, immigration and customs charges). While there was considerable concern at the possible proliferation of these charges, the Conference did not feel able to recommend to Council that states should not impose charges for functions not previously charged for as that would be an unwarranted restriction on states' ability to respond to changing circumstances, such as the need for measures to alleviate problems of facilitation, congestion or security. The Conference instead recommended two basic principles which the Council has accepted and incorporated in its revised *Statements to Contracting States on Charges for Airports and Air Navigation Services* (Doc. 9082/4, 4th edn, 1992). In this document, the Council recommends that in the field of international civil aviation states should (a) impose charges only for services and functions which are required for international civil aviation; and (b) refrain from imposing charges which discriminate against international civil aviation in relation to other modes of international transport.

The principle in (b) above addresses the types of charges referred to in the previous paragraph (for example, immigration and customs charges) and aims to curb the proliferation of such charges where they are imposed in a manner which discriminates against international civil aviation. The principle in (a) above addresses charges levied to cover the cost of services and functions *not required for* civil aviation (for example, promotion of tourism, national museums or books for a university library). The Conference recognized that these latter 'charges' are in effect taxes on aviation and not within the scope of the Council Statements on Charges in Doc. 9082.

Developments with Regard to ICAO Policy

In accordance with Assembly Resolution A26-15 which instructed the Council to review compliance with the three resolutions and one recommendation contained in Sections I-IV of Doc. 8632, the ICAO Council proposed certain revisions to existing policies of ICAO in the field of international air transport as they appeared in Doc. 8632. These revisions were placed before the 29th Session of the ICAO Assembly in September 1992 and were approved by the Assembly. The revisions to the four Sections of Doc. 8632 carry the following additions and rationales.

Section I

1 The Resolution in Section I relating to the taxation of fuel, lubricants and other consumable technical supplies now also applies to aircraft designated by a contracting state (in addition to aircraft registered in a contracting state).
2 The same Resolution highlights the fact that international air transport plays a major role in the development and expansion of international trade and travel in furtherance of the objectives of ICAO. Therefore the Resolution holds that the imposition of national and local taxes and customs and other duties on the acquisition of fuel, lubricants and consumable technical supplies for use by aircraft in connection with international air transport is an

impediment to the sound, economical and orderly development of international air transport operations. The term 'local' in this context relates to political subdivisions of a state such as states, provinces and municipalities.

3 Customs and other duties referred to in (2) above include import, export, excise, sales, consumption and internal duties and taxes of all kinds.

4 The duties and taxes described above, while including those levied by any taxing authority within a state, whether national or local, shall not be or continue to be imposed on the acquisition of fuel, lubricants or consumable technical supplies used by aircraft in connection with international air services except to the extent that they are based on the actual costs of providing airports or air navigation facilities and services and used to finance the costs of providing them.

5 In adopting this Resolution the Council endorsed the policy of reciprocal exemption from, or refund of, customs and other duties on certain fuel, lubricants and other consumable technical supplies used in international air transport. It did so upon the bases of, inter alia, longstanding maritime practice and the established policy of many states. The Council recognized the obvious practical difficulties inherent in adopting any other course of action and pointed out that its policy as set forth in the Resolution appeared to be the only one available in the foreseeable future which would, in a simple and effective manner, assure equitable treatment for international aviation throughout the many jurisdictions in which it operated.

6 The Resolution includes, in addition to fuel and lubricants, consumable technical supplies such as de-icing fluid, hydraulic fluid and cooling fluid which, in their usage, furnish a precise parallel with fuel and lubricants. The Resolution goes somewhat further than Article 24(a) of the Chicago Convention in that the fuel, lubricants and other consumable technical supplies on board upon arrival of the aircraft, so long as they are not off-loaded, remain exempt from customs and other duties and can be consumed without any obligation that they or their equivalent be 'retained on board on leaving the territory' of the state granting the exemption. More importantly, the Resolution also provides for exemption or refund for the fuel, lubricants and other consumable technical supplies taken on board at the final international airport of call in a customs territory of a state, whether or not such airport is located at the border of the customs territory.

7 The Resolution is applicable to all aircraft engaged in international operations, that is those performing scheduled, non-scheduled and private flights, and including those aircraft leased

or chartered by an operator of another state even though the aircraft concerned may be registered in the state from which the exemption is sought. The Council concluded that all types of operations were entitled to equal treatment in this respect and this had been the basis upon which Article 24(a) of the Chicago Convention was drafted. Those contracting states which, thus far, have granted exemption from duties on fuel and so on to one type of operation only (for example, scheduled international flights) have therefore been invited to make special efforts in bringing their national practices into line with this clause of the Resolution. It is clear that fuel, lubricants and so on should be exempt from any kind of duties and taxes regardless of the names attached to such levies in different countries.

8 While the term 'local' relates to political subdivisions of a state such as states, provinces and municipalities, and there are difficulties which might arise in some states where such entities have the constitutional right to levy duties and taxes on their own behalf, the inclusion of this term has been intended to encourage such states to seek the necessary internal arrangements for the benefit of international air transport. If such arrangements cannot reach complete fruition, the other state concerned can still determine whether sufficient reciprocity is available to warrant its entry into an agreement.

9 The Council recognized that 'throughput' charges imposed by government or airport authorities on fuel companies in return for facilities or services provided can in certain circumstances become, in practical effect to those engaged in international air navigation, the equivalent of another tax payable by them. However, taxes and customs or excise duties on fuel differ in essence from charges (however they may be levied) for the use of certain facilities and the Council has recommended in its Statement on Airport Charges in Doc. 9082 (*Statements by the Council to Contracting States on Charges for Airports and Air Navigation Services*) that 'where fuel "throughput" charges are imposed they should be recognized by airport authorities as being concession charges of an aeronautical nature. ("Concession charges" are fees for the right to operate a commercial activity at an airport.)' In general, to clarify what is a charge and what is a tax, the basic message conveyed is that, when any levy on consumption of fuel (a) falls on aircraft operators of other states engaged in international air navigation, (b) is in the form of a compulsory contribution to the support of the government, and (c) is not then used for airports or air navigation facilities and services, it is in reality an excise tax and comes within the terms of the Resolutions of Council set forth in Sections I and II of Doc. 8632.

Section II

1 The Recommendation in Section II on the taxation of fuel, lubricants and other consumable technical supplies when an aircraft registered in one state or is designated by that state makes successive stops at two or more airports in one customs territory of another state has been upgraded to a Resolution and carries the same revisions applicable to Resolution 1 in Section I. The upgrading was due to information supplied to ICAO by states concerning their practices, whereby the Council noted that there was evidence of a more general acceptance in recent years for granting exemption from duties to international air transport for this fuel. Taking this into account, the Council decided to upgrade the original Recommendation to a Resolution as it was convinced that compliance with its terms would result in a considerable amount of facilitation to international aircraft operations with, in most cases, little loss of revenue to states. This Resolution, like the Resolution in Section I, is based on reciprocity.

2 This Resolution also deals with the exemption from duties and taxes on the fuel and so on in the tanks of an aircraft when it arrives in another state and on the fuel taken on board in that state prior to departure for another customs territory of the same or the territory of another state. Council's Resolution in this section goes one step further, calling on states to grant such exemptions also for the fuel and other consumable technical supplies taken on board an aircraft engaged in international air navigation when it makes successive stops at two or more international airports in a single customs territory. Council has endeavoured to make it clear in the above Resolution that the fuel in question is that taken on board at international airports in the state concerned prior to the last international airport of call.

The revised version of Doc. 8632 (*ICAO's Policies on Taxation in the Field of International Air Transport*, Doc. 8632-C/968, 2nd edn, January 1994) was distributed to states on 11 August 1994, where the Secretary General of ICAO addressed a State Letter to all member states of ICAO, drawing their attention to the revised Doc. 8632 and calling for their positions on the ICAO policies on taxation as contained in this document by 31 December 1994. On 18 November 1994, the Director General of IATA, in his letter to presidents and chief executives of IATA member airlines, enclosed the ICAO Secretary General's State Letter and urged them to contact their civil aviation authorities to ensure that their responses reached ICAO by 31 December 1994. In his letter, the Director General of IATA further encouraged all member airlines to take an active role in advocating the full implementation of ICAO's taxation policies by appropriate government departments.

At its 32nd Session, held from 22 September to 2 October 1998, the ICAO Assembly adopted Assembly Resolution A32-17 (Consolidated statement of continuing ICAO policies in the air transport field), Appendix E to which contains ICAO policy on taxation. The resolution, which recognizes that international air transport plays a major role in the development and expansion of international trade and travel and the imposition of taxes on aircraft, fuel inter alia may have an adverse economic and competitive impact on international operations. A32-17 urges contracting states to follow the resolutions of the Council as contained in Doc. 8632 (*ICAO's Policies on Taxation in the Field of International Air Transport*) and requests the ICAO Council to ensure that the guidance and advice contained in Doc. 8632 is current and responsive to the requirements of contracting states.

The ICAO Council, at its 156th Session in February 1999, adopted a Consolidated Resolution on Taxation of International Air Transport.[21] This Resolution, which is fully consistent with existing policy in both Doc. 9082 and Doc. 8632 states that, with respect to taxes on fuel, lubricants and other consumable technical supplies, taxation on aviation fuels inter alia may have an adverse economic and competitive impact on international air transport operations. The Council resolved accordingly that, when an aircraft registered in one contracting state, or leased or chartered by an operator of that state, is engaged in international air transport to, from or through a customs territory of another contracting state its fuel, lubricants and other consumable technical supplies shall be exempt from customs or other duties on a reciprocal basis, or, alternatively, in the cases of fuel, lubricants and other consumable technical supplies taken on board in consonance with (b) and (c) below, such duties shall be refunded, when

a the fuel and so on is contained in the tanks or other receptacles on the aircraft on its arrival in the territory of the other state, provided that no quantity may be unloaded except temporarily and under customs control;
b the fuel and so on is taken on board for consumption during the flight when the aircraft departs from an international airport of that other state either for another customs territory of that state or for the territory of any other state, provided that the aircraft has complied, before its departure from the customs territory concerned, with all customs and other clearance regulations in force in that territory; or
c the fuel and so on is taken on board the aircraft at an international airport in one customs territory of another state and the aircraft makes successive stops at two or more international air-

ports in that customs territory on its way to another customs territory of that state or to the territory of any other state.

The above three provisions shall apply whether the aircraft is engaged in an individual flight or in the operation of an air service and whether or not it is operating for remuneration.

The foregoing exemption is based on reciprocity, and therefore, no contracting state complying with the Resolution is obliged to grant to aircraft registered in another contracting state or aircraft leased or chartered by an operator of that state any treatment more favourable than its own aircraft are entitled to receive in the territory of that other state. Notwithstanding the underlying principle of reciprocity, the Council, by its Resolution, encourages contracting states to apply the exemption, to the maximum extent possible, to all aircraft on their arrival from and departure for other states.[22]

Emissions Trading

The essential philosophy of emissions trading in environmental protection is based on a certain flexibility allowed to market forces to reach the lowest cost involved in an operation while at the same time achieving an environmental target which has already been set. The word 'trading' correctly denotes an exchange, and when applied to the aviation context means a certain trade-off between airlines whose fleets pollute more than others and low polluting airlines. The trade-off could take the form of a 'purchase' by the high polluting airline of the reduction level of a low polluting airline. Emissions trading would encourage airlines to seek innovation in technology and to reduce their emission levels.

Emissions trading of levels of pollution between airlines differs fundamentally from the existing expectation of each airline maintaining a standard level of emission by its aircraft. When airlines trade emission levels, the rates at which their aircraft pollute the atmosphere will be taken as a whole and applicable to a whole fleet, so that an airline which is over and above its permitted pollution level could join with another airline which is below the standard level of pollution required of it, thus making the average pollution between the two more acceptable than if taken individually. This mechanism encourages a low polluting airline to achieve even lower standards, in order to trade its levels with high polluting airlines.

The Third Conference of the Parties to the United Nations Framework Convention on Climate Change (Climate Change Convention)[23] was held from 1 to 11 December 1997 at Kyoto, Japan. Significantly, the states parties to the Convention adopted a protocol (Kyoto

Protocol)[24] on 11 December 1997 under which industrialized countries have agreed to reduce their collective emissions of six greenhouse gases[25] by at least 5 per cent by 2008–12. Ambassador Raul Estrada-Oyuela, who had chaired the Committee of the Whole established by the Conference to facilitate the negotiation of a protocol text, expressed the view that the agreement will have a real impact on the problem of greenhouse gas emissions and that 11 December 1997 should be remembered as the 'Day of the Atmosphere'.[26]

The Kyoto Protocol, in Article 1(*a*)(v) calls on each state party to achieve progressive or phasing out of market imperfections, fiscal incentives, tax and duty exemptions and subsidies in all greenhouse gas-emitting sectors that run counter to the objective of the Convention and application of market instruments. The subject of emissions leading to trading is addressed initially in Article 3 of the Protocol which requires states parties to ensure that their aggregate anthropogenic carbon dioxide equivalent emissions of the greenhouse gases listed in Annex A do not exceed their assigned amounts, calculated pursuant to their quantified emission limitation and reduction commitments inscribed in Annex B. The provision also requires states parties to the Protocol to reduce their overall emissions of greenhouse gases by at least 5 per cent below 1990 levels in the commitment period 2008–12. Article 3(6) goes further, in providing that states parties shall be allowed a certain degree of flexibility in implementation of Article 3 and the reduction of their emission standards.

The subject of emissions trading is explicitly addressed in Article 6, which states that, for the purpose of meeting its commitments under Article 3, any party included in Annex 1 may transfer to or acquire from, any other such party emission reduction units resulting from projects aimed at reducing anthropogenic emissions by sources or enhancing anthropogenic removals by sinks of greenhouse gases in any sector of the economy provided the parties concerned approve of such trading and, inter alia, such trading actually results in a reduction in emission by sources.

Article 17 sets out that the Conference of the Parties shall define the relevant principles, modalities, rules and guidelines, in particular for verification, reporting and accountability for emissions trading. It also provides that the parties included in Annex B to the Protocol may participate in emissions trading for the purposes of fulfilling their commitments under Article 3. Such trading shall be supplemental to domestic actions for the purpose of meeting qualified emission limitation and reduction commitments under Article 3.[27]

Once the Protocol has entered into force,[28] Annex 1 parties must submit an annual inventory of emissions to the Convention Secretariat,[29] enabling expert review teams to provide a full assessment of such parties' compliance with the Protocol.[30] These expert assessments will be reviewed by the Conference of the Parties serving as the meeting of the parties to the Protocol,[31] which will adopt decisions on implementation.[32]

Article 12 of the Protocol is also noteworthy in that it defines a clean development mechanism (CDM) which introduces the concept of joint implementation by a developed country and a developing country.[33] The mechanism admits of the advantage afforded to the parties concerned, in developed countries gaining the benefit of the partnerships in emissions trading with developing countries which are more cost-effective in financing such projects. The CDM achieves the dual goal of enabling developing countries to operate projects which result in emission reductions which contribute to the objectives of the UNFCCC,[34] and also enabling countries specified in Annex 1 of the Kyoto Protocol which finance such projects through the CDM to use emissions reductions to reduce their own emissions *in toto*.[35]

The mechanism is supervised by an executive board and the responsibility of establishing procedures to make certain that proper verification of projects is achieved in a transparent manner devolve upon to the Conference of the Parties to the Protocol.[36] By virtue of Articles 12(10) and 3(12), Annex I countries could contribute to their own emission reduction targets under the Protocol by using emission reductions from jointly implemented projects under the CDM during the period 2000–2008.

A watershed provision of the Kyoto Protocol lies in Article 2.2 which stipulates that parties included in Annex 11 shall pursue limitation or reduction of emissions of greenhouse gases not controlled by the Montreal Protocol[37] from aviation and marine bunker fuels, working through the International Civil Aviation Organization and the International Maritime Organization, respectively. This lays the regulatory responsibility for emissions trading with regard to aircraft engine emissions squarely on ICAO.

ICAO's Role in Emissions Trading

At the 32nd Session of the ICAO Assembly, Resolution A32-8, containing a consolidated statement of continuing ICAO policies and practices related to environmental protection, was adopted. This Resolution urges states to refrain from unilateral environmental measures that would be harmful to the development of international civil aviation.

On the subject of aircraft engine emissions, the Resolution, in its Appendix F, makes mention of the fact that the Kyoto Protocol calls for developed countries to pursue limitation or reduction of greenhouse gases from aviation bunker fuels, working through ICAO, and invokes Appendix A which calls upon the ICAO Council to maintain the initiative in developing policy guidance on all aviation matters related to the environment and not leave such initiatives to other organizations.

Appendix H of A32-8 refers to ICAO's policies on charges and taxes,[38] and the policy statement issued by the ICAO Council on 9 December 1996 in the form of a Council Resolution of an interim nature, and urges states to follow the current guidance of the Council on emission-related levies. The Council is similarly exhorted by the Assembly, through A32-8, to continue to pursue the question of emission-related levies with a view to reaching a conclusion prior to the next Ordinary Session of the Assembly in 2001.

The policy statement of the Council dated 9 December 1996 takes into consideration the fact that a number of states consider it desirable to use a levy to reflect environmental costs associated with air transport, while other states do not consider it appropriate to impose such a levy under the present circumstances. The Council goes on to state that it considers the development of an internationally agreed environmental charge or tax on air transport that all states would be expected to impose would appear not to be practicable at the time, given the differing views of states and the significant organization and practical implementation problems that would be likely to arise.

According to the Council Statement, ICAO is seeking to identify a rational common basis on which states wishing to introduce environmental levies on air transport could do so. The Council strongly recommends in its statement that any environmental reviews on air transport which states may introduce should be in the form of charges rather than taxes and that the funds collected should be applied in the first instance to mitigating the environmental impact of aircraft engine emissions, for example by (a) addressing the specific damage caused by these emissions, if that can be identified, (b) funding scientific research into their environmental impact, or (c) funding research aimed at reducing their environmental impact, through developments in technology and new approaches to aircraft operations.

Finally, the Council urges states that are considering the introduction of emission-related charges to take into account the non-discrimination principle in Article 15 of the Convention on International Civil Aviation and the work in progress within ICAO and, in the meantime, to be guided by the general principles in the *Statements by the Council to contracting States on Charges for Airports and Air Navigation Services* (Doc. 9082/4) and the following principles adapted from those agreed by the 31st Session of the ICAO Assembly: that there should be no fiscal aims behind the charges, the charges should be related to costs, and the charges should not discriminate against air transport as compared with other modes of transport.

As part of its efforts to monitor the issue of emissions and economic instruments in that regard, and also to reach a conclusion prior to the next Assembly Session of ICAO in the year 2001, the Council of ICAO is actively pursuing the issue also through its Committee on Aviation Environmental Protection (CAEP). CAEP, at its 4th meeting (CAEP/4) held in April 1998, identified as an integral part of its work programme the need to address emissions inventories for future scientific assessments; long-term emissions burden estimates used for quantifying benefits of regulatory charges; and the effectiveness of operational measures to reduce aircraft emissions or their effect on the atmosphere.[39] The meeting also noted that further work on market-based options for reducing emissions was necessary.

The CAEP/4 Report, which was considered by the 32nd Session of the ICAO Assembly, presented a report on emissions-related levies which was quite extensive. CAEP/4 basically envisaged four options for levies: a fuel levy, ticket levy, route levy and an airport levy. With regard to the application of a levy, the Report considered a revenue neutral application, a general taxation application, a levy application based on a preventive-cost approach and an application involving paying damages or compensation for third party injury. The Report also considered the efficacy of each levy option and application as well as implementation aspects of environmental levies in the context of their relation both to levy collection and to the application of levies. As a pivotal point to the whole exercise, CAEP/4 examined the role of ICAO with regard to such levies.

Another critical area of work in regard to emissions trading is IPCC's Special Report on Aviation and the Global Atmosphere, released in June 1999.

Legal Issues concerning Emissions Trading

There will most likely be three types of emissions trading: country-to-country trading between national governments, company-to-company trading within domestic trading schemes, and company-to-company trading internationally.

Country-to-country trading Trading between countries would essentially involve bilateral or multilateral treaties to be signed by the states concerned. These would be governed by the principles of public international law. Liability for breach of agreement would be based on principles of state responsibility and would be deemed enforceable through the International Court of Justice (ICJ).

International responsibility of states relates both to breaches of treaty provisions and to other breaches of legal duty. In the *Spanish*

Zone of Morocco Claims case, Huber J observed: 'Responsibility is the necessary corollary of a right. All rights of an international character involve international responsibility. If the obligation in question is not met, responsibility entails the duty to make reparation.'[40] In the *Barcelona Traction* case, the ICJ held:

> an essential distinction should be drawn between the obligations of a State towards the international community as a whole, and those arising *vis-à-vis* another State in the field of diplomatic protection. By their very nature, the former are the concerns of all States. In view of the importance of the rights involved, all States can be held to have a legal interest in their protection; they are obligations *erga omnes*.[41]

The International Law Commission has observed of the ICJ decision: 'in the Court's view, there are in fact a number, albeit limited, of international obligations which, by reason of their importance to the international community as a whole, are – unlike others – obligations in respect of which all States have legal interest'.[42] The views of the ICJ and the International Law Commission, which has supported the approach taken by the ICJ, give rise to two possible conclusions relating to *jus cogens* and its resultant obligations *erga omnes*: (a) obligations *erga omnes* affect all states and thus cannot be made inapplicable to a state or group of states by an exclusive clause in a treaty or other document reflecting legal obligations without the consent of the international community as a whole; (b) obligations *erga omnes* pre-empt other obligations which may be incompatible with them. Examples of obligations *erga omnes* cited by the ICJ include prohibition of acts of aggression, genocide, slavery and discrimination.[43] It is indeed worthy of note that all these obligations are derivatives of norms which are *jus cogens* at international law.

In its Report to the General Assembly, the International Law Commission recommended a draft provision which required: 'Every State has the duty to conduct its relations with other States in accordance with international law and with the principle that the sovereignty of each State is subject to the supremacy of international law.'[44] This principle, which forms a cornerstone of international conduct by states, provides the basis for strengthening international comity and regulating the conduct of states both internally – within their territories – and externally, towards other states. States are effectively precluded by this principle from pursuing their own interests untrammelled and with disregard to principles established by international law.

At public international law *de lege ferenda*, a state should not be entitled to cite provisions of its own laws or inadequacies in its laws as its response to a breach of its obligations imposed by international law. Called the monistic theory, jurisprudence supporting this premise is monotonously consistent, as is reflected in the *Free Zones* case,[45] where the Provisional Court of International Justice (PCIJ) ruled that France was precluded from using its own legislation to desist from performing its international obligations. In the earlier case of *Polish Nations in Danzig*[46] the PCIJ held:

> It should ... be observed that ... a State cannot adduce as against another State its own Constitution with a view to evading obligations incumbent upon it under international law or treaties in force. Applying these principles to the present case, it results that the question of the treatment of Polish nationals or other Persons of Polish origin or speech must be settled exclusively on the basis of the rules of international law and the treaty provisions in force between Poland and Danzig.[47]

The above judicial theory holds that there is a general duty incumbent upon all states to bring their internal laws into conformity with obligations and responsibilities imposed by international law.[48] This is an implied obligation which a state has *erga omnes*.

Company-to-company trading Company-to-company trading under a domestic setting will be dealt with by the laws of the jurisdiction concerned. In common law countries, liability for breach of contract would be essentially dependent upon the *cursus curiae*. At a fundamental level, the principle of contract law, enunciated by Lord Diplock, still functions as the basis of understanding between the parties: 'The law is concerned with legal obligations only, and the law of contract only with legal obligations created by mutual agreement between contractors – not with expectations, however reasonable, of one contractor that the other will do something that he has assumed no legal obligation to do.'[49] In the seminal case of *Hadley* v. *Baxendale*,[50] decided in 1854, Alderson B set the above principle in a framework of damages for breach of contract when he said:

> Where two parties have made a contract which one of them has broken, the damages which the other party ought to receive in respect of such breach of contract should be such as may fairly and reasonably be considered either arising naturally, i.e. according to the usual course of things, from such breach of contract itself, or such as may reasonably be supposed to have been in the contemplation of both parties, at the time they made the contract, as the probable result of the breach of it.[51]

The aggrieved party is only entitled to recover such part of the loss actually resulting as at the time of the contract was reasonably foreseeable as liable to result from the breach.[52] What was at the time reasonably foreseeable depends upon the knowledge then possessed by the parties or, at all events, the party who commits the breach.

There is also the remedy of specific performance at equity under the common law, where a decree of specific performance is issued by the court which constrains a contracting party to do that which he has promised to do. The concept of specific performance has its genesis at early law, where courts had to address many instances where the remedy available at common law was not adequate. Although the normal remedy at common law for breach of contract is damages, and in most cases the award of damages affords adequate compensation, there are instances, for example when performance promised to an aggrieved party would not be available anywhere else, where specific performance is enforced.[53]

A mandatory injunction is another equitable remedy at common law which directs the defendant to take measures positively to undo what he has already done to breach a contract. The case of *Lord Manners* v. *Johnson*[54] reflects the ability of a court vested with powers of adjudication under a common law jurisdiction to compel a defendant to demolish a house which he has constructed contrary to an existing contract. Analogically, a person who refuses, or fails, to perform an emissions trading contract could be compelled to perform the contract by injunction.

Company-to-company trading internationally The analogy to companies trading with each other internationally on emissions trading in the modern-day context is the typical trans-boundary contract, such as a cyber contract performed on the Internet where two or more jurisdictions are at play. In a cyber contract, the contract is established by offer and acceptance in two different places through the Internet and liabilities and rights of parties are determined on a choice of jurisdiction and according to the principles of the chosen jurisdiction.

Usually, such a contract is concluded when, in response to an offer made by an offeror, the offeree indicates acceptance to the offeror. In cases of simultaneous communication of the offer and acceptance, made face-to-face by the offeror and offeree, the essentials of a contract are clear. However, when parties are not in close proximity to each other and communicate their dealings over the telecommunications medium, the process may become slightly more complicated, in that it may not always be clear as to what constitutes an offer or an acceptance. In such instances, it largely becomes a matter of interpretation as to whether both the offeror and the offeree had the intent to conclude the contract.

The element of intention to contract and to conclude the process on the part of both the offeror and the offeree is initial to the formation of the contract. Courts have insisted that proof of an offer to enter into legal relations upon definite terms must be followed by the production of evidence from which the courts may infer an intention by the offeree to accept that offer. Thus the statements made by the parties in the process of negotiations are of extreme importance in the determination of a concluded contract. The 1840 case of *Hyde* v. *Wrench*[55] offers the seminal principle that a series of communications from either party may impinge on an original offer. In the *Hyde* case, the defendant, on 6 June offered to sell an estate to the plaintiff for £1000. On 8 June in reply, the plaintiff made an offer of £950, which was refused by the defendant on 27 June. However, on 29 June, the plaintiff wrote to the defendant that he was now willing to pay £1000.

The importance of the *Hyde* decision lies in the fact that the court held that no contract existed. The plaintiff had, by rejecting the offer made on 6 June, precluded himself from reviving the offer later. In other words, once an offer is rejected by the offeree, he cannot go on on the basis that the offer would still stand in its original form. When this principle is applied to an auction situation where the airline is offering to consider offers over the Internet from the public, any offer made by a member of the public for a seat on a flight cannot be rejected by the airline and later revived.

Of course, a counter-offer situation is different, where an airline nominates an alternative sum as acceptable. For example, if A offers over the Internet $100 as a price he would pay for a seat from Montreal to Toronto, the airline concerned can counter-offer the seat at $125, thus making itself the offeror. Unlike in the *Hyde* case, here there is no outright rejection of the offer.

In the instance of an auction carried out over the Internet, the primary issue at stake in the determination of a contract is whether the parties intended the contract to be concluded. For instance, if a person offers a certain price to the airline over the Internet and the airline gives him a reference number, the allocation of that number may not necessarily indicate acceptance of the offer by the airline. The 1989 US case of *Corinthian Pharmaceutical Systems Inc.* v. *Lederle Laboratories*[56] is a good analogy. In the *Corinthian* case, a person dealing in medicinal drugs on a wholesale basis ordered a consignment of drugs through a computerized telephone ordering system. The order was placed strategically a day before a price increase was to take effect. The wholesaler ordered through the manufacturers' automated telephone order system and, after the order message was placed by him, he was allocated a 'tracking number' by the manufacturer's computer system. There was absolutely no human interaction in the transaction. Subsequently, when the manufacturer refused to sell the consignment of drugs as ordered by the wholesaler at the pre-increase price as ordered, the court held with the manufacturer's position that the tracking number issued by the manufacturer's computer was not an acceptance of the offer, but merely an acknowledgment of the receipt of the order – or offer in contractual law terms. The court concluded that no contract had been concluded, and the wholesaler was denied purchase of the goods at the lower price.

There is no doubt as to when and where the contract comes into being when parties sign a contract simultaneously in a face-to-face setting. It is often not a trivial legal task to determine when and where, when either an offer or an acceptance, or both, are sent by telegraph, telex, fax, electronic data interchange (EDI), e-mail, or via the Internet, or are communicated by telephone. The uncertainty began even before the advent of the telegraph, with the mail delivery system. The general contract law principle is that an offer is not considered accepted until the acceptance of the offer is received by the offeror. In England in the 19th century, an exception to this rule was developed by judges for offers and acceptances sent by the mail. The so-called 'post box rule' or expedition theory prescribes that, where an offer is made in the mail, the contract takes effect immediately at the time acceptance is posted in the mail (rather than when the acceptance is actually received by the offeror) where use of the mail is reasonable in the circumstances or expressly contemplated by the parties. This rule effectively precludes the need to hold the offeree responsible for delays in communications and places the burden of uncertainly of the waiting period on the offeror; that is, the offeror does not know that it has earlier concluded a binding contract until it receives the offeree's acceptance in the mail, whereas the offeree knew the contract came into existence the moment it posted its reply letter. Shifting this risk to the offeror, and giving the concomitant assurance to the offeree, was reasonable because of the increased reliability of the Royal Mail in the 1800s, to the point where multiple deliveries a day in larger urban centres were the norm. The expedition theory is a good example of a legal doctrine being firmly grounded in the communication environment and commercial processes of its day.

As the telegraph, telephone and other new communications technology evolved into widespread use, cases established principles as to when and where contracts were concluded. In *Carow Towing*, an early Canadian case, courts held that a contract entered into by telephone should be treated like a letter and should follow the expedition theory, with acceptance occurring at the place the acceptance is spoken and not where the offeror hears the acceptance.[57] By contrast, in the *Entores*[58] case, a later British decision, Lord Denning concluded that, for simultaneous communications like the telephone, the place where the contract is concluded is where the offeror hears the acceptance, and thus, if the line goes dead during the telephone conversation, the onus is upon the offeree to call back the offeror to ensure the words of acceptance had been communicated to the offeror. Subsequent cases in Canada have followed the decision in *Entores* rather than the approach in *Carow Towing*,[59] with the exception of Quebec where, until recently, the preponderance of case law has followed the principle that telephone contracts arise when and where the offeree speaks its acceptance;[60] since the enactment of the current Civil Code of Quebec in January 1994, Article 1387 explicitly provides that in respect of telephone contracts acceptance occurs when and where the acceptance is received. It is interesting to note that the *Entores* decision was also followed in two fax cases, one in Nova Scotia[61] and one in New Zealand,[62] where each held that a contract made by fax arises when the offeror receives by fax the acceptance of the offeree.

Courts in the *Entores* case also held that telex technology results in instantaneous communications with the result that acceptance occurs when the message is received by the offeror. This approach was confirmed in a decision by the House of Lords in the *Brinkibon* case.[63] In this case the court held that, although telex communications should be categorized as simultaneous, in each case the specific constituent elements and factors in the communications system concerned need to be carefully considered:

> The senders and recipients may not be the principals to the contemplated contract. They may be servants or agents with limited authority. The message may not reach, or be intended to reach, the designated recipient immediately; messages may be sent out of office hours, or at night, with the intention, or on the assumption, that they will be read at a later time. There may be some error or default at the recipient's end which prevents receipt at the time contemplated and believed in by the sender. The message may have been sent and/or received through machines operated by third persons. And many other variations may occur. No universal rule can cover all such cases; they must be resolved by reference to the intentions of the parties, by sound business practice and in some cases by a judgment where the risks should lie.[64]

The recognition of the above facts in the *Brinkibon* case raise a number of emerging issues in respect of EDI, e-mail and Internet communications. Certain EDI transmissions, for example will fall into the simultaneous communications category. Much of EDI is effected, not between the trading principals, however, but by use of intermediaries, so-called value-added networks (VAN) or service providers. An EDI message could likely go through the message sender's VAN, then through the recipient's VAN, and finally to the recipient. Similarly, e-mail messages over the Internet may be routed to electronic mailboxes from which the recipient has then to download. In such instances, it may be more difficult to conclude that the simultaneous communication rules should apply. Also it may be difficult to determine when exactly an electronic message arrives at the recipient's location for purposes of being recognized as legally effective: for instance, an early British case that held that a letter sent in a sealed envelope is not considered received until it is opened by the addressee personally.[65] Whether such a rule should apply in the case of e-mail, or whether an e-mail message should be deemed received when it is available to be viewed by the intended recipient, regardless of the time at which the recipient actually reads the message, is a moot point. Another question is when should a telex or fax be deemed to have arrived at a workplace? In one case,[66] the answer suggested when the message was received by the recipient's machine (on a Friday after business hours and not three days later on a Monday morning when a person actually reads the telex).

Given these ambiguities, prudent users of electronic commerce should try to avoid having to refer these issues to a judge by providing, in their EDI Trading Partner Agreement (TPA) or other similar document, precisely what electronic message must be received by which computer (that is, the recipient's or the recipient's VAN) in order for a contract to arise, thereby bringing clarity to the questions as to when and where the electronic contract arose. As to the 'where' question, the parties to the TPA would be well advised to select a governing law in advance, and to make sure the VAN agreements contain the same jurisdiction, so that there is no question which law would apply if it were ever considered necessary to resort to adjudication. This is particularly true for EDI and Internet transactions where each trading partner's VAN, or Internet service provider, may be in a jurisdiction different from the customer, and therefore possibly the laws of four different jurisdictions may apply if the parties remain silent on the governing law question. In such circumstances, as Lord Denning observed in the *Entores* case concerning two parties in different jurisdictions, the problems arise because the laws of the respective jurisdictions are different. Therefore, predicting a court's probable response is difficult, given that the court will invariably try to seek the most just remedy under the circumstances, but in some cases this is truly a difficult task. As an example, consider the court's commentary in the *Export Packers* case, where the judge recommended that the various rules developed by the law over the years, such as the simultaneous communication rule in the *Entores* case, should not be applied in a rigid fashion:

> When the common law rules relating to offer and acceptance were under development the telephone did not exist. At that time agree-

ments were made by two or more persons getting together and reaching a common understanding. As the postal system came into being elaborate rules were made by the courts covering the mechanics of reaching a bargain by mail. Today a person ordinarily resident in British Columbia may telephone from Japan where he is on a business trip to a person ordinarily resident in Ontario but who is also then visiting Italy. They may agree to the same kind of contract which is the subject-matter of this writ. It does not necessarily follow the place where the contract was made was Japan and that Japanese law governs its interpretation. Alternatively, it would be hard to argue the place where the contract was made was Italy and the law of that country ought to apply to its interpretation.[67]

This dictum clearly confirms the benefit accrued to users of electronic commerce in crafting their own rules for dealing with issues of formation of contract. Making commercial relationships more secure and predictable through contract, however, can be a costly and time-consuming exercise. Therefore this may be an area for law reform. In the United States, the National Conference of Commissioners of Uniform State Law are already working toward establishing new rules under the Uniform Commercial Code that would take the view that Internet communications are instantaneous in nature and that therefore a contract comes into existence when the sender of the offer receives an electronic message signifying acceptance. This does not, however, answer the question as to when the acceptance is effective if the offeror was not present before the computer; in other words, does receipt require a human intervention and acknowledgement? In resolving this question, the following should be observed: the purpose and function of the rule, who would be prejudiced by a particular holding, what are the reasonable expectations of the parties, and on whom it is reasonable to place a burden for helping to 'fix' the system, if indeed it needs it.

Perhaps the single most important issue in trans-boundary contracts is that which pertains to jurisdiction. Given the World Wide Web and its global application, the most compelling question in this regard would pertain to the trans-boundary applicability of an Internet contract. In this regard, the most convenient analogy comes from the two jurisdictions of Canada and the United States. Would an offeror in Canada, who offers $500 over the Internet for a round trip between Toronto and Miami, be able to enforce an auction agreement against a US airline at its home base in Florida? In a case decided in 1952,[68] in Canada, where the plaintiff brought a case to the Ontario High Court against an American radio broadcasting station which was broadcasting, from across the border, allegedly libellous statements which could be heard over the air waves in Canada, the defendant radio station brought up a motion of dismissal, alleging that the Ontario Court in Canada had no jurisdiction to hear a case against a party to the action which was an enterprise based in the United States. The court disagreed, and held:

> A person may utter all the defamatory words he wishes without incurring any civil liability unless they are heard and understood by a third person. I think it a 'startling proposition' to say that one may, while standing south of the border or cruising in an aeroplane south of the border, through the medium of modern sound amplification, utter defamatory matter which is heard in a Province in Canada north of the border, and not be said to have published a slander in the Province in which it is heard and understood. I cannot see what difference it makes whether the person is made to understand by means of the written word, sound-waves or ether-waves in so far as the matter of proof of publication is concerned. The tort consists in making a third person understand actionable defamatory matter.[69]

In the more recent case of *Pindling* v. *National Broadcasting Corporation*[70] in respect of an American television broadcast received in Canada, the Ontario High Court held that the Prime Minister of the Bahamas was held entitled to bring the case to Canada, instead of the United States. The *Pindling* decision illustrates well the principle of 'forum shopping' which can be culled from the television context and be held applicable to the analogous situation of a contract transacted over the Internet.

The above principle may be derogated only in an instance where the court seized of the case could invoke the principle of 'forum non convenience' which allows the transfer of a suit from an originally filed jurisdiction to some other jurisdiction which is better placed to hear the case concerned. In the 1996 case of *National Bank of Canada* v. *Clifford Chance*[71] the Canadian courts which were charged with hearing a case where a Toronto-based firm had contracted with a law firm in the United Kingdom, transferred the case to the United Kingdom although the contract was concluded in Toronto, on the grounds that the contract concerned a United Kingdom-based project and the legal advice obtained had been UK law given by lawyers in the United Kingdom. On the basis of the *Clifford Chance* principle, it would not be unusual for a common law court to determine that, in an auction for an airline seat, where the offer emanates from, say, Canada over the Internet for a seat out of the United Kingdom on a United Kingdom based carrier, the applicable jurisdiction would lie with the courts in the United Kingdom, although the contract itself may have been concluded in Canada.

There is a dichotomy in the judicial thinking with regard to cases involving contracts concluded over the Internet. On the one hand, courts are refusing to bring a person into a jurisdiction purely because he contracted with a business entity which is based in that jurisdiction. This approach is illustrated by the 1994 US decision in the case of *Pres-Kap, Inc.* v. *System One, Direct Access Inc.*,[72] where the court refused to grant jurisdiction to Florida where a resident in New York had used a Florida-based on-line network information service merely to gain access to a database. Similarly, the court in the famous 1997 *SunAmerica* case[73] refused to find jurisdiction in a trademark case solely on the basis of the defendant's operation of a general access web site:

> Plaintiffs ask this Court to hold that any defendant who advertises nationally or on the internet is subject to its jurisdiction. It cannot plausibly be argued that any defendant who advertises nationally could expect to be hauled into Court in *any* state, for a cause of action that does not relate to the advertisements. Such general advertising is not the type of 'purposeful activity related to the forum that would make the exercise of jurisdiction fair, just or reasonable'.[74]

The principle of universal application of jurisdiction has been invoked in other instances, where courts have accepted jurisdiction on the basis of sales made to customers through the defendant's web site,[75] or based on soliciting donations,[76] or based on subscribers signed up by the defendant for services delivered over the Internet,[77] or for having follow-on contacts, negotiations and other dealings in addition to, and often as a result of, the initial Internet-based communication.[78] The common thread which runs through the fabric of judicial thinking in this regard is that parties who avail themselves of technology in order to do business in a distant place should not then be able to escape that place's legal jurisdiction. These cases are all-embracing, from contract breach claims to tort, including trade libel; in several cases, courts have even found jurisdiction in trademark infringement matters merely on the basis of a defendant's general access web site,[79] or linking to a national ATM network through a telephone line indirectly through an independent data processor in a third state.[80]

An overall evaluation of the US civil cases discussed above concludes that, while the general trend is for courts to assert jurisdiction over non-residents on the basis of their Internet activities, there are still a few situations where some courts may not apply jurisdiction.

Although the choice of forum may extend universally, it does not necessarily mean that enforcement from a judgment would automatically follow. In the case of *Bachchan* v. *India Abroad Publications Incorporated*,[81] the plaintiff, who was a national of India who had won the right to have his case heard in the United Kingdom, was unable to enforce judgment in New York. The New York courts held that the

UK law applicable to the case did not accord with US law and therefore the decision could not be recognized as enforceable in the United States.

Notes

1 See Ozone Science News, *The Newsletter of the UNEPIE Ozone Action Programme*, 26, April 1998, 7.
2 Ibid.
3 See 'A New Threat', *Acid News*, 2, June 1997, 15. In 1997, four European airlines launched a programme to measure ozone levels during flights to assess the impact of pollution on the environment (*Air Letter*, Wednesday 13 August 1997, 13 (805), 2).
4 'A New Threat' (*supra*, n.3).
5 Scientist David Fahey believes that aerosols of aircraft plumes could form the complex chemistry required for formation of cirrus clouds. See Fred Pearce (1997), 'Aircraft Wreck Havoc on Ozone Layer', *New Scientist*, 15 February, p.18.
6 Another significant project carried out in Europe was the AERONOX project of the European Union which was in three stages. The first stage calculated an exact worldwide inventory of aircraft emissions; the second examined how the pollutants in the exhaust plume change from immediately after their emission from the engine until they reach a 'stable' condition; the third stage calculated the probable effects by means of models on the diffusion in the atmosphere and on chemical and physical changes. The key focus is on the nitrogen oxide emissions and their effects on the concentrations of ozone at high altitudes. This project has already been concluded.
7 Martin Hindley (1996), 'Emission Control', *Flight International*, 31 January–6 February, p.69.
8 See 'Global Atmospheric Effects of Aviation', Report of the Proceedings of the Symposium, Virginia Beach, Virginia, USA, 15–19 April 1996, NASA, p.1.
9 Ibid., p.4.
10 A Pigouvian tax is a specific rate tax on units of emission or damage.
11 Black's Law Dictionary (1951).
12 *New London* v. *Miller*, 1941, *Connecticut Reporter* at 112.
13 1956 *Southern Reporter* at 81.
14 *In re. Mytinger*, DC: Tex., 31 F. Supp. 977 at 979.
15 See *Aviation Daily*, 16 November 1990, 328, where IATA Director General calls the one-dollar 'Facilitation Fee' proposed by the USA and which was to be imposed on aliens visiting the USA a 'tax'. See also *Aviation Daily*, 11 January 1990, 71 where he makes a strong plea to the US Secretary of Transport to urgently review the taxation of international transport. This tax was later withdrawn by the US authorities, largely as a response to the effective lobbying against the imposition of this tax by such organizations as IATA. See R.I.R. Abeyratne (1993), 'Air Transport Tax and its Consequences on Tourism', *Annals of Tourism Research*, 20(3), 450–60.
16 See, generally, Hainer Hinshaw (1939), 'The Protection of Aviation from Inequitable Taxation', *Journal of Air Law*, 9, 75–94.
17 Ibid.
18 William K. Tell (1931), 'Taxation of Aircraft Motor Fuel', *Journal of Air Law*, 2, 347. See also *Lowell* v. *Boston*, III Mass. 454 (1873).

19 Statute of the International Court of Justice, United Nations, New York, Article 38.

20 Hainer Hinshaw (*supra*, n.16).

21 Consolidated Resolution on Taxation of International Air Transport, C-WP/11072, 5/2/99.

22 The expression 'customs and other duties' shall include import, export, excise, sales, consumption and internal duties and taxes of all kinds levied upon the fuel, lubricants and other consumable technical supplies; and the duties and taxes shall include those levied by any taxing authority within a contracting state, whether national or local. These duties and taxes shall not be or continue to be imposed on the acquisition of fuel, lubricants or consumable technical supplies used by aircraft in connection with international air services except to the extent that they are based on the actual costs of providing airports or air navigation facilities and services and used to finance the costs of providing them.

23 (1992) 31 I.L.M. 849. On the negotiations and text of the Climate Change Convention, see D. Bodansky (1993), 'The United Nations Framework Convention on Climate Change: A Commentary', *Yale Journal of International Law*, 18, 451–558. See also J. Barrett (1991), 'The Negotiation and Drafting of the Climate Change Convention', in R. Churchill and D. Freestone (eds), *International Law and Global Climate Change*, Hamburg: Werner, pp.183–200.

24 Kyoto Protocol to the United Nations Framework Convention on Climate change, UN Doc. FCCC/CP/1997/L.7/Add.1.

25 Carbon dioxide, methane, nitrous oxide, hydrofluorocarbons, perfluorocarbons and sulphur hexafluoride.

26 UN Environment Programme (UNEP) Press Release, 11 December 1997.

27 The subject of emissions trading falls within the purview of the Intergovernmental Panel on Climate Change (IPCC), which was established in 1988 by the World Meteorological Organization and the United Nations' Environment Programme (UNEP) to assess the scientific basis and impact of climate change. The IPCC's first scientific report was published in 1990 and recommended the negotiation of a framework convention to combat global warming. The United Nations Framework Convention on Climate Change (UNFCCC) was adopted on 9 May 1992 and the treaty entered into force on 21 March 1994. This chapter, being a legal one, will not address details of these bodies. For an extensive treatment of the IPCC's work and the UNFCCC, see Colin Warbrick and Dominic McGoldric (eds) (1998), 'Global Warming and the Kyoto Protocol', *ICLQ*, 47, April, 446–62.

28 The Protocol will enter into force 90 days after 'not less than 55 Parties to the [Climate Change] Convention, incorporating Parties included in Annex 1 which accounted in total for at least 55% of the total carbon dioxide emissions for 1990 of the Parties included in Annex 1' have ratified (Art. 24 of the Protocol).

29 Ibid., Art. 7(1). The Secretariat is located in Bonn, Germany. Its postal address is P.O. Box 260 124, D-53153, Bonn, Germany.

30 Ibid., Art. 8(1).

31 Ibid., Art. 8(5). When the Conference of the Parties meets as the meeting of Parties to the Protocol, those states that are party to the Convention but not to the Protocol may participate but only as non-voting observers (ibid., Art. 13(1) and (2)). Parties to the Protocol will meet annually (Art. 13(6)) to review the implementation of the Protocol (Art. 13(4)).

32 Ibid., Art. 8(6).

33 See J.K. Parikh (1995), 'Joint Implementation and North South Cooperation for Climate Change', *International Environmental Affairs*, 7(1), 22–41.

34 *Supra*, n.27.

35 See Article 12(3) of the Kyoto Protocol.
36 Article 8 of the Protocol.
37 'Montreal Protocol on Substances that Deplete the Ozone Layer' (1987), *I.L.M.*, 26, 1550. The Montreal Protocol controls gases such as chlorofluorocarbons, which not only have ozone-depleting characteristics but also contribute to the greenhouse effect. The Kyoto Protocol has, by explicitly excluding the Montreal Protocol's role in ICAO's mandate, included carbon dioxide, nitrogen oxides and compounds of sulphur emissions within ICAO's purview.
38 As contained in Doc. 9082 (*Statements by the Council to Contracting States on Charges for Airports and Air Navigation Services*) and Doc. 8632 (*ICAO Policies on Taxation in the Field of International Air Transport*).
39 CAEP/4, Committee on Aviation Environmental Protection, Fourth Meeting, Montreal, 6–8 April 1998, Montreal ICAO, pp.1–8.
40 *1925 RIAA ii* 615 at 641.
41 *Barcelona Traction, Light and Power Company Limited, I.C.J. Reports*, 1974, 269–70.
42 *Yearbook of International Law Commission*, 1976, Vol. II, Part One, at 29.
43 *I.C.J. Reports*, 1970, at 32.
44 *Report of the International Law Commission to the General Assembly on the Work of the 1st Session*, A/CN.4/13, 9 June 1949, at 21.
45 (1932) PCIJ, Ser. A/B No. 46, 167.
46 (1931) PCIJ, Ser. A/B No. 44, 20.
47 Ibid., 24.
48 See Fitzmaurice (1957), *Hague Recueil*, 92 (II), 89.
49 *Lavarack* v. *Woods of Colchester, Ltd.* [1967] 2 QB 278; [1966] 3 All ER 683.
50 (1854) 9 Exch. 341 at 354.
51 Ibid., at 355.
52 *Victoria Laundry (Windsor) Ltd.* v. *Newman Industries Ltd.* [1949] 2 KB 528.
53 See *Cuddee* v. *Rutter* (1720) I.P. Wms. 570, where specific performance of an agreement to transfer £1000 company stock was refused.
54 (1875) 1 Ch.D. 673.
55 (1840), 3 Beav. 334.
56 724 F. Supp. 605 (S.D. Ind. 1989).
57 *Carow Towing Co.* v. *The 'Ed. McWilliams'* (1919), 46 D.L.R. 506 (Ex. Ct.).
58 *Entores, Ltd.* v. *Miles Far East Corporation* [1955] 2 All ER 493 (C.A.).
59 See, for example, *McDonald & Sons Ltd.* v. *Export Packers Co. Ltd.* (1979), 95 D.L.R. (3d) 174 (B.C.S.C.). See also *Re Viscount Supply Co. Ltd.* (1963), 40 D.L.R. (2d) 501 (Ont. S. C.); *National Bank of Canada* v. *Clifford Chance* (1996), 30 O.R. (3d) 746 (Gen. Div.).
60 *Rosenthal & Rosenthal Inc.* v. *Bonavista Fabrics Ltd.* [1984] C.A. 52 (Que. C.A.).
61 *Balcom (Joan) Sales Inc.* v. *Poirier* (1991), 288 A.P.R. 377 (N.S. Co. Ct.).
62 *Gunac Hawkes Bay (1986) Ltd.* v. *Palmer* [1991] 3 N.Z.L.R. 297 (H. Ct.).
63 *Brinkibon Ltd.* v. *Stahag Stahl and Stahlwarenhandelsgesellschaft mbH* [1982] 1 All ER 293 (HL).
64 Ibid., 296.
65 *Arrowsmith* v. *Ingle* (1810), 3 Taunt. 234.
66 The *'Pendrecht'* [1980] 2 Lloyd's Rep. 56 (QB).
67 *McDonald and Sons Ltd.* v. *Export Packers Co. Ltd.* (1979), 95 D.L.R. (3dl 174) (B.C.S.C.) at 180.
68 *Jenner* v. *Sun Oil Co. Ltd.* (1952) 16 C.P.R. 87 (Ont. H.C.J.).
69 Ibid., 98–9.
70 (1984) 49 O.R. (Ed) 58 (H.C.J.).
71 (1996) 30 O.R. (3d) 746 (Gen. Div.).
72 636 So. 2d. 1351 (Fla. App. 1994).

73 *IDS Life Insurance Co.* v. *SunAmerica, Inc.*, 958 F. Supp. 1258 (N.D. III. 1997), aff'd in part, vacated in part, 1998 WL 51350 (7th Cir.) (Westlaw).

74 Ibid., 268.

75 *Digital Equipment Corporation* v. *AltaVista Technology, Inc.* 960 F. Supp. 456 (D. Mass. 1997). See also *Cody* v. *Ward*, 954 F. Supp. 43 (D. Conn. 1997), where a court took jurisdiction based on telephone and e-mail communications that consummated a business relationship begun over *Prodigy's* 'Money talk' discussion forum for financial matters. In partially justifying this decision, the court noted that the use of fax technology, and even live telephone conferences, can greatly reduce the burden of litigating out-of-state.

76 *Heroes, Inc.* v. *Heroes Foundation*, 958 F. Supp. 1 (D.D.C. 1996).

77 *Zippo Manufacturing Company* v. *Zippo Dot Com, Inc.*, 952 F. Supp. 1119 (W.D. Pa. 1997).

78 *Resuscitation Technologies, Inc.* v. *Continental Health Care Corp.*, 1997 WL 148567 (S.D. Ind.) Weslaw). The court in this case was not concerned that the defendants had never visited the forum state in person and concluded at para. 5: 'Neither is the matter disposed of by the fact that no defendant ever set foot in Indiana. The "footfalls" were not physical, they were electronic. They were, nonetheless, footfalls. The level of Internet activity in this case was significant.' See also *EDIAS Software International, L.L.C.* v. *BASIS International Ltd.*, 947 F. Supp. 413 (D. Ariz. 1996). In this case the court summed up the essence of many of the Internet jurisdiction cases by stating at 420: 'BASIS [the defendant] should not be permitted to take advantage of modern technology through an Internet Web page and forum and simultaneously escape traditional notions of jurisdiction.' See also *Gary Scott International, Inc.* v. *Baroudi*, 981 F. Supp. 714 (D. Mass. 1997).

79 *Panavision International, L.P.* v. *Toeppen*, 938 F. Supp. 616 (CD- Cal. 1996); *Maritz, Inc.* v. *CyberGold, Inc.*, 947 F. Supp. 1328 (E.D. Mo. 1996); *Inset Systems, Inc.* v. *Instruction Set, Inc.*, 937 F. Supp. 161 (D. Conn. 1996). In the latter case the court observed, at 165:

> In the present case, Instruction has directed its advertising activities via the Internet and its toll-free number toward not only the state of Connecticut, but to all States. The Internet as well as toll-free numbers are designed to communicate with people and their businesses in every state. Advertisement on the Internet can reach as many as 10,000 Internet users within Connecticut alone. Further, once posted on the Internet, unlike television and radio advertising, the advertisement is available continuously to any Internet user. ISI has therefore, purposefully availed itself of the privilege of doing business within Connecticut.

80 *Plus System, Inc.* v. *New England Network, Inc.*, 804 F. Supp. 111 (D. Colo. 1992).

81 585 N.Y.S. 2d 661 (Supp. 1992).

PART II
LIABILITY ISSUES

11 Turbulence and Personal Injury

Introduction

Turbulence is defined as a state of fluid flow in which the velocities exhibit irregular and random fluctuations. It may occur in an unstable air mass as hot air rises, which is called convective turbulence, or in a stable air mass caused by strong wind shears, which is called mountain wave turbulence or clear air turbulence.[1]

A study, the results of which were published by the Flight Safety Foundation in October 1994,[2] reveals that for the 35-year period between 1958 and 1993, turbulence was the cause of the largest number of aircraft accidents which did not involve aircraft equipment, crew or flight operational procedures as causes.[3] The same study showed that turbulence had been the cause of aircraft accidents in the above category in the same proportion for the period 1989–93 as in the 35-year period referred to above.

Apart from turbulence caused by naturally occurring wind movements, there is also the danger posed to aircraft from wake turbulence, or turbulence caused in the wake of one aircraft in close proximity to another. A study conducted by the National Transportation and Safety Board (NTSB) of the United States in February 1994 reveals that 51 wake turbulence accidents and incidents were reported in the United States between 1983 and 1993.[4] The same study confirms that wake turbulence affects small aircraft and large aircraft alike.[5]

The threat posed to air travel by turbulence was addressed by the International Civil Aviation Organization as far back as 1950, when the Third Session of the ICAO Meteorology Division recommended a programme of research which included arrangements for collecting data from the crews of civil aircraft and the development of turbulence-measuring devices for use in radiosonde and radio/radar wind ascents. Following these recommendations, the Fourth Session of the Division, held in 1954, simultaneously with the first session of the

Commission for Aeronautical Meteorology of the World Meteorological Organization (WMO), made recommendations that WMO encourage its members to continue research on the distribution of turbulence and gusts both geographically and with altitude and also on the physical structure of these phenomena, and, inter alia to make the findings available to ICAO[6] and that, among other things, ICAO be requested to maintain a high level turbulence report form (ICAO model) whereby both ICAO and WMO could urge states to see the closest cooperation between meteorological services and airline operators in obtaining from aircraft commanders reports on turbulence experienced during flight.[7]

From a legal perspective, turbulence per se does not pose any challenges. However, injury caused to passengers as a result of turbulence may have legal connotations in terms of carrier liability. The direct source of handling turbulence is always the airline pilot, as the 1993 study[8] showed for 80 per cent of the total number of citations from 1958–93.[9] All modern aircraft are fitted with weather radar which enables the flight crew to circumvent severe turbulence. Assuming the turbulence is inevitable, given the exigency of a situation which makes it impossible to avoid turbulence, there still remains the question of crew conduct: how the crew dealt with the aftermath of the turbulence encounter and whether the necessary precautions had been taken to prepare the passengers for the approaching ordeal.

This chapter will address principles of air carrier liability under the existing Warsaw System in instances of injury or death caused to passengers as a result of turbulence, with special emphasis on the conduct of airline crew.

Turbulence

Turbulence is a property of most fluids – liquids and gases – encountered in nature. Simply put, it is 'bumpiness in flight' which can be mitigated by manoeuvring by the pilot, usually by the introduction of accelerations of speed at the occurrence.[10] The overall effects of turbulence have been best summed up by McLean, who states:

> Fortunately, flight is smooth much more frequently than it is turbulent. In fact, the chance that an aircraft flying anywhere in the troposphere or lower stratosphere will encounter noticeable turbulence is only about one in twenty. The risk can be significantly greater or less depending on geographical location, altitude, season, local weather conditions, and time of day, but even in regions with high frequencies, most turbulence intensities are light. For greater intensities, the chances become very small. The odds of a random encounter with severe turbulence is one in several hundred, or less. In fact, in 2775 weather-

related U.S. Civil Aviation accidents between 1982 and 1984, only 222 (8%) were caused by turbulence.[11]

These statistics by no means reflect the full impact of turbulence on flight, although they convey the general idea that injury and death caused to passengers by turbulence have not been unconscionably frequent.

Turbulence may occur at lower intensities, causing passenger discomfort and pilot fatigue – conditions which may not *ipso facto* be causes of action at law – but may still lead to dangerous consequences if persistent, leading to accidents. Such lower intensity turbulence, if coupled with poor visibility, heavy precipitation and icing, may contribute to serious flight consequences. In a 1991 study on Canada, it was found that turbulence was a contributing factor in 38 per cent of the cases resulting in aircraft weather-related accidents during the period 1977 to 1983.[12]

Turbulence, although actually part of the natural state of the atmosphere, often acts like a stream and becomes fluid in motion. It has eddies and countercurrents, bubbles and smoother spots, and may affect different parts of an aircraft in diverse ways. For example, in 1995, a large aircraft in cruise mode experienced turbulence where the flight deck crew and the flight attendants in the front of the aircraft only experienced a brief lightness on the feet but no other adverse effects. However, the same incidents produced severe gyrations in the back of the aircraft, resulting in several crew members having to be hospitalized with multiple fractures.[13]

Pilot reports of turbulence (PIREPS) play a critical role in helping investigators analyse and forecast turbulence incidents. These reports are the only tangible evidence which remains after the fact which could prove that turbulence exists and gives dimensions of its extent and intensity in a given reported incident. The only drawback to PIREPS is that the pilot determines the degree of intensity of turbulence, and it has been claimed that there appears to be little uniformity in reports of pilots who observe and report incidents of turbulence.[14] Of course, this is not the fault of the pilot, who has to rely on his powers of observation while concentrating on coping with the incident in the absence of specific instruments on board to measure the intensity and extent of the turbulence.

ICAO, through its Automatic Air Reporting Study Group (ATARSG) has emphasized the importance of dissemination of information on turbulence as being an essential factor in aeronautical meteorology and air traffic control.[15] The ICAO position is fully reflected in Annex 3[16] to the Convention on International Civil Aviation[17] and Rules of the Air and Air Traffic Services,[18] and states the existence of an operational requirement to report turbulence in every air report. However, unfortunately, this requirement does not have automatic global approval and ICAO has, through its Air Navigation Commission, charged ATARSG to monitor and study the development of methods to measure and report turbulence in automated air reporting in order that proposals may be developed in an appropriate manner. These proposals are expected to enable revision of the ICAO documentation accordingly, taking into account automated reports of turbulence.

Legal Liability of the Carrier

Legal liability of the carrier would prima facie arise if death or injury to passengers results from an accident caused by turbulence. Article 17 of the Warsaw Convention[19] states: 'The carrier shall be liable for damage sustained in the event of the death or wounding of a passenger, if the accident which caused the damage so sustained took place on board the aircraft or in the course of any of the operations of embarking or disembarking.' To control the floodgates of litigation and discourage spurious claimants, the Convention admits of certain defences the airline may invoke and, above all, limits the liability of the airline to passengers and dependants of deceased passengers.

General Definition of 'Accident'

The Warsaw Convention stipulates that an 'accident' should cause injury or death to a passenger[20] if it were to be considered for liability. At common law, the word 'accident' is defined by Halsbury, who states:

> the word accident (or its adjective accidental) is no doubt used with the intention of excluding the operation of natural causes such as old age, congenital or insidious disease, or the natural progression of some constitutional, physical or mental defect, but the ambit of what is included by the word is not entirely clear… What is postulated is the intervention of some cause … so as to be fairly describable as fortuitous … it covers any unlooked-for mishap or an untoward event which is not expected or designed.[21]

Perhaps the first known attempt at definition was in a case reported in England in 1900,[22] where a man, in the course of lifting heavy machinery, vomited blood as a result of an abnormality of his internal organs. Smith LJ interpreting section 1(1) of the Workmen's Compensation Act of 1897 under which the action was brought for compensation under a personal accident insurance policy, held that the death of the man was due to disease and therefore did not accord with the true sense of the word 'accident'.[23] Collins LJ agreeing with the view expressed by Smith LJ decided that an accident should be fortuitous and unexpected and in this case the event which led to the death of the worker was not fortuitous.[24] In a case which followed,[25] where a workman had to balance a beam in such a way as to avoid falling and in the course of which precarious exercise he strained the muscles of his back, Collins MR held that an accident, to be compensated, should be fortuitous and unexpected,[26] to which Matthew LJ added that the criterion should be to determine what would happen within the course of employment and what would not.

Both the cases cited seem to accord with Halsbury's inclination to treat accident as a fortuitous event. Analogically, the approach of the judges to an accident caused to an airline passenger would seemingly have included the dual criteria of there being an unexpected or fortuitous event not contributed to by the inherent ill health of the passenger and which should have occurred within the course of his carriage by air. The later case of *Fenton* v. *Thorley and Co. Limited*[27] qualified the somewhat restrictive definition of the word 'accident' adopted in the earlier cases. Lord Macnaughten, while recognizing that an accident should be an unlooked-for mishap or an untoward event which is not expected or designed,[28] observed that the earlier definition could even make a stupid act performed by a person compensable, if such was fortuitous. In this case an appeal of an apparently healthy man who ruptured himself by an act of over exertion during employment was deemed by the House of Lords to have qualified to be allowed compensation under the rubric of 'accident'. Perhaps the most significant statement on the position was by Lord Robertson, who said: 'No one out of a law court would ever hesitate to say that this man met with an accident … the word "accident" is not made inappropriate by the fact that the man hurt himself.'[29] Lord Lindley, dealing with the term 'accident' in the same case, held that 'The word "accident" is not a technical legal term with a clearly defined meaning. Speaking generally, but with reference to legal liabilities, an accident means any unintended occurrence which produces hurt or loss.'[30] His Lordship went on to say:

> every injury must have a cause. The proximate cause may be an internal strain; but if, as in this case, the strain is occasioned by an effort to overcome an obstacle accidentally presented to a workman in the course of his employment I am not prepared to say that the Act[31] does not apply.[32]

Viscount Haldane LC in a later case,[33] while agreeing with Lord Macnaughten's view in *Fenton* v. *Thorley*,[34] qualified the decisions further by stating that Lord Macnaughten did not exclude intentional acts of third parties from the purview of the term 'accident'. In this case, where a schoolmaster was killed by a premeditated assault of two schoolboys, the assault was considered an accident and compensation was allowed.

In *R.* v. *Morris*, a more recent case decided in 1972, the term 'accident' was interpreted to mean in the broadest possible terms 'any unintended occurrence'. This was a case where two cars interlocked in pursuance of the driver of one vehicle pushing the other which had refused to start. Lord Widgery CJ in examining the word 'accident' seemingly depended upon the quantum of damage more than on anything else to determine whether an accident had occurred. If this approach were to be followed, the English law would show a decided inconsistency with the more laudable approach taken in *Fenton's* case.[35]

A valid criticism which may lie against the English common law is that at no point has there been an attempt to define the term 'accident' in concrete terms. The only positive step seems to have been that which was taken by Lord Lindley in *Fenton's* case, where his Lordship stated that, although there is no technical definition of the term itself, an occurrence may be considered accidental in the case of a workman if an obstacle presents itself within the course of the activity which led to the occurrence. In assessing the term 'accident', American law is not as explicit as the English law, although it is noteworthy that American courts have excluded unforeseen and unexpected incidents from the purview of the word 'accident'. In *Kinavey* v. *Prudential Insurance Co. of America*,[36] where the deceased fell after intoxicating himself and placing himself in a position of grave risk on a railway bridge, the court held that nothing unusual or unforeseen occurred as the risk was extremely likely to have been realized under the circumstances. Accordingly, compensation was not required to be paid to the deceased's dependants by the insurance company covering the life of the deceased.

In a later case[37] decided in 1957, the principles applied by the court were substantially the same as in *Kinavey's* case, where the operative criterion applied was that any act of the deceased or wounded in which he voluntarily undertook a grave risk would effectively preclude the dependants of the deceased from invoking the word 'accident' in their claim. In this case the deceased had lain down on a busy highway and been killed by a vehicle. He was of sound mind and had been warned by his companions of the grave danger of his act. The court held that death was due to the voluntary assumption of risk by the deceased and that the incident did not occur accidentally.

Voluntary assumption of risk appears to be the prominent factor which excludes compensation in the United States of America for claims relating to death or injury by accident. In a 1951 case,[38] this principle had been expressly laid down by a court which denied the award of compensation in an instance where the insured died as a result of participating in 'Russian Roulette'. Similarly, in a case decided earlier,[39] the courts had held that, even if it assumed that a person was not aware of a particular susceptibility to risk, no award of compensation would be available to the injured person by the person who allegedly causes him the injury. It appears to be clear therefore that American law seems to run parallel to the English common law to insist on unexpected events being classified as accidental. The heavy reliance on voluntary assumptions of risk underscores this fact.

The common law of Canada has, in more than one instance, expressly recognized the principle enunciated by Lord Macnaughten in *Fenton's* case that the word 'accident' can be attributed to an unexpected incident or one which is undesigned. In a 1940 decision,[40] Crocket J spelt out the fact that an accident is an untoward event.[41] In this case a worker incurred internal injury in the course of her duties while operating a new hand embossing machine. The decision is very clear, in that, as in *Fenton's* case, the claim was found to be compensable notwithstanding the risk, since the employee had to take the risk involved to perform her duties. Courts in Canada have refused compensation in instances where consequential damage is caused by a person's voluntary behaviour which leads to the injury. In *Travellers' Insurance Company* v. *Elder*,[42] where a customer in a restaurant used abusive language and was assaulted as a result, the court held that the injuries were effected directly and independently of causes other than through accidental means.

A noteworthy feature in the *Travellers' Insurance Company* case is that the court had relied upon the fault of the claimant as a basis for rejecting his claim[43] and on the fact that the claimant had placed himself in a position that would objectively be considered to have brought about an assault upon himself. This approach was seen in another case[44] where a deer poacher shot at another while poaching, which invited retaliation resulting in the death of the first poacher. The Nova Scotia Supreme Court held that death had not been caused accidentally since the deceased, by his act of firing at the other, had invited the retaliatory shot. The rationale in the case appears to be that, if the injury caused is calculated to be foreseeable by the injured, such injury would not be considered accidental.

The test of foreseeability has been strongly applied in the case of *Candler* v. *London and Lancashire Guarantee and Accident Company of Canada et al.*,[45] where the court had pronounced that an injury which is the reasonable consequence of a voluntary act of the injured cannot be considered as having been caused by accidental means. In this case the deceased met with his death by falling from the twelfth floor of a hotel. The insurance company with whom the deceased had held a life insurance policy denied compensation on the grounds that the deceased had been in an advanced state of intoxication. Grant J stated:

> The purpose of his [the deceased's] action to show his friend that he had sufficient nerve to take the risk of falling, that was obviously associated with his actions, was so evident to Simmonds [the friend] that, to use his words, he was petrified at the display. His efforts to dissuade Candler from engaging in such act consisted partly in telling him that he need not so act.... His statement that he would show he still had nerve is the conclusive evidence that he appreciated the risk involved.[46] His acts on the night in question in assuming the dangerous position he did on the top of the coping could have no useful purpose whatever except the obvious opportunity to convince Simmonds that he possessed sufficient nerve to accept the challenge that was associated therewith ... His conduct was foolhardy and attended with the most obvious danger.... I therefore hold that Candler's death was not caused either by accidental means or by accident.[47]

Grant J seems to have assiduously followed the objective test of foreseeability and attributed the cause of death to consequential injury arising from the initial act of intoxication of the deceased. This interpretation has precluded the death of the deceased from being considered an accident.

There are two assumptions that emerge from the decision in the *Candler* case. One is that in determining the occurrence of an 'accident' the courts in Canada would inevitably consider the cause of the accident as a relevant fact. The other is the incontrovertible assumption that, if the incident arises out of the foreseeable consequences of an act of the deceased or injured person, the incident itself would not be considered for compensation.

It is very clear that the three jurisdictions of the United Kingdom, the United States and Canada recognize at common law certain basic facts in determining whether a given incident can be termed an 'accident'. They are that the incident should constitute the following: (a) an unexpected, fortuitous or untoward happening; (b) it should not be a consequence of irrational conduct of the deceased or injured person; and (c) the incident should be one which is not reasonably foreseeable by the deceased or injured. Perhaps the only exception is *Fenton* v. *Thorley*,[48] where it was recognized that an injury may be compensable even if caused with foreseeability if the risk was foreseen but was inevitable. Be that as it may, the most critical problem in this area where all three jurisdictions are concerned is that the common law has not offered an acceptable definition of the word 'accident'.

'Accident' in Air Law

In commercial aviation, the word 'accident' is sometimes given as broad a definition as those just considered. The Chicago Convention of 1944 defines accident as 'occurrence associated with the operation of an aircraft'.[49] The Warsaw Convention in Article 17 speaks of the 'the accident which caused the damage', reducing the accident to the cause rather than to the death or injury.[50] The United States Supreme Court has held that *in limine* an accident must be unexpected and external to the passenger.[51] It is not sufficient that the plaintiff suffers injury as a result of his own internal reaction to the usual, normal and expected operation of the aircraft.[52] Such incidents as hijackings, terrorist attacks and bomb threats have been considered to be accidents, together with aircraft crashes.[53] An accident could even involve such lesser incidents as tyre failure on take-off[54] and the supply of infected food causing food poisoning of passengers.[55]

In 1982, a passenger travelling from New York to Manila suffered a massive coronary seizure in flight. The allegation against the airline was that, as a result of the failure of the employees of the airline to render medical assistance, the patient's condition suffered irreparable deterioration resulting in death. Responsibility devolved upon the court to fit this incident to that of an 'accident' within the meaning of the Warsaw Convention. The court readily did this by deeming that the word 'accident' in air law in this instance was not the heart attack itself but the failure on the part of the airline to render medical assistance in flight. The court said: 'After all, it is no different from an airline's liability in a hijacking incident where the accident is not the acts of the hijackers but the alleged failure on the part of the carrier to provide adequate security.'[56] The airline was accordingly found liable for damage so sustained by the deceased passenger.

In a contemporaneous case, a passenger brought action in the US District Court of Puerto Rico for a hernia sustained by the lifting of a heavy suitcase from the conveyor belt. A baggage handler of the defendant airline had refused to carry the suitcase and the plaintiff had solicited aid from her relatives, who were not allowed to enter the baggage area by a guard on duty. The action against the airline was dismissed by the court primarily on the grounds that the plaintiff did not suffer an unexpected injury, as she had previously undergone a gall bladder operation and would have known her condition to be delicate.[57]

In 1983, a medical practitioner suffering from a head cold and respiratory infection boarded an aircraft. He disembarked completely deaf. The plaintiff averred that he suffered discomfort in his ears at descent probably due to sudden pressure changes that may have occurred. He alleged that the airline knew or ought to have known that passengers suffering from head colds would risk losing their hearing. In addition, it was alleged that the airline owed a duty to warn the passenger that it was dangerous to travel with a head cold. The airline denied the existence of such a duty. The US District Court for the Southern District of New York reasoned that it would be incongruous to impose a duty on an airline to envisage all possible human afflictions and assess their effect in air travel and warn passengers accordingly. In any event, the airline was in this instance not aware that the passenger was suffering from a head cold. In this decision the court clearly indicated that the presumption of liability imposed by the Warsaw Convention on airlines and the highest-degree-of-care doctrine applicable thereto should not be taken advantage of by plaintiffs.[58] Similarly, there would be no cause of action against an airline where a passenger's ill health is aggravated as a result of acceleration at take-off or deceleration on landing.[59]

In April 1984, an intermediate Appellate Court in New York was faced with the task of deciding whether an airline can be held liable for the death of a passenger who chokes to death owing to his intoxication. The decision was in the affirmative and the court in enforcing judgment against the airline drew the analogy between a dispensing druggist and an airline. The airline serves its passengers with drink and thus undertakes the responsibility not to serve in excess and to exercise reasonable care for the safety of passengers. In addition, in the event of excessive intoxication of a passenger, the airline is under a legal duty to render such medical assistance as is necessary to revive the passenger or in any event to keep him out of danger. In the light of this principle, the airline has a further duty to protect others from a drunken passenger who gets out of control.[60]

In *Air France* v. *Saks*,[61] the United States Supreme Court interpreted the word 'accident' in the context of the Warsaw Convention to mean an occurrence whereby a passenger is injured owing to an unexpected or unusual event or happening that is external to the passenger,[62] and that, where the injury results from the passenger's own internal reaction to the normal exigencies of air travel, such injury would not be construed as having resulted from an accident. In this case, the plaintiff was a passenger on an Air France flight from Paris to Los Angeles. During the descent the plaintiff suffered severe pain in her left ear which was aggravated thereafter. The plaintiff – who consulted a doctor after the plane landed – was informed that she was rendered completely deaf in her left ear. The plaintiff brought an action in a California State court on the grounds that her hearing loss was due to the negligent maintenance by the airline of the pressurization system of the aircraft which transported her. Air France moved that the allegation of the plaintiff could not be sustained within the meaning of the word 'accident' of Article 17 of the Warsaw Convention, which was meant to be an unusual and unexpected happening. Further, the airline alleged that at all times the pressurization system of the aircraft had been normal. The District Court granted summary judgment to the plaintiff on the basis that 'accident' in Article 17 was meant to be an unusual and unexpected happening. The Supreme Court rejected the rationale adopted by the lower court on the ground that Article 17 refers to an accident which causes an injury and therefore it is the cause and not the effect that is the determinant. Accordingly, the Supreme Court held that air carriers would be liable only if an accident caused the passenger injury. Thus an injury that was in itself an accident was insufficient to satisfy the requirements of Article 17 of the Warsaw Convention.

There will be no accident if in a normal flight free of turbulence a passenger suffers discomfort from a condition he suffers from, such as a hiatus hernia[63] or thrombophlebitis.[64] In *Abramson* v. *Japan Airlines*, an airline passenger suffered an aggravation of a pre-existing hiatus hernia shortly after take-off from Anchorage on a flight to Tokyo. The passenger, who was under medication for his condition for six years, had not informed the carrier prior to boarding. The passenger, however, claimed that, had he been given occupation of a few empty seats, he could have massaged his stomach back to normal. The airline had claimed that there were no empty seats in flight, contrary to the passenger's claim that there were in fact nine empty seats in flight in the first class section of the aircraft. The passenger claimed that his hernia attack constituted an 'accident' within the provisions of Article 17 of the Convention. The court rejected this claim and held that the plaintiff's difficulty was not in any way related to his transportation by air and, accordingly, there was no accident under Article 17.

It would have been interesting if the court had applied the principle of *Seguritan's* case,[65] where failure to render medical assistance by the airline was construed as falling within the purview of the word 'accident'. After all, the airline did not make any attempt at rendering assistance to the passenger in *Abramson's* case. The court's reasoning in the latter case contradicts the earlier decision and leads to a logical absurdity. The intention of the Convention was seemingly to provide a uniform system of compensation for passengers bringing claims against airlines operating international air services. To suggest that the failure of an airline to render required assistance is excusable under the Convention is completely at odds with earlier decisions and also arguably with the intention and purpose of the Convention itself.

Insofar as the word 'wounding' of a passenger in Article 17 is concerned, courts have initially held that such would only be in instances of 'bodily injury' and consequently would be palpably conspicuous physical injury.[66] This excluded mental injury. However, a later decision[67] held that types of injuries enumerated should be construed expansively to encompass as many types of injury as are colourably within the ambit of the enumerated types, including mental and psychosomatic injuries. This decision has been followed consistently in a strong line of cases.[68] In the United States, mental injury is now entrenched in most jurisdictions as an independently compensable head of damages.[69] As indeed Burnett CJ said in *Medlin* v. *Allied Investment Co*:[70]

> Memory and empathy tells us that 'hurt' perceived through sensory media other than that of touch may be just as painful if not more than the hurt perceived by the tactile sense. Moreover, physicians tell us that the consequences of invasion of the person accomplished through the perceptory media of sight and sound may be also as damaging if not more damaging than invasions of the persons accomplished through the sense of touch.[71]

Indeed, mental anguish or injury would now be recognized by most jurisdictions as falling within the purview of 'wounding' of a passenger under Article 17 of the Warsaw Convention.

It is apparent from the *cursus curiae* that a stringent standard of proof of the nature of the occurrence is insisted upon by the courts if liability of the carrier is to be established under Article 17 of the Warsaw Convention. In *Salce* v. *Aer Lingus Airlines*,[72] the District Court for the Southern District of New York required of the plaintiff to show that the landing of the aircraft in which the plaintiff travelled was anything other than a normal landing. The plaintiff averred that he had received personal injuries due to the hard landing of the aircraft. In the absence of clear evidence of a hard landing, the court would presume that the landing performed by the aircraft in this instance was not an unexpected or unusual event that would satisfy the requirements of an 'accident' under the Warsaw Convention.

However, when facts are self-evident, as in the case of *Salerno* v. *Pan American World Airways*,[73] the courts would not hesitate to award damages to a plaintiff passenger. In this case, the District Court for the Southern District of New York held that knowledge of a bomb threat which subsequently caused a miscarriage to a passenger came within the meaning of scope of the word 'accident'. The plaintiff, together with her two children, were passengers aboard a PANAM flight from Miami to Uruguay. The cockpit crew, after take-off, instructed the cabin crew to look for a bomb which the former had been informed by air traffic control to be on board. The crew notified the passengers, including the plaintiff. She suffered a miscarriage 24 hours after being informed of the alleged bomb on board and having watched the cabin crew looking for the object. The court held that an 'accident' within the meaning of the Warsaw Convention caused the plaintiff's injuries because a bomb threat is 'external to the passenger' and is an unexpected and unusual event outside the usual, normal and expected operation of the aircraft.[74]

The above discussion reveals the salutary principle that the word 'accident' has been considered far more liberally in modern air law than is done under other areas of common law. It also underscores the fact that courts have been more inclined to treat acts of omission on the part of airlines as an 'accident', as was shown in *Seguritan's* case.[75] The airline is presumed liable for an 'accident' where a drunken passenger assaults another, or where a passenger suffers a heart attack and is not given the necessary medical attention in flight, as is possible, just to name two instances.

Defences Available to the Airlines

The foregoing discussion involved two key factors which govern the civil liability of airlines: the presumption of liability that is imposed upon the airline and the liability limits that apply to protect the airline from unlimited liability and spurious claimants. There are two other factors which operate as adjuncts to the initial concepts. They are that the airline may show certain facts in its defence to rebut the presumption, and that, if the airline is found to be guilty of wilful misconduct, it is precluded from invoking the liability limits under the Warsaw Convention. Viewed at a glance, the said four concepts seem to be grouped into two sets of balancing measures. The end result is that, whilst on the one hand the airline is subject to stringent standards of liability, on the other, it is protected by two provisions which limit its liability in monetary terms and allow a complete or partial defence in rebuttal of the presumption.

Article 20(1) of the Warsaw Convention provides that the airline shall not be liable if it proves that the airline and its agents had taken all necessary measures to avoid the damage or that it was impossible for the airline and its agent to take such measures. Shawcross and Beaumont are of the view that the phrase 'all necessary measures' is an unhappy one in that the mere happening of the passenger injury or death presupposes the fact that the airline or its agents had not in fact taken all necessary measures to prevent the occurrence.[76] The airline usually takes such precautions as making regular announcements to passengers on the status of a flight, starting with instructions on security and safety measures that are available in the aircraft. These measures are taken by the airline to conform to the requirements of the Warsaw Convention that the airline has to take all necessary measures to prevent an accident in order that the presumption of liability is rebutted. Thus, in a case decided in 1963,[77] it was held that a passenger who leaves her seat when the aircraft goes through turbulent atmosphere is barred from claiming under the Warsaw Convention for personal injury. Here it was held that an admonition of the airline that the passengers were to remain seated with their seat belts fastened during the time in question was proof of the airline having taken the necessary measures as envisaged in the Warsaw Convention.[78] This case also established the fact that 'all necessary measures' was too wide in scope and that a proper interpretation of the intention of the Warsaw Convention would be to consider the airline to require taking all 'reasonably necessary measures'. In a more recent case, Chapman J imputed objectivity to the phrase 'reasonably necessary measures' by declaring that such measures should be considered necessary by 'the reasonable man'.[79] A similar approach was taken in a subsequent case where the court held that the airline should show more than the fact that it was not negligent in order to invoke Article 20(1) of the Warsaw Convention.[80] The United States also follows this approach of objectivity. In *Manufacturers Hanover Trust Co.* v. *Alitalia Airlines*,[81] it was emphasized that the airline must show that all reasonable measures had been taken from an objective standpoint in order that the benefit of the defence be accrued to the airline. Some French decisions have also approached this defence on similar lines and required a stringent test of generality in order that the criteria for allowing the defence be approved.[82]

The airline which has the burden of proof cannot seek refuge in showing that normal precautions were taken. For example, normal precautions in attending to the safety of the passengers prior to a flight are not sufficient. If, therefore, the airline cannot adduce a reasonable explanation as to why the accident occurred despite the reasonably necessary precautions being taken, it is unlikely to succeed in its defence.[83] Insofar as the requirement of impossibility to take precautions is concerned, the courts have required clear evidence of the difficulties faced by the airline in avoiding the disaster. In one case of a crash landing the court decided that it was insufficient for the airline to show that the aircraft was in perfect condition and that the pilot took all steps to effect a good landing. The airline had to show that the weather conditions were so bad that the aircraft could not land in another airport.[84] In *Haddad* v. *Cie Air France*,[85] where an airline had to accept suspicious passengers who later perpetrated a hijacking, the court held that the airline could not deny boarding to the passengers who later proved to be hijackers. In that instance, the airline had found it impossible to take all necessary precautions and was considered sound in defence under Article 20(1).

A similar approach was taken in the case of *Barboni* v. *Cie Air France*,[86] where the court held that, when an airline receives a bomb threat while in flight and performs an emergency evacuation, a passenger who is injured by evacuation through the escape chute cannot claim liability of the airline since it would have been impossible for the airline to take any other measure.

If the airline proves that the damage was caused by or contributed to by the negligence of the injured person the court may, in accordance with the provisions of its own law, exonerate the carrier wholly or partly from his liability.[87] Contributory negligence under the Warsaw Convention has been treated subjectively as and when cases are adjudicated. The courts have not set an objective standard, as in the earlier defence. For instance, in *Goldman* v. *Thai Airways International Ltd.*,[88] it was held that a passenger is not guilty of contributory negligence if he keeps his seat belt unfastened throughout the flight and suffers injury when there is no sign given by the aircraft control panel to keep the seat belt on. However, if a passenger removes a bandage or brace that he is required to keep on for an existing injury and he suffers injury in flight owing to the removal of the support, he will be found to have contributed to the negligence resulting in his injuries.[89]

Article 25(1) of the Warsaw Convention states that the airline shall not be entitled to avail itself of the provisions of the Warsaw Convention which excludes or limits its liability, if the damage is caused by the wilful misconduct or by such default on the part of the airline as, in accordance with the law of the court to which the case is submitted, is considered to be equivalent to wilful misconduct. Article 25(1) extends this liability to acts of the agent of the airline acting within the scope of his employment and attributes such wilful misconduct to the airline. Such actions as the failure of the technical crew of the aircraft to monitor weather conditions and the failure to execute a proper approach in adverse weather conditions are examples of wilful misconduct of the airline.[90] Similarly, the failure of a crew which is going off duty to inform the incoming crew of a defect in the aircraft or any such relevant issue which would affect the safety of the aircraft could be construed as an act of wilful misconduct on the part of the airline.[91]

The effect of Article 25 is that the plaintiff becomes entitled to lift the limit of liability of the airline as prescribed in Article 22 of the Warsaw Convention if he proves that the airline was guilty of wilful misconduct. Thus the burden of proof falls on the plaintiff and, if he succeeds, he may claim an amount over and above the prescribed limits of airline liability.

The limitation of liability of the carrier that the Warsaw Convention imposes could be circumvented by the plaintiff proving that the carrier was guilty of wilful misconduct in causing the injury. Wilful misconduct as an exception to the limitation of liability rule appears in all three air law conventions that admit of liability limitations.[92] The original French text of the Warsaw Convention states that, if the carrier causes the damage intentionally or wrongfully or by such fault as, in accordance with the court seized of the case, is equivalent thereto, he shall not be entitled to claim the limitation of liability.[93] Drion[94] maintains that the English translation inaccurately states that the liability limitations of a carrier will be obviated if the damage is caused by his *wilful misconduct* or by such *default*.[95] The contentious issue in this question is, what kind of misconduct is required? Drion is of the opinion that, by approaching the issue in terms of conflicting concepts, the question whether *faute lourde* as proposed originally in the French text, and for which there was an English equivalent of 'gross negligence', was in fact more appropriate than the word *dol*, which now occupies the document, and for which no accurate English translation exists, has emerged as to what standards may be used in extrapolating the words 'dol' or 'wilful misconduct'. Miller[96] takes a similar view when she states that the evils of conceptualistic thinking that had pervaded the drafting of Article 25 which rendered it destitute of coherence has now been rectified by the Hague Convention which has introduced the words 'done with intent to cause damage or recklessly and with knowledge that the damage would probably result'.[97]

This confusion was really the precursor to diverse interpretations and approaches to the concept of wilful misconduct under Article 25 of the Warsaw Convention. The French government took steps by its Air Carrier Act of 1957 to rectify ambiguities in this area by interpreting *dol* in the Convention as *faute inexcusable*, or deliberate fault, which implies knowledge of the probability of damage and its reckless acceptance without valid reason,[98] making a strong analogy with the Hague Protocol's contents. This interpretation, needless to say, brought out the question whether such reckless acceptance would be viewed subjectively or objectively.

The Belgian decision of *Tondriau* v. *Air India*[99] considered the issue of Article 25 of the Convention and the Hague interpretation. The facts of the case were usual, involving the death of a passenger and a consequent claim under the Convention by his dependants. The significance of the case lay, however, in the fact that the Belgian court followed the decision of *Emery and others* v. *SABENA*[100] and held that, in the consideration of the pilot's negligence under Article 25, an objective test would apply, and the normal behaviour of a good pilot would be the applicable criterion. The court held: 'Whereas the plaintiffs need not prove, apart from the wrongful act, that the pilot of the aircraft personally had knowledge that damage would probably result from it, it is sufficient that they prove that a reasonably prudent pilot ought to have had this knowledge.'[101] The court rationalized that a good pilot ought in the circumstances to have known the existence of a risk and no pilot of an aircraft engaged in air transport ought to take any risk needlessly. The Brussels Court of Appeal, however, reversed this judgment and applied a subjective test, asserting that the Hague Protocol called for 'effective knowledge'. Professor Bin Cheng seems to prefer the objective test in the interpretation of 'wilful misconduct' in Article 25, on the grounds that a subjective test would defeat the spirit of the Convention and that judges would be 'flying in the face of justice in search of absolute equity in individual cases'.[102]

Peter Martin, analysing the Court of Appeal decision in *Goldman* v. *Thai Airways International Ltd.*,[103] agrees with Bin Cheng and criticizes the lower court decision which awarded Goldman substantial damages for injuring his hip as a result of being thrown around in his seat in turbulence, in an instance where the captain had not switched on the 'fasten seat belt' sign.[104] Martin maintains that Goldman failed to prove that the pilot knew that damage would probably result from his act, as envisaged in the Hague Protocol principle. Being an aviation insurance lawyer, Martin is concerned that, while the English courts have a proclivity towards deciding Article 25 issues subjectively, insurance underwriters could view the breach of the limits stringently. Both on the count of the need for objectivity and on the count of the adverse effects on insurance, it is difficult to disagree with Cheng and Martin.

Recent jurisprudence recognizes that wilful misconduct of the carrier need not be deduced from a single act, but rather that the jury may consider the effect of a series of actions or inactions by the carrier. This approach is particularly significant in the instance of damage caused by turbulence, where the flight crew may be required to take a series of measures to cope with the physical threat caused by turbulence to the aircraft and persons onboard. In a 1996 decision,[105] rendered by the Court of Appeal of the United States for the Sixth Circuit, the court held:

> We do not agree ... that the jury should have been prohibited from viewing the airline's individual mistakes together as a 'series of actions or inactions' exhibiting reckless disregard for the safety of the passengers. No principle of law or logic requires a jury evaluating wilful misconduct to focus exclusively on discrete acts, without regard for the complete chain of events leading to the accident. This is especially true if those acts, though individual, nevertheless reflect an overall frame of mind or course of conduct which led to them.[106]

The case of *Koirala* v. *Thai Airways International*,[107] decided in the same year, offers an analogous situation where damage to persons on board was caused by the crash of Thai Airways flight TG-311 on 31 July 1992 near Kathmandu, Nepal. The pilot in this instance was attempting a controlled flight into terrain (CFIT) landing amidst adverse weather. The court concluded that the accident had occurred inter alia as a result of the flight crew's conscious failure to monitor their navigational instruments during the lengthy period of time. The court also found that the captain and the first officer knew or should have known that failing to perform their duty to continuously monitor the aircraft's navigational instruments could create a grave danger under circumstances which involved flying in bad weather with poor visibility. According to the court, the conduct of the crew was tantamount to reckless disregard of the probable circumstances, and the wilful misconduct of the crew was the proximate cause of the damage caused to aircraft and persons on board.

Notes

1 For a detailed account of the nature of turbulence, see Carl Knable (1995), 'Atmospheric Turbulence', *Flight Deck*, 16, Summer, 17–22.
2 'Turbulence Accidents Increased in 1993 Over Previous Five Years', *Flight Safety Digest*, Flight Safety Foundation, October 1994, 26.
3 The year 1958 was identified by the study as approximately the year in which the jet transport era commenced. The study reveals that for the period 1958–93 turbulence caused 164 accidents, as against 56 caused by pushback (forced deceleration of the engine), 51 by emergency evacuation, 29 at boarding and deboarding, 27 by vehicle collision, 12 by jetblast, seven by test flight and seven by passengers. (Ibid., 28.)
4 Capt. Tom Duke (1996), 'Training to Beat Wake Turbulence', *FAA Aviation News*, March, 1.
5 Ibid.
6 See 'Atmospheric Turbulence in Relation to Air Navigation', *ICAO Circular 44-AN/39*, Recommendation No. 41, p.3.
7 Ibid., Recommendation No. 42, p.4.
8 Ibid., note 2.
9 The captain was not necessarily the sole source of the accidents cited.
10 Peter F. Lester (1994), *Turbulence, A New Perspective by Pilots*, New York: Jeppessen, pp.1–3.
11 J. McLean (1986), 'Determining the Effect of Weather in Aircraft Accident Investigations', Paper A1AA-86-0323, AIAA 24th Aerospace Sciences Meeting, Reno, p.7.
12 See T.B. Shaw (1991), 'Weather Related Accidents in the Canadian Aviation Industry, An Analysis of the Chief Contributing Factors', *Reprints of the Fourth International Conference on Aviation Weather Systems*, Paris: American Meteorological Society, pp.137–57.
13 Major Timothy H. Minor (1997), 'Turbulence from Shearing and Gravity Waves', *Flying Safety*, June, p.7.
14 *FAA Aviation News*, May–June 1992, 24.
15 ATARSG/3 Study Note No. 11, 4/3/97, 5.

16 Meteorological Service for International Air Navigation and Procedures for Air Navigation Services.
17 Convention on International Civil Aviation, signed at Chicago, 7 December 1944, ICAO Doc. 7300/7, 7th edn, 1997.
18 PANS-RAC, Doc. 4444.
19 Convention for the Unification of Certain Rules Relating to International Carriage by Air, signed at Warsaw on 12 October 1929. See *Annals of Air and Space Law*, Vol. XVIII, 1993, Part II, pp.323–50 for the text of the Convention.
20 Ibid., Article 17.
21 See *Halsbury, Laws of England*, 3rd edn, Vol. 22, para. 585, p.293.
22 *Hensey* v. *White*, 1900 1 KB 481.
23 Ibid., 484.
24 Ibid., 485.
25 *Boardman* v. *Scott and Witworth* (1902) 1KB 43.
26 Ibid., 46.
27 (1903) AC 433.
28 Ibid., 446–7.
29 Ibid., 452.
30 Ibid., 453.
31 Workmen's Compensation Act, 1897.
32 (1903) AC 443 at 455. See also *Trim Joint District School Board of Management* v. *Kelly*, 1914 AC 667 at 669 and, generally, *Anderson* v. *Balfour* (1910) 2 I.R. 497 and *Nisbett* v. *Rayne* (1910) 2 KB 689.
33 *Trim Joint District School Board of Management* v. *Kelly*, 1914 AC 667.
34 *Supra*, n.27.
35 Ibid., 231.
36 (1942) 27 A. 2d 286.
37 *Allred* v. *Prudential Insurance Co. of America*, 100 S.E. 2d 226.
38 *Thompson* v. *Prudential Insurance Co.*, 66 S.E. 2d 119.
39 *Evans* v. *Metropolitan Life Insurance Co.* (1942), 174 p. 2d 961.
40 *Workmen's Compensation Board* v. *Theed* (1940) 3 DLR 561.
41 Ibid., 557.
42 (1940) 2 DLR 444.
43 Ibid., 448, 449.
44 *Turner* v. *Northern Life Ass'ce Co.* (1953) 1 DLR 427.
45 (1963) 40 DLR 408.
46 Ibid., 422.
47 Ibid., 423.
48 *Supra*, n.27.
49 Convention on International Civil Aviation signed in Chicago, 1944 (*supra*, n.17), Annex 13.
50 *Shawcross and Beaumont* (1988), *Air Law*, 4th edn reissue, VII, 153.
51 *Air France* v. *Saks*, 105 S. Ct. 1338 (1985).
52 Ibid.
53 *Husserl* v. *Swiss Air Transport Co. Ltd.*, 485 F. 2d. 1240 (2nd Circ. 1975); *Day* v. *Trans World Airlines Inc.*, 528 F. 2d 31 (2nd Circ. 1975); *Evangelinos* v. *Trans World Airlines Inc.*, 550 F. 2d 152 (3rd Circ. 1976). See also *Salerno* v. *Pan American World Airways*, 19 Avi Cas 17, 705 (SDNY 1985).
54 *Arkin* v. *Trans International Airlines Inc.*, 19 Avi Cas 18, 311 (EDNY 1985).
55 *Abdulrahman Al-Zamil* v. *British Airways Inc.*, 770 F. 2d 3 (2nd Circ. 1985).
56 *Seguritan* v. *Northwest Airlines Inc.*, 86 A.D. 2d 658 (2d Dept. 1982). See also *Lloyds Aviation Law*, 1(4), 1 August 1982, 1.
57 *Vincenty* v. *Eastern Airlines*, 528 F. Supp. 171 (D.P.R. 1982). Also *Lloyds Aviation Law*, 1(3), 15 July 1982, 2.

58 *Sprayregen* v. *American Airlines Inc.*, 570 F. Supp. 16 (SDNY 1983). See also *Warshaw* v. *Trans World Airlines Inc.*, 443 F. Supp. 400 (ED Pa. 1977); *Pironneau* v. *Cie Air-Inter* (Pan CA 03 July 1986). Cf. *De Marines* v. *KLM Royal Dutch Airlines*, 586 F. 2d 1193 (3rd Circ. 1978).
59 See *Warshaw* v. *Trans World Airlines Inc.* (*supra*, n.58) 408.
60 *O'Leary* v. *American Airlines*, 475 NYS 2d 285 (A.D. 2d Dept. 1984).
61 *Supra*, n.51.
62 Ibid., 1345.
63 *Abramson* v. *Japan Airlines Company Ltd.*, 739 F. 2d 130 (3rd Circ. 1984).
64 *Scherer* v. *Pan American World Airways Inc.*, 387 NYS 2d. 581 (1976).
65 *Supra*, n.56.
66 *Rosman* v. *Trans World Airlines Inc.*, 34 NY 2d 385 (1974).
67 *Husserl* v. *Swiss Air Transport Co. Ltd.*, *supra*, n.53.
68 *Krystal* v. *BOAC*, 403 F. Supp. 1332 (DC Cal. 1975); *Karfunkel* v. *Cie Nationale Air France*, 427 F. Supp. 971 (SDNY 977); *Borham* v. *Pan American World Airways Inc.*, Avicas. 18, 236 (SDNY 1977).
69 See R.I.R. Abeyratne (1986), 'The Human Stress Factor and Mental Injury in American Tort Law – A Patchwork Quilt?', *The Anglo American Law Review*, 15 (4), 338–60.
70 398 S.W. 2d 170.
71 Ibid., 273–4.
72 19 Av. Cas (CCH) 17, 377 (SDNY 1985).
73 606 F. Supp. 656 (SDNY 1985).
74 Ibid.
75 *Supra*, n.56.
76 Shawcross and Beaumont (*supra*, n.50), VII (116).
77 *Chisholm* v. *British European Airways* (1963) 1 Lloyds Rep. 626. Also *Grein* v. *Imperial Airways Ltd.* (1937) 1 KB 50 CA at 69–71 *per* Greer LJ.
78 See *Chisholm* v. *British European Airways*, (*supra*, n.77), 629.
79 *Goldman* v. *Thai Airways International Ltd.* (1981) 125 Sol Jo 413 (High Ct). Also in (1983) 1 All ER 693.
80 (1986) 2 All ER 188.
81 429 F. Supp. 964 (SDNY 1977).
82 *Preyvel* v. *Cie Air France* (1973) 27 RFDA 198. Also *Rivière-Girret* v. *Ste-Air Inter* (1979) Uniform L.R. 173.
83 *Panalpina International Transport Ltd.* v. *Densil Underwear Ltd.* (1981) 1 Lloyds Rep. 187.
84 *Mandreoli* v. *Cie Belge d'Assurance Aviation*, Milan 1972 (1974) Dir Mar 157.
85 (1982) 36 RFDA 342.
86 (1982) 36 RFDA 355.
87 Warsaw Convention (*supra*, n.19), Article 21.
88 (1983) 3 All ER 693.
89 *Bradfield* v. *Trans World Airlines Inc.* 152 Cal. Rptr 172 (Ca. CA 1972).
90 *Butler* v. *Aeromexico*, 774 F. 2d 499 (11th Cir. 1985).
91 *Piano Remittance Corp.* v. *Varig Brazilian Airlines Inc.*, 18 Av. Cas (CCH). 18, 381 (SDNY 1984).
92 The Convention for the Unification of Certain Rules Relating to the Assistance and Salvage of Aircraft at Sea, Brussels, 1938; The Rome Convention, 1933; and the Warsaw Convention, 1929.
93 Article 25.
94 H. Drion (1954), *Limitation of Liabilities in International Air Law*, The Hague: Martinus Nijhoff, p.195.
95 Ibid.

96 Georgette Miller (1979), *Air Carrier's Liability Under the Warsaw System*, Amsterdam: Kluwer, p.200.
97 Hague Protocol, 1955, Article XIII.
98 Miller (*supra*, n.96), p.202.
99 *Revue Française de droit aérien* (R.F.D.A.) 1977, 193.
100 5 December 1967; R.F.D.A. 184.
101 Transcript of judgment, p.4.
102 Bin Cheng (1977), 'Wilful Misconduct, From Warsaw to the Hague and From Brussels to Paris', *Annals of Air and Space Law*, II, 99.
103 (1983) *Law Society's Gazette*, 8 June 1983, 1485.
104 Peter Martin (1983), 'Intentional or Reckless Misconduct, From London To Bangkok and Back Again', *Annals of Air and Space Law*, VIII 145–9.
105 *In re Air Crash Disaster, Polec* v. *Northwest Airlines*, Inc. 86F. 3d 498 (6th Cir. 1996).
106 Ibid.
107 1996 Westlaw 40243 (N.W. Calif. Jan. 26, 1996).

12 The Spread of Tuberculosis in the Aircraft Cabin

Introduction

When there is incontrovertible evidence of a person contracting a disease such as tuberculosis as a result of being infected in an aircraft while on board, liability issues pertaining to the airline arising from the incident may involve principles of private air carrier liability. The Warsaw Convention of 1929[1] provides that the carrier is liable for damage sustained in the event of death or wounding of a passenger, or any other bodily injury suffered by a passenger, if the accident which caused the damage so sustained took place on board the aircraft or in the course of any of the operations of embarking or disembarking. Of course, on the face of the provision, the words 'wounding' and 'bodily injury' do not necessarily lend themselves to being associated with infection. A fortiori, according to the Warsaw Convention, the wounding or injury must be caused by 'accident', which is not typically a synonym for 'infection'. However, the recent decision in *El Al Israel Airlines Limited* v. *Tseng*[2] introduced a new dimension to the word 'accident' under the Warsaw Convention by giving it pervasive scope to include such acts as security body searches performed by the airlines. In this context, the word 'accident' loses its fortuity and it becomes applicable to an expected or calculated act. Thus, if an airline knows or ought to have known that an infected passenger was on board its flight, causing others on board to be infected, it may well mean that the act of the airline would be construed by the courts as an accident within the purview of the Warsaw Convention.

Given the above circumstances, an evaluation of the principles of legal liability that may apply to air carriers with regard to passengers contracting tuberculosis while in flight in their aircraft would be relevant. This evaluation, which will follow, will be made under both the common law principles of tort law and the liability principles contained in the Warsaw Convention.

Tuberculosis

Mycobacterium tuberculosis was identified in the 19th century as causing tuberculosis (TB) which now ranks as the world's most deadly infectious disease. An estimated three million people die from it annually and scientists have yet to find a vaccine for the prevention of the disease. The World Health Organization (WHO) records that approximately one-third of the world's population is infected with the TB bacterium and it is estimated that nearly eight million cases may have occurred worldwide in 1996.[3]

The bacteria settle in a person's lungs and destroys them over time. It can move to other organs such as the brain, liver, kidney and spine, triggering a battle between the bacteria and the body's immune system. The bacteria are conveyed from the infected persons through a sneeze or cough, through the air in what are known as 'droplet nuclei', to be inhaled by others. Although the confined space of an aircraft cabin would be a conducive environment for the transmission of airborne bacteria, there is no medical evidence which concludes that transmission of the bacteria can occur on short flights.[4]

In 1996, three medical scientists investigated the likelihood of transmission of tuberculosis from a highly infectious passenger with pulmonary/laryngeal tuberculosis to others on board two short flights of approximately 75 minutes' duration. The scientists followed up the event with questionnaires addressed to all 146 passengers on the flights. Their conclusions, based on the responses received, were that, although the possibility of transmission cannot be excluded, there was a very low likelihood of the transmission of the disease during the flights in question.[5]

One commentator[6] records that the attention of the air transport industry was focused on the ramifications of the spread of tuberculosis in the aircraft cabin only in 1996, when a 32-year-old woman succumbed to TB as a result of contracting the disease during a flight on a Boeing 747-100 aircraft from Chicago to Hawaii. On this flight, six passengers in the rear of the aircraft, 13 rows away from the identified carrier of the disease, had been infected.[7] Be that as it may, the air transport industry has not been found wanting in its cooperation with health officials in handling the aftermath of infection, as was seen in the autumn of 1998, when an infected passenger on board an eight-hour flight from Paris to New York was found to be suffering from a particularly virulent form of tuberculosis; and the health authorities received every cooperation from the airline concerned in tracking down the 13 passengers who had been infected during the flight.[8]

Air Carrier Liability at Tort Law

Principles of liability of air carriers with respect to negligence in the spread of tuberculosis in their aircraft cabins are no different from liability principles pertaining to the spread of other diseases transmitted through food, such as salmonella poisoning, cholera and staphylococcal food poisoning.[9] In the case of the transmission of the TB bacterium in the aircraft cabin, as with the other diseases mentioned, the air carrier has a two-phased prospect of facing a claim for damages: prevention and contingency planning.

Prevention

Any airborne disease such as tuberculosis is affected by the environment, particularly if this is an enclosed one, as in an aircraft cabin. The ventilation system plays a critical part in this regard and, therefore, it is crucial to an air carrier's conduct to determine the manner in which the carrier decides on ventilation systems in its aircraft. For instance, early jet aircraft until the 1980s offered 100 per cent fresh air in the cabin. However, in the 1990s, ironically with more evolved technology, ventilation systems in aircraft were built in such a way as to recycle stale air, thus increasing the chances of survival of bacteria in the aircraft cabin. Even if such a practice were ineluctable, in that recycling is a universal practice which is calculated to conserve fuel, a prudent airline would take other measures, such as change of air filters through which ventilation is provided.

Air in the cabin is usually dry and lacking in humidity since the outside air at cruising altitudes has an extremely low water content. The humidity level in the air of an aircraft cabin at cruising level has been recognized as being of 10–20 per cent humidity, which is approximately the same as desert air.[10] The lack of humidity per se does not facilitate the transmission of bacteria, but makes breathing difficult, particularly for persons suffering from respiratory diseases, such as asthma. When dry air becomes stale through recycling, the chances of removing droplets of air which is usually accomplished by fresh air becomes remote. A suggested solution for a prudent airline to take in this regard is to reintroduce 100 per cent fresh air which is humidified.[11]

Contingency Planning

The other limb under which an airline could face a liability claim lies in the area of contingency planning through effective communications. Although it is incontrovertible that an airline cannot know beforehand whether one of its passengers carries the TB bacterium, it can, once advised of the fact, take effective measures to ensure fullest cooperation with the health authorities involved.

Although, usually, the health department is advised of an airline passenger who had travelled while being infected, there may be instances where a passenger or his physician may contact an airline first. In such instances the airline is obligated to advise the health authorities immediately of all details, not only of the patient concerned but of all passengers who were in the flight with the infected person.

An essential prerequisite of airline contingency planning is the establishment of a link between the medical centre of the airline and its central booking or reservations system whereby, when necessary, the reservations department of the airline can transmit full information to the medical centre to follow up instances of possible infections, particularly in the airline's home base. It is not sufficient for the airline merely to wash its hands of an infected flight by merely giving the passenger manifest to the health authorities. The airline's reservation system should be sufficiently well equipped to have all data relating to passengers' addresses, telephone numbers and so on, which can be given to both the airline medical staff and the state health authorities.

A prudent airline would follow up diligently the list of infected passengers to ensure that they receive proper medical care and documentation necessary for the obtaining of whatever assistance is required. It is critical that the airline, at every moment, keeps its own medical staff involved in instances where its passengers have been or may have been infected, in order for the proper clinical determination of quarantine times and isolation to be followed professionally.

In case of potential exposure of passengers to tuberculosis, airlines should have a mechanism in place that would advise the health authorities of the state concerned immediately. Airlines should give special training to its crews in using first aid for precautionary purposes. All necessary medical equipment should be stored in the aircraft. In case of possible infection, airlines should vigorously maintain all contact with those who may have been infected, offering them medical attention in addition to that which may be provided by the state authorities. In stations other than their own home stations, airlines should maintain their own medical contacts to assist infected persons from a flight.

Legal Issues

The pre-eminent legal provision which governs this issue is contained in the Convention on International Civil Aviation (Chicago Convention);[12] Article 14 of which states:

> Each contracting State agrees to take effective measures to prevent the spread by means of air navigation of cholera, typhus (epidemic), smallpox, yellow fever, plague, and such other communicable diseases as the contracting States shall from time to time decide to designate, and to that end contracting States will keep in close consultation with the agencies concerned with international regulations relating to sanitary measures applicable to aircraft. Such consultation shall be without prejudice to the application of any existing international convention on this subject to which the contracting States may be parties.

This provision explicitly devolves primary responsibility on states to take effective measures to prevent airborne diseases in aircraft and implicitly requires states to issue guidelines for airlines, by liaising with the international agencies concerned. *Non obstante*, airlines have to face certain legal issues themselves in terms of their conduct. Primarily, airlines are expected to conform to applicable international health regulations and the laws of the countries in which their aircraft land.[13] Furthermore, the airline owes its passengers a duty of care to exercise all caution in protecting their rights, so that a blatant instance of a person who looks sickly and coughs incessantly at the check-in counter cannot be ignored. Common law principles of tort law vigorously distinguish between negligence, recklessness and wilful blindness. Of these elements of liability, wilful blindness is particularly relevant since it brings to bear the need for an airline to be vigilant in observing passenger profiles in potentially dangerous or threatening situations. The Canadian Supreme Court has stated:

> Wilful blindness is distinct from recklessness because, while recklessness involves knowledge of a danger or a risk and persistence in a course of conduct which creates a risk that the prohibited result will occur, wilful blindness arises when a person who has become aware of the need for some inquiry declines to make the inquiry because he does not wish to know the truth. He would prefer to remain ignorant. The culpability in recklessness is justified by consciousness of the risk and by proceeding in the face of it, while in wilful blindness it is justified by the accused's fault in deliberately failing to inquire when he knows there is reason for inquiry.[14]

Civil wrongs which are exclusively breaches of trust or of some other merely equitable obligation are one of four classes of wrongs.[15] Therefore the tort of misfeasance (deliberate wrong) and nonfeasance (failure to take action to perform a duty of care owed) such as wilful blindness to a possible wrong that may be committed, both of which an imprudent and careless airline may be guilty of in the case of the spread of disease in the aircraft cabin, becomes 'a civil wrong for which the remedy is a common law action for unliquidated damages, and which is not exclusively the breach of a contract or the breach of a trust or other merely equitable obligation'.[16]

Therefore, in general terms, a tort arises from an act performed by the defendant whereby he or she has without just cause or excuse caused some harm to the plaintiff.[17] This rationale is grounded on the classical juridical maxim *sic utere tuo ut alienum non laedes* which essentially means that no one can hurt another by word or deed. It follows naturally, therefore, that a person aggrieved as a result of a tort of another can claim pecuniary compensation in respect of damage suffered. A person who contracts tuberculosis, for example, while travelling in an aircraft which carried an infected person whose disease was transmitted to that person can, under this principle, expect compensation from the airline concerned if the airline is found to have breached its duty of care by either positively contributing to the damage (by knowingly allowing the infected person to travel or by knowingly installing a ventilator system in the aircraft which is not effective in preventing the spread of airborne disease) or by wilfully blinding itself to the potential danger of a sickly person entering the aircraft cabin without making further inquiry.

It is incontrovertible that proof of negligence of the airline, whether through wilful neglect or through wilful blindness, would be extremely difficult to establish in the case of the spread of an airborne disease such as tuberculosis, as against such diseases as cholera. The former cannot be linked to unsanitary conditions in the cabin per se, whereas the latter can readily be determined through an ex post facto examination of the cabin. The only instance imaginable, where an airline can be held reprehensible and consequently liable for pecuniary compensation, is when an obviously sickly passenger is checked in by the airline without making an inquiry; when the airline knows beforehand that a particular passenger is positively infected with the disease; or when the aircraft cabin is not properly equipped to prevent the spread of disease. Therefore, air carrier liability for this particular tort would invariably be addressed after the fact: that is, after passengers have been infected with the disease, when action taken by the airline to assist both those infected and the health authorities concerned would become relevant.

In an instance where an airline is found liable, courts would be charged with quantifying the personal loss incurred by a person contracting the disease. In the 1964 case of *H. West & Son* v. *Shephard,*[18] decided in the House of Lords in Britain, Lord Morris of Borth-y-

Gest rejected the argument that courts should decide whether a person who was so debilitated by disease was in a position to enjoy monies awarded in compensation. His Lordship was of the view that the award of compensation was symbolic of reparation made, irrespective of its practical importance to the plaintiff:

> I consider that it is sufficient to say that a money award is given by way of compensation and that it must take into account the actual consequences which have resulted from the tort ... if damages are awarded to a plaintiff on a correct basis it seems to me that it can be of no concern to the court to consider any question as to the use that will thereafter be made of the money awarded.[19]

Lord Morris of Borth-y-Gest made the distinction between money given in the form of compensation as above in recognition of the damage caused, and compensation given to cover financial loss, such as payment for nursing and medical services and the cost of medicine, as two different elements of compensation. The overall point made by the *Shephard* decision is that compensation should be substantial and not merely a token, irrespective of whether the plaintiff was able to enjoy the money or not. In this sense, compensation is awarded for what is suffered by the plaintiff and is not based on an evaluation of a thing lost. In the Australian case of *Skelton* v. *Collins*,[20] Taylor J of the High Court of Australia observed: 'compensation cannot be based on evaluation of a thing lost. It must surely be based upon solace for a condition created, not upon payment for something taken away'.[21] Taylor J's reasoning was further developed by the House of Lords three years later in the case of *Baker* v. *Willoughby*,[22] where Lord Reid said:

> A man is not compensated for the physical injury; he is compensated for the loss which he suffers as a result of that injury. His loss is not having a stiff leg; it is in his inability to lead a full life, his inability to enjoy those amenities which depend on freedom of movement and his inability to earn as much as he used to earn or could have earned.[23]

The issue of quantum of damages for personal injury has been addressed by courts on the basis that the damages awarded should be such that the ordinary rational man would not instinctively regard them as either mean or extravagant, but would consider them to be sensible and fair.[24] Indeed, as Lord Denning MR observed in 1966: 'the award of damages in personal injuries cases is basically a conventional figure derived from experience and from awards in comparable cases'.[25] In addition to the compensation for damage caused, the plaintiff is also entitled to compensation with regard to pre-trial pecuniary loss as a result of expenses actually and reasonably incurred on account of the injury. Compensation under this heading may cover clothing and medical expenses[26] and nursing expenses.[27] As for future pecuniary loss, the usual consideration is towards loss of future income, although, if the injured person dies, there could also be a claim for lost dependency.[28] Future pecuniary loss is usually calculated by the multiplier method, which is based on a calculation of the plaintiff's net annual loss multiplied by a figure chosen so as to produce an overall sum which is intended to provide, by withdrawals of both interest and capital, compensation for the lost income in the years ahead. The multiplier is not dependent upon the number of working years the plaintiff would have had ahead if not for the illness, since allowance is made in the calculation for contingencies such as illness which might have struck the plaintiff in any event. Therefore, in practice, the multiplier rarely exceeds 18, even in very young plaintiffs.

Of course, in the case of tuberculosis, the court will also assess the period during which the incapacity will continue. Invariably, there will be consideration in this regard whether there will be total incapacity for a particular period, followed by partial incapacity for a further period. The following four considerations would be critical to a court's assessment of future income loss: (a) for what period income would probably be lost; (b) what the average loss of income would be through that period; (c) what is the appropriate multiple to give the value an annuity of that loss for the period concerned; and (d) what sum should be deducted from the multiple for contingencies.

In the case of a young child not yet in employment, and who is expected to be adversely affected by the disease contracted, the courts would have to determine whether the child could be permanently or temporarily disabled as a result of ill-effects of the disease. In addition, courts would have to hazard a conjecture as to the child's future progression had he or she not contracted the disease. In the 1975 case of *Taylor* v. *Bristol Omnibus Co. Ltd*,[29] the court assumed that the child's earning capacity would be similar to that of the father's and assessed the loss at 16 years' purchase, and reduced it by 50 per cent to give current value. In a later case,[30] where a child of five years was expected to live only up to the age of 27 years owing to a disease contracted, the court awarded a modest sum for that period concerned but refused to recognize that compensation should be awarded for 'lost years', which the court found to be nebulous and therefore valued at nil. In the 1981 case of *Croke* v. *Wiseman*,[31] which concerned a child aged two with brain damage who would live up to the age of 40, the court assumed that the child would earn the national average wage for 22 years and valued this figure at just under nine years' purchase, reducing the multiple to five to arrive at the current value.

Irrespective of the plaintiff's age, the rationale for determining future income loss was well laid down in the 1977 case of *Moeliker* v. *A. Reyrolle & Co. Ltd.*,[32] where the court seized of the case gave the correct criteria for determining compensation. According to this decision, what has to be quantified is the present value of the risk of future financial loss. If there is no actual loss of earnings sooner or later, there should be no award. If, however, there is a significant risk, its value would depend on the magnitude of the risk and how far in the future. Based on this premise, another case[33] decided in the same year ended with the award of substantial compensation to a young man with an arm injury, on the basis that he was likely to suffer from osteo arthritis later in life, although this would be many years ahead.

Loss of career which a person injured or infected is already in is another significant consideration. Of course, some occupations are more attractive than others, not necessarily in monetary terms but rather in the job satisfaction they offer. When a person is already enjoying such a career, for instance as an airline pilot or surgeon – two professions for which there are stringent health requirements – infection by a disease such as tuberculosis could be critical. In such instances courts would be compelled to take into account the damage caused by total loss of career.[34]

As for loss of earning capacity which the plaintiff avers he or she would have had if not for the injury (and which the plaintiff did not have at the time of injury) the observation obiter of Diplock LJ in *Browning* v. *War Office*[35] is relevant: 'A plaintiff is not entitled to damages for loss of capacity to earn money unless it is established that he would, but for his injuries, have exercised that capacity in order to earn money.'[36] In every claim for specific compensation concerning earning capacity, the plaintiff has the burden of showing clearly and convincingly that there was actual loss of future income owing to the injury or illness caused.

Liability under the Warsaw Convention

It is an incontrovertible principle of tort law that tortious liability exists primarily to compensate the victim by compelling the wrongdoer to pay for the damage he has done.[37] The second international conference on Private International Law[38] which led to the introduction of the Warsaw Convention[39] obviously followed this basic principle but deviated to align the provisions of the Warsaw Convention with existing exigencies of civil aviation. The Conference based its approach towards air carrier liability on the fault theory of tort, which has its genesis in the Industrial Revolution, where common law adopted the principle that a wrongdoer or tortfeasor must be at fault for him to be compelled to compensate the injured. The fault theory was introduced as a solution to the problems caused by injury to persons by the proliferation of machinery during the Industrial Revolution and on the basis that those responsible for introducing faulty machinery should pay those who are injured by them.

One of the fundamental deviations from the fault liability principle in the context of the Warsaw Conference was that, instead of retaining the basic premise that the person who alleges injury must prove that the injury was caused by the alleged wrongdoer, the Conference recognized the obligation of the carrier to assume the burden of proof. This was done seemingly to obviate the inherent difficulties which are posed in situations of air carriage where it would be difficult, if not impossible, to determine fault from evidence which is reduced to debris and wreckage after an aircraft accident. The Conference succinctly subsumed its views on liability in the words of its Reporter:

> These rules sprang from the fault theory of the liability of the carrier toward passengers and goods, and from the obligation of the carrier to assume the burden of proof. The presumption of fault on the shoulders of the carrier was, however, limited by the nature itself of the carriage in question, carriage whose risks are known by the passenger and consignor. The Conference had agreed that the carrier would be absolved from all liability when he had taken reasonable and ordinary measures to avoid the damage ... one restriction on this liability had been agreed upon.
>
> If for commercial transactions one could concede the liability of the carrier, it did not seem logical to maintain this liability for the navigational errors of his servants, if he proves that he himself took proper measures to avoid a damage.[40]

The Conference went on to suggest that, if the damage arises from an 'intentional illicit act' for which the carrier was liable, he should not have the right to avail himself of the provisions of the Convention.[41] The words 'intentional illicit act' were later changed to 'wilful misconduct' by the Conference at the request of the British delegate, Sir Alfred Dennis, and the Greek delegate, Mr Youpis.[42]

Deeming that it was not equitable to impose absolute liability upon the carrier, the Conference admitted that the carrier's responsibility would be limited to liability limits of monetary value and, furthermore, he could be freed of all liability when he had taken the reasonable and normal measures to avoid the damage.[43]

The Conference obviously based the Warsaw Convention on tort law principles of liability, where tort duties are primarily fixed by law, in contrast to contractual obligations which can arise only from voluntary agreement.[44] More than 70 years after the Warsaw Convention was introduced, however, there has been a palpable shift towards introducing a contractual element by the 1995 IATA Inter-Carrier Agreement which, although not having the legal status of a Convention but remaining an agreement among air carriers, retains the basic presumption of air carrier liability of the Convention but rejects the liability limitations of the Warsaw Convention and its protocols by recognizing that the compensatory amount that a carrier should pay for personal injury or death may be contractually agreed upon by the carrier and claimant according to the law of the domicile of the claimant.

Admittedly, this is not what the Conference envisaged. However, it must be borne in mind that the Conference recognized that the Warsaw Convention applied only to the unification of 'certain' rules, as proposed by the delegate of Czechoslovakia. Also the underlying purpose of the IATA initiative, which is to allow for greater flexibility for insurance underwriters, on the one hand, and more leverage for airlines in their risk management, on the other, is fundamentally consistent with the views of the Warsaw Conference. At the same time, the Convention does not preclude the right of a carrier to enter into agreement with a claimant on the issue of compensation. The Warsaw Conference itself recognized that:

> in reality, this Convention creates against the air carrier an exceptional system, because in the majority of the countries of the world, contracts of carriage are concluded under a system of free contract. The carrier is free to insert in the contract clauses which exclude or reduce his liability, as much as for goods as for travellers.[45]

The Inter-Carrier Agreement, which was approved by IATA carriers at their Annual General Meeting in Kuala Lumpur in October 1995, claims to preserve the Warsaw Convention, but carriers agree to take action to waive the limitation of liability on recoverable compensatory damages in claims for death, wounding or other bodily injury so that recoverable compensatory damages may be determined and awarded by reference to the law of the domicile of the passenger. This provision in effect introduces a contractual element to an otherwise pure tortious liability regime. The agreement attacks the monetary limits of liability of the Convention and retains all other provisions of liability, which are essentially the presumption of liability of the carrier and his defences against such a presumption.

With the rejection of the liability limits, the provision relating to breaking such limits in instances where the carrier is guilty of wilful misconduct has also been rejected. Therefore, effectively, certain elements of tortious liability that the Convention had have been expunged. In the final analysis, the principle of fault which the architects of the Warsaw Convention entrenched in it has been rejected by the IATA agreement. Lee Kreindler observes:

> The fault system is extremely important to the public. It is a public protection. It has improved aviation safety and security. While I don't profess to understand what the international airlines are now up to, it is clear to me that one of their purposes is to put an end to the tort system, in international airline transportation, at least as between the passenger and the airline, and that I oppose.[46]

Kreindler points out the ambivalence of the IATA Agreement in designating the law of the domicile of the passenger as being applicable for the award of compensatory damages, while it retains the provision of the Warsaw Convention which designates jurisdictions.[47] Sean Gates picks up the issue of 'domicile' and observes that the IATA agreement refers to Article 28 of the Warsaw Convention which it claims relates to 'domicile' but in actual fact does not. In fact, Gates questions whether 'domicile' would cover personal or corporate domicile and holds that this is another area where the IATA Agreement has not shown clarity.[48]

The ICAO Draft Convention

Integral to the agenda of the Diplomatic Conference on Private Air Law of the International Civil Aviation Organization (ICAO) of May 1999 is the Draft Convention for the Unification of Certain Rules For International Carriage by Air. This document seeks to replace the existing Warsaw Convention of 1929[49] in its totality.

However, the new Montreal Convention[50] does not make any provision for specific instances of damage caused as a result of mental injury. Instead, it states in Article 16 that the carrier is liable for damage sustained in case of death or bodily injury of a passenger upon condition only that the accident which caused the death or injury took place on board the aircraft or in the course of any of the operations of embarking or disembarking. It seems that the Convention left it open to courts to interpret whether mental injury is 'bodily injury'. In this context, the adjudications under the Warsaw system become extremely relevant.

Article 17 of the Warsaw Convention states that the carrier is liable for damage sustained in the event of the death or wounding of a passenger or any other bodily injury suffered by a passenger, if the accident which caused the damage so sustained took place on board the aircraft or in the course of any of the operations of embarking or disembarking. From its inception, this provision has proved contentious in its application as courts adjudicating a claim under Article 17 have been consistently constrained to interpret the words 'bodily injury' either as pure physical injury or as mental suffering accompanied by physical injury where the latter was a causative factor in bringing about the former. These rulings held that there could not be compensation under Article 17 for pure mental shock, psychic trauma, anxiety or mental discomfort. In the 1991 case of *Eastern Airlines Inc.* v. *Floyd et al.*,[51] the United States Supreme Court concluded that there must at least be physical manifestation of injury, if not death or physical injury, in order for a claimant to sue successfully an air carrier under Article 17. The court, however, did not address the issue as to whether mental injury accompanied by physical injury was a compensable element. The *Floyd* decision is consistent with its precursor – the 1974 case of *Rosman (and Herman)* v. *Trans World Airlines*,[52] which related to a hijacking incident – holding that there have to be palpable, objective bodily injuries, including those caused by psychic trauma related to the incident, and for the damage flowing from the bodily injuries and not from the trauma per se. The *Rosman* decision followed in the wake of a 1973 decision[53] which held the same.

The inclination of the courts to insist on pure physical injury as an essential element of compensability is arguably due to the fact that courts took refuge in the original French terminology of the Convention which was *'lésion corporelle'*, which means 'physical wound', as against *'lésion mentale'* which means 'mental wound'.[54] A diametrically opposed view emerged in a *cursus curiae* which ignored the connotations of the French language and visited the original intention of the draughters of the Convention. In *Husserl* v. *Swiss Air Co. Ltd.*,[55] also a case concerning the hijacking of an aircraft, the court observed the lacuna relating to the absence of reference to emotional injury in Article 17 and deemed fit to construe the provision broadly, to include injuries other than pure physical injury.

This polarization of views will be moot once courts start to apply the new ICAO Convention, which has gone through several drafts through the ICAO Legal Committee. In its first draft, the new Convention, under Article 16, provided as follows:

> The carrier is liable for damage sustained in case of death or bodily injury or mental injury of a passenger upon condition only that the accident which caused the damage so sustained took place on board the aircraft or in the course of any of the operations of embarking or disembarking. However, the carrier is not liable if the death or injury resulted solely from the state of health of the passenger.[56]

This draft, which was the result of the deliberations of the ICAO Study Group on the subject in 1995, underwent further 'surgery' at a later stage of the Group's deliberations, which introduced the element of 'personal injury' into the provision to cover both physical and mental injury. However, the final draft submitted to the May 1999 Diplomatic Conference reads that the carrier is liable for damage sustained in case of death or *bodily injury* (my emphasis) of a passenger upon condition only that the accident which caused the damage so sustained took place on board the aircraft or in the course of any of the operations of embarking or disembarking. However, the carrier is not liable to the extent that the death or injury resulted from the state of health of the passenger.[57]

The reintroduction of the words 'bodily injury' and the removal of 'personal and mental injury' could be interpreted either way: that the final draft intended retaining exclusively physical injury with no hint of mental injury, or that mental injury is imputed to 'bodily injury', taking into consideration the emergent trend of equating mental injury with a tangible bodily injury.

Although courts have been somewhat preoccupied with the term 'bodily injury' as against 'mental injury', the crux of the matter essentially lies earlier in the provision which speaks of 'damage' caused. The 1996 Supreme Court decision in *Zicherman* v. *Korean Air Lines*[58] ruled that it was quite evident that the English word 'damage' or 'harm', which was reflected in the official French text of the Convention as 'dommage', has a wide application and was, in fact, used by the Warsaw Convention draughters in its classical French law sense of 'legally cognizable harm'. The *Zicherman* decision incontrovertibly brings to bear the compelling significance of legally cognizable harm as being a compensable element and therefore admits of mental injury as 'damage' under Article 17, if the domestic law applicable to a case were to deem mental injury as such. The operative issue therefore remains as to whether mental injury is a legally cognizable harm.

The ICAO Draft Convention has been preoccupied, quite understandably, with the two most contentious and frequent issues within air carrier liability: physical and mental injury. However, if the Draft Convention retains the words 'personal injury', it would certainly be arguable that it may give courts wider scope to examine whether the infliction of a disease would be determinable as a personal injury.

General Principles

Generally in law an accusation has to be proved by the person who alleges it. Therefore a presumption of innocence applies to an accused person until he is proven guilty. However, in the instance of carriage by air of passengers, the airline is presumed liable if a passenger alleges personal injury or if his dependants allege his death as having been caused by the airline.[59] Of course, the airline can show in its defence that it had taken all necessary measures to avoid the damage[60] or that there was contributory negligence[61] and obviate or vitiate its liability. This curious anomaly of the law imposing on the airline a presumption of liability is contained in the Warsaw Convention, Article 17. The Warsaw System therefore presents to the lawyer an interesting and different area of the law which is worthy of discussion.

Article 17 of the Warsaw Convention was analysed in some detail in the previous chapter in order to clearly identify the circumstances in which a claim may be sustained against an airline for passenger injury or death. The defences available to the airline and the monetary limits of liability were also discussed there.

Embarking and Disembarking

Article 17 further provides that the accident which causes the damage should take place on board the aircraft or in the course of any of the operations of embarking or disembarking. The first alternative – that of being on board – is self-explanatory and does not require discussion. The second, which involves the operations of embarking or disembarking has been subject to sustained judicial discussion and analysis. Although *ex facie*, the words 'on board the aircraft' are not problematical, the phrase has been interpreted at least once to engulf time spent by passengers in a hotel consequent to a hijacking.[62] The argument in this case was that the passengers would have been on board if not for the hijacking. This is an extreme interpretation which seems to say that the airline is liable for all accidents within that period of time from the start of the embarkation process to the end of the disembarkation.

Current law on the subject seems to favour the test known as the 'Day–Evangelinos test', which was developed as a consequence of a series of terrorist acts on passengers in airport departure lounges. This is a tripartite test which has three elements of consideration: the location of the passenger, the nature of his activity at the time of the accident and the degree of control exercised by the airline at the relevant time. A number of US cases have accepted this test.[63] This test clearly establishes the fact that, unless the passenger is under the control or direction of the airline at the terminal, there is no liability for injury or death caused to the passenger under the provisions of the Warsaw Convention. A case which brings out the significance of this test is *Adler* v. *Austrian Airlines*, where a passenger slipped on some ice and fell between the terminal building and the aircraft bus. The bus was operated by the airport staff and not by the airline. A Brussels court, applying a test similar to the Day–Evangelinos test, held that the passenger was not under the control of the airline and was thereby precluded from invoking the provisions of Article 17 of the Convention.

The test itself obviates the need to go painstakingly through every possible exigency in the light of the requirement that the accident should occur during the process of embarkation or disembarkation. Prior to the adoption of this test, there was no uniformity in the judicial reasoning behind the definition of embarkation and disembarkation. It was left to each individual court to determine whether a given situation would fall within the scope of chronology of these two extremities. Now the tripartite test has made the task of the courts much easier.

Liability Limits

The Montreal Convention of 1999 stipulates in Article 20.1 that, for damages arising under paragraph 1 of Article 16 not exceeding 100 000 special drawing rights for each passenger, the carrier shall not be able to exclude or limit his liability. The provision goes one step further to set up a two-tier system of liability in Article 20.2, stating that the above strict liability amount does not apply if the carrier proves that such damage was not due to the negligence or other wrongful act or omission of the carrier or his servants or agents or such damage was solely due to the negligence or other wrongful act of a third party. Since these provisions would only come into force after the required number of ratifications were received by ICAO, the Warsaw provisions would remain in force until then. The Warsaw Convention states in Article 22:

> In the transportation of passengers the liability of the carrier for each passenger shall be limited to the sum of 125,000 francs. Where, in accordance with the law of the court to which the case is submitted, damages maybe be awarded in the form of periodic payments, the equivalent capital value of such payments shall not exceed 125,000 francs. Nevertheless, by special contract, the carrier and the passenger may agree to a higher limit of liability.

The currency of denomination of the franc refers to the French franc consisting of 65.5 milligrams of gold at the standard of fineness of nine hundred thousandths. These sums may be converted into any national currency in round figures.[64] At the time the Convention was signed in 1929, twelve and a half french francs made the US dollar which makes the airline liability for passenger death or injury a maximum of US$20 000. The question arises today as to what conversion rate applies to the French franc as stipulated at the Warsaw

Convention. Admittedly, the currency fluctuations of today would not make the old conversion standards practicable. This has given rise to much debate, particularly in the United States.

The Supreme Court of Puerto Rico in 1982 held that the limits of liability of the Warsaw Convention should be converted from francs to dollars by reference to the last official price of gold in the United States, as set forth in the last Civil Aeronautics Board (CAB) order dealing with the dollar equivalents of the Warsaw Convention limits of liability.[65] The most significant recent development on this point is seen in the 1984 case of *Trans World Airlines Inc.* v. *Franklin Mint Corp*,[66] where the US Supreme Court held that the limits of liability under Article 22 of the Warsaw Convention which are expressed in French gold francs are to be converted into US currency by using the last official price of gold.[67] The facts of the case were that Franklin Mint paid for the transportation of certain numismatic material to TWA from Philadelphia to London. The cargo was lost and Franklin Mint sought US$250 000 as damages from the defendant airline. The Court of Appeals for the Second Circuit somewhat unexpectedly pronounced that TWA's liability was limited under Article 22 of the Warsaw Convention but the liability limits were unenforceable owing to the inapplicability of the Convention and impracticability of converting currency as envisaged by the Convention in 1929.[68] The Supreme Court found the limits enforceable and cited with approval the decision of the Civil Aeronautics Board of the United States to use the last official price of gold as the basis for conversion within the authority of that agency and consistent with the US Constitution.[69]

The *Franklin Mint* case concerned the carriage of cargo and the question arose whether the decision would apply to passenger liability as well in terms of the applicability of the provisions of the Warsaw Convention to cases of passenger liability. In 1984, this problem was solved when the United States District Court for the Central District of California held that the principle of the *Franklin Mint* decision shall apply to personal injury and wrongful death claims.[70] The *Franklin Mint* standards however, are not absolute and static. In other words the US Supreme Court considered that the use of a limit based, for example, on gold was designed to deal with the fluctuations of inflation and in an inflationary economic environment a fixed limit in national currency might just fail to meet the desired result as envisaged by the Convention. To give effect to the objective of Article 22 and the envisaged economic uniformity, the court recognized that it may be necessary for periodic adjustments of the limit to be made, as converted into dollars. The CAB was charged with making such adjustments to accord with values of other Western currencies and of changes in conversion rates of currencies of other Warsaw signatories. Since the US Supreme Court considered the last valuation of the CAB in 1978 for its decision in the *Franklin Mint* case, such was taken to apply at the time the case was adjudicated in 1984.

It has also been suggested that a successful solution to the problem of matching the franc with the dollar would be to seek parity of the US dollar with special drawing rights (SDR), a basket of currencies which would adjust themselves with currency fluctuations of different countries. This, it is argued, would also allow a ready conversion of the SDR to any currency of any jurisdiction hearing a case of passenger death or injury under the Warsaw Convention. There is no logically compelling argument for either the *Franklin Mint* principle or the SDR principle. In most jurisdictions, courts may have to interpret the Convention on this point as best as they can, particularly in the absence of specific legislation.

The question of air carrier liability and the approach taken in its context by the Warsaw Convention has seen the emergence of the scholarly analysis of two issues: should liability of the carrier be based on fault and consequently on the principles of negligence and limited liability or should liability be based on strict liability? Drion, in his 1954 treatise on liability,[71] inquires into the various rationales and scenarios that may come up in an intellectual extrapolation of the subject. He examines the fact that an insurance system for liability, which would inextricably be linked to a strict liability concept, would be desirable, as a plaintiff would be able to claim compensation from an impecunious defendant through the latter's insurer, on the deep pocket theory,[72] and that insurance underwriters may, in their own interest, be impelled to formulate aviation accident preventive schemes, strengthening the effects of accident prevention.[73] Drion also puts forward eight rationales for the rebuttable limitation of liability presumption that appears in Article 17, quantified by Article 22 of the Convention: maritime principles carry a limitation policy; the protection of the financially weak aviation industry; the risks should be borne by aviation alone; the existence of back-up insurance; the possibility of the claimants obtaining insurance; limitation of liability being imposed on a *quid pro quo* basis on both the carrier and operator; the possibility of quick settlement under a liability limitation regime; and the ability to unify the law regarding damages.[74]

These rationales, and whatever else forms considerations of policy in the assessment whether a liability system should be based on negligence or strict liability should be addressed with the conscious awareness that, while the Convention imposes a rebuttable presumption of limited liability on the carrier, the contributory negligence of the plaintiff can exculpate the carrier and obviate or apportion compensation. More importantly, wilful misconduct of the carrier transcends liability limits and makes the liability of the carrier unlimited.

Strict liability, on the other hand, as proposed in the Montreal Protocols 3 and 4, does not admit of breaking liability limits, sets a maximum limit of compensation that the carrier has to pay, and makes this limit unbreakable by such extraneous factors as the carrier's wilful misconduct.

The ultimate question therefore is, does one keep the Warsaw–Hague concept of fault and limited liability, or does one embrace a system of strict liability which assures the aggrieved party of pecuniary or reipersecutory recompense, while obviating the need for lengthy determinations of who was at fault after the fact. In other words, does one point a finger at the carrier in the first instance, then limit his liability and again break the limit if he is at fault, or make the carrier pay a sum of money, the maximum limits of which have been set, with the assurance that such limits would not shoot up unconscionably if the carrier was negligent?

The Convention unified legal principles relating to air carrier liability, thus precluding the application of scores of differing domestic laws.[75] It did not succeed, however, in presenting to the world unequivocally objective and quantified rules of liability. This precludes a plaintiff from knowing that, as a rule, he would be compensated if he was injured in an air accident, since the Convention admits of challenge on the grounds of the plaintiff's conduct before, during or after the accident. The strict liability principle introduced by the Guatemala City Protocol and carried through by the Montreal Protocols, on the other hand, has been applauded on the following grounds:

> First, it gets money into the hands of the passengers much more quickly. Second, it saves transaction expenses which include legal fees and other substantial litigation costs. Third, it provides compensation to passengers in those factual situations where no responsible party is at fault, such as in an act of terrorism.[76]

Alexander Tobolewski points out very validly that actual aviation practice in terms of aviation insurance by the airlines has nothing to do with limitation of liability and claims, since airlines insure their fleets and liabilities for colossal amounts in the insurance market.[77] He suggests, therefore, the harmonization of the law and actual practice (presumably by infusing a more specific quantum in damages) and simplification of the system of recovery, inter alia, both of which strongly suggest a regime such as the one envisaged in the Montreal Protocols.[78] Werner Guldimann concludes:

> The most important and urgent matter in the present decade is the continuation of the efforts undertaken by ICAO to re-establish the former universality and uniformity of the Warsaw system by having

> the Montreal Protocols No 3 and 4 rapidly ratified by the greatest possible number of contracting States.[79]

Although Professor Bin Cheng holds the view that the Montreal Protocols are heavily weighted towards the carrier, that the limits therein are inadequate and that the unbreakability of the limit of the SDR value is undesirable,[80] the view that strict liability should be embraced seems more sensible, in view of the inconceivable number of passengers carried every year by air, the possible eradication of legal contingency fees and, above all, giving teeth to the meaning and purpose of law: that it should be an instrument of solace, not an opportunity for debate.

In an evaluation of the Warsaw System,[81] it was said in 1979 that, during the first 25 years of the existence of the Warsaw Convention, it had served the aviation community satisfactorily.[82] Peter Martin bases this observation on the argument that, when the Hague Protocol was being drafted in 1955, it was recorded that only 55 Warsaw cases had been adjudicated, and that is a very small number of cases for an instrument of the stature of the Warsaw Convention.[83] The unifying process of the liability of an air carrier, started by the Warsaw Convention, dealt with liability concepts, the quantum of compensation, exceptions on liability, jurisdictional issues and prescription of action. It is sad, however, that, together with the original Warsaw Convention, there are now seven other international agreements, few of which have ever seen the light of day. This means that the unification process started by the Warsaw Convention had been criticized and found wanting at various stages of its chequered history. The original document has been excoriated many times, prompting Professor Cheng to call it the 'Warsaw shambles',[84] although it remained, when these comments were made of it, the most widely implemented private international law convention.[85]

Ex facie, from a strictly practical standpoint, it would appear that many facets of unification of the Warsaw Convention have come under interpretation by different philosophies, presumably owing to the lack of specificity of the principles of unification and, a fortiori, the language used. For instance, the delivery of the passenger ticket and the attendant carrier liability came under a series of confounding judicial thought processes, where in two cases[86] the courts decided that the ticket had to be delivered in such a manner as to afford the passenger a reasonable opportunity to take measures to protect himself or herself against liability insurance, only to decide in *Chan* v. *Korean Airlines*[87] that the only requirement of Article 3 of the Convention was that a ticket be delivered. *Goldman* v. *Thai Airways International Limited*[88] was another case where two confusing issues were decided upon. The first involved the question whether the concept of 'wilful misconduct' as reflected in Article 25 of the Convention was to be interpreted objectively or subjectively. The second issue concerned compensatory limits which were so confusing to both the courts and the parties to litigation that an outside settlement was effected on a mutually acceptable basis.[89] The issue regarding compensatory limits for death or personal injury has had a consistent evolution, starting from the Warsaw Convention at Approximately US$8300, increased twofold by the Hague Protocol 1955, increased again by the Guatemala City Protocol to 100 000 special drawing rights (SDR) (about US$130 000) with the Montreal Protocols going even higher. The currency conversion to gold value has been another bone of contention of many parties to litigation and the case of *Franklin Mint* v. *TWA*[90] left the situation in fiscal anarchy by deciding that, in the United States, the Poincaré gold franc has to be converted to the last official price of gold before the United States left the gold market, and not the free market price of gold. This not only made the overall American attitude towards seeking enhanced compensation turn 360 degrees, but also awarded unrealistically low compensation to the plaintiff. Further, a case in Australia has given a new interpretation to the notion of carrier negligence in the carriage of cargo[91] and a New Zealand case has decided that any interested party can now claim compensation under a cargo claim.[92]

The Montreal Agreement of 1966, a private agreement between carriers plying the United States, was also the result of failure by contracting states to reach an international solution to the problem of unifying principles of liability, particularly insofar as the quantum of damages was concerned. The Montreal Agreement amply demonstrates, as an ICAO document[93] points out, that a private agreement between air carriers, sponsored by IATA, can unhinge and question the credibility of a multilateral international treaty between sovereign states. Mankiewicz attributes this chaotic state of disagreement to the stand taken by the United States when he states:

> Indeed, there is real irony in the history of the Warsaw Convention. For more than thirty years, the United States of America have steadily and successfully fought for, and obtained and signed, six protocols to amend the Warsaw Convention as well as a 'Convention Supplementary to the Warsaw Convention'. But they have ratified not one of these Warsaw instruments. In spite of the huge amounts of time and money spent all these years by ICAO and its member States, the US judiciary is still saddled with the awkward task of applying, construing constructively or destructively, misinterpreting and circumventing a convention which is now 60 years old.[94]

There is only one viable alternative to rectify this anomaly and preserve the unification efforts of the Warsaw Convention, and that comes in the nature of ratifying the Montreal Protocols 3 and 4. As Professor Michael Milde states :

> There is hardly any viable alternative to a determined effort to bring the Montreal Protocols Nos 3 and 4 into force. If that aim is not accomplished in the very near future, we may witness a trend to denunciation of the Warsaw System by several States with the ensuing chaotic conflicts of laws, conflicts of jurisdiction, unpredictably high compensation claims and skyrocketing increase in insurance premiums.[95]

The civil liability of an airline for the causing of death or injury to passengers has been established by international treaty and entrenched in law by judicial interpretation. The courts have attempted to balance the interests of the airline and the passenger, as indeed has been the perceived intention of the Warsaw Convention. The predominant feature of this area of civil liability is that air transport in terms of the commercial transportation of passengers is incontrovertibly the mode of transport that involves the highest levels of technology. Therefore courts may find difficulty in ascertaining negligence, wilful misconduct and the overall liability of the airline in the face of complex technical arguments and defence. However, this reason alone should not justify obviating the tortious element that has so carefully been entrenched in the Warsaw Convention by its founders and used by courts over the last 66 years. As the foregoing discussions reflect, liability issues under the Warsaw Convention has been consistently addressed by the courts on the basis of their interpretation of negligence, wilful misconduct and contributory negligence, all of which are exclusively issues involving principles of tort law.

An Analysis

It is clear that the conventional interpretation of the term 'accident' in tort liability has been extended in aviation cases under Article 17 of the Warsaw Convention where the courts have imputed intention to the carrier in certain instances. To this extent, both the *Seguritan*[96] case – which addressed the issue of the carrier's liability in not being able to provide regular medical assistance when necessary – and the *O'Leary* case[97] – where a passenger was given more liquor than he could consume in flight – perforce prove that the courts have interpreted the Warsaw Convention to enforce liability of the carrier on the principles of intention. Wilful misconduct, has therefore played an important role in establishing that, in certain circumstances at least, it would be justified to consider that the extent of the carrier's fault is a valid consideration in the award of damages.

Fault liability as enforced by the Warsaw Convention may also be adequately reflected in intentional negligence, where the carrier intentionally breaches the duty of care he owes the passenger. Determination of a breach of a duty or care as a distinct evidentiary tool by the courts would act towards accident prevention, in that instances of carrier liability which emerge from accident investigations could then be used as admissible evidence.

The new trend, in doing away with fault liability and introducing a system of liability that may apply irrespective of fault but aligned to monetary compensation based upon subjective assessments of jurisdictional liability, has its genesis in the decade between 1960 and 1970. During this period civil law liability in tort entered a new phase, effectively superannuating the existing system of liability and replacing it with a system of liability insurance. Tortious liability was no longer considered cost effective, and was no match for less expensive insurance. Jurists thought it more equitable and, above all, practical to embrace a legal system that espoused loss distribution, which acted as the national precursor to liability insurance. This system of liability was assisted along the way by three reasons which militated against fault liability and acted as catalysts towards the successful launch of liability insurance. Firstly, a tort system based upon fault was expensive to administer, when compared with any system of insurance; secondly, litigation was fraught with delay, which a plaintiff could often ill afford; thirdly, the unpredictability of the result of cases based upon fault liability often put plaintiffs under pressure to settle their claims for amounts less than they would receive if their claims went successfully to trial.

The question that now arises is whether the international aviation community should retain fault liability or embrace strict liability which is designed to obviate adjudication for tortious liability and settle claimants on a subjective basis.

Rationales for the limitation of liability in private air law had been discussed by Drion in 1954,[98] when he discussed nine reasons, listed earlier in this chapter. The task which now has to be accomplished is to inquire whether private air law needs the concept of limited liability or whether another system could be recommended. The most compelling arguments for the limitation of liability in private air law are that it protects the financially weak aviation industry, unifies private air law against draconian domestic laws and expedites the payment of compensation. It is interesting to analyse these concepts in today's aviation context. We live in a world where complex litigation issues emerge, carefully thought out by contingency-fee lawyers who have an inexplicable capacity to produce a variety of defendants out of a hat. For instance, now, there is a conscious awareness that there are co-liable parties: manufacturers of component parts, air traffic controllers, and even government agencies such as airports authorities. Would it be fair to limit the liability of the carrier and expose these three categories of defendants to unlimited liability? There may also be the instance where the deceased or injured may have had enormous capacity to earn during his working life, which would be interrupted or terminated by an air accident. Does this mean that such a defendant settles for a limited sum of money as compensation and bears his losses? Professor Bin Cheng claims that the SDR 100 000 of the Montreal System is woefully inadequate and implies that a higher limit should be considered or the possibility of breakability of the limits should be endorsed, on the lines of the Warsaw Convention.[99]

It is prudent to approach this question with due emphasis laid on the economic ramifications of this strictly legal consideration since, at its core, the question addresses not principles of legal rectitude, nor issues of justice, but matters of financial interest to the parties concerned. It is inevitable therefore to consider the effect of limitation of liability as against unlimited liability and rationalize between the two and arrive at a synthesis of the concepts or (if possible) a totally new concept. To determine this situation, it is necessary to assess the Warsaw Convention, with its principles of limitation of liability as coupled with unlimited liability in the event of gross negligence of the carrier, the Montreal Protocols with their strict liability and higher limits of liability with no possibility to accommodate unlimited liability under any circumstances; and a pure instance of general liability with no inhibitions whatever. Of course, it is needless to say that these three alternatives would be viewed from the standpoint of the plaintiff passenger or his dependant and the defendant airline. The operative theme of this inquiry would be money and not complex legal issues, since it is money that both parties are ultimately interested in.

It is incontrovertible that aviation insurers, when faced with increasing levels of claims and declining premium income, would naturally increase their policy deductibles and seek to incorporate exclusions of cover. The aviation insurance market increasingly feels that there is no closeness at all between the underwriters and brokers, on the one hand, and the insured (airline), on the other.[100] One commentator recommends either a substantial increase in voluntary limits of liability or total abandonment of limiting air carrier liability, implying that either would benefit both the plaintiff and the defendant.[101] Peter Martin suggests that the best future for the Warsaw system would be the abandonment of limitations.[102] He states:

> There are very good reasons for imposing on carriers at least a very high standard of care, and even strict liability. Strict liability without

> limitations already applies in many States to third party liability to persons other than passengers and that is generally believed to be right ... why should a passenger, therefore, be in a worse position than a person or owners of property on the ground?[103]

The insurance lawyers obviously need higher liability limits and specificity in this area. The steady disintegration of the Warsaw System, which is mainly attributable to its incompetence in providing for satisfactory compensatory limits, has been proved by figures which were released by the Rand Corporation showing that, in a cross-section of cases studied, Warsaw–Montreal tickets obtained a per capita compensation of US$184 000, while non-Warsaw–Montreal tickets had received double this amount. This amount has further increased over the years, demonstrating that the Warsaw limits are rapidly being left behind.[104] It is clear, therefore, that one of the viable alternatives to the IATA Inter-carrier Agreement's strict liability and private contract proposal is to consider the extension of the Warsaw limits and the first step towards this goal is the ratification by states of the Montreal Protocols. If such a measure is accepted, it is also imperative that the scope of the Convention be extended to third parties such as air traffic controllers and manufacturers of component parts of aircraft to seek consistency and to give the insurance market a clear picture and more accurate assessment. By bringing these parties under the Warsaw umbrella, both the plaintiff and the defendant would be well served, in that the plaintiff would be assured of quick settlement and the defendant would be comfortable with the thought that his liability is limited. This could also preclude contingency-fee appearances by lawyers.

At the same time, one must not lose sight of the importance of the insurance aspect to liability under the Warsaw Convention. It must be noted that, when the subject of insurance was addressed at the Warsaw Conference, the president of the drafting committee, Mr Gianini, observed:

> I may remind you that, under present conditions of air navigation, we have arrived at the conclusion that the problem is not yet ripe. But, given the importance of the problem, given that no one is disposed to consider the work already done as an end, we have expressed, on my proposal, wishes by which we indicate that the study of the problem deserves to be pursued. That is to say that we leave the door open for later discussions. In order to advance the solution of this problem, we have also expressed a wish, signed by all governments, by which we ask the governments to bring insurance into practice as much as possible. It is only then that one will be able to envisage the possibility of setting up an international rule.[105]

These words of more than 70 years ago, which show vision and deep understanding of the future of civil aviation, should not be disregarded. It is time that the international aviation community looked hard at emerging trends relating to the Warsaw Convention and attempted a balanced and workable solution.

Emerging Trends in Wilful Misconduct of the Carrier

Of the two instances in which the Warsaw Convention provides that the carrier's liability is unlimited, one relates to the absence of documentation (absence of the passenger ticket and baggage check or air waybill) on the grounds that the document of carriage evidences the special regime of limited liability as prescribed in the Warsaw Convention. The other, which has turned out to be contentious, deals with instances where the damage is caused by the carrier's wilful misconduct, or such default on his part as, in accordance with the law of the court which exercises jurisdiction in the case, is considered to be the equivalent of wilful misconduct. Article 25 of the Warsaw Convention provides:

> The carrier shall not be entitled to avail himself of the provisions of this Convention or exclude or limit his liability, if the damage is caused by his wilful misconduct or by such default on his part as, in accordance with the law of the Court seised of the case, is considered to be equivalent to wilful misconduct.[106]

The provision further stipulates that the carrier shall not be entitled to avail himself of the above provisions if the damage is caused as aforesaid by any agent of the carrier acting within the scope of his employment.[107]

The primary significance of Article 25 is that it addresses both wilful misconduct and the *equivalent* (my emphasis) of wilful misconduct. The authentic and original text of the Warsaw Convention, which is in French, uses the words '*dol*' and '*faute … equivalente au dol*'. There is a palpable inconsistency between the English translation of the original text and the original text itself, in that the French word '*dol*' personifies the intention to inflict an injury on a person, whereas the English words 'wilful misconduct' require the defendant carrier to be aware of both his conduct and the reasonable and probable consequences of his conduct, in the nature of the damage which may ensue from the carrier's act. Wilful misconduct, therefore, may not necessarily involve the intention of the carrier, his servants or agents, and remains wider in scope as a ground of liability.

Most civil law jurisdictions have equated '*dol*' with 'gross negligence'. Drion[108] dismisses the element of intention by citing examples such as the theft or pilferage of goods or baggage (which are more frequent in occurrence than aircraft accidents) which may not necessarily always occur with the concurrence or knowledge of the carrier and cites a list of possible instances where gross negligence would form more justification for the invocation of Article 25. Notable examples are assault or indecent behaviour by personnel of the carrier, accidents caused by the conduct of personnel, serving bad food, bumpy rides causing passenger injury, and failure to instruct passengers of rough weather and so on.[109] Drion also makes the valid point of citing delay in carriage as having many dimensions which may be accommodated within the purview of Article 25 without warranting the consideration of intention.[110]

Common law jurisdictions, on the other hand, have separated 'wilful misconduct' from 'negligence' and insisted that the conduct of the carrier has to be 'wilful' or intentional for a successful case to be grounded on Article 25 of the Warsaw Convention. This approach is consistent with the original contention of the British delegate to the Warsaw Conference, who claimed that wilful misconduct should pertain to 'acts committed deliberately or acts of carelessness without any regard for the consequences'.[111] In the 1952 British case of *Horabin* v. *British Overseas Airways Corporation*, the court held:

> To be guilty of wilful misconduct the person concerned must appreciate that he is acting wrongfully, or is wrongfully omitting to act and yet persists in so acting or omitting to act regardless of the consequences, or acts or omits to act with reckless indifference as to what the result may be.[112]

In the same year, in the United States, the New York Supreme Court Appellate Division held that wilful misconduct was

> dependent upon the facts of a particular case, but in order that acts may be characterized as wilful there must be on the part of the person or persons sought to be charged, a conscious intent to do or to omit doing the act from which harm results to another, or an intentional omission of a manifest duty. There must be a realization of the probability of injury from the conduct and a disregard of the probable consequences of such conduct.[113]

The above approach has been followed by subsequent American decisions which have classified wilful misconduct as requiring 'conscious intent to do or omit doing an act from which harm results to another'[114] and 'wilful performance of an act that is likely to result in damage or wilful action with a reckless disregard of the probable consequences'.[115]

As to the second limb of Article 25.1, which provides that the equivalent of wilful misconduct would suffice to impose liability, the Convention leaves the scope of the provision wide open to include such topical issues as substance abuse at the workplace and air crew fatigue. A discussion of these issues will follow in Chapter 13.

Recent Judicial Decisions on Wilful Misconduct

Arguably the watershed decision on the notion of wilful misconduct in recent times was contained in the case *In re Korean Airlines Disaster of September 1, 1983,*[116] where the trial court considered wilful misconduct to be 'The performance of an act with knowledge that the act will probably result in an injury or damage, or in some manner as to imply reckless disregard for the consequences of its performance.' This pronouncement was used by the American courts in the 1994 decision of *Pasinato* v. *American Airlines Inc.,*[117] concluding that the act in question of a flight attendant did not constitute wilful misconduct within the purview of Article 25.2 of the Warsaw Convention. In the *Pasinato* case, a passenger of an American Airlines flight which was bound for Chicago from Italy was struck on the head when a heavy tote bag fell from an overhead bin in the cabin. The incident was the outcome of an initial request by the passenger for a pillow immediately after take-off, where the flight attendant, in a bid to open the overhead bin above the passenger to retrieve the pillow, was unable to prevent a tote bag falling from the bin onto the passenger's head. The passenger and her husband sued American Airlines under Article 25 on the grounds of wilful misconduct. The trial court was of the following view:

> there is no dispute that the flight attendant opened the overhead bin to get a pillow for another passenger. The flight attendant's disposition indicates that she opened the bin with one hand, in her customary manner, with the other hand placed defensively above her head near the bin to prevent an object from falling upon her or a passenger sitting below. Further, the flight attendant stated that she tried to catch the totebag that fell from the bin (and may have touched it as it fell), but that it fell too quickly.[118]

The court took cognizance of the contention of American Airlines that the technical and cabin crews give reported warnings to passengers of the dangers of opening overhead bins, both over the public address system of the aircraft and by personal messages. The evidence of the flight attendant – that incidents of objects falling from overhead bins were infrequent and generally harmless – based on her experience, was also considered relevant. The court found difficulty in applying the criterion of the *Korean Airlines Disaster* case,[119] in that it was difficult if not impossible, for the court, to envisage how the flight attendant's actions could amount to wilful misconduct. It was of the view that the pivotal criterion for determining the existence of wilful misconduct – knowledge that the act would probably result in an injury or damage – was absent. A fortiori, the court observed that the other criterion established in the *Korean Airlines* case, that of an act which is performed in a manner indicating reckless disregard for the consequences, was also missing in the *Pasinato* case.

In the 1994 case of *Baba* v. *Compagnie Nationale Air France*,[120] involving damage to cargo, a Federal trial court in Washington found for the plaintiff and awarded damages against the act of the defendant carrier for improperly packing and storing hand-woven Persian carpets, as a result of which some of the carpets were damaged owing to the seepage of rain water when the carpets were kept outside by the carrier pending their loading onto the aircraft. The court in this instance followed the bench in *Pasinato* by reiterating the criteria for the proof of wilful misconduct as established by the *Korean Air* litigation. A compelling piece of evidence which enabled the court to arrive at its conclusion in the *Baba* case was the fact that the air carrier had disregarded its own cargo-handling regulations in storing the carpets outdoors, in the rain. In its findings the court held: 'In short, through a series of acts, the performance of which were intentional, the carrier has demonstrated a reckless disregard of the consequences of its performance, This disregard is emphasized by the fact that no damage report was ever produced.'[121]

The court, while waiving the liability limits of the Warsaw Convention in the *Baba* case, noted that a combination of facts can, taken together, amount to wilful misconduct. It was sufficient, in the court's view, for an act to be intended, and not necessary for the resulting injury or wrongfulness of the act to reflect intention or knowledge. It was also significant that the court further observed that a finding of wilful misconduct was appropriate when the act or omission constituted a violation of a rule or regulation of the defendant carrier itself.

Courts in the United States have been cautious to determine the parameters of 'scope of employment' as envisaged in Article 25.2 of the Warsaw Convention, which imputes liability to the carrier with regard to acts of its employers acting within the scope of their employment. In the 1995 case of *Uzochukwu* v. *Air Express International Ltd.*,[122] where a New York Federal trial court had to decide on a case of theft by two airline employees of cargo of the carrier, it was held that the fact that the employees had used forged documents to perpetrate the offence of theft was sufficient to conclude that the act was outside the scope of employment and that the carrier could not be held liable under Article 25.2. It is arguable that the conclusion of the court was based on the fact that generally, in the United States, 'wilful misconduct' is regarded as the intentional performance of an act with knowledge that the performance of that act would probably result in injury or damage or intentional performance of an act in such a manner as to imply reckless disregard of the probable consequences.

In *Robinson* v. *Northwest Airlines Inc.*,[123] a case decided in March 1996 and involving circumstances similar to the *Pasinato* case, the United States Court of Appeals dismissed the appeal of the plaintiff who had lost judgment in the trial court against the carrier. The trial court had allowed a motion of the carrier that the plaintiff's claim in relation to her being injured by a piece of hand luggage falling from an overhead bin while the plane was taxiing, and additional injuries caused to her by a passenger striking her on the head with the latter's baggage, were not valid at law.

The Court of Appeals, in affirming the dismissal of the action of the plaintiff, noted that, while a common carrier (a carrier which opens itself to the world to conduct business in the carriage by air of passengers, baggage and goods) owes a high degree of care to its passengers, it cannot be considered an insurer of the passenger's safety. The court found that the plaintiff failed to raise an issue of fact regarding the carrier's breach of duty towards her. The court was of the following view:

> Short of physical constraint of each passenger until each is individually escorted off the plane, we fail to see what Northwest could have done to prevent this accident. At best, that is precisely what the plaintiff has established; the fact that an accident occurred. However, as noted above, common carriers are not insurers of their passengers' safety.[124]

A similar approach can be seen in the contemporaneous case of *Bell* v. *Swiss Air Transport Co. Ltd.*,[125] where an Intermediate Appellate Court in New York State refused to allow the plaintiff's claim that the loss of his laptop computer during a security check of the airline was due to the airline's wilful misconduct. In the court's view, the plaintiff had failed to prove that the airline intentionally mishandled his baggage with knowledge or reckless disregard for the probable consequences of its conduct. The court also noted that it was the local police, and not the airline, who had required the carrying out of the security check.

The case of *Singh* v. *Pan American World Airways*,[126] decided in May 1996, offers a helpful insight into the rationale for determination of wilful misconduct. In wrongful death and personal injury actions arising out of the 1995 hijacking of a Pan Am flight between Bombay and New York, the jury concluded that the carrier had been guilty of wilful misconduct on the reasoning that the management of the carrier knew, or ought to have known, of serious lapses in its security programme. In fact, there had been representations made by the carrier's staff to the management on several occasions prior to the hijacking. Furthermore, the jury was influenced in its conclusion by the fact that the carrier was aware of terrorist activity at European, Middle Eastern and Asian high-risk airports and that very little had been done by the carrier to provide enhanced security at these airports.

In the case of the crash of Thai Airways Flight TG-311 near Kathmandu, Nepal, in July 1992,[127] the question at issue was whether the air crew had been guilty of wilful misconduct in flying into terrain. The fatal crash occurred during approach to Kathmandu airport, an airport known to be one of the most difficult in the world to land.[128] Evidence had revealed that the captain had given the bearings of the aircraft to the control tower shortly before the crash, and that such were inconsistent with instruction previously given by the tower to the crew in the cockpit of the aircraft. The court concluded that the plane had veered towards terrain surrounding the airport as a result of the crew's conscious failure to monitor their navigational instruments. The court held:

> the captain and the first officer knew or should have known that failing to perform their duty to continuously monitor the aircraft's navigational instruments would create a grave danger under the circumstances … both the captain and the first officer were well aware that their duty to consciously monitor navigational instruments was an act *necessary for safety* … their duty to perform this crucial act was so obvious under the circumstances that failing to perform it was *reckless in the extreme* … .[129]

The *Thai Airways* case therefore marks an instance where the elements of wilful misconduct were imputed to the crew on the basis that, owing to their expertise, they knew or ought to have known the reasonable and probable consequences of their act.

A further dimension to the notion of wilful misconduct was added in the *Northwest Airlines Air Crash* case[130] of August 1996, where the Court of Appeals of the Sixth Circuit added that a finding of wilful misconduct may be based upon consideration of a series of actions or inactions. The court was of the view that, since many complex safety systems interact during an aeroplane flight, an air disaster would usually require multiple acts. In other words, the court held that it was permissible for a jury to consider an airline's individual errors or a series of errors and not restrict itself to the only act which seemingly caused an accident.

If one were to analyse the rationale of wilful misconduct in the light of the *cursus curiae* so far discussed, one would conclude that wilful misconduct hinges itself on knowledge of the perpetrator that damage would result or reckless disregard for consequences of an act on the part of the perpetrator. The question which then arises is whether such issues as substance abuse in the workplace and air crew fatigue would subscribe to the notion of wilful misconduct as it is perceived at the present time. This will be addressed in Chapter 13.

Notes

1 Convention for the Unification of Certain Rules Relating to International Carriage by Air, signed at Warsaw on 12 October 1929.

2 1999 Westlaw 7724 (Jan. 12 1999).

3 *Tuberculosis and Air Travel, Guidelines for Prevention and Control*, WHO/TB/98-256 Geneva: World Health Organization, 1998, p.7.

4 M. Moore, K.S. Fleming and L. Sands (1996), 'A Passenger with Pulmonary Laryngeal Tuberculosis: No Evidence of Transmission on Two Short Flights', *Aviation Space Environment Medicine*, 67, 1097–1100.

5 Ibid., 1097.

6 Farrol Kahn (1998), 'Sick Aircraft', *The Aviation Quarterly*, Part 3, July, 167.

7 Ibid.

8 'World's Next Epidemic: Resistant Tuberculosis', *The Montreal Gazette*, Wednesday 17 March 1999, B1.

9 See A.S.R. Peffers, J. Bailey, G.L. Barrow *et al.* (1973), 'Vibrio parahemolyticus gastroenteritis and international air travel', *Lancet*, 1, 143–5. See also R.G.A. Sutton (1974), 'An Outbreak of Cholera in Australia due to Food Served in Flight on an International Aircraft', *Journal of Hygiene*, 72, 441–51; M.S. Eisenberg, K. Gaarslev, W. Brown *et al.*, (1975), 'Staphylococcal Food Poisoning During Air Travel', *Lancet*, 2, 595–9; and F.R. Ratzinger (1965), 'Disease Transmission by Aircraft', *Aeromedical Review*, 4, pp.1–10.

10 Tuberculosis and Air Travel (*supra*, n.3), p.23. The humidity level of a home or office building is usually 40–60 per cent.

11 See Farrol Kahn, 'Sick Aircraft', (*supra*, n.6), 166.

12 Convention on International Civil Aviation, signed at Chicago on 7 December 1944, 7th edn, 1997, Doc. 7300/7.

13 World Health Organization, *International Health Regulations*, 3rd annotated edn, Geneva: WHO, 1983.

14 *R.* v. *Sansregret* (1985) 18 C.C.C. (3d) 223 (S.C.D.).

15 The other types of wrongs are wrongs exclusively criminal; civil wrongs which create no right of action for unliquidated damages, but give rise to some other form of civil remedy exclusively; and civil wrongs which are exclusively breaches of contract.

16 This definition of a tort was cited with approval in the case of *Anglo-Saxon Petroleum Co. Ltd.* v. *Damant* [1947] KB 794 at 796, and in *Philip Morris Ltd.* v. *Airley* [1975] V.R. 345 at 347.

17 See A. Seavey (1942), 'Harm is the Tort Signature Principles of Torts', *Harvard Law Review*, 56, 73.

18 [1964] AC 326, [1963] 2 All ER 625.

19 Ibid., 348, 633.

20 (1966) 39 ALJ 480.
21 Ibid., 486. This view was endorsed at English common law in 1980 in the case of *Lin Poh.choo* v. *Camden and Islington Area Health Authority* [1980] AC 174, [1979] 2 All ER 910.
22 [1969] 3 All ER 1528.
23 Ibid., 1532.
24 See *Fletcher* v. *Autocar and Transporters Ltd.* [1968], 1 All ER 726 at 750 *per* Salmond LJ.
25 *Ward* v. *James* [1966] 1 QB 273, [1965] 1 All ER 563.
26 *Gage* v. *King* [1961] 1 QB 188.
27 *Shearman* v. *Folland* [1950] 2 KB 43.
28 See *The Esso Malaysia Case* [1975] QB 198. In the case of loss of future income, courts may take into account the sums that might have been payable in the future by the plaintiff as income taxes, which would naturally be deducted from the compensation payment. See *British Transport Commission* v. *Gourley* [1956] AC 1985.
29 [1975] 2 All ER 1107, [1975] 1 WCR 1054.
30 *Conolly* v. *Camden and Islington Area Health Authority* [1981] 3 All ER 250.
31 [1981] 3 All ER 852, [1982] 1 WLR 71.
32 [1977] 1 All ER 9, [1977] 1 WLR 132.
33 *Cook* v. *Consolidated Fisheries Ltd.* [1977] 1 All ER 36.
34 See *Morris* v. *Johnson Matthey & Co. Ltd.* (1967) 112 Sol. Jo 32, CA and *Hearnshaw* v. *English Steel Corporation Ltd.* (1971) 11 K1R 306.
35 [1963] IQB 750, [1962] 3 All ER 1089.
36 Ibid., 754; 1093.
37 John G. Fleming (1983), *The Law of Torts*, 6th edn, London: The Law Book Company, 1.
38 Warsaw, 4–12 October 1929.
39 Convention for the Unification of Certain Rules Relating to International Carriage by Air, Warsaw, 1929 (*supra*, n.1).
40 *Second International Conference on Private International Law*, 4–12 October 1929, Warsaw, Minutes (translated by Robert C. Horner and Didier Legrez), New Jersey: Fred B. Rottman & Co. 1975, p.21.
41 Ibid., 58.
42 Ibid., 59–66.
43 Ibid., 251–2.
44 Fleming (*supra*, n.37), 2.
45 Horner and Legrez (*supra*. n.40), 47.
46 Lee S. Kreindler (1996), 'The IATA Solution', *Lloyd's Aviation Law*, 14(21), 1 November, 5.
47 Ibid., 6.
48 Sean Gates, 'IATA Inter Carrier Agreement – The Trojan Horse for a Fifth Jurisdiction?' *Lloyd's Aviation Law*, 14(23), 1 December, 2.
49 Convention for the Unification of Certain Rules Relating to International Carriage by Air, signed at Warsaw on 12 October 1929. (49 Stat. 3000, *T.S.* No. 876 (1934) reprinted in note following 49 U.S.C. App. 1502, 1988 edn.). Also published in *Annals of Air and Space Law*, XVIII, 1993, Part II, pp.323–49.
50 International Conference on Air Law, Montreal, 10 to 28 May 1999, ICAO Doc. 55, 27/5/99.
51 17 April 1991, 23 Avi. 17,367.
52 358 N.Y.S. 2d 97 (1974), 13 Avi. 17,231.
53 368 F Supp. 1152 (1973), 12 Avi. 18,405.
54 For a detailed discussion on this subject see, Caroline Desbiens (1992), 'Air Carrier's Liability for Emotional Distress Under Article 17 of the Warsaw

Convention: Can it Still be Invoked?', *Annals Air and Space Law*, XVII, Part II, pp.159–66.
55 (D.C.N.Y. 1972) 351 F. Supp. 702.
56 See 'Report of the Rapporteur on the Modernization and Consolidation of the Warsaw System', *The Aviation Quarterly*, Part 5, July 1997, p.313.
57 Draft Convention for the Unification of Certain Rules for International Carriage by Air, Reference Text, DCW Doc No. 4, 5/3/99, Article 16.1.
58 116 S. Ct. 629 (1996).
59 Shawcross and Beaumont (1988), *Air Law*, 4th edn, 1 reissue, VII, 152.
60 Ibid., VII (116).
61 Ibid., VII (117).
62 *Husserl* v. *Swiss Air Transport Co. Ltd.*, 485 F. 2d 1240 (2nd Circ. 1975). See also *People of the State of Illinois* v. *Gilberto*, 383 NE 2d 977.
63 *Day* v. *Trans World Airlines Inc.*, 528 F. 2d 31 (2nd Circ. 1975); *Evangelinos* v. *Trans World Airlines Inc.*, 550 F. 2d 152 (2d. Circ. 1977); *Leppo* v. *Trans World Airlines Inc.*, 392 NYS 2d 660 (AD 1977); Rolnick v. *El Al Israel Airlines Ltd.*, 551 Supp. 261 (EDNY 1982).
64 Warsaw Convention, Article 22(4).
65 *Delgado* v. *Pan American World Airways Inc.*, nos. R-81-12, R-80-318 (Sup. Ct P.R. 18 March 1982).
66 104S. Ct. 1776 (1984).
67 Ibid., 1784–9.
68 *Franklin Mint Corp* v. *Trans World Airlines Inc.*, 690 F. 2d 303, 304 (2nd Cir. 2982).
69 104 S. Ct. at 1784–9.
70 In re Aircraft at Kimpo International Airport, Korea, on 18 November 1980, MDL-482 (D.C. Ca. 1984), reversing the court's earlier decision at 558 F. Supp 72 (C.D., Cal. 1983).
71 Drion (1954), *Limitation of Liabilities in International Air Law*, The Hague: Martinus Nijhoff, p.7.
72 Ibid., p.8.
73 Ibid.
74 Ibid., pp.12–13.
75 *Reed* v. *Wiser*, 555 F. 2d 1079 (2nd Cir.) at 1090.
76 Nicholas Mateesco Matte (1983), 'The Warsaw System and the Hesitation of the United States Senate', *Annals of Air and Space Law*, VIII, 164.
77 Alexander Tobolewski (1978), 'Against Limitation of Liability, A Radical Proposal', *Annals of Air and Space Law*, III, 263.
78 Ibid., 266.
79 Werner Guldimann (1991), 'A Future System of Liability in Air Carriage', *Annals of Air and Space Law*, XVI, 104.
80 Bin Cheng (1989), 'What is Wrong with the Montreal Additional Protocol No. 3?', *Air Law*, XIV(6), 232.
81 The Warsaw Convention of 1929 was amended by The Hague Protocol 1955, the Guadalajara Convention 1961, The Guatemala City Protocol 1971, and the Montreal Protocols 1, 2, 3, 4, of varying dates. It should also be noted that the Montreal Agreement of 1966, a private arrangement between air carriers, also purported to amend the Warsaw Convention. Hereafter, joint references to all these instruments will be referred to as the Warsaw System.
82 Peter Martin (1979), '50 Years of the Warsaw Convention, A Practical Man's Guide', *Annals of Air and Space Law*, IV, 234.
83 Ibid.
84 Bin Cheng (1977), 'Wilful Misconduct, From Warsaw to the Hague and from Brussels to Paris', *Annals of Air and Space Law*, II, 99. Rene Mankiewicz also

uses the word 'shambles' when he describes the Warsaw Convention. See Rene H. Mankiewicz (1989), 'From Warsaw to Montreal With Certain Intermediate Stops', *Air Law*, XIV(4), 26.

85 Martin (*supra*, n.82), 239.

86 *Warren* v. *Flying Tiger Line Inc.*, 352 F. 2d 494 (CA 9 1965); *Mertens* v. *Flying Tiger Line Inc.*, 341 F. 2d 841 (CA 2 1965).

87 21 Avi 18, 228, (1989).

88 1983 1 All ER 693.

89 D.A. Kilbride (1989), 'Six Decades of Insuring Liability Under Warsaw', *Air Law*, XIV(4/5), 187.

90 18 Avi 17, 778, 1984.

91 *SS Pharmaceutical Co. Ltd.* v. *Qantas Airways Limited*, 1988 1 Lloyds Law Reports 319.

92 *Tasman Pulp and Paper Co. Ltd.* v. *Pan American World Airways Inc. and others*, see X1 *Annals of Air and Space Law*, XI, 1987 323 for a detailed account.

93 Ref. LE 3/27, 3/28 – 91/3, at 5.

94 Mankiewicz (*supra*, n.84).

95 Michael Milde (1989), 'ICAO Work on the Modernization of the Warsaw System', *Air Law*, XIV(4/5), 206.

96 *Seguritan* v. *Northwest Airlines Inc.*, 86 A.D. 2d 658 (2 Dept. 1982). See also *Lloyds Aviation Law*, 1(4) 1 August 1982, 1.

97 *O'Leary* v. *American Airlines*, 475 N.Y.S. 2d 285 (A.D. 2d Dept. 1984).

98 H. Drion (*supra*, n.71), p.12.

99 Bin Cheng (*supra*, n.80), 232.

100 Kilbride (*supra*, n.89), 191.

101 Ibid., 192.

102 Martin (*supra*, n.82), 248.

103 Ibid.

104 Guldimann (*supra*, n.79), 96.

105 Minutes of the Second International Conference on Private Aeronautical Law (*supra*, n.40), 183.

106 See Convention for the Unification of Certain Rules Relating to International Carriage by Air, signed at Warsaw on 12 October 1929, reproduced in *Annals of Air and Space Law*, XVIII, 1993, Part II, 339.

107 Ibid., Article 25, 2.

108 Drion (*supra*, n.71), para. 181, p.212.

109 Ibid., para. 181.2, p.213.

110 Ibid., paras 181.4 and 5, p.213.

111 Horner and Legrez (*supra*, n.40), p.42.

112 (1952) 2 All ER 1016 at 1022.

113 *Goepp* v. *American Overseas Airlines*, New York Supreme Court, Appellate Division (1st Dep) 16 December 1952; [1952] US Av R 486; IATA ACLR, No. 12.

114 *Grey* v. *American Airline Inc.* 4 Avi. 17, 811 (2d Cir. 1955).

115 *Wing Hang Bank Ltd* v. *Japan Air Lines Co.* 12 Avi. 17, 884 (S.D.N.Y. 1973).

116 932 F. 2d 1475, 1479 (D.C. Cis), cert denied, 1125.ct.616 (1991).

117 No. 93 C 1510, 1994 Westlaw 171522 (N.D. Ill. 2 May 1994).

118 Ibid.

119 *Supra*, n.116.

120 866 F. Supp. 588 (D.D.C. 1994).

121 Ibid.

122 1995 Westlaw 151793 (E.D.N.Y. 27 March 1995).

123 No. 94-2392 (6 cir., 15 Mar. 1996).

124 Ibid.

125 25 Avi. Cas (CCH) 17, 259 (Sup. Ct. App. Tm. N.Y. 1st Dept. 1996).

126 920 F. Supp. 408 S.P.N.Y. (1996).
127 See *Koirola* v. *Thai Airways International*, 1996, Westlaw 402403 (N.D. Calif. 26 Jan. 1996).
128 See 'Article 25 – Thai Airways found guilty of Wilful Misconduct in 1992 Kathmandu Crash Litigation', *Lloyd's Aviation Law*, 15(6), 15 March 1996, 1.
129 Ibid., 2–3.
130 86 F. 3d 498 (6th Cir. 1996).

13 Wilful Misconduct of the Airline

Introduction

Common law principles relating to professional negligence of the air carrier in aviation accidents and determination of their validity in the light of rapidly emerging trends in the area of safety and security in aviation are steadily becoming important in the rapid evolution of air transport. (See Chapter 12, p. 191, 'Liability under the Warsaw Convention'.)

Medical Emergencies on Board

The notion of wilful misconduct has frequently been associated with the inability of the carrier to provide medical assistance in an emergency and, a fortiori, the failure on the part of the carrier to take adequate measures to ensure that such emergencies would be handled diligently and professionally on board.[1] A development in the field of aviation medicine, introduced in the summer of 1996, indicated a seminal innovation in this area, when United Airlines announced the fitting of a telemedicine unit on one of its commercial aircraft. The unit, which is the size of a large briefcase, is called Telemedic Systems Equipment and was fitted in one of the carrier's Boeing 767 aircraft on a three-month trial basis.[2] It is designed to improve the crew's response to a medical emergency by measuring a number of the body's vital signs, including ECG, blood pressure and heart rate and transmitting them, in real time, to a doctor on the ground.

The implications of this development could be far-reaching at law. Future attempts made by air carriers at equipping their aircraft with such medical facilities as telemedicine would effectively preclude the invocation by a plaintiff of Article 25, if such measures are taken, or are perceived to be taken, as a genuine attempt by the carrier to ensure that a medical emergency could be diligently handled through such means. It must be emphasized, however, that the very installation of sophisticated technical equipment would be insufficient to convince a court that the carrier took all necessary precautions and measures to treat a medical emergency. On a more conceptual basis, the carrier has to show in such instances that it trained its personnel to use the equipment installed in an aircraft properly and, more importantly, that it instilled in the employees the significance of medical assistance on board a flight.

Air Crew Fatigue

Another issue which has aroused much interest is air crew fatigue, where flight safety experts have been involved in using scientific methods to study the contentious issue of pilot fatigue as a cause of incidents and accidents. Although a complete determination of fatigue-causing factors which may have an adverse effect on performance of technical crew on a flight has yet to be made, the limited information and data which are currently available are being used by the experts to establish a system of working guidelines and rules.

Sleep deprivation is considered a major factor in air crew fatigue, which can produce loss of concentration, slow reaction time, visual illusions, disorientation and, more seriously, misinterpretation of flight instrument information. Fatigue may cause loss of interest in a pilot, making him neglect the task of completing flight procedures and necessary routines in flight.[3] Useful countermeasures to combat pilot fatigue have been identified by Airbus Industrie in its research where measures such as monitoring cockpit workload, flight crew alertness, sleep loss, and snoozing habits of crew and recommendations were being made to airlines at the time of writing.[4] A contemporaneous study by Boeing, who followed the basis of an 'alertness management' philosophy, identifies pre-planned cockpit naps, assigning relief crew members to a flight, electronic crew activity monitors and scheduled interaction with cabin crew as effective measures in combating crew fatigue.[5]

Analyses of confidential reports to NASA's Aviation Safety Reporting System reflect that approximately 21 per cent of all report aircraft accidents are related to fatigue.[6] From a legal perspective, this necessarily means that fatigue could be a serious factor for consideration on the issue of wilful misconduct, particularly if it can be shown that the defendant airline did not make any serious attempts at addressing the problem. Legal connotations of fatigue as an identifiable element of wilful misconduct may possibly emerge, particularly in instances relating to ultra long-haul flights (where flight duty of a technical crew member in charge of a flight exceeds 16 hours).

Michael Bagshaw, senior aviation physician of British Airways, has observed: 'As soon as we fly, we are venturing beyond our natural environment and compromising our health and safety, so it is a question of minimizing risks by maintaining a sense of proportion. The whole of aviation is based on a risk benefit analysis, and ultra long-haul flying is no exception.'[7]

From a regulatory standpoint, ICAO has made provision for flight time and flight duty period limitations in Annex 6 to the Chicago Convention. In the Annex, flight time and flight duty period limitations are established for the sole purpose of reducing the probability of fatigue of flight crew members which may adversely affect the safety of flight.[8] The Annex identifies types of fatigue that may have an impact upon the performance of technical crew on a flight,[9] and defines flight duty periods. The definition of a flight duty period in the Annex is intended to cover a continuous period of duty which inevitably includes a flight or a series of flights. The period of duty is calculated to include all duties a flight crew member may be required to carry out from the moment he reports at his place of employment on the day of a flight until he is relieved of duties, after he completes his flight or series of flights.[10] The Annex specifies that rest periods are meant to serve as periods of time for air crew to recover from fatigue and the way in which this recovery is achieved is the responsibility of the individual.[11] The most salutary provision in the Annex relates to guidelines in the formulation of regulations or rules governing flight time limitations and provides that the size of the crew complement and the extent to which the various tasks to be performed can be divided among the members should be taken into account. The provision further provides the necessity for adequate horizontal rest periods to be indulged in by air crew if duty time is to be extended. Some of the critical factors identified as affecting crew performance are traffic density, navigational and communication facilities, rhythm of the work/sleep cycle, number of landings and take-offs, aircraft handling, performance characteristics and weather patterns.[12] Similar provisions are contained in Part III of Annex 6 in regard to helicopter performance and operating limitations.[13]

In 1994, the Air Navigation Commission of ICAO considered a review of proposed amendments to Parts I and III of Annex 6 in the light of comments by states and international organizations[14] received as a result of a survey conducted by ICAO.[15] The overall comments of states were tantamount to a recognition of the importance of setting universal regulatory standards on flight crew duty time.[16]

With the evolution of medical knowledge, which has shown rapid progress over the years, it would seem that carriers would have to take serious cognizance of the effect of fatigue on air crew as a potential element of liability under Article 25 of the Warsaw Convention. It is now known that symptoms of jet lag (which the air crew is constantly subject to) are very similar to those of fatigue. Furthermore, the length of the trip, crossing of time zones and disruption of sleep cycles lead to excessive fatigue and the pilot may well show signs of disorientation, irritability and confusion, and exhibit severe physical symptoms such as constipation and aches and pains.[17] In this respect, air carriers may obviate any possible accusations under Article 25 by following, or at least seeming to follow, some guidelines which have already been suggested, such as stringent pre-planned cockpit rests, strategic flight crew scheduling and, more importantly, flight deck automation which may assist in ensuring more expedient cockpit management.[18]

Substance Abuse in the Workplace

Although the use of drugs, psychotropic substances and alcohol in the workplace is collectively perceived as substance abuse in the workplace, alcohol abuse is a major source of concern in the area of flight safety. With the increasing awareness and steady development of statistics and data which prevail on this subject, it is becoming increasingly difficult for carriers to ignore the problem or to deny its existence. Moreover, in an instance where an accident occurs as a result of substance abuse by the air crew, the carrier would probably be a prime target as a defendant under Article 25.2 of the Warsaw Convention. In fact, arguably, the carrier may even be found accountable under Article 25.1 by itself, for not taking adequate precautions to prevent substance abuse in the workplace in certain circumstances.

The abuse of alcohol by air crew is a general aviation problem and, admittedly, the reported alcohol involvement rates in fatal general aviation accidents have decreased consistently from the 1960s through to the present time.[19] Nevertheless, carriers have to take adequate precautions to ensure that no incidents related to alcohol consumption by their air crew result in claims under the notion of wilful misconduct. In the United States, pilots became part of the 7 460 000 workforce in transport who became subject to the Alcohol Misuse Prevention Programme which commenced on 1 January 1995. The United States Department of Transportation (DoT) inaugurated new rules along with this programme which prohibit any person acting or attempting to act as a crew member of a civil aircraft within eight hours of consuming any alcoholic beverage or while having a blood alcohol concentration of 0.04.[20]

On a global scale, the United Nations General Assembly, on 11 March 1994, adopted Resolution 48/112 on International Action to

Combat Drug Abuse and Illicit Production of Trafficking.[21] This resolution addresses the overall problem on a general basis and seemingly relates to narcotic drugs and psychotropic substances. However, on a more specific scale, ICAO, at its 27th Session of the Assembly in 1989, adopted Resolution A27-12[22] (Role of ICAO in the suppression of illicit transport of narcotic drugs by air) which inter alia urges the ICAO Council to elaborate with a high degree of priority concrete measures in order to prevent and to eliminate possible use of illicit drugs and abuse of other drugs or substances by crew members, air traffic controllers, mechanics and other staff of international civil aviation. The ICAO Assembly followed its action by adopting, at its 29th Session in 1992, Resolution A29-16[23] (Role of ICAO in the prevention of substance abuse in the workplace) and, while making mention of Resolution A27-12, the Assembly expressed its grave concern that substance abuse by civil aviation employees may seriously compromise aviation safety and urged the Council to maintain its vigilance over the problem of substance abuse in the field of civil aviation.

As a result of the above action by the ICAO Assembly, ICAO has produced its manual on the prevention of problematic use of substances in the aviation workplace,[24] which has been developed by the Aviation Medicine Section of the ICAO Secretariat. The purpose of the document, as stated in its Foreword, is to 'provide States with a tool for decision-making to use when deciding on the best policy for user States and for State licensing authorities when planning national strategies'.[25] The manual also suggests that it can be used by airlines and other employers to implement, on a practical level, established policies and strategies in a cost-effective way, with due regard for aviation safety and personal welfare of employees.

The manual comprises five chapters, cohesively woven together to give the reader a detailed account of substance abuse and its consequences. Its main thrust and strength lie in Chapter 1, which is dedicated to education of the aviation workforce, and Chapter 2, which identifies the problems and recommends suitable treatment and rehabilitation. The document also contains some useful attachments on strategic planning and testing. The legal significance of this document and its relation to Article 25 of the Warsaw Convention is apparent. Air carriers can no longer plead lack of guidance or ignorance of the problem of substance abuse in the workplace in the face of such a development in the regulatory field of civil aviation; nor can they ignore the recommendations of the document in terms of the training programmes and strategic planning it offers. In the ultimate analysis, therefore, the existing consciousness and regulatory material would indeed act as effective tools towards convincing a court of law of an air carrier's wilful misconduct in the case of an adjudication of a plaintiff's rights under the Warsaw Convention.

Air Crew Communication in the Aircraft

Several dramatic accidents have emphasized certain deficiencies which may exist in cockpit–cabin coordination and communication. The reasons for poor communication between pilots and members of cabin crew are multifarious, in that they are historical, organizational, environmental, psychosocial and regulatory. The basic problem between these two categories of airline staff who are thrust together on a flight involves the fact that the two crews represent two distinct and separate cultures, which may often inhibit satisfactory teamwork. Although the role of the technical crew in flight safety has been well documented,[26] the flight attendant's role on safety has been treated at best with ambivalence, with the flight attendant being considered as 'back-end crew' (as opposed to 'front-end crew', referring to the pilot), keeping a fairly orderly cabin and serving coffee. Of course, the flight attendant may assist in instances involving terrorism or emergency evacuation, but customarily the role of the flight attendant has been feminized and, often, trivialized. Perhaps the main reason for the perceived bifurcation of the two types of crew is their geographic locations, where the cockpit and the cabin remain as two distinct geographic and social environments.[27] As there are different areas of responsibility which devolve upon technical crew members and cabin crew members, it is inevitable that two separate cultures will exist in the aircraft. Often, through no fault of their own, and owing to their particular responsibilities, the technical crew in the cockpit may isolate itself from the cabin crew, leading to serious lapses of communication between the two. Australian accident investigator David Adams observes:

> If you look at almost any company [airline], you will usually find that the cabin attendants and the flight crew are very clearly separated. They work for different branches of the company in most cases. The culture is one of almost complete separation. Yet the fact of the matter is, in a safety situation, these two sections of the company have to work together. And the consequences of not working together quite often means a bunch of people get killed.[28]

One commentator's study of crew members' attitudes in flight reflects significant differences between personality dimensions of US pilots and flight attendants. The study attributes these psychosocial differences to pilots being task-oriented and preferring a cognitive style of problem solving based on logic and systems-oriented reasoning. Flight attendants, on the other hand, were identified as preferring an affective cognitive style and orientation to decision making.[29]

Whatever be the relationship between the flight attendant and passenger, on the one hand, and flight attendant and pilot, on the other, they have a common denominator. With regard to accidents caused as a direct or indirect result of the flight attendant's conduct – be it an injury to a passenger or aircraft accident precipitated by the conduct of the flight attendant affecting pilot performance – the legal consequences of air carrier liability would revolve round whether the act of the flight attendant or the pilot, as the case may be, was tantamount to wilful misconduct on the part of the carrier.

Should Wilful Misconduct be Expunged from a New Liability Regime?

From the above discussion of medical emergencies, air crew fatigue, substance abuse and air crew communication, it may seem that the conduct of an air carrier may be prima facie brought into question under any of the four elements, should the carrier overtly disregard or ignore the inherent dangers presented by each individual element. The inevitable question that would arise then would be, 'Should wilful misconduct be removed from a new liability regime under such compelling emergent factors?' If the answer to this question is in the affirmative, the question arises, 'Would a realm of strict liability give carriers the independence to conduct themselves as they please, knowing that they are covered for all acts, whatever their nature, by a preconceived and established scheme of insurance?' In other words, the bottom line, or ultimate question, would be, 'Should carriers be held accountable for their acts when they wilfully and with knowledge cause damage, or should they be absolved from accountability as to their fault under all circumstances?'

As discussed earlier, Lee Kreindler offers a direct response to the above questions by saying that the fault system is important to the public and that it is a public protection. He maintains that it has improved aviation safety and security. On the other hand, it has been contended that Article 25 is a provision which provokes litigation and that it should be removed and replaced by a system which automatically guarantees a certain negotiable guarantee of compensation.[30]

A pre-funded system of injury compensation may tend to disregard the role played by and contribution made by a person who causes injury to another. In direct contrast to this approach, a sustained body of judicial thought has established a group of basic concepts and terms, which consist of theories of culpability and defence on the premise of responsibility of the individual. Called 'tort law', this thought process reflects a judicial desire to reduce the number and severity of accidents. Often called 'deterrence', this approach is best illustrated in the case of *Brizendine* v. *Visador Co.*,[31] where the court held that tort law should provide 'a healthy incentive to manufacturers to make their products safe'.[32] To this principle courts have also added the requirement that a person who causes an accident should show that he took 'all possible means' and every precaution to prevent the accident from occurring. *Taylor* v. *Superior Court*,[33] a case addressing the deterrence rationale that drunk driving may constitute 'malice' if performed under circumstances which disclose a conscious disregard of the possible dangerous circumstances.[34] In a previous case,[35] the court stressed the paramount need to deter people from driving cars after drinking.

The pervasive reliance of common law on the paradigm of reciprocity, whereby a person who injures another knowing the consequences his act may cause is called upon to compensate for the damage caused, is grounded in its very fundamental sense in Aristotelian corrective justice. In Book V, Chapter 4 of his *Nicomachean Ethics*, Aristotle advocates justice in the distribution by the state of mores, honours and other items of value on the basic postulate of merit. According to Aristotle, it made no difference if a good man defrauded a bad man, or a bad man a good one – the law should only look to the distinctive character of the injury and treat the parties as equal. The judge would, in the Aristotelian sense, attempt to equalize things by means of the penalty, taking away from the gain of the assailant or wrongdoer. The term 'gain' is applied in a general sense where suffering is estimated as loss. The duty to rectify under corrective justice is based not on the fact of injury but on the conjunction of injury and wrongdoing. The person who injures must do wrong as well as do harm, and the person who is injured must be wronged as well as harmed. For example, a person who drives a bad bargain has no access to corrective justice since he has been harmed but not wronged.

The system of corrective justice as propounded by Aristotle, and used by common law courts, is compatible with the economic theory of law in that the economic theory of law, which is a means of bringing about an efficient allocation of resources by correcting externalities and other distortions of the market's allocation of resources, requires that, if the person who injures does not pay, he will have no incentive to take precautions in the future, and there will be more accidents than is optimal.

Judge Learned Hand, in 1947, addressed the social function of liability for wrongful acts and adumbrated an economic meaning of a wrongful act. In *United States* v. *Carroll Towing Co.*,[36] Judge Hand identified three issues: the magnitude of the loss where an accident occurs, the probability of the accident occurring, and the burden of taking precautions that would avert it. According to His Honour, if the product of the first two issues exceeded the third one, the failure to take precautions would be a wrongful act. There is therefore a certain moral disapproval and even indignation attached to a wrongful act.

Notes

1 See R.I.R. Abeyratne (1997), 'The Notion of Wilful Misconduct in the Warsaw System: Emerging Trends at Common Law', *Annals of Air and Space Law*, XXII(1), 187–205.

2 'Doctor on Board', *Aeronautical Satellite News*, October–November 1996, 5. Although telemedicine has been used for a considerable time, this is the first known instance of its use in flight. Telemedicine has been defined by the European Commission as 'rapid access to shared and remote medical expertise by means of telecommunications and information technologies, no matter where the patient or relevant information is located' (Ibid).

3 Pierre Sparaco (1996), 'Combating Fatigue to Enhance Safety', *Aviation Week and Space Technology*, 4 November, 49.

4 Ibid.

5 Ibid., 54.

6 See Phillippa H. Gander *et al.* (1995), 'A NASA Study shows How Age and Circadian Rhythm affect Sleep Loss', *Airline Pilot*, April, 20.

7 'Sleepless Flights', Report of the Royal Aeronautical Society Aviation Medicine Group Conference, 'Aeromedical Aspects of Ultra Long-Haul Operations', published in *Aerospace*, September 1994, p.22.

8 Annex 6 to the Convention on International Civil Aviation (Operation of Aircraft) Part 1, 5th edn, July 1990, Attachment A, 1.1.

9 Ibid., 1.2.

10 Ibid., 2.2.1.

11 Ibid., 2.3.

12 Ibid., 3.2.

13 Annex 6 to the Convention on International Civil Aviation, Part III, 2nd edn, July 1990, Attachment C, 3 and 4.

14 AN-WP/6888, 28/2/94.

15 Ibid., Appendix A. See also State Letter AN 11/9-93/77.

16 AN-WP/6888 (*supra*, n.14), Appendices B and C.

17 See 'Out of Synch Jet Lag', *Airworthy Aviator*, August 1992, 1. See also David F. Dingles, 'Crew Rest and Sleep Deprivation', Flight Safety Foundation, 35th Corporate Aviation Seminar, 18–20 April 1990, Montreal; Leonard J. Thompson (1986), 'Disorders of Circadian Rhythm with Air Travel', *Patient Management*, December, 13; also P. Davenport and D. Jensen, 'Fatigue Factors on Two Man Crews', *Pilot*, December, 23.

18 Curtis Graeber, 'Fatigue in Long Haul Operations – Sources and Solutions', *U.K. Flight Safety Focus – Spring 1992*, Part 2, 1.

19 See J.R. Dille and E.W. Morris (1967), 'Human Factors in General Aviation Accidents', *Aerospace Medicine*, 38, 1063–6; also H.L. Gibbons (1988), 'Alcohol, Aviation and Safety Revisited: A Historical Review and a Suggestion', *Aviation Space Environmental Medicine*, 59, 657–60; C.C. Ryan and S.R. Mohler (1972), 'Intoxicating Liquor and the General Aviation Pilot in 1971', *Aerospace Medicine*, 43, 1024–6.

20 Suzanne L. Kalfus (1994), 'Alcohol Testing Begins', *Airline Pilot*, October 16.
21 A/RES/48/112, 11 March 1994.
22 Doc. 9662. Assembly Resolutions in Force (as of 4 October 1995), 1–36, 1–37.
23 Ibid., 11–24.
24 Doc. 9654-AN/945, 1st edn, 1995.
25 Ibid., iii.
26 See E.L. Wiener (1988), 'Cockpit Automation', in E.L. Wiener and D.C. Nagel, *Human Factors in Aviation*, San Diego: Academic Press, pp.433–59.
27 Rebecca D. Chute (1995), 'Cockpit–Cabin Communication: I. A Tale of Two Cultures', *The International Journal of Aviation Psychology*, 5(3), 258.
28 Cited in V.P. Moshansky (1992), *Commission of Inquiry into the Air Ontario Crash at Dryden, Ontario*, Toronto: Minister of Supply and Services, p.1087.
29 See M.J. Vandermark (1991), 'Should Flight Attendants be Included in CRM Training? A Discussion of a Major Air Carrier's Approach to Total Crew Training', *The International Journal of Aviation Psychology*, 1, 87–94. See also A. Merritt (1993), 'Human Factors on the Flight Deck; the Influence of National Culture', paper presented at the Seventh International Symposium on Aviation Psychology, Columbus, Ohio, April.
30 Gerald M. Mayo, 'Implementation of the IATA Intercarrier Agreement', *Lloyd's Aviation Law*, 15(7), 1 April, 2.
31 305 & Supp. 157, (D. Or. 1969).
32 Ibid., 160.
33 24 Cal. 3d 890 (1979).
34 D. 892.
35 *Harrell* v. *Ames*, 265 Or. 183 at 190 (1973).
36 159 F. 2d 169 (2d Cir. 1947).

14 Mental Injury

Introduction

This chapter will discuss scientific and forensic implications of mental injury as interpreted by the medical and legal professions, with a view to extrapolating the possible future outlook for the damage as a compensable element in private air carrier liability.

The Nature of Mental Distress

The law, as any other human discipline, has treated the mind as an unfathomable abstraction. Through the years, this attitude has led to a blend of caution and curiosity.[1] This led to a compromise: to give legal recognition to an injury to the human mind[2] only when it was accompanied by some physical attribute perceptible to the senses. To the lawyer, it remains a mere legal platitude which still exerts a strong influence on the attitude of the courts towards tortious liability.

Although it can be seen that this attitude has acted as a pervasive influence in restricting the award of damages for pain of mind, a closer study of recent trends reveals an interesting development. Legal writing, sociological change and scientific development have prompted the courts in the United States of America[3] to show signs of recognizing the infliction of mental distress as being compatible with the legal definition of a tort. Mere pain of mind has hitherto been recognized as being abstract and indefinable in terms of visual assessment. It is this quality which has cautioned the courts against fraudulent and frivolous actions. However, it is clear that mental distress, once identified and defined, can be considered a damage for the purpose of the law of torts.

It is a curious fact that the courts in the United States and the United Kingdom have been used to recognizing a set of torts as actionable wrongs. Had they pondered over a suitable definition of a tort, they would have realized that defining a tort is as difficult as defining mental distress. Conceptually, a tort remains a breach of duty which grounds an action for damages. This excludes contractual or quasi-contractual duty. Thus far, the courts have not been overtly concerned about the question 'What is a tort?' Rather, they have been seeking an answer to the question, 'What are torts?' A treatise on tort says: 'A "tort" is simply the Norman word for "wrong", but "torts" have typically been distinguished from wrongs identified with contractual relations. Tort law, then, is concerned with civil wrongs not arising from contracts.'[4]

Normally, definitions of tort refer to harm or damage caused to the injured as a requirement for the award of damages. As mentioned earlier, generally, the courts have been hesitant to consider mental distress as damage, as it has been considered to be incapable of assessment. In sharp contrast is the view, taken by some early writers,[5] that mental suffering is indeed damage and an injury upon the human being and therefore should be considered a tort. It is submitted that such a view is more acceptable as it is based on both scientific and sociological studies.

The society we live in today is far more complex and variegated than the ones before the 20th century. More population, expanded industry and production, have exposed man to many more hazards than before. The incidence of mental injury in today's society can be expected to be more frequent than before. As White says, 'mental injury was the stuff of "real" life in twentieth-century America and hence the stuff of tort law'.[6] It is no surprise, therefore, that, when Prosser called the infliction of mental distress 'the birth of a new tort',[7] he was acutely aware of the reluctance of the courts to consider mental distress as a damage or harm, and thus regard its infliction as a tort. Whether mental distress causes damage and whether it can be assessed is worthy of discussion.

In the area of tortuous liability, it cannot be disputed that an imbalance of a person's mental equilibrium is inextricably related to fear. If one looks at a definition of 'fear', its relationship with pain of mind caused by a civil wrong becomes immediately apparent: 'The word "fear" comes from the old English "Faer" for sudden calamity or danger and was later used to describe the emotion of uneasiness caused by the sense of impending danger',[8] which is: 'A normal response to active or imagined threat in higher animals and comprises an outer behavioural expression, an inner feeling and accompanying physiological damage.'[9]

Much has been written in detail of the aggression committed by the feeling of fear and anxiety on the internal organs of the human body. Fear is said to have been 'born of innumerable injuries in the course of evolution ... developed into portentous foreshadowing of possible injury ... capable of arousing in the body, all of the offensive and defensive activities that favour the survival of the organism'.[10] Emotional agitation, anxiety or fear is known to bring about an imbalance in the digestive process,[11] dryness of the mouth,[12] an increase in blood sugar[13] and a general disruption of the internal organs of the human body. This feeling of discomfort, even though temporary, is a positively unpleasant experience.[14]

The observations made so far by medical authorities seem to recognize clearly the deleterious effects of pain of mind. There is no justification, therefore, for rejecting this notion *in limine*, as being beyond human perception. However, it is difficult to reject totally the point made by the courts in the United States that mental distress when inflicted should not be recognized as an actionable tort, as it is difficult to prove and therefore would give rise to arbitrary and frivolous suits. The notion of mental distress, even though easily recognizable as damage, has to be considered with care. The plaintiff's case has to be viewed with circumspection, which could be done by imposing stringent standards of proof of injury on the plaintiff.

Although the early view taken by the courts that the infliction of mental distress should not be entertained at all owing to its vagueness was totally acceptable to them in the context of the time it was followed, modern science, which has drawn a distinct relationship between the human mind and the body, has proved the view to be inconsistent with the needs of the present day. At the present time, the US courts have veered away from the original state of apprehension they were in, and have recognized mental distress as an injury, while setting standards of proof to be complied with by the plaintiff in order that the defendant be equally protected. This approach is both progressive and reasonable, although an overt emphasis on the protection of the defendant can easily act to the detriment of the plaintiff's case.

Legal Theory and Mental Distress

The early view taken by the courts in the United States, that mental injury is incapable of being visualized or proved, was the result of the influence of English common law.[15] Heavy reliance was placed by the English courts in the 10th century on the fact that mental injury was beyond the realm of human understanding. Therefore, although not mentioned in specific language, it is evident that the courts, acknowledging the futility of defining mental distress as damage, attributed to the tortfeasor the same quality of being unable to realize and foresee the distinct mental injury that he could cause one who is injured by him. One can only surmise that it had been considered logical that, if the courts could not identify mental distress as damage, the tortfeasor certainly could not either. Therefore, originally, as a tortfeasor could not be expected to be conscious of the possibility of mental injury which his victim might suffer, he would not be held liable unless he actually intended the mental injury, or was conscious that his act would result in causing the victim pain of mind that would lead to an observable physical injury. The courts have been concerned with two main problems: whether physical injury should necessarily follow mental injury and whether such mental injury should be intentionally caused for it to be recognized as damage. To both these questions, the answer has been in the affirmative.

Mental Injury Intentionally Caused

After the decision in *Lynch* v. *Knight*, the case of *Wilkinson* v. *Downton*[16] followed, introducing the principle in England that the courts would recognize an act calculated to cause mental injury, which leads to consequent physical injury, as a wrong. The words 'calculated to' mean 'likely to', which immediately calls for the requirement that the tortfeasor should be consciously aware of the likelihood of mental injury to the injured. These two cases were heavily relied upon in the United States. The influence has been so significant that it has pervaded academic opinion as well. Prosser, in 1937, defined the infliction of mental distress as 'the intentional outrageous infliction of mental suffering in an extreme form'.[17] A conspicuous feature of the definition is the inclusion of the word 'intentional'. Does this mean that mental distress unintentionally inflicted is no damage at all in terms of a tort? The answer lies in the dictum in *Wilkinson's* case itself, which recognizes as actionable damage which is likely to be caused by the act of the tortfeasor. When compared with the element of intention which implies deliberation and a desire to cause a particular injury, the former is more suited to the context of modern tort law.

A prominent aspect of the law of torts has been its adherence to the principles of the common law in the award of damages. For example, in cases of negligence, the courts, both in the United States and in England, have not restricted the award of damages for injuries only caused intentionally. It is certainly true that an act deliberately intended to cause mental injury is much more heinous than an unintentional infliction of mental distress. However, it does not necessarily follow that mental injury, to be recognized as a damage, should be solely intentionally inflicted. Judicial and academic reasoning in support of insisting on an intentional infliction of mental injury has been so far based on the fact that the mind is not easily observable, and an injury to it is not easily envisaged by an injurer. Today, the mind and the body are considered a composite system, connected to one another. An injury to the mind is as apparent as an injury to the body, so that there is no longer a need to insist on the element of intention to establish the culpability of the tortfeasor. Therefore a tortfeasor may be held responsible for the damage caused to the mind of the injured even though he did not actually intend to inflict mental injury.

Academic and Judicial Opinion on Mental Distress as a Physical Injury

Although Prosser dealt only with the intentional infliction of mental distress,[18] he was quite emphatic that mental distress is similar to physical damage: 'mental suffering is no less a real injury than physical pain … and it is … the business of the courts to make precedent where a wrong calls for redress'.[19] One of the earliest in England to observe the significance of mental distress as a positive injury was Kennedy J, when he said: 'I should not be surprised if the surgeon or the physiologist told me that nervous shock is or may be in itself an injurious affection of the physical organism.'[20] This statement is an acknowledgment that mental injury may lead directly to physical injury which, though not externally visible, may be evident to a trained medical mind. However, it is interesting to note that such opinion did not radically change the attitude of the courts in this respect. The basic difficulty was that the conventional view of tort liability could not be shaken. The commission of a tort had to be ascertainable externally. Judges, being laymen from the medical point of view, have been consistently hesitant to adjudicate upon anything which was not apparent or proven on an empirical basis. While it is true that the effects of mental injury could not be scientifically proved by way of a general test, the overwhelming opinion of medical science should have at least made the courts acknowledge the plausibility of what was stated. This makes the judicial approach on this subject a trifle disconcerting.

Once the courts recognize that mental distress per se is an actionable wrong when inflicted, they can devise a viable basis for determining who is entitled to damages. The guidelines for awarding damages and the role played by the courts will be discussed later in this work. For the present, it can be stated that, by adopting a rigid attitude towards the infliction of mental distress, the courts do not exhibit a full appreciation of mental distress as an injury.

Failure to accord recognition to the infliction of mental distress as an actionable injury raises the interesting point whether it would constitute a violation of a fundamental human right in the context of American society. It cannot be doubted that the fundamental rights of man in the United States are the right of personal liberty and security, reputation and property,[21] the invasion of which constitutes a tort. It is fair to assume that no court will deny this principle. If this be so, it seems clear that the infliction of pain of mind, under any circumstances, is an erosion of the right to liberty and security. To establish therefore that mental distress when inflicted upon a person can be regarded as a tort, the only element needed seems to be to ascertain definitely that mental distress ensued from a particular act. This should be done with caution.

That a tort is a wrong committed against a person is undisputed. To what extent this definition can be applied is seen in the statement that 'particular torts, as Trespass or Violence, Defamation, Nuisance and the like can be defined well enough, but the term "tort" is also used to denote wrong in general. It includes the unclassified residuum as well as specific definable wrongs'.[22] The infliction of mental distress falls into the 'unclassified residuum' and is certainly a wrong. Though not often, it has been judicially recognized that mental distress is synonymous with a state of anxiety caused by stress. Stanford J said, 'mental distress ... includes sorrow and grief',[23] to which Rainey J added humiliation, mortification and shame as sensibilities of the mind which show mental distress.[24] This view is seen in one instance where a person who was subjected to a state of intense worry was held to be suffering from mental distress.[25] On the one hand, it is evident that anxiety induced by stress in any form is both an injury and an infringement of a right. On the other, the courts definitely stand circumscribed, as they have not been able to visualize the damage and assess it. It is a dichotomy difficult to resolve. The only way out of this tangle is for the courts to view mental injury as a definite injury on the following lines.

It is a common human feature to undergo a mental reaction under stress. For instance, if a person is involved in an accident directly or indirectly by witnessing the accident, the thought process of that person will be far from pleasant. The thoughts that run through his mind threaten his sense of security. Therefore a person who causes the accident commits a wrong against anyone who is either directly involved in it or who witnesses it and is shocked by what he sees. However, this does not necessarily mean that liability attaches in respect of everyone in the vicinity of the accident. A clear burden of proof should rest on the plaintiff to show that he in fact suffered mental injury as a result of an act of the defendant.

A gradual awakening to the problem which veered away from the initial attitude of regarding the infliction of mental distress along the lines of the English common law, which rejected the notion as being abstract and vague, was seen with the emergence of American realist thinking. It brought out new perspectives to the concept of tort. This was done by acknowledging that the dispensation of justice was dependent – if not totally, to some extent at least – on allied disciplines. Medical science, economics and technology were used to deduce facts which were outside the purview of the law. In this light, mental distress ceased to be vague. It was found that mental distress could be assessed.

The infliction of mental distress has been recognized by writers for a considerable period of time as an actionable wrong. The emphasis so far has been on the intention of the person who causes it. In fact, legal thinking has not been generally used to associate the infliction of mental distress with an unintentional act. This was due to regarding the human mind as totally unrelated to the functions of the human body. A duty not to upset the mental stability of a person to his detriment does not seem to tie up with the duty of care not to injure one's neighbour,[26] the fundamental premise on which negligence is based. As a result of this, the majority of jurisdictions in the United States have insisted that mental distress is parasitic and should be the outcome of an intentional act causing visible physical injury. Yet there are some jurisdictions which recognize the infliction of mental distress per se as actionable. This has been done with no uniformity. Courts have digressed from one concept to another, ranging from foreseeability in negligence[27] to the extreme measure of imposing strict liability.[28] The profusion of legal writing, which has dealt mostly with the principles of negligence as applicable to the infliction of mental distress, and the general policy laid down in most states to award damages in tort to the most deserving have left the courts worse confounded. To inquire into this situation, the judicial trends which evolved into the existing position have to be traced.

Some Judicial Trends in the Treatment of Mental Distress

Mental Distress Intentionally Inflicted Accompanied by Physical Injury

In the United States, mental distress has been the subject of much litigation. The cases, most of which are similar in facts, are innumerable. It would be both fruitless and difficult to analyse each case in order to arrive at a general conclusion as to what the law is on the subject. It is proposed in this chapter to analyse the case law selectively, on the basis of how important the cases are in portraying the overall judicial attitude towards the subject.

The recognition of the infliction of damage in the field of torts evolved gradually. As mentioned earlier, the courts were hesitant to identify mental distress as compensable and as an isolated head of liability. Therefore the common law recognized mental distress as actionable only if intentionally inflicted or if accompanied by physical impact. Generally, the assessment was made by determining whether the two elements mentioned above caused some observable physical injury to the plaintiff. Most states in the United States relied heavily upon these criteria as guidelines in the award of damages.

The Physical Impact Theory

Mental distress has been regarded in many states as being merely the outcome of a physical injury which results from a physical impact upon the human body. The insistence on recognizing the actionability of mental distress if inflicted only as a result of an actual physical impact on the plaintiff was so prominent that it was known as the 'Physical Impact Theory'. In legal parlance, the states which adopt this theory are called 'impact states'. The theory itself is best illustrated by the case of *Beaty* v. *Buckeye Fabric Furnishing Co.*,[29] decided in Arkansas in 1959. One of the plaintiffs brought an action against the driver of a tractor which struck the plaintiff's vehicle. Consequently, the plaintiff's father was crushed and killed when the trailer rolled back from a stationary position owing to brake failure. The deceased was heard to groan and cry out after the impact, which made the court conclude that the distress caused to the deceased was more mental than physical, though it lasted for a short duration. The court awarded damages of $1000, to be distributed among the children of the deceased. Henley CJ, delivering judgment, said: 'it is a well settled principle in Arkansas law that no recovery can be had for negligently inflicted mental anguish, fright, shock or grief, unless the same is produced by a physical injury ... that rule extends to physical symptoms resulting from the emotional shock in question'.[30]

This approach is also reflected in other decisions cited by His Honour, where physical injury was considered to be a natural precursor to mental injury.[31] An exception is seen in cases involving the right of privacy, where courts have, while recognizing the necessity of the impact theory, deemed it fair to award damages for injury to the personality.[32] The law seems to recognize public humiliation to be more of a mental injury than the infliction of death on a person. *Ex facie*, the demarcation sounds ludicrous, as both humiliation and death can involve continuous mental suffering. It is time to review this attitude and treat both equally, as torts involving the human mind which cause acute discomfort. The ramifications of the impact theory and the developments which followed will be discussed later.

The Intentional Infliction of Mental Distress

Some jurisdictions regard the infliction of mental distress as parasitic or dependent upon the element of intention, in the absence of physical impact. The dependence upon intention has almost been taken for granted. In many states, the infliction of mental anguish, pain of mind and apprehension are still heavily burdened with the necessity of being accompanied by an intentional act on the part of the defendant. In Connecticut, it has been recognized that 'a cause of action in tort may be created for a plaintiff's emotional distress which is the foreseeable and proximate result of the defendant's intentional, wanton or wilful wrongful conduct'.[33] It is clear in this instance that the court meant that emotional distress caused to a person is damage recognizable in tort if the defendant could foresee the possible infliction of mental distress that could be caused by his intentional wrongful conduct. The act itself, though intentionally caused, need not be performed with the specific intention of causing mental distress to the victim.

In Florida, which shows consistent litigation on the subject of the infliction of mental distress, the law is in sharp contrast to the broad rationale mentioned above. There is no single instance of the infliction of pain of mind being regarded as independent of intention.[34] The most recent pronouncement comes from *Steiner & Munach* v. *Williams*,[35] decided in 1976, in which it was decided that the law in Florida still remains that there is no recovery for mental or emotional injuries unless there are other factors present. These were named as either a physical impact or such injuries produced as a result of a deliberate and calculated act performed with the intention of producing such an injury by one who knows that his act will in fact cause injury. This insistence on intention as a requisite for the award of damages for mental distress is seen in Maryland,[36] Kansas[37] and South Carolina.[38] There is almost an implied recognition that mental security or stability need not be taken into account by a reasonable man as a protected right of an individual. Most states have followed the rule that, for the infliction of mental distress to be recognized as a damage, it has to be the outcome of physical injury caused by physical impact, or it has to be the result of an intentional act by the defendant. This attitude can be observed in Massachusetts,[39] as well as in Pennsylvania,[40] Ohio,[41] New Jersey,[42] Mississippi,[43] Missouri,[44] Michigan,[45] Washington,[46] Virginia[47] and Texas.[48] The heavy reliance placed on the element of intention is due to the fact that the courts do not regard mental distress as an injury for which a tortfeasor could be held liable unless he desires such injury to be inflicted on the injured.

A far less stringent criterion is observed in Nebraska, which recognizes that physical injury is not an essential prerequisite for awarding damages for the infliction of mental distress, if mental injury is a reasonably certain result of the act of the tortfeasor. There are some states which rely so much on the element of intention that they have recognized the infliction of mental distress to be solely dependent on whether the defendant's act was intended to cause mental injury to the plaintiff. New Jersey[49] has gone a step further in saying that the only factor necessary is the defendant's conduct when he inflicted the injury on the plaintiff. Undeniably, in this case the courts would inquire whether the defendant's conduct shows a disregard for the possible mental pain that could be caused to the plaintiff by the defendant's act.

One conspicuous feature which stands out in the above instances is that much is left to judicial discretion. To elaborate further, while all jurisdictions have stated that mental distress has to be accompanied either by physical injury or by an intentional act on the part of the defendant, the methods adopted and the criteria laid down to determine whether mental distress can result from particular circumstances have differed. This is especially so in the case of intention. While some courts have laid down requirements to determine the nature of the act, others have determined the existence or non-existence of an intentional act without laying down specific guidelines for doing so. This is an interesting feature which warrants discussion.

Determining the conduct of the plaintiff has been approached in two different ways. The first is both stringent and direct. An example of the first category is Iowa, which has categorically stated that the element required is a wilful act which is carried out against the plaintiff. This approach was first seen in 1932 in the case of *Barnett* v. *Collection Service Co.*[50] It concerned the claim of an elderly widow who had been repeatedly sent letters of demand by a coal company for $28.75, which she owed them. She claimed that she suffered mental distress as a result of the letters. There was no evidence of physical injury whatever. The court held that an action would lie for the infliction of mental distress on the plaintiff, as she was the subject of a wilful act committed by the defendant company. Almost the same terminology was followed in 1967,[51] where a court decided that mental distress is recognized only if it is inflicted in the course of a wilful act on the part of the defendants. The courts do not definitely say whether by a wilful act they mean an act committed wilfully with a desire to cause mental distress in particular, or whether the act alone has to be deliberate with no specific intent to cause mental injury. Academic opinion favours the view that it should be a wilful act with desire to cause mental distress.[52]

The second approach is where the requirement of intention has yielded to the element of foresight. In Oklahoma, the element required is neither a wilful act nor intention to cause mental injury, but mere foreseeability. This obviates the insistence on volition on the part of the defendant. In pursuance of this policy, an Oklahoma court held that an action could be successfully grounded against a defendant whose act had inflicted traumatic neurosis on the plaintiff, if the circumstances enabled the defendant to have reasonable foresight of the result of his act.[53]

Judicial Recognition of Mental Distress as Damage

Generally, mental distress is inflicted as a result of an accident. It may be caused as a result of the negligence of the persons involved in the accident, or even by a third party who is not physically present at the accident. For example, an accident may be caused by a defective product which fails to function properly. In that case it may be entirely the fault of the manufacturer. The attitude of the courts has thus far been to insist either on a physical impact on the plaintiff or on an intentional act on the part of the defendant. In both cases observable physical symptoms were the basis of the courts' assessment of the mental injury. In this sense the infliction of mental distress has always been dependent on one of the two accompanying factors mentioned above.

This attitude prevailed as late as 1958. In Ohio, where a court rejected a claim for damages for emotional distress and embarrassment caused by threats,[54] Stewert J, citing precedent,[55] observed that 'the damages sought to be recovered are too remote and speculative. The injury is more sentimental than substantial. Being easily simulated and hard to disprove, there is no standard by which it can be justly or even approximately compensated'.[56] This total rejection of mental distress unaccompanied by any other element was largely due to heavy reliance being placed on the accepted view that 'mental suffering and its consequences are so evanescent and intangible that they cannot be foreseen or anticipated and for that reason, have no proximate causal connection with the defendant'.[57]

The view that mental distress, to be recognized as inflicted on a person tortiously, has to be fortified by other elements has led to uncertainty in Florida. In 1972, a court pronounced on a general basis that, in the area of tort, the infliction of mental distress is compensable. Two years later, in a suit brought by a person against the manufacturer of an aeroplane, for mental suffering caused to his wife as a result of an accident, the court held that the infliction of mental pain and anguish, in the absence of physical impact, could not be recognized.[58] This makes Florida fall into the category of an impact state. In the 1972 case, Mager J stated that, if mental distress was the outcome of a tort committed against a person, it was compensable.[59] There was no further expansion or explanation. If one were to accept the view that a tort is a civil wrong against a person which is not contractual, as stated earlier, the statement of Mager J would mean that, if mental distress is inflicted as a result of a breach of duty which one owed to another, it is compensable. All that the plaintiff need show is that the defendant owed the plaintiff a duty of care which was breached, as a result of which the plaintiff suffered damage. The only difficulty lies in determining what damage is. To Florida and the other impact states, it should be the outcome of an actual physical impact on the plaintiff. In other words, the damage should be perceptible to the senses and be caused by a physical impact alone. The essential weakness of the impact theory is that its proponents considered the infliction of mental injury to be actionable only if it showed its ill effects after being caused by a physical impact on the body of the victim. There arises cause for the criticism that the theory does not envisage that mental injury can be caused by hearing or by seeing something unpleasant. In the modern context, a person who witnesses an accident caused by a defective product such as faulty aircraft, or who hears a loud sound which a defective product causes and suffers mental distress as a consequence, would not have any remedy against the person responsible for the product. The main reason for the narrow outlook taken by the impact theory is that no consideration has been given to the real nature of mental distress and how differently it can be caused.

The Infliction of Mental Distress as an Independent Head of Damage

The component states of the United States are divided on the question of the status of mental distress per se. By mental distress per se is meant mental distress independent of observable physical injury caused by either physical impact upon the plaintiff or an intentional act on the part of the defendant. Generally, it can be said that most states still adhere to the traditional common law approach of requiring one or the other. The states which have deviated from this trend, though few in number, have been more specific in asserting the recognition of the infliction of mental distress as an independent tort.

Illinois is an example of a state which, though an adherent to the common law principle that physical injury is essential for the award of damages, has digressed radically to change its law. In *Bushers* v. *Graceland Cemetery Association of Albion Illinois*,[60] decided in 1958, where the infliction of mental distress was averred by the plaintiffs, this approach was clear. The plaintiffs objected to oil drilling in a cemetery in which a relative of theirs was buried. Platt CJ stated that there was a recognized breaking away from the general rule on this point.[61] His Honour cited a previous decision where it was stated that 'the Common Law, it is said, grants recovery only for injuries either to the person or the purse and not for mere mental suffering. This reasoning no longer portrays the law'.[62] This brought Platt J to the conclusion that the trend in the United States was to give increasing protection to the interests of freedom from emotional distress.[63] The same line of judicial thinking is observed in Maine, where the overriding consideration has been for the recognition of the freedom from mental assault. In *Wallace* v. *Coca Cola Plants Inc.*,[64] where the plaintiff brought an action against a soft drink bottler for injuries caused to him when he drank from a bottle containing a prophylactic, the court discounted a previous decision[65] which held that bodily injury was essential to an action in mental distress. The decision in the *Wallace* case was heavily influenced by the advances made by medical science in this area. Pomeroy J summed up by saying that mental damage, to be actionable, must be substantial and manifested by objective symptomatology.[66] By this is meant that the courts have every right to assess the circumstances of a case and to conclude whether mental distress has been inflicted on a plaintiff or not. This decision was later cited with approval by McKusick CJ in *Vicnire* v. *Ford Motor Credit Co.*,[67] where His Honour said that any person merits protection from even an unintentional act which produces mental distress.[68]

Medical science has done much to present the notion of mental distress in a new perspective. This is one reason why some jurisdictions recognize mental distress even though it is caused independently of physical impact. The statement of Arterburn J, in 1956, illustrates the subtlety that 'mental anguish for which recovery may be had in an action for personal injury is something more than mental sensation or pain resulting from physical injuries'.[69] The same criterion has been followed rigidly in Kansas, which has accepted the view that neither physical injury nor an intentional act is necessary to award damages for inflicted mental distress.[70] The policy behind such reasoning is that mental distress is no longer an unidentifiable concept, but a definite, independent wrong when inflicted on a person.

Louisiana is yet another jurisdiction which has been emphatic about the recognition of the infliction of mental distress as an independent head of compensation. In *Gremilion* v. *C&L Construction Co. Inc. et al.*,[71] decided in 1960, the court positively stated that the infliction of mental distress warrants damages. The plaintiff suffered shock when heavy equipment owned by the defendant and insured by the co defendant ran out of control and crashed into the plaintiff's truck. Hood J observed, 'In Louisiana, damages for mental anguish and shock resulting from trespass or damages to property are considered as actual damages and as such are compensatory.'[72] His Honour cited the case of *McGhee et al.* v. *Yazoo & M.V.R. Co.*,[73] which expressed the same principle more elaborately. The court in the *McGhee* case said:

> we see no reason why damages for mental anguish or suffering cannot be recovered in addition to property damage. Mental anguish or suffering is a distinct element of damages and is not merely an incident to be taken into consideration in addition to a pecuniary loss suffered by reason of a wrongful or negligent injury to persons and property.[74]

This gradually evolved into the recognition that the concept of mental distress as an independent head of damage is an integral part of contemporary jurisprudence in Louisiana.[75] Once the infliction of mental distress is established by the circumstances, the courts award damages without going into whether there was an intentional act of the defendant, or whether there was a physical impact on the plaintiff.

In the state of New York, the rule set out in *Michel* v. *Rochester Railway Co.*[76] in 1986, that mental anguish caused by the fault of a person is not actionable against him in the absence of contemporaneous physical impact, has since been abrogated. In *Battalla* v. *State*,[77] it was held that a nine-year-old girl could recover for psychic injury caused to her by the act of an operator of a chair lift who failed to fasten the safety bar in the chair. However, this reasoning has been cautiously applied so as not to apply on an overtly general basis. This is because of an apprehension that it would prima facie act to the detriment of the defendant. The courts in New York have insisted on stringent evidence of mental suffering before a claim for damages can be allowed. While conceptually it has been recognized that mental injury without attendant physical injury is allowable as a head of damage,[78] the courts have stated the general law to be based on the criterion of whether the act which inflicted mental anguish was intentionally caused or not.[79] However, in *Battalla's* case neither of these elements was mentioned, as the courts decided to award damages on the circumstances of the case. It is envisaged that in New York a decision would largely depend on the facts of a case. Where the negligence was gross and the injury caused was considerable, the courts would have no hesitation in making an exception, as in *Battalla's* case.

Under Montana law, the courts have taken a different approach. The application of the law itself is liberal. It recognizes as a compensable injury any detriment caused by a person. Pursuant to this principle, the courts on two occasions have recognized an independent cause of action for mental injury inflicted.[80] The identical judicial policy is seen in the application of the law in Michigan, where courts have unreservedly accepted the infliction of mental distress as an independent tort. *Stewart* v. *Rudner*[81] was a case where the parents of a still-born child suffered pain of mind as a result of the failure on the part of the surgeon to perform a caesarian operation on the mother. The mother sued the surgeon for failure to perform his contractual obligations. The court held that recovery for mental disturbance is actionable both in contract and in tort. Smith J said:

> although the law in this field is in a state of marked transition and fluidity, it is not too early to state that there is a marked trend towards recovery ... We have come to realize, slowly, it is time that law protects interests of personality as well as physical integrity of the person, and that emotional damage is just as real and as compensable as physical damage.[82]

In Iowa and Colorado, the infliction of mental distress is *in limine* considered a viable head of injury, provided there exists a causal nexus between the act and the injury caused.[83] However, the interesting feature in these two jurisdictions is that, while the infliction of mental distress is accorded considerable independence from other wrongs, the courts have approached the subject taking into consideration the circumstances and the seriousness of a case. Courts have been emphatic about the need for a definite connection between the act of the defendant and the injury caused. In this respect, the law in these two states is not dissimilar to that in New York which was discussed earlier. The discretion exercised by the courts in assessing the infliction of mental distress in relation to the act of the defendant is so wide that, in *Meiter* v. *Cavanagh*,[84] decided in Colorado in 1978, in which the purchaser of a house sued the vendor for not vacating the house and indulging in outrageous conduct, the court awarded damages to a plaintiff for mental distress caused by the action of the defendant, without laying down the criteria it followed.

The history of the notion of mental distress has undergone a steady evolution in California. The prominent feature in this jurisdiction is that the case law seems to have been decided on the initial premise that mental distress is an independent injury. It has been differentiated from physical injury as being self-existent and *sui generis*.[85] In *U.S.* v. *Hatahley et al.*,[86] Pickett CIR. J stated the view by recognizing mental distress as an independent injury if it is the result of extreme circumstances of the defendant's behaviour.[87] However, a division of opinion exists in some instances where the courts have stated that the infliction of mental distress is not in itself a tort, but a form of injury resulting from tortious conduct.[88] There is yet another view which says that mental distress should be severe to be compensated[89] and must result in physical injury. This reflects the Californian attitude that, while mental distress is considered to exist independently, the courts have been circumspect about awarding compensation owing to the absence of a precise definition of the phrase 'mental distress'. Much is left to the discretion of the courts to award damages. This is due to two factors. The first is that the courts, in assessing mental distress, have not embarked upon a serious study of the notion of mental distress from a psychological standpoint. If this was done, arriving at a conclusion in each case would have been made much easier. The second is that the courts have always regarded the measure of damages to be altogether incapable of being assessed. The result of this attitude brought about a great deal of diversity within the courts.

The case of *Vanoni* v. *Western Airlines*,[90] decided in 1967, demonstrates a new approach to the treatment of mental distress. In an instance in which some passengers of a flight operated by Western Airlines sued for nervous disorders experienced by them because of the negligent landing of the aircraft, Elkington J took a more liberal view:

> the real question … is whether the subsequent nervous disturbance of the plaintiff was a suffering of the body or of the mind. The interdependence of the mind and the body are [*sic*] in many respects so close that it is impossible to distinguish their respective influences upon each other … It is a matter of general knowledge that an attack of sudden fright or an exposure to imminent peril has produced in individuals a complete change in their nervous system and rendered one who was physically strong and vigorous, weak and timid. Such a result must be regarded as an injury to the body rather than to the mind … Whatever may be the influence by which the nervous system is affected, its action under that influence is entirely distinct from the mental process which is set in motion by the brain. The nerves and the nervous centres of the body are part of the physical system, and are not only susceptible to lesion from external causes, but are also liable to be weakened and destroyed by causes primarily acting upon the mind. If these nerves and the entire nervous system is thus effected, there is a physical injury thereby produced; and if the primal cause of this injury is tortious, it is immaterial whether it is direct … or indirect through some action upon the mind.[91]

The judgment, unlike the others previously delivered, has apparently been arrived at without regarding mental distress as an unknown quantity, coupled with a more liberal view of the biophysical interpretation of the concept. In addition, the court took the view that the causal connection between the act of the defendant and the injury suffered by the plaintiff may be established either directly or indirectly through the mind. The basis of the decision was that, if the initial act of the defendant is tortious, in that it amounts to a breach of a duty of care owed to the plaintiff, it matters not whether the mental injury which follows occurs directly or indirectly through some reaction upon the mind. This has shed an entirely new light on the notion of mental distress as it has been judicially recognized by the common law. While it is not disputed that stringent standards have to be set in measuring the harm done to a person physically in assessing the mental injury suffered, it must be acknowledged that a basic recognition of the damage done to the human being in terms of Elkington J's evaluation would raise the concept of mental distress from the quagmire of dormancy it has been placed in by the courts.

Some Definite Trends towards the Recognition of the Infliction of Mental Distress as an Independent Head of Liability

There are a few states previously cited, which show unequivocally that the infliction of mental distress is purely an independent head of liability. Such states have recognized that the common law subscribes to this view. In order that their attitude be seen in more detail, a broader discussion is warranted.

Perhaps the most enlightening view in favour of treating the infliction of mental distress per se as a separate head of liability is the line of judicial authority in Louisiana. A clear view that mental distress need not in any way be accompanied by any other factor for it to be considered eligible for redress prevails over all other considerations.[92] Its independence as a separate entity is well illustrated by Lottinger J in *Trahan* v. *Perkins*,[93] where His Honour stated:

> It is well established in our jurisprudence that a tort which gives rise to mental anguish or emotional upset or other mental suffering on the part of the injured party creates a claim for damages which is separate and distinct from any claim for physical pain or suffering resulting from physical injury.[94]

This statement unquestionably demonstrates that the established law in Louisiana favours the independence of the infliction of mental distress as a tort.

Oregon too has recognized the viability of the infliction of mental distress as a separate head of liability. In *Horis* v *City of Burns*,[95] where a widow brought an action against a city council which disinterred the remains of her husband, Holman J said that the infliction of mental distress was definitely an invasion of a legal right and therefore a wrongful act. He concluded that no physical injury or other factor is necessary to award damages.[96] An encouraging factor in these two jurisdictions is that the courts are not unmindful of the risk of falling into difficulty if this view is practised without reservation. To counter the problem, the courts have, while recognizing the necessity of giving significance to the mental element in human beings, exercised the maximum caution. The courts have done this by considering the two factors of tracing liability to the defendant and assessing the measure of damages. With regard to the former, the requirement has been that a definite nexus be established between the plaintiff and the defendant in order that it be clearly shown that the defendant caused injury to the plaintiff.[97]

After much uncertainty, the law in New York seems to favour the broad view accepted by both Louisiana and Oregon. Unlike what happened in most other states, the case law in New York has evolved steadily. The original requirement of physical injury was totally rejected by the view that the infliction of mental distress is independently compensable. This has been dealt with earlier. The principle enunciated by this view is that there is recovery for pain of mind arising out of a breach of a duty of care owed to the plaintiff by the defendant. On the point of treating the concept of freedom from mental distress as a legal right, there is much authority.[98] This is based on the view that there need not be physical impact or an observable physical injury. The infliction of mental distress can result directly from a negligent act which is accompanied by foresight on the part of the defendant. A conspicuous feature in New York, as compared with Louisiana, is that, although both recognize mental distress as a separate injury eligible for redress, it is difficult to ascertain the policy of the former state from the cases at hand. The reason is that the New York courts have dealt with cases the circumstances of which clearly establish prima facie liability on the defendant. In *Lula* v. *Sivaco Wire and Nail Co.*,[99] Van Pelt Bryan DJ stated that, although New York has recognized the concept independent of other factors, little has been said on the subject.[100] The most recent decision is the case of *Corso* v. *Crawford Dog and Cat Hospital Inc.*,[101] decided in 1979. The owner of a pet poodle, who had paid for an elaborate funeral for her pet, opened the casket in which the poodle's remains were to be and found a dead cat inside. She sued the funeral director alleging, inter alia, mental distress. Friedman J considered the element of mental distress per se and awarded damages.[102] This decision was based on the fundamental principle enunciated in *Battalla* v. *State*,[103] that mental distress could be recognized alone if it was the outcome of a negligent act by the defendant.

If an assessment is to be made on the number of jurisdictions which do not consider the infliction of mental distress as independent as against those which regard the existence of the concept separately, it could be said that in the United States, still, there are more states which regard mental distress as parasitic. Even among the jurisdictions which have shown a liberal attitude, apart from Louisiana and Illinois, the law is uncertain and only partially developed. Apart from this, there is an overwhelming majority of jurisdictions the attitudes of which are totally repugnant to the sustenance of the infliction of mental distress as a separate area of compensable injury. The inexorable conclusion that can be arrived at from these factors is that the law in the United States in this area has still not expanded to accommodate the notion of pain of mind fully. However, the vehement minority has broken all barriers. Perhaps the most liberal view so far has been taken in a Tennessee case in which, although the court required both outrageous conduct of the defendant and serious mental injury to the plaintiff, Burnett CJ said:

> memory and empathy tells us that 'hurt' perceived through sensory media other than that of touch may be just as painful if not more than the hurt perceived by the tactile sense. Moreover, physicians tell us that the consequences of invasion of the person accomplished through the perceptory media of sight and sound may be also as damaging if not more damaging than invasions of the person accomplished through the sense of touch.[104]

A prominent feature in the minority view is that, although it recognizes mental distress as independent and compensable, the courts have considered the gravity of the injury, showing a sensible balance of equities, as it would be dangerous to award damages for the mere reason that mental distress is inflicted on a person. For the present, the most encouraging thought is that at least a few states have recognized the nature of mental distress. Once this is done, establishing criteria to protect against arbitrary actions should not be difficult.

Emotional Injury under the Warsaw System of Liability

It is incontrovertible that, in a discussion of whether mental injury is a 'wounding' or 'bodily injury' as reflected in the Warsaw Convention, a 'personal injury', as referred to in the Guatemala City Protocol,[105] or a fortiori 'lésion corporelle' as appearing in the French text of the Convention, its nature has to be both medically and forensically determined in order that the concept of mental distress be assigned its place in the Convention. No judge could presume to comprehend the nature of mental injury in all its pathological and medical connotations – a necessity if a juridical basis for mental injury were to be determined under the Warsaw System.

Medical jurisprudence is greatly assisted by the pioneering research of Sigmund Freud, who first analysed mental injury and traced its origins to a combination of fear and anxiety that caused physical changes in the human body.[106] It is now well established from a medical standpoint (if not from a medical-jurisprudence standpoint) that fear and anxiety cause 'unpleasant subjective feelings of terror, a pounding heart, muscular tenseness, exaggerated startle, dryness at the throat and mouth, a sinking feeling in the stomach, nausea, perspiration, an urge to urinate and maybe to defecate … difficulty in breathing etc'.[107]

Forensically speaking, the terms 'bodily injury', 'wounding' and 'lésion corporelle' have been obfuscated by the preconceived juridical notion that there is a strict difference between mental and bodily injury. The confusion seems to have been worse confounded by the interpretation of the French term of 'lésion corporelle' as strictly bodily injury (which indeed it may well be) and therefore the erroneous basis of the two being mutually exclusive had prevailed in some instances. *Burnett* v. *Trans World Airlines*[108] is one such case where the court held that the French version of the Convention should prevail and therefore only a bodily injury (and not mental injury) must be considered as compensable. Although the case of *Rosman* v. *Trans World Airlines*[109] rejected this view that the French text prevails as the primal document, its ultimate decision was that mental injury per se was not compensable under Article 17 of the Convention. The courts in this line of cases seem to have adopted the archaic views of *Lynch* v. *Knight*[110] without consulting the prevalent findings of forensic medicine. A second line of thinking emerged in the case of *Husserl* v. *Swiss Air Transport Co.*,[111] where the court held that mental injury was 'included' in bodily injury, claiming that the words 'bodily injury' in the Convention really covered mental injury. Here again, the court refused to identify a medical similarity between the two terms but, rather, went on to read the words 'mental injury' into the Convention.[112] Miller concludes that, if a court adopted the line of thinking in the *Husserl* and *Karfunkel* decisions, a plaintiff would recover for mental distress, while if the *Rosman* decision were to be followed, no award of damages would ensue.[113]

The operative point here is not whether the French text prevails over the English translation of the Convention. Nor is it, for that matter which of the two lines of the *cursus curiae* is acceptable. The matter at issue is whether mental injury is actually a 'physical injury' in a medical sense. If this question is decided in the affirmative, there will be no need to sustain the debates that have prevailed over the thread of cases that have run through this contentious issue.

It is interesting to note that, in the case of *Floyd* v. *Eastern Airlines*,[114] the Eleventh Circuit Court of Appeals of New York examined 'lésion corporelle' in the original French text and decided that the legislative history of the Convention and the case law admitted of mental injury, even without accompanying physical injury, being compensable under Article 17. This is the only early instance of a court transcending the bounds of judicial parochialism and actually recognizing that there are other fields of human expertise that become relevant in the adjudication of human disputes.

Mankiewicz, in a well reasoned and *au fait* paper, refers to the concept of 'personal injury' in the Guatemala Protocol (which was also suggested at the Hague Protocol of 1955) and suggests a viable compromise: 'The legislative history of Article 17 compels the conclusion that, at least as far as American courts are concerned, the expression "lésion corporelle" should be understood to mean "personal injury".'[115] It is somewhat disturbing that some recent cases have still held on to the need for accompanying physical injury in order for emotional injury to be compensable. In the 1997 Australian case of *Kotsambasis* v. *Singapore Airlines*,[116] the New South Wales Court of Appeal followed the *Floyd* decision and held that, without accompanying bodily injury, the plaintiff could not recover for pure psychological injury. The plaintiff in this case had claimed that she had suffered acute nervous shock and feared for her life following a fire which broke out in the engine of the aircraft in which she was travelling, while at Athens Airport. The Court of Appeal went on the basis that the signatory states to the Warsaw Convention, in 1929, had no specific intent to include pure psychological or emotional distress within the purview of Article 17 of the Convention.[117] The Court of Appeals in the *Kotsambasis* case disagreed with the lower court judges' finding with an earlier Australian decision,[118] which was in the appellate process at the time the *Kotsambasis* case was being decided. Although the New South Wales Court of Appeal conclusively decided at the appeal of the *Georgopoulos* case that pure mental distress was comparable, without there being a need for accompanying physical injury, the *Kotsambasis* decision overruled it.

In the United States, although few instances of judicial determination which follows *Floyd* v. *Eastern Airlines*[119] support the view that plaintiffs could recover only for physical injuries and for emotional injuries flowing from those injuries,[120] the 1996 decision regarding the case of *Zicherman* v. *Korean Airlines Co. Ltd*[121] gave the United States Supreme Court the opportunity to confirm that the Warsaw Convention itself contained no specific or particular preclusion from recovering compensation from any damages, be it physical or mental. The *Zicherman* decision allowed the plaintiff to claim for 'legally cognizable harm' to be determined by local law in accordance with otherwise applicable choice of law principles. A year later, the 1997 decision of the *Roselawn* case[122] held with the Supreme Court findings in the *Zicherman* case, stating:

> Article 17 does not say that a carrier will only be liable for damage caused by a bodily injury, or that passengers can only recover for mental injuries if they are caused by bodily injuries.[123]

The aviation community has now reached a stage where the *cursus curiae* at common law, such as the *Floyd* and *Zicherman* decisions, would be moot when the ICAO Draft Convention for the Unification of Certain Rules for International Carriage by Air is discussed at Montreal through a diplomatic Conference for the purpose of its adoption, to be held on 10–28 May 1998. If adopted, this Convention would blaze a new trail, and provide the judiciary with the *travaux préparatoires* of the Conference as resource material. Courts would no longer have to inquire as to the intent of the makers of the original Warsaw Convention of 1929, since the 1999 ICAO Convention would supplant its predecessor.

In terms of the element of 'mental injury', it is very clear that the working papers of the Study Group, which was appointed by the ICAO Court in November 1995 for the specific purpose of developing a mechanism within the framework of ICAO to accelerate the modernization of the Warsaw System, are explicit in reflecting the Group's intentions. Vijay Poonoosamy, the rapporteur of the Study Group, in his report states:

> the expression 'personal injury' would open the door to non-physical personal injuries such as slander, libel, discrimination, fear, fright and apprehension and this could be neither desirable nor acceptable. Use of 'bodily injury' would be more acceptable but would exclude mental injuries such as shock. Recent Court decisions in the U.S. demonstrate how difficult an area this is and a clear statement must be agreed upon which is not limitless in scope. Since it would be clearly fair and equitable to compensate for impairment of health (i.e. both physical and mental/psychic injuries) it may be preferable to define personal injury as such.[124]

It is interesting to note that the rapporteur, on behalf of the ICAO Study Group, categorizes fear, fright and apprehension, which are symptoms of injury that bring about physical results, as shown in the scientific evidence in the introduction of this chapter, as non-physical 'injuries'. He then goes on to identify 'shock' as a mental injury.

The ICAO Legal Committee, which examined the report of the Study Group, retained the term 'mental injury' in Article 16 of the ICAO Draft Convention.[125] However, final versions of the Draft Convention,[126] which were the document in issue at the May 1999 Diplomatic Conference at ICAO, gives Article 16 of the Draft Convention as follows:

> *Article 16.1*
> The carrier is liable for damage sustained in case of death or bodily injury of a passenger upon condition only that the accident which caused the death or injury took place onboard the aircraft or in the

> course of any of the operations of embarking or disembarking. However, the carrier is not liable to the extent that the death or injury resulted from the state of health of the passenger.[127]

In the draft, the words 'personal' and 'or mental' have been stricken from the original phrase, 'personal bodily or mental injury', making it incontrovertible that the new Convention does not intend to encompass mental injury as a compensable element in Article 16. This exclusion, ipso facto, would give the courts a clear direction as to the way to proceed in an adjudication involving mental injury in the carriage by air of a person, except that it is not clear whether, by the exclusion of the words 'mental injury', the Convention also wished to exclude 'the impairment of mental health', which can be imputed as being inclusionary in the working papers of the ICAO Study Group. It would not be surprising if this dichotomy were to create, in the future, two schools of judicial thought, as indeed existed under the 1929 Warsaw Convention and its Protocols.

There could also well be a line of reasoning, as in the *Zicherman* case, which would insist on interpreting 'bodily injury' as extending to 'legally cognizable harm', thereby extending the phrase to mental injury.

There is no doubt that medical science has clearly identified mental disturbance. Modern science has debunked the legal attitude which was brought about by the requirement that physical injury is an essential prerequisite of mental injury. It is now believed by medical science that the mental injury that a victim suffers can be extreme. Although it is caused by fear, in most cases it is not mere fright or nervous shock but also an extreme form of neurosis[128] which follows the traumatic event of an accident. Neurosis in its extreme form is a psychogenic disorder following a psychic injury with or without physical harm.[129] It results in considerable impairment of ability to function in ordinary life. Generally, it is precipitated by a traumatic incident and is solely due to psychological reactions, which makes external physical injury a totally unrelated factor.

It is not surprising that, as far back as 1939, the courts pronounced that any person 'needs the privilege of being careless whether he inflicts mental injury to another or not'.[130] The courts viewed mental injury as no redressable injury. The unfortunate thing is that, although in many areas of the law, academic opinion and judicial decisions have been symbiotic, the courts did not heed the comments of Prosser,[131] Bohlen[132] and many others[133] who, at an early stage, recognized mental injury as an independent injury which infringes the interest of peace of mind. The only conclusion that can be reached is that the courts have not taken the trouble to seek a definition for mental injury and this has made their treatment of the injury misguided and often erroneous. As has been pointed out earlier, a minority of jurisdictions have, notwithstanding this general attitude, been courageous enough to say that it is a definite and identifiable injury.

The courts should primarily consider the meaning and purpose of the law when dealing with mental injury and accident liability. To say that it is the business of the law to remedy wrongs that deserve it,[134] is a legal platitude. If the injury suffered by a plaintiff is proved by connecting it to an accident, there is no doubt that the injury is a wrong that needs correction by way of awarding damages to the plaintiff.

There is little room for doubt that most common law courts would readily regard post-traumatic stress disorder (PTSD), which is a relatively new phenomenon (earlier referred to by the medical profession as 'whiplash injuries'), as a legally cognizable harm per se. PTSD excludes mental injury caused as a result of a person's death by natural causes (such as witnessing the death of a family member under natural circumstances). It includes mental injury or distress caused by witnessing sudden events such as accidents, natural disasters and instances of armed combat. Typical symptoms of PTSD are recurrent and persistent experiencing of an event in question; exclusion of the outside world when experiencing such recurrences of events in one's mind; avoidance of circumstances needing change; and increased confusion and disturbance of mind, resulting in such experiences as lack of sleep and temper tantrums.[135] The *facta probanda*, or elements of proof, needed to establish PTSD are, in an aircraft accident, the fact that the claimant is suffering from PTSD; such PTSD has been brought about by shock caused by experiencing the event of an accident or other incident calculated to induce such a psychiatric disorder; and the close proximity of the claimant to the accident site.

The issue as to whether the courts would associate PTSD with 'bodily injury' as envisaged in the present Warsaw structure or even the new regime reflected in the Convention proposed by ICAO, would largely depend on the extent to which courts would be ready to embrace the compelling scientific findings with regard to mental distress and its application within the term 'bodily injury'.

In the United States, torts became a distinct area of the law only in the late 19th-century. It has been regarded as a flexible discipline where rigid distinctions are impossible to make. Inflexible principles and conservatism have no place in the rapidly evolving tort law in America.[136] One writer[137] has aptly commented that, as a consequence of this progressive evolution of tort law, the common law in time to come would entertain mental distress actions freely. The immunities given to the injurer under fault liability would gradually disappear.

The reason for this is quite clear. In a civil wrong such as a tort, the law now seeks to correct a wrong rather than punish a wrongdoer. For this purpose there is no need to depend on fault liability as the sole criterion of deciding an action in mental distress. The only thing necessary is to determine that the victim is free of fault and that the defendant was responsible in some way for the injury caused. The law itself on this matter should be based heavily on social welfare. It is inevitable that, eventually, the courts will follow this trend, taking into account social policy and the interests of society as a whole, and compensate injury, whether mental or physical, in an appropriate manner.

Notes

1 See *Lynch* v. *Knight* (1861) 9 H.L.C. 577, 598, where Lord Wensleydale said: 'mental pain or anxiety the law cannot value, and does not pretend to redress, when the unlawful act complained of causes that alone'.
2 Hereafter, injury to the human mind, mental distress, pain of mind, emotional distress and other similar references mean any influence on the human mind which would temporarily or permanently upset the mental stability of a person, sufficient to cause discomfort to the mind.
3 Hereinafter referred to as the United States.
4 G.E. White (1980), *Tort Law in America*, XI.
5 See W. Prosser (1971), *Handbook of the Law of Torts*, 4th edn; also, Prosser (1939), 'Intentional Infliction of Mental Suffering – A New Tort', *Michigan Law Review*, 37 n.14), pp. 874; White (*supra*, n.14), p.102.
6 See White (*supra*, n.14), pp.102, 103.
7 See *Michigan Law Review*, 37 (1939) 874.
8 I.M. Marks (1969), *Fears and Phobias*, p.1.
9 Ibid.
10 *Boston Medical and Surgical Journal*, CL XIII (1910), 893.
11 W.B. Cannon (1932), *Bodily Changes in Pain, Hunger, Fear and Rage*, 253–4.
12 Ibid., 325–6.
13 W.B. Cannon (1967), *The Wisdom of the Human Body*, p.276.
14 For internal changes causing discomfort, see generally *The Physiology of Emotions*, Report of the Third Annual Symposium of the Kaiser Foundation Hospitals, Northern California (1961), 16–16, at 17–15.
15 The attitude is typified by the strong approach taken in *Lynch* v. *Knight* (*supra*, n.1).
16 (1897) 2 QB 57.
17 Prosser, 37 *Michigan Law Review* (*supra*, n.14).
18 See. Prosser, *Handbook of the Law of Torts* (*supra*, n.15), p.328.
19 Ibid.
20 *Dulieu* v. *White* (1901) 2 KB 669 at 677.
21 Jeremiah Smith (1920–21), 'Torts Without Names', *University of Pennsylvania Law Review*, 69, 91.
22 Street, *Foundations of Legal Liability*, London: Butterworths, XXV–XXVI.
23 *Davis* v. *Hill*, 291 S.W. (1927) 681, at 684.
24 *International & G.N.R. Co.* v. *Hood*, 118 S.W. (1909) 1119, at 1122.
25 *Waller* v. Keller, 218 S.W. (1920) 792, at 794.

26 See *Donoughue* v. *Stevenson*, 1932 A.C. 562.
27 See *Dillon* v. *Legg*, 69 Cal. Rptr. 72.
28 See *Shepard* v. *Superior Court*, 142 Cal. Rptr. 612.
29 179 F. Supp. 688.
30 Ibid., 697.
31 See *Taxakarna & F.T. Smith Railway Co.* v. *Anderson*, 53. S.W. 673. For Columbia law, see *Gilber* v. *Kiemesha Concord Inc.*, 302 A. 2d 740 at 745; also *Garber* v. *United States*, 578 F. 2d 414 at 416, per Leventhal CIR. J. For Indiana law based on the same impact principle, see *Leatherman* v. *Gateway Transportation Co.*, 331 F. 2d 241 at 245; also *Berrier* v. *Beneficial Finance, Inc.*, 234 V. Supp. 204 at 205, *per* Echbach J.
32 *Olan Mills Inc. of Texas* v. *Dodd*, 353 S.W. 2d 22, where the defendant used a photograph of the plaintiff without permission, which the court felt gave rise to a cause of action irrespective of physical injury or *mala fides*. See the judgment by McFadden J at 24.
33 *United Services Automobile Association* v. *Glens Fall Insurance Co.*, 350 F. Supp. 869 at 872, *per* Zampano DJ.
34 See *Slocum* v. *Food Fair Stores of Florida*, 100 So. 2d 396, where a customer alleged mental distress culminating in coronary failure. Drew J at 396, accepted that recovery may be had for intentionally inflicted mental injury without physical impact. In *Korbin* v. *Berlin*, 177 So. 2d 551, it was held that malice and mental distress are complementary factors. See also *Jackson* v. *Rupp*, 228 So. 2d 916, and *Ellington* v. *U.S.*, 404 F. Supp, 1165 at 1167, where Reed DJ implied that, for an action in mental distress to be sustained, there has to be both physical impact resulting in a physical injury and the element of intention.
35 334 So. 2d 39.
36 *Zeiglar* v. *F. Street Corporation*, 235 A. 2d 703 at 705.
37 *Dawson* v. *Associates Financial Serv. Co. of Kansas Inc.*, 529 A. 2d 104.
38 *Whitten* v. *American Mutual Liability Insurance Co.*, 468 F. Supp. 470.
39 *Cohen* v. *Lion Products Co.*, 177 F. Supp. 486; *Sullivan* v. *H.P. Hood & Sons*, 168 N.E. 2d 80, at 84; *In Re. Petition of United States*, 418 F. 2d 264, at 268.
40 *Becker* v. *Borough of Schylkill Haven*, 189 A. 2d 764, at 767.
41 *Barnett* v. *Sun Oil Co.*, 172 N.E. 2d 734, at 735; *Heid* v. *Red Malenit Inc.*, 231 N.E. 2d 356, at 358.
42 *Greenberg* v. *Stanley*, 143 A. 2d 588.
43 *Aldregh* v. *Johnson*, 318 So. 2d 870, at 873 *per* Robertson J, who said that, although the court would not insist on physical injury, the injury must be capable of assessment. Also *Lyons* v. *Zale Jewellery Co.*, 150 So. 2d 154, at 162; *Johnson* v. *Ford Motor Co.*, 354 F. Supp. 645, at 648; *State Farm Mutual Automobile Insurance Co. et al. Johnson* v. *Ford Motor Co.*, 35 F. Supp. 645, at 648; *State Farm Mutual Automobile Insurance Co. et al.* v. *Village of Isle*, 122 n.W. 2d 36.
44 *Gambill* v. *White*, 303 S.W. 2d 41, at 42; *Langworthy* v. *Pulitzer Publishing Co.*, 368 F. Supp. 385; *Smith* v. *Aldridge*, 356 S.W. 2d 532; *Franscisco* v. *Traveller's Insurance Co.*, 363 F. Supp. 761, at 762.
45 *Maine* v. *Matson Oldsmobile-Cadillac Co.*, 148 N.W. 2d 779; *Frishett* v. *State Farm Mutual Automobile Insurance Co.*, 143 N.W. 2d 612.
46 *Browning* v. *Slenderella Systems of Seattle*, 341 P. 2d 85.
47 *Womack* v. *Eldridge*, 210 S.E. 2d 145, at 148, where four elements were required to satisfy the requirement to award damages for mental distress without physical injury: (a) an intentional and reckless act, (b) outrageous conduct on the part of the defendant, (c) a causal connection between the act and the pain of mind caused, and (d) severe emotional distress.
48 *Houston-American Finance Corporation* v. *Travis*, 343 S.W. 2d 323; *Stafford* v.

Steward, 295 S.W. 2d. 665, at 667, *per* Long J; *Fisher* v. *Carousel Motor Hotel Inc.*, 414 S.W. 2d 774; *Pat H. Foley and Co.* v. *Wyatt*, 442 S.W. 2d 904, at 906, *per* Johnson J; *Ledisco Financial Services Inc.* v. *Viracola*, 533 S.W. 2d 951, at 957, *per* Cornelius J.

49 *Gray* v. *Serruto Builders*, 265 A. 2d 404, at 413, per Herbert JSC. One can contrast this attitude with that of Virginia law which insists on an intentional infliction of mental distress. See *Williams* v. *Pine Line Service Inc. et al.*, 126 S.E. 2d 384, at 384, *per* Browning J. (See also the cases cited *supra*, n.57.) *Sprouse* v. *Clay Communications*, 211 S.E. 2d 674, and *Perlin* v. *Chappel*, 96 S.E. 2d 805, at 806, are two more cases which rigidly followed the same approach. For the same approach in Missouri, see *Warren* v. *Parrish*, 436 S.W. 2d 670.

50 242 N.W. 25.

51 *Leahy* v. *Morgan*, 275 F. Supp. 424.

52 See *Drake Law Review*, 7 (1957), 60; also *Iowa Law Review*, 18 (1952), 370.

53 *Buckner* v. *Freight Liner Corp.*, 403 F. Supp. 671.

54 *Parmalee* v. *Ackerman*, 252 F. 2d 721.

55 See *Grill* v. *Abele Funeral Home Inc.* 42 N.E. 2d 788; *Bartow* v. *Smith*, 78 N.E. 2d 735; *Reed* v. *Fort*, 112 S.W. 600.

56 *Parmalee* v. *Ackerman* (*supra*, n.64), 740.

57 *Bartow* v. *Smith* (*supra*, n.55), *per* Hart J, 740.

58 See *Henry Morrison Flagler Museum* v. *Lee* (1978) 268 So. 2d. 434.

59 Ibid.

60 171 F. Supp. 205.

61 Ibid., 212.

62 *Sick* v. *Perk Dog Food Co.*, 106 N.E. 2d 742 at 745.

63 Ibid., 746.

64 269 A. 2d 117.

65 Ibid., 120, citing *Herrick* v. *Evening Pub Co.*, 113 A. 116.

66 Ibid., 121.

67 401 A 2d 148.

68 Ibid., 154.

69 *New York Chicago and St. Louis Railroad Co.* v. *Henderson*, 137 N.E. 2d 744 at 746.

70 *Monroe* v. *Daw* 559 P. 2d 332, at 327, *per* Prager J.

71 125 So. 2d 198.

72 Ibid., 201.

73 19 So. 2d 21.

74 Ibid., 24, *per* Rogers J. See also *Fontenot* v. *Magnolia Petroleum Co. et al.*, 80 So. 2d 845, at 850, *per* Simon J.

75 See *American Steel Building Co. Inc.* v. *Brezner* 158 So. 2d 623, at 631, *per* Tate J; also *Nickens et ux* v. *C.A. McGehee et ux*, 184 So. 2d 271, at 278, *per* Landry J.

76 151 N.Y. 107.

77 176 N.E. 2d 729.

78 *Ferrara et al.* v. *Galluchio et al.*, 176 N.Y.S. 2d 996.

79 *Canverien* v. *De Metz*, 188 N.Y.S. 2d 627, at 631, *per* Nathan J.

80 See *Wilson* v. *Northland Greyhound Lines*, 166 F. Supp 667 at 676.

81 84 N.W. 2d 816.

82 Ibid., 822. For the same point, see *Jankowski* v. *Mazzotta*, 152 N.W. 2d 49.

83 *Northrup* v. *Miles Homes Inc. of Iowa*, 204 N.W. 2d 850, at 860, *per* Reynoldson J; also *Towns* v. *Anderson*, 579 P. 2d 1163; *Hopper* v. *U.S.*, 244 F. Supp. 314.

84 Colo. App. 580 P. 2d 399.

85 *Altman* v. *Manhattan Savings Bank*, 148 Cal. Rptr. 100, at 103, *per* Hastings AJ.

86 257 F. 2d 920.

87 Ibid., 925. Extreme circumstances have been interpreted to mean plaintiff's outrageous conduct in *Perati* v. *Atkinson*, 28 Cal. Rptr. 898, at 899, *per* Draper J,

and in *Renteria* v. *County of Orange*, 147 Cal. Rptr. 447. In *Leavy* v. *Cooney*, 29 Cal. Rptr. 580, at 584, Shinn J said that extreme circumstances would mean the plaintiff's wrongful and intentional conduct. *Spackman* v. *Good*, 54 Cal. Rptr. 78, at 84, held the same as *Leavy's* case on the point. In *Mack* v. *Hugh W. Comstock Association Inc.*, 37 Cal. Rptr. 466, at 469, it was held that wantonness and malice on the part of the defendant constituted extreme circumstances.

88 *Gauthier* v. *General Telephone Co.*, 48 Cal. Rptr. 78, at 90.

89 *Fletcher* v. *Western National Life Insurance Co.*, 89 Cal. Rptr. 78, at 90.

90 56 Cal. Rptr. 115.

91 Ibid., 117.

92 See *Clegg* v. *Hardware Mutual Casualty Co.* 264 F. 2d 152, at 155; also *Salme* v. *United States Fidelity and Guarantee Co.*, 320 F. 2d 18, at 20, where Bell J said: 'It has been the law in Louisiana that recovery may be had for fright or nervous shock unaccompanied by physical injury evidenced by objective symptoms.' There are six other cases which upheld the same point: *Stewert* v. *Arkansas Southern Railway Co.*, 36 So. 676; *Klien* v. *Medical Building Realty Co. Inc.*, 147 So. 122; *Holland* v. *St. Paul Mercury Insurance Co.*, 135 So. 2d 145, at 157, *per* Landry J; *Ford* v. *State Farm Mutual Automobile Insurance Co.*, 139 So. 2d 798; *Taylor* v. *All State Insurance Co.*, 205 So. 2d 80, at 811, *per* Lottinger J; *Booty* v. *American Finance Corporation of Shrive Port Ia.*, 224 So. 2d 512 at 515.

93 La. 197 So. 2d 96.

94 Ibid., 99.

95 415 P. 2d 29.

96 Ibid., 31; also see *Senn* v. *Bunick*, Or. App. 594 P. 2d 837.

97 *Chriss* v. *Manchester Insurance & Indemnity Co.*, La. App. 308 So. 2d 803, at 805, *per* Lemmon J.

98 *Galella* v. *Onassis*, 487 F. 2d 986; *Cohen* v. *Varig' Airlines, S.A. Empresa etc.*, 380 N.Y.S. 2d 450, at 459; *Brown* v. *Fifth Avenue Coach Lines Inc.*, 185 N.Y.S. 2d 923; *Halio* v. *Lurie*, 222 N.Y.S. 2d 759, at 763; *Grimm* v. *Bam*, 195 N.Y.S. 2d 36.

99 265 F. Supp, 222.

100 Ibid., 225.

101 415 N.Y.S. 2d 182.

102 Ibid., 183.

103 176 N.E. 2d 729.

104 Ibid., 273, 774.

105 Protocol to Amend the Warsaw Convention signed at Guatemala City, 1971, hereafter referred to as the Guatemala Protocol.

106 S. Freud (1959), *Inhibitions, Symptoms and Anxiety*, p.12. Sigmund Freud identified herein that while fear per se was identified as neurotic anxiety, a combination of fear with anxiety produced mental injury, which he said was the result of unrecognized internal sources of threat that produced adverse physical changes in the human body. Also C.E. Izard and S.S. Tompkins (1966), *Anxiety and Behaviour*, p.125, C.D. Spielberger (1972), *Anxiety – Current Trends in Theory and Research*, vol. 2, p.263, R. May (1950), *Meaning of Anxiety*, p.53, *The Physiology of Emotions* (*supra*, n.14), 15–16 and F. Dunbar (1954), *Emotions and Bodily Changes*, 4th edn, p.685, give similar views on the pathological effects of mental distress on the human body.

107 Marks (*supra*, n.8). 'The experience of fear and anxiety is known to cause a person to bend his body, jerk his head forward, blink his eyes' (May, *supra*, n.106, pp.46–8). *The Psychosomatic Journal of the American Medical Association* (1947, 1527) recorded that half the cases of acute illnesses and recovery problems are attributable to the mental state of the patient. Anxiety is also known to bring about an imbalance in the digestive process, (Cannon, *supra*, n.20, pp.253–4). Cannon (*supra*, n.22) p.276 states that mental distress would in-

crease blood sugar levels of a subject bringing about a positively unpleasant experience.

108 12 Avi. 17, 603 (S.D.N.Y. 1975).

109 13 Avi. 17, 231 (N.Y. Ct App 1974).

110 *Supra*, n.1.

111 13 Avi. 17, 603 (S.D.N.Y. 1975).

112 This somewhat parochial view was followed in the cases of *Karfunkel* v. *Air France*, 14 *Avi*. 17, 674 (S.D.N.Y. 1977) and *Krystal* v. *British Overseas Airways Corporation*, 14 *Avi*. 17, 128 (C.D. Cal 1975). *Herman* v. *TWA*, 12 *Avi*. 17, 304 (1972) and *Palagonia* v. *TWA* 13 *Avi*. 17, 478 (1974) were two further instances of mental injury being 'included' in the rubric of physical injury.

113 Georgette Miller (1979), *Air Carrier's Liability Under the Warsaw System*, Amsterdam: Kluwer.

114 872 F. 2d 1462 (11th Cir. 1989).

115 Rene H. Mankiewicz (1979), 'The Application of Article 17 of the Warsaw Convention to Mental Suffering Not Related to Physical Injury', *Annals of Air and Space Law*, IV, 192.

116 See David B. Johnston (1997), 'Australian Court Holds that Damages for Pure Psychological Injury are not Recoverable in Warsaw Convention Cases', *Aviation Insurance and Law*, 16, No. (9), September, p.166.

117 Ibid.

118 *Georgopoulos* v. *America Airlines* [1994] I.A.S.L.R. 38 (N.S.W. Sup. Ct).

119 *Supra*, n.123.

120 See *Jack* v. *Transworld Airlines, Inc.*, 854 F. Supp 654 (N.W.Cal. 1994), *Burnett* v. *Transworld Inc.*, 975 F. 2d 35; also *Tseng* v. *El Al Israeli Airlines Ltd.*, 919 F. Supp. 155 (S.D.N.Y. 1996).

121 11b S.Ct. 629 (1996).

122 *In re Aircrash Disaster Near Roselawn, Indiana* on 31 October 1994, 954 F. Supp. 175 (N.D. Ill. 1997).

123 Ibid., at 179.

124 'The Modernization of the "Warsaw System" – The ICAO Draft Convention on the Liability of the Air Carrier', *The Aviation Quarterly*, Part 5, July 1997, pp.298–9.

125 Ibid., 313.

126 Draft Convention for the Unification of Certain Rules for International Carriage by Air, Reference Text, DCW Doc. No. 5. 5/3/99, Montreal: ICAO.

127 Ibid., p. 8.

128 See J.M. Hart (1978), 'Neurosis Following Trauma', *Cumberland Law Review*, 8, 495.

129 Ibid., 497.

130 *Clark* v. *Associate Retail Credit Men*, 105 F. 2d 62, at 64.

131 See Prosser, *Handbook of the Law of Torts* (*supra*, n.5), p.327.

132 G.Bohlen (1902), 'Developments in Tort Law', *American Law Register*, 51, 141.

133 See J. Harper and G. McNeely (1938), *Wisconsin Law Review*, 426; D. Goodrich (1922), *Michigan Law Review*, 20, 497; E. Magruder (1936), *Harvard Law Review*, 49, 1033.

134 Prosser, *Handbook of the Law of Torts* (*supra*, n.5), p.54.

135 See Mark Franklin (1997), 'Liability in Negligence for Post Traumatic Stress Disorder', *The Aviation Quarterly*, Part 3, January, 173.

136 N. Green, *Proximate and Remote Cause* (in essays) at 1.

137 W.H. Pedrick (1974), 'Does Tort Law Have A Future', *Ohio Law Journal*, 39, 784.

15 Negligence of the Airline Pilot

Introduction

A professional pilot is a person who engages in such flying as makes it necessary that he or she holds a valid airline transport pilot's licence (ATPL). This chapter will therefore not address the professional conduct of persons who are holders of private pilots' licences and use such licences for non-remunerative flights, or flights which do not involve payment of monies for services rendered in flying aircraft. Also excluded are holders of ATPLs who happen to fly on particular occasions under circumstances where a private pilot's licence would be adequate, for instance when a person flies for recreation or on personal business although he may hold an ATPL.

There are several provisions of law in the United Kingdom which apply to the professional commercial pilot. Firstly, Article 81(1) of the Civil Aviation Act of 1982 provides that, where an aircraft is flown in such a manner as to be the cause of unnecessary danger to any person or property on land or on water, the pilot or the person in charge of the aircraft, and also the owner thereof, unless he proves to the satisfaction of the court that the aircraft was flown without his actual fault or privity, shall be liable and on summary conviction to a fine not exceeding a particular scale[1] or to imprisonment for a term not exceeding six months, or to both.

In addition to the above provision, Articles 55 of the Air Navigation Order of 1995 stipulate that a person shall not recklessly or negligently act in a manner likely to endanger an aircraft or any person on board. Article 56 provides that a person shall not recklessly or negligently cause or permit an aircraft to endanger any person or property.

Legal requirements notwithstanding, assessments carried out from 1977 to date reveal that pilot decision making is a significant factor in aircraft accidents. In 1977, Jensen and Benel[2] reported that 35 per cent of all non-fatal and 52 per cent of all fatal general aviation accidents in the United States during the period from 1970 to 1974 could be attributed to faulty pilot decision making. In 1991, Diehl,[3] another researcher, using the methodology of Jensen and Benel, concluded that 56 per cent and 50 per cent of aircraft accidents in commercial aviation and non-commercial aviation, respectively, were attributable to pilot error with regard to decisions taken by the pilot.

Commercial airline pilots operate in a highly complex environment, particularly in single pilot operations. The difficulties faced by pilots in the work environment are compounded by the fact that, often, inadequate information aggravates the problem. Pilots rely heavily on their visual and auditory senses while flying, and it is of paramount importance that accurate information be available to the pilot at all times. Most importantly, pilots usually have a predilection for completing their given schedule no matter what: completing a flight as planned, meeting schedules, impressing their employees and pleasing the people they carry. Therefore negligent issues concerning the professional conduct of a pilot are quintessential elements for a highly esoteric legal debate. This chapter will examine and analyse judicial attitudes with regard to negligence of the airline pilot and make observations as to their relevance to the general area of professional negligence.

Negligence of the Airline Pilot

The tenets of international aviation law attribute to the pilot (hereafter also referred to as the commander) of an aircraft absolute responsibility for the safe operation of his aircraft. Often this principle is seen to defeat its purpose in the determination of a single instance of professional conduct of the pilot when such is considered to have endangered the safety of the aircraft, its passengers and property. The main reason for this confusion is the clear dichotomy which exists between statutory provisions and international conventions, on the one hand, which unequivocally lay down the fact of absolute responsibility of the pilot, and the treatment of single instances of negligent professional conduct of the pilot in their isolation, on the other. So far, no attempt has been made either by international law and local statute or by judicial decisions to recognize that the conduct of the pilot in the aircraft should be viewed in its entirety, due regard being given to fundamental principles of law, the conduct of the pilot as a professional in whose hands lie the lives of hundreds of passengers and who takes on his job assuring his employer that his special skills and expertise would transport the passengers and their property safely under normal circumstances, and to any special circumstance which would render the effect of that assurance nugatory.

The law as it exists lays down a presumption of absolute responsibility of the pilot. In sharp contrast, the adjudication of instances of professional conduct of the pilot shows a clear demarcation between good airmanship and bad airmanship. Of these, the latter shows clear evidence of having been decided on individual merits and not on a general criterion or principle of recognizing the elements of law, special circumstances and the human factor as a composite whole. Therein lies the problem.

The following analysis will examine the question of bad airmanship of the pilot in its entirety, thereby seeking to introduce certain general principles based on the presumption of responsibility that the law imposes. Such general principles could then be applied to special circumstances which would thus give rise to special rules pertaining to the professional conduct of the pilot. To achieve this end, an examination and analysis of legal principles, judicial decisions and special circumstances is necessary.

Applicable Laws and Consequences

According to accepted principles of law as laid down by international convention, it is incontrovertible that the final responsibility for the safe operation of an aircraft lies with the pilot. The Convention on International Civil Aviation[4] provides that 'The pilot-in-command shall be responsible for the operation and safety of the aeroplane and for the safety of all persons on board, during flight time.'[5] This presumption of responsibility has influenced most states which have signed or ratified the Convention and is reflected clearly in their air navigation laws.[6] These laws have been observed to list requirements which any pilot with a sense of good airmanship would naturally comply with. Failure to comply with such regulations has been clearly interpreted to be bad airmanship which renders the pilot liable for prosecution on a criminal charge.[7] In any event, the fundamental postulate which imposes prima facie responsibility on the pilot has been accepted as a general principle of liability of the pilot which sets the base for determining his legal status and responsibility.[8]

The legal responsibility placed on the commander of the aircraft is therefore inextricably linked with the expectation of good airmanship. Airmanship has been regarded as an indefinable quality and has been used to describe the intuitive faculty of the pilot where he concerns himself with what is right or wrong in the operation of an aircraft, which is acquired by sustained experience in flying.[9] Whilst it is

> the proper conduct of the normal flight to avoid creating hazard, it is also the ability to overcome potential hazard where failure has occurred.

> With procedures laid down, drills to cover eventualities and the installation of duplicated equipment it is not surprising that crew error is seen as an element in so many accidents.[10]

The above analysis seems to suggest that the pilot should be held absolutely responsible for the safety of his flight, not only as he lays claim to special expertise, but also as he has been given the benefit of sophisticated duplicate equipment which makes his job easier. Thus the stringent legal responsibility placed upon the pilot is seen to be further justified.

The absolute responsibility cast upon the pilot inevitably carries with it absolute and final authority from take-off to landing.[11] The status of the pilot therefore entails far-reaching consequences, making an instance of his negligent act open to be interpreted as a dangerous and unlawful act which could justify a charge of manslaughter at the least.[12] Criminality of the act of the pilot lies quite independently of the incontrovertible liability in negligence[13] which would follow from such act.

Yet another consequence that the pilot would face is loss of employment. The pilot who holds a valid licence is considered to be responsible both to the state and to his employer. The employer of the pilot has been recognized as demanding of his employee the right to decide whether to continue the employment of a pilot if he constitutes a threat to air safety in the course of his employment.[14] This principle is obviously followed on the basis that the product that the aircraft operator offers the passenger would lose its value totally if his credibility as a safe operator was lost by the negligent act of his pilot. In this perspective, no reputation, however glamorous, would obviate adverse publicity regarding the safety standards of an airline. Further, the pilot naturally hinges his entire capability and eligibility for employment on his ability to transport his passengers and cargo safely from one point to another. To achieve at least minimum standards of safety, the employer should ascertain the competence of the pilot on his record at the point of employment and the pilot should justify his employment by the professional conduct that is expected of him and not regard his employer as one who suspiciously watches the performance of his duties. The ideal relationship between the pilot and his employer was expressed by Captain A. J. Burridge, when he said:

> If the suspicions of pilots can be allayed, and if an atmosphere of mutual trust between pilots and airline managements can be created, I think that responsible pilots could be persuaded to accept that the standard of flight safety we all want requires that Draconian remedies must be applied to cases of really bad airmanship in order to prevent their recurrence.[15]

Negligence

The basis of liability in negligence is founded on the principle that, when a person owes a duty of care to another, a breach of such duty grounds an action in negligence against the offender.[16] The elements of negligence relevant in the case of a pilot is the duty or standard of care he owes and whether that duty has been breached. While the law imposes an objective test of how the 'reasonable man' would execute that duty of care in ordinary circumstances which do not require of him some special skill, in the case of a pilot the standard applicable would be that of the reasonable professional pilot. In the words of McNair J:

> Where you get a situation which involves the use of some special skill or competence then the test as to whether there has been negligence or not is not the test of the reasonable man because he has not this special skill; a man need not possess the highest of expert skill; it is well established law that it is sufficient if he exercises the ordinary skill of an ordinary competent man exercising that particular art.[17]

The degree of negligent conduct required of a person in charge of transporting passengers and cargo has been set out in clear terms in cases concerned both with the responsibility of a captain at sea and with that of a pilot in command of an aircraft. Brett LJ, delivering judgment on a captain of a ship said: 'Captains of ships are bound to shew such skills as persons of their position with ordinary nerve ought to shew under the circumstances.'[18] Perhaps the most significant case involving the negligence of a pilot is the decision in *Taylor* v. *Alidair Limited*,[19] which related to an unfair dismissal action in which a pilot appealed against his dismissal following a heavy landing leading to an uncorrected bounce and the collapse of the nosewheel assembly of the Viscount aircraft he was flying. The aircraft made a heavy touchdown, bouncing 10 feet into the air and touching down heavily again on all three wheels on the runway. There was considerable damage to the engines and air-frame. Bristow J held that:

> there are activities in which the degree of professional skill which must be required is so high and the potential consequences of the smallest departure from that high standard are so serious that one failure to perform in accordance with those standards is enough to justify dismissal. The passenger-carrying airline pilot, the scientist operating the nuclear reactor, the chemist in charge of research into possible effects of, for example, thalidomide, the driver of the Manchester to London express, the driver of an articulated lorry full of sulphuric acid, are all in the situation in which one failure to maintain

the proper standard of professional skill can bring about a major disaster.[20]

This decision, which was upheld on appeal in the Court of Appeal,[21] stems largely from the approach that fundamental principles of tortious liability relating to the duty of care are extended to expect a greater degree of care from a person who undertakes a profession which not only requires special skill but also involves the fact that resultant damage caused by a breach of duty on the part of the professional would be so great as to reasonably expect him to exercise more care than that exercised by the ordinary employee who performs less responsible functions. This rationale has so far been virtually unanimous: that one single instance of irresponsible conduct which could cause serious damage would justify stringent legal measures being imposed on the professional.

The position of the pilot in command of an aircraft therefore seems to be governed by the application of three presumptions: (a) the special skill and expertise the pilot is presumed to possess, (b) the enhanced duty of care expected of the pilot in view of such special skill and expertise; and (c) the magnitude of the damage that may be caused in the eventuality of a breach of the duty of care by the pilot. These three principles are no doubt inextricably connected to one another in that, in a high-risk profession such as that of the pilot of an aircraft, the risks of flying are significant and require the special skills and expertise that a pilot not only possesses but should also use to preclude any eventuality of danger. Indeed, there is strong opinion that it is arguable that a duty would be cast on the employer to remove the pilot at the first clear sign of inefficiency.[22]

Cases on Negligence

In interpreting the rudiments of liability for negligence, judicial decisions have maintained that there is no liability for negligence unless in a particular instance a legal duty is owed by the defendant to the plaintiff, such duty to be one which is owed to the plaintiff himself and to no other.[23] The standard of conduct of the defendant which is required by the common law is that of the reasonable man.[24] However, courts have recognized that in exceptional circumstances a person may hold himself out as possessing a special skill or believing on reasonable grounds that he possesses the required skill to perform his duties.[25]

If such person, having held himself out to claim such special skills, does not possess such, or if he exhibits conduct showing lack of such skills, he will be subjected to the application of the maxim *imperitia culpae adnumeratur*. The maxim requires professional conduct of a higher degree than that expected of the reasonable man. McNair J states:

> the test is the standard of the ordinary skilled man exercising and professing to have that special skill. A man need not possess the highest expert skill at the risk of being found negligent. It is well established law that it is sufficient if he exercises the ordinary skill of an ordinary competent man exercising that particular art.[26]

The 'ordinary skill' approach adopted in instances where such professionals as doctors, surgeons, chemists and other similar categories have appeared as defendants has not been accepted in its entirety by the courts in cases concerning negligence of the pilot. While the degree of care required of the pilot has been interpreted to be more a question of fact to be decided bv the jury,[27] the courts have gone so far as to hold that to establish negligence of the pilot the plaintiff would have to present clear evidence of what exactly happened in the aircraft at the time of the alleged negligence of the pilot.[28] However, if facts are clear and need no elucidation, the plaintiff need not further enlighten the court on the circumstance of the case[29] as it can be judged: 'What was done by the pilot that he ought not to have done, what was left undone by him that he ought to have done.'[30] However, if the plaintiff is unable to plead clear evidence in instances of ambiguity, even persuasive circumstantial evidence would suffice.[31]

Taylor v. *Alidair Ltd*[32] is perhaps the most important decision which sets out the principles of liability for negligence of the pilot. In this case, an employment appeal tribunal which examined the appeal of a company which suspended a pilot from flying who had successfully argued against his suspension at an industrial tribunal held that one failure to maintain the proper standard of professional expertise expected of an aircraft commander could bring about a major disaster. Such risk, it was held, was so great that a pilot had to exercise the highest standards of care and skill to ensure the safety of his aircraft, its passengers and property.

Taylor's case, which concerned the hard landing of an aircraft by the pilot, was one which the appeal tribunal found to contain clear facts which enabled the tribunal to assess the conduct of the pilot. The pilot had, as a result of unskilled handling, hit the runway in a way that it bounced off and could, at that moment, have landed in the proper manner had the pilot exercised his skill as expected of him. There was indeed no evidence to show that after the bounce the situation was irretrievably hopeless. It would not be incorrect to conclude that the findings of the appeal tribunal in *Taylor's* case clearly laid down the principles that (a) in the instance of an error of omission or commission by a pilot which results in some damage, negligence can be imputed to the pilot, (b) if clear facts unequivocally demonstrate the commission of the error, negligence is presumed, and (c) such negligence would incontrovertibly justify the suspension *in limine* of the pilot.

There have been many cases where, on objective criteria, negligence of the pilot has been established. Such instances as the omission to check quantities of fuel carried,[33] failure to comply with established proper procedure in pre-flight checks[34] and rules of air in flight,[35] improper handling of the controls[36] and negligence during take-off[37] have all been decided on the basis that the professional ability and skill professed by the pilot would presuppose the justifiable expectation of the pilot's exercising due standards of care. At the least, negligence would be imputed to the pilot and at the most, when facts are clear *in limine,* negligence would be presumed, which might result in the most drastic measures being taken against the pilot.

It is clear that *Taylor's* case and others of similar circumstances have taken up where provisions of conventions and local laws have left off. The stringent presumption of responsibility placed upon the pilot by written laws has been extended by the *cursus curiae* to impose a presumption of liability. So far the uniformity of this trend has been undisturbed. Perhaps the only other factor which competes with this proclivity towards uniformity is the immutable objectivity with which the pilot's actions are viewed in determining his liability.

With regard to Articles 55 and 56 of the Air Navigation Order, one can notice that implicit in these provisions is a need for reasonable care or due diligence on the part of the pilot. In the 1994 case of *R.* v. *Adomako,*[38] Lord McKay seemingly followed the earlier rationale of Lord Diplock in *R.* v. *Caldwell*[39] where His Lordship observed:

> 'Reckless' as used in the new statutory definition of the mens rea of these offences is an ordinary English word. It had not, by 1971, become a term of legal art with some limited esoteric meaning than which it bore in ordinary speech, a meaning which surely includes not only deciding to ignore a risk of harmful consequences resulting from one's acts that one has recognized as existing, but also failing to give any thought to whether or not there is any such risk in circumstances where, if any thought were given to the matter, it would be obvious if there was.[40]

Although the interpretation given by Lord Diplock in the *Caldwell* case has been followed in later cases, to the effect that recklessness would cover both an attendant disregard of the reasonable and probable consequences of one's act by a person who professes special skill, such as a pilot, and a negligent act by a 'reasonable man', the offences envisaged in Articles 55 and 56 of the Air Navigation Act do not necessarily need 'recklessness' as an element for culpability of the pilot. Mere negligence is sufficient, on the ground that the pilot does not always have to be grossly negligent or reckless to be held liable under the Act. To support this premise, there is scholarly opinion[41] that both recklessness and negligence involve a common inability or failure on the part of the miscreant to comply with objective conduct. The following definition, which brings negligence on a par with recklessness for the purpose of finding a person liable, is relevant to ascertaining possible future judicial attitudes towards the determination of negligence of the airline pilot:

> Negligence is conduct which departs from the standard to be expected of a reasonable man. This is not to say that a person's state of mind is always irrelevant when negligence is in issue. He may, for example, have special knowledge which an ordinary person would not possess. The question then is, whether a reasonable man, with that knowledge, would have acted as he did.[42]

It would appear from this emergent trend that the contentious *November Oscar* case of 1991,[43] which was decided on the recklessness of the pilot, may now be viewed within the parameters of negligence as well. The case involved the conduct of a pilot who, while attempting to make a category II landing in diminished visibility at London Heathrow Airport, made a deviation from the centre line of landing, necessitating a turn around which took the plane just five feet higher than the top of a nearby hotel. The reasoning of the jury involved the decision making of the captain, and whether the decision taken was timely and appropriate and whether the captain had acted in an appropriate manner in taking the plane around for a second landing attempt.

Substance Abuse and Crew Communication

Substance abuse by airline crew, whether pilots or cabin attendants, may also contribute to one of the most critical aspects of flight safety: crew communication. On 27 March 1998, the United States Food and Drug Administration approved the use of Viagra (Sildenafil Citrate) as an oral medication for the treatment of male impotency. Viagra, the first known medication of its kind, can be obtained only by prescription. It acts by enhancing the effect of nitric oxide in the human body (which is released in response to sexual stimulation) thereby relaxing smooth muscle, which in turn increases blood flow to certain areas of the male genitalia, facilitating enhanced ability of the male to perform sexual intercourse.

If abused (or used in excess), Viagra can cause dangerous side-effects such as increased sensitivity of the eyes to light and blurred vision, headaches and lowering of the blood pressure, all of which could result in seriously endangering the safety of an aircraft if they affect the pilot. The Federal Aviation Administration (FAA) of the United States permits flight crew members to use Viagra, provided they do not use the medication less than six hours before they commence flight duty.[44] The Administration further requires that airline pilots strictly adhere to the manufacturers' dosage recommendations, which is 50 mg, to be taken one to four hours prior to sexual activity, and not more than once a day.[45]

Viagra is by no means the only medication which comes with conditions attached. The FAA does not approve the use of the antihistamine Zystec (while approving the use of Sudafed, Seldane, Hismanal, Clariton and Allegra) and approves treatment with desensitization injections (allergy shots). Also approved by the FAA are certain antacids/stomach medications, antibiotics, certain antidepressants and psychoactive medications, anti-hypertension medications which reduce blood pressure, asthma medication, cholesterol medications and other medications calculated to reduce cholesterol, and chemotherapy. The FAA also approves hypoglaemic and diabetic medications and certain herbal treatments.[46]

The advent of Viagra once again brings into focus the issue of substance abuse at the workplace in civil aviation, with particular emphasis on emergent issues of negligence of the airline pilot, the aviation professional who admittedly performs the most responsible function in civil aviation. The profession of aeronautics, particularly relating to the piloting of aircraft, remains one of the most responsible, particularly in the context of the many lives that are entrusted to the airline pilot at any given time. The realization that pilots should be fit and well to perform their professional duties has gradually evolved, from the initial requirement of a medical certificate issued according to the standards laid down by the International Civil Aviation Organization (ICAO) to a ground breaking concept introduced in 1982 by cardiologist, Professor Hugh Turnstall-Pedoe, who, while working at Ninewalls Hospital in Dundee, suggested that the health of pilots should be assessed the same way as engines are assessed by engineers.[47] One of the measures suggested was the permanent requirement of having a co-pilot in the cockpit. The hypothesis submitted in support of this requirement was that, if an average flight lasted 60 minutes and the critical take-off and landing phases are taken as the first and last three minutes of a flight, having a second pilot reduces the risk of incapacitation of the first pilot causing a fatal accident by a thousandfold.[48]

There is no doubt that cabin crew form an integral part of commercial aviation, and they should also come under universal training methods and codes of conduct, as do the pilots, mechanics, aeronautical engineers and other professionals who are involved with the successful operation of a commercial flight. There is a compelling need for the international aviation community to be the subject of a serious study relating to the feasibility of introducing a unified system of rules relating to the conduct of cabin crew, which could, inter alia, include principles of protection of cabin crew and provide for compensation in case of injury. After all, they are the only ones who deal with the 'human factor' of a flight, which could be most unpredictable at the best of times.

The lack of attention paid by the aviation community to the importance of the flight attendant's role in a commercial flight has led to recurring instances of breakdown of communication between cabin crew and technical crew. Inevitably, this anomaly may pose serious problems in the area of air carrier liability. It is heartening to note, however, that there is now a growing awareness of the status of the flight attendant in commercial aviation. For instance, in 1994, the United States officially recognized that flight attendants have demonstrated a critical role in the safety of passengers, by limiting the length of their duty times and introducing mandatory rest periods under federal law. Under FAA regulations, flight attendants must be given at least nine hours' rest for duty periods lasting up to 14 hours in any 24 hour period. For longer periods, the FAA prescribes specific rest periods and larger cabin crews. The rules also give flight attendants a full 24 hours of rest for every seven calendar days. Federal law had previously mandated minimum rest periods for air traffic controllers and technical crew.[49]

There have been innumerable complaints in the past by technical crews (pilots and flight engineers) relating to unacceptable cabin crew conduct that has allegedly jeopardized flight safety. A commentary published in March 1995 reported that, during a hectic night approach to a busy airport in the United States, a flight attendant had opened the door to the flight deck to remove dinner trays, flooding the cockpit with light and distracting the flight crew. The flight attendant had refused the captain's earlier request to bring meals forward early in the flight, and the food was brought in only after the descent had begun.[50] In his report, the captain had written that 'the approach was unsafe' and described a serious breakdown in communication between the cockpit crew and the cabin crew. Confirming a near miss with a smaller aircraft which was claimed by the captain to have occurred as a result of the commotion caused by the unfortunate entry of the flight attendant in the cockpit, the captain had gone on to record:

> The captain is helpless to plan the approach any more. The flight attendants ignore requests and directions from the captain. They work for the marketing department and don't hesitate to tell pilots they don't have to listen to them. On this flight, the flight attendant's blatant disregard of the captain's request resulted in an unsafe approach. If the flight attendant had listened to the captain's request to bring meals up, she would not have been in the cockpit at low altitude causing a distraction.[51]

There have also been instances where cabin crew members have been instrumental in causing involuntary injury to passengers. One such instance was when a passenger on board an American Airlines flight from Italy to Chicago was injured when a heavy tote bag fell on her from the overhead bin in the aircraft. This injury had been caused as a result of the flight attendant opening the overhead bin to retrieve a pillow at the request of the passenger. One of the considerations the court had to decide upon was the plaintiff's contention that American Airlines had failed to provide adequate instructions to its crew on the operation of aircraft apparatus.[52]

Clearly, the conduct of cabin crew members during the course of their employment will affect two classes of persons: passengers in the cabin and technical crew in the cockpit. In both instances, any adverse conduct on the part of cabin crew which would in turn result in claims for damages would affect the employer airline adversely, bringing to bear the intrinsic and incontrovertible link between the airline and its cabin crew members. Also any liability that would arise out of the conduct of cabin crew would involve air carrier liability on principles of vicarious liability at tort.

Whatever be the relationship between the flight attendant and passenger, on the one hand, and flight attendant and pilot, on the other, the relationships have a common denominator. With regard to accidents caused as a direct or indirect result of the flight attendant's conduct – be it an injury to a passenger or an aircraft accident precipitated by the conduct of the flight attendant affecting pilot performance – the legal consequences of air carrier liability would revolve round whether the act of the flight attendant or the pilot, as the case may be, was tantamount to wilful misconduct on the part of the carrier.

Notes

1 Consequent to the enactment in the United Kingdom of the Criminal Justice Act of 1982, section 37 of the Act provides that maximum fines that may be imposed by a magistrate's court are fixed by and with reference to standard scales. The intent of this provision is to accord some flexibility to the Home Secretary to vary the scales in accordance with currency fluctuations.

2 R.S. Jensen and R.A. Benel (1977), *Judgment Evaluation and Instruction in Civil Pilot Training* (Tech. Rep. No. FAA-RD-78-24), Springfield, VA: National Technical Information Service. See also Stephen R. Murray (1997), 'Deliberate Decision Making by Aircraft Pilots: A Simple Reminder to Avoid Decision Making Under Panic', *The International Journal of Aviation Psychology*, 7(1), 84.
3 A. Diehl (1990), *The Effectiveness of Aeronautical Decision Making Training, Proceedings of the 34th Meeting of the Human Factors Society*, Santa Monica, CA: The Human Factors Society.
4 Convention on International Civil Aviation, signed on 7 December 1944 (Chicago Convention). See ICAO Doc. 7300/7, 7th edn, 1997.
5 See Annex 6 to the Convention on International Civil Aviation signed in Chicago on 7 December 1944 (*supra*, n.4), para. 4.5.1. Popularly called the Chicago Convention, this Convention sets out universal principles governing international civil aviation; it came into effect on 4 April 1947.
6 See The British Air Navigation Order (1985) Article 32, which states, inter alia: 'The Commander of an aircraft registered in the United Kingdom shall satisfy himself before the aircraft takes off … that the flight can safely be made, taking into account the latest information available as to the route and aerodromes to be used, the weather reports and forecasts available and any alternative course of action which can be adopted in case the flight cannot be completed as planned.' See also, generally, U.S. Federal Aviation Regulations FAR 91.3(a), Australian Air Navigation Regulations, Regulation 219 and New Zealand Civil Aviation Regulations (1953), Regulation 59.
7 See N. Price (1976), *Pilot Error*, New York: Random, pp.238–9. See also generally the findings of the New Zealand Royal Commission of Inquiry into the 1979 Buenos Aires, Mt. Erebus DCIO Disaster.
8 See N.M. Matte (1875), *The International Legal Status of Aircraft Commander*, p.34. See also Videla Escalada (1979), *Aeronautical Law*, pp.210–11; S.M. Speiser and C.F. Krause (1978), *Aviation Tort Law*, Vol. 1, New York: Random, 473.
9 A.J. Burridge (1977), 'The Dismissal of a Pilot for Poor Airmanship – The Employer's Point of View', *Aeronautical Journal*, May, 206.
10 See H.A. Hopkins (1977), 'The Dismissal of a Pilot for Poor Airmanship', *Aeronautical Journal*, May, 203. See also, generally, Videla Escalada, (*supra*, n.8), p.210; A. Van Wijk (1975–6), 'Responsibilities of Airline Pilots', *Air Law*, 302.
11 See Matte (*supra*, n.8), p.34.
12 N.D. Price (1991), *Essential Law for Pilots and their Crew*, pp.72–3. See also, generally, P.J. Kolczvnski (1985), 'The Criminal Liability of Aviators and Related Issues of Mixed Criminal – Civil Litigation: A venture in the Twilight Zone', *Journal of Air Law & Commerce*, 51 (1), 4.
13 See, generally, Shawcross and Beaumont, *Air Law*, 4th edn, reissue, V/86–V/90. The concept of negligence will be discussed at some length later in this chapter.
14 See M. Edwards (1977), 'The Continued Employment of Pilots Involved in Incidents or Accidents: The Operator's Responsibilities and Liabilities', *Aeronautical Journal*, May, 211.
15 Burridge (*supra*, n.9), 208.
16 See *M'Allister (Donoghue)* v. *Stevenson*, 1932 AC 562.
17 *Bolam* v. *Friern Hospital Alanagement Committee* (1957) 2 All ER 118 at 121. See also *Phillips* v. *Whiteley* (1938) 1 KB 566 at 570.
18 *The Bywell Castle* (1879) 4 P.D. 219 at 226.
19 (1976) IRLR 420.
20 Ibid., 423. See also generally, *Australian National Airlines Commission* v. *The Commonwealth of Australia and Canadian Pacific Airlines* (1974–75) 132 CLR 582.
21 See (1978) IRLR 82 CA; *Air Law*, 1978, p.49.
22 See Shawcross and Beaumont, (*supra*, n.13), V/84.

23 See *Palsgraf* v. *Long Island R.R. Co* (1928) 284 N.Y. 339. See also *Le Lievre* v. *Gould* (1893) 1 QB 491; *Bourhill* v. *Young* (1943) AC 92.
24 See *Vaughan* v. *Menlove* (1837) 3 Bing. N.C. 468.
25 See *Daly* v. *Liverpool Corporation* (1939) 2 All ER 142 at 144; *Whiteford* v. *Hunter* (1950) W.N. 533; *Randall* v. *Tarrant* (1955) 1 WLR 255 at 259; *Bolam* v. *Friern Hospital Management Committee* (1957) 2 All ER 118 at 120; *Wells* v. *Cooper* (1958) 2 QB 265.
26 See *Bolam* v. *Friern Hospital Management Committee* (1957) 2 All ER 118 at 121. See also, generally, *Phillips* v. *William Whiteley Ltd.* (1938) 1 KB 566 at 569.
27 *Steinbock* v. *Schiewe*, 330 F. 2d 510 (1964) at 512.
28 *United States* v. *Vigderman*, 194 F. 2d 977, affirmed on appeal in *Vigderman v United States*, 175 F. Supp. 802 at 807.
29 *Vigderman* v. *United States* (*supra*, n.28), 807–8.
30 Ibid., 810.
31 Ibid.
32 *Supra* (n.19).
33 *Steinbock* v. *Schiewe* (*supra*, n.27); also *Keenan* v. *Martin*, 13 Avi 18, 037 (N.Y. 1975).
34 *Union Trust Co* v. *Eastern Airlines*, 211 F. 2d 62.
35 *Herrick and Olsen* v. *Curtiss Flving Service Inc.* (I 932) US Av 110 (NY).
36 See *Nichols* v. *Jones*, 260 So 2d 748 (La. 1972). See also *Israel* v. *U.S.*, 247 F. 2d 426 (2nd Circ., 1957), *Robart* v. *Brehmer*, 207 P. 2d 898 (Cal. 19491).
37 *Hovden* v. *Boyle*, 254 P. 2d 813 (Kan., 1953).
38 (1994) 3 All ER 79.
39 (1981) 1 All ER 961.
40 Ibid., 966.
41 See J.C. Smith and Brian Hogan (1992), *Criminal Law*, 7th edn, p.92.
42 Ibid.
43 For a detailed account of the case, see, Mervyn E. Bennun (1995–6), 'Prosecuting Professional Pilots in the United Kingdom after *November Oscar*: Reflections in the Law and Policy', *Journal of Air Law and Commerce*, 341.
44 See W. Keith Martin (1998), 'Impotence, Gallstones, EKGs and Sleep Apnea', *Airline Pilot*, May, p.5.
45 Ibid.
46 For a detailed discussion of FAA-approved medication for pilots, see W. Keith Martin (1997), 'What Can I Take and Still Fly?', *Airline Pilot*, June/July, pp.14–16.
47 Tony Evans (1995), 'How Fit is the Pilot, Doctor?', *Focus on Commercial Aviation Safety*, 18, Spring, 8.
48 Ibid., 9.
49 *Air Letter*, no. 13,060, Wednesday 17 August 1994, p.1.
50 Rebecca D. Chute (1995), 'On a Collision Course', *Air Line Pilot*, March, p.20.
51 Ibid.
52 *Pasinato* v. *American Airlines, Inc.*, No. 93 C 1510, 1994 Westlaw 171522 (N.D. ILL. 2 May 1994). For a more detailed report and analysis of this case, see *Lloyd's Aviation Law*, 13(11), 1 June 1994, pp.4–5.

16 Unruly Passengers

Introduction

When 'Bala', an intoxicated passenger on board a Delta Airlines flight, made numerous unwanted and unsolicited verbal and physical advances to Stephania Tsevas who was seated next to him, Bala's romantic overtures became so annoying to Stephania that the cabin attendants had to relocate Bala elsewhere in the aircraft cabin. Later, when Stephania and her husband sued the airline for damages[1] sustained by her as a result of sexual assault by Bala, it was revealed that Bala had been served with wine and alcoholic beverages to the point that he became intoxicated. The plaintiff had repeatedly brought Bala's inebriated state to the attention of the cabin attendants before she had suffered Bala's advances.

The ordeal Stephania Tsevas suffered is by no means an isolated one in present-day airline travel. In the same year, a passenger on board a Virgin Atlantic Airways flight terrorized passengers almost throughout the nine-hour flight he was on from Orlando in the United States to Manchester in the United Kingdom. The offender had been drinking for four hours prior to embarkation and was clearly not in a fit state to undertake travel in a locked space for a sustained length of time. Similar instances recorded describe a cabin attendant being stabbed by a passenger on board a KLM flight from Bangkok to Amsterdam; the cabin of a United Airlines flight being defecated upon by a passenger on refusal of service of alcohol by the cabin staff; and the assault on a cabin attendant by a passenger who had kicked her in the small of her back when she had asked her son to stop smoking.[2]

Unruly passengers in aircraft are not always habitual natural undesirables and convicts; it is generally thought that the majority of incidents take place in the first class cabin.[3] The growth rate of the problem is alarming, and one study suggests that an estimate taken recently reflects an increase of 400 per cent since 1995.[4] A further intriguing fact is that there have been instances where passengers who, for all purposes, are rational respectable persons, have blown up in the face of a mere trifle such as the refusal from the airline to upgrade the passenger to first class. Offensive conduct on board aircraft is not unlike 'road rage', where a respectable person, driving a vehicle on a highway, could react on the spur of the moment with violence. On board an aircraft, as in a motor vehicle, people have to react to situations in a confined space. As Lee Fjelstad analysed: 'The passengers are out of touch with their businesses, their normal surroundings. They are out of sync, there is nothing comfortable around them. They are sitting next to people they don't know or don't like, with habits they may not approve of.'[5]

This chapter will trace the extent to which the world community is aware of the problem, address its legal implications at international law and suggest action to be taken both by states and by airlines to combat the problem.

Regulatory Measures

At the 32nd Session of the Assembly of the International Civil Aviation Organization, held in Montreal from 22 September to 2 October 1998, the Legal Commission of the Assembly recognized that the existing international conventions relating to the offences on board aircraft serve primarily to prevent and prosecute acts of hijacking, sabotage and terrorist attacks endangering the safety of international civil aviation. However, certain lesser types of offences committed on board aircraft, such as assault, battery or alcohol-related riotous behaviour, have become a growing concern to the international aviation community because of their increasing frequency and lack of prosecution. The Commission noted that, in reviewing this matter, the ICAO Council had, on 3 June 1996, approved the inclusion of the subject in the General Work Programme of the Legal Committee. Consequently, the 30th Session of the Legal Committee had recommended to the Council that a working group be established if the Council deemed this appropriate. During its 151st Session, the Council decided on 6 June 1997 that this item be given the fifth priority in the General Work Programme of the Legal Committee and that a Secretariat Study Group be established for this item.

At the same session of the Assembly, the International Air Transport Association (IATA),[6] presented a working paper for discussion,[7] which presented two general causes as leading to unruly conduct: (a) the widespread banning of smoking on board, which frustrate smokers and provokes petulance; and (b) the intake of alcohol by passengers both immediately before the flight and on board. In its working paper, IATA addressed the issue of drafting a new international treaty to deal with the issue of unruly passengers, and concluded that a more efficient measure to combat the problem would be for ICAO to urge member states to enact stringent legislation within their territories to permit prompt and effective intervention in apprehending and prosecuting offenders who arrive immediately after commission of an offence on board an aircraft.

The International Transport Workers' Federation (ITWF) presented its own paper[8] at the ICAO Assembly, calling offences committed by unruly passengers 'acts which, whether or not they are offences, may or do jeopardise safety of the aircraft or of persons or property therein or which jeopardise good order and discipline on board'.[9] The ITWF, which has a membership of over 170 000 cabin crew and 85 000 check-in staff and several thousands of security workers at airports around the world, emphasized to the Assembly that over and above the injuries caused to cabin crew, check-in and security staff by unruly passengers, the most serious element of the issue was the jeopardizing of the safety of an entire flight. In this context the Federation identified the following areas as worthy of attention and made the recommendations appearing below.

1 Passenger management and operating procedures. This involves the process of dealing with airline passengers: pre-boarding, on board the aircraft and at disembarkation. Guidance and recommendations are required for measures and procedures aimed at dealing with incidents or preventing them occurring, such as denied boarding procedures, passenger information policies, alcohol policies, special training for airport and airline personnel (for example, training in conflict avoidance, passenger restraint, collection of evidence) and crew–police liaison procedures.
2 Facilitation of legal and judicial measures. Guidance and recommendations are required for putting into place laws which ensure that the national jurisdiction of the country of disembarkation applies to all passengers on all flights entering that country, providing appropriate police powers (and resources) at airports, and appropriate judicial and police responses to all degrees of offense which violate the Tokyo Convention. A number of countries, including the United States and the United Kingdom, have already put in place laws intended to implement the Convention as applied to cases of disorderly passenger behaviour.
3 Improvements to the air travel environment and experience. This should address the wider environment of air transport services which contribute to the increase in such incidents. Guidance and recommendations are required to identify and address factors which cause passenger stress and/or aggression, such as

overbooked flights, delayed flights, lack of passenger information, overcrowded aircraft seating, aircraft design, the understaffing of airport and airline services, as well as unmet passenger expectations.

The ITWA endorsed IATA's call for states to adopt national laws which ensure them adequate legislative and judicial powers to deal with an offender in their territories. In a similar manner to the IATA conclusion, the ITWA called for appropriate ICAO guidelines for states, to be developed through a study group of experts.

At its 104th Meeting of Directors General of Civil Aviation, held in Paris on 16–17 December 1998, the European Civil Aviation Conference (ECAC) addressed the issue of legal action to be taken with regard to unruly passengers[10] and decided that an expert be nominated from the United Kingdom on behalf of ECAC, to participate in the work of the ICAO Study Group to be established.

ICAO has already responded to the various views from the above international organizations and its 32nd Assembly, by having the first meeting of the ICAO Secretariat Study Group on Unruly Passengers in Montreal on 25–7 January 1999. At this meeting, the Group discussed the various options available to the international community to address the problem. The work of the Group is continuing.

Work of ICAO

ICAO's work on the issue of unlawful acts committed on board aircraft, though not related explicitly to the conduct of unruly passengers, goes back to 1950, when the Legal Committee of ICAO, upon a proposal from the Mexican Representative on ICAO Council for study of the legal status of airports, referred the subject to the ad hoc Sub-Committee established by the Legal Committee.[11] After a survey had been made of all the problems relating to legal status of aircraft, it was decided by the Committee that the best course would be to confine the work to a detailed examination of some particularly important matters, namely crimes and offences committed on board aircraft, jurisdiction relating to such crimes and the resolution of jurisdictional conflicts. The Sub-Committee thought that resolving these problems was of vital importance for the following reasons:[12]

1 One characteristic of aviation is that aircraft fly over the high seas or over seas having no territorial sovereign. While national laws of some states confer jurisdiction on their courts to try offences committed on aircraft during such flights, this was not the case in others, and there was no internationally agreed system which

would coordinate the exercise of national jurisdiction in such cases. Further, with the high speed of modern aircraft and having regard to the great altitudes at which they fly as well as other factors, such as meteorological conditions and, in certain parts of the world, the fact that several states may be overflown by aircraft within a small space of time, there could be occasions when it would be impossible to establish the territory in which the aircraft was at the time a crime was committed on board. There was, therefore, the possibility that in such a case, and in the absence of an internationally recognized system with regard to exercise of national jurisdiction, the offender might go unpunished.

2 National jurisdictions in respect of criminal acts are based on criteria which are not uniform; for example, on nationality of the offender, or nationality of the victim, on the locality where the offence was committed, or on nationality of the aircraft on which the crime occurred. Thus several states may claim jurisdiction over the same offence committed on board aircraft, in certain cases. Such conflict of jurisdictions could be avoided only by international agreement.

3 The possibility that the same offence may be triable in different states might result in the offender being punished more than once for the same offence. This undesirable possibility could be avoided by a suitable provision in the Convention.

After sustained deliberation and contradiction, the Sub-Committee on Legal Status of Aircraft produced a draft convention which was submitted to the Legal Committee on 9 September 1958.[13] The Legal Committee in turn considered the draft convention at its 12th Session held in Munich in 1959,[14] undertaking a substantial revision of the draft. The revised text was subsequently submitted to the ICAO Council, who in turn submitted the draft to member states and various international organizations for their comments. A new sub-committee was formed in 1961 to further review the issue. Its report was studied by the Legal Committee in its 14th Session, held in Rome in 1962. A final text of a convention was drawn up at this meeting and communicated to member states with a view to convening a diplomatic conference in Tokyo with a long-term prospect of adopting a convention on aerial rights. This convention[15] was signed in Tokyo on 14 September 1963 by the representatives of 49 ICAO member states, and entered into force after six years, on 4 December 1969.[16] This slow process of ratification of the convention was by no means due to the ineptitude of the convention, as has been claimed,[17] but was solely due to the fact that the convention was drafted prior to the series of hijackings in the late 1960s and was not implemented with due dispatch by most states. Another reason for the delayed process was the complicated legal and political issues facing many countries at the time of the adoption of the Convention.[18] A significant feature of the Tokyo Convention is that although at first states were slow in acceding to or ratifying it, 80 states did ratify it within one year, presumably in response to the spate of hijackings that occurred during that period.

The Tokyo Convention

The main purpose of the Tokyo Convention was to secure the collaboration of states in restraining terrorist activity – hijacking in particular – directed at air transport. It has therefore been said that 'The first action taken by the international community to combat hijacking was the Tokyo Convention 1963. This Convention was originally designed to solve the problem of the commission of crimes on board aircraft while in flight where for any number of reasons the criminal might escape punishment.'[19] The focus on hijacking notwithstanding, the convention was a general charter of rights of states on any crime or offence committed on board aircraft.

The objectives of the Tokyo Convention may be divided into four principal areas.

1 The convention makes it clear that the state of registration of the aircraft has the authority to apply its laws. From the standpoint of states such as the United States, this is probably the most important aspect of the convention, since it accords international recognition to the exercise of extraterritorial jurisdiction under the circumstances contemplated in the convention.
2 The convention provides the aircraft commander with the necessary authority to deal with persons who have committed, or are about to commit, a crime or an act jeopardizing safety on board his aircraft through use of reasonable force when required, and without fear of subsequent retaliation through civil suit or otherwise.
3 The convention delineates the duties and responsibilities of the contracting state in which an aircraft lands after the commission of a crime on board, including its authority over, and responsibilities to, any offenders that may be either disembarked within the territory of that state or delivered to its authorities.
4 The crime of 'hijacking' has been addressed in some depth.[20]

The convention applies to any act that is an offence under the penal laws of a contracting state, as well as to acts which, whether or not they are offences, may jeopardize safety, good order and discipline on board. The convention thus does not define the offence at the international level, nor does it explicitly explain the nature of the offence. Alona E. Evans has observed: 'The offence is not made a crime under international law; its definition is to be determined by the municipal laws of the contracting state.'[21] Admittedly, there are some limitations placed upon the scope of the application of the convention. Firstly, the convention excluded from its operation aircraft used in military, customs or police services. It should be noted that reference is not made in the convention to 'State aircraft', as mentioned in Article 3 of the Chicago Convention, which does not apply to such aircraft. This difference in terminology is explained by the fact that state aircraft provide air transport that is usually provided by civil aircraft and civil transport in some cases. Secondly, offences against penal laws of a political nature or those based on racial or religious discrimination are not covered by the convention except to the extent that the convention addressed such acts which jeopardize safety or good order and discipline on board. The reason for excluding those offences from the scope of the convention could be attributed to the following view:

> Penal laws forbidding various forms of racial and religious discrimination take many and varied forms, and the views of the Courts of the Contracting States may differ on the issue of whether one or the other is within or without the Convention. Even more divergence of view can be expected in decisions which involve the question of whether a particular offence is of a 'political nature'.[22]

Although the convention does not define the offence of hijacking or any offence committed by an unruly passenger, Article 11 specifies the circumstances that would constitute such offence as 'When a person on board has unlawfully committed by force or threat thereof an act of interference, seizure or other wrongful exercise of control of an aircraft in flight or such an act is bound to be committed'. According to this definition, an offence committed by an unruly passenger as a result of his disreputable conduct could be classified as an act of interference. Therefore when such an offence is committed in the above manner, the state in which the aircraft lands has two obligations which it must satisfy according to the terms of the convention. The first obligation is that the landing state 'shall take all appropriate measures to restore control of the aircraft to its lawful commander or to preserve control of the aircraft and shall return the aircraft and its cargo to the person lawfully entitled to possession'.

R.P. Boyle emphasized the above contention in his view on hijacking and the restoration of the aircraft to the pilot:

> The obligation assumed by a State under the Tokyo Convention with respect to the disposition of the hijacker *or other offender* … is to take all appropriate measures to restore control of the aircraft to its lawful commander and to permit the passengers and crew to continue their journey as soon as practicable and to return the aircraft and cargo to persons lawfully entitled.[23] (Original emphasis)

This view could equally apply to any other offence calculated to endanger the safety of an aircraft.

Powers Given to the Aircraft Commander and Others in Order to Combat Offences on Board

The convention gives wide powers to the aircraft commander to control an offence committed on board the aircraft which he commands. Article 6 enables the aircraft commander to use reasonable measures, including restraint, to protect the safety of the aircraft, and maintain good order and discipline, when he has a reasonable ground to believe that a person has committed an offence contemplated in Article 1(1): (a) offences against penal laws; (b) acts which, whether or not they are offences, may jeopardize the safety of the aircraft or of persons or property therein or which jeopardize good order and discipline on board.

An interesting observation to be made in respect to (a) above is that, according to the provision, the aircraft commander will have the power to take measures and restrain a passenger even if his act did not amount to jeopardizing the safety of the aircraft or the person or the property therein. In addition, (b) directly leads to an analogous situation of an offensive act perpetrated by an unruly passenger. If, for example, the conduct of two or more passengers, while on board the aircraft, appear to be leading to the commission of some illegal act (the conduct of a drunken sporting team on board would be a good example), then, according to (a) above, the commander can restrain them on the suspicion that they are conspiring to commit an act which may jeopardize good order and discipline on board. This seems to be totally consistent with the general thrust of the convention and its principal objective, which is to ensure the maintenance of safety and good order 'on board' the aircraft.

The aircraft commander, in discharging his duties according to the convention, can require or authorize the assistance of the crew and request the assistance of passengers for that purpose. Even passengers and crew members are authorized under Article 6(2) to take reasonable preventive measures without any authorization from the aircraft commander whenever they have reasonable grounds to believe that such action is immediately necessary for safety reasons.

Although this clause is wide enough to give powers to other people beside the aircraft commander in order to tighten the measures that lead to the thwarting of acts of unlawful interference with civil aviation, some delegates at the Tokyo Conference attacked this approach on the ground that passengers normally would not be qualified to determine whether a particular act jeopardized the safety of the aircraft or persons and property therein, and, for this reason, it was unwise to give this authority to passengers.[24] However, this argument was rejected 'on the ground that this provision contemplated an emergency type of situation in which the danger to the aircraft or persons and property on board was clearly present, and in fact no special technical knowledge would be required to recognize the peril'.[25]

The powers entrusted to the commander in order to suppress any unlawful act that threatens the safety of the aircraft go as far as requiring the disembarking of any person (who commits any of the acts referred to in Article 1(1) and discussed above) in the territory of any state in which he lands and delivering him to its competent authorities.[26] The state is under an obligation to allow the disembarkation and to take delivery of the person so apprehended by the aircraft commander, but such custody may only be continued for such time as is reasonably necessary to enable the criminal extradition proceedings (if any) to be instituted. In the meantime, the state of landing should make a preliminary enquiry into the facts and notify the state of registration of the aircraft.[27]

In any event, the commander as well as the crew members and passengers are given immunity from suits by the alleged offender against whom they acted. Article 10 expressly provides:

> Neither the aircraft commander, any member of the crew, any passenger, the owner or operator of the aircraft, nor the person on whose behalf the flight is performed shall be held responsible in any proceedings on account of the treatment undergone by the person against whom the actions were taken.

This protection was given to the aircraft commander and other persons in order to encourage them to fight the wrongful acts contemplated by the convention.

Jurisdiction to Punish the Offender

The major problem that states often face in the process of combating an offence committed on board an aircraft is the issue of jurisdiction. This is most evident in cases where the crime often takes place outside the jurisdiction of the receiving state, although in most, if not all, of the cases it could be argued that the offence is of a continuing nature. Under international law, states' jurisdiction to prosecute is founded upon two traditional concepts. First, there must exist a substantial link between the person or the act and the state claiming sovereign jurisdiction and, second, this theoretical basis must be actualized through a sovereign act, that is legislation for implementation of this theoretical act. In an act of an international nature, such as an offence committed by an unruly passenger, two or more states involved may possess jurisdiction to prosecute. As a result, jurisdictional conflicts are eminent, since two or more of those states can claim the right to prosecute and press claims against each other through diplomatic channels. In order to eliminate these conflicts, the jurisdictional rules incorporated in the Tokyo Convention were preferred. The Tokyo Convention was adopted to grant powers to states to establish jurisdiction which would be uncomplicated by diplomatic claims over criminal acts committed on board aircraft.

Jurisdiction over offences and acts committed on board appertain primarily to the state of registration of the aircraft (Article 3(1)). The adoption of this rule guarantees to the flights over the high seas the assured presence of criminal law. It provides a sound legal basis for extraterritorial exercise of criminal jurisdiction extending even to cases of flight within foreign airspace. Mendelsohn has observed:

> As a matter of international law, therefore, any crime aboard an international carrier, no matter where, by or against whom it is committed, can be punished by at least one sovereign – the State of registration of the carrier. All doubts are removed on the question whether the flag will henceforth follow the aircraft as it traditionally has followed a vessel.[28]

Article 3(2) of the Convention provides: 'Each Contracting State shall take measures as may be necessary to establish its jurisdiction as State of registration over offenses committed on board aircraft registered in such State.' It is clear that the fundamental objective of this sub-paragraph was to make the act of combating an offence committed in an aircraft an international issue in which all states must take part when need arises.

Article 3(3) went further to give more grounds of jurisdiction in order to eliminate the gravity of the obstacles that hinder the prosecution of offenders. It provides that the convention does not exclude criminal jurisdiction exercised in accordance with the national law. Mendelsohn has commented on this sub-paragraph:

> Its objectives are (a) to retain all existing jurisdiction presently asserted by the various States; (b) to enable them to enact further legislation providing for even more extensive jurisdiction; and most

> important, (c) to require the State of registration to extend at least some of its criminal laws to its aircraft and to provide an internationally accepted basis for the application and enforcement of these laws.[29]

The convention also authorizes a contracting state which is not a state of registration to intervene in the case of an aircraft in flight in five cases in which the offence (a) has an effect on the territory of state; (b) has been committed by or against a national or permanent resident of state; (c) is against the security of the state; (d) consists of a breach of any rules or regulations relating to the flight or manoeuvre of aircraft in force in such state; e) that the exercise of such jurisdiction is necessary in order to ensure the observance of any obligation of such state under a multilateral international agreement.

As regards the geographic scope of the convention for jurisdictional purposes, Article 1 provides that the convention applies in respect of acts or offences committed while the aircraft is 'in flight' or on the surface of the high seas or on another area which does not have a territorial sovereign. The term 'in flight' is defined in Article 1(3) as 'from the moment when the power is applied for the purpose of take-off until the moment when the landing run ends'. Hence attempts at the commission of offences initiated during the time the aircraft is parked or taxi-ing are not considered to be within the ambit of the convention. As a consequence, the provisions of the Tokyo Convention fell short of curbing offences against air transport facilities. This shortcoming of the Tokyo Convention, inter alia, led to the adoption of the Montreal Convention (1971), which will be discussed later in this chapter.

Powers and Duties of States

It is a basic obligation of a state to cooperate with other states in order to ensure the safety of international civil aviation. Article 11 of the Tokyo Convention, which is referred to above, provides that contracting states have certain obligations whenever a person on board an aircraft has unlawfully committed by force or threat thereof an act of interference, seizure or other wrongful exercise of control. The question of whether a particular act is lawful or unlawful is to be judged by the law of the state of registration of the aircraft or the law of the state in whose airspace the aircraft may be in flight. Paragraph 1 of Article 11 imposes on all the contracting states the obligation to take appropriate measures to restore or to preserve the aircraft commander's control of the aircraft. The words 'appropriate measures' are intended to mean only those things which it is feasible for a contracting state to do and also only those which it is lawful for a contracting state to do. Thus a contracting state which is situated thousands of miles away from the scene of the offence is not under any obligation to take any action, because it would not be feasible for it do so.

Article 12 imposes another obligation on each contracting state. This Article is a corollary to Articles 6 and 8 of the Convention. The latter two Articles authorize the aircraft commander to disembark any person who has committed, or is about to commit, an act of the type described in Article 1 of the convention. Article 12 obliges a contracting state to allow the commander of an aircraft registered in another contracting state to disembark the alleged offender. Article 12 provides: 'Any Contracting State shall allow the commander of an aircraft registered in another contracting state to disembark any person pursuant to Article 8, paragraph 1.' Thus it is clear that the obligation of a contracting state to permit disembarkation of a hijacker, at the request of the aircraft commander, is an unqualified obligation.

Article 13 of the convention deals with the obligation of a contracting state to take delivery of a person from the aircraft commander. This provision should be contrasted with the authority of the aircraft commander to disembark. The obligation of the contracting state under this Article is a corollary to the authority given to the aircraft commander under Articles 6, 7 and 9. Paragraph 1 of Article 13 states the primary unqualified obligation of each contracting state to 'take delivery'. Paragraph 2 addresses the obligation of a contracting state, having taken delivery, to take custody. It provides that the contracting state is under an obligation to take 'custody' only if it is satisfied that the circumstances warrant such action. Thus the state is left free to judge for itself whether the act is of such a nature as to warrant such action on its part and whether it would be consistent with its law since, under paragraph 2, any such custody is to be affected only pursuant to the law of the state taking custody. However, such custody may only be continued for that period of time which is reasonably necessary to enable criminal proceedings to be brought by the state taking custody, or for extradition proceedings to be instituted by another interested or affected state. On the other hand, any person taken into custody must be given assistance in communicating immediately with the nearest appropriate representative of the state of which he is a national (Article 13(3)).

Extradition

Article 16 of the convention provides that offences committed on aircraft registered in a contracting State are to be treated, for the purpose of extradition, as if they had been not only in the place where the offence has occurred, but also in the territory of the state of registration of the aircraft. Without prejudice to this provision it is declared that 'nothing in this Convention shall be deemed to create an obligation to grant extradition'. A commentator observes:

> The Tokyo Convention does not oblige the Contracting State to punish an alleged offender upon his disembarkation or delivery. Ironically, the landing State must set him free and let him proceed to the destination of his choice as soon as is practicable if it does not wish to extradite or prosecute him. The Contracting States are obliged to extradite the offenders, if at all, only under provisions of other treaties between them.[30]

The failure to provide for a machinery of mandatory extradition if prosecution was not conducted was considered a major shortcoming of the Tokyo Convention. However, the above loopholes from which the convention suffers severely are not the only ones:

> Looking from the vantage point of today, it is obvious that the Tokyo convention left major gaps in the international legal system in attempting to cope with the scope of aircraft hijacking. There was no undertaking by anyone to make aircraft hijacking a crime under its national law, no undertaking to see to it the crime was one punishable by severe penalties and, most important, no undertaking to either submit the case for prosecution or to extradite the offender to a State which would wish to prosecute.[31]

This principle is also true of other offences committed on board aircraft.

Responsibilities of States

As has been mentioned, all states party to the convention undertake to permit disembarkation of any person when the commander considers that it is necessary to protect the safety of the flight or for the maintenance of good order and discipline on board. States also commit themselves to take delivery of any person the commander reasonably believes has committed a serious offence on board.[32] In this case, when they have taken delivery, states concerned must make an immediate inquiry into the facts of the matter and report the findings to both the state of registration and the state of which the person is a national.[33] Where the state considers the circumstances warrant such action, it shall take custodial or other measures, in accordance with its laws, to ensure that the person delivered to it remains available while the inquiry is conducted. Such measures may be continued for a reasonable time to permit criminal or extradition proceedings to be instituted when such proceedings follow from the inquiry.[34]

Although the convention is unequivocal in providing clearly that all contracting states should ensure their legal competence in respect of aircraft on their register, thus addressing jurisdictional issues with regard to crimes on board aircraft, there are a number of lapses in the convention which make it open to criticism. Firstly, the convention does not apply to 'aircraft used in military, customs or police services'.[35] This is a topical issue which requires clarity as, in modern exigencies of airlines, there are instances when civilian aircraft are called upon to carry military personnel or supplies, as much as military aircraft are sometimes deployed to execute civilian flights.[36]

Problems concerning registration, particularly when the convention insists on registration as a pivotal issue, may also change the circumstances, although commanders could be totally ignorant of the laws of the state in which the aircraft they are flying is registered. The commander may be required to determine whether a certain action on his aircraft does in fact constitute a crime and, more particularly, a serious crime. Since, at most, a commander may have some familiarity with the laws of the state of the operator, the United Kingdom[37] has elected to incorporate the terms of the convention into its domestic legislation, thereby widening its scope to cover any aircraft controlled by its own nationals.

The convention could also be improved upon in terms of chronology of the offences in that its applicability extends to the period from 'the moment when power is applied for the purpose of take-off until the moment when the landing run ends',[38] and in relation to the powers of the commander, who has authority, for the purposes of the convention, only from the time at which external doors close following embarkation to the time when doors open for disembarkation.[39] These parameters are far from satisfactory. In relation to the first, courts have been inconsistent in interpreting similar definitions of flights used in insurance policies. It has been contended that power is first applied 'for the purpose of take-off' when the aircraft first begins to move under its own power to the take-off position.[40] In relation to the second, the terms 'all its external doors' also leaves confusion worse confounded in that it makes unclear whether 'all its external doors' includes, for example, cargo or baggage hold doors, or doors giving access to such areas as the electronic compartment of the aircraft. It is not difficult to envisage circumstances in which these areas could be of significance. The main problem, however, is that the convention does not provide for the manner in which the offender should be dealt with after he has been removed from the aircraft. The somewhat poor and inadequate drafting in Articles 14 and 15 seems to suggest that it is only when the person disembarked or delivered cannot or does not wish to continue his journey that the State of landing can take action.[41] They do not offer a state any guidance as to questions arising from requests for extradition of an offender or extradition by the state's own initiation.

The convention also fails to identify the 'offenses and certain other acts committed on board' which are its subject matter as extraditable offences, and therefore all requests for extradition arising out of an offence under the convention must be dealt with under existing extradition arrangements. Even where those agreements are existing between the two states concerned, this could often lead to confusion and delay. Furthermore, in any case, many 'jeopardising' acts are unlikely to be recognized as forming a basis for extradition. A marked omission of the convention is that, while it creates and defines 'jeopardizing' acts, it does not require States to treat these as 'serious crimes', although the convention's procedures in respect of delivery and extradition are applicable only to serious crimes.

With respect to extradition, the state of registration of a leased aircraft which is involved in an offence will have little interest in pursuing a matter in which none of its nationals have been involved. A dry lease can further complicate the issue of extradition, since often in these circumstances such a state which is not directly involved in the offence is unlikely to be enthusiastic about incurring the trouble and expense associated with extradition and subsequent trial.

The Montreal Convention

The Montreal Convention[42] of 1971 was another attempt by the world community to address the problems caused by unlawful acts against civil aviation and to ensure aviation safety. In view of the concern at the present time that the acts of unruly passengers may jeopardize the safety of aircraft, the Montreal Convention is relevant to the subject under discussion. The objectives of the Montreal Convention are best summarized as follows:

> The primary aim of the Montreal Convention was to arrive at a generally acceptable method of dealing with alleged perpetrators of acts of unlawful interference with aircraft. In general, the nations represented at the Montreal Conference agreed that acts of sabotage, or violence and related offenses interfering with the safety and development of international civil aviation constituted a global problem which had to be combatted collectively by concerned nations of the international community. A multilateral international convention had to be adopted which extended both the scope and efficacy of national legislation and provided the legal framework for international co-operation in the apprehension, prosecution and punishment of alleged offenders.[43]

A noteworthy approach adopted by the Montreal Convention in its endeavours to curb hostile acts against civil aviation is to define the offence broadly in order to embrace all the possible acts that might occur. The first issue which faced the draughters of the convention in this respect related to the provision of substantial coverage of serious offences, at the same time avoiding the difficulties that may arise in connection with the listing of specific crimes in a convention intended for adoption by a great many states. After much debate and deliberation, this issue was settled and the final conclusion of the meeting is reflected in Article 1. Gerald Fitzgerald described the method of enumerating the offences in the Convention as being 'novel': 'Article I is novel in that it describes a number of penal offenses within the framework of a multilateral convention.'[44]

Article 1 of the Convention defines and enumerates the offences of unlawful interference with aircraft as follows:

1 Any person commits an offense if he unlawfully and intentionally:
   (a) Performs an act of violence against a person on board an aircraft in flight if that act is likely to endanger the safety of that aircraft in flight, or
   (b) Destroys an aircraft in service or causes damage to such an aircraft in flight if that act is likely to endanger its safety in flight, or
   (c) Places or causes to be placed on board an aircraft in service, by any means whatsoever, a device or substance which is likely to destroy that aircraft, or to cause damage to it which renders it incapable of flight, or to cause damage to it which is likely to endanger its safety in flight, or
   (d) Destroys or damages air navigation facilities or interferes with their operation, if any such act is likely to endanger the safety of aircraft in flight, or
   (e) Communicates information which he knows to be false, thereby endangering the safety of an aircraft in flight.
2 Any person also commits an offense if he:
   (a) Attempts to commit any of the offenses mentioned in paragraph 1 of this Article;
   (b) Is an accomplice of a person who commits or attempts to commit any such offense.

It should be noted that, while Article 1 delineates several different offences, the dual requisites of unlawfulness and intent apply to the offences enumerated. Fitzgerald observes:

> The introductory language of paragraph 1 makes it clear that the dual element of unlawfulness and intention must be present in all of the acts covered by sub-paragraphs (a) to (e); otherwise those acts will not

be offenses. The dual element would also apply to attempts and complicity covered by sub-paragraph 2.[45]

Sub-paragraph (a) of Article 1 is designed to deter and punish acts of violence committed against persons on board aircraft in flight. It should be noted that not all acts of violence come within the scope of the offence, but only those likely to endanger the safety of the aircraft. The notion of an act of violence referred to in this sub-paragraph includes armed attack and also attack against the lives of persons by other means, such as by blows, strangling, poisoning or lethal injection.

The word 'violence' used in sub-paragraph (a) can be interpreted as including not only an armed attack or physical assault, but also verbal assault and intimidation.[46] The act of violence perpetrated upon a person on board an aircraft according to sub-paragraph (b) may come from within or without the aircraft. The manner in which sub-paragraph 1(a) is worded, when it is read with the opening language of Article 1, would lead one to conclude that the person performing the act of violence does not have to be on board the aircraft in order to come under the convention. This means that the convention would apply to a person who, being outside the aircraft (for example a low-flying and slow-moving helicopter or light aircraft) in flight or who, while on the ground, has poisoned food which is later consumed by a person on board such aircraft.[47]

According to this sub-paragraph, the act of violence is not restricted to those acts which imperil the life of the victim. Any act of violence perpetrated against a person on board and which is likely to interfere with the safety of the aircraft falls within the scope of the offence. Hence the standard for determining whether the convention is applicable in a given situation does not hinge on the gravity or the heinousness of the act but rather on its effect on the safety of the aircraft in flight. It is to be noted that the same definition as given in Article 3 of the Hague Convention for an 'aircraft in flight' applies in (Article 2(a) of the Montreal Convention).

Article 1(2) covers the case of an attempt to commit an offence and the case of being an accomplice to commit one of the offences listed in the sub-paragraphs of Article 1. During the debate on the Montreal Convention, there was an attempt to include conspiracy in the definition, but some delegations, including France, were of the view that, since conspiracy was not an offence under their national systems of penal law, it should not be included in the convention. After long deliberations, it was decided by a vote that reference to conspiracy would not be made in the convention.

Penalties and the Scope of the Convention

The Montreal Convention provides for the undertaking by each contracting state to make the offences covered by the convention punishable by 'severe penalties'. Article 3 of the Montreal Convention states that each contracting state undertakes to make the offences mentioned in Article 1 punishable with severe penalties. Unlawful acts against the safety of civil aviation are thus considered to be serious crimes which the contracting states must punish with severe penalties. The term 'severe penalties', however, is not defined.

Article 4 of the Convention stipulates which flights are to be covered by the convention. Paragraph 1 excludes from the operation of the convention aircraft used in military, customs or police services.[48] According to paragraph 2 of Article 4, the scope of the convention is determined primarily in terms of the international element of aviation. In the case of the offences contemplated in clauses (a), (b), (c) and (e) of Article 1(1), the convention applies irrespective of whether the aircraft is engaged in an international or domestic flight only if, as stated in Article 4(2):

(a) the place of take-off or landing, actual or intended, of the aircraft is situated outside the territory of the State of registration of that aircraft; or
(b) the offence is committed in the territory of a State other than the State of registration of the aircraft.

The convention also applies in cases of international flights if the offender or the alleged offender is found in the territory of the state other than the state of registration of the aircraft.

Jurisdictional Powers Given to States under the Montreal Convention

Article 5 of the convention, which concerns jurisdiction, provides that each contracting state shall take such measures as may be necessary to establish its jurisdiction over offences in three instances: when the offence is committed in the territory of that state; when the offence is committed against or on board an aircraft registered in that state; and when the aircraft on board which the offence is committed lands in its territory with the alleged offender on board. This convention, like its predecessor,[49] does not exclude any criminal jurisdiction exercised in accordance with national law. Fitzgerald states: 'A controversial topic in the Montreal Convention is that of jurisdiction, since, like the Hague Convention, this Convention attempts to establish a form of universal jurisdiction over the alleged offender.'[50]

Article 5 of the Montreal Convention provides that each contracting state shall take such measures as may be necessary to establish its jurisdiction over the offenders in the following cases:

1 (a) when the offence is committed in the territory of that state;
  (b) when the offence is committed against or on board an aircraft registered in that state;
  (c) when the aircraft on board which the offence is committed lands in its territory with the alleged offender still on board; and
  (d) when the offence is committed against or on board an aircraft leased without crew to a lessee who has his principal place of business or, if the lessee has no such place of business, his permanent residence, in that state.

2 Each contracting state shall likewise take such measures as may be necessary to establish its jurisdiction over the offences mentioned in Article 1, paragraphs 1(a), (b) and (c) and in Article 1, paragraph 2, in so far as that paragraph relates to those offences, in the case where the alleged offender is present in its territory and it does not extradite him pursuant to Article 8 to any of the states mentioned in paragraph 1 of this Article, that is, Article 5.

3 This convention does not exclude any criminal jurisdiction exercised in accordance with the national law.

An analysis of Article 5 would lead to the conclusion that at least four states are specifically empowered to exercise concurrent jurisdiction over an alleged offender: (1) the state within whose territorial boundaries the offence is committed (whether the offence takes place on its territory or within its airspace), this reaffirming and codifying the traditional basis of territoriality; (2) the state of registration of the aircraft (hence such state is empowered to exercise its jurisdiction over offenders who commit their crimes on board aircraft registered in those states); (3) the state of landing, if the offender is on board the aircraft; and (4) any party to the convention within whose boundaries the alleged offender is present, if that state refuses to extradite the offender to any of the states having jurisdiction under Article 5(1).

Article 5(2) adopts the interpretation of universal jurisdiction as contained in the Hague Convention. Furthermore, Article 5, paragraph 3, provides that the jurisdictional basis delineated by the convention does not supersede any criminal jurisdiction that has derived from national laws of the parties to the convention. Consequently, the jurisdictional relation to nationality may be asserted by the state of nationality of the alleged offender, and the states which are the targets of the offence or whose nationals are threatened, maimed or killed by the offender may invoke the protective principle or the lesser recognized jurisdictional basis of passive nationality. These additional bases of jurisdiction are expected to further increase the possibility of suppressing the offenders.

In his concluding remarks, Professor Fitzgerald has observed: 'Thus, the Montreal Convention breaks new ground and goes beyond codification in providing for the international legal action to be taken by States in respect of many acts.'[51] By adopting the Montreal Convention, concerned states attempted to provide a framework which would substantially widen the scope and application of national legislation and thereby both penalize and deter unlawful interference with aircraft.

Extradition or Prosecution

Article 7 of the Montreal Convention embodies the principle of *aut dedere aut judicare*, which is the basis of the whole draft. It reads as follows:

> The State party in whose territory the alleged offender is present shall, if it does not extradite him, submit without exception whatsoever and without undue delay, the case to its competent authorities for the purpose of prosecution, through proceeding in accordance with the laws of that State.

According to this provision, a contracting state has an obligation either to extradite the alleged offender found in its territory or to submit his case to the competent authorities for the purpose of prosecution. It appears from the overall reading of 'without exception whatsoever' that the convention makes prosecution mandatory. However, a deeper analysis of the Article brings to bear the fact that it does not mandate the actual prosecution of the offender but merely the submission of the case to the competent domestic prosecuting authorities. This contention is supported by the fact that, during the Montreal Conference, the Israeli delegation proposed that the convention include a mandatory prosecution provision, although this proposal was defeated by vote of 35 to two with six abstentions.

The failure of the Montreal Convention to provide for an objective to prosecute, when the offender is not extradited, was considered a weakness regarding the system of sanctions *aut dedere aut punire*. A commentator observes:

> The lack of a mandatory system of prosecution with respect to aerial terrorism must be emphasized. Despite the repeated efforts of some delegations during the Hague and Montreal Conferences, the existing texts on aerial terrorism do not recognize the system of mandatory

prosecution in case of denial of extradition requests. On the contrary, the State authorities in charge of the handling of prosecution may well decide that, according to their domestic law, the alleged offender should not be prosecuted at all.[52]

Extradition and Other Principles

Although the Montreal Convention was considered a breakthrough in combating terrorism and other offensive acts against air transport, it remains, like its predecessors, tenuous and destitute of real effect. It would be a platitude to state that the effectiveness of any convention, however well draughted and universally accepted, would depend on the willingness and ability of states to enforce within their own territory the rule of law.

> Even if it is widely ratified, a small number of States can undermine [a treaty's] effectiveness by actively supporting or condoning acts of unlawful interference and by providing havens for the perpetrators of such acts. Because of conflicting ideologies and political exegesis, such events have in fact occurred.[53]

Another problem is that, although both the Tokyo and the Montreal Conventions have entered into force, barely half of the world community subscribes to either one or all of these agreements, and therefore their total impact has been less than inhibiting. At the time of writing, 166 states had ratified the Tokyo Convention, and 169 states had ratified the Montreal Convention of 1971. This rate of ratification of the conventions, when compared to the number of 185 member states of ICAO, has drastically reduced their effectiveness: 'Whether the Convention will fulfil its aims is dependent upon the breadth of support it obtains, indicated in part by the number of ramifications it receives. For the Convention to be effective, it must be acceded to by almost all nations.'[54]

Some states have not only failed to ratify the conventions, but have also undermined the conventions' effectiveness by providing sanctuaries for alleged offenders. Motivated by political and economic interests, other states have granted tacit support, and occasionally even active aid, to the perpetrators.

As a direct effect of the failure of the international community to provide an effective machinery for combating offences against air transport, threats to international civil aviation have consistently become more alarming and grave. New facets, and more spectacular types of offences, have evolved as a result. In an effort to redress the situation, concerned actions, under the auspice of ICAO, have attempted to formulate and adopt a multilateral international accord which would compel recalcitrant states into adherence both to customary and international law and to the provisions of the Tokyo, Hague and Montreal Conventions.

Notes

1 *Tsevas* v. *Delta Airlines, Inc.*, 1997 WL 767278 (N.A. Ill. 1997).
2 See 'Unruly Passengers', *Aviation Security International*, 2(2), 1997, 4.
3 For more detailed information on this particular issue, see Stephen R. Ginger (1998), 'Violence in the Skies: The Rights and Liabilities of Air Carriers when Dealing with Disruptive Passengers', *Air and Space Law*, XXIII(3), 106. This discussion gives a detailed account of US regulations on the conduct of unruly passengers.
4 See Douglas W. Nelms (1998), 'As More Passengers Fill More Aircraft, the Airlines are Finding the Skies Decidedly Unfriendly', *Air Transport World*, 3/98, 35.
5 Ibid., p. 39.
6 IATA, like ICAO, has recognized the problem for some time, and formed a Working Group on Disruptive and Unruly Passengers comprising professionals from the fields of aviation security, safety and in-flight services employed in IATA's member airlines, assisted by the legal expertise available in IATA and its member airlines. This working group has already accomplished considerable work of a significant nature, including the identification of the problem itself, and the development of a recommended practice for use by IATA member airlines. For more details see '"Unruly Some" to Bring One Rule for All', *Airlines International*, 4 Issue (6), November/December 1998, 38–9.
7 See 'Unruly Passengers' (working paper submitted by IATA), A32-WP/72, LE/7, 21/7/98.
8 See 'Unruly Passengers', A32-WP/167, LE/12, 23/9/98 (information paper submitted by ITWF).
9 Ibid., 1.
10 'Legal Action on Unruly Passengers', DGCA/104-WP/9, 8/22/98.
11 See R.P. Boyle (1964), 'The Tokyo Convention on Offenses and Certain Other Acts Committed on Board Aircraft', *Journal of Air Law & Commerce*, 30, 305–28, for a detailed analysis of the Tokyo Convention.
12 Report of the Sub-Committee, LC/SC, 'Legal Status', WD No. 23, 10 October 1956.
13 Boyle (*supra*, n.11), 320.
14 Ibid., at 321.
15 'Convention on Offences and Certain Other Acts Committed on Board Aircraft', ICAO Doc. 8364.
16 R.P. Boyle (1981), 'International Action to Combat Aircraft Hijacking', *Lawyers of the Americas*, 463.
17 Ibid., 463.
18 A. Abramovsky (1974), 'The Hague Convention', *Columbia Journal of Transnational Law*, 3(3), 389.
19 Boyle (*supra*, n.11).
20 Boyle (*supra*, n.16), 329.
21 A.E. Evans (1969), 'Hijacking: Its Cause and Cure', *The American Journal of International Law*, 63, 708.
22 Boyle (*supra*, n.16) 333.
23 Ibid., 331.

24 Ibid., 340.
25 Ibid.
26 See Articles 8 and 9 of the Tokyo Convention.
27 See Articles 12 and 13 of the Tokyo Convention.
28 A.I. Mendelsohn (1968), 'In Flight Crime, The International and Domestic Picture under the Tokyo Convention', *Virginia Law Review*, 53, 515.
29 Ibid., 514.
30 D.Y. Chung (1976), *Some Legal Aspects of Aircraft Hijacking in International Law*, New York: Kluwer, p.150.
31 Boyle (*supra*, n.16), 320.
32 Article 13(1).
33 Article 13(5).
34 Article 13(2).
35 Article 1(4).
36 See generally, Ruwantissa I. R. Abeyratne (1997), 'The Use of Civil Aircraft and Crew for Military Purposes', *Annals of Air and Space Law*, XXII, Part II, 1–24.
37 Civil Aviation Act 1982, Section 92.
38 Article 1(3).
39 Article 6(2).
40 For a discussion of this issue, see R.D. Margo (1987), *Aviation Insurance*, 2nd edn, London: Butterworths, p.154. The editors of the fourth edition of *Shawcross and Beaumont, Air Law* (London: Butterworths) consider that there is now no doubt that the 'meaning, as suggested by the natural and ordinary meaning of the words used', that is, 'the period between starting to accelerate down the runway and turning off it after landing is the correct one' (although on many occasions pilots would consider that their landing run had been completed long before taxiing to the turning off point). See *Shawcross and Beaumont*, para. VIII (2), note (3).
41 Article 16(2).
42 Convention for the Suppression of Unlawful Acts Against Safety of Civil Aviation, signed at Montreal on 23 September 1971. See ICAO Doc. 8966.
43 A. Abramovsky (1975), 'The Montreal Convention', *Columbia Journal of International Law*, 14(2), 278.
44 G.F. Fitzgerald (1971), 'Toward Legal Suppression of Acts Against Civil Aviation', *International Conciliation*, 585, 57.
45 Ibid., 68.
46 Ibid.
47 Ibid.
48 See Abeyratne, (*supra*, n.36).
49 Convention for the Suppression of Unlawful Seizure of Aircraft (Hague Convention) signed at The Hague on 16 December 1970. The Hague Convention addressed the issue of hijacking of aircraft and therefore is not relevant to this chapter.
50 Fitzgerald, quoted in Abramovsky (*supra*, n.43), 73.
51 Ibid., 75.
52 Declan Costello, 'International Terrorism and the Development of the Principle Aut Dedere Aut Judicare', *Journal of International Law & Commerce*, 11(11), 488.
53 A. Abramovsky (1975), 'Multilateral Convention for the Suppression of Unlawful Seizure and Interference with Aircraft, Part II of the Montreal Convention', *Columbia Journal of Transportation Law*, 14, 300.
54 Ibid.

17 Transportation of Abducted Children

Introduction

Elizabeth Pittman, a minor child, was kidnapped by her mother in defiance of a court order prohibiting the mother's access to her child as a result of the mother's divorce. The mother, Erna Pittman, used the services of Icelandair to remove her daughter from the United States to Iceland. The father of the child, Frederick Pittman, who had lawful custody of Elizabeth, filed action[1] against Icelandair, Erna and other defendants concerned, on the grounds that they collectively conspired to abduct his daughter. As a defendant, Icelandair found itself charged with tortious interference with parental rights, conspiracy, intentional infliction of emotional distress, false imprisonment and negligence. In the context of the above allegations the plaintiffs – father and daughter – averred the following against Icelandair: the carrier allowed Erna and her daughters to board its flight under false names; the carrier falsified its passenger manifest to conceal the fact that Erna was travelling with her two children; and the employees of the carrier surreptitiously escorted Erna and her daughters to the aircraft departing for Iceland. The defendant airline denied all allegations.

The plaintiffs contended that they had called the offices of Icelandair to inform them that Erna might attempt to kidnap her daughter in violation of an existing court order and seek transportation from New York to Keflavic with her daughter on Icelandair. The plaintiffs had given Icelandair physical descriptions of Erna, Elizabeth and Elizabeth's sibling, Anna, over the phone, without setting such details down in writing. The issue at hand before the Court of Appeals for the Second Circuit of New York, which was adjudicating upon Icelandair's request to set aside an order in favour of the plaintiffs for US$ 15 million, was whether the airline had been given adequate notice to cause it to know that Erna was committing a tort because her travel to Iceland was prohibited by a court order. In other words, was the airline aiding and abetting in the kidnapping of the child? The Court of Appeals held in favour of the airline, on the basis that Icelandair's duty as a common carrier to transport persons who presented tickets was not replaced on the basis of 'mere oral representations such as those made on the telephone by the plaintiffs'.[2]

The *Pittman* case brings to bear the significance of the position of a commercial carrier who may be perceived to connive with, and aid and abet, a kidnapper of a minor child. This chapter will address liabilities of the carriers in such a situation and measures taken by Canadian authorities to manage the problem.

Child Abduction and Trans-boundary Transportation of Abducted Children

Curiously, international civil aviation has been a key player in contributing to the growth in immigration, which has provided opportunity for relationships leading to marriages between different nationalities and cultures. These marriages, like homogeneous marriages being contracted by persons wherein cross-cultural aspects were not relevant, are susceptible to economic and social phenomena of the modern age such as rising divorce rates, domestic violence and the speed with which the global economy is plummeting towards expansion as one single concept. A child who suffers a divorce or separation of his natural parents will incontrovertibly suffer significant emotional stress and psychological damage. A fortiori, a child who is forced under abduction by one parent to go to a country which is foreign to her faces severe dislocation of environment in terms of the change in cultural, linguistic and living arrangements in the new country. In addition, the separation from the absent parent often results in the child undergoing severe psychological trauma which frequently results in confusion, fear, despair and even anger.[3] If, as is often the case, an abducting parent keeps moving the displaced child constantly to avoid detection, the impact of such change on the child will be devastating.

An expert in the International Social Service of Canada has observed: 'International child abduction is the most serious violation of a child's rights. Children are the chief victims of child abduction. However, in the end, everyone loses.'[4] The logical conclusion one could arrive at, in the context of the offence of child abduction, is that it is a violation of a child's rights and a form of child abuse.

When viewed in the above context, the thought that airlines who are perceived to aid and abet child abductors may also be perceived as aiding and abetting child abuse, is indeed a frightening one.

The Hague Convention

Twenty years ago, on an initative of Canada, 30 countries met to search for an international solution to child abduction. The result was the Hague Convention on the Civil Aspects of Child Abduction, adopted by the Hague Conference on Private International Law.[5] This convention, the only multilateral instrument providing assistance in the cross-border abduction of children, came into force on 1 December 1983.

The Hague Convention is based on the fundamental postulate that the best interests of children are met by ensuring their prompt return to the state of habitual residence. To this end, the convention provides that each signatory state undertakes to return a child who has been abducted into that state to legal custody in that child's pre-abduction home state. The act of abduction, according to the Hague Convention, is the physical removal, without the consent of the other parent, of a child below the age of 16, typically by a non-custodial or joint custodial parent with a background of upbringing in another country. The convention aims at securing the swift return of children unilaterally taken to or from a foreign country and at promoting cooperation among nations and among the competent authorities in their respective states and, most importantly, at deterring child abduction. Article 13(b) of the convention gives four exceptions to the otherwise absolute requirement for the return of the abducted child to his or her home state, including an exception if there is a grave risk that the child's return would expose the child to physical or psychological harm or otherwise place the child in an intolerable situation.

As of October 1998, only 44 countries had ratified the Hague Convention and 26 countries had acceded to it. Although this is a modest record, the 1997 special commission appointed to review the operation of the Hague Convention shows that, when compared with statistics on the outcome of child abduction cases involving non-Hague countries, the Hague Convention countries seem to be doing better in solving their abduction cases.[6] A study done in 1994 showed that, in the United States, 43 per cent of incoming Hague abduction cases and 40 per cent of outgoing Hague cases were resolved satisfactorily, whereas only 20–25 per cent of non-Hague cases had been resolved during the same period.[7]

One of the shortcomings of the Hague Convention is that it is structured to accommodate a cumbersome administrative process. This fact was recognized by the second meeting of the special commission which reviewed the operation of the Hague Convention, in 1993. The meeting concluded:

> Delay in legal proceedings is a major cause of difficulties in the operation of the Convention. All possible efforts should be made to expedite such proceedings. Courts in a number of countries normally decide on requests for return of a child on the basis only of the application and any documents or statements in writing submitted by the parties, without taking oral testimony or requiring the presence of the parties in person. This can serve to expedite the disposition of the case. The decision to return the child is not a decision based on the merits of custody.[8]

A further difficulty which the Hague Convention has not addressed is the problem faced by a parent seeking the return of his or her child who has been abducted to a country where legal representation may not be as effective as in the country from where the child was abducted.[9]

Air Carrier Liability

The Hague Convention, which is essentially a treaty between contracting states, is restricted to the securing of the prompt return of children wrongfully removed to or retained in any contracting state and to ensure that rights of custody and of access under the law of one contracting state are effectively respected in other contracting states. Therefore the convention does not apply to an airline (even if one were to impose nationality on the airline and link it to the convention as an instrumentality of state) which may be charged with the offence of aiding and abetting a non-custodian parent in removing a child from his habitual residence.

The responsibility of securing the objectives of the Hague Convention falls squarely on the state concerned,[10] which, by virtue of Article 6, is required to designate a Central Authority to discharge the duties which are imposed by the convention. Therefore an airline could argue *in limine* that the central authority of a state (if the abduction took place in a signatory state to the Hague Convention) had a legal obligation to advise the airlines operating in the territory of the state concerned of possible incursions of the law by non-custodian parents.[11]

The United Nations Convention on the Rights of the Child,[12] adopted in New York on 20 November 1989, in Article 9 requires:

> States Parties shall ensure that a child shall not be separate from his or her parents against their will, except when competent authorities subject to judicial review determine, in accordance with applicable law and procedures, that such separation is necessary for the best interests of the child.[13]

Furthermore, Article 11 imposes upon states parties the duty to take measures to combat the illicit transfer and non-return of children abroad and requires states parties to promote the conclusion of bilateral or multilateral agreements or accession to existing agreements. The convention has two other provisions, Articles 35 and 37(b), which provide respectively that states parties shall take all appropriate national, bilateral and multilateral measures to prevent the abduction or sale of or traffic in children for any purpose or in any form, and that no child shall be deprived of his or her liberty unlawfully or arbitrarily.

The liability of an airline in the transportation by air of an abducted child would therefore arise only in an instance where the airline aided and abetted the commission of the offence volitionally or through its own negligence in not taking into account a tangible warning by an aggrieved party.

Aiding and Abetting

When considering the *Pittman* case as a paradigm, it is clear that the airline did not receive adequate warning from the plaintiff on the possible commission of the abduction of Elizabeth Pittman by her mother. The United States International Parental Kidnaping Crimes Act,[14] in Section 1204(a) states: 'Whoever removes a child from the United States or retains a child (who has been in the United States) outside the United States with intent to obstruct the lawful exercise of parental rights shall be fined under this title or imprisoned for not more than 3 years, or both', thereby requiring from the airline the element of intent in order for it to be held liable for removing a child from his or her country of residence. To be found guilty of aiding and abetting an abduction, an airline must not only assist the principal, but intend to assist the principal. A person who unwittingly delivers a bomb or administers a poison will not be guilty as a party to an offence even though that person may have committed the act of assisting the commission of the offence.[15] In the case of *R.* v. *Dunlop*,[16] Dickson J admonished: 'A person cannot properly be convicted of aiding and abetting in the commission of acts which he does not know may be or are intended … One must be able to infer that the accused had prior knowledge that an offence of the type committed was planned.'[17]

The *mens rea* or mental element needed for aiding and abetting an offence extends to intent required to complete the crime. In the 1990 case of *R.* v *Kirkness*,[18] which concerned a murder, the Canadian Supreme Court recognized that an accused aiding and abetting a murder must intend that death ensue or that the act of aiding and abetting would contribute to the occurrence of the death or at least be reckless whether death ensue or not.[19] If this principle were to be applied to the instance of an airline which is made aware in the appropriate manner of the airline being an accessory to an offence, either the airline, by its actions, must will the end result of the offence, such as the injury caused to an abducted child, or be reckless as to whether such injury occurred or not.

Recklessness

Recklessness is a lower form of *mens rea* than intent, purpose, wilfulness or knowledge, but, in common law jurisdictions, it is still a form of subjective *mens rea*. In criminal law a person acts recklessly if he or she has adverted to or become aware of the risk of the prohibited conduct. In *R.* v. *Sansregret*,[20] the Supreme Court stressed the importance of distinguishing recklessness from negligence:

> In accordance with well-established principles for the determination of criminal liability, recklessness, to form a part of the criminal *mens rea*, must have an element of the subjective. It is found in the attitude of one who, aware that there is danger that his conduct could bring about the result prohibited by the criminal law, nevertheless persists, despite the risk. It is, in other words, the conduct of one who sees the risk and who takes the chance.

Recklessness requires subjective advertence to the prohibited risk and can be distinguished from negligence, which requires only that a reasonable person in the accused's circumstances would have recognized the risk.[21] A person recklessly aids and abets if he recognizes the risk that his act would facilitate the offence, while a person would negligently aid and abet if a reasonable person in his circumstances would have known there was a risk that the injury would be caused. As will be seen later in this chapter, the actual fault element for aiding and abetting falls somewhere in between recklessness and negligence.

Recklessness is a common form of subjective *mens rea*. Martin JA has stated that 'the general *mens rea* which is required and which suffices for most crimes where no mental element is mentioned in the definition of the crime, is either the intentional or reckless bringing about of the result which the law, in creating the offence, seeks to prevent'.[22] Recklessness requires only subjective awareness of the risk of the prohibited act, as opposed to knowledge of the likelihood of the prohibited act.

Wilful Blindness

A more recent and controversial form of subjective *mens rea* is wilful blindness. There is no consensus about its definition, but the Canadian Supreme Court has stated:

> Wilful blindness is distinct from recklessness because, while recklessness involves knowledge of a danger or a risk and persistence in a course of conduct which creates a risk that the prohibited result will occur, wilful blindness arises when a person who has become aware of the need for some inquiry declines to make the inquiry because he does not wish to know the truth. He would prefer to remain ignorant. The culpability in recklessness is justified by consciousness of the risk and by proceeding in the face of it, while in wilful blindness it is justified by the accused's fault in deliberately failing to inquire when he knows there is reason for inquiry.[23]

In the instance of an airline being advised of a possibility of its transporting an abducted child, and if the airline does not exercise appropriate caution and take all measures possible to avert such carriage, it may be arguable that the airline could be considered as having blinded itself wilfully to the possibility of the offence and to the reasonable and probable consequences of its act of not acting on a complaint received.

The test which would ultimately determine whether an airline wilfully blinded itself to a possible situation of cross-border abduction where the airline itself would play a part in the offence would indeed have to be a subjective one, particularly in an instance where the only evidence the airline would have would be a mere telephone call, such as in the *Pittman* case.

In *Tutton*,[24] McIntyre J stated that criminal negligence involved proof of conduct which required a marked and significant departure from the standard required from a reasonable person under such circumstances. His Lordship proposed that an accused's subjective perception of circumstances could be relevant in determining whether he or she acted with criminal negligence. He warned that the application of an objective test may not be made in a vacuum for the following reasons:

> Events occur within the framework of other events and actions and, when deciding on the nature of the questioned conduct, surrounding circumstances must be considered. The decision must be made on a consideration of the facts existing at the time *and* in relation to the accused's perception of those facts. Since the test is objective, the accused's perception of the facts is not to be considered for the purpose of assessing malice or intention on the accused's part but only to form a

> basis for a conclusion as to whether or not the accused's conduct, *in view of his perception of the facts*, was reasonable.[25] (Original emphasis)

Although the accused must conduct himself like a reasonable person, that standard of conduct could be determined on the basis of the accused's own perception of the circumstances.

In a subsequent case dealing with the offence of dangerous driving causing death, Cory J observed that objective fault must be determined in the context of the events surrounding the incident. However, His Lordship did not insist, as McIntyre J had, that the accused's own perception of the facts should be considered. Cory J stated:

> Although an objective must be applied to the offence of dangerous driving, it will remain open to the accused to raise a reasonable doubt that a reasonable person would have been aware of the risks in the accused's conduct. In order to convict, the trier of fact must be satisfied that a reasonable person in similar circumstances ought to have been aware of the risk and danger involved in the conduct manifested by the accused.[26]

If the reasoning of Cory J were to be made applicable to an airline faced with a mere telephone call from an unidentified source claiming himself to be the father of a child about to be abducted, one could argue that the objective test of 'the reasonable man' would be to require any prudent airline to check as a matter of course, at the point of check-in of passengers, whether a child unaccompanied by both natural or adoptive parents carried sufficient legal documentation to justify boarding. Such an objective test would apply to the airline principles of negligence as enunciated in the British case of *Bourhill* v. *Young*,[27] where Lord McMillan said:

> The duty to take care is the duty to avoid doing or omitting to do anything the doing or omitting to do which may have as its reasonable and probable consequence injury to others, and the duty is owed to those to whom injury may reasonably and probably be anticipated if the duty is not observed.[28]

However, in order to apply negligence and objectivity, the airline concerned would have to be adequately warned and aware of the danger.

Cooperation between State Authorities and Airlines

In order for the courts of common law jurisdictions to impute absolute responsibility, on an objective basis, to an airline for the carriage of an abducted child, state authorities may have to provide airlines with details of possible infractions of the law by non-custody parents through their passport and consular offices. States should insist that, when applying for a child's passport or visa, both parents should be required to present themselves at the passport or consular office or, in the alternative, one parent could apply, together with a notarized letter from the other, giving consent to the application for the passport or visa.

An annotation in the child's passport or, if the child is included in a parent's passport, in that parent's passport, to the effect that the child cannot be accompanied by him or her (if the parent does not have custody) would ensure that the onus is on the airline at the check-in stage to take a look at the passports concerned and make its own judgment. In such an instance the airline would allow the carriage of a child unaccompanied by both parents only if the non-travelling parent has issued a notarized document giving his or her permission for the child to travel.

In any event, it is extremely important that, on this issue, all concerned, that is, state authorities and airlines, work together to prevent the removal of a child from his or her natural residence by a parent who does not have custody of a child. It is equally important for state authorities and airlines to work together to reinstate the child in his natural residence once the offence has been committed. With regard to the return of the child to his home country, the recipient state should have the legal obligation to examine the documentation of a child travelling with a single parent or other in order to determine whether the child is carrying any legal document from the non-accompanying parent(s) giving the escort authorization to accompany the child on a cross-border trip without them. If the child does not carry such documentation, the recipient state should consider the child an inadmissible passenger.

The Return of an Abducted Child as an Inadmissible Passenger

The Chicago Convention of 1944[29] in its Article 13 provides that the laws and regulations of a contracting state with regard to the admission to or departure from such state of passengers, crew or cargo of aircraft, in relation to their entry, clearance, immigration, passports, customs and quarantine, should be complied with by or on behalf of such passengers, crew or cargo, upon entrance into or departure from, or while within the territory of, that state. This provision prima facie imposes a legal duty on the airline passenger concerned or her parent/guardian to comply with the legislation of the country he is attempting to enter, presumably by ensuring inter alia that he carries all necessary legal documentation to enter that country. The provision also carries the implied requirement that, if the passenger fails to comply with such laws, they should be complied with on behalf of the passenger. By this, Article 13 of the Chicago Convention, without explicitly stating that it is the airline's responsibility to ensure, on behalf of the passenger, compliance with laws of the country of arrival, imputes to the airline that responsibility. Of course, one can argue that, in the absence of explicit mention in the provision, the airline is not responsible for ensuring that a passenger is admissible in the country to which it carries that passenger, particularly since the Chicago Convention is a treaty establishing the obligation of states towards each other. Therefore, logically, it may be arguable that, when Article 13 uses the words 'on behalf of', it may well be applicable to the duty devolving upon the authorities of the state in which the person embarked on his flight.

Annex 9 to the Chicago Convention – on facilitation of air transport – dedicates Section E of its Chapter 3 to inadmissible persons carried by air. The Annex provides that the operator (airline) which carries a passenger to a country shall be responsible for the custody and care of passengers and crew until they are accepted for examination for the purposes of immigration[30] which that country is obligated to do without unreasonable delay.[31] The authorities take responsibility for such passengers and crew once they are so accepted for examination, until a determination is made whether they are admissible to the country or not.[32]

A person found inadmissible is required to be handed over by the authorities who find him so inadmissible to the operator (airline) who brought him in.[33] The airline is then responsible for taking the person back to his country of origin (where he commenced his flight) or to any other place which accepts him.[34]

The Annex casts a burden on a state in which a person has stayed for a period of time (not merely in transit) prior to his landing in another state which finds him inadmissible, to accept such person for examination, subject to the fact that, by doing so, the state which accepts the person for examination does not jeopardize his life or freedom.[35] The most relevant provision of Annex 9 to the question at issue is Standard 3.40.1, which stipulates: 'Contracting States shall not fine operators in the event that passengers are found inadmissible unless there is evidence to suggest that the carrier was negligent in taking precautions to the end that passengers complied with the documentary requirements for entry into the receiving State.' There is also the provision that contracting states and operators shall cooperate, where practicable, in establishing the validity and authenticity of passports and visas,[36] with a recommendation that, where operators cooperate with the control authorities to the satisfaction of those authorities, contracting states should mitigate fines and penalties that might otherwise be applicable to the operators for inadmissible passengers carried to those states.[37]

A strict interpretation of regulatory provisions on air carrier liability for the carriage of inadmissible persons seems to suggest that there is no prima facie presumption of guilt on the airline. On the contrary, Article 13 of the Chicago Convention, which is strictly an international treaty containing provisions setting out legal obligations between states, provides that applicable laws have to be complied with by the passenger, *or on behalf of the passenger* (my emphasis), which may be interpreted as saying that state authorities, such as customs and immigration or consular authorities, would have a greater burden of ensuring compliance with Article 13 than the airlines.

A fortiori, Annex 9, by Standard 3.40.1, explicitly requires that, in the absence of evidence of the carrier's negligence, the carrier shall not be fined. Although the linkage between the convention and annex is at times doubted, in view of the statement in Article 54(l) in the convention that the annexes to the convention are so named for convenience, nonetheless it is an incontrovertible fact that Annex 9 draws its authority from the convention and therefore is an integral part of it. Standard 3.40.1, which has been developed by the Council of ICAO with the approval of ICAO member states, is therefore international in scope and not diminished in its legal authority, but rather acts as an explanatory note to Article 13 of the convention.[38]

Passport Fraud

The possibility of passport forgery in order to avoid detection, by a person abducting a child, is a real one. In such instances, the security and integrity of the passport,[39] which is usually recognized as the fundamental legal document of travel between countries, becomes a critical issue in the determination of liability. The passport carries details of a person's identity, country of citizenship and entitlement to travel privileges. Above all, and in the context of inadmissible passengers, the passport will serve as assurance, to the country in which a person is found inadmissible, that he can return to the country which issued the passport.

Unless otherwise specified, a passport remains the property of the state of issue, and therefore misuse or destruction of a passport becomes an infringement of law against that state. Conversely, a grave responsibility devolves upon states to ensure that their property is secure from such misuse or fraud – particularly the commonest known abuse or fraud in the nature of forgery. The use of forged or counterfeit passports, the use of valid passports by imposters, and the misuse of valid passports by their rightful owners in the perpetration of an offence are some of the common ways in which passport fraud is perpetrated today.[40]

At its 32nd Session, held in Montreal between 22 September and 2 October 1998, the ICAO Assembly adopted a resolution which requests the Council of ICAO to study specific actions and measures for enhancing the effectiveness of controls on passport fraud, including the possible preparation of necessary Standards and Recommended Practices (SARPs) and guidance material, to be implemented by contracting states in the interests of maintaining the integrity and security of passports and other travel documents. The resolution also calls upon all contracting states to intensify their efforts to safeguard the security and integrity of their passports, to protect their passports against passport fraud, and to assist one another in these matters.[41]

The United Nations General Assembly, at its 85th Plenary meeting in December 1993, adopted a resolution[42] concerning the prevention of smuggling of aliens, wherein the General Assembly condemned the practice of smuggling of aliens in violation of national and international law and, inter alia, requested states that had not done so to make special efforts to prevent their airports, means of ground transport and air carriers from being used by smugglers of aliens.

The resolution also requested the relevant specialized agencies (ICAO being mentioned as one) to consider ways and means, within their respective spheres of competence, to enhance international cooperation to combat the smuggling of aliens.

In a subsequent (1997) resolution,[43] the United Nations General Assembly, at its 51st session, inter alia, recognized that international criminal groups often convinced individuals to migrate illegally by various means for enormous profits and that socioeconomic factors influenced the problem of the smuggling of aliens and also contributed to the complexity of current international migration. The Assembly requested states to cooperate bilaterally and on a multilateral basis to prevent the use of fraudulent documents and reaffirmed the need to fully observe international and national law in dealing with the smuggling of aliens, including the provision of humane treatment and strict observance of all human rights of migrants.

Notes

1 *Pittman* v. *Icelandair*, No. 97-9066, 1998 US App LEXIS 13642 (2d Cir 26 June 1998). For a discussion of the case, see 'Parental Kidnapping Verdict', *Aviation Insurance and Law*, 17(9), September 1998, 7–8.

2 'Parental Kidnapping Verdict' (*supra*).

3 See J. Kiedrowski, C.H.S. Jayawardene and M. Dalley (1994), 'Parental Abduction of Children: An Overview and Profile of the Abductor', Royal Canadian Mounted Police, Ottawa, October, 22–5.

4 See 'International Child Abduction: Issues for Reform, Fourth Report of the Standing Committee on Foreign Affairs and International Trade, First Report of the Sub-Committee on Human Reports and International Development', Ottawa, April 1998, 7.

5 Done at The Hague on 25 October 1980. See *International Legal Materials*, XIX(6), November 1980, 1501.

6 D. Ngabonziza (1997), 'Mediation in International Family Disputes', International Symposium on Globalization of the Rights of the Child: The Role of The Hague Convention, The Hague, 13 September, p.2.

7 L. Silberman (1994), 'Hague International Child Abduction Convention: A Progress Report', *Law and Contemporary Problems*, 57(3), Summer, 217.

8 Cited in A. Dyer and S. Detrick (1997), 'Checklist of Issues to be Considered at the Third Meeting of the Special Commission to Review the Operation of the *Hague Convention on the Civil Aspects of International Child Abduction*', Hague Conference on Private International Law, January, p.10.

9 A. Dyer (1993), '*The Hague Convention on the Civil Aspects of International Child Abduction* – Towards Global Cooperation: Its Successes and Failures', *International Journal of Children's Rights*, 1, 287–8.

10 Article 1(a) and (b).

11 Article 2.

12 *International Legal Materials*, XXVIII(6), November 1989, 1448.

13 Article 9(1).

14 18 USC 1204.

15 See the Canadian Case of *R* v *Berryman* (1990) 57 C.C.C. (3d) 375 (B.C.C.A).

16 1979), 47 C.C.C (2d) 93 at 111 (S.C.C.).

17 Ibid., 110.

18 1990), 60 C.C.C, (3d), 97.

19 Ibid., 127.

20 (1985) 18 C.C.C (3d) (S.C.D.).

21 *O'Grady* v. *Sparling* (1960), 128 C.C.C 1 at 13 (S.C.C.).

22 *R.* v. *Buzzanga* (1979) 49 C.C.C (2d) 369 at 381.

23 *R.* v. *Sansregret* (1985) 18 C.C.C. (3d) 223 (S.C.D.).

24 See *R.* v. *Tutton* (1989) 48 C.C.C. 3d 129 at 140.

25 Ibid., 141.

26 *R.* v. *Handal* (1993) 79 C.C.C. (3d) 97 (S.C.C.).

27 [1942] 2 All ER 396 at 402.

28 Ibid., 408.

29 Convention on International Civil Aviation, signed at Chicago on 7 December 1944. For full text, see ICAO Doc. 7300/6, 7th edn, 1997.

30 Annex 9 (Facilitation), Chapter 3, Section E, 3.38.1.

31 Ibid., 3.38.

32 Ibid., 3.38.2.

33 Ibid., 3.39.

34 Ibid.

35 Ibid., 3.39.1.

36 Ibid., 3.40.3.

37 Ibid. Recommended Practice, 3.40.2.

38 It is noteworthy that the ICAO Facilitation Panel, which met in Montreal from 17 to 21 November 1997, has suggested two new Recommended Practices to Annex 9 which provide:

- the appropriate public authorities of Contracting States either singly or jointly should enter into co-operative arrangements such as memoranda of understanding with the airlines providing international services to and from that State, setting out guidelines for their mutual support and co-operation in countering the abuses associated with travel document fraud. Such arrangements should assign mutual responsibilities to the public authorities and to the airlines, in the ascertainment of the validity and authenticity of the travel documents of embarking passengers, and in the necessary steps to prevent the loss or destruction of documents by passengers enroute to their destinations; and
- Contracting States are encouraged to make arrangements such as memoranda of understanding (MOUs) with other Contracting States with the intention of permitting the positioning of 'liaison officers' at airports or to establish other forms of international co-operation in order to assist airlines to establish the validity and authenticity of the passports and visas of embarking passengers. (See 'Facilitation Panel Report', First Meeting, Montreal, 17–21 November 1997, 1–4.)

The above two recommendations were adopted *inter alia* as Amendment 17 to Annex 9 by the ICAO Council at its 155th Session, on 8 December 1998. At the time of writing, the Amendment had been sent to Contracting States by ICAO for their comments.

39 For a more detailed discussion of the legal nature of the passport, see R.I.R. Abeyratne (1992), 'The Development of the Machine Readable Passport and Visa and the Legal Rights of the Data Subject', *Annals of Air & Space Law*, XVII, Part II, 12–14.

40 In conformity with Article 22 of the Chicago Convention, which confirms the agreement of all contracting states to adopt all practicable measures to prevent unnecessary delays to aircraft, passenger and crews especially in the administration of laws relating to immigration, quarantine customs and clearance, ICAO is actively seised of the development of a machine readable travel document which uses various devices to secure the passport, visa and other travel documents against fraud.

41 The full text of the resolution is as follows:

International co-operation in protecting the security and integrity of passports

Whereas the passport is the basic official document which denotes a person's identity and citizenship and provides an assurance for the State of transit or destination that the bearer can return to the State which issued the passport;

Whereas international confidence in the security and integrity of the passport is of prime importance in the functioning of the international travel system;

Taking into account the resolution adopted by the United Nations General Assembly which requests that ICAO consider ways and means to enhance international co-operation to combat the smuggling of aliens, while emphasizing that such efforts should not undercut the protection provided by international law to refugees;

Taking into account the resolutions adopted by the United Nations General Assembly and the Economic and Social Council which request that Member States establish or improve procedures to permit the ready discovery of false travel documents, that States co-operate bilaterally and on a multilateral basis to prevent the use of fraudulent documents, and that States take measures to provide penalties for the production and distribution of false travel documents and the misuse of international commercial aviation; and

Whereas high level co-operation among States is required in order to strengthen resistance to passport fraud, including the forgery or counterfeiting of passports, the use of forged or counterfeit passports, the use of valid passports by imposters, the misuse of authentic passports by rightful holders in furtherance of the commission of an offence, the use of expired or revoked passports, and the use of fraudulently obtained passports.

The Assembly:

1. *endorses* the actions taken by the Council through the Air Transport Committee to strengthen and approve specifications for machine readable passports as they relate to security of such documents;
2. *requests* the Council to study specific actions and measures for enhancing the effectiveness of controls on passport fraud, including the possible preparation of necessary SARPs and guidance material, to be implemented by Contracting States in the interests of maintaining the integrity and security of passports and other travel documents; and
3. *calls upon* all Contracting States to intensify their efforts to safeguard the security and integrity of their passports, to protect their passports against passport fraud, and to assist one another in these matters.

42 A/RES/48/102.
43 A/RES/51/60.

18 State Liability for the Global Navigation Satellite System

Introduction

The Global Navigation Satellite System (GNSS) is essentially a system of satellite technology which, when applied to aviation, determines the position, velocity and components of an aircraft in flight. GNSS has its origin in the ground-breaking ICAO mechanism devised some 10 years ago, called the Future Air Navigation System (FANS) which paved the way for the now ultra-modern air navigation management system called Communications, Navigation, Surveillance/Air Traffic Management (CNS/ATM). GNSS has been aptly described as the most exciting technological shopping trip of the 20th century that will provide many safety and efficiency specials for both the developed and the developing world.[1] Safety and efficiency features promised by GNSS include advanced screening of mountainous regions in countries such as Japan, New Zealand and Nepal (which are currently finding it difficult with available radar screening technology) and visual surveillance of vast desert areas of the Middle East and countries such as Australia and the United States.[2]

Ever mindful of the legal implications that such a gigantic stride in satellite technology may bring the world of civil aviation, ICAO has prepared a draft charter setting out the legal issues of GNSS. The document was developed through a panel of legal and technical experts and embodies the fundamental postulates driving the implementation and operation of GNSS within the parameters of certain accepted international law norms such as sovereignty of states and international accord through cooperation. The main thrust of the GNSS mechanism is of course the ensuring of safety in aviation through precision in CNS/ATM which is the pre-eminent consideration of international civil aviation at the present time.

At ICAO's first ever World-wide CNS/ATM Systems Implementation Conference, held in Rio de Janeiro from 11 to 15 May 1998, the conference considered the above mentioned ICAO draft Charter[3] on the Rights and Obligations of States Relating to Global Navigation Satellite Systems, as an interim legal framework for CNS/ATM systems. The Rio Conference, which was identified by the President of the ICAO Council, Dr Assad Kotaite, as one which succeeded in focusing the attention of the world aviation community on key issues of financing and management of CNS/ATM systems and crystallized the needs and available resources for the safe and orderly growth of civil aviation into the next millennium,[4] expressed its support for the adoption of the draft charter.

The draft charter embodies the most compelling elements that would affect the operation of GNSS, such as aviation safety, global accessibility by users of GNSS, accuracy, reliability, continuity, availability and integrity of GNSS, sovereignty and compatibility with relevant global planning and implementation. Of these elements, the issue of sovereignty is the most fundamental and essential. It is the core issue which affects the philosophy of GNSS, unlike the other elements, which are technical and procedural.

The draft charter, which was presented to the 32nd Session of the ICAO Assembly in September/October 1998, states that it is driven by the need to ensure safety in aviation in the context of the use and operation of GNSS and the underlying principle, inter alia, that every state preserves its authority and responsibility to control operations of aircraft and to enforce safety and other regulations within its sovereign airspace. It further elaborates that the implementation and operation of GNSS shall neither infringe nor impose restrictions upon states' sovereignty, authority or responsibility in the control of air navigation and the promulgation and enforcement of safety regulations.

Whatever may be the contribution of ICAO and the rest of the global aviation community towards successfully implementing GNSS, ultimately the overall responsibility of implementing GNSS falls on states themselves. The genesis of state responsibility lies in Article 28 of the Chicago Convention,[5] which states inter alia that each contracting state undertakes, to the extent practicable, to provide in its territory, airports, radio services, meteorological services and other air navigation facilities to facilitate international air navigation, in accordance with the standards and practices recommended or established from time to time, pursuant to the convention. This provision incontrovertibly brings to bear the need for states not only to take all practicable measures to provide air navigation facilities in their respective territories but also to be associated with implementation of GNSS through standards and recommended practices adopted under the umbrella of the Chicago Convention. Article 28 also imputes to states the responsibility of international cooperation in this regard and their attendant responsibility of ensuring the success of that implementation.

Principles of legal liability of states in the operation of GNSS have been discussed elsewhere[6] and it is not the intent of this chapter to re-examine them. Instead, this chapter will examine the fundamental principles of state responsibility under Article 28 of the Chicago Convention and build on the significant observation made by the President of the ICAO Council on this subject:

> The activities of non-governmental entities in outer space shall require authorization and continuing supervision by the appropriate State. The implications of this provision, which has been regarded as a part of general international law, will have to be studied in the context of GNSS. While an air law instrument may impose responsibility directly on non-governmental service providers of GNSS in the sense of private law, the general responsibility of the relevant States in the sense of public law has not been obviated.[7]

GNSS, which comes within the purview of aerospace law, will command a place in the law of outer space, which is perhaps the most dramatic example of new international law. There is no doubt that GNSS will involve part option, part practice and part treaty in space law practice, defying orthodox and dogmatic classification. By its very nature, and being a product of new economic and technological pressures, GNSS will demand a stringent test of the elasticity of international and municipal law, requiring a harmonious blend between the two legal systems and making their boundaries less clearly defined. The use of the common term 'transnational law', which is now freely used to define this grey area, is a good example of a possible jurisprudential approach to GNSS.

The 1989 British case involving the International Tin Council[8] stressed the importance of international law and its application on a community basis. Lord Oliver observed:

> A rule of international law becomes a rule – whether accepted into domestic law or not – only when it is certain and is accepted generally by the body of civilized nations; and it is for those who assert the rule to demonstrate it, if necessary before the International Court of Justice. It is certainly not for a domestic tribunal in effect to legislate a rule into existence for the purposes of domestic law and on the basis of material that is wholly indeterminate.[9]

The thrust of Lord Oliver's observation is that a municipal tribunal, when it is confronted with the need to apply a principle of international law, should determine whether such a principle has been widely accepted by the international community. A municipal tribunal certainly does not possess the jurisdiction to impose an international norm which it creates for the purpose, even if such a fictitious principle is to apply only domestically.

In order to examine the principles of state responsibility, this chapter will address the most fundamental postulates of jurisprudence at air and space law which establish such responsibility.

Principles of State Responsibility under Space Law

The legal and philosophical bases of space law form the antithesis of those applicable to air law in that space law is grounded on the principle that outer space is the common heritage of mankind and that no state or individual can therefore claim rights *in rem* to any portion of outer space. Air law, on the other hand, is firmly entrenched in the principle of sovereignty of states, so that a state may lay claims to rights over the airspace above its territory.[10] This essentially means that, while the implementation of air law is heavily influenced by municipal law, space law is solely grounded on legal principles binding on the community of nations. Principles of public international law therefore play an exclusive part in the application of space law principles.

In terms of jurisprudence, space law represents the idealist school which supports community interest over national interest, while air law represents the realist school which advocates that national interests are pre-eminent considerations for all purposes. The idealist school believes that individual interests should best be served by collective intercourse and is best illustrated by the view of Lauterpacht, who was of the view that 'a community may be said to be the body of a number of individuals more or less bound together through such common interests as to create a manifold intercourse between single individuals'.[11] Legal principles relating to the international community necessarily emanate collectively from that community as a body of rules which require the consent of the community. An examination of the philosophy of space law therefore essentially requires an examination of the nature of public international law itself. This chapter will discuss the philosophical basis of the common heritage principle of space law, through an evaluation of public international law and their relation to each other.

Space law is one of the most recent additions to international jurisprudence. That it pertains to one of the most highly technology-intensive activities is an incontrovertible fact and was made evident with the successful launch of the Space Shuttle 'Columbia' on 12 April 1981, when the world entered a new age of space exploitation, leaving behind the period of space exploration which seemingly started in 1957 with the launch of the Russian 'Sputnik'. Understandably, the world was elated in 1981 at the phenomenon of the space shuttle, to the extent that a space technologist at NASA said, 'I am convinced that by 1990 people will be going on the shuttle routinely – as an aircraft.'[12] Of course, it has not happened quite that way yet. One must concede, however, that the expert's prophecy was at least partially correct, in that by 1990 we were actively involved with the concept of the aerospace plane, of which the space shuttle was a precursor.

The emergent philosophical problem posed by space law, in its offer to mankind of a new dimension of transport law and property law, was succinctly summarized by Professor Bockstiegel in 1983, when he said that space law

> is the newest main field of international law … and it depends more than most other fields on probable and fast technical progress … [13] It is obvious that the application of space technology will lead to the growing commercialization of space activities, since such service – at least in the long run – can only be maintained and expanded if it is self financing.[14]

The blending of high technology with a new forensic code of conduct on hitherto unchartered territory has brought to the fore the need for the community of nations to formulate a sustainable legal theory that will ensure non-exploitation of space resources by individuals or states, while at the same time incorporating the element of responsibility and liability for individual and state conduct in outer space.

As mentioned earlier, the basic principle of space law is the 'common interest' (or common heritage) principle which emerged as a result of the first specific resolution on space law of the United Nations General Assembly in 1958.[15] The 'common interest' principle has since been incorporated in subsequent multilateral treaties, particularly the Outer Space Treaty of 1967,[16] Article 1(1) of which provides: 'the exploration and use of outer space, including the moon and other celestial bodies, shall be carried out for the benefit and in the interest of all countries, irrespective of their degree of economic or scientific development, and shall be the province of all mankind.' This provision, which binds signatory states, is seemingly a departure from the traditional 'national interest' approach of international air law and has represented a moral obligation to some,[17] while to others the provision has represented a *jus cogens* or mandatory legal principle.[18]

The International Court of Justice (ICJ), in the *North Sea Continental Shelf* case,[19] held that legal principles that are incorporated in treaties, such as the 'common interest' principle, become customary international law by virtue of Article 38 of the 1969 Vienna Convention on the Law of Treaties. Article 38 recognizes that a rule set forth in a treaty will become binding upon a third state as a customary rule of international law if it is generally recognized by the states concerned as such. Article 1(1) of the Outer Space Treaty, which declares that the use of space technology is achieved under the 'common interest' principle for the common good of humanity, therefore becomes a principle of customary international law, or *jus cogens*. Obligations arising from *jus cogens* are considered applicable *erga omnes*, which means that states using space technology owe a duty of care to the world at large in the provision of such technology. The ICJ, in the *Barcelona Traction* case, held:

> an essential distinction should be drawn between the obligations of a State towards the international community as a whole, and those arising *vis-à-vis* another State in the field of diplomatic protection. By their very nature, the former are the concerns of all States. In view of the importance of the rights involved, all States can be held to have a legal interest in their protection; they are obligations *erga omnes*.[20]

The International Law Commission has observed of the ICJ decision: 'in the Court's view, there are in fact a number, albeit limited, of international obligations which, by reason of their importance to the international community as a whole, are – unlike others – obligations in respect of which all States have legal interest'.[21] The views of the ICJ and the International Law Commission, which has supported the approach taken by the ICJ, give rise to two possible conclusions relating to *jus cogens* and its resultant obligations *erga omnes*: (a) obligations *erga omnes* affect all states and thus cannot be made inapplicable to a state or group of states by an exclusive clause in a treaty or other document reflecting legal obligations without the consent of the international community as a whole; (b) obligations *erga omnes* pre-empt other obligations which may be incompatible with them.

Examples of obligations *erga omnes* cited by the ICJ are prohibition of acts of aggression, genocide, slavery and discrimination.[22] It is indeed worthy of note that all these obligations are derivatives of norms which are *jus cogens* at international law. If it can be accepted that a principle of *jus cogens* creates obligations *erga omnes*, it becomes an undeniable fact that Article 1(1) of the Outer Space Treaty could be considered a peremptory norm or *jus cogens*, since it generates obligations towards the international community as a whole. Christol observes:

> Article 1 Paragraph 1 of the Space Treaty, with its adoption of the common benefits and interests guarantee, can be supported (as an example of peremptory norms) because the provisions conform to

> moral law in the sense that all humankind is to benefit unconditionally, and because the terms are consistent with the spirit and the purposes identified in Article 1 pars 1 through 3 and Article 2 pars 1 through 4 of the UN Charter, as well as with complementary international agreements of lesser authority. To the extent that the terms are beneficial to individuals, the larger community, and States, and when the provisions are founded on the fundamental moral principles contained in the foregoing paragraphs of Article 1 and 2 of the UN Charter, such basic principles qualify for the status of peremptory norms of general international law.[23]

The effect of this observation is that the content and nature of Article 1(1) confirms that it is a *jus cogens*. There is seemingly no reason why the international community should not give such recognition to the 'common interest' principle as enshrined in Article 1(1) which is aimed at the protection of the interests of the international community as a whole. A fortiori, on the same basis, Article IX of the Outer Space Treaty, which requires that states should avoid harmful contamination and adverse change in the environment of the Earth which may result from the exploration of outer space, would incontrovertibly be considered *jus cogens*.

Article VI of the Outer Space Treaty provides in part that state parties to the treaty shall bear international responsibility for national activities in outer space, whether such activities are carried out by governmental agencies or non-governmental agencies. This provision clearly introduces the notion of strict liability *erga omnes* to the application of the *jus cogens* principle relating to outer space activities of states, and could be considered applicable in instances where states hold out that they have a responsibility to the international community as providers of technology achieved and used by them in outer space, which is used for purposes of air navigation. Article VI further requires that the activities of non-governmental entities in outer space shall require authorization and continuing supervision by the appropriate state party to the treaty, thus ensuring that the state whose nationality the entity bears will be vicariously answerable for the activities of that organization, thereby imputing liability to the state concerned. Article VII makes a state party internationally liable to another state party for damage caused by a space object launched by that state.

The Registration Convention of 1974[24] in Article II(1) requires a launching state of a space object that is launched into earth orbit or beyond to register such space object by means of an entry in an appropriate registry which it shall maintain and inform the Secretary General of the United Nations of the establishment of such a registry. This provision ensures that the international community is kept aware of which state is responsible for which space object and enables the

United Nations to observe outer space activities of states. Article VI of the convention makes it an obligation of all state parties, including those that possess space monitoring and tracking facilities, to render assistance in identifying a space object which causes damage to other space objects or persons. Justice Manfred Lachs reads these provisions of the Registration Convention as meaning that the state of registry and the location of the space object would govern jurisdictional issues arising out of the legal status of space objects.[25] On the issue of joint launching of space objects, Justice Lachs observes:

> No difficulties arise whenever a State launches its own object from its own territory; the same applies to objects owned or launched by non-governmental agencies registered in that State. However, in cases of joint launching, agreement between the parties is required as to which of them is to be deemed the 'State of Registry'. A similar agreement is also necessary when a launching is carried out by an international organization.[26]

The above provision ensures the identification of parties responsible for specific activities in outer space and thereby makes it easier to impose liability for environmental damage caused.

The Outer Space Treaty,[27] while expostulating the fundamental principle in its Article I that the exploration and use of outer space, including the moon and other celestial bodies, shall be carried out for the benefit and in the interests of all countries, explicitly imposes in Article VII international liability and responsibility on each state party to the treaty, for damage caused to another state party or to its populace (whether national or juridical) by the launch or procurement of launch of an object into outer space. In its preceding provisions the treaty imposes international responsibility on states parties for national activities conducted in outer space. The treaty also requires its states parties to be guided by the principle of cooperation and mutual assistance in the conduct of all their activities in outer space.[28] This overall principle is further elucidated in the same provision: 'States Parties to the Treaty shall pursue studies of outer space, including the moon and other celestial bodies, and conduct exploration of them so as to avoid harmful contamination and also adverse changes in the environment of the Earth resulting from the introduction of extraterrestrial matter.'[29]

The Moon Agreement[30] of 1979 provides that, in the exploration and use of the moon, states parties shall take measures inter alia to avoid harmfully affecting the environment of the earth through the introduction of extraterrestrial matter or otherwise.[31] The Liability Convention[32] contains a provision which lays down the legal remedy in instances of damage caused by space objects. Article II provides:

'A launching State shall be absolutely liable to pay compensation for damage caused by its space objects on the surface of the Earth or to aircraft in flight,'[33] thereby imposing a regime of absolute liability on the state that launches space objects such as satellites, which provide technology and communication that is used for air navigational purposes. Although, admittedly, neither the Outer Space Treaty and the Liability Convention explicitly provides for damage caused by technology and communication provided by space objects, culpability arising from the 'common interest' principle and liability provisions of the two conventions can be imputed to states under these conventions.

Gorove states that, in the field of international space law, two clearly connected terms have been used: liability and responsibility.[34] Although 'responsibility' has not been cohesively interpreted in any legal treaty relating to outer space, 'liability' occurs in the Liability Convention and is sufficiently clear therein. This, however, does not mean that state responsibility is not relevant to the obligations of states law as, in international relations, the invasion of a right or other legal interest of one subject of the law by another inevitably creates legal responsibility. Professor Brownlie observes:

> today, one can regard responsibility as a general principle of international law, a concomitant of substantive rules and of the supposition that acts and omissions may be categorized as illegal by reference to the rules establishing rights and duties. Shortly, the law of responsibility is concerned with the incidence and consequence of illegal acts, and particularly the payment of compensation for loss caused.[35]

Brownlie adds:

> The nature of State responsibility is not based upon delict in the municipal sense, and 'international responsibility' relates both to breaches of treaty and to other breaches of legal duty. There is no harm in using the term 'international tort' to describe the breach of duty which results in a loss to another State, but the term 'tort' could mislead the common lawyer. The compendious term 'international responsibility' is used by tribunals and is least confusing.[36]

International responsibility relates both to breaches of treaty provisions and to other breaches of legal duty. In the *Spanish Zone of Morocco Claims* case, Justice Huber observed: 'responsibility is the necessary corollary of a right. All rights of an international character involve international responsibility. If the obligation in question is not met, responsibility entails the duty to make reparation'.[37] The provision and use of GNSS by states within their territories carries with it the fundamental responsibility not to cause damage to international users of such services. This raises the delicate issue of *culpa* or fault on the part of the state concerned and whether knowledge of the damage can be imputed to the provider state even in instances where knowledge cannot be clearly established. In the *Corfu Channel* case,[38] which involved damage to British vessels in Albanian waters caused by mine laying by Albania, the court said:

> it cannot be concluded from the mere fact of the control exercised by a State over its territory and waters that that State necessarily knew, or ought to have known, of any unlawful act perpetrated therein, nor yet that it necessarily knew, or should have known, the authors. This fact, by itself and apart from other circumstances, neither involves *prima facie* responsibility nor shifts the burden of proof.
>
> On the other hand, the fact of this exclusive territorial control exercised by a State within its frontiers has a bearing upon the methods of proof available to establish the knowledge of that State as to such events. By reason of this exclusive control, the other State, the victim of a breach of international law, is often unable to furnish direct proof of facts giving rise to responsibility. Such a State should be allowed a more liberal recourse to inferences of fact and circumstantial evidence …
>
> The Court must examine therefore whether it has been established by means of indirect evidence that Albania has knowledge of mine-laying in her territorial waters independently of any connivance on her part in this operation. The proof may be drawn from inferences of fact, provided they leave *no room* for reasonable doubt. The elements of fact on which these inferences can be based may differ from those which are relevant to the question of connivance.[39]

There is also explicit recognition that principles of international law apply to space law. The General Assembly of the United Nations in 1961 adopted the view that international law, including the Charter of the United Nations, applies to outer space and celestial bodies.[40] It is also now recognized as a principle of international law that the breach of a duty involves an obligation to make reparation appropriately and adequately.

General Comments

There is no room for doubt that, in the formulation of space law as a new legal regime, the international community has paid attention to the most significant influence over this discipline of the two superpowers which existed at the time. The two great power blocs, the United States of America and the Union of Soviet Socialist Republics were then the main protagonists (supported by their allies and a few neutral European states and the Third World). This polarization created an environment whereby an ideological balance was required to counter the possibility of encroachment by realist thought which was calculated to establish an outer space legal regime that would have admitted of the creation of real property rights by one power bloc over the other in outer space to the detriment of humankind in general.

The detriment envisaged was not only in its physical attributes and apprehension for the physical welfare of humanity, but also in the economic imbalance a realist approach to space law would have brought to bear. The segmentation of space law into municipal regimes would have resulted in the inexorable endorsement of realist theory, that states are egotistical utility enhancers and that the freedom of internal legislation would have given states a legal licence to maximize their freedom of outer space activities, thereby obviating any possibility of cooperation with other states. The inevitable corollary to this scenario would have been the avoidance of spreading the benefits of outer space exploration and exploitation throughout the world.

The general delineation of outer space as a common area rather than as an area which could be conquered therefore rested on the more traditional ground of international cooperation. However, the decision of the two power blocs to settle on commonality rather than on appropriation as the basis for the philosophy of space law is by no means the result of hard bargaining: it was the preferred choice of both parties. History records that there was no coercion or imposition of one system at the expense of another at the time of law making. One commentator says: 'it resulted from a process of weighing competing proposals based on different analogies and converging on the view that one of the underlying analogies was better than the other'.[41] Be that as it may, it is not possible to dismiss the pervasive influence exerted by the international legal order in the late 1950s when space law was being promulgated. It was this influence which made it possible for the philosophy of space law to be primarily founded upon the concept that, unlike the situation in the formulation of air law in 1944, where states were aware of the economic and technical implications of a tried and tested product, outer space was an unknown quantity, controlled exclusively at that time by two power blocs who had ominous war power, and therefore its philosophy was destined to spread across the globe equally, ensuring commonality and responsibility.

Principles of State Responsibility at Air Law

Inherent in the GNSS mechanism is the critical role played by air traffic management which is not regulated by international convention owing to the permeating influence of the principles of state sovereignty. Therefore responsibility of states for their air traffic management rests heavily on the concept of sovereignty upon which air law has been built.

Air law is based entirely on the concept of state sovereignty in air space and is essentially related to land. The concept dates back to early Roman times, when 'States claimed, held, and in fact exercised sovereignty in the air space above their national territories … and … the recognition of an existing territorial airspace of States by the Paris Convention of 1919[42] was well founded in law and history'.[43]

The Roman State adopted an all-embracing approach in ensuring the protection of private and public rights of its citizens. It could not have assumed full jurisdiction to lay down rules for its citizenry unless it exercised rights of sovereignty in airspace as well as on land. The genesis of the concept of sovereignty in airspace is traced back to Justinian's *Corpus Juris Civilis*,[44] where the concept seemed rather to be the work of some gloss upon a passage in the 'Digest'. Accordingly, airspace at that time became, in international law, a contentious issue when it came to justifying the removal of projections from adjoining property over a place of burial.[45] Bouve added the view that airspace was new space added to accommodate man's ability to fly.[46] Thus the right bestowed by the private law maxim, *Cujus est Solum, Ejus est Usque ad Coelum* was firmly entrenched as an absolute right of a person under ancient Roman law. This maxim, which means that a right of land ownership brings with it rights of ownership of airspace above the land, was later found to be unacceptable as an absolute rule. Blacklisted as a 'product of some black letter lawyer',[47] the rule was later adapted to mean that no nation acquired any domain in what was known as navigable airspace until such domain was needed to protect subjacent territory.[48]

The doctrine of sovereignty was introduced to the Western world by the French philosopher Bodin. At a time when political attitudes were in transition from the dominance of the universal church to a universal legal order, Bodin introduced sovereignty as a supreme power over citizens and subjects that was not itself bound by laws.[49] Bodin elaborated that every independent community had to consider that, while acknowledging the authority of the law, a state was above the law if it wished to govern successfully. Other jurists who supported the theory of exclusive sovereignty were Hugo Grotius, who maintained that sovereign states were independent of foreign control, and Thomas Hobbes, who said that sovereignty was absolute and its misuse was unthinkable. John Locke attempted to compromise the absolute quality of sovereignty by opining that sovereignty was not absolute and unquestionable, in that it was an exchange of social trust between the government and the people. Accordingly, there was an inarticulate premise that a breach of the social trust between the two parties would erode the concept of sovereignty. John Austin, in his *Province of Jurisprudence Determined* (1892) defined sovereignty as emanating from a person: 'a determinate human superior not in the habit of obedience to a like superior, receives habitual obedience from the bulk of a given society, that determinate superior is sovereign in society and that society is therefore sovereign and independent'.[50]

The important question is, how is sovereignty determined? Both juristic and judicial opinion favour the view that sovereignty of airspace should be determined on the role played by the importance of subjacent airspace in its relation to land and sea. In other words, a symbolic possession of the airspace is necessary in order that states can claim sovereignty over their airspace. Therefore the concept of sovereignty becomes compatible with the concept of ownership of property with possession by the owner, to the exclusion of others. To determine sovereignty in airspace, three elements would have to be resolved: the use of airspace, the nature of its possession, and the nature of its control to the exclusion of others.

The use of airspace is inextricably linked to the social needs that the airspace in question would subserve. Roscoe Pound envisaged that one of the fundamental bases for the control and use of property was its sociological importance.[51] There is no difficulty in establishing a nexus between the sociological value of territorial land and sea and the protection offered to them by the subjacent air space of a country. The next element – symbolic possession – has its roots in the early Roman law concept of *traditio longa manu*,[52] where possession was transferred by a symbolic act such as the handing over of a key to a premises when continued and consistent access was impracticable. Savigny elaborates on this classical theory by infusing three elements into the concept of possession: detention with *animus domini* or the will to hold as owner, *animus possidendi* or the will to exclude others from one's property, and *animus rem sibi habendi* or the will to hold for oneself. Savigny's concept of the need to blend detention with *animus* (intention) for the establishment of possession is satisfied by the modern concept of sovereignty in airspace, since all these elements can be seen in a state's claim to sovereignty over airspace where the three elements impute the physical fact of de facto *dominium* to the intention to retain possession of the object.[53] Jhering went a step further by claiming that detention was not necessary; only the will of the possessor was. Weber and Erlich both contended that the law is not a formal set of rules but a prime method of establishing order in society and accordingly required a person merely to show incontrovertible reason for the need to possess property. The final element – the nature of control of airspace – can be subsumed in modern juristic thought: that the modern interpretation of the concept of sovereignty is not the ability to make war or to exploit others, but to legislate over a given state or community.[54]

Perhaps the most convincing justification for the acceptance of sovereignty in airspace as the fundamental legal norm in air law is seen in Hans Kelsen's pure theory of the law.[55] Kelsen considered that all international laws derived their basis from a *grundnorm*, or a basic legal postulate, derived purely from law and not from morality. This basic norm was international custom. In this context, the philosophy of air law is founded on the concept of sovereignty in airspace and would sustain its credibility through this customary concept. The idea of sovereignty is then taken to its final conclusion and ultimate justification by Pound, when he states: 'Men must be able to assume in civilized society that they may control, for purposes beneficial to themselves, what they have created by their own labour and what they have acquired under existing social and economic order. This is a final postulate of civilized society.'[56] If Pound's view – that man must control what he has created for his benefit, under the existing social and economic order – were to prevail, it is logical to say that the element of control that man exercises as 'sovereignty' must essentially be viewed on a collective basis, and that the interest of the world community must necessarily be considered.

Judicial Decisions and Academic Views on Sovereignty

The linkage between the use of airspace and the protection of a subjacent territory was supported by American and English decisions[57] where the *ad Coelum* maxim was called 'a fanciful phrase ... a glittering generality which has not arisen out of contested law suits and not therefore received close judicial scrutiny'.[58] American judicial opinion is exemplified in the decision in *Hinman* v. *Pacific Air Transport*,[59] where the court said: 'Title to the airspace unconnected with the use of land is inconceivable. Such a right has never been asserted. It is a thing not known to the law.'[60] The court in this instance applied the overall doctrine as modified and ruled that the plaintiff, who claimed ownership of 150 feet above his land, had no rights in superjacent airspace over the defendant, who operated his plane 100 feet above the plaintiff's land. The *ad Coelum* maxim was therefore no longer regarded as the law. On the one hand, the formula that it extended from the centre of the earth to the skies was judicially tenuous. On the other, the fact that a landowner had unlimited rights relating to the air space above his land was considered retrogressive and indefinable. There was no evidence of customary acceptance of the maxim for jurists to consider it as a scholastic doctrine of practical acceptance.

The *ad Coelum* formula therefore became a figurative phrase, never to be taken literally but used to express complete ownership of land, and the right to superjacent airspace only to the extent as was necessary or convenient to the enjoyment of land. The owner of land owns as much of the airspace above him as he uses, but only so long as he uses it.

By the end of the 19th century, the private law concept of absolute ownership of airspace over land was antiquated. The beginning of the 20th century saw the emergence of states' sovereignty in airspace. The impetus for public international law to take over the issue of rights over airspace was given by the August 1904 aerial incident where Russian guards shot down the German balloon 'Tschudi' when it was flying outside Russian territory and the two unrelated but similar incidents that occurred in 1908 and 1910.[61] The French government hastened to call a conference of European powers in 1910. For the first time, participating states at this conference recognized airspace belonging to individual states on the basis that 'The upper air is a national heritage common to all of the people, and its reasonable use ought not to be hampered by an ancient artificial maxim of law.'[62] The consensus of opinion of the European states in 1910 followed the landmark US decision of *Erickson* v. *Crookston*,[63] decided in 1907, where the court said: 'Common law rules are sufficiently flexible to adapt themselves to new conditions arising out of modern progress, and it is within the legitimate province of the courts to so construe and apply them.'[64]

The First World War decided the issue of public rights over airspace, when Germany alleged that the *casus belli* was the penetration of German airspace by French aviators. The experience of the war (1914–19) strongly reinforced the view of the British delegation (supported by Holland, Denmark and Switzerland) at the European Air Law Conference of 1910 that states' sovereignty extended *usque ad coelum* and that belligerent aircraft cannot go over the territory of another at will.[65] By the end of the war, air law was regarded as a discipline that accepted air as being a free commodity except when it was connected to owned property (subjacent airspace) and seen to be used to protect that property.[66]

Professor Bin Cheng addresses the principles governing post-Second World War sovereignty over airspace as enunciated in Article 1 of the Chicago Convention[67] and concludes: 'The now firmly established rule of international law that each State possesses complete and exclusive sovereignty over the airspace above its territory means that international civil aviation today rests on the tacit acquiescence or express agreement of States flown over.'[68]

Shawcross and Beaumont define sovereignty in international law as the right to exercise the functions of a state to the exclusion of all other states in regard to a certain area of the world.[69] In international aviation the concept of sovereignty is the fundamental postulate upon which other norms and virtually all air law are based.[70] Post-1944 attitudes towards the concept of sovereignty in airspace and the philosophy of air law range between the unlimited public law right of a state to exercise sovereignty over its airspace and the idea of free movement of air traffic. Professor Goedhuis identifies the idea of 'free traffic' as opposed to the exclusivity of the sovereignty principle as being considered by jurists as a constructive element of aviation which furthers life and raises it to a higher level.[71] This view is supported by the claim that general principles of international law demand that sovereignty of states should be limited by the principle of freedom of peaceful traffic.[72] Be that as it may, a view advocating the free use of airspace of a country by aircraft of foreign nationalities would give rise to a dichotomy: that there should be freedom of aviation with a minimum of restrictions or none at all, or that international air traffic should be firmly regulated. Professor Lissitzyn analyses the concept of sovereignty in its modern development as having three basic principles: that each state has exclusive sovereignty over its airspace; each state has complete discretion as to the admission of any aircraft into its airspace; and that airspace over the high seas and other areas not subject to a state's jurisdiction is *res nullius* and is free to the aircraft of all states.[73]

H.A. Wassenbergh lists seven objectives of a state's policy in respect of modern civil aviation:

a to contribute to the functioning of the international community of states as a total legal order by upholding and further developing the rule of international law;
b to protect the integrity and identity of the national society;
c to promote the nation's participation in man's activities in the air and space;
d to create the best possible conditions and opportunities for use by the public of aviation and space activities;
e to increase the benefits to be derived from the use of the air and outer space for its nationals;
f to promote the further development of technology and the knowledge of man;
g to cooperate with other states on the basis of equal rights in order

> to bridge conflicting national interests and achieve the aims mentioned above.[74]

Paul Steven Dempsey attributes the insistence of man on sovereignty to the fact that the human being is a territorial beast whose primordial imperative was to satisfy his thirst for control over a given area.[75] This view seems compatible with the early trends in the context of which the Paris Convention[76] provided that each state enjoys complete and exclusive sovereignty over the airspace above its territory.[77] Accordingly, from 1919, transit and landing rights for airlines became notionally subject to the explicit or tacit approval of the state in which the aircraft landed. Later, in August 1945, at the first meeting of the Opening Session of the Interim Council of the Provisional International Civil Aviation Organization (PICAO), the Hon. C.D. Howe, Minister of Reconstruction, Canada said: 'We [Canada] believe that there must be greater freedom for development of international air transport and that this freedom may best be obtained within a framework which provides equality of opportunity and rewards for efficiency.'[78] Edward Warner, Representative of the United States of America (later the first President of the ICAO Council) said at the same meeting:

> Our first purpose will be to smooth the paths for civil flying wherever we are able. We shall seek to make it physically easier, safer, more reliable, more pleasant; but I believe it will be agreed also that we should maintain the constant goal that civil aviation should contribute to international harmony. The civil use of aircraft must so develop as to bring the peoples closer together, letting nation speak more understandingly unto nation.[79]

Dr Warner had notably stressed the purpose of civil aviation as being the promotion of international harmony and dialogue between nations. He had also made it clear that the seminal task of civil aviation is to bring the people of the world together through understanding and interaction. It is clear that, at this stage at least, civil aviation was recognized more as a social necessity than as a mere economic factor. In addition, through the statements of Minister Howe and Dr Warner, one can glean the attitude of the international community towards aviation at that time: that civil aviation was based on equality of opportunity and that it was a social need rather than a fiscal tool.

Jurisprudential aspects of state responsibility for ensuring that there is no damage or loss to others caused by the use and operation of GNSS lie essentially in the importance one could place in the thrust of public international law principles of international cooperation and comity, on the one hand, and municipal law which may be calculated to obviate such obligations, on the other. The theoretical dichotomy is well reflected in the clash of ideology between dualism and monism.

Dualism (or pluralism) recognizes that international law and municipal law are two distinct forces, one representing law between sovereign states and the other representing the internal or domestic law of a state, whereby relations between citizens and citizens and the executive of the state concerned are determined. Typical dualist theory leaves the two regimes severely alone, holding that, while municipal law may decree certain international laws to be part of municipal law, it is certainly not a rule-of-thumb issue to import international law to be part of municipal law. Based on this logic, dualist doctrine would expect municipal courts to apply municipal law.

Monism, on the other hand, accepts unreservedly the supremacy of international law and bases itself on its distrust of the state in its role of protecting human rights. At least in the context of the relation between obligations of states and municipal law, monism is given more credibility than dualism, in that a state cannot plead provisions of its own laws or inadequacies in its laws as its response to a breach of its obligations imposed by international law. Jurisprudence supporting this premise is monotonously consistent, as is reflected in the *Free Zones Case*,[80] where the Provisional Court of International Justice (PCIJ) ruled that France was precluded from using its own legislation to desist from performing its international obligations. In the earlier case of *Polish Nations in Danzig*,[81] the PCIJ held:

> It should ... be observed that ... a State cannot adduce as against another State its own Constitution with a view to evading obligations incumbent upon it under international law or treaties in force. Applying these principles to the present case, it results that the question of the treatment of Polish nationals or other Persons of Polish origin or speech must be settled exclusively on the basis of the rules of international law and the treaty provisions in force between Poland and Danzig.[82]

There is a compelling school of thought which is consistent with the above judicial theory and holds that there is a general duty incumbent upon all states to bring their internal laws into conformity with obligations and responsibilities imposed by international law.[83]

If the concept of state sovereignty were still to preclude consensus on international accord with regard to state responsibility for air traffic control services provided within states' territories, one could expect that the responsibility of states in this field would have to be determined by the principles of public international law. State responsibility at air law would be restricted not only to the instance of provision of air traffic control services but also to other aspects which involve GNSS. In all such instances both air law and space law are inextricably interwoven by the principle of state responsibility *erga omnes* enumerated in the *Barcelona Traction* case, which Professor Brownlie elaborates as a general principle of international law and Justice Huber identifies as the necessary corollary of a right.

In the ultimate analysis, therefore, one could only agree with Wassenbergh when he said that one of the seven objectives of a state's policy with regard to modern civil aviation is to cooperate with other states on the basis of equal rights in order to bridge conflicting national interests. GNSS should form no exception to this thinking process.

Notes

1 Rosalind Dubs (1996), 'Selection of GNSS Solutions for Australia and the Region', *Journal of Air Traffic Control*, July–September, 64.
2 See Anne Paylor (1994), 'Asia Prepares for GNSS', *Airports International*, May, 33–5.
3 See 'ICAO working paper, WW/IMP-WP/10, 11/5/98, item 5, Appendix.
4 See ICAO World-wide Conference Produces Strong Recommendations for Financing and Managing CNS/ATM Systems Implementation', *ICAO News Release*, PIO 3/98, p.1.
5 Convention on International Civil Aviation, signed at Chicago on 7 December 1944, Doc. 7300/7 7th edn, 1997, Montreal: ICAO.
6 See B.D. Kofi Henaku (1996), 'International Liability of the GNSS Space Segment Provider', *Annals of Air and Space Law*, XXI, Part I, 143–79; also Assad Kotaite (1996), 'ICAO's Role with Respect to the Institutional Arrangements and Legal Framework of Global Navigation Satellite Systems (GNSS) Planning Implementation', *Annals of Air and Space Law*, XXI, 202–3.
7 Kotaite (*supra*, n.6, 203).
8 (1989) 3 WLR 969 (HL).
9 Ibid., 1014.
10 See R.I.R. Abeyratne (1992), 'The Philosophy of Air Law', 37 *American Journal of Jurisprudence*, 135–44.
11 H. Lauterpacht (1955), *International Law*, 8th edn, p.11.
12 *National Geographic*, March 1981, p.317.
13 Karl-Heinz Böckstiegel, 'Prospects of Future Development in the Law of Outer Space', *Annals of Air and Space Law*, VIII, 305.
14 Ibid., 314.
15 UNGA Resolution 1348 (XII), 13 December 1958.
16 Treaty on Principles Governing the Activities of States in the Exploration and Use of Outer Space, Including the Moon and Other Celestial Bodies, opened for signature at Moscow, London and Washington on 27 January 1967, 610 UNTS 205.
17 D. Goedhuis (1976), 'Some Substantive and Procedural Issues Presently at Stake in Space Legislation', *Zeitschrift für Luft-und Weltraumrecht*, 25 German Journal of Air and Space Law, 198–9; also Bin Cheng (1968), 'The 1967 Space Treaty', *Journal du Droit International*, 95, 578.

18 M.G. Markoff (1976), 'Disarmament and "Peaceful Purposes" Provisions in the 1967 Outer Space Treaty', *Journal of Space Law*, 4, 3; also N.M. Matte (1980), 'Aerospace Law: Telecommunications Satellites', *Recueil des Cours* 166(1), 147; R.S. Jakhu, *Developing Countries and the Fundamental Principles of International Space Law* (Girardot *et al.*, ed.), p.351; C.Q. Christol (1983), *The Jus Cogens Principle and International Space Law*, XXVI Colloquium, 1.
19 *I.C.J. Reports*, 1970, 32.
20 *Barcelona Traction, Light and Power Company Limited, I.C.J. Reports*, 1974, 269–70.
21 *Yearbook of International Law Commission* (1976), Vol. II, Part One, p.29.
22 *I.C.J. Reports*, 1970, 32.
23 Christol (*supra*, n.18), 6.
24 Convention on Registration of Objects Launched into Outer Space, adopted by the General Assembly of the United Nations, New York, 12 November 1974, 1023 UNTS 15.
25 Manfred Lachs (1972), *The Law of Outer Space, An Experience in Contemporary Law Making*, Leiden: Sijthoff, p.70.
26 Ibid.
27 *Supra*, n.16.
28 Ibid., Article IX.
29 Ibid.
30 Agreement Governing the Activities of States on the Moon and other Celestial Bodies, signed on 5 December 1979, UN Doc. A/RES/34/68 of 5/12/1979.
31 Ibid., Article 7.
32 Convention on International Liability for Damage Caused by Space Objects, 29 March 1972, 24 U.S.T 2389, T.I.A.S No. 7762.
33 Article II(a) defines damage as including loss of life, personal injury or other impairment of health; or loss or damage to property of states or of persons natural or juridical, or property of international governmental organizations.
34 Stephen Gorove (1983), 'Liability in Space Law: An Overview', *Annals of Air and Space Law* VIII, 373.
35 Ian Brownlie (1990), *Principles of Public International Law*, 4th edn, Oxford: Clarendon Press, p.433.
36 Ibid., p.434.
37 1925 RIAA ii 615 at 641.
38 *ICJ Reports*, 1949, at 4.
39 Ibid., 18.
40 Resolution 1721 (XVI), adopted on 20 December 1961. See also Article 3 of the Outer Space Treaty.
41 M.J. Peterson (1997), 'The Use of Analogies in Developing Outer Space Law', *International Organization*, 51(2), Spring, 266.
42 The Paris Convention of 1919 will be discussed later on in this chapter.
43 John Cobb Cooper, 'Roman Law and the Maxim *"Cujus Est Solum"* in International Law', cited in *Explorations in Aerospace Law*, 55(102), 1968.
44 42 tit. 24, pr 22 S.4.
45 A.K. Kuhn (1910), 'Beginnings of an Aerial Law', *American Journal of International Law*, 4, 123.
46 G. Bouve (1930), 'The Development of International Rules of Conduct in Air Navigation' *Air Law Review*, 1(6).
47 S.E. Baldwin (1910), 'The Law of the Airship', *American Journal of International Law*, 4, 97.
48 Cooper (*supra*, n.43), 29.
49 C.B. Weeramantry (1982), *An Invitation to the Law*, Sydney: Butterworth, p.175.
50 Ibid., 176.

51 Roscoe Pound (1961), *Introduction to the Philosophy of the Law*, New Haven: Yale University Press, p.114.
52 Weeramantry (*supra*, n.49), p.165.
53 Roscoe Pound (1959), *Jurisprudence*, Vol. V, Part 8, St Paul, Minn.: West Publishing Company, p.95.
54 Dennis Lloyd (1964), *The Idea of the Law*, Harmondsworth: Penguin Books, p.171.
55 See Leon L. Fuller (1949), *The Problems of Jurisprudence*, Brooklyn: The Foundation Press.
56 Roscoe Pound (1922), *An Introduction to the Philosophy of Law*, New Haven: Yale University Press, pp.192–3.
57 *United States* v. *Curtiss-Wright Export Corp et al.*, 299 US 3904 (1936): *United States* v. *State of California*, 322 US 19 (1947); for English law, see *Wandsworth Board of Works* v. *United Telephone Company*, 13 QB 904. See also Robert R. Right (1968), *The Law of Airspace*, New York: Bobbs-Merril Company, p.65, for comments on the *ad Coelum* principle as used in the USA and UK. In English law, the *ad Coelum* principle at private law can be traced to Lord Cooke (Liber 1, S.1 p. 4). This doctrine was approved in *Fay* v. *Prentice* (1845) 1 CB 827, *Corbett* v. *Hill* (1874) 9 L.R. eq 671 and *Ellis* v. *Loftus* (1874) L.R. 10, C.P. 10.
58 *Wandsworth Board of Works* v. *United Telephone Company* (*supra*, n.57), 905.
59 84 F. 2d 411 (2d Cir 1937).
60 Ibid., 417.
61 Visty C. Gunatilaka (1972), 'Problems of Airspace Sovereignty in the Seventies', LLM thesis, Institute of Air and Space Law, McGill University, Montreal, p.5.
62 W. Jefferson Davis (1930), *Aeronautical Law*, London: Parker, Stone and Baird, p.30.
63 100 Minn. 481 (1907).
64 Ibid., 484.
65 N.H. Mollere (1963), *The Law of Civil Aviation*, London: Sweet and Maxwell, p.4.
66 Carl Zollman (1927), *Law of the Air*, Milwaukee: The Bruce Publishing Company, p.3.
67 Convention on International Civil Aviation, signed at Chicago, 7 December 1944. See ICAO Doc. 7300/7, 7th edn.
68 Bin Cheng (1962), *The Law of International Air Transport*, London: Stevens and Sons, p.3. See also pp.3–17 for a discussion on the manner in which air rights devolve upon air carriers under the sovereignty doctrine of the Chicago Convention.
69 Shawcross and Beaumont (1977), *Air Law*, London: (Butterworth & Company, p.15.
70 Ibid.
71 D. Goedhuis (1947), *Idea and Interests in International Aviation*, quoted in Z. Joseph Gertler (1979), 'Order in the Air and the Problem of Real and False Options', *Annals of Air and Space Law*, IV, 100.
72 Ibid.
73 O.J. Lissitzyn (1983), *International Air Transport and National Policy*, New York & London: Garland Publishing, p.365.
74 H.A. Wassenbergh (1978), 'Reality and Value of Air and Space Law', *Annals Air and Space Law*, III, p.352.
75 Paul Steven Dempsey (1987), *Law and Foreign Policy in International Aviation*, Dobbs Ferry, New York: Transnational Publishers, p.7.
76 Convention Relating to the Regulation of Aerial Navigation, signed 13 October 1919 (hereafter referred to as the Paris Convention).
77 Paris Convention, Article 1.
78 *PICAO Documents*, 1945, Volume 1, Doc. 1, p.3, Montreal.

79 Ibid., Doc. 2, p.2.
80 (1932) PCIJ, Ser. A/B No. 46. 46 at 167.
81 1931) PCIJ, Ser. A/B No. 44 at 20.
82 Ibid., at p.24.
83 See Fitzmaurice (1957), *Hague Recueil*, 92 (II), 89.

19 Liability Issues: Prevention of Controlled Flight into Terrain

Introduction

Controlled flight into terrain (CFIT) or, in simple terms, crews unwillingly flying their aeroplanes into the ground, still remains the single most frequent contributor to and causative factor of aircraft accidents.[1] In 1998, 24 CFIT driven accidents occurred, resulting in at least 17 total hull losses and 385 fatalities.[2] The previous year's records reflect that 50 CFIT-related accidents occurred, resulting in 31 hull losses and 770 fatalities. Going back further, it is recorded that, during the 1978–96 period, there were an average of 42 accidents per year, resulting in 29 hull losses and 510 fatalities.[3]

Despite these demoralizing figures, the International Civil Aviation Organization has been carrying out a sustained programme and prevention campaign, particularly in the 1990s. Two noteworthy and signal achievements of ICAO in this field have been the numerous recommendations incorporated into Annex 6 to the Chicago Convention[4] as a result of work carried out by a CFIT task force led by ICAO and the Flight Safety Foundation, culminating in 1995, and the ICAO Accident Investigation and Prevention (AIP) Divisional meeting held in Montreal from 14 to 24 September 1999. At this meeting, some 151 world aviation experts agreed on a series of recommendations designed to strengthen aircraft accident prevention through enhanced reporting systems and more efficient sharing of safety-related information.[5]

In opening the meeting, the President of the ICAO Council, Dr Assad Kotaite succinctly drew attention to the pervasive and all-encompassing factors prevailing upon modern aviation as being significant in the prevention and investigation of CFIT accidents. Dr Kotaite observed:

> Fundamental to prevention in aviation safety is the thoroughness of accident and incident investigations, and the timely reporting of the findings ... Our [ICAO's] investigation policies, procedures and techniques must keep pace with developments in aviation technology, worldwide expansion of air services, increased competition among airlines, liberalization of access to markets and the continuing trend of partnerships among airlines and manufacturers.[6]

Dr Kotaite makes the very relevant point of there being a compelling need for work on accident prevention and investigation in order to keep pace with the prolific advances of commercial aviation and aviation technology. In the spirit of this observation of the President of the ICAO Council, the September 1999 meeting proposed a new chapter in Annex 13 to the Chicago Convention,[7] containing requirements, inter alia, for states to establish mandatory incident-reporting systems to facilitate the collection of information on actual or potential safety deficiencies, and to establish voluntary incident-reporting systems to complement the information captured by mandatory reporting systems.

Also among ICAO's contributions to the prevention of CFIT-related accidents is the requirement for the installation of Ground Proximity Warning Systems (GPWS) worldwide in large jet aircraft. It is reported that GPWS reduces CFIT risk by 95 per cent.[8] Of course, prevention of aircraft accidents, whether CFIT-related or otherwise, does not depend entirely on technology. The human factor is equally important, as emphasized by Earl F. Weener, chief engineer for aircraft reliability at the Boeing Commercial Airplane Group.[9] This view is supported by the Flight Safety Foundation (FSF) which emphasizes that, as soon as a GPWS warning occurs in an aircraft in flight, pilots should, immediately and without hesitation, evaluate the warning and execute the pull-up action recommended in the company procedure manual. If such a manual is not available, the FSF recommends that pilots should immediately initiate a maximum-performance full power climb until the GPWS warning signal stops. The only exception to this procedure is when clear meteorological conditions prevail enabling 100 per cent visibility, which would entitle the pilots to determine whether a warning signal is false. The final step in the procedure is for the pilots to notify air traffic control, as soon as possible, when a pull-up is executed consequent to a GPWS warning signal.

It is incontrovertible that CFIT involves a delicate balance between the involvement of technology and human professional conduct in the cockpit. In this context, the CFIT checklist developed by the FSF in 1994 and endorsed by ICAO is all-encompassing and effective. The checklist is capable of being used both to evaluate specific flight operations and to enhance pilot awareness of the CFIT risk. The checklist's most salient and positive attribute is that it enables the pilot, through a system of positive and negative scoring, to evaluate the risk with the greatest precision possible. It has as the last line of defence the GPWS signal, before which, if a pilot follows the three-part document faithfully, a ground proximity warning could be obviated. From a legal perspective, the availability of such a document imputes good airmanship to the pilot as a matter of course and the GPWS and the global requirement of its installation in aircraft places a responsibility on the carrier.

The following discussion will address regulatory and legal issues involving CFIT accidents and the liabilities of the parties responsible for the avoidance of such accidents.

Regulatory Issues

The seminal pronouncement on aviation safety is contained in the Preamble to the Convention on International Civil Aviation[10] wherein states parties agree on certain principles and arrangements of the Convention in order that international civil aviation may be developed in a safe and orderly manner.

The Chicago Convention also establishes ICAO whose aims and objectives are, inter alia, to ensure the safe and orderly growth of international civil aviation throughout the world;[11] meet the needs of the people of the world for safe, regular, efficient and economical air transport;[12] and promote safety of flight in international air navigation.[13] In pursuance of these aims and objectives, ICAO, at its 29th Assembly, held from 22 September to 8 October 1992, adopted Assembly Resolution A29-13 on the improvement of safety oversight, which reaffirms a state's responsibility for safety oversight and calls member states to reconfirm their safety oversight obligations, among other things.[14]

The 31st Assembly, held in Montreal in 1995, adopted Resolution A31-9 on the Implementation of the ICAO Program for the Prevention of Controlled Flight into Terrain (CFIT). The resolution makes reference to the updating of ICAO standards relating to GPWS and the objective of the CFIT task force of a 50 per cent reduction in the global CFIT accident rate by 1998, and directs the ICAO Council to continue to develop the ICAO programme for the reduction of CFIT accident rates as a matter of priority. It also urges states to implement ICAO's CFIT prevention programme, particularly in terms of the installation and carriage of GPWS in aircraft, and to take all necessary measures towards achieving the 50 per cent reduction rate of CFIT accidents.[15]

At its 32nd Assembly, held in 1998, ICAO saw the adoption of Resolution A32-15 on the ICAO Global Aviation Safety Plan (GASP) which, inter alia, noted with concern that CFIT continues to be a very significant cause of accidents in airline operations and stressed the need for a reduction in the rate of fatal accidents in airline operations. The resolution reiterates the need for full implementation of the ICAO programme for the prevailing CFIT, as outlined in Resolution 31-9.[16]

As guidance material for states on the prevention of CFIT accidents, the latest edition of Annex 6 to the Chicago Convention, which is on the subject of operations of aircraft, requires *in limine* under the subject of international general aviation that aeroplanes when operated across land areas which have been designated by the state concerned as areas in which search and rescue would be especially difficult shall be equipped with such signalling devices and life saving equipment (including means of sustaining life) as may be appropriate to the area overflown.[17] The annex also makes the recommendation that all turbine-engined aeroplanes of a maximum certified take-off mass in excess of 15 000 kg or authorized to carry more than 30 passengers should be equipped with a ground proximity warning system.[18]

There are other provisions in the annex which require the installation of a GPWS in other types of aircraft.[19] The annex also emphasizes the need,[20] from 1 January 1999, for a GPWS to provide warnings of an excessive descent rate; excessive terrain closure rate; excessive altitude loss after take-off or go-around; unsafe terrain clearance while not in landing configuration when the gear is not locked down or flaps are not in a landing position; and excessive descent below the instrument glide path.

For international commercial air transport, the annex stipulates that an aeroplane engaging in commercial air transport should be equipped with instruments which will enable the flight crew to control the flight path of the aeroplane, carry out any required procedural manoeuvres and observe the operating limitations of the aeroplane in the expected operating conditions.[21] Commercial aircraft are also required to be equipped with GPWS and, from 1 January 1999, the same criteria for warning requirements[22] as are contained in the annex for general aviation would apply.[23]

ICAO's Safety Oversight Programme

The ICAO Dilemma

There are three provisions in the Chicago Convention which affect the subject of safety. Primarily, Article 12 requires each contracting state to maintain uniform aviation regulations in conformity, to the greatest possible extent, with those established under the Convention. Article 31 stipulates that every aircraft engaged in international aviation shall be provided with a certificate of airworthiness issued or rendered valid by the state in which it is registered. The following provision (Article 32) requires the pilot of every aircraft and the other members of the operating crew of every aircraft engaged in international navigation to be provided with certificates of competency. More importantly, Article 32(*b*) empowers states to refuse to recognize, for the purposes of flight above their own territories, certificates of competency and licences granted to any of its nationals by another contracting state.

All these provisions really mean one thing: maintain uniform standards in certification so that safety of civil aviation can be ensured. The question is whether such uniformity is ensured in the case of an airline which makes prolific use of leased aircraft or a 'virtual' airline where most services are outsourced and largely unsupervised by the airline itself. There is also the question whether some airlines may be tempted to accept the lowest cost in terms of contracted out engineering and maintenance services. The answer, of course, lies in one thesis: ensuring that regulation in the area of safety is uniformly carried out. Incontrovertibly, such a responsibility should fall on the entire world civil aviation community. The methodology for this proposition is already in place, in the form of ICAO Standards and Recommended Practices (SARPs). The solution, however, is elusive, purely because ICAO SARPs do not have absolute powers of enforceability under international law.

Basically, ICAO promulgates its SARPs through its 18 annexes to the Chicago Convention. Article 54(l) of the Chicago Convention prescribes the adoption of international standards and recommended practices and their designation in annexes to the convention, while notifying all contracting states of the action taken. The fundamental question which has to be addressed *in limine*, in the consideration of the effectiveness of ICAO's SARPs, is whether SARPs are legislative in character. If the answer is in the affirmative, then, at least theoretically, one can insist upon adherence to SARPs by states.

The adoption of SARPS was considered a priority by the ICAO Council in its Second Session (2 September–12 December 1947)[24] which attempted to obviate any delays to the adoption of SARPs on air navigation as required by the First Assembly of ICAO.[25] SARPs inevitably take two forms: a negative form, for example that states shall not impose more than certain maximum requirements, and a positive form, such as that states shall take certain steps as prescribed by the ICAO annexes.[26]

Article 37 of the convention obtains the undertaking of each contracting state to collaborate in securing the highest practical degree of uniformity in regulations, standards, procedures and organization in relation to international civil aviation in all matters in which such uniformity will facilitate and improve air navigation. Article 38 obligates all contracting states to the convention to inform ICAO immediately if they are unable to comply with any such international standard or procedure, and to notify differences between their own practices and those prescribed by ICAO. In the case of amendments to international standards, any state which does not make the appropriate amendment to its own regulations or practices shall give notice to the Council of ICAO within 60 days of the adoption of the said amendment to the international standard or indicate the action which it proposes to take.

There is no room for doubt that the annexes to the convention or parts thereof lay down rules of conduct both directly and analogically. In fact, although there is a conception based on a foundation of practicality that ICAO's international standards that are identified by the words 'contracting states shall' have a mandatory flavour (imputed by the word 'shall'), while recommended practices identified by the words 'contracting states may' have only an advisory and recommendatory connotation (imputed by the word 'may'), it is interesting that at least one ICAO document requires states, under Article 38 of the convention, to notify ICAO of all significant differences from both standards and recommended practices, thus making all SARPS regulatory in nature.[27]

Another strong factor that reflects the overall ability and power of the council to prescribe civil rules of conduct (and therefore legislate) on a strict interpretation of the word is that, in Article 22 of the convention, each contracting state agrees to adopt all practical measures through the issuance of special regulations or otherwise, to facilitate and expedite air navigation. It is clear that this provision can be regarded as an incontrovertible rule of conduct that responds to the requirement in Article 54(l) of the convention. Furthermore, the mandatory nature of Article 90 of the convention – that an annex or amendment thereto shall become effective within three months after it is submitted by the ICAO Council to contracting states – is yet another pronouncement on the power of the council to prescribe rules of state conduct in matters of international civil aviation. A fortiori, it is arguable that the ICAO Council is seen to possess not only the attribute of the term 'jurisfaction' (the power to make rules of conduct) but also the term 'jurisaction' (the power to enforce its own rules of conduct). The latter attribute can be seen where the convention obtains the undertaking of contracting states not to allow airlines to operate through their air space if the council decides that the airline concerned is not conforming to a final decision rendered by the council on a matter that concerns the operation of an international airline.[28] This is particularly applicable when such airline is found not to conform to the provisions of Annex 2 to the convention that derives its validity from Article 12 of the convention relating to rules of the air.[29] In fact, it is very relevant that Annex 2, the responsibility for the promulgation of which devolves upon the council by virtue of Article 54(l), sets mandatory rules of the air, making the existence of the legislative powers of the council an unequivocal and irrefutable fact.

Academic and professional opinion also favours the view that, in a practical sense, the ICAO Council does have legislative powers. Milde says:

> The Chicago Convention, as any other legal instrument, provides only a general legal framework which is given true life only in the practical implementation of its provisions. Thus, for example, Article 37 of the Convention relating to the adoption of international standards and recommended procedures would be a very hollow and meaningless provision without active involvement of all contracting States, Panels, Regional and Divisional Meetings, deliberations in the Air Navigation Commission and final adoption of the standards by the Council. Similarly, provisions of Article 12 relating to the rules of the air applicable over the high seas, Articles 17 to 20 on the nationality of aircraft, Article 22 on facilitation, Article 26 on the investigation of accidents, etc., would be meaningless without appropriate implementation in the respective Annexes. On the same level is the provision of the last sentence of Article 77 relating to the determination by the Council in what manner the provisions of the Convention relating to nationality of aircraft shall apply to aircraft operated by international operating agencies.[30]

Milde concludes that ICAO has regulatory and quasi-legislative functions in the technical field and plays a consultative and advisory role in the economic sphere.[31] A similar view had earlier been expressed by Buergenthal, who states:

> the manner in which the International Civil Aviation organization has exercised its regulatory functions in matters relating to the safety of international air navigation and the facilitation of international air transport provides a fascinating example of international law making … the Organization has consequently not had to contend with any of the post war ideological differences that have impeded international law making on politically sensitive issues.[32]

Dempsey endorses, in a somewhat conservative manner, the view that ICAO has the ability to make regulations, when he states:

> In addition to the comprehensive, but largely dormant adjudicative enforcement held by ICAO under Articles 84–88 of the Chicago

> Convention, the Agency also has a solid foundation for enhanced participation in economic regulatory aspects of international aviation in Article 44, as well as the Convention's Preamble.[33]

One of the issues that is being addressed by ICAO is the need for a formulation by the Organization of a comprehensive response of ICAO to Resolution A29-3, taking into account the related tasks already in hand or planned by the subsidiary bodies. Therefore one of the main goals of ICAO at present is to find ways to create a greater interest and participation in the formulation of SARPs by states and to strengthen the organization's capability of monitoring the actual status of differences from or compliance with standards on the basis of its own findings. The latter element is especially important, as differences filed by states do not always appear to be representative of the reality.

ICAO believes that there are a number of reasons that prevent states from indicating their compliance, or otherwise, with ICAO SARPs. These may include the following:

1. insufficient communication between ICAO and recipient states; loss of documentation by recipients and delays in delivering the documentation to the responsible party beyond the target date for replies; organizational structures of civil aviation authorities which render difficulties in identification of, and routing to, the responsible party;
2. insufficient resources within states to consider expeditiously and process ICAO documentation and to implement the relevant standards into their national legislation;
3. difficulty in comprehending and interpreting annex material as well as subject matter which is beyond the level of expertise of the recipient administration; and
4. possible lack of understanding about the role of states in the consultation phase of the development of ICAO standards.[34]

More fundamentally, it is always a possibility that states may have insufficient resources either to implement standards or to advise ICAO of non-compliance with the relevant standards. It should be noted, in this context, that recent initiatives by states, in an effort to address the concerns raised by the 29th Session of the Assembly and to assure the safety of their citizens, have raised fundamental questions about the effectiveness of the multilateral safety assurance afforded by the Chicago Convention.

ICAO feels that the need to remind contracting states continually of their obligation to notify the organization of any differences from the standards in the annexes to the Convention remains a critical factor in its advances towards more state participation in its regulatory process. Furthermore, the level of implementation of those standards by states into their national legislation and procedures has to be improved. These two elements complement each other; if too many states simply notified ICAO of their non-implementation of the safety standards, states could no longer assume a mutual level of minimum safety standards and would have to resort to a bilateral or regional approach in order to ensure an acceptable safety oversight between themselves.

Some catalysts for the global implementation of standards and the harmonization of national rules have been identified as the bilateral and multilateral cooperation of states. As will be discussed in Part III, organizations such as the European Civil Aviation Conference, the African and Latin American Civil Aviation Commissions have already taken initiatives in this area. Other organizations, such as the Conference of Directors General of Civil Aviation of the Asia and Pacific Regions, the Commonwealth of Independent States and other groups, including trading blocs, may be considered as effective vehicles for the promulgation and adoption of agreements and understandings in this regard.

Another significant issue is that there is an increasing need for cooperation in the regulatory field for states in a particular geographic setting and with certain common regulatory needs which are dictated by technical, operational and environmental needs and motives. Recent years have witnessed the growing significance of regional organizations that are addressing traditional ICAO activities such as technical harmonization, standardization and regulatory matters. These activities are likely to intensify in the near future and may well affect the role of ICAO as the principal intergovernmental organization responsible for the regulation and coordination of international civil aviation.

ICAO's strategy for the development and implementation of ICAO Standards and Recommended Practices purports to make use of available modern technological tools, but at the same time aim at more basic issues:

1 to ascertain and document the actual status of implementation of ICAO SARPs and the extent of differences from standards, improving communication channels amongst headquarters, regional offices and states to facilitate this objective;
2 to improve the awareness on the part of states of the vital role they play in the multilateral safety assurance provided for in the Chicago Convention, which is founded upon the effective implementation of ICAO SARPs;
3 similarly, to create or improve the awareness on the part of states

of their role in the development of ICAO SARPs, with a view to encouraging more states to be actively involved in the formulation process;

4 to pursue systematic analysis of the reasons for any non-implementation of SARPs and differences from standards;

5 to develop realistic programmes, including the ICAO technical cooperation programmes, and their funding, to assist states in implementing SARPs, where necessary; and

6 to establish adequate coordination and cooperation with states in a regional context in the field of rule harmonization and the implementation of standards.

ICAO is a United Nations agency and the United Nations was created, in more senses than one, during the Second World War. Although, originally, there were questions asked by the international community about whether this wartime union of states could satisfactorily and appropriately be converted into a peacetime organization for international cooperation, these questions were solved by the creation within the Economic and Social Council (ECOSOC) of the United Nations of various specialized agencies (ICAO being one) which were brought into relationship with the United Nations.[35] The ECOSOC may enter into agreements with any of these specialized agencies, coordinate activities of the agencies through consultation, and define terms on which the agency concerned would be brought into relationship with the United Nations.[36]

Therefore ICAO conceptually shares the international status of the United Nations, while members of the ICAO Secretariat are international civil servants. The establishment of ICAO as the specialized agency of the United Nations which is responsible for regulation of international civil aviation brings to bear the need to inquire why such specialized agencies are created instead of conferring functions which are to be performed by them upon the United Nations itself. One of the reasons that have been adduced is that the general organization of the United Nations and its personnel could not take on all specialized activities that are handled by the various specialized agencies. Another is that a single organization with greatly increasing administrative personnel would have been too cumbersome a bureaucracy. Be that as it may, the question as to what status ICAO holds in the international community, which in turn would shed some light on the status of its regulations, would largely lie in the definition of the word 'agency'. On the term 'specialized agency' one commentator has observed:

> They are Specialized as to subject-matter, of course, but the implications of the second term may not be so clear. These Agencies are in

> fact, as the general UN is not, examples of international administrative agencies ... whose chief function is the administrative one, although the conference or representative organs associated with them (or with which they are associated), and the legislative or policy determining activities of the latter, are not to be disregarded...
>
> The relationships to be developed between Specialized Agencies and the UN constitute a major problem of international statesmanship. As in the case of regional organizations, whatever the value of the special institutions, the situation would be difficult and dangerous unless adequate measures for coordination of the various elements could be worked out. This is a problem for searching analysis in principle and for careful application in practice. If the Specialized Agencies are created by the UN suitable coordination should be possible, but if it be a question of coordinating with the UN an Agency created independently the task is more difficult.[37]

The above comment supports the view that a certain coordination exists between specialized agencies and the United Nations on the basis of their relationship ipso facto. Hence it may be inferred by this argument that the regulations promulgated by a specialized agency should have similar status and leverage to that of any created by the parent United Nations.

Over the years, ICAO has played a seminal and alert role in monitoring safety in civil aviation and has diligently endeavoured to enhance ICAO SARPs and obtain state compliance of these provisions. At the 31st Session of the ICAO Assembly, held in Montreal from 19 September to 4 October 1995, ICAO contracting states adopted Resolution A31-2[38] on increasing the effectiveness of ICAO. The Resolution inter alia recognizes the new and rapidly evolving technological, social, economic and legal challenges in the field of civil aviation and directs the ICAO Council and Secretary General, within their respective competencies, to intensify efforts to develop a strategic action plan for the organization. The plan is required to be implemented by a systematic planning process which develops the financial progress and utilization of the organization. It also directs the Council, among other things, to ensure the effectiveness of the ICAO safety oversight mechanism.

On 22 May 1997, ICAO officially launched its Strategic Action Plan in accordance with the directives of the Assembly in Resolution A31-2. At the launch, the President of the ICAO Council, Dr Assad Kotaite, renewed calls for increasing powers which would enable ICAO to oversee the implementation of aviation safety and security standards worldwide.[39] Dr Kotaite identified ICAO's role in the present context succinctly:

> Never has there been a greater need for a strong and active ICAO ... In civil aviation, globalization, commercialization of government service

> providers, liberalization of economic regulation, increasing environmental controls and the emergence of new technologies all have significant implications for safety and security. Addressing these issues effectively requires an unprecedented level of co-operation among countries and a corresponding level of global co-ordination which extends beyond borders.[40]

The President of the Council concluded by suggesting that ICAO's goal should be to become the recognized worldwide auditor of safety and security standards for international civil aviation. His message echoes the fundamental truth that nothing in international civil aviation is parochial and disconnected.

Recent ICAO and Regional Initiatives

In order to address the issue of aviation safety, the Council of the International Civil Aviation Organization (ICAO) convened in Montreal, from 10 to 12 November 1997, an international conference for Directors General of Civil Aviation to review the ICAO Safety Oversight Programme and to consider its expansion.[41] Almost simultaneously with this event, ICAO released its preliminary accident and security statistics for 1996, which show that scheduled air carriers from the 185 ICAO contracting states reported 23 fatal aircraft accidents in 1996, compared with 26 in the previous year.[42] Although the incident rate declined in 1996, the number of passenger deaths reported rose dramatically, to 1135, compared with 710 in 1995.

The Conference concluded inter alia that ICAO should continue to fulfil its leading role with a view to making the Safety Oversight Programme more assertive and effective; that there should be a harmonized approach in conducting safety audits; and that the ICAO Safety Oversight Programme should be expanded to other technical fields at the appropriate time, initially to include air traffic services, aerodromes, support facilities and services.[43]

Although the statistics of CFIT portend a certain perceived gloom, the silver lining comes with the awareness of the enormity of the problem and identification of factors contributing to the aircraft accident rate. These factors include underdeveloped aviation infrastructure, poor airline operating practices, inadequate national aviation oversight of varying degrees, poor air traffic control capability, lack of navigational aids and radar coverage, and substandard airport equipment. Unsatisfactory meteorological facilities have also been identified as possible causes of aircraft accidents.

For its part, ICAO, through its Air Navigation Commission, completed within the period 1995–8 the development of a framework which encapsulates the seminal ICAO activities in pursuit of aviation safety. The Commission created a comprehensive document which encompassed a Global Aviation Safety Plan (GASP) which aims at giving ICAO leadership to gain a commitment from states and the industry to enhance aviation safety worldwide. Safety is the primary concern of the world aviation community at the present time. This is not only because the fundamental postulates of the Chicago Convention of 1944[44] call for the safe and orderly development of international civil aviation[45] and mandate ICAO to ensure the safe and orderly growth of international civil aviation throughout the world,[46] but also because the aviation world faces a critical era where, in the words of Dr Assad Kotaite, President of the ICAO Council, 'the international aviation community cannot afford to relax its vigilance ... ICAO would continue to take timely action to ensure safety and security standards are in effect, and that deficiencies are properly and efficiently addressed'.[47]

The compelling need for higher standards in aviation safety was formally recognized when the ICAO Council adopted ICAO's Strategic Action Plan on 7 February 1997. The basic strategic objective of the plan is to further the safety, security and efficiency of international civil aviation. ICAO plans to accomplish this task by assisting states in identifying deficiencies in the implementation of annexes to the Chicago Convention, in particular those that contain provisions which ensure safety in aviation. One of the core elements of ICAO activity on safety, according to its Strategic Action Plan, is to carry out assessments by teams of experts of the capacity of participating states to control effectively the level of safety for which they have responsibility. ICAO's Safety Oversight Programme would implement this activity, extending to personnel licensing, operation of aircraft and aircraft airworthiness. ICAO may, in the foreseeable future, extend this programme to cover areas such as air traffic control and the operation of airports.

Taking their cue from ICAO, several regional aviation organizations have formally incorporated safety provisions in their documentation. The African Civil Aviation Commission (AFCAC), at its Thirteenth Plenary Session (Abuja, 11–18 May 1995), discussed the matter of safety oversight in Africa, which led to the Commission adopting Decision S13-3,[48] on safety oversight. This decision recognizes that states must take appropriate means to ensure compliance with international safety standards contained in the relevant annexes to the Chicago Convention and that most African states may not have the necessary infrastructure to fully implement such standards. The Commission refers to the ICAO Safety Oversight Programme in Decision S13-3 and instructs the AFCAC Bureau to improve safety oversight in AFCAC activities and promote cooperation among African states in the field of safety oversight. Through the Decision,

AFCAC has also requested ICAO's assistance for African states in order that they may effectively introduce the Safety Oversight Programme in Africa.

The Fifteenth Plenary Session of AFCAC, held in Abuja on 20–24 April 1998, followed earlier action of AFCAC in the field of safety by adopting Resolution S15-5, which recognized that there were increasing numbers of private airlines licensed and operating in Africa following the liberalization policies adopted by some African countries. In this context, the Assembly recognized that aviation safety in Africa is of paramount importance to African civil aviation and that, to this end, there was a need for African states and airlines to enhance safety awareness amongst themselves. Resolution S15-5 therefore urges all African member states to enhance safety awareness within their respective organizations through increased training of flight crews and technicians and strict adherence to safety regulation and operations within the prescribed safety standards. The resolution further calls upon all African member states to make every endeavour to reaffirm their commitment to safety oversight.[49]

The European Civil Aviation Conference (ECAC) at its 100th Meeting of Directors General of Civil Aviation (Paris, 14–15 May 1997) discussed an ECAC Recommendation on Safety of Foreign Aircraft[50] which calls for increased ramp checks on aircraft and rigid adherence, on a bilateral basis, by states to the provisions of the Chicago Convention on licensing of personnel and certification of aircraft.[51] The ECAC bilateral safety clause calls *in limine* for consultations to be called for at any stage where such consultations would relate to safety standards of aircrew, aircraft or the operation of aircraft. The provision allows for the revocation of the clause, if one party to the agreement finds that the other does not maintain minimum ICAO standards. The clause also admits of the need to conduct random ramp checks in order for one party to determine whether aircraft conform to Article 33 of the Chicago Convention, which relates to certification of airworthiness.

At the same meeting, ECAC also discussed a recommendation[52] on leasing of aircraft and safety, which calls for standards as prescribed in Annex 6 (Operation of Aircraft) to the Chicago Convention and minimum conditions on the use of leased aircraft, to ensure that they are maintained in accordance with ICAO Standards of Safety. It must be noted that safety regulations of the European Community are generally stringent on product liability,[53] stipulating that any person who imports into the community a product for leasing is considered a manufacturer of that product for purposes of product liability.

At the 103rd Meeting of the Directors General of Civil Aviation in Paris on 1–2 July 1998, ECAC further considered safety issues of the European region and discussed issues related to ICAO's Safety Oversight Programme and its follow-up of oversight assessments of the European region.[54] More recently, at its 108th Meeting of Directors General of Civil Aviation, held in Paris in December 1999, the ECAC DGCAs endorsed the principle of an annual discussion of the ECAC Programme for Safety Assessment of Foreign Aircraft (SAFA) and agreed to the publication early in the year 2000 of the SAFA Annual Report.[55] An earlier SAFA Report, applicable to 1996–8, records that some of the common deficiencies observed by ECAC pertaining to flight decks of foreign aircraft were the non-availability of flight crew licences, absence of a noise certificate on board, absence of required manuals on board or such manuals being out of date, and deficiencies in the calculation of load distributions.[56]

Another regional civil aviation organization which has recognized the compelling need for the implementation of safety oversight in its region is the Latin American Civil Aviation Commission (LACAC). At LACAC's Eleventh Assembly (Manaus, 7–10 November 1994) some LACAC member states adopted the 'Manaus Declaration', which expressed its support of the role of the ICAO Council to establish a safety oversight programme and requested ICAO to implement the programme as quickly as possible.[57] At the 12th LACAC Assembly, held in Panama on 5–8 November 1996, the Assembly adopted Resolution A12-4, which made reference to the Manaus Declaration as being the basis of aviation safety policy in the region and resolved to support ICAO efforts at safety oversight. The resolution also urged all member states to take the necessary measures to achieve technical perfection, to the extent possible in the implementation of aviation safety measures in their territories.[58]

Both ICAO and the regional aviation organizations have focused their attention on the air navigational aspects of safety oversight. This is understandable, since safety of civil aviation primarily depends on safe air navigation. However, safety of civil aviation does not stop at air navigation. There are other extraneous factors which may affect aviation safety, such as human conduct in the aircraft and air traffic controller liability.

On 2 October 1998, ICAO concluded its 32nd Session of the Assembly, which commenced in Montreal on 22 September. The Assembly endorsed the establishment of a universal Safety Oversight Programme which would comprise regular, mandatory, systematic and harmonized safety audits. These audits, which commenced on 1 January 1999, are being carried out by ICAO in all its 185 contracting states, with their consent and at their request, under a Memorandum of Understanding signed by and between each state concerned and ICAO. The ICAO safety audit is aimed at determining whether individual states have the capacity to provide safe air navigation services to aircraft which traverse their airspace. It comes at a critical time in aviation history when international civil aviation is at the beginning of a new millennium which, in its first 15 years, portends a virtual doubling of current air traffic both in the upper and the lower airspace.

At its 32nd Session, the ICAO Assembly recognized that the ICAO Safety Oversight Programme had reached a saturation point in terms of policy and sought to address policy in developing the programme further. It was considered at this session that there were regional deficiencies and shortcomings in the field of air navigation and that contracting states had to correct such problems. In its deliberations, the Assembly found useful the development of the United States safety programme in April 1998 through its Federal Aviation Administration (FAA), called 'Safer Skies', which was designed to achieve a fivefold reduction in fatal accidents. Through this programme, the FAA intends to address inter alia the CFIT issue, matters pertaining to engine failures, and weather and loss of control.

Taking the above into consideration in the context of its own Global Aviation Safety Plan, the ICAO Assembly adopted Resolution A32-15, which recognized that the primary objective of the organization is to continue promoting the safety of international civil aviation, noting that the expected increase in the volume of international civil aviation would result in an increasing number of aircraft accidents unless the accident rate was reduced. The Assembly also adopted Resolution A32-1 on increasing the effectiveness of ICAO. While the former Resolution endorses the ICAO plan urging contracting states to examine and revise their laws if necessary to achieve a proper balance among the various elements of accident prevention efforts and to encourage increased voluntary reporting of events that could affect aviation safety, the latter endorses continuing work by the ICAO Council along the lines of Resolution A31-2, which has been referred to earlier.

Legal Issues

With all the exhortations of the ICAO resolutions and ICAO's work in establishing standards, recommended practices and guidelines, responsibility primarily devolves on the states concerned to recognize that the flight crew in CFIT accidents is but the final link in a chain of events caused by systemic factors.

In order to significantly reduce CFIT accidents, states should ensure that aviation systems are improved. State responsibility in the field of preventing CFIT accidents should be two-pronged. The first need is to ensure that adequate training is given to crews of airlines over which a particular state has control. Since few operators have instituted training on CFIT accidents,[59] which fact has been gleaned from seminars conducted by ICAO in 1998 and 1999, states have the responsibility of taking cognizance of the fact that, although ICAO has distributed more than 3000 copies of its *CFIT Education and Training Aid,* both in paper and in CD Rom format, and more than 6000 copies of a video on the subject, all personnel concerned in CFIT accidents are yet to receive comprehensive training. States should ensure that personnel concerned are trained on standard operating procedures and have the benefit of conducting route and familiarization checks of terrain; that they are trained on available ATC radar services and departure and approach procedures and charts; and that there are third party audits of training procedures used by airlines. States must also make operators aware of the enormity of the CFIT problem and establish an effective risk management programme concerning the prevention of CFIT-related accidents.

One of the biggest responsibilities imposed upon states is their commitment to updating communication facilities such as radio communication and radar in civilian air traffic control through regulatory agencies, including governmental authorities. If states are decision makers and creators of policy for airlines, they should also ensure total compliance with the CFIT checklist. Airline management has a pre-eminent role in ensuring safety of their flights. Management-level decision makers of the airlines have an inherent duty to fully endorse recommended regulations on CFIT prevention and concentrate on risk management of the human error factor. It is ineluctable that airline management creates and sustains the safety culture of the organization concerned. One of the fundamental measures that could be taken in this regard is the proper allocation of crew duties. Since most of CFIT-related accidents have been known to occur at night,[60] airline managements have a responsibility of ensuring proper management of flight crew duties during the night. Proper monitoring of approaches and landing at night, monitoring of the effective use of autopilot during approaches and follow-up of Aeronautical Information Circular (AIC) clearance by air crew are also implicit in the airlines' list of responsibilities in the field of safety.

Another important strategy for a prudent airline to follow lies in communication, where the airlines concerned should establish clear and functional links between management, policy makers and flight crew. The liability of an airline consequent upon a CFIT accident would significantly lie in any absence of teamwork and effective and proper communication systems. It is primarily for the airline to determine and appreciate that CFIT accidents may occur as a result of both human and environmental factors. The latter may involve inadequate air traffic control services and radar malfunction, proximity of landing facility (airports) to mountainous terrain, and poor runway lighting. Flight crew awareness of these risk factors and their education on preventive techniques should be ensured by airlines through comprehensive training programmes run by the organizations' flight operations departments.

One of the most constructive recommendations on flight crew training with regard to the prevention of CFIT accidents has been made by Boeing's Chief Engineer of Aircraft Reliability, Earl F. Weener, who states: 'Flight crew training must emphasize approach planning and the criteria for acceptable approach stabilization. Moreover, there must be a clear management philosophy that does not penalize crews for making missed approaches.'[61] At the air crew level, an extremely heavy responsibility lies on the pilots – in particular the command pilot – to ensure that all measures of CFIT prevention are taken on the flight. The CFIT checklist identifies some of these as follows:

a) fly the way you train. Do not deviate from Standard Operating Procedures rehearsed during practice flights;
b) conduct route and familiarization checks for new pilots – especially on international flights. Use visual training aids such as videotapes of instrument approaches into unfamiliar airports;
c) use ATC radar services to the maximum extent possible and know when they are limited or not available;
d) furnish all cockpit crew with departure and approach charts, including adequate chart-holders and proper illumination;
e) use supplemental instrument charts that have colors or shaded contours depicting topographical features (similar to British Airway's Aerad or Lufthansa's Atlas charts);
f) thoroughly review the entire instrument departure or approach prior to commencing the procedure;
g) complete the approach checklist prior to starting the instrument approach procedure;
h) make the cockpit a distraction-free, 'sterile' environment during the instrument departure or approach procedure;
i) have the second-in-command crewmember fly the departure or approach procedure during night or IMC (Instrument Meteorological Certificate) and use the pilot-in-command to monitor the procedure;
j) have the PNF (pilot-not-flying) crosscheck all critical altitudes, including the initial approach fix, glideslope intercept altitude, step-down fixes on non-precision approaches and the final approach fix;
k) have the PNF provide a 500-foot altitude callout and other altitude cues during the final stages of the approach; and
l) whenever possible, have a qualified observer occupy the jump seat to help monitor terrain avoidance during instrument approaches in IMC or at night.

Ultimate responsibility for the safety of passengers and others on board lies with the captain and such responsibility extends towards declaring and exercising emergency authority, exerting managerial authority and control over the rest of the crew, directing crew member actions and assigning duties and responsibilities. The captain is also in charge of 'conflict resolving' communications between flight crew in instances where the captain and co-pilot differ in opinion on a particular move in coping with an emergency situation such as CFIT.

The overall responsibility of a flight which devolves upon a captain does not in any way derogate the accountability at law of a co-pilot or any other technical crew member responsible for the operation of a flight. In the cockpit a certain mutual responsibility exists among crew members according to the varying amount of experience they may have. For example, inasmuch as a senior pilot is required to guide and instruct his less experienced colleagues in flight, an experienced first officer may also be expected to assist a newly appointed captain.

Conclusion

At the root of the issue of aviation safety in general and the prevention of CFIT accidents in particular lies the fundamental question as to whether ICAO Assembly resolutions and other declarations are binding on states. Of course, neither the United Nations nor its specialized agencies were conceived as legislative bodies. Both the United Nations Charter and the Chicago Convention contemplate as their objectives the coordination or harmonizing of states' activities through recommendations and guidelines, however termed. However, this does not in any way preclude the United Nations or a specialized United Nations agency such as ICAO from acting like legislatures through the traditional processes of treaty law making and declarations of law. The various resolutions, standards and recommendations adopted through the ICAO mechanism are the result of the exercise of the collective will of governments and therefore incontrovertibly become law ipso facto. The United Nations law-making process involves a certain 'democratization' of law making, on the basis that, as against traditional law making, the United Nations system operates on the principle that all member states have an equal right to participate in the 'adoption of law' process where decisions are taken on a single or two thirds majority or consensus basis.

ICAO Assembly resolutions, provisions of the various annexes to the Chicago Convention and other declarations are certainly reflective of binding international law on the basic postulate that they are authentic interpretations of the Chicago Convention as agreed by all ICAO contracting states. They are also affirmations by states of recognized autonomy law and are expressions of general principles of law accepted by states. Therefore there is no room for doubt that the criteria set by Article 38 of the Statute of the International Court of Justice for a given rule to be recognized as public international law are met by ICAO 'law'. This philosophy is further supported by the recognition of the ICJ of the legal force of several United Nations resolutions and other declarations within the scope of the court's advisory opinions.[62]

State responsibility regarding adherence to ICAO declarations becomes, in view of the above discussion, non negotiable. A fortiori, in the case of aviation safety, even non-contracting states become bound to follow the ICAO legislative process, on the same lines as the applicability of the United Nations Convention on the Law of the Sea of 1982 and the various United Nations covenants on human rights which affect all states. Adherence by states may be ensured through periodic reports from states on the status of adherence; facilitation by ICAO of the adherence by states, for example by the conducting of safety oversight audits and checks; and even more drastic measures that may seriously jeopardize the membership of a non-compliant state. There is also the availability of the measure of adjudication and judicial enforcement through such an organ as the International Court of Justice.

State responsibility percolates to all instrumentalities operating air services, whether they belong to the state concerned or not, to the extent that states have overall responsibility and accountability to ensure that airline managements and their flight operations departments take all necessary measures in compliance with international regulations on safety.

Notes

1 A CFIT accident is defined as an event where a mechanically normally functioning aeroplane is inadvertently flown into the ground, water or an obstacle. See Flight Safety Foundation, *CFIT Checklist*, Section 3, para. 3.1.

2 R.T. Slatter (1999), 'CFIT Training Material Provides Basis for Developing Effective Prevention Programmes', *ICAO Journal*, January/February, 17. See also Reinhard Menzel (1998), 'Analysis Shows that CFIT Continues to Account for the Heaviest Loss of Life Worldwide', *ICAO Journal*, April, 5.

3 Ibid.

4 Annex 6, *Operations of Aircraft*, 7th edn of Part I (July 1998) and 6th edn of Part II (July 1998). The provisions of the Annex relating to CFIT will be addressed in detail later in this discussion.

5 'Accident Prevention Recommendations Complement Recent Global Safety Initiatives', *ICAO News Release*, PIO 12/99, p.1.

6 Ibid.
7 Annex 13, *Aircraft Accident and Incident Investigation*, 8th edn, July 1994.
8 Capt. Tom Duke (ret.) (1996), 'Conquering CFIT', *Airline Pilot*, March, 10.
9 'More moves on CFIT', *World Air News*, September 1993, 35.
10 Convention on International Civil Aviation, signed at Chicago on 7 December 1944. See ICAO Doc. 7300/7, 7th edn, 1997, 1.
11 Ibid., Article 44(*a*).
12 Ibid., Article 44(*d*).
13 Ibid., Article 44(*h*).
14 See Doc. 9730, 'Assembly Resolutions in Force' (as of 2 October 1998) at pp.1–47.
15 Ibid., pp.1–49.
16 Ibid., pp.1–49 to 1–50.
17 Annex 6, *Operations of Aircraft*, 6th edn of Part II (*International General Aviation*) *Aeroplanes*, July 1998, Standard 6.4.
18 Ibid., Recommendation 6.9.1.
19 Ibid., Recommendations 6.9.2 and 6.9.5.
20 Ibid., Recommendation 6.9.4.
21 Annex 6, *Operation of Aircraft*, 7th edn of Part I (July 1998), *International Commercial Air Transport, Aeroplanes*, Standard 6.2.1.
22 Ibid., Standard 6.15.
23 See *supra*, n.20.
24 Proceedings of the Council, 2nd Session, 2 September–12 December 1947, Doc. 7248 – C/839, 44–5.
25 ICAO Resolutions A-13 and A-33, which resolved that SARPS relating to the efficient and safe regulation of international air navigation be adopted.
26 ICAO Annex 9, *Facilitation*, 9th edn, July 1990, Foreword.
27 *Aeronautical Information Services Manual*, ICAO Doc. 8126-0 AN/872/3. ICAO Resolution A1-31 defines a standard as 'any specification for physical characteristics … the uniform application of which is recognized as necessary … and one that States will conform to'. The same resolution describes a recommended practice as 'any specification for physical characteristics… which is recognized as desirable …and one that member States will endeavour to conform to'. T. Buergenthal (1969), *Law Making in the International Civil Aviation Organization*, p.10, also cites the definitions given in ICAO's Annex 9 of SARPS.
28 Article 86 of the Convention.
29 Article 12 stipulates that, over the high seas, the rules in force shall be those established under the Convention, and each contracting state undertakes to ensure the prosecution of all persons violating the applicable regulations.
30 Michael Milde (1984), 'The Chicago Convention – After Forty Years', *Annals of Air and Space Law*, IX, 126. See also Jacob Schenkman (1955), *International Civil Aviation Organization*, Geneva: Librairie E. Droz, p.163.
31 Milde, *supra*, 122.
32 Buergenthal, *supra*, n.27, p.9.
33 Paul Stephen Dempsey (1987), *Law and Foreign Policy in International Aviation*, Dobbs Ferry, New York: Transnational Publishers.
34 Ibid., p.5.
35 *Charter of the United Nations and Statute of the International Court of Justice*, United Nations: New York, Article 57.
36 Ibid., Article 63(1) and (2).
37 Pitman B. Potter (1935), *An Introduction to the Study of International Organization*, 5th edn, New York and London: Appleton Century-Crofts, pp.273–4.
38 See *Resolutions Adopted by the Assembly*, 31st Session, Montreal, 19 September–4 October 1995, ICAO: Montreal, 1995, p.2.

39 See 'ICAO Releases Strategic Action Plan, President Renews Call for Empowerment', *ICAO News Release*, PIO 10/97, p.1.
40 Ibid.
41 ICAO Doc. P10 16/97, p.1.
42 ITA Press 284, 1–5 April 1997, p.10.
43 See Directors General of Civil Aviation Conference on a Global Strategy for Safety Oversight, Montreal, 10–12 November 1997, DGCA/97, Conclusions and Recommendations.
44 Convention on International Civil Aviation, signed at Chicago on 7 December 1944. See ICAO Doc. 7300/6, 6th edn, 1980.
45 Ibid., Preamble, p.1.
46 Ibid., Article 44(a).
47 ITA Press (*supra*, n. 42), p.10.
48 Decision S13-3: Safety Oversight. See African Civil Aviation Commission, Thirteenth Plenary Session, Abuja, 11–18 May 1995, AFCAC/13 Report, p.25.
49 African Civil Aviation Commission, Fifteenth Plenary Session, Abuja, 20–24 April 1998 (AFCAC/15), p.20.
50 DGCA/100-DP/7, 21/4/97, Appendix.
51 Article 31 provides that every aircraft engaged in international navigation shall be provided with a certificate of airworthiness issued or rendered valid by the state in which it is registered. Article 32 provides for the issuance of a certificate of competency to technical crew of aircraft and prescribes minimum standards. Article 33 stipulates that certificates of airworthiness issued to aircraft by one state should be acceptable by another, provided certain minimum standards are followed.
52 DGCA/100-DP/8, 28/4/97, Appendix.
53 EU Council Directive 85/374/EEC of 25 July 1985.
54 Report of the 103 Meeting of Directors General of Civil Aviation (DGCA/103), Paris, 1–2 July 1998, p.5.
55 DGCA/108-SD, 16/12/99, p.3.
56 See *ECAC/JAA Programme for Safety Assessment of Foreign Aircraft*, Report 1996/1998, Paris: ECAC, p.7.
57 ICAO Doc. 9637, *Annual Report of the Council*, 1994, Montreal: ICAO ch. III, pp.45–6.
58 Comision Latinoamericana de Aviacion Civil, XII Asamblea Ordinaria (Ciudad de Panama, 5 al 8 de Noviembre de 1996), CLAC/12, Sumario de Decisones (30/12/96), p.14.
59 Slatter (*supra*, n.2), 17.
60 'Management Has a Responsibility to Ensure a Viable CFIT Accident Prevention Program is in Place', *ICAO Journal*, March 1997, p.11.
61 See 'More moves on CFIT', (*supra*, n.9), 35.
62 See, for example, Legal Consequences for States of the Continued Presence of South Africa in Namibia (South West Africa) notwithstanding Security Council Resolution 276 (1970), 1971 ICJ Rep 16 (16 June). See also Advisory Opinions on Western Sahara, 1975 ICJ Rep 12 (16 October).

PART III
THE FUTURE OF AVIATION IN THE REGIONS

20 The American Region

Introduction

For the purposes of this work, the Americas are considered as comprising Canada, Mexico and the United States. The American continents are by themselves large regions, both geographically and in terms of traffic volume carried within the territory of the region. As for South America and the Caribbean, the region is heavily interlinked with North America and Mexico, and is progressively advancing towards policies in aviation which are consistent with coexistence with North America. Therefore this chapter will not address aviation challenges faced by the South American aviation industry separately. There will be a separate chapter to follow on South American Aviation. The United States stands both as initiator of global policy pertaining to civil aviation and as the most prolific contributor to aviation in the region. Its influence, therefore, on civil aviation in the next millennium will be significant. The above notwithstanding, the importance of the roles played by Canada, Mexico and the South American and Caribbean nations in shaping the destiny of aviation in the years to come cannot be underestimated.

The United States has been actively promoting the virtues of a liberalized international air transport structure since 1978. This is reflected by the signing of 23 bilateral agreements by the United States between 1978 and 1982, based on a liberal formula.[1] This trend has continued vigorously, prompting Secretary of State Rodney E. Slater to say, in 1997, that the accelerated movement towards achieving open-market aviation agreements in 1997 has put the US Department of Transportation (DoT) on a fast track toward making open skies the worldwide standard.[2] In 1997, the United States reached open-skies agreement with 15 countries, more than in all previous 10 years combined.[3]

Canada, on the other hand, has been less market-driven and more cautious. Some scholars have reported that Canadian bilaterals tend to restrict, rather than facilitate, international competition.[4] One reason given for this cautious approach is that it is the belief of Canada that a traditional international aviation strategy, which was more protective of airline interests, would obviate the 'destructive impact of competition'.[5] Canada and the United States negotiated and entered into an open-skies agreement in 1995. The negotiations, which commenced in the latter part of 1994, were smooth compared to nearly 30 years of difficult negotiations the two countries had in settling their ideological differences regarding traffic rights.[6] The open-skies agreement is viewed as being successful beyond the expectations of its strongest proponents and it is indeed worthy of inquiry as to whether this agreement impelled Air Canada, which was essentially a protectionist carrier, to move towards aggressive competition in the trans-border air transport market.[7] Another corollary was the dramatic growth of traffic between the two countries in the first three years after the signing of the agreement. Both Canadian carriers, Air Canada and Canadian Airlines, benefited by the agreement which gave these carriers opportunities to embark upon new routes between Canada and the United States and use code sharing agreements with US carriers.[8]

Although Canada still exercises a somewhat cautious approach towards South America, Central America and the Caribbean, the United States is proceeding quickly with these countries by encouraging them into liberal agreements in air transport. In 1997, the United States signed its first open-skies agreement with a Latin American country by signing for an open-skies aviation regime with Panama. On this occasion, DoT Secretary Slater said:

> This first open-skies agreement in Latin America represents the opening of an important market for U.S. citizens, businesses and airlines. It also is an important step for Panama and the Central American region as these countries move to develop further their economic resources and create new tourist destinations.[9]

Secretary Slater, identifying South America as one of the world's fastest growing economic regions, hoped that the United States–Panama agreement would be a precursor to other agreements between the United States and South American countries.[10] This was realized just two months later, when he signed open-skies agreements with six Central American countries in May 1997.[11]

The most fundamental issue that has to be addressed in the context of aviation in the Americas is whether a liberalized structure leading ultimately to open skies between carriers of the Americas and other parts of the world will have consequences on a global scale. On the one hand, an open-skies regime will infuse more air transport services to where there is demand, irrespective of considerations for market share and protection of carriers who are unable to compete. On the other, uncontrolled proliferation of air transport may bring about ecological problems, tourism problems and other infrastructural difficulties to small nations developing tourism potential. The issue therefore boils down to the question: would open competition be beneficial to civil aviation on a global basis, as advocated by the more prolific air transport service regions such as North America, South America and Europe.

Trading Policies of Canada, Mexico and the United States

Canada

Canada has prolific foreign ownership in the private sector of the country's economy and therefore has approached the regulation of foreign investment somewhat cautiously.[12] This situation and the trends that are the corollaries of it have kindled the regulation of foreign investment, particularly with the help of appropriate measures that have been adopted.[13] With the establishment of the Foreign Investment Review Agency (hereafter FIRA),[14] Canada adopted a restrictive policy on foreign direct investment, screening every foreign investment through FIRA, regardless of resources offered and wealth and size of the investment, and allowing only foreign investments of significant benefit for Canada.[15]

FIRA was subject to sustained criticism from all parties who had dealings with the Agency. Complaints concerned the inordinate delay in the completion of processing (which usually took from 12 to 18 months), its indiscreet screening process, the lack of care in considering relevant information, the seemingly arbitrary selection criteria and, above all, the fact that foreign investors were required to negotiate with an Agency which, in the end, was not the one having powers to take the final decision with regard to the investment proposal under consideration. FIRA was therefore perceived by Canada's trading partners as a discretionary organ impeding the free flow of trade and investments.[16] One of the examples of discontent among Canada's trading partners is seen in the formal complaint brought by the United States against certain requirements imposed by FIRA on foreign investors to the GATT in 1982, resulting in a GATT panel concluding that domestic sourcing requirements of the Agency were inconsistent with Canada's obligations as stipulated in Article III:4 of the GATT.[17] However, FIRA does not appear to have been as ominous in its negative approach to foreign investment as it was perceived to have been, since the average approval rate of investment proposals was at that time 90 per cent. It is worthy of note, however, that the level of foreign ownership in Canada declined from 37 per cent in 1971 to 24 per cent in 1987 under FIRA.

In 1984, Canada implemented a major reversal of the status quo by adopting its 'Open for Business' Policy. The newly elected Conservative government and its enactment of the Investment Canada Act[18] (hereafter ICA) ensured the repeal of the FIRA, replacing it with the Investment Canada Agency and an altogether new philosophy.[19] The ICA has conceptually encouraged foreign and domestic investment since basing its philosophy on the legislative recognition that foreign investment was beneficial to Canada.[20] The Act abolished the mandatory review process for the establishment of all new Canadian businesses and required a review in the case of direct acquisitions of $5 million or more, indirect acquisitions of over $150 million, and those investments relating to the advancement of culture.[21]

As a response to FIRA, ICA's investment review process was streamlined and given a lower profile than that enjoyed by FIRA. Under the new system, the investor received an answer to his investment proposal within 45 days of his proposal being deposited.[22] ICA adopts the criterion of selection that the reviewed instrument must be of net benefit to Canada.[23] This criterion has not impeded the successful review in any of the reviewed transactions brought before Investment Canada since its creation.[24]

There were also restrictions on foreign ownership in Canada in specific sectors of the economy, as is the case in many other countries. These sectors included aviation,[25] banking,[26] fisheries,[27] agriculture,[28] shipping,[29] oil, gas and uranium production[30] and broadcasting and cable distribution.[31]

The United States

Compared with the experience of Canada, foreign investment has caused much less political upheaval in the United States. The United States had been, up to the 1980s, a strong net exporter of capital and did not have much to fear from foreign influence in trade issues within the country. In the earlier 1970s, however, with the burgeoning oil crisis, petrodollars were invested in the United States, leading to a 38.3 per cent and 22.3 per cent increase in foreign direct investment in 1973 and 1974, respectively. This figure can be contrasted with a 6 per cent increase on average in the decade between 1962 and 1972. This quantum leap in foreign investment caused grave concern in Congress and led to a national inquiry being instituted which called for measures affecting foreign investors in the United States. The 27-volume and 9000 page long final report, describing comprehensively the regulations facing foreign investors, concluded that a sufficient number of sectors were appropriately regulated, and recommended that substantial change to the existing policy was unnecessary.[32]

Unlike Canada's comparably restrictive foreign investment policy, the United States has a liberal 'open door policy' on foreign direct investment and is one of the most open economies in this respect. The United States International Investment Policy Statement of 1983 confirmed:

> The United States has consistently welcomed foreign direct investment in this country. Such investment provides substantial benefit to the United States...We provide foreign investors fair, equitable and non-discriminatory treatment under our laws and regulations. We maintain exceptions to such treatment only as far as necessary to protect our security and related interests which are consistent with our international legal obligations.[33]

The United States has adopted the approach that the absence of regulation encourages investment and is beneficial to the US economy,[34] and has therefore generally adopted a non-discriminatory treatment for foreign investors.[35] A commentator adds:

> Foreign nationals and companies are treated as favourably as nationals or companies of the United States with respect to the establishment and operation of enterprises in this country... Further, on the basis of the national treatment principle investors from other countries can generally make investments in this country on the same legal terms as American investors.[36]

The 'open door policy' and national treatment principle, however, do not give an accurate picture of the status of foreign investment in the United States. In contrast to what the 'open door policy' is perceived to be, there are numerous laws that effectively preclude this policy from taking full effect, thus impeding foreign investments in the country. An example of this inhibitive approach is the 1988 'Exon-Florio Amendment' which provided the president with broad powers to review investments of foreign investors on his own initiative for any reason including those those investments which directly or indirectly affect national security. The president may also review a foreign investment following the complaint of a third party.[37]

Investors may, by their own volition, serve notice on the Committee on Foreign Investment in the United States (CFIUS). In addition, the CFIUS can also decide to inquire into an investment by itself. It then advises the president of its decision with regard to an investment and the president ultimately decides whether or not the investment is contrary to national security interests. The notion of 'national security' is ambivalent in the context, lacking a precise definition, and this hiatus has left great discretion to the executive in the implementation of the Act. The Act is used infrequently and each case is evaluated individually.[38]

In addition, many other sectors which operate through a fixed maximum level of foreign participation are excluded from foreign investor participation entirely or partially. These restrictions are seen at the federal level in the fields of communications,[39] transportation,[40] aviation,[41] energy and national resources,[42] banking[43] and defence.[44] Federal laws such as antitrust regulations contained in the Clayton Act of 1981[45] – which prohibits direct or indirect acquisition of shares of a company when it would affect or lessen competition in such a way as to make way for the creation of a monopoly – and the Sherman Act of 1981,[46] – which prohibits monopolies created by contract, conspiracy or other ways that restrain trade, may also bring to bear serious effects on the foreign investors' investments in the United States.

Mexico

Any trading enterprise conducting business in Mexico is subject, *in limine*, to all laws and regulations applicable in Mexico, including environmental[47] and labour laws.[48] The regulatory philosophy applicable to business conducted in Mexico follows a policy of internal growth in order to achieve self reliance and freedom from dependence on industrialized countries. In order to follow this philosophy, Mexico has, in the past, regulated heavily on foreign enterprises conducting business in Mexico, with the exception of foreign exchange controls. One of the forerunners of this regulatory structure is the Foreign Investment Law, which admits of tighter control of businesses, thereby ensuring maximum benefits to Mexico. Investors had to go through a stringent review process and are curbed to a maximum of 49 per cent of participation. They were also required to operate their businesses strictly within the commercial restraints imposed by Mexico. This policy worked in the period 1950–70, when food exports acted as a catalyst to Mexico's commercial policy. The period which followed Mexico's burdensome public debt due to this policy called for the creation of public enterprises, to buttress the crisis-laden agricultural sector and supplement inadequate oil revenues which could not per se sustain Mexico's economic programme.[49] The government of President Salinas therefore obviated the stringent regulatory trade policy in order to align Mexico with industrialized policy trends. Foreign investors are now given the opportunity to take advantage of Mexico's *Programa de Intercambio de Deuda Publica por Capital* or Debt-for-Equity Swap Programme,[50] which has been designed to allow a foreign investor to buy a part of the debt owed by Mexico to private banks at a discounted rate of 40 per cent. The foreign investor may then liquidate the value of the debt in pesos through the Mexican government so that he can finance his local investments. A similar programme had been in existence since 1986, but was suspended in early 1988 as the increased cash flow caused by the influx of foreign investors caused further inflation in the country.[51]

The system of investment which followed operated on an auction basis, where a foreign investor secures a deposit and presents a detailed bid, proposing the nature of investment and the value of debt. This programme is also available to public enterprises being privatized. The bidder who secures the contract is announced within 60 days of the closing of the bidding.[52] The US$3.5 billion which were set aside for the auction programme was accounted for in two auctions. This was more encouraging than envisaged and the government has not decided to apply this programme to other debts.

The Mexican Constitution prohibits foreign ownership of lands in a zone which represents close to half of the country's entire surface. This zone stretches for 100 kilometres along the borders and 50 kilometres along the shores of the country. Owing to this prohibition, foreign investment in the tourism and hotel industry has been circumscribed. This constitutional impediment has been subject to much interpretation, one of which admits of foreigners holding beneficiary rights through a Mexican trust, in which a Mexican bank acts as trustee. This mechanism has been used for a sustained period of time, leading to its legal recognition since 1971. The first legal allowance made was in the nature of a presidential decree which allowed a fiduciary ownership by foreigners for a maximum period of 30 years.

The Foreign Investment Law which came into effect in 1973 provided for conditions and requirements for the establishment of a trust and required the Foreign Investment Commission to institute guidelines governing the criteria and procedures by which such trusts could be established.[53] The Ministry of Foreign Affairs had final power to approve a project on a case-by-case basis. The Mexican financial institution acting for a foreign investor must apply for the permit on behalf of that foreign investor who wishes to buy tourism or industrial facilities within the prohibited zone. Once permission is granted, a certificate of immovable participation is issued to the foreign investor. This certificate does not grant the beneficiary rights in any real property on the land or in the building he uses. The certificate, which is valid for 30 years, cannot be amortized.[54] The foreign investor was, however, given the option of leasing the premises from the trustee for a maximum period of 10 years. At the end of the period, all property rights of *utendi* and *fruendi* (use and enjoyment) on the premises were transferred to a Mexican national.[55]

The 1989 regulations introduced by the Salinas government did not change the Constitution. They merely gave beneficiaries of land trusts the right to renew the certificate for periods of 30 years by establishing consecutive trusts.[56] Renewal was granted if the Foreign Investment Law and the first obligation of the foreign corporation were respected. The new regulations also provided for an issuance of permits from the Ministry of Foreign Affairs for investments admissible without review from the Commission and for *Maquiladoras*.[57] The land trusts system does not seem to have discouraged foreign investment in Mexico, since a 30-year renewable trust is in most cases more advantageous than being a tenant.

During the era of strict restriction of foreign investment, the import of any product into Mexico required a licence. This requirement ensured the implementation of Mexico's economic policy of internal growth and import substitution and made access to the Mexican market for imported products difficult. Importation involved high customs duties and, therefore, the level of imports was very low.[58] When Mexico acceded to GATT in 1986, the decision was taken to adhere to most of GATT's principles and incorporate them in Mexican law.[59] By a law of 1988, the import licence scheme was abolished.[60] Consequent to this measure being taken, only agricultural and food products such as wheat, powdered milk, cheese, coffee, seafood and automobile industry products – approximately 3 per cent of goods imported into Mexico – required an import licence.

The foreign investor is not bound by the Foreign Investment Law to limit himself to domestic sources in the purchase or use of raw materials. Mexico has made concrete efforts to harmonize import classification by becoming party to the United Nations Convention on Contracts for the International Sale of Goods[61] and giving the foreign investor in Mexico an environment favourable to obtaining external goods necessary for the conduct of his business.

The only other element the foreign investor is required to comply with in the operation of a business in Mexico is the law relating to foreign exchange. Mexico, which has a history of liberal exchange control laws which required no exchange control from 1929 to 1982, had to enact a decree on exchange control in 1982.[62] This decree sought to eliminate the outflow of hard currency and to obtain more binding effect of small investment arrangements. This law, however, was effective only for a few months before being superseded by the *Decreto Control de Cambio*.[63] This decree diversified the status quo of generalized control of trade to a scheme of restricted control, creating two foreign exchange markets: a controlled and a free market. The former, which was operated by banks, was regulated by government and had restricted access. The latter was an untrammelled free market based on the principles of supply and demand. The goal of this dual system was to replenish Mexico's treasury with as much foreign exchange as possible and to use this resource where it was most needed. The free market alternative, also known as 'coyote', has been designed to eliminate the black market and give people an alternative way to deal with their needs pertaining to currency.

The controlled market is regulated so that specific types of foreign currency income must be exchanged on the controlled market, such as income from the export of goods,[64] and the funds used by *maquiladoras* to cover local costs and loans received from banks. This inflow of foreign currency, which is directed to foreign banks, is used for the repayment of debts in foreign currency, the purchase of merchandise imports and payment of royalties and technical assistance, and compliance with other contractual obligations. While the other controlled market uses foreign currency influx for debt servicing, the free market is used for pure currency operations. Since the difference between the exchange rates is approximately 2 per cent, the foreign investor does not necessarily find himself restricted by the above regulations. He can use the free market for all capital operations, investments, remittance of dividends, payment of royalties and intercompany loans. Furthermore, there are no exchange control regulations for travellers.

Competition Options

The Transatlantic Common Aviation Area

Whether there should be absolute, untrammelled competition within the Americas and between the Americas and Europe is a critical issue for the coming years. Of course, one recent suggestion has been to crystallize a 'convergence of regulatory principles' between Europe and the United States in competition by establishing a Transatlantic Common Aviation Area (TCAA). This concept, suggested by the Association of European Airlines (AEA) in a policy statement,[65] puts forward detailed and realistic proposals on how to bring about an ideal regulatory convergence between the European region and the United States, addressing three areas: matters in respect of which harmonization is necessary, those in respect of which convergence could take the form of mutual recognition, and those which could in principle be left at the discretion of each party.

The TCAA concept advocates the freedom of the parties to provide services, addresses issues pertaining to airline ownership and the right of establishment, provides recommendations with regard to competition policy, and offers guidelines on the leasing of aircraft. Since the TCAA aims at replacing traditional governmental regulatory control of such aspects of competition as market entry and pricing, the issues emerging from competition policy are by far the most complex and difficult to deal with within the parameters of the TCAA. Although the fundamental postulates of competition in Europe (as followed through by EU regulations) and the United States are broadly similar in intent, and both depend to a certain extent on the application of extraterritoriality in their regulations, there are obvious differences, such as those embodied in the different approaches to transatlantic airline alliances. Also the United States stringently relies on a principle of 'public interest' in its air transport policy; European competition rules are not as explicit in their policies. The basic essence of a TCAA would therefore establish the principle that matters of route sharing, capacity, pricing and frequency of services should be driven by market forces rather than be determined by governmental intervention. This way a certain commonality could be established between air transport of the two regions.

Another option, of course, is to allow absolute open competition between Europe and North America. Although globalization of competition in trade is a reality, in the case of air transport it may be premature, since the current bilateral air services negotiations structure still seems to work, and absolute globalization of air transport will involve the question of air transport being encompassed in the General Agreement on Trade in Services (GATS) which contains the Most Favoured Nations (MFN) treatment clause under the General Agreement on Tariffs and Trade (GATT) which later came within the purview of the World Trade Organization (WTO). Under the MFN clause, a GATS member could be required, immediately and unconditionally, to accord to the services and service suppliers of any other member treatment no less favourable than it accords to like services and service suppliers of any other country. This is not practicable, as the application of the MFN principle to international air transport would adversely affect and hold back the current process of liberalization between like-minded states.

Competition between the Americas and the Rest of the World under the World Trade Organization

Although no state in the Americas or Europe has advocated or recommended the inclusion of air transport services in the GATS, it is worthwhile to inquire whether globalization of trade in air transport would lead to a situation where it would be discussed under the GATS umbrella. At the 31st Session of the ICAO Assembly, which held deliberations from 19 September to 4 October 1995, the Assembly adopted a resolution which recognizes ICAO as the multilateral body in the United Nations system competent to deal with air transport and develop inter alia, on a continuing basis, policy guidance on the regulation of international air transport for contracting states. The thrust of this resolution is that ICAO is charged on a continuing basis with recommending policy on the economic regulation of air transport.[66] It remains to be seen how this mandate would be affected by the conservatism which still attaches to commercial air transport.

There has been sustained interest in the world of commerce aimed at bringing international air services within the GATS under the umbrella of GATT. The above resolution of the 31st Session of the ICAO Assembly addresses this issue by recognizing that ICAO has actively promoted an understanding by all parties concerned of the provisions of the Chicago Convention[67] and of ICAO's particular mandate and role in international air transport. The resolution also requests WTO and its member states to accord due consideration to the fact that ICAO has a constitutional responsibility to international air transport which could be discharged through the results of ICAO's World-wide Air Transport Conference and ICAO's continuing work on economic regulation of international air transport.[68]

At its 32nd Session, The ICAO Assembly, in September 1998, adopted Assembly Resolution A32-17 containing a consolidated statement of continuing ICAO policies in the air transport field. This resolution, in Appendix A, Section IV, reaffirms the primary role of developing policy guidance on the regulation of international air transport and, inter alia, requests the WTO and its member states to accord due consideration to ICAO's constitutional responsibility for international air transport. The resolution also requests the ICAO Council to continue to monitor the developments in trade in services and keep the contracting states advised.[69]

At its 158th Session in November 1999, the Council considered and adopted a resolution[70] which inter alia affirmed that the exclusion of 'traffic rights'and 'services directly related to the exercise of traffic rights' from the GATS is consistent with the aviation communities' general goal of gradual, progressive, orderly and safeguarded change towards market access as well as the effective and sustained participation of all states in international air transport. The resolution also urges ICAO contracting states that are members or prospective members of WTO to examine carefully the implications of any proposed inclusion of an additional air transport service or activity in GATS, while requesting WTO to take full cognizance of ICAO's policy on trade in services as contained in Assembly Resolution A32-17. The Council also considers that ICAO should be actively engaged in any review of the classification of international air transport activities for the purposes of negotiation or application of the GATS to air transport.

Earlier, in the process of its deliberations, the ICAO Colloquium of 1992 considered the views of experts on whether air traffic rights should be considered trade in services and brought within the purview of GATT, a proposal that had been included in the Agenda of GATT under GATS. There has been sustained debate in the aviation world on whether air services performed by commercial airlines – operating both scheduled and unscheduled flights – should be included in the General Agreement on Trade in Services (GATS) of the General Agreement on Tariffs and Trade (GATT).[71] GATS seeks to establish a multilateral framework of principles and rules for trade in services with a view to expansion of such trade under conditions of transparency,[72] national treatment[73] and *progressive liberalization*.[74] The fundamental principle of GATT is its Most Favoured Nation (MFN) Treatment clause,[75] whereby each party to the agreement accords immediately and unconditionally to services and service providers of any other party treatment no less favourable than that it accords to like services and service providers of any other country. These provisions reflect the basic philosophy of GATS and play a vital role in affecting the decision of the international community on whether or not air transport services should be brought under its purview. Other features of GATS which have attracted discussion in relation to air services are provisions relating to increasing participation of developing countries within GATS[76] and dispute settlement.[77]

The issue of trade in services in general was discussed in GATT's latest round of multilateral trade negotiations launched by ministers of GATT contracting states who met in September 1986 in Punta del Este, Uruguay. The Uruguay Round was the eighth round of multilateral trade negotiations held by GATT so far,[78] and by far one of the most complex. This round of negotiations was assisted by the Group of Negotiators on Services (GNS) which the GATT established in 1986 to follow the services negotiations. The GNS had drafted a detailed agreement comprising 35 articles and five annexes, with one of the annexes comprising provisions on air transport services. The Annex on Air Transport Services applies both to scheduled and to unscheduled air services and generally excludes its application: (a) to air traffic rights covered by the Chicago Convention, including the five freedoms of the air[79] and bilateral air services agreements; and (b) to directly related activities which would limit or affect the ability of parties to negotiate, grant or to receive traffic rights or which would have the effect of limiting their exercise.[80]

Notwithstanding the above provisions, GATS applies inter alia to computer reservations systems in air transport, the selling or marketing of air transport services, and transactions in civil aircraft.[81] The proposition, that GATS would not apply to air traffic rights covered by the Chicago Convention but apply to the selling or marketing of air transport services, creates *in limine* a dichotomy that has to be resolved. Air traffic rights that result from the Chicago Convention's provisions are the tool with which the selling or marketing of air transport services are carried out and the two are inextricably linked. Confusion is worse confounded by Article 1 of GATS, which defines trade in services as inter alia the supply of a service from the territory of one party into the territory of another party. The application of this definition to the provision of air transport services by an air transport enterprise would lead one to the inexorable conclusion that the definition of trade in services provided in GATS refers implicitly to the exercise of air traffic rights – which are obtained by virtue of the Chicago Convention. The explicit exclusion of air traffic rights in GATS is therefore ambivalent.

For the present, the overall purpose of including air transport services in GATS seems to be to apply the broad principles of market access and the MFN philosophy to the selling or marketing of air traffic services. The purview of GATS in controlling air transport services would therefore be considered only in situations where air traffic rights are exercised multilaterally or plurilaterally. GATS would not apply in instances where states elect to use Article 6 of the Chicago Convention, which governs all bilateral air services agreements and states that the permission of a grantor state is necessary for a commercial air transport enterprise to operate air services into or out of a state. In any event, the Annex on Air Transport Services to GATS does not reflect confidence in itself by providing in Article 6 of the Annex that the operation of the Annex shall be reviewed periodically, or at least every five years.

There are two provisions in the Annex on Air Transport Services in GATS which are also worthy of mention. One is on the access to and use of publicly available services offered by a party on reasonable and non-discriminatory terms,[82] and the other is on dispute settlement procedures which could be invoked only where dispute settlement procedures provided for in bilateral air services agreements, or under the Chicago Convention itself, have been exhausted.[83]

The regulation of air transport services lies within the purview of ICAO, which maintains in its Legal Bureau a register of all bilateral air transport agreements. The bilateral air transport agreement usually includes a reciprocal agreement between states for their carriers to have fair and equal opportunity in operating air services between their territories without unduly affecting the air services operated by each other. Under a bilateral agreement, capacity offered by carriers must bear close relationship to the needs of the people using air transport.[84] These regulatory provisions have so far succeeded in protecting carriers of lesser developed states by obtaining for them fair and equal opportunity to operate air services in routes that are shared by more established carriers of wealthier nations.[85]

Since GATS cannot sustain air transport services within a bilateral framework, it now remains to be seen whether the aviation community will move in the future towards placing air traffic rights in a multilateral or plurilateral system. In such an eventuality, GATS would doubtless rejuvenate its efforts at seeking to include air transport services within its purview under liberalized market access and the MFN treatment clause. In this context, the role played by ICAO – the guardian and mentor of international civil aviation – becomes relevant.

ICAO has the mandate (under the Convention on International Civil Aviation signed in Chicago in 1944), experience and expertise in a wide range of air transport matters: technical, economic and legal. Issues of operating arrangements, market access, pricing and capacity for the designated airlines of each state are the subject of bilateral air transport agreements between states, except for arrangements within the European Economic Community for mutual relations between member states. International air transport is, in effect, conducted under an extensive network of some 1800 separate bilateral agreements or treaties. ICAO has taken the position that international air transport is an economic activity in which there is a strong national interest and involvement, as well as a long-established, comprehensive and detailed structure of standards, principles and operating arrangements.

ICAO believes it is important to draw to the attention of GATS and its member states certain critical features of international air transport which are relevant to any present or future consideration of how air transport should be treated in the context of the trade in services negotiations. The main consideration that impels ICAO to maintain steadfastly its position as the guiding force behind air transport services is that it feels that bilateralism at the operating level has over the decades proved to be a flexible system which allows states to pursue their objectives, whether these be open and competitive or more protective or restrictive regimes for their airlines. ICAO strongly maintains that any external multilateral framework which sought general or limited application would need to recognize and be compatible with this existing structure of air transport.

Nevertheless, multilateralism in the form of a broad-based consensus on principles and guidance to states in the conduct of their air transport activities has enjoyed renewed interest in ICAO in recent years. While seeking to develop progressively positions and guidance to assist states in their regulatory/economic activities, ICAO recognizes the sovereignty of states in pursuing their own national air transport policies and objectives. ICAO's role in this sphere is therefore merely consultative and recommendatory, without being incompatible with liberalization in this sector. ICAO has also expressed its resolve to continue to cooperate with GATT and the GNS in its trade in services discussions in order that ICAO's views and concerns and the particular features of the international air transport sector are properly taken into account by GATT and the GNS.

The Organization's position on the regulation of air transport services was formally adopted at its 7th Assembly, held in June/July 1953, where Assembly Resolution A7-15 resolved that there was no prospect at the time of achieving a universal multilateral agreement, although ICAO acknowledged that the achievement of multilateralism in commercial rights remained an objective of the organization. This resolution is still in force and reflects ICAO's commitment to achieving an acceptable multilateral basis for air transport services.

Later, at its 26th Session in September/October 1986, the ICAO Assembly adopted Resolution A26-14, which reaffirmed that ICAO was the multilateral body in the United Nations system competent to deal with international air transport and urged contracting states which participated in any multilateral negotiations on trade in services where international air transport was included to ensure that their representatives were fully aware of potential conflicts with the existing legal system for the regulation of international air transport. The resolution also requested the ICAO Council to actively promote a full understanding by international bodies involved with trade in services of the role of ICAO in international air transport and the existing structure of international agreements regarding air transport. This resolution helped sensitize states and GATT regarding the air transport sector. Although this resolution is no longer in force, it reflects adequately ICAO's philosophy on the subject. In view of the significant recent and possible future developments in the trade in service negotiations, the question arises however, whether this policy is fully adequate to continue to serve the interests of ICAO and international air transport over the next few years or whether it requires reassessment and additional directives from the Assembly.

Assembly Resolution A26-14 gave guidance to states and the Council and expressed certain concerns, but it did not set out an organizational view on the inclusion of international air transport in a multilateral agreement on trade in services. A future session of the Assembly may consider developing such a view for transmission to GATT and the GNS as well as to contracting states. One possible view the Assembly may consider is that air transport should not be included in a services agreement. The adoption of such a position by ICAO could be grounded on two of the concerns found in Resolution A26-14: one is the organization's concern about ICAO's role as the United Nations specialized agency responsible in air transport matters; the other is the organization's concern for the integrity of the Chicago Convention principles and arrangements and the widespread system of bilateral air transport agreements that are a consequence of those principles.

At ICAO's air transport Colloquium of April 1992, at least two speakers expressed the need to exercise caution on the subject of handing over air transport services to GATS. The International Air Transport Association (IATA)'s Director General, Gunter Eser, informed the Colloquium that most international airlines categorically opposed the inclusion of air transport services in GATS. Dr Eser, while recognizing that national interests clearly exist in air traffic rights issues, drew the attention of the Colloquium to the economic concerns of the airline industry. He saw the need for a balance between economic regulations and a free market, on the basis that bilateralism per se cannot exist on its own in view of multilateral practices in such areas as tariff coordination which have proved that plurilateralism has a distinct edge over bilateralism in commercial air transport.[86] Dr Eser's assessment was that any such plurilateralism would be best developed by ICAO and not a trade institution such as GATT.[87]

Another speaker at the Colloquium, Vijay Poonoosamy, said:

> The underlying premise of GATT is that free trade in the air transport sector will promote economic growth and development. I beg to differ. To enable international air transport to deliver its many and varied goods in a safe and orderly manner we must steer a commonsense and enlightened course between regularity overkill and destructive laissez-faire. For more than 45 years, ICAO has provided a means for governments to co-operate in the development and maintenance of an effective trading environment for international air transport. Today ICAO provides the proper forum for charting such a vital course for survival.[88]

Gary Sampson, Director, GNS Division GATT, expressed the view that the airline industry over the last decade had changed dramatically, moving towards reduced administrative regulation of airlines and the promotion of competition through greater reliance on market forces, as opposed to government fiat, in determining service levels such as fares, capacities and frequencies. Sampson further stated that, although there was clear distinction between 'hard' rights such as air traffic rights and 'soft' rights such as as marketing and sales rights, the application of GATS both to hard and soft rights would enable participants to concentrate their efforts on doing business without restraint under the GATS agreement.[89] David Buckingham, the Australian delegate to the Colloquium, was of the view that what the international community needed was not a simplistic affirmation of the relevance to aviation of the GATT principles of free trade, but a broad-based agreement that liberalized trade in aviation rights.[90] Daniel M. Kasper, author,[91] stressed that fundamental GATT principles such as the unconditional MFN and market access clauses were likely to impede rather than advance liberalization. Instead, he advocated a conditional MFN treatment scenario under a plurilateral system where only those parties willing and able to accede to terms of the said agreement would be required to comply.[92]

The main strength of the GATT approach to air transport services lies in its commitment to liberalization within a defined time scale. The discipline of GATT in accomplishing its objectives also acts as a positive factor. In a general sense, GATT is viewed with favour by those who see some merit in its role as custodian and guide of air transport services, for two reasons. First, the modern trend of aviation towards globalization, privatization and cross-border alliances and computer reservations systems (CRS) conglomerates, and the overall tendency of air transport operators to seek market access, have made bilateralism obsolete. The changing structure of international civil aviation needs to consider multilateralism, which is the ideal of GATT. Second, the Uruguay Round which intends to envelop air transport services in the GATT concept advocates a process of gradual liberalization (firstly only of 'soft' rights), negotiated market access and an efficient dispute settlement system.[93]

Arguments against the GATT's role in air transport services are, however, more compelling, the most basic being that aviation issues must essentially come within the purview of an organization specialized in international civil aviation, such as ICAO. The strongest objection is aimed at the principles of GATT, such as the unconditional MFN treatment philosophy, which is calculated to lead to competitive imbalances between airlines, and the long and tedious process of GATT which would take years to resolve disputes, whereas under the existing bilateral system more expeditious measures are available.[94] To overcome this problem, experts have suggested that GATT's MFN rule should apply only to 'soft' trading rights in aviation (such as ground handling, CRS systems and sales) and 'hard' rights should be included in a multilateral agreement outside GATT.[95] Kasper opposes the application of the MFN philosophy to air services:

> unconditional MFN would deprive air service negotiators of essential flexibility. Trade barriers in air services vary widely in form and impact across markets, forcing even liberal nations to discriminate when granting traffic rights in order to counteract the sometimes severe restraints their carriers encounter in foreign markets. Due to the nature of these non-tariff barriers and to the fact that they often arise in ancillary markets, a universal solution, such as the elimination of the

> ancillary restraints by all signatories, would be exceedingly difficult to negotiate and to enforce.
>
> Under these circumstances, adopting unconditional MFN would undermine the ability of governments to tailor packages of economic rights that offset the mix of restraints in particular foreign markets. It would be especially troubling for those markets characterised by a high degree of cooperation between the national airline and the government.[96]

There is also the disturbing thought that, unlike what happens in a bilateral negotiation for air traffic rights, where two states can readily analyse the economic implications of sharing air traffic rights between points of the two states, the MFN principle would create a free-for-all, the consequences of which would not be capable of being economically assessed or controlled.

IATA has suggested that ICAO adopt GATT principles with regard to all aspects of the air services agreement except in the area of air traffic rights and frequency of operations of aircraft. This suggestion has been strongly resisted by the International Chamber of Commerce (ICC), which argues that the aviation field should retain its purity of having characteristics and attributes that are susceptible to negotiation, although air traffic rights should be negotiated under a more efficient system than the prevailing bilateral system. Kasper shares a compatible view: 'To achieve true liberalization in air services, a new approach will be required, one that focuses on securing agreement among a relatively small group of liberal trading partners willing to abide by a strict condition on a reasonably level playing field.'[97]

Although GATS does not seek control over air traffic rights, it is appropriate to consider this subject as a future consideration of the overall GATT philosophy. It is evident that the principles of GATT are inconsistent with the present legal regime that applies to air traffic rights. The Chicago Convention is the sole legal document that governs the principle of air traffic rights and explicitly recognizes the principles of state sovereignty in Article 1. The sovereignty of a state reserves for that state the right to control activities within its territory and, a fortiori, the convention strengthens this concept by requiring that special permission of a state must be obtained for the operation of air services into and out of its territory by an air transport operator of another state.

The foregoing discussion reflects the fact that, ever since the question of commercial air traffic rights arose as a corollary to the principle of sovereignty as recognized in the Paris Convention and, later, in the Chicago Convention, air transport has been viewed as a social need, run on equality of opportunity that is not a mere theoretical concept but one that can be practically enjoyed by states.[98] To these qualities have been added the view of Dr Wassenbergh, that state policy in civil aviation must protect the integrity and identity of the national society.[99] The Chicago Convention, in its Preamble, calls for cooperation between nations and peoples so that international air transport services may be established on the basis of equality of opportunity and operated soundly and economically. The Chicago Convention further charges ICAO with the task of ensuring the prevention of economic waste caused by unreasonable competition[100] and ensuring that the rights of contracting states are fully respected and that every contracting state has a fair opportunity to operate international airlines.[101] The critical question therefore is whether multilateral liberalization of the bilateral air services agreement would preclude some states from having a fair opportunity to operate international airlines on an equal-opportunity basis. It is only logical to conclude that the answer to the question of whether multilateralism should ultimately replace bilateralism would lie in a clear perception of what is meant by the term 'multilateralism' in this context, and whether multilateralism would interfere with the states' right to the practical enjoyment of fair and equal opportunity in the operation of air services.

Nature of WTO's Competition Rules

The World Trade Organization which, unlike GATT, is not an agency of the United Nations, has reached an understanding with ICAO to address the issue of air traffic rights at an appropriate time in the future.[102] It is therefore very relevant to examine the competition rules of WTO.

The genesis of competition law in trade, and, therefore, of WTO rules on competition, may well lie in the United Nations Conference on Trade and Employment, held in Havana in November 1947. This conference laid the ground for the International Trade Organization (ITO), the charter of which had two chapters relating to competition. Chapter III of the Charter of the International Trade Organization provided that no member shall impose unreasonable or unjustifiable impediments that would preclude other members from obtaining, on equitable terms, facilities for economic development. Chapter V, which provided for the elimination of restrictive business practices, requires that each member will take appropriate measures, individually or through collective involvement, to prevent business practices from affecting international trade, thereby leading to restrained competition, limited access to markets or fostered monopolistic practices.[103] The ITO competition rules were embellished with controls over price fixing and other forms of anti-competitive practices endemic to private enterprises. However, the functioning of ITO never attained fruition and these provisions remained academic. A second attempt was made by the United Nations Economic and Social Council (ECOSOC),[104] but this effort too was destined to fail. The third attempt, made by GATT in 1959, also failed to elicit a concrete proposal. Later, the Organization for Economic Cooperation and Development (OECD) established a system of exchange of information and a procedure for consultation of competition rules among enforcement authorities.

WTO, established on 1 January 1995, will administer the new global trade rules, agreed in the Uruguay Round, which came into effect on the same day. These rules, which are the result of seven years of negotiations among member states of GATT, establish the rule of law in international trade, estimated at $5 trillion in 1995. The WTO involvement in world trade is estimated to raise the fiscal proportions of trade to $500 billion by the year 2005.[105] The WTO has a membership of 150 states and is far wider in scope than its predecessor, bringing into the multilateral trading system trade in services, intellectual property protection and investment. Unlike GATT, which was a provisional treaty serviced by an ad hoc secretariat, WTO is a full-fledged international organization in its own right and administers a unified package of agreements to which all member states are committed. In other words, it is an improved version of GATT and serves as an effective watchdog of international trade and a management consultant. Its economists are required to keep a close watch on the pulse of the global economy and provide studies on the main trade issues of the world.

WTO considers that four fundamental factors are shaping the world economy: the broader integration of the world economy; the sharply different trends in the developed and developing countries; the spread of market-oriented reforms; and the end of the cold war.[106] On the subject of market-oriented reforms, WTO believes:

> If there are no rules in trade then the resulting anarchy will inevitably lead to conflict. International norms not only ensure freedom for economic agents to operate in their commercial interest across national frontiers. They also enhance the freedom of governments in their trade policy interventions, by defining the scope of actions permissible within the confines of international law. The behaviour of all governments becomes more predictable when all accept the rules of the game.[107]

Obviously, WTO believes that a coherent set of rules followed in conformity with the accepted norms of international law should govern competition. This does not necessarily mean that WTO is against free trade. It merely means that free trade has to be conducted according to accepted universal norms, and these norms have been explicitly laid out in the WTO Agreement. The trade in services portion of the agreement carries specific rules of competition.

Transparency is another concept which has been recognized for practical applicability in the WTO rules. Accordingly, each member is required to publish promptly and, except in emergency situations, at the latest by the time of their entry into force, all relevant measures of general application which pertain to or affect the operation of the agreement.[108] There is also the requirement of publication of international agreements pertaining to or affecting trade in services to which a member is a signatory.[109] Article XVII of the WTO Agreement lays down the principle of national treatment which requires each member to accord to services and service providers of any other member, in respect of all measures affecting the supply of services, treatment no less favourable than it accords to its own like services and service suppliers. This provision is effectively tied up with the principle of elimination of all discrimination from the applicability of the WTO Agreement, as reflected in Article V, achieving the dual goal of elimination of existing discriminatory measures and prohibition of new or more discriminatory measures. The requirement for equality of treatment is also reflected in provisions related to market access, whereby the agreement requires, in Article XVI, treatment no less favourable from any member to others than that uniformly provided under WTO rules.

It is claimed that, since the primary purpose of the WTO system is to achieve trade among members as liberally and fairly as possible while retaining the essence of non-discrimination in trade practices, the WTO system should guarantee a fair and equitable opportunity for market access by enterprises of members to the national markets of other members. This is done mainly through the removal of government barriers to the extent possible and the convergence of national regulatory regimes such as those which relate to intellectual property rights.

One of the most serious challenges faced by WTO in this regard is the claims by some states of 'unfair trade' by others, where the claimant states feel victimized by private business practices of enterprises of other states. The corollaries of anti-dumping are one such example, where the exporter is faced with the situation in which imports to his country are precluded by his country, with a view to compelling the consumption of the exporter's goods within the country of production. This practice often leads to price increases and protectionism within a market. The WTO rules therefore strive for fair and equal opportunity in competition, in the same way the bilateral air services agreement requires.

One of the major considerations of the WTO is the perceived incompatibility between business practices of countries and uniform competition rules which are required to be enforced globally. There is an obvious link between business systems and corporate behaviour, on the one hand, and competition rules (or the lack thereof), on the other. There is also probably a functional relationship between them, in that competition rules partly reflect existing business systems and corporate behaviour (a regulatory system functions well only if it is fundamentally accepted). Also business systems and corporate behaviour often adjust to, and take advantage of, the possibilities opened by competition rules. To that extent, the disparities between competition rules, on the basis that what is permitted in one state may be prohibited in another, may influence disparities in business systems and corporate behaviour and may constitute an impediment for enterprises which seek entry into another market. Some examples are cited below.

In the European Community, where government barriers such as tariffs and import restrictions have been removed, competition policy measures play a vital role in ensuring that the common market operates without hindrance by private restrictive business practices. In the EC, the role of competition policy has increased dramatically with the progressive integration of the common market.

In the Structural Impediment Initiative (SII) negotiated between the US government and the Japanese government in 1989–90, business customs and corporate behaviours were the major issues. The US government has claimed that restrictive business customs and corporate behaviour were the major impediments which restricted effective market access to the Japanese market by foreign enterprises. In accordance with the SII, the two governments have agreed that an increase in competition rules in Japan would increase market access to the Japanese market by foreign enterprises by removing private restrictive business practices. A number of reforms of the Japanese Anti-monopoly Law resulted from this agreement, including an increase in administrative surcharges and criminal fines to be imposed on enterprises when they engage in cartels.[110] This functional relationship between competition rules and business systems and corporate behaviour, rooted as they are in cultural, economic and political traditions, may, however, often place limitations upon possible achievements attained by the applicability of partial harmonization of competition rules. Differences in business systems and corporate behaviour are generally wide-ranging and complex, and the application of competition rules may often fail to bridge the gap between the two elements. This notwithstanding, a vigorous enforcement of competition rules in trading nations may still be able to play a useful role in preparing common rules which could be made applicable to trading nations. The adoption of common rules of conducts for enterprises may well reduce undue imbalances in different business systems and could pave the way for enterprises to compete for roles in markets of trading states outside their own market-place.

WTO should also take into consideration the fact that, as globalization of national economies is achieved through the removal of governmental barriers to trade such as tariffs and import restrictions, new trade issues may arise. One such issue is the possible incompatibility between different regulatory/business systems among trading states. Differences in domestic regulatory systems and in business customs and behaviours often emerge as barriers to transnational business activities. These differences may take the form of inconsistencies between technical standards, taxation, environmental protection measures, labour standards and other barriers which hamper enterprises seeking to engage in trans-boundary trade. Such differences obviously create disparity among the states concerned.

Extraterritoriality is one concept which could affect more than one jurisdiction in the application of domestic trade policy. The United States, the European Community and Germany are proponents of extraterritoriality where competition rules are applied to commercial conduct of foreign enterprises which conduct business in places other than those whose domestic markets are affected by such trade. In the seminal *Alcoa* case[111] of 1945, the US courts established the 'effects' theory, whereby commercial conduct carried out overseas but intended or calculated to affect the United States would be subject to US antitrust laws. This doctrine has been followed by the courts in the United States with an unfailing consistency, culminating in recent guidelines on international commercial operations adopted by the United States Justice Department.[112] These guidelines contain principles that give the United States a wide scope of extraterritorial jurisdiction in respect of anti-competitive practices which foreign enterprises follow in countries outside the United States, provided such activities adversely affect the United States' market in that particular commercial activity. One of the most compelling features of this legislation is its emphasis on 'market access' relating to US businesses in foreign countries. A number of hypothetical examples incorporated in these guidelines indicate that the Department of Justice would challenge the conduct of foreign enterprises in foreign countries if such enterprises would hinder US enterprises from using opportunities to export goods to a foreign country or investing in a foreign country.

In the famous *Woodpulp* case,[113] the Court of Justice of the European Communities decided that the EC competition rules apply to agreements of foreign enterprises which are entered into outside the European Community as long as they are implemented within the common market.

One cannot deny that, in this era of global economy, some degree of extraterritoriality in the enforcement of national competition rules is inevitable. A state would therefore be seen as being justified in applying its competition rules to the conduct of foreign enterprises abroad when conduct which occurs in a foreign country affects its economy adversely, particularly where the state in which such conduct occurs has no competition rules or has no intention to prohibit such conduct. This phenomenon is easily reflected by transnational business entities who may engage in restrictive business practices in a 'twilight zone' where no state can fully exercise jurisdiction and yet harmful effects of such restrictive business practices may be felt in one or more states. To say that there should be no extraterritoriality of any kind in the application of competition rules would mean that such transnational entities can engage in anti-competitive conduct with impunity.

There is of course the consideration that an extraterritorial application of competition rules is a costly business both for the enforcement agency and for the foreign defendants, and is often a second-best solution to a problem which essentially examines how to cope with transnational anti-competitive conduct. An extraterritorial application of competition rules is often not as effective as it would be if applied domestically. A state which attempts to apply its anti-competitive laws extraterritorially to a defendant enterprise located abroad could always face difficulties of enforcement and considerations of forum and jurisdiction. There could also be disabling legislation in a foreign state which may effectively preclude extraterritoriality.

The *Watchmakers of Switzerland* case[114] of 1955 exemplifies the essential commercial law principle of the United States, that applicability of antitrust laws on foreign enterprises may often entail conflict with legislation of other states. The court in this case held that a watch repair enterprise, conducted in the United States by two Swiss corporations, could be subjected to the domestic laws of the United States. The court further held that, in order for a foreign corporation to be present within the jurisdiction of a court for purpose of service of process, there must be proof of continuous local activities and a showing that, under all circumstances of the case, the forum is not unfairly inconvenient. Even though the two Swiss entities had no property in the United States and did not carry out their activities directly (the business activities of the Swiss corporations were carried out by an American corporation in the United States), since the Swiss corporations determined the prices and terms of the business enterprise, the court further held that the Swiss corporations could be subjected to antitrust statutes and tariff laws of the United States.[115]

In the watershed case of *Laker Airways Limited* v. *SABENA Belgian World Airlines*,[116] it was held that territoriality-based jurisdiction allows states in the United States to regulate conduct or status of individuals or property physically situated within a territory even if effects of conduct are felt outside that territory, and, conversely, conduct outside a territory, which is calculated to have a substantial effect on that territory, may also be similarly regulated. It was also held that a state has jurisdiction to prescribe law governing conduct of its nationals whether such conduct takes place inside or outside the territory of that state. Accordingly, the plaintiff, Laker Airways Limited, a British corporation seeking remedy in the United States, whose activities in question took place in countries other than the United States, was deemed to be subject to US antitrust legislation on the basis that such activities gravely impaired US interests.[117] In deciding upon the contentious question whether the law of the United Kingdom should apply to the plaintiff, the court compared the diametrically opposed antitrust legislations of the United Kingdom and of the United States and held:

> We find no indication in either the statutory scheme or prior judicial precedent that jurisdiction [by the United States] should not be exercised. Legitimate United States interests in protecting consumers, providing for vindicating creditors' rights, and regulating economic consequences of those doing substantial business in our country are all advanced under the congressionally prescribed scheme. There are more than sufficient jurisdictional contacts under *United States* v. *Aluminium Co. of America*[118] and subsequent case law to support the exercise of prescriptive jurisdiction in this case.[119]

In the United States, the scope of antitrust legislation and protection thereby extends to those persons who are either directly or indirectly affected adversely by antitrust violations by third parties. The adverse effect on the plaintiff must be one that the laws were written to guard against. An example of this principle can be seen in the *Uranium antitrust litigation* of 1979,[120] where a business entity which indulged in a 'tying arrangement'[121] to sell its product was considered in violation of antitrust legislation. The tie-in resulted in a drop in demand for the product concerned, giving way to a drop in prices and adversely affecting other competitors of the product in the market.

The role of WTO in extraterritoriality becomes significant when one considers the eventuality where the extraterritorial application of competition rules becomes too costly or burdensome on states concerned. WTO offers the alternative of its own dispute settlement process and a framework within which members may seek positive comity and a certain convergence or harmonization of competition rules. There have been several proposals for convergence, the most practical and well-thought-out of which is the Draft International Antitrust Code, which is referred to as DIAC, proposed by a group of competition law scholars, called the Munich Group. The DIAC proposes that there should be a comprehensive international antitrust code covering the major areas of competition law, such as horizontal agreements, vertical agreements, mergers and acquisitions, the relationship between competition law and industrial policies and others. It also recommends the establishment of an international antitrust agency which shares the responsibility of enforcement of international competition rules with the national governments.

Ideas expressed in the DIAC are similar to those in Chapter V of the WTO Charter, giving one the impression that the DIAC may well have been drafted along the lines of the schemes of international antitrust enforcement contemplated by the WTO Charter. The DIAC remains the most ambitious of the proposals made in recent years.

Another attempt at international antitrust regulations is reflected in the work of a task force established by the American Bar Association which issued a report (ABA Report) advocating an agreement among states with regard to some basic principles on unlawfulness of cartels and unification of filing requirements under the merger laws of various states. The report contains a modest recommendation seeking partial harmonization through an agreement among states on basic principles, and does not seek the establishment of a comprehensive international authority to enforce international rules.

Professor Eleanor Fox of New York University Law School has taken the idea of the DIAC further, proposing a scheme in which states would agree on 'a few fundamental world-linking principles' of competition policy such as, inter alia, prohibition of cartels and positive comity.[122] Fox's proposal basically requires each state to carry out convergence of competition rules while adopting fundamental principles established in an international agreement.

The advantage of the DIAC approach to establish an international code is that, in such an instrument, rules and obligations of member states would be clear and member states would have a clear goal to achieve. It must be mentioned that a somewhat similar approach has been made within the framework of the WTO, in the area of intellectual property. In the Agreement on Trade-related Intellectual Property Rights (TRIPs), principles with regard to the minimum protection of intellectual property rights and the enforcement of the rights under intellectual property laws are clearly laid out and members are obligated to incorporate these principles in their domestic legislation, while allowing for a grace period in the case of developing countries. It would not be incorrect to say, therefore, that, in this respect, the DIAC approach already has a precedent in the WTO system.

The disadvantage of a comprehensive international code approach may be that it lacks flexibility. It is often true that, when comprehensive principles are already declared, member states have no choice but to accept them, when there may well be justification for considering principles other than those declared in the code which may be more feasible. There could even be possibilities of applying different combinations of such principles. As mentioned earlier, the TRIPs agreement is an attempt to accomplish convergence of intellectual property laws of members. If it proves to be successful, an international code approach may be a good prospect as a model for international competition laws. Since the TRIPs agreement was formally initiated only at the beginning of 1995, it is premature to predict the prospect of domestic implementation of such a scheme by members at the present time.

Yet another approach is the 'instalment' or 'evolutionary' approach, for which there is an important precedent in WTO. This precedent, which is adopted in GATS, provides for a general scheme for future negotiations in the liberalization of trade in services within the general principles of the most-favoured nation treatment clause and transparency clause. At the present time, the liberalization of trade in services is largely left to future negotiations and GATS only provides for a scheme of negotiation. This is largely due to the fact that trade in services is a complicated field involving complex and diverse issues. Admittedly, however, it is encouraging that the GATS scheme could be drawn on by members if the need arises in the future.

Concluding Comments

It must be stringently maintained that neither the United States nor any other country has, in its pursuit of open skies, advocated the GATS umbrella. The US approach has been in keeping with its policy of 'public interest' and of maximizing air transport as a service industry to confront the challenges of the coming decades. The GATS example served only to show a certain similarity of equal opportunity and competition under the MFN clause, which would be reflective of the philosophy of an open skies regime, where all states participating in an open skies policy with each other would enjoy absolutely equal air traffic rights on a reciprocal basis.

As to the question whether the GATS negotiating scheme should be adopted with regard to international competition policy, the main consideration should be that, if such is ever considered, it should be contemporaneous with the consideration of a scheme within the WTO for negotiating international antitrust principles. Negotiations may be on a total harmonization or a partial harmonization basis. Such an approach would have the advantage of the possibility of introduction by members of a variety of international competition agreements out of which they could select one which was suitable. Also, if this approach were adopted, it would be important for members to have a firm commitment to promoting competition law and policy both internationally and domestically. Such commitment should be clearly declared. Also it may be necessary to establish, as in GATS, a time schedule within which negotiations should be carried out.

A declaration of fundamental principles of competition would also be necessary. This declaration should contain analogous provisions to most favoured nation treatment, national treatment and transparency. Consideration should also be given to prohibition in principle of cartels, resale price maintenance, boycotts and others. At the same time, one should be cautious that, given a wide variety of principles that are followed by members with regard to other areas such as mergers and acquisitions, vertical non-price restraint and predatory pricing, it may be feasible merely to declare general and abstract principles which require members to promote competition policy in such areas.

Although, admittedly, WTO is not the only forum in which a scheme of convergence of competition laws can be accommodated (the OECD, for example, is to every purpose an appropriate forum) there is compelling reason for such a scheme to be considered under the WTO umbrella owing to the volume of membership that WTO carries. Among the more than 125 states which participated in the Uruguay Round leading to the establishment of the WTO Agreement, not all have competition laws and many are not ready for them yet. When an international competition code is draughted, it is only logical to expect a certain degree of universality in its principles and such could be accomplished on a wider scale, given WTO's membership.

Professor Petersmann has recommended[123] that an international competition code be accommodated as an agreement of Annex 4 of the WTO Agreement, which contains optional agreements. Petersmann examines the idea of a smaller number of nations entering into such an agreement initially, such as the United States, Japan and members of the European Community, with Canada and Australia joining in subsequently. A grace period for developing states to join the agreement has also been addressed. He believes that, at least in the initial stage, an international competition code among a smaller number of members may work more effectively. Such an agreement may, according to Petersmann, address 'market access' issues effectively.

Generally, it is felt that the inclusion of an international competition code in the WTO Agreement would have the advantage that coordination between competition policy and other policies embodied in WTO agreements such as TRIPS, the Safeguard Agreement and the Antidumping Agreement would be accomplished more easily than it would be if a competition code were established separately from WTO. Another envisaged advantage is that the dispute settlement process incorporated in Annex 2 of the WTO Agreement could be utilized when a dispute arises relating to the enforcement of competition laws.

Perhaps the only similarity between the competition rules of the existing bilateral structure relating to the air services agreement and WTO competition rules is the insistence by both systems on the requirement of fair and equal opportunity. The current bilateral structure of the air services negotiations will remain in force as long as states consider subjectively the potential of air traffic that their carriers would have over others by excluding others from given market segments. This the states can do, not only because of Article 6 of the Chicago Convention but also by virtue of the underlying principle of sovereignty which legally entitles a state to prohibit a carrier from flying into or out of its territory without that state's permission. As the preceding discussion has revealed, the protectionist attitude that pervades commercial air transport is not limited to struggling carriers of developing nations but applies to mega-carriers who 'protect' what they believe to be a legitimate share of their market. Against this backdrop, the term 'market access' can only be used with the word 'reciprocity'. The status quo in commercial aviation is therefore by no means consistent with the competition principles advocated by WTO.

If the concept of 'market access' of commercial aviation is to be in consonance with WTO competition rules, the first step that the aviation community will have to take is to change its overall philosophy and consider all international air traffic as international property rather than national property. This calls for a radical change in international policy on the subject of air traffic rights, where individual states would be considered as having an overall duty towards their citizens and whereby citizens are considered as units of an international community of nations, rather than units of that particular state. In other words, states would represent citizens as nationals of an international society. The international traffic market would then be taken as a whole and nations would adapt themselves to an extranational approach in sharing international air traffic. Once the extranational philosophy was in place, it would not be difficult to consider extraterritoriality in competition in a manner compatible with WTO competition rules, particularly in the context of the latter's emphasis on uniformity. The principles of transparency, most favoured nation treatment and dispute resolution could then all fall into place.

Although, theoretically, the above proposal may sound logical and workable, in practicality, it cannot be denied that states have jealously guarded their historical rights to air traffic over the past 54 years and would therefore be reluctant to embrace a multilateral approach to enter into open competition.

Notes

1 P.P.C. Haanappel (1983), *Pricing and Capacity Determination in International Air Transport*, Amsterdam: Kluwer Deventer, p.27.
2 US DoT News Release, Monday 12 January 1998.
3 Ibid.
4 Marlin Dresner and Michael Trethaway (1987), 'Policy Choices for Canada International Air Transport, Proceedings of the Administrative Sciences Association of Canada', *International Business*, 83–94.
5 See Donna Mitchell (1997), 'Canadian International Air Transport Historical Background and Current Policy', Ministerial Task Force on International Air Transport.
6 See Raymond J. Kaduk (1997), 'Canadian Carrier Strategies and the 1995 Open-Skies Agreement', *Journal of Air Transport Management*, 5(3), 145.
7 Ibid., 152.
8 Carole A. Shifrin (1998), 'Open-Skies Pact Boon to Canada, U.S.', *Aviation Week and Space Technology*, 2 March, p.43.
9 'United States Panama reaches Open-Skies Agreement', DoT Press Release 33-97, Friday 14 March 1997.
10 Ibid.
11 'Secretary Slater signs Open-Skies Agreement with Central American countries', DoT Press Release 67-97, Friday 9 May 1997.
12 See the *Gordon Commission Report*, which analysed the extent of foreign ownership in Canada. This report proposed that foreign investment in Canada be controlled in four ways, including control by a central review board (*Report of the Royal Commission on Canada's Economic Prospects*, Ottawa: Queen's Printer, 1958). A subsequent study, *the Gray Report*, concluded that it was necessary to regulate foreign investment in Canada in view of the very high level of foreign ownership in Canada. According to this report 76 per cent of the energy sector and 90 per cent in various other sectors were under foreign ownership. See *Foreign Direct Investment in Canada*, Ottawa: Information Canada, 1972.
13 For material on investment between Canada and the United States, see H.I. MacDonald (1972), 'Nationalism in Canada', T.E. Reid (ed.), *Foreign Ownership: Villain or Scapegoat*, in Toronto: Holt, Rienhart & Winston, p.71; T.F. Frank and K.S. Gudgeon (1975), 'Canada's Foreign Investment Control Experiment: The Law, The Context and the Practice', *New York University Law Review*, 50, 76; D. McDowall (1984), 'A Fit Place for Investment?', *Study No. 81*, Ottawa: Conference Board of Canada; S. Wex (1984), *Instead of FIRA: Autonomy for Canadian Subsidiaries?*, Institute for Research on Public Policy Montreal; G. Dewhirst and M. Rudiak (1986), 'From Investment Screening to Investment Development: The Impact of Canada's Foreign Investment Review Agency (FIRA) and Investment Canada in Canada's Technological Development', *Can. U.S. L.J.*, II, 149. For material on investment similarities in Canada and Mexico, see J.H. Hodgson (1975), 'Las Inversiones Estranjeras en el desarollo de Canada y de America Latina', R.B. Farell (ed.), *America Latina y Canada Frente a la Politica Exterior de los Estados Unidos*, Mexico: Fondo de Cultura Economica, p.56.

14 Foreign Investment Review Act, S.C. 1973–4. See also J. Turner (1983), 'Canadian Regulation of Foreign Direct Investments', *Harv. Int'l L.J.*, 23, 333; M. Dewhirst (1984), 'The Canadian Federal Government's Policy in Foreign Direct Investment', in E. Fry and L. Radebaugh (eds), *Regulation of Foreign Direct Investments in Canada and the United States*, Provo, Utah: Brigham University, p.27.

15 Foreign Investment Review Act (*supra*, n.14), Article 2(1). Small investments of $5 million which employed no more than 200 employees, however, required only the formality of registration.

16 See J. Albrecht (1984), 'Canadian Foreign Investment Policy and the International Politico Legal Process', *Canadian Yearbook of International Law 1982*, Vancouver: University of British Columbia Press, p.149.

17 Article III.4 of GATT provides:

> The products of the territory of any contracting party imported into the territory of any other contracting party shall be accorded treatment no less than that accorded to like products of national origin in respect of all laws, regulations and requirements affecting their internal sale, purchase, transportation, distribution or use. The provisions of this paragraph shall not prevent the application of differential internal transportation charges which are based exclusively on the economic operation of the means of transport and not on the nationality of the product.

See also 'Administration of the Foreign Investment Review Act', Report of the Panel, 25 July 1983, BISD 30th Supp., 140 (1982–3).

18 Investment Canada Act, R.S.C. 1985, c 28 (1st Supp.).

19 See, generally, M. Heinz Juergen (1986), 'Regulation of Foreign Investment in Canada' LLM thesis, McGill University. The author analyses comparatively the FIRA and ICA in his thesis. See also J. Baker (1984), 'From FIRA to Investment Canada', *Canada–U.S. Economic Relations in the Conservative Era of Mulroney and Regan*, Provo Utah: Brigham University, in E. Fry and L. Radebaugh (eds), p.47; also generally, J.M. Spence (1986), 'Current Approaches to Foreign Investment Review in Canada', *McGill L. J.*, 31, 507.

20 *ICA* (*supra*, n.18), Article 2.

21 Ibid. Article 14(1)(*a*). This regulation obviated the review of 90 per cent of the transactions that were required to be reviewed by FIRA. See, however, G.C. Glover, D.C. New and M.M. Lacourciere (1985), 'The Investment Canada Act: A New Approach to Foreign Investments in Canada', *Bus. Lawyer*, 4, 98, where the authors claim that the 10 per cent of the investment categories that were retained from the FIRA days comprised 90 per cent of the total transactional value of investments in Canada and therefore this apparent achievement of the ICA is merely illusory.

22 Ibid., Article 21(1). This period is extendable to a maximum of 75 days, unless the investor agrees to the contrary. Both the FIRA and the ICA considered the review of a proposal to be based on policy rather than law. See E. J. Arnett (1985), 'From FIRA to Investment Canada', *Alb. L.R.*, 24, 26.

23 Ibid., Article 21. The criteria determining 'net benefit to Canada' are similar to those followed by FIRA and vest the minister responsible for the implementation of the ICA with a large discretion. Article 20 provides that these criteria should be based upon the effect of investment on labour and employment, productivity, human and other resources, technological development and benefit, national and international market competition, the extent of participation by Canada and the consistency of the investment with national, economic and cultural policies of Canada.

24 Three-quarters of the 5266 investment proposals received up to the end of 1990 were not subject to review, and the 25 per cent that were reviewed had all been approved. See Investment Canada (1991), *The Opportunities and Challenges of North American Free Trade: A Canadian Perspective*, Ottawa: Investment Canada, 44. See also Investment Canada (1991), *Annual Report 1990–1991*, Ottawa: Investment Canada.
25 Aeronautics Act 1985, R.S.C. Ch. F-2.
26 Bank Act 1985, R.S.C., Ch B-1.
27 Fisheries Act 1985, R.S.C., Ch F-14.
28 Western Stabilization Act, 1985, R.S.C. Ch W-7.
29 Canada Shipping Act 1985, R.S.C. Ch S-9.
30 Territorial Lands Act 1985, R.S.C., Ch F-7; Canadian Petroleum Resources Act 1986, Can. Stat., Ch 45; Canada Oil and Gas Act, S.C. 1981 C 81. The Canadian energy policy has often been subject to criticism on the basis that the Canadian government adopted a policy of inordinate appropriation and that such policy was calculated to 'Canadianize' the industry. See C.J. Olmstead, E.J. Krauland and D.F. Orentlicher (1984), 'Expropriation in the Energy Industry: Canada's Crown Share Provisions as a Violation of International Law', *McGill L.J.*, 439. Also, for a descriptive analysis of Canada's energy programme, see E. Mendes (1981), 'The Canadian Energy Program: An Example of Assertion of Economic Sovereignty or Creeping Expropriation in International Law', *Vand. J. Trans.*, 475.
31 Broadcasting Act 1985 R.S.C. Ch B-1.
32 Foreign Direct Investment Study Act of 1974, 15 U.S.C. 786 (1982); *Foreign Direct Investment in the United States: Report of the Secretary of Commerce to the Congress in Compliance with the Foreign Investment Study Act of 1974*, Montreal: McGill, 1976.
33 International Investment Policy Statement 19 *Weekly Comp. Pres. Doc.* 1214 (September 1983) cited in J. Raby (1990), 'The Investment Provisions of the Canada–United States Free Trade Agreement: A Canadian Perspective', *A.J.I.L.*, 400.
34 See, generally, E.M. Graham and P.R. Krugman (1989), *Foreign Direct Investment in the United States*, Washington: Institute for International Economics.
35 The United States is limited by its Constitution and by the treaty provisions governing the country in its capacity to regulate foreign investment. There are built in guarantees that are offered to foreign investors in the *Friendship, Commerce and Navigation Treaties* (FCN) and the *OECD Code of Liberalization of Capital Movements*, which have a direct effect on the US legal system, and the guarantee of due process and non-discrimination entrenched in the United States Constitution.
36 H.E. Bale Jr. (1985), 'The United States Policy Towards Inward Foreign Direct Investment', *Van J. Trans. L.*, 18, 207.
37 Omnibus Trade and Competitiveness Act of 1988, Pub. L. No. 100-418, 102 Stat 1107 (West Supp. 1989). See J.A. Knee (1989), 'Limiting Abuse of Exon-Florio by Takeover Targets', *Geo. Wash. J. Int'l L & Econ.*, 23, 475. Also M. Sandstrom and C. Coccuza (1989), 'The Omnibus Trade and Competitiveness Act of 1988: an Overview', *Rev. Int'l Bus. L.*, 3, 65; M. Prichard (1988), 'Status of the Omnibus Trade Bill and the Canada–U.S. Free Trade Agreement', *Rev. Int'l Bus. L.*, 2, 95.
38 On 1 February 1990, President Bush issued an order, based on the Exon-Florio Amendment, to the China National Technology Import and Export Corporation to divest its holdings in MAMCO, a US manufacturer of aircraft components. MAMCO was a firm which fabricated custom made metal components for the use of manufacturing civilian aircraft and helicopters. See J. Mendenhall

(1991), 'Recent Developments: U.S. Executive Authority to Divest Acquisitions Under the Exon-Florio Amendment – the MAMCO Divestiture', *Harv.J. Int'l L.*, 32, 294. See also D.S. Nance and J. Wasserman (1990), 'Regulation of Imports and Foreign Investment in the United States on National Security Grounds', *Michigan J. Int'l L.*, 11, 926 for a discussion of presidential powers on the regulation of foreign investments on national security grounds.

39 The Federal Communications Commission may refuse to grant a broadcasting licence if the corporation applying for the licence is owned by foreigners and if it is in the national interest to refuse the grant of such licence. See Federal Communications Act, 47 U.S.C. 734 (1976).

40 Jones Act of 1920, 46 U.S.C. 802 (1976 & Supp. V 1981).

41 Federal Aviation Act, 49 U.S.C. 1301 (1976 & Supp. V 1981).

42 Atomic Energy Act, 42 U.S.C. 2133, 2134 (1982); Mineral Leasing Act, 30 U.S.C. 22 (1982); Agricultural Foreign Investment Disclosure Act, 7 U.S.C. 3501 (1978). See also P. Scarborough (1985), 'The Foreign Investor in the United States: Disclosure, Taxation and Visa Laws', *Int'l Lawyer*, 19, 94.

43 National Bank Act, 12 U.S.C. 1974. The restrictions aimed at under the banking laws of the United States are based on the nationality of the directors of a foreign investment company and not on foreign ownership.

44 One of the most compelling elements of state control of foreign investment in the United States is based on national defence under the Defence Production Act of 1950, 50 U.S.C.A. App. 2170 (West Supp. 1989).

45 Clayton Act, 15 U.S.C. 1981.

46 Sherman Act, 15 U.S.C. 1981. See J. Davidow (1976), 'Extraterritorial Application of U.S. Antitrust Law in a Changing World', *L & Pol. Int'l Bus.*, 8, 895; P.N. Swan (1984), 'International Antitrust – The Reach and Efficacy of United States Law', *Oreg. L.R.*, 63, 177; J.A. Kraft (1988), 'Recent Development, Antitrust Law: Extra-Territoriality: In re: Uranium Anti Trust Litigation', *Harv. J. Int'l L.*, 21, 515.

47 Law to Achieve Ecological Balance and to Protect the Environment by Preventing and Controlling Pollution of the Atmosphere, D.O., November 1988; Law to Protect the Ecology and Environment from Dangerous Substances, D.O. November 1988. These laws are implemented and enforced by the Secretariat of Urban Development and Ecology (SEDUE).

48 See 'Free Trade Negotiations with Mexico: Environmental matters', *Int'l Environment* Affairs,3, 1991, 219. See also S.P. Mumme *et al.* (1998), 'Political Development and Environmental Policy in Mexico', *Latin American Research Review*, 23, 7; T.C. du Mars and S. Beltran el Rio (1988), 'A Survey of the Air and Water Quality Laws of Mexico', *Natural Resources Journal*, 28, 787, for an overview of environmental legislation in Mexico. See also Labour Canada (1991), *Comparison of Labour Legislation of General Application in Canada*, the United States and Mexico, Ottawa: Labour Canada for an analysis of the labour laws of Mexico. For NAFTA issues on the labour and environmental position of Mexico, see J. McCambly (1991), 'North American Free Trade Requires a Charter of Labour', *Canadian Speeches/Issues*, 4, 47; S.T. Reyes (1991), 'Labour Market Interdependence Between Mexico and the United States', in C.W. Reynolds (ed.), *The Dynamics of North American Trade and Investment – Canada, United States, Mexico*, Stanford: Stanford University Press, p.241.

49 See, generally, A.T. Kate (1978), *La politica de protection en el desarollo de Mexico*, Mexico: Fondo de Cultura Economica.

50 *Programa de Intercambio de Deuda Publica por Capital*, D.O. 30 March 1990. This programme is an integral part of the understanding between banks in Mexico and the Mexican government which resulted from the Brady Plan. Banks

have undertaken to write off Mexico's medium- and long-term debt, while providing new loans to the government and reducing interest rates.

51 See M.B. Baker (1988), 'Debt–Equity Swaps and Mexican Law: the Interplay between Law and Regulation', *North West J. Int'l L.*, 9, 333.

52 J.F. Torres Landa (1990), 'Report on the New Rules for Operation of Debt–Equity Swaps in Mexico', *Int'l Lawyer*, 25, 734.

53 *Ley para Promover la Inversion Mexicano y Regular la Inversion Estranjera*, D.O. 9 March 1973. The text of this law was reproduced in *International Legal Materials*, 12, 1973, 643.

54 According to Article 20 of the Foreign Investment Law (*supra*, n.53), there was no option to renew this permit.

55 Ibid., Article 20.

56 Ibid.

57 *Maquiladoras* are in-bond assembly plants where only a fraction of their production is allowed to be sold on the domestic market. The parts are imported into Mexico, to be assembled and then exported to other countries. See Article 17 of the *Foreign Investment Law* (*supra*. n.53).

58 It is noteworthy that, in the first five years of the decade between 1980 and 1990, imports into Mexico amounted to an average value of US$12 billion per year, whereas, in 1990, imports amounted to a value of US$32.8 billion.

59 Mexico adhered to GATT's Antidumping Code of 1979, Code on Import Licences of 1979, Code on Customs Valuation of 1979 and the Regulations Against Unfair Trade Practices.

60 *Ley del Impuesto General de Importation*, D.O. 12 February 1988.

61 U.N. Doc. A/CONF.97/18, Annex 1, reprinted in *International Legal Materials*, 19, 1980, 668.

62 *Decreto que establece el control generalizado de cambios*, D.O. 1 September 1982. The imposition of foreign exchange control was exceptional in the context that the peso had not been subject to control.

63 *Decreto Control de Cambio*, D.O. 10 December 1982.

64 This does not apply, however, to exports of small value, or to the *maquiladora* industries. It is also noteworthy that the Mexican exporter is legally obliged to require that exports be paid for in a foreign currency.

65 Aeropolitical News, IATA,REf.744-18.11.99.

66 A31-WP/224, P/57, Report on Agenda Item 36.1-5.

67 Convention on International Civil Aviation, signed at Chicago on 7 December 1944. See ICAO doc. 7300/7 7th edn, 1977.

68 Ibid.

69 See 'Assembly Resolutions in Force (as of 2 October 1998)', ICAO Doc. 9730, p.III-4.

70 See C-WP/11247, 2/11/99, Appendix.

71 GATT was a multilateral body established in Geneva on 1 January 1948 on coming into force of the General Agreement on Tariff and Trade (GATT) negotiated and signed by 23 countries. GATT functions as the principal international body concerned with negotiating reduction of trade barriers and with international trade relations. While being an organization to which member states belong, where they could use it as a forum in which they can discuss and overcome their problems and negotiate to enlarge world trading opportunities, GATT is also a code of rules which is calculated to liberalize world trade. GATS is an Annex to the main GATT agreement and has a special segment on air transport services as trade in services.

One of the agreements contained in the Final Act of the Uruguay Round (*infra*, n.108) establishes a World Trade Organization which will serve as single institutional framework for the GATT as well as all the agreements and arrangements concluded under the Uruguay Round. This permanent organizational framework, which replaces the GATT structure, will be headed by a ministerial conference at least once every two years and will include a General Council to oversee the operation of the Agreement and to act as both a dispute settlement body and a trade policy review mechanism. Therefore all references to GATT in this chapter will infer references to the World Trade Organization.

72 Article III of GATS requires each party to publish promptly all relevant laws, regulations, administrative guidelines and all other decisions, rulings or measures of general application, by the time of their entry into force.

73 GATT's national treatment philosophy provides foreign services and services suppliers with treatment no less favourable than that accorded to a country's own services and service suppliers.

74 Since GATS is an Annex to the GATT agreement, it should be noted that the provisions of GATS are governed by those of GATT and that the two documents incorporate the same basic principles.

75 Article II of GATS. Article XVI extends the MFN principle to market access.

76 Article IV of GATS provides that the increasing participation of developing countries in world trade shall be facilitated through negotiated specific commitments by different parties. It also requires developed member states to establish contact points within two years from the entry into force of the GATS agreement to facilitate the access of developing states' service providers to information related to their respective markets concerning commercial and technical aspects of the supply of services; registration, recognition and obtaining of professional qualifications; and the availability of service technology. The provision also states that special priority would be given to the least developed States in the implementation of Article IV and particular account would be taken of the difficulties experienced by developing states in accepting negotiated commitments in view of their special economic situation and their development, trade and financial needs.

77 Article XXIII on dispute settlement is considered to be well balanced and equitable and provides that, if any party should consider that another party fails to carry out its obligations or commitments under the agreement, it may make written representations or proposals to the other party or parties concerned and the latter should give sympathetic consideration to the representations or proposals so made. If no satisfactory settlement could be arrived at, the GATT agreement provides for a formal dispute settlement procedure in Articles XXII and XXIII.

78 There have been six rounds of trade agreements so far: 1947 in Geneva; 1949 in Annecy, France; 1951 in Torquay, United Kingdom; 1960–62 in Geneva (the Dillon Round); 1964–7 in Geneva (the Kennedy Round); 1973–9 in Geneva (the Tokyo Round) where negations were launched at a ministerial meeting in September 1973 in Tokyo. The Tokyo Round produced the most comprehensive agreements of the round of negotiations where 99 member states participated. Negotiations of the Tokyo Round were concluded in November 1979 with agreements covering an improved legal framework for the conduct of world trade (including recognition of tariff and non-tariff treatment in favour of and among developing countries as a permanent legal feature of the world trading system); non-tariff measures (subsidies and countervailing measures); technical barriers to trade; government procurement; customs valuation; import licensing procedures; a revision of the 1967 GATT anti-dumping code; bovine meat; dairy products; tropical products; and an agreement on free trade in civil aircraft. The agreements contained special and more favourable treatment for developing countries.

79 The five freedoms of the air were created at the Chicago Conference of 1944 and comprise the following:

1 the right to fly over the territory of a state without landing;
2 the right to land in the territory of a state for non-traffic purposes;
3 the right to put down passengers, mail and cargo taken on in the territory of the state whose nationality the aircraft possesses;
4 the right to take on passengers, mail and cargo destined for the territory of the state whose nationality the aircraft possesses; and
5 the right to take on passengers, mail and cargo destined for the territory of any other contracting state and the right to put down passengers, mail and cargo coming from any such territory.

80 Annex on Air Transport Services, General Agreement on Trade in Services, MTN. TNG/W/FA Article 2.
81 Ibid., Article 3.
82 Annex on Air Transport Services, GATS, (*supra*, n.80), Article 4.
83 Ibid., Article 5.
84 These conditions are the result of an agreement reached on 11 February 1946 by the United States and the United Kingdom in Bermuda. For a clear analysis of the Bermuda Agreement, see Ramon de Murias (1989), *The Economic Regulation of International Air Transport*, McFarland, pp.52–72.
85 See, generally, R.I.R. Abeyratne (1993), 'The Air Traffic Rights Debate – A Legal Study', *Annals of Air & Space Law*, XVIII–I, 3.
86 ICAO WATC-1.10, 6/4/92 at 1. See also *Airline Business*, June 1992, 37; Ron Katz (1992), 'ICAO Montreal Colloquium, the Future of Air Transport Regulation', *IFALPA International Quarterly Review*, 10, June, 13–15.
87 *Aviation Daily*, 9 April 1992, p.56.
88 ICAO Doc. WATC-3.11, 8/4/92 at 4.
89 ICAO Doc. WATC-3.13, 8/4/92 at 4.
90 ICAO Doc. WATC-3.15, 8/4/92 at 5.
91 See Daniel M. Kasper (1988), *Deregulation and Globalization, Liberalizing International Trade in Air Services*, Ball.
92 ICAO Doc. WATC-3.17, 8/4/92 at 5.
93 Geoffrey Lipman (1990), 'Is GATT just another Four Letter Word?', *Aerospace World*, IV, September, 98. See also Daniel M. Kasper (1989), 'The GATT approach – Applying the GATT to Air Services – Will it Work?', *ITA Magazine*, November/December, 9–12.
94 Kathryn B. Creedy (1990), 'Should Air Transport be in or out of GATT?', *Interavia*, 9, 717.
95 Ibid.
96 Kasper (*supra*, n.91), p.96.
97 Ibid., Preface.
98 See John C. McCarrol (1963), 'The Bermuda Capacity Clauses in the Jet Age', *Journal of Air Law and Commerce (JALC)*, 29(2), Spring, 119, where the author says: 'fair and equal opportunity… to operate should mean … equality of practical capability to operate'. See also P. Van Der Tuuk Adriani (1955), 'The Bermuda Capacity Clauses', *JALC*, 22(406), Autumn, 413.
99 Dr. H.A. Wassenbergh lists seven objectives of a state's policy in respect of modern civil aviation:

a) to contribute to the functioning of the international community of States as a total legal order by upholding and further developing the rule of international law;
b) to protect the integrity and identity of the national society;

c) to promote the nation's participation in man's activities in the air and space;
d) to create the best possible conditions and opportunities for use by the public of aviation and space activities;
e) to increase the benefits to be derived from the use of the air and outer space for its nationals;
f) to promote the further development of technology and the knowledge of man;
g) to cooperate with other States on the basis of equal rights in order to bridge conflicting national interests and achieve the aims mentioned above.
H.A. Wassenbergh (1978), 'Reality and Value of Air and Space Law', *Annals Air and Space Law*, III, 352.

100 Chicago Convention (*supra*, n.67, Article 44(*e*).
101 Ibid., Article 44(*f*).
102 A31-WP/224, P/57, 2/10/95 at 36.1:17.
103 For a detailed discussion of the ITO, see Robert R. Wilson (1947), 'Proposed ITO Charter', *American Journal of International Law*, 41(4), October, 881 and 882.
104 U.N. Economic and Social Council, Official Records, 134th Session, 546th meeting (5/SR.546 11 September 1951 . See also Report of the ad hoc Committee on Restrictive Business Practices, E/2380, 30 March 1953.
105 *Focus Newsletter*, Geneva: WTO, January/February 1995, p.2.
106 See speech of Peter D. Sutherland, Director General of WTO, World Trade Organization Press Release PRESS/1, 27 January 1995 (95-0156), p.1.
107 Ibid., at p.5.
108 Ibid., Article III.
109 Ibid.
110 See H. Matsushita (1991), 'The Structural Impediments Initiative: an Example of Bilateral Trade Negotiation', *Michigan Journal of International Law*, 12(2), Winter, 436–49.
111 *United States* v. *Aluminium Company of America*, 148 F. 2d 416 (2d Cir. 1945).
112 See *BNA, Antitrust and Trade Regulation Report*, 67 (1685), 20 October 1994, pp.488 *et seq*.
113 *Ahlstrom Osakeyhtio* v. *Commission* (1988) ECR 5193.
114 *United States* v. *The Watchmakers of Switzerland Information Center Inc. et al.*, 133 F. Supp. 40.
115 Ibid., 41.
116 731 F. 2d 909 (1984).
117 Ibid., 910.
118 *Supra* (n.111).
119 *Supra* (n.116).
120 *In re Uranium Antitrust Litigation, Westinghouse Electric Corporation* v. *Rio Algom Limited et al.*, 473 F. Supp. 393 (1979).
121 A tying arrangement is the sale of one item (the tying product) only on condition that the buyer would take the second item (the tied product) from the same source. Such arrangements are per se unreasonable and violative of antitrust laws if the tie-in involves two distinct products, and the party has sufficient economic power in the tying market to impose significant restraints in the tied product market.
122 See, generally, Eleanor Fox (1998), 'Antitrust, Trade and the 21st Century – Rounding the Circle, *Record of the Association of the Bar of the City of New York*, pp.535–88.
123 E.U. Petersmann (1994), 'Proposals for Negotiating International Competition Rules in the GATT–WTO World Trade and Legal System', *Aussenwirtschaft*, 49, Heft II/III: Ruegger S. 231–77.

21 The Asian Region

Introduction

The Asian financial crisis of the late 1990s also affected the airline industry in Asia. While bills for fuel, overflight fees and aircraft purchase were mounting, Asian airlines reacted differently to the crisis. Garuda of Indonesia became technically bankrupt, Merpati and Sempati of the same country shut down,[1] but Singapore Airlines did well to record a healthy increase in post-tax profit for the year ending 31 March 1998. However, the latter's business success during the crisis – which was largely due to a healthy balance sheet acquired just before the crisis befell Asia – is by no means an indicator of the effect of the crisis on airlines in Asia. Overall, forecasts of growth in passenger traffic to and from Asia fell drastically and all airlines flying to and from the region experienced reduced load factors, especially on routes to and from Seoul, Hong Kong, Bangkok, Kuala Lumpur and Jakarta.

Asian aviation is unique in many ways. Firstly, there is no regional organization looking after the interests of aviation in Asia as a whole. Secondly, international mega-carriers and much smaller international airlines coexist harmoniously without devouring each other. Thirdly, the Asia/Pacific Region has the largest share of the world economy,[2] experiencing the highest rate of growth among the regions in the aviation industry. Many Asian airlines reached strategic alliances in 1997, the most noteworthy of them being Japan Airlines with Air France, Singapore Airlines with Air New Zealand and Ansett Australia and Air India with Air France. Separately an 'Olympic Alliance' was formed, involving Air New Zealand, United Airlines, Thai Airways, Malaysia Airlines, South African Airways and Lufthansa, to serve as official airlines for the Sydney 2000 Olympic Games in Australia.[3]

The key to successful aviation business in Asia has always been a three-cornered concept: low costs, quality service, and the increasingly competitive business environment in the continent. Many business enterprises in Europe and North America have been looking towards establishing bases in Asia, which offers them growth and increased opportunities.[4] Asian economies are generally strong, and the region relatively peaceful since the end of the Vietnam War in the 1970s. The busiest international route in the world is Hong Kong – Taipei and 50 per cent of all B747-400S delivered in the mid 1990s were to Asian carriers.

Despite all the fancy figures, aviation's bottom line is that it is a business, and profit making is the main objective. As an industry, aviation has an enormous appetite for investment, which should be cautiously balanced with the multifarious problems and challenges faced by the industry. Airport congestion, intense competition among carriers, airspace congestion and the need for injection of resources for advanced navigational equipment are common issues for the aviation industry in any region of the world. Asia is no exception. Another compelling issue is market access and the question whether multilateralism will prevail in Asia or whether the region will proceed cautiously, as it does with managed liberalization.

Leaving the Asia/Pacific Region and proceeding west towards the Middle East, one finds that, despite the affluence, Middle East carriers are also just coping with the emerging challenges of modern aviation. The International Monetary Fund (IMF) reports an overall stunted year in 1999–2000 for the Middle East in terms of growth and passenger carriage, which in 1998 fell in the region for the first time since 1991.[5] More significantly, capacity growth has overtaken demand in the Middle East and, according to the Arab Air Carriers Organization (AACO), Arab airlines in 1998 suffered a serious decline in passenger load factors, descending to six points lower than the average set by the International Air Transport Association (IATA).[6]

Despite the downturn, Arab carriers have managed to reduce their unit costs by 10 per cent over the past few years and costs are continuing to drop. Airlines such as the fledgling dynamo Qatar Airways are building their fleets and others, such as Royal Air Maroc and Saudia, are renewing their wide-body fleets and enlarging them. In related air transport fields, nine airline members of AACO are making savings of $200 million through a joint computer reservations system called 'Arabi' through the Galileo network. Other airlines are joining forces in the West Asian Region in fuel-saving agreements.

Although a single Arab market still remains a distant possibility, Arab carriers are becoming more open to alliances with carriers of other regions: for example, Royal Air Maroc has bonded together with Air France, Iberia and TWA on a code-sharing basis and Qatar Airways has an arrangement with Lufthansa. This trend shows a significant move on the part of the Arab carriers to link their commercial interests with European carriers in order to keep the East–West link alive and optimize market access and the sharing of revenues with European carriers.

Political Considerations

Any political analysis of Asian aviation will inevitably commence with the claim that the regime of bilateralism, which has existed through the 55 years of regulated commercial aviation in the world, is preferred by developing nations since it allows their airlines to overcome their inherent vulnerabilities which have emerged from the economic and political underdevelopment of these states.[7] Baldev Raj Nayar adds that, although the developing nations are comfortable with this status quo, they owe nothing to the process which introduced bilateralism, which was the result of the stalemate between the developed nations in their endeavour to protect their own national interests.[8] Although Nayar's claim can be accepted as valid, it has been questioned whether it would be correct to attribute consistency between the nationalistic interests of the developed world and interests of the airlines of the developed nations.[9] In taking these factual analyses further, it would be relevant at the present time to inquire whether the hypothesis that Asian airlines are still comfortable with the conservative protectionism of controlled market access is valid. A fortiori, the most critical question to be addressed now relates to what Asian airlines should be doing in the future to compete in the global market.

Arguably, the most sensitive issue faced by Asian carriers is the prospect of total liberalization or entering 'open skies' with their counterparts of the developed world. A significant development of the open skies concept is the multilateral agreement looming ahead between the United States and the European Union (with Canada, Mexico and/or Latin America included). Many believe that this is just a precursor to a worldwide open skies regime, involving Asia as well.[10] However, Barbara Beyer, President of Avmark, has cautioned that Asian carriers could be seriously affected if they were to be subjected to open skies agreements in their operations between Asia and the United States.[11] Beyer focused particularly on the adverse impact of Asia–United States open skies agreements on countries with large domestic populations spread out over a vast geographic area, such as Thailand, Indonesia, the Philippines, Malaysia and China. The rationale behind this philosophy is that Asian carriers, however large by their standards, are not comparable in size to US carriers and therefore would not be able to gain access to US domestic markets as much as their US counterparts would be able to exploit domestic Asian markets. Conversely, however, smaller countries such as Singapore and Brunei, with no domestic markets, would stand to gain from a large US domestic market without having to offer reciprocity in their territories to the US carriers.

A manifestation of the recommended cautious Asian approach to the open skies concept is seen in the ongoing relationship between Japan and the United States in their bilateral air services negotiations. Japan Airlines, the largest Asian carrier, has a fleet of 128 aircraft, almost the same as TWA and way below Northwest, which has a fleet of 400 aircraft. Japan has claimed that an absolutely liberalized market access arrangement between the two countries for their airlines would result inevitably in overall dominance by alliances formed by US carriers to operate air services into Japan.[12]

Be that as it may, the stage is now set for regional open skies arrangements, from European market liberalization[13] to Central American Open Skies,[14] with the United States encouraging vigorously those who are willing to enter into open skies arrangements from other parts of the globe. Against this backdrop, the entire juggling act of opening the skies in Asia seemingly hinges on the delicate balance between the prospect of unlimited market access, on the one hand, and protectionism, on the other. The primaeval fear of losing in open competition and being annihilated in the process has naturally and inevitably pervaded the weaker segments of commercial aviation, who feel they do not have the tools to withstand the colossus of airline alliances and mega-carrier strategy.

A compromise between the two extremes has emerged through the work of the Air Transport Regulation Panel of ICAO, which, at its Ninth Meeting (Montreal, 10–14 February 1997), reported to the ICAO Council that it would be impracticable for states to follow a code of conduct which would define actions of unfair competition in all situations. The panel was of the view that, as a safeguard mechanism, states should agree on basic principles that would constitute unfair competition when two or more states agree to move from a rigid bilateral scheme of market access to a more liberalized regime. These principles involve practices related to airlines charging excessive, fares and rates and adding excess capacity or frequency of service on routes, such practices being sustained and dominant and resulting in an adverse economic impact on the carrier who is affected by the practices.

Justification for maintaining a bilateral system of negotiation is firmly rooted in the principles of the Chicago Convention that every state has complete and exclusive sovereignty over the air space above its territory[15] and that international air transport services may be established on equality of opportunity.[16] It is logical therefore to anticipate that any proponent of bilateralism would argue that a multilateral system would erode the requirement of equality of opportunity. Susumu Yamaji, Chairman, Japan Airlines, was one of the speakers at the ICAO Worldwide Colloquium on Air Transport held in 1992 who supported this school of thought when he said:

> My conversation is supporting evidence that American mega-carriers have established an advantageous position over foreign carriers in the international market by offering frequent flier and hub-and-spoke systems. Those programs become doubly effective through integration with their huge domestic market, which provides mega-carriers with 70 to 80% of their revenue. On the other hand, although foreign carriers can get some access to the US domestic market through code-sharing arrangements or marketing cooperation with smaller domestic carriers, it is quite impossible to secure the same competitive level as the mega-carriers. In some sense, American passengers are restricted in their choice of airlines by frequent flyer and hub-and-spoke systems. It is ironic that, while allegedly seeking freer and more open competition, passengers find themselves fettered with limited choice in reality.[17]
>
> …
>
> Most Asian countries, including Japan, are not in a position to accept the sort of 'law of the jungle' competition in which, I am sure, the strong mega-carriers would be the only survivors in control of the market and the consumer. I cannot think of any country which will allow the loss of their airline to excessive freedom of competition, for in allowing so, they would be losing their own independent access to third and fourth freedom transport. If liberalization abandons the adjustment of differences in competitive ability among carriers, it will only result in the demise of smaller carriers.[18]

Aruna Mascarenhas of Air India, while emphasizing that the economic philosophy of equality of opportunity was a logical counterpart to the political notion of sovereignty, pointed out that postwar aircraft technology, marketing and distribution techniques had flourished under the bilateral system, proving its flexibility. She critically analysed the multilateral system for its counterproductive nature:

> Multilateralism has been held to be a panacea for these problems. In concept, a global multilateral framework for the exchange of traffic rights (and I am not referring here to the recent attempt to include civil aviation in the General Agreement on Trade in Services) will provide all signatories immediate and unrestricted access to the international markets covered by the agreement with no restrictions (other than airline licensing standards) on designation of airlines, airline ownership, capacity or fares … Ironically, in practice, it could work exactly in reverse. The last decade has witnessed the emergence of

> mega-carriers who have cornered a large part of the world's fleet, and have built formidable barriers to entry in the form of hubs, computerized reservations systems and brand loyalty programs. Bilateral agreements alone could prevent a total take-over of the industry by a dozen or so mega-airlines.[19]

Mascarenhas observed that the only common denominator in the issue of air traffic rights amongst all nations of the world is what she calls the 'national interest'. She further concluded:

> This national interest has led all countries – however small – to have their own airlines, be it to promote trade and tourism, provide national security or simply show the flag. National interest has now led some of the larger countries, whose airlines are positioned to dominate the industry, to push for liberalization, and to 'go beyond' the bilateral system.
>
> The point is that national sovereignty and national pride are as relevant today as they were in 1944. And governments need airlines, almost as much as airlines need governments. As the Gulf crisis has shown, even the strongest airlines cry for help from their governments when the going gets rough. And even when they are protected (such as the case of the US megas, by statute, from foreign take-over) the recent relaxations in ownership rules are partly motivated by the need to protect them from financial distress.[20]

The conclusion that Mascarenhas arrived at at the Colloquium was similar to that of Yamaji: that multilateralism would only serve the economic interests of countries that have strong, competitive and powerful international airlines. Their view is summarized in the statement of Mascarenhas:

> If one were to pick horses for courses, the multilateral is an obvious choice for the one or two countries in the world who have strong airlines but limited home markets and who have very little left to offer in return for additional rights under a bilateral exchange. Not surprisingly, Singapore, which typifies this category, is amongst the strongest supporters of a global multilateral.
>
> Conversely, bilateralism would appeal to the vast majority of countries like India, with substantial markets but whose airlines are at a disadvantage in terms of size and staying power in any global free-for-all.[21]

Challenges and Responses

Whatever the political stage in Asia and the rest of the world, commercial exigency dictates that the foremost challenge faced by Asian aviation is competition among carriers. The primary responses to this challenge lie in information technology and competitive strategy. With the information revolution sweeping the world today, business competition in Asia in general and airline competition in particular should focus mainly on achieving dramatic reductions in the cost of obtaining, processing and transmitting information in order to maximize radically on profit bases.

Most Asian carriers have already realized that information technology is more than just computers. Information relates not only to stored databases but to management of information through convergent and integrated technologies ensuring optimal information usage. With the current growth rate being experienced by Asian carriers, proper management of information would accomplish for them (a) competitive edge and ways to outperform rival competition, (b) opening out of new businesses within parent companies, and (c) radical change in industry structure consistent with emergent challenges posed by the industry.

The airline product has both a physical and an information dimension. The information dimension or component broadly represents a systematic spectrum of knowledge to be acquired by the purchaser of the product and made maximum use of. For example, convenient, convincing and accessible information on the particular product concerned would be important to the airline passenger or consignor.

It is an incontrovertible fact that the airline industry's structure in Asia is composed of five competitive forces which may eventually decide on profitability: the power of the purchaser of the product; the power of the provider (airline) of the product; threats caused by new entrants; threats caused by other modes of transport; and the rivalry among existing competitors. Information technology can radically affect all these factors. For instance, information technology could create automated tickets and airway bills, produce pop-up computer reservations information on the Internet, and create direct telecommunication links between airline and passenger. In addition, airlines could develop differentiated travel services for corporate customers through the use of information technology, which could arrange travel and monitor expenses incurred by a corporate entity on its travel budget. This could be accomplished by any competitive airline by searching for the lowest air fares and arranging for intermodal travel when the passenger gets off the aircraft at his destination.

Information technology also has the capability of enhancing an airline's scope regionally and globally by increasing its ability to conduct business in its international offices in coordination with the head office. Above all, the use of information technology can give rise to derivative and generic business enterprises such as computer reservation systems and frequent flyer clubs. Airlines which use information technology prudently could also manage it in such a manner that excess capacity could be 'sold' to other similar businesses.

The second tool which Asian airlines could use effectively is competitive strategy, which is essentially the genus of which strategic alliances between airlines is a species. Competitive strategy means being different. Harvard Business School Professor Michael Porter states that competition strategy is composed of calculated business acts which deliberately choose a different set of activities to deliver a unique mix of value.[22] Present-day commercial strategies of airlines relating to their in-flight service – such as installing a video system in every seat, or offering gambling activities in aircraft – are as relevant as analogies in this regard as the case of IKEA, the global furniture retailer based in Sweden, which focuses on young furniture buyers who look for style at low cost. Other good examples are Southwest Airlines in the United States, which offers short-haul, low-cost, point-to-point services between mid-size cities and secondary airports in large cities; Singapore Airlines, which perpetuated the in-flight myth of the 'Singapore Girl' and Emirates, which became an aggressive competitor in Asia with its superior quality in-flight service.

Arguably, the strongest commercial tool now used in the airline industry, and one which is used with great effect in the developing world, is the strategic alliance between airlines. The rationale behind the strategic alliance is to increase revenue and decrease or reduce costs in order to maximize profits. Lufthansa has reported that it gained over $250 million from its alliance in 1998, a figure obtained mainly from revenue earned. More importantly, it is expected that this figure will be further improved by an additional amount of $44 million in cost savings.[23]

From an Asian and European route perspective, QANTAS and British Airways are already showing significant profit on capacity coordination on the Kangaroo route (between Australia and the United Kingdom) and on routes between Europe and Australia. So is Thai Airways International, in its participation in the 'Star Alliance'. These airlines have shown that the answer to success in strategic arrangements between airlines does not lie in flooding an existing market with capacity. Rather, airlines who operate services in conjunction have to assess cautiously the market potential and the market share enjoyed by each prior to an alliance being arranged. This is because the fundamental structure of a strategic alliance for market share lies in one major airline tapping into additional traffic flows of a 'home' market fed by a carrier who in turn gains access to a network of new destinations through its alliance with the major operator.

Airlines could do well (particularly those airlines who, in the 1980s and early 1990s, relied heavily on determining market share on a given route through historical statistics in order to protect such share) to abandon overt reliance on statistics which 'define' and demarcate market share. There is no magic number in market shares; rather, within the concept of market share lies a real need to maximize profitability. Another compelling need in Asian aviation is the ability to attract potential customers and to retain existing ones. Perhaps the most important factor is the relevance of tapping dormant markets rather than redistributing existing traffic. One stratagem that airlines, particularly in regions of Asia which have untapped business and tourism potential, could adopt is to create excess demand in areas where tight oligopolies may exist and to attempt to cater to such demand by supplying capacity.

Conclusion

There are several strategic measures that Asian airlines should adopt for the future. Firstly, they must continue to embrace globalization on the foundation of a unique competitive position. The first step towards effectively continuing to participate in a global market is to gain a competitive advantage over other carriers wherever possible. Airlines should globalize also in areas (such as computer reservation systems) where they have the most telling advantages.

Secondly, airlines of Asia must concentrate on having a consistent policy in penetrating international markets. In order to achieve this objective, airlines must make a comprehensive assessment of market shares that can be tapped in foreign markets, with or without the assistance of other carriers involved in these markets. In order to establish business effectively in foreign markets, an airline would need to establish a clear home base from which to run its business. The home base should be located in the country which has the most favourable demand for the business. However, diverse activities of an airline should essentially be dispersed in appropriate markets in order to optimize fully on generic or derivation products.

Another gem of wisdom that can be effectively used by Asian airlines lies in the fact that alliances need not all be strategic and exclusively calculated to yield profits. There could be alliances which, where formed, merely ensure the global presence of an airline which can be developed into a viable business prospect at a later stage when market demands more capacity.

The basic challenge faced by Asian airlines, particularly those from developing countries, is to shift from the mere competitive advantage they may have in certain areas to an overall competitive advantage. To achieve this, airlines must adopt distinctive strategies. As a starting point, they must form alliances to the extent possible on a regional basis and build regional networks as far as possible. These regional networks could develop distinctive product varieties for which the airlines could become known. With the passing of time, these airlines would be able to build innovative capacity sufficient to enter more and more markets. It is then that most Asian airlines would gain the competitive advantage they are looking for.

Notes

1 See 'Pall Over Asia', *Air Transport World*, 9, 1998, p.30.
2 *Annual Reports of the Council*, Montreal: ICAO, 1998, p.1.
3 'The World of Civil Aviation', Montreal: ICAO, 1997–2000 (Circular 273-AT/113), p.17.
4 See 'A Bright Future for Aviation', *Aerospace*, June 1994, 8.
5 Tom Gill (1999), 'Opening Arab Skies', *Airline Business*, June, p.47.
6 Ibid.
7 See Stephen D. Krasner (1985), *Structured Conflict: The Third World Against Global Liberalism*, Berkeley, California: University of California Press, pp.3–97.
8 Baldev Raj Nayar (1994), *The State and International Aviation in India*, New Delhi: Manohar, pp.1–2.
9 John E. Richards (1999), 'Toward a Positive Theory of International Institutions: Regulating International Aviation Markets', *International Organization*, 53(1), Winter, pp. 7–8.
10 'U.S. Anticipate Open-Skies Treaties between Asian Economies', *Aviation Daily*, 16 September 1997, p.475.
11 'Asia Warned over Open Skies Pact with U.S.', *Air Letter*, no. 13, 838, Tuesday, 30 September 1997, p.2.
12 'Japan says U.S. holds up Aviation Deal', *Air Letter*, no. 13, 800, Wednesday, 6 August 1997, p.1.
13 See 'European Market Liberalization Moves to Centre Stage', *Aviation Daily*, 8 January 1997, p.4.
14 'Honduras, El Salvador, Guatemala, Join Panama in Open Skies', *Aviation Daily*, 30 April, 1997, p.185.
15 Convention on International Civil Aviation, signed at Chicago in 7 December 1944, ICAO Doc. 7300/7, 1997, Article 1.
16 Ibid., Preamble.
17 ICAO WATC-1.13, 6/4/92 at 4.
18 Ibid.
19 ICAO WATC-1.17, 6/4/92, at 2.
20 Ibid., at 5.
21 Ibid., at 3.
22 Michael E. Porter (1998), *On Competition*, Harvard Business Review Book Series, Cambridge, Mass.: Harvard University Press, p.45.
23 See Chris Tarry (1999), 'Playing for Profit', *Airline Business*, June, p.90.

22 The African Region

Introduction

Regulatory responsibility for civil aviation in Africa generally falls under the broad umbrella of the International Civil Aviation Organization, which is charged with global regulatory responsibility in the field of civil aviation. At regional level, and through cooperation with ICAO, the African Civil Aviation Commission (AFCAC) – the regional specialized agency of the Organization of African Unity (OAU)[1] which is charged with the responsibility for development of civil aviation in Africa – takes responsibility for assisting member African states in their endeavour towards developing civil aviation in their territories. At its Fifteenth Plenary Session held in Abuja in April 1998, AFCAC sought to face reality squarely in the eye, by addressing the key issues which may affect the African states in the next millennium in attaining success as a competitive force in the world of civil aviation.

At the meeting, AFCAC addressed *in limine* the cornerstone of African civil aviation – the Yamoussoukro Declaration – which is the fundamental postulate containing the strategies considered by the Africans as inherent in their aviation philosophy. As its commitment towards the development of African civil aviation, AFCAC resolved to play a more prominent role in the implementation of the Declaration, together with such other organizations as the African Airline Association (AFRAA).

This chapter will analyse the microcosm of the issues which AFCAC, AFRAA and other concerned African civil aviation bodies need to address in order to attain their objectives and goals.

The History of Civil Aviation in Africa

One of the watershed events of African civil aviation history occurred in 1961 when 10 African nations[2] signed the Treaty on Air

Transport in Africa.[3] Popularly known as the Yaounde Treaty, it has its roots in Articles 77 and 79 of the Chicago Convention of 1944,[4] which provides for the setting up by two or more states of joint or international operating organizations and for the participation of the states in these organizations. Based on these principles, the Yaounde Treaty established perhaps the oldest surviving jointly owned airline – Air Afrique – to operate on behalf of its contracting states international services between their territories and from their territories to non-contracting states' territories,[5] and also domestic air services within the territories of the contracting states.[6] These services are now operated by the airline consequent to the negotiations between contracting states carried out through a body named the Comité Multinational de Négociation des Etats Signataires du Traité de Yaounde (CMN). At the present time, contracting states to the Yaounde Treaty include states of Western and Central African sub-regions.

The second major event in African civil aviation history occurred in 1988, when African civil aviation ministers gathered in Yamoussoukro in the Republic of the Ivory Coast on 6 and 7 October and signed the Yamoussoukro Declaration on a New African Air Transport Policy.[7] This declaration was the result of a collective consensus in Africa that African nations must, inter alia, prepare for the effects of deregulation in the United States on other countries and the potential adverse effects on African airlines of the air transport liberalization policies of Western Europe, especially the application by the EEC of the Treaty of Rome to air transport services and the creation of a single internal European market by 1993. The Declaration also responds to the fact that many aircraft owned by African airlines are obsolete and thus in need of replacement at great cost, particularly with regard to the need for African airlines to comply with Chapters 2 and 3 of Annex 16 to the Chicago Convention concerning aircraft noise. Another compelling issue addressed at Yamoussoukro and incorporated into the Declaration concerned the liberal exchange of air traffic rights by African states and the need for African airlines to market their product competitively through an unbiased computer reservation system.

The Yamoussoukro Declaration committed African states, both individually and collectively, to achieve the total integration of their airlines under the above policies within a period of eight years. The eight years were divided into three phases of two years, three years and three years, respectively. A review of the Declaration, conducted by African experts at a meeting held in Mauritius in September 1994, resulted in a series of solutions for achieving the implementation of the Yamoussoukro Declaration, recommended by the experts.[8] The overall recommendation of the experts was to incorporate the Declaration as an integral part of national air transport policy in each

African state.[9] The incorporation was to be provisionally effective immediately after the Mauritius meeting.

Later in April 1997, the Banjul Accord for an Accelerated Implementation of the Yamoussoukro Declaration, adopted by Ghana, Sierra Leone and the Gambia, Cape Verde, Guinea Bissau and Nigeria, recognized the region representing these states as a single geographical commercial air transport operations zone for the purpose of implementing the Yamoussoukro Declaration through a joint secretariat established for the purposes of aeronautical cooperation within these states, offering specialized services in air traffic services, safety oversight, market access, engineering and maintenance, communications, aeronautical information services and meteorology.

Since the Yamoussoukro Declaration in 1988, some progress has been made in the aeropolitical scene in Africa. For example, there is increasing cooperation among airlines of the Southern African Development Community (SADC) countries. These airlines and their countries concerned have already discussed possibilities of operating air transport services by SADC: country airlines under a common logo. At the time of writing, a protocol was being considered for the establishing of a Southern Africa Regional Air Transport Authority (SARATA) which is a new entity that would formulate and coordinate air transport policies within the SADC region and cope with emergent changes in the air transport industry in the region.

Another recent initiative has been the Air CEDEAO project which would set up a joint airline to serve the western sub-region of Africa. The Northern African states have their own contemporary contribution to the evolving air transport scene in Africa in the form of Air Maghreb, a consortium for consolidating and operating air transport services in Northern Africa more efficiently. Separately, in the western sub-region, three states have initiated the establishment of Air Mano, a multinational airline. States in the African continent have made significant strides in the field of computer reservation systems (CRSs) by joining together to develop GETS (the Gabriel Extended Travel Service), a CRS launched by the Société Internationale de Télécommunications Aéronautiques (SITA). Another great stride in African civil aviation has been made towards facilitating the implementation of the Yamoussoukro Declaration with the opening out of South Africa to intra-African aviation. The developed aviation infrastructure of South Africa is now made available to African states, particularly in areas such as leasing of aircraft, engineering and maintenance services and the training of personnel.

In the area of air navigation services and the provision of air navigation facilities to aircraft, ASECNA (Agence pour la Sécurité de la Navigation Aérienne en Afrique et Madagascar) which is the agency for the safety of air navigation in Africa and Madagascar,[10] has created

ASECNA services, a subsidiary agency which explores and facilitates numerous concomitant activities related to air transport and air navigation in Africa. Some of the significant areas in which ASECNA services are involved are fleet financing and management under leasing and sale agreements.[11] This activity could well give rise to the formation of an African aircraft leasing company, in conformity with the objectives stipulated in the Yamoussoukro Declaration.

The Air Tariff Coordination Forum of Africa (ATCOF) – a new forum – has been charged with assisting the air transport industry of Africa in coping with and adapting to the vicissitudes and vacillations of international air tariff policy on fares and rates. This is yet another area where the African air transport and civil aviation scene is showing signs of conforming to the objectives of the Yamoussoukro Declaration.

In spite of the many strides made by the African nations, there are still challenges ahead with regard to a proper implementation of the Yamoussoukro Declaration in full. These challenges are mostly in the economic field, and are seemingly being addressed. The involvement of non-African investors in civil aviation in Africa, both from the public and the private sectors, is an example of the positive approach so far adopted in this regard. In the legal field, considerable work has been accomplished towards bringing about the implementation of the Yamoussoukro Declaration, particularly after the Mauritius meeting of 1994. This chapter will examine some of the more critical legal issues that should be addressed by African states in seeking the full implementation of the provisions of the Yamoussoukro Declaration, as they approach the new millennium.

Legal and Economic Issues

Simply stated, the Yamoussoukro Declaration is anchored upon the fundamental postulate of cooperation in air transport brought about by the integration of African airlines. Toward this end, the first phase of implementation of the Declaration – which is given a life of two years – carries the objective inter alia of carrying out studies and research on air transport issues in order to integrate African airlines harmoniously with the rest of the world air transport industry to ensure fair competition at market access. The second phase, which is given three years to implement the objectives of the Declaration, is dedicated to commercial aspects of air transport such as the integration of CRS, joint purchase of spare parts, maintenance and overhauling of equipment, training of personnel and so on. The third phase, which is also allotted a span of three years, concerns the actual implementation of the overall integration of African airlines into a consortium of competitive commercial entities that would bring about sustained progress in air transport in Africa that would be capable of withstanding rapidly evolving world trends in aviation.

The Yamoussoukro Declaration brings to bear the inexorable fact that economic and legal issues in African civil aviation are inextricably linked together, and cannot be addressed in isolation. The primary consideration and concern facing civil aviation in Africa is incontrovertibly the economic factor. However, the legal infrastructure which is needed to place economic issues in their right order follows inevitably, making it essential that the two areas of interest are addressed together.

Although some of the objectives of the Yamoussoukro Declaration have already been achieved at least partially (such as by the participation by most African airlines in the GETS CRS system), the most critical areas involving overall airline management and the use of modern commercial tools, such as the merger of airlines and effective fleet financing, have yet to be addressed in a comprehensive way. Although not specifically mentioned in the Declaration, safety oversight is a factor of critical interest to African civil aviation, and has to be addressed realistically, along with other issues raised by the Yamoussoukro Declaration.

The Need for New Aircraft Fleets in Africa

There are two types of mega-trends affecting the airline industry today: country mergers and airline mergers. Both these trends affect the airline industry profoundly. Of these, the unification of Europe is the largest single influence on international airlines. From 1 January 1993, 12 European countries commenced sharing their air traffic rights and strengthening their airlines' marketing potential. There is also a possibility that Australia and New Zealand will form a more crystallized and intensified joint aviation market. At intraregional level, the most ominous development in recent years was the proposed British Airways–KLM merger. If this merger materialized, the two megacarriers, who would ordinarily benefit from the economic unification of their two countries in the European Community, would have further consolidated their positions in the aviation world by joining forces. This could have only meant more aggressive competition by them using the usual cost-cutting synergy of joint purchasing of equipment, elimination of management duplication and the sharing of resources. Each would also have had mutually eliminated a strong competitor in the other and shared access to new markets more effectively. The proposed British Airways–KLM merger was, however, not the only one that was significant on a regional basis. SAS,

Sabena, Austrian Airlines and Swissair were also involved in grouping together in Europe to form a strategic alliance called the 'European Quality Alliance'. The threat posed even at interregional level with current commercial arrangements between British Airways and American Airlines, and KLM and NorthWest, are real issues that affect the commercial viability of African airlines adversely.

Within the two mega-trends are smaller trends that individual airlines have to follow just to remain competitive: privatization, the use of information technology, removing infrastructure constraints and governmental restraints and most importantly, changing travel patterns. These trends have given rise to the new phenomenon in the global aviation scene that survival (if not success) of airlines is now dependent not on pricing but on service. This new phenomenon calls for the airline product to be similar to one from the entertainment industry, bearing in mind that a passenger spends 70 per cent of his total travel time in the aircraft on long-distance flights. To counter strong alliances between countries and airlines, the smaller carriers (as well as the big ones) are now going in more for glamour and in flight-luxury to score on the 70 per cent in flight time. Personal video screens for every seat, satellite assisted telephone facilities and teleconference services are some of the luxuries offered. Indeed, as David Shoenfeld, International Marketing Vice President of Federal Express said, 'If you view your services as flying between terminals, you miss the point.'

The view that 'marketing is determined from the view of the customer' is becoming more valuable now than ever before. To survive, airlines have to build 'brand recognition'. There are 12 important factors influencing passenger choice: flight punctuality, excellence of in-flight service, superiority of aircraft, comfortable seats, clean cabins, seats and washrooms, good food and beverages, superior first class, superior business class, efficient reservations systems, pricing, good check-in service and attractive frequent flyer programmes. At least seven of these factors are entirely dependent on the quality of the aircraft. Indeed, the foremost important factor – punctuality – cannot be achieved with aged aircraft. The matter becomes more crucial to a relatively small airline, running a small fleet of aircraft, where, if one aircraft is grounded for reasons of repair or maintenance, the entire flight schedule of the airline will be in disarray, leading to delays down the line. Connecting services will be disrupted and passengers stranded. It is easy to envisage the effect this catastrophe would have on the airline's good name. No amount of superior in-flight service would atone for a six-hour delay where a connecting passenger has to sit inside an unknown airport terminal. It is therefore necessary for any airline to seriously consider removing one of its most burdensome infrastructural constraints – its ageing aircraft.

Another compelling reason for airlines to modernize their fleets is that ageing aircraft do not conform to noise restrictions imposed by many countries and thus face being barred from certain airports. Noise has become a crucial environment issue in the world aviation community. At the 27th Session of the Assembly of the International Civil Aviation Organization (ICAO) held in Montreal in 1989, when the matter of possible noise restrictions on subsonic jet aircraft was taken up, the main concern of the Assembly was to achieve a balance between the desire to protect the environment around airports against unnecessary noise and the desire to avoid excessive costs associated with accelerated replacement of noisier aircraft, particularly where these aircraft were registered in countries which did not themselves intend to introduce noise-related operating instructions. In one of their past sessional discussions, Airports Council International (ACI) noted that aircraft noise represents a major constraint upon the future viability and capacity of the aviation system. Unless concerted international action was taken, there would be a proliferation of various local legislation banning noisy aircraft from their airports, a measure that would have a devastating effect on air commerce. The International Air Transport Association (IATA) representing the airlines at the Session noted that the airline industry recognized the need in many states to address political and other concerns relating to the environment and the fact that the noise climate in areas adjacent to airports is linked to the ability of airports to provide expanded travel facilities to meet the growing demand for air travel. The ICAO Assembly ultimately decided that further time was necessary for consultation and analysis with a view to reaching consensus, and deferred the issue to the 28th (Extraordinary) Session of the Assembly which was held in Montreal in October 1990.

At its 28th (Extraordinary) Session, the ICAO Assembly, by its Resolution A28-3, urged states not to commence phasing out noisy aircraft until 1 April 1995, and to spread out the phasing in period over seven years, from 1 April 1995, so that airlines would have time to renew their aircraft fleets or 'hush-kit' them (silence the engines of aircraft) to conform to prescribed noise levels. ICAO further urged States not to restrict before the end of the phase-in period the operations of any aircraft less than 25 years of age from the date the aircraft was issued with its first certificate of airworthiness and to assist aircraft operators in their efforts to accelerate fleet modernization.

The standards of the international community on ageing aircraft are now clear. States have been given the right by the international civil aviation community to start phasing out aircraft from 1 April 1995, completing it by the year 2002. What this means is that airlines that have in their fleets ageing aircraft would have to commence modernizing their fleets soon. If they fail to modernize their fleet their ageing aircraft would not be admitted to countries which have phased them out by legislation. The need for modernizing ageing aircraft fleets has become more compelling than ever, and is amply reflected by the recommendations made by the Fourth Meeting of ICAO's Committee on Aviation Environmental Protection (CAEP) which was held from 6 to 8 April 1998. CAEP has recommended the reduction by an average of about 16 per cent levels of nitrogen oxides (NO_x) that aircraft engines are currently allowed to emit under Annex 16 to the Chicago Convention.[12] CAEP has also recommended that states implement ICAO's new Communications, Navigation, Surveillance and Air Traffic Management systems (CNS/ATM), thereby implicitly requiring aircraft to be equipped with the modern facilities on board to comply with the satellite navigation systems introduced by the CNS/ATM systems.

Another measure taken by CAEP at its Fourth Meeting which would seriously affect African airlines, needing them to consider the modernization of their fleets, was CAEP's commitment to carry out more work in the future to establish new noise standards for jet aeroplanes that would be more stringent than the present Chapter 3 standards in Annex 16.[13]

Despite a Gulf war in 1990, and the recession in the early 1990s, industry growth remained strong throughout the decade. European traffic growth is estimated at 5 per cent and growth forecasts for the Asia–Pacific region are 8.6 per cent per annum. McDonnell Douglas, a major aircraft manufacturer, in its 'Outlook for Commercial Aircraft 1988–2002', forecasts a sustained growth rate of worldwide commercial passenger traffic at 5.7 per cent per annum. Worldwide cargo capacity demand has been forecast at a 6 per cent annual rate up to the year 2002. During the next 15 years, worldwide generic demand for new passenger aircraft is forecast at 5888 units, with an estimated value of US$302 billion, and a total generic demand at 413 full cargo freighters up to the year 2002.

Apart from the compelling marketing reasons and environmental factors discussed above, a modernized fleet in an African airline would succeed in sweeping the airline to success if the acquisition of aircraft was managed prudently. For example, the new aircraft would have to be placed in the fleet just before the airline reaches peak utilization of its aircraft. New air traffic rights of the airlines would have to be negotiated beforehand and existing ones reviewed for maximum utilization. The fixed costs of the new aircraft would have to be analysed well beforehand to maximize profits. The resale value of the aircraft, when they are ultimately phased out in order that newer aircraft may be brought in, should also be given serious consideration. Engineering and maintenance facilities and costs thereof of new aircraft also have to be carefully thought out.

To capitalize on changes in their competitive environment, competent airline managers now need to know that, in the foreseeable future, there will be a few mega-carriers operating in America, Europe, Asia and the Pacific Rim and that these carriers will probably be composites of strong strategic alliances between powerful airlines and powerful regional states. They will be well equipped to offer the quality of service and punctuality that the glamour of modern air travel requires. To compete with these carriers for a fair share of the market, a smaller African airline would have to offer a comparable product. In order to offer this type of product, airline managers in Africa have to consider the global issues now facing the world of civil aviation and, above all, the ways and means to adapt to the sweeping trends of the rest of the world in aviation.

Although the standards of management in African airlines are currently of a high standard, these airlines need constantly to update their management profile to adapt to the rapidly changing global aviation scene as envisaged by the Yamoussoukro Declaration. For this purpose, airline managers have to be constantly trained in such issues as market access and benefits that could be derived through Africa's strategic position in the world, market resources available, the efficient use of commercial torts such as outsourcing[14] and franchising,[15] and the ensuring of aviation safety within Africa.

With the trend of liberalization sweeping the world, African airline managers have to be particularly mindful of the various arrangements between mega-countries which now accept 'open skies'.

Market Access

At the time of writing, the United States and the United Kingdom were discussing deregulating air transport between the countries. The talks were aimed at replacing the UK–USA bilateral air services agreement with an open-skies agreement, which would allow the market to determine prices, routes and scheduling. The United States has already signed open-skies agreements with the Netherlands and Germany, although an agreement for open skies with the United Kingdom could be on a much larger scale, considering the frequency of air services between the two countries. One of the problem areas that were being ironed out at the discussions was the reported apprehension of the UK authorities that an open-skies policy between the United Kingdom and the United States, if fully implemented, would give American carriers access to countries beyond the United Kingdom with full commercial traffic rights (that is, the right to carry passengers between the United Kingdom and third countries), whereas British carriers had no rights to fly between destinations in the United States.[16]

According to a study carried out in the United States, a liberalized open-skies agreement with the United Kingdom will provide a five-year, $108 billion boost to the US economy and create 152 000 new jobs. The study projects a five-year period of steady growth and an estimated 9.4 million new passengers a year, who would take advantage of the 86 per cent increase in air services between the two countries if an open-skies policy was implemented[17] and help introduce US–UK air services from 12 new US cities.[18] American Airlines chairman Robert Crandall sums up the view of the US carriers on an open-skies policy between the two countries: 'This study confirms what we have been saying for some time – open skies with the UK will be good for passengers, shippers and communities across the country by providing new service, more competition and lower fares in the transatlantic market.'[19]

Earlier, in June 1996, Japan rejected a proposal by the United States for an open-skies agreement on somewhat similar grounds to the British, that US carriers have unlimited rights to fly beyond Japan under the current bilateral air services agreement which was signed in 1952 by the two countries. In return, Japan Airlines, the only Japanese airline at that time, has no comparable benefit.[20] Japan has openly claimed that it does not support the US version of open skies, for two reasons: (1) Japan would not have access to the large US domestic market, and (2) open skies does not take into account inconsistencies created by capacity constraints in airports such as Narita and Kansai.[21] The United States, on the other hand, maintains that Japanese authorities seem more intent on protecting intra-Asian air service markets for Japanese carriers by blocking US carrier competitors than they are in opening the US–Japan aviation market.[22]

The US carriers have, in their favour, consistently advocated an open-skies policy throughout the world. In May 1996, Delta Airlines' Chief Executive, Ronald Allen called upon the European Union to enter into an open-skies agreement with the United States. Allen contended that open skies are useful because they remove government restrictions on every aspect of aviation except for safety and predatory market behaviour, and concluded that an open-skies policy would result in a more vibrant market-place where consumers were allowed to select among the best, most efficient and most competitive operators.[23]

The United States has also sought open skies agreements with some Asian countries. In September 1995, US authorities signed a Memorandum of Understanding with the authorities of Hong Kong which liberalized to a large extent existing arrangements for the carriage of cargo by air between the two countries.[24] Singapore Airlines has been a staunch supporter of the open-skies policy and has openly called for its implementation between Asia and the United

States. According to Singapore Airlines' Chairman, Cheong Choong Kong:

> The US and Singapore agree that liberalizing aviation is in the best interests not only of the consumers but of the economy generally through the stimulation of trade ... I hope therefore that the US will extend its open skies to cover the Asia–Pacific region, which, based on traffic forecasts is going to be the largest aviation market within 15 years.[25]

Later, in December 1996, Cheong was critical of the stance taken by the United States in response to the offer of open skies by Singapore and Malaysia. He said:

> it was 'no secret' that open skies bilaterals with Singapore and Malaysia were attainable right away... but unfortunately it was all or nothing with them [the United States]; they insisted on a critical mass of willing countries before they would proceed. Apparently, Malaysia and Singapore did not constitute such a critical mass.[26]

He also extended his comments on liberalization to Australia and New Zealand, claiming that those countries should open their markets so that tourists can fly in and out of, and, more importantly, within their territories more conveniently,[27] thus suggesting that such markets should not be protected and preserved only for the national carriers of Australia and New Zealand.

On the subject of critical mass in Asia, which in the United States is alleged to be interested in an 'all or nothing' principle, the suggestion made by the prime minister of Malaysia in October 1995, that Asia–Pacific nations should adopt a common stand in talks with the United States, is significant. The key contention of Asian countries against most developed countries in the West is that the latter's enthusiasm for open skies is tainted by their refusal to lay open their domestic markets within the open-skies package. This refusal, it is claimed, only reflects a cosmetic balance between countries which do not have extensive domestic markets and those, such as the United States, which do, when open skies are discussed on an international basis. Prime Minister Mohamad declared: 'Asia–Pacific nations must be prepared to act in concert and adopt a co-ordinated stance in negotiating with the EU and the US ... the consequence of not doing so will likely be the domination of the aviation industry by the mega-carriers from the US and Europe.'[28]

In January 1997, officials from the United States and Singapore reached an open-skies aviation deal, making Singapore the first Asian country to sign an open-skies deal with the United States.[29] The US–Singapore deal followed a preliminary meeting in October 1996 which included South Korea, Taiwan, Malaysia and Brunei. On 10 January 1997, the United States also reopened its negotiations with Japan and was expected to sign an open-skies agreement in 1997.

In the above context, it cannot be claimed incontrovertibly that an open-skies policy, as advocated by the various proponents, is not totally lacking in overprotectiveness. Most nations still give an unusually high priority to the marketing policies of their airlines, which are naturally geared to world protectionism and exploitation. An ideal open-skies policy should be such as the one practised by Dubai, where, irrespective of reciprocity, unlimited access to air traffic rights is given to anyone who wishes to operate air services. Maurice Flanagan, Group Managing Director of Emirates (the airline of Dubai) writes:

> Open skies describes the situation in which a country allows unlimited traffic rights to the airlines of other countries, almost always on a reciprocal basis and is not all [sic] common. Open skies usually results from bilateral negotiation. Singapore, however, places open skies on the table immediately, and, if the other side reciprocates, there the negotiations end. Holland is much the same. But Dubai grants open skies unconditionally, i.e. without requesting reciprocity, which is unique for a place which has its own airline.[30]

Whichever way the open skies policy is interpreted, and whatever the nature of the practice is, it is inevitable that liberalization would affect market forces and affect airlines differently. With free market competition expanding around the globe in the recent past and the emergence of free trade agreements such as NAFTA (North American Free Trade Agreement), EFTA (European Free Trade Agreement) and free market forces within the European Union, the collapse of the communist economy in most countries including the former USSR and increasingly new consumer demands in Japan, it is a necessary corollary that protectionism in commercial aviation should give way to some degree of liberalization at least.

African airlines are therefore faced with the imminent prospect of the future realm of commercial aviation being controlled by a group of air carriers which may serve whole global regions and operated by a network of commercial and trade agreements. Regional carriers will be predominant, easing out niche carriers and small national carriers whose economics would be inadequate to compare their costs with the lower unit costs and joint ventures of a larger carrier. It is arguable that a perceived justification for 'open skies' or unlimited liberalization exists even today in the bilateral air services agreement between two countries, where *fair and equal opportunity to operate* air services is a *sine qua non* for both national carriers concerned. This has been reinterpreted to mean *fair and equal opportunity to compete* and, later still, *fair and equal opportunity to participate effectively* in the international air transport as agreed.[31] Of course, there has been no universal acceptance of this evolution in interpretation, and most carriers and states whose nationality such carriers have, continue to maintain their positions tendentiously.

ICAO has suggested the following preferential measures for the consideration and possible use of its member states who are at a competitive disadvantage when faced with the mega-trends of commercial aviation and market access:

a the asymmetric liberalization of market access in a bilateral air transport relationship to give an air carrier of a developing country more cities to serve, fifth freedom traffic rights[32] on sectors which are otherwise not normally granted, flexibility to operate unilateral services on a given route for a certain period of time, and the right to serve greater capacity for an agreed period of time;
b more flexibility for air carriers of developing countries (than their counterparts in developed countries) in changing capacity between routes in a bilateral agreement situation, code sharing to markets of interest to them, and changing gauge (aircraft types) without restrictions;
c the allowance of trial periods for carriers of developing countries to operate on liberal air service arrangements for an agreed time;
d gradual introduction by developing countries (in order to ensure participation by their carriers) to more liberal market access agreements for longer periods of time than developed countries' air carriers;
e use of liberalized arrangements at a quick pace by developing countries' carriers;
f waiver of nationality requirement for ownership of carriers of developing countries on a subjective basis;
g allowance for carriers of developing countries to use more modern aircraft through the use of liberal leasing agreements;
h preferential treatment in regard to slot allocations at airports;
i more liberal forms for carriers of developing countries in arrangements for ground handling at airports, conversion of currency at their foreign offices and employment of foreign personnel with specialized skills.[33]

These proposed preferential measures are calculated to give air carriers of developing countries a head start which would effectively ensure their continued participation in competition with other carriers for the operation of international air services. Furthermore, improved market access and operational flexibility are two benefits which are considered as direct corollaries to the measures proposed.

While the open skies policy sounds economically expedient, its implementation would undoubtedly phase out smaller carriers who are now offering competition in air transport and a larger spectrum of air transport to the consumer. Lower fares, different types of services and varied in-flight service profiles are some of the features of the present system. It is desirable that a higher level of competitiveness prevail in the air transport industry and, to achieve this objective, preferential measures for carriers of developing countries would play a major role.

In addition to addressing the preferential measures proposed by ICAO, which would be of immense assistance to carriers of developing countries if implemented, it would be prudent for the international aviation and trading community to consider the larger issue of funding, whereby long-term low-interest loans could be made available to carriers of developing countries through such institutions as the World Bank and the International Monetary Fund. Some consideration could also be given to a balanced distribution of aircraft throughout the world, whereby developing countries could have access to aircraft which have been discarded by their more affluent counterparts. An equitable system of leasing these aircraft is a possibility that could be considered in this regard.

The exemption of aircraft operated by carriers of developing countries from technological standards (to the extent possible) which may apply to modern aircraft is another useful tool which could be addressed under the umbrella of preferential measures. Aircraft engine emission standards and noise regulations are some examples which could be examined in this regard.[34]

Preferential measures may also be considered on a collective basis whereby air traffic rights could be used by a carrier of one country on behalf of another carrier representing another country. This would help, particularly in the event of a developing country not being able to launch its own airline or being unable to allocate its national carrier on a particular route for economic reasons. This principle could also be extended to cover instances where airlines from developing countries could combine their operations by using their collective air traffic rights. For example, airlines of countries A and B who have been granted air traffic rights to operate air services from their countries to countries C and D, respectively would be able to operate one joint service to countries C and D in one flight, using their collective traffic rights under this scheme.

It could be argued on behalf of the African airlines that, as far as possible, developing countries should be released from the obligation to own and control their air carriers or to have their carriers substantially owned and controlled by their nationals. It is only then that countries which cannot fully finance their carriers could maintain them and provide a well rounded competition in the air transport industry.

Aviation Safety

Safety is the primary concern of the world aviation community at the present time. This is not only because the fundamental postulates of the Chicago Convention[35] call for the safe and orderly development of international civil aviation[36] and mandate ICAO to ensure the safe and orderly growth of international civil aviation throughout the world,[37] but also because the aviation world faces a critical era where, in the words of Assad Kotaite, President of the ICAO Council: 'the international aviation community cannot afford to relax its vigilance ... ICAO would continue to take timely action to ensure safety and security standards are in effect, and that deficiencies are properly and efficiently addressed'.[38]

The compelling need for higher standards in aviation safety was formally recognized when the ICAO Council adopted ICAO's Strategic Action Plan on 7 February 1997. The basic strategic objective of the plan is to further the safety, security and efficiency of international civil aviation. ICAO plans to accomplish this task by assisting states in identifying deficiencies in the implementation of annexes to the Chicago Convention, in particular those which contain provisions which ensure safety in aviation.

One of the core elements of ICAO activity on safety, according to its Strategic Action Plan, is to carry out assessments by teams of experts of the capacity of participating states to control effectively the level of safety for which they have responsibility: ICAO's Safety Oversight Programme, which would implement this activity, extends to personnel licensing, operation of aircraft and aircraft airworthiness. ICAO may, in the foreseeable future, extend ICAO's Safety Oversight Programme to cover areas such as air traffic control and the operation of airports.

Taking a cue from ICAO, several regional aviation organizations have formally incorporated safety provisions in their documentation. At its Thirteenth Plenary Session (Abuja, 11–18 May 1995) AFCAC discussed the matter of safety oversight in Africa, which led to the Commission adopting Decision S13-3[39] on Safety Oversight. This decision recognizes that states must take appropriate steps to ensure compliance with international safety standards contained in the relevant annexes to the Chicago Convention and that most African states may not have the necessary infrastructure to fully implement such standards. The Commission refers to the ICAO Safety Oversight Programme in Decision S13-3 and instructs the AFCAC Bureau to improve safety oversight in AFCAC activities and promote cooperation among African states in the field of safety oversight. Through the Decision, AFCAC has also requested ICAO's assistance for African states in order that they may effectively introduce the Safety Oversight Programme in Africa.

The European Civil Aviation Conference (ECAC) at its 100th Meeting of Directors General of Civil Aviation (Paris, 14–15 May 1997) discussed an ECAC Recommendation on Safety of Foreign Aircraft[40] which calls for increased ramp checks on aircraft, and rigid adherence, on a bilateral basis, by states to the provisions of the Chicago Convention on licensing of personnel and certification of aircraft.[41]

The ECAC bilateral safety clause calls *in limine* for consultations to be called for at any stage where such consultations would relate to safety standards of aircrew, aircraft or the operation of aircraft. The provision allows for the revocation of the clause, if one party to the agreement finds that the other does not maintain minimum ICAO standards. The clause also admits of the need to conduct random ramp checks in order for one party to determine whether aircraft conform to Article 33 of the Chicago Convention, which relates to certification of airworthiness.

At the same meeting, ECAC also discussed a recommendation[42] on leasing of aircraft and safety, which calls for standards as prescribed in Annex 6 (Operation of Aircraft) to the Chicago Convention and minimum conditions on the use of leased aircraft, to ensure that they are maintained in accordance with ICAO standards of safety.

It must be noted that safety regulations of the European Community are generally stringent on product liability,[43] stipulating that any person who imports into the community a product for leasing is considered a manufacturer of that product for purposes of product liability. Another regional civil aviation organization which has recognized the compelling need for the implementation of safety oversight in its region is the Latin American Civil Aviation Commission (LACAC). At LACAC's Eleventh Assembly (Manaus, 7–10 November 1994) some LACAC member states adopted the 'Manaus Declaration', which expressed its support of the role of the ICAO Council to establish a Safety Oversight Programme and requested ICAO to implement the programme as quickly as possible.[44]

Both ICAO and the regional aviation organization have focused their attention on the air navigational aspects of safety oversight. This is understandable, since safety of civil aviation primarily depends on safe air navigation. However, safety of civil aviation does not stop at air navigation. There are other extraneous factors which may affect aviation safety, such as human conduct in the aircraft and air traffic controller liability. The management of these areas of activity is as crucial to African civil aviation as the overall ensuring of aviation safety through satellite communication systems.

Taking the above analogies into consideration, the African states should, in the final analysis, consider that one of the most important management issues for Africa concerns the safety of civil aviation. Regulation in Africa on this subject should be introduced on the fundamental basis that air transport is now a high technology-intensive industry, and any regulation promulgated must be focused on a proactive and not reactive approach. Aviation management must address through regulation such aspects as cross-culture communications in the cockpit and cabin, enhanced automation in the cockpit, and a common policy on crew conduct based on available statistics on disruptive passenger conduct. For the last measure to attain fruition, a unified system of collecting information on disruptive behaviour must be implemented. The most important step, at this juncture, is for the African aviation community to support studies which may be initiated by ICAO in the necessary and relevant areas related to the overall issue of aviation safety.[45]

Conclusion

The principal instrumentality of airline cooperation in Africa is the African Airline Association (AFRAA), which is the only such organ in the region that enables African airlines to collaborate in their services and the services provided by any air transport enterprise within Africa, in the pursuit of the airline integration envisaged by the Yamoussoukro Declaration.[46] On the regulatory side, the African Civil Aviation Commission (AFCAC) coordinates policy, technical and coordination issues with ICAO and IATA without actually involving itself with airline issues directly. This two-pronged modality has somehow to converge at the focal point of the Yamoussoukro Declaration's airline integration policy, if a meaningful adaptation by the African airlines to the global trends in aviation is to attain fruition.

The fact that such an integration is possible is amply evidenced by the 1961 Yaounde Treaty and the African Joint Air Services (AJAS) accord signed by and between Tanzania, Uganda and Zambia. The latter provided for the establishment of an independent air transport operating agency within Article 77 of the Chicago Convention to operate air services in intercontinental routes on behalf of Air Tanzania, Uganda Airlines and Zambia Airways, together with Air Maghreb (which is actually a combination of the airlines of Algeria, the Libyan Arab Jamahiriya, Mauritania, Morocco and Tunisia) and Air Mano, consisting of the carriers Air Guinea, Air Liberia and Sierra Leone Airways.

In addition to this airline integration, it is encouraging to note that the restructuring and commercialization which started in Africa in 1992 has yielded positive results. More African airlines are veering from the 'flag carrier' notion and going in for self-reliance, privatization and delinking themselves from governmental control. The privatization of Kenya Airways and the turnaround of Air Tanzania and Uganda Airlines are good examples of a progressive African air transport industry.

However, considered *in toto*, African civil aviation, with the exception of the few airlines already mentioned, has failed to show that it could contribute positively to national economic integration and development. Moreover, African airlines in general have shown over the past few years the need for a management approach that could cope with global trends in civil aviation. Nonetheless, the prognosis for the future of African air transport is far from gloomy. Although African airlines do not yet contribute to the regional economy, it is encouraging that, over the 1985–95 period, the scheduled airlines of the African region showed an annual increase in operating revenues in US dollars at the rate of 5.4 per cent[47] compared with a world annual average of 9.1 per cent, and positive overall operating results have been achieved by these airlines since 1992.[48] During 1996, ten airlines in the world, five of which were from Africa,[49] showed progress towards privatization.

Obviously, the potential for achieving full maturity within the global challenges faced by Africa remains within the African states and their airlines themselves. Autonomy in civil aviation authorities, the aggressive development of infrastructure, and personnel training are the key that could open the door to strategic African airline management within the Yamoussoukro Declaration.

Notes

1 The Organization of African Unity was set up as the regional organ for Africa primarily for the purpose of promoting peace and security in the African region. OAU is set up under Article 52(1) of the United Nations Charter which states: 'Nothing in the present Charter precludes the existence of regional arrangements of agencies for dealing with such matters relating to the maintenance of international peace and security as are appropriate for regional action, provided that such arrangements or agencies and their activities are consistent with the purposes and principles of the United Nations.'

2 Central African Republic, Republic of the Congo, Republic of the Ivory Coast, Republic of Gabon, Republic of Dahomey, Republic of Upper Volta, Islamic Republic of Mauritania, Republic of Niger, Republic of Senegal and the Republic of Chad.

3 See ICAO Circular 98-AT/19, 1970, for text of the Treaty.

4 See Convention on International Civil Aviation, signed at Chicago on 7 December 1944. See ICAO Doc. 7300/7, 7th edn, 1997, for text of the Convention.
5 Yaounde Treaty (*supra*, n.4), Article 2.
6 Ibid., Article 3.
7 See 'Report of the African Civil Aviation Commission, Eleventh Plenary Session (AFCAC/11), Blantyre, 22–31 May 1989', Dakar: AFCAC, 1990, Appendix, for the text of the Yamoussoukro Declaration.
8 See United Nations Economic Commission for Africa, TRANS/EXP/94-07 Annex 1.
9 Ibid., para. 2.1.
10 ASECNA was created by the Convention of St. Louis de Senegal, which was signed on 12 December 1959. ASECNA's objective is to provide services that are designed to guarantee the regularity and safety of flights in the designated territories. The Agency manages the en-route and air navigation installations and services pooled by the signatory states. The convention establishing ASECNA was signed by Chad, Cameroon, Central African Republic, the Congo, Dahomey, Gabon, Ivory Coast, Malagasy Republic, Mauritania, Niger, Sénégal and Upper Volta. Mali and Togo were later signatories.
11 ASECNA services collaborate in fleet financing with the Banque Ouest Africaine de Développement (BOAD) and the Caisse Française de Développement (LCFD).
12 See 'ICAO Environmental Experts Recommend Stricter Noise and Emissions Standards', ICAO News Release, PIO 02/98, p.1.
13 Ibid., p.2.
14 For a detailed discussion on this subject, see R.I.R. Abeyratne (1997), 'Outsourcing and the Virtual Airline – Legal Implications', *Air and Space Law*, XXII(4/5), October, 182–93.
15 See R.I.R. Abeyratne (1997), 'Franchising in the Airline Industry, Some Implications at Common Law', *Air and Space Law*, XXII(6), December, 284–90.
16 See 'US, UK to Restart Open Skies Talks in London', *Air Letter*, no. 13, 633, Monday 2 December 1996, p.2.
17 The current bilateral air services agreement between the two countries, known as the Bermuda 2 Agreement, permits only two US carriers, American and United, to serve London's Heathrow Airport from a limited number of cities.
18 See 'US–UK Open Skies to add $108bn to Economy', *Air Letter*, no. 13, 621, Thursday 14 November 1996, p.3.
19 Ibid.
20 'U.S.–Japan, Fairplay Comes First', *Airlines International*, Jan./Feb. 1996, 7.
21 *Aviation Daily*, 326 (56), Monday 23 December 1996, p.4.
22 'No surprise in Japan's Rejection of Open Skies', *Aviation Daily*, 28 June, 1996, p.529.
23 'Delta Calls for Open Skies with Europe', *The Air Letter*, no. 13, 400, Friday 24 May 1996, p.1.
24 'US Hong Kong in MOU; DOT Presses to Liberalize Asian Markets', *Aviation Daily*, 2 October 1995, p.3.
25 'SIA Chief Seeks Open Skies between US, Asia', *Air Letter*, no. 13, 519, Monday 24 June 1996, p.3.
26 'Singapore Airlines CEO says Singapore, Malaysia Ready for Open Skies', *Aviation Daily*, 326 (45), Friday 6 December 1996, p.377.
27 Ibid.
28 'Asian Airlines Urged to Adopt United Stand', *Air Letter*, no. 13, 363, Wednesday 1 November 1995, p.1.
29 'U.S., Singapore agree to end air restrictions', *Air Letter*, no. 13, 667, Monday 27 January 1997, p.3.

30 Maurice Flanagan (1996), 'Open Skies and the Survival of the Fittest', *Aerospace*, August, 16.
31 Henri Wassenbergh (1996), 'De-Regulation of Competition in International Air Transport', *Air and Space Law*, XII, 2 November, 80.
32 The right to take on or discharge passengers, mail and cargo in a country other than the grantor state.
33 See 'Study on Preferential Measures for Developing Countries', ICAO Doc. AT-WP/1789, 22/8/96 at A-7–A-9.
34 For a detailed discussion of regulations on aircraft noise and engine emissions, see R.I.R. Abeyratne (1996), *Legal and Regulatory Issues in International Aviation*, New York: Transnational Publishers, pp.271–313.
35 Chicago Convention (*supra*, n.5).
36 Ibid., Preamble, p.1.
37 Ibid., Article 44(*a*).
38 ITA Press, 284, 1–5 April 1997, p.10.
39 Decision S13-3: Safety Oversight. See African Civil Aviation Commission, Thirteenth Plenary Session, Abuja 11–18 May 1995, AFCAC/13 Report, p.25.
40 DGCA/100-DP/7, 21/4/97, Appendix.
41 Article 31 provides that every aircraft engaged in international navigation shall be provided with a certificate of airworthiness issued or rendered valid by the state in which it is registered. Article 32 provides for the issuance of certificates of competency to technical crew of aircraft and prescribes minimum standards. Article 33 stipulates that certificates of airworthiness issued to aircraft by one state should be acceptable by another, provided certain minimum standards are followed.
42 DGCA/100-DP/8, 28/4/97, Appendix.
43 EU Council Directive 85/374/EEC of 25 July 1985.
44 ICAO Doc. 9637, *Annual Report of the Council*, Montreal: ICAO, 1994, pp.45–6.
45 See R.I.R. Abeyratne (1997), 'International Obligations as regards Safety in International Civil Aviation', *The Aeronautical Journal*, 101 (1010), December 461–6.
46 African Airline Association, Articles of Association, Article 4B.
47 See 'The World of Civil Aviation, 1996–1999', ICAO Circular 271-AT/112, p.88.
48 Ibid., p.89.
49 Ibid., p.13.

23 The European Region

Introduction

Air transport in the European Community is fundamentally regulated by two treaties: the treaty which establishes the European Coal and Steel Community (ECSC Treaty) and the treaty which establishes the European Economic Community (EEC Treaty). The former, which was signed in Paris in 1951, addresses issues related to the carriage of coal and steel through the media of rail, road and inland waterways, and as such is not directly relevant to aviation. The latter, on the other hand, admits of issues relating to all modes of transport in the carriage of persons and goods and is of some relevance to aviation.

The EEC Treaty, which was signed in Rome on 25 March 1957,[1] has at its core a Common Transport Policy (CTP) concept which is calculated to achieve the fundamental purposes of the European Community.[2] One of the most salient features of the EEC Treaty is that the tasks of the Community are set out succinctly in Article 2, which provides inter alia for the adoption of a CTP, as provided for in Article 3(1) of the treaty. This provision is linked to Article 74 which in turn provides that the objectives of the Treaty in relation to issues of transport would be pursued by state parties within the parameters of the CTP, which is established by the Council of Europe through secondary legislation.

The rights and duties of the Council of Europe in establishing the CTP, particularly in the fields of air and maritime transport, can be attributed to a 1986 case[3] and to Article 189 of the EEC Treaty which admits of the Council adopting such measures as common rules attributable to international transport to or from the territory of a member state or passing across the territory of one or more member states, the conditions under which non-resident carriers may operate transport services within a member state, and any other appropriate provisions.

Article 84(1) of the EEC Treaty makes the provisions of the title of the section relating to transport apply to rail, road and inland waterway, with a qualifier in Article 84(2) which gives the discretion to the Council to decide whether, and to what extent and by what procedure, appropriate provisions may be laid down for sea and air transport. This is immediately followed by the discretion given to the Council to decide unanimously whether, to what extent and by what procedure appropriate provisions may be laid down for maritime and air transport. Although explicit mention of air and maritime transport is made in Article 84, implicit in the treaty is the understanding that the transport title will not ipso facto apply to the two modes of transport. The applicability of the treaty to air and maritime transport was examined in some detail in the 1974 case of *Commission* v. *France*,[4] where the court observed: 'Whilst under Article 84(2), therefore, sea and air transport, so long as the Council has not decided otherwise, is excluded from the rules of Title IV Part Two of the Treaty relating to the CTP, it remains, on the same basis as other modes of transport, subject to the general rules of the Treaty.'[5] The court subsequently confirmed this view in a later case,[6] decided in 1977. Both the 1974 and 1977 decisions make it incontrovertible that the general rules of the treaty apply *per-force* to transport in general, if the Council, acting under Article 84(2), does not decide to the contrary. This means essentially that the Commission has upon it a legal duty[7] as well as a political duty[8] to ensure that the general provisions of the treaty are applied to air and maritime transport.

The Treaty on European Union (TEU) is a supplemental treaty which embellishes the provisions of the EEC Treaty, particularly by adding that the Council shall lay down measures to improve transport policy, in addition to its duties in Article 75(1). The TEU also laid down the principle that the Council is obligated in all instances to act on proposals from the Commission, consequent to obtaining the opinion of the European Parliament. This procedure is laid out in Article 189C of the EEC Treaty and the TEU merely enforced the need for Council to act according to the provision. The TEU also requires that the European Community should contribute to the establishment and development of trans-European networks in the fields of transport, telecommunications and energy infrastructures, as per Article 129b(1) of the Treaty of the European Community.

The Joint European Council, in October 1997, confirmed the creation of a European Common Aviation Area (ECAA) which would encompass the European Community states, member states of the European Economic Area (EEA) and the Associated States of Central Europe. The common aviation area is based on the *acquis communautaire* in air transport and is founded in a multilateral agreement which contains transitional provisions on market access and environmental protection, with particular emphasis on noise. European Community legislation is extended by the ECAA Agreement in areas relating to market access and ancillary issues, competition rules, air traffic management, safety, environmental protection, social aspects and consumer protection.

The perceived dichotomy of wide ranging powers of the European Union in terms of its external relations in air transport on the one hand and the inhibitions cast upon the Union by the seminal legislative instrument, the Treaty of Rome[9] (EEC Treaty), by not explicitly granting the Union competence, has led to sustained examination by the adjudicatory process. The European Court of Justice (ECJ) in 1971 decided that the Community has both external competence and internal competence on an intra-Europe basis. This judgment gave implicit external competence to the European Union to take over control of negotiations on behalf of European member states in matters relating to international air transport agreements. Although this implicit right has not been used by the Union extensively, it was indeed used in the 1990s when the European Community adopted internal rules pertaining to computer reservations systems (CRS) on an intra-Europe basis. This right does not, however, extend to trade in services, on the basis of a 1994 ECJ judgment which decided that trade in services including trade relating to air transport services is beyond the jurisdiction of the Union.

With the advent of the Maastricht Treaty of 1992,[10] which provided that the European Community may decide to cooperate with third countries to promote projects of mutual interest, it was possible to encompass the countries of Central and Eastern Europe within the purview of the European Union, thus extending some flexibility to the rigid treaty law governing Europe, particularly in relation to trade in services and commercial competition in air transport. In January 1993, when the third and final phase, or third package, of European Community air transport liberalization took effect, there were in place regulations covering areas such as market access, slot allocation and scheduling.

Competition within Europe

The tightly woven pan European legislation on competition reflects the desire of the European nations to band together as a collective force, rather than compete individually with other nations or among themselves in the field of air transport. The combined European markets rank third worldwide and, in 1996–2000 it was expected that European air carriers would be responsible for approximately 8 per cent of world aviation[11] in passenger kilometres. Although a combined

Europe is more populous than North America, airlines of the European Union countries have not optimized this potential market, primarily owing to their high operating costs. A few airlines were on top, such as British Airways, KLM and Lufthansa in the mid-1990s, while most other European carriers were operating at below break-even levels.[12] However, as a result of the rapidly evolving collectiveness of the European states and their competitive banding together, particularly in the liberalization of intra-European markets, European Union carriers have now entered more intra-European routes and several airlines of European states have established subsidiaries in other Union member states.

The success of the European Union states in tightening their air transport legislation and liberalizing air transport within Europe is a classic example of the 'cluster' theory which is based on the competitive advantage of a cluster of nations which are geographically proximate to each other. In this case, the air carriers of a cluster of European states, interconnected and linked by commonalities and complementaries, are given the opportunity of forming alliances, sourcing their capital, goods and technology to locate their operations within the European continent, wherever it may be cost-effective. The prevalence of clusters in economies, as against isolated competition, brings to bear new concepts about national, municipal and international economies and opens a whole new dimension of competition centred on liberalization on an intracontinental legal structure.

Clustering in European air transport in areas of slot allocation and market access has created new management agendas for European carriers, giving them a tangible stake in key business areas such as taxation, utility cost sharing and wages. The European Union states, in their macroeconomic vision, have created a driving force in the European air transport industry, not only by maximizing air transport potential within the Continent, but also by creating new types of dialogues between air transport enterprises within Europe.

The essential theory of clustering is founded upon interaction of economic potential of a group of enterprises. Clusters of European airlines operating within Europe would affect competition by increasing the productivity across the board of constituent partners, by increasing the capacity of commercial partners' innovation and growth in productivity, and by stimulating new business strategy that expands business and the dimensions of the cluster. Clusters also effectively maximize economies of agglomeration by promoting proximity of operation while minimizing costs and increasing proximity to markets. Together with the overall thrust of the cluster phenomenon in Europe brought about by tight legislation on liberalization, European nations also have the advantage of the immense capacity of their air transport industry to innovate and upgrade. Europe has retained competition advantage within the Continent through a highly localized process.

Competition outside Europe

For the European Union nations, what is the most important is arguably the North Atlantic air transport market between the United States and Europe. A primary commercial tool which European carriers have used in participating in this market is the air carrier alliance. The North Atlantic market was by far the largest in the world in the mid-1990s, with 34 million passengers carried in 1993.[13] The largest country pair in this market link is the United States–United Kingdom, which accommodated 43 per cent of all United States–Europe traffic in 1997.[14]

Although postwar trends of Bermuda I and Bermuda II bilateral understandings which had certain restrictions on capacity and tariffs were perceived as inhibiting the hidden potential in air transport between the US and Europe, the United States external aviation policy of liberalization, which was launched in 1978, paved the way for more competition between the two. The Netherlands, which blazed the trail with the first liberalized bilateral in 1978 with the United States,[15] was followed by Belgium[16] and Germany[17] in quick succession.

One of the most significant commercial considerations, which has sometimes been a contentious issue with regard to transatlantic air transport, has been the extraterritorial application of EU and US competition law. Understandably, both the Union and the United States have explicit policy pertaining to air transport which is carried out by legislation. It is not unusual, therefore, that the laws applicable to transnational air transport – from both ends – may be questioned by either side as being extraterritorial. Such a contention does not necessarily reflect *mala fides* on the party against whom extraterritoriality is alleged. Usually, the question of extraterritorial application of national laws arises in instances where, in the absence of an international framework of competition rules, the extraterritorial application of national competition laws is perceived to be necessary to patch up loopholes emerging from the territorial reach of national jurisdiction.

The United States, for its part, has, through its courts, applied US antitrust laws to commercial activities conducted outside the United States if such activities impinged upon the equilibrium of commercial activities within the United States by having a direct, substantial and reasonably foreseeable effect within the country.[18] The Foreign Trade Antitrust Improvement Act of 1982,[19] which grants the US courts jurisdiction over aspects of foreign conduct, grants the US Department of Transport jurisdiction over air routes between the country and a foreign country, including routes which are entirely outside the United States if competition on such routes is reasonably likely to have an adverse effect on the United States. As a result of this legislative possibility, courts in the United States have jurisdiction over antitrust actions brought by private entities in a court in the United States even where such actions may concern foreign entities.[20]

In a laudable and fair attempt at balançing harmoniously the stringent application of US law to foreign conduct with external cooperation, the United States has enacted the 1994 International Antitrust Enforcement Assistance Act which broadly admits of arrangements with foreign authorities to investigate antitrust violations through the exchange of information and common and reciprocal retrieval of evidence.

European Union rules on extraterritoriality are not explicit and therefore are not incorporated in the competition provisions of Articles 85 and 86 of the EEC Treaty. Although at best an inference may be drawn from an interpretation of these provisions and extraterritoriality may be imputed to the provisions, the European Court of Justice in the 1988 *Woodpulp* case[21] applied the principle of the *lex situs* to jurisdiction and held that it is the place where the anticompetitive arrangements take effect that determines the jurisdiction of the Union in matters relating to competition. Since Article 87 of the EEC Treaty requires appropriate regulations or directives to give effect to the principles as set out in Articles 85 and 86, it flows logically that implementing legislation is necessary to give effect to Articles 85 and 86[22] in the instance of issues arising from air transport in routes between the European Union and a third country or in routes that are entirely outside the community. Mention must be made in this regard to the case of *Ahmed Saeed*,[23] where the German Federal Court of Justice sought the ruling of the European Court of Justice on a matter pertaining to the selling in Germany of air tickets to the public at prices below the level approved by the Federal Minister of Transport, in contravention of local German municipal law. The issue was whether Article 86 of the EEC Treaty had overriding jurisdiction over local laws of Union states, and the ECJ held that Article 86 is directly applicable in national courts even in the absence of implementing legislation.

In the field of air transport, the European Union has shown that national prosperity is created, not inherited, and that, contrary to popular belief, a commercially successful enterprise within a nation does not necessarily grow because of that nation's natural endowments, its cheap labour force or its currency values, but rather by the capacity of that industry to innovate and upgrade. As the winds of change swept commercial aviation towards the new millennium, European nations showed that, at least in air transport, nations have become more, not less, important. They have created competitive advantages for themselves through a highly localized process.

Individual states of Europe must reconcile themselves to the fact that, unlike large nations such as the United States, Canada and Russia, they are relatively small. Geographic magnitude of a country becomes a relevant consideration in air transport in terms both of the volume of traffic generated by a particular country and of the negotiating leverage it has in bartering air traffic rights and points of departure and landing. If a country is small, it is usual for that country to have lesser airports than a larger country and the latter would consequently have more opportunity to bargain. Therefore, incontrovertibly, European states have to band together in order to optimize their collective potential.

Strict EU legislation should continue in product performance, product safety and environmental impact to promote a competitive advantage and stimulate and upgrade domestic demand. The last element – environmental impact – should be particularly addressed in harmony with global regulations as promulgated through the International Civil Aviation Organization. As a future measure, European states should also continue limiting direct cooperation in the air transport field among industry rivals in order to obviate anti-competitive conduct. As a supplemental measure, competition should be deregulated and state monopolies (which are already discouraged in the Union) should be eschewed. Finally, governments should pursue vigorously an open market policy which veers from managed trade that has a tendency to deal with the fall-out of national competitiveness.

As for European airlines, they should continue to look for pressure and challenge in order to innovate commercially towards more achievements while seeking out their most capable competitors as motivators. More importantly, and as prudent airlines must, airlines of European nations should establish early warning systems which would indicate any hint of change in the air transport market both within and without Europe. Airlines could find and serve passengers and consignors who have the most anticipated needs, find places whose regulations foreshadow emerging regulations elsewhere, bring outside expertise into their management teams if needed and constantly conduct research on market access.

In the quest for globalization of European air transport activity, airlines should tap selectively sources of advantage in other nations' airlines. However, airline alliances have to be used only selectively in order to minimize cost bases and obviate relinquishing profits that would accrue to an airline without the alliance concerned. Inevitably, an airline alliance shows the partners' mediocrity to an extent, particularly if profits are not optimized and alliances are formed on core activities.

The central theme for European nations and their airlines for the future is 'leadership', which they currently hold in air transport regulation by being second to none and equal to the best.

Notes

1 Treaty Establishing the European Economic Community, signed in Rome on 25 March 1957, 298 UNTS 11.
2 The word 'Community' alludes to the European Economic Community which is now called the European Community consequent upon the signing of the Treaty of the European Union on 1 November 1993.
3 Case 18/83, *European Parliament* v. *EC Council*, (1986) 1 CMLR 138 ECJ.
4 Case 167/73, (1974) ECR 359.
5 Ibid., 367.
6 Case 156/77, *EC Commission* v. *Kingdom of Belgium*, judgment of 12 October 1977, [1978] ECR 1881.
7 Article 175 of the EEC Treaty addresses issues pertaining to recourse for failure to act.
8 As per the powers of the European Parliament, provided for in Articles 137 to 144 of the EEC Treaty.
9 *Supra*, note 1.
10 Treaty on European Union, 7 February 1992, 1 CMLR 719.
11 *Association of European Airlines Yearbook, 1996*, Brussels: Association of European Airlines, 1996, p.19.
12 Ibid., p.15.
13 *US International Air Passenger and Freight Statistics, 1993*, 1(5), Washington: 1994, p.21.
14 *U.S. Internal Air Passenger and Freight Statistics, 1998*, 1(8), Washington: 1998, p.32.
15 See Amendment of March 31, 1978 (1123 U.N.T.S. 345, T.I.A.S. 8988) to the Air Transport Agreement between the Government of the United States and the Government of the Kingdom of the Netherlands, 3 April 1957, 410 U.N.T.S. 193; T.I.A.S. 4787.
16 US–Belgium Agreement, T.I.A.S. 9231.
17 See D. Bartkowski and E. Byerly (1997), 'Forty Years of U.S.–German Relations', *Zeitschrift für Luft und Weltraumrecht* (German Journal of Air & Space Law), 46(1), 8.
18 *United States* v. *Aluminium Co. of America* (Alcoa), 148 F. 2d 416 (2d Cir. 1945). See also Ludwig Weber (1995), 'Modern Trends in the Antitrust/Competition Law Governing the Aviation Industry', *Air & Space Law*, XXII, 101.
19 Also known as the Sherman Act 37, 15 V.S.C. § 6a.
20 See Weber (*supra*, n.18), 103.
21 *Ahlstrom Osakeyhtio* v. *Commission* ('Woodpulp') 1988, reported in L. Giemulla *et al.*, *European Air Law*, The Hague, 1997, c.4a.
22 Article 86 provides that, in certain circumstances, any abuse by one or more undertakings of a dominant position within the common market or in a sub-

stantial part of it shall be prohibited as incompatible with the common market insofar as it may affect trade between member states.

23 Case 66/86, *Ahmed Saeed Flugreisen and Silver Line Reiseburo GmbH* v. *Zentrale zur Bekämpfung unlauteren Wettebewerbs E.V.*, [1989] ECR 803, [1990] 4 CMLR 102.

24 The South American Region

Introduction

When the year 2000 dawned, a salutary trend in South American air transport was the move towards 'open skies' with the United States. This millennium trend, which saw 12 states in South America signing such agreements up to January 2000, and having more in the offing, augurs more competitive activity for the airlines of the region and stimulation of market growth. As an example, Mexico, which is the closest Latin American partner having a common border with the United States, is claimed to have generated an income of 8 billion US dollars from tourist arrivals in 1999, with a tourism-promotion budget of 80 million.[1] South America's sustained effort at initiating open-skies agreements is arguably an enthusiastic response of the South American region to spur sagging traffic figures of tourist arrivals originating from the United States. Statistics have shown that traffic from Europe to South America far outweigh traffic generated by the North American neighbours, especially the United States.[2]

Another move towards developing air transport in the South American region originated from the regional organization – the Latin American Civil Aviation Commission (LACAC), which, at its 13th Assembly held in July 1998, adopted Resolution A13-1,[3] aimed at the expansion of the geographic area of LACAC. This resolution, which is calculated to radically alter the composition of LACAC, detracts from the membership of LACAC which existed until 1998, comprising states in South America, Central America including Panama, Mexico and the Caribbean states, and amends article 2 of the Commission's statute which identified its geographic bounds in terms of LACAC membership. The new article of the statute, as amended by Resolution A13-1, changes existing text which reads:

> The Latin American Civil Aviation Commission, hereinafter referred to as either the Commission or LACAC, may be made up solely by the

> States located in South America, Central America including Panama, Mexico and the Caribbean States, a geographical area which, for purposes of this document shall be referred to as Latin America

to read:

> The Commission ... , which hereinafter shall be known as the Pan American Civil Aviation Commission, the Commission or PACAC, shall be made up by the States located in the American Continent and the Caribbean, a geographical area which, for the purposes of the present document shall be called the Region.[4]

A significant move towards regional cooperation in South America was seen in initiatives taken at the Cartagena meeting which resulted in the adoption of the Cartagena Agreement of 1989.[5] The Agreement represented five nations[6] which had common goals for air transport. The Mercosur Agreement[7] on Common Markets, adopted in 1991, although containing principles of trade and commerce in general, is another influential treaty which drives the commercial trends in aviation in South America.

An earlier agreement also signed in Cartagena, Colombia, in May 1969 established the Andean Community (ANCOM).[8] The Community's mission was to constitute a conscientious global plan of mutual region trade, progressively establish external common tariffs, equitably share the cost of regional investment programmes, harmonize internal economic policies, including foreign investment, and give special treatment to Bolivia and Ecuador as the two least developed states in the region.

With the new developments in the South American region such as the adoption of the LACAC resolution expanding the geographic scope of South American civil aviation to encompass and be included in a Pan American Organization, a transformation in South American air transport policy could well take place, making air transport operators in the region more involved in commercial activity in a more global sense. The real sustenance of South American aviation under a wider American umbrella would be predicated upon the essential need for airlines of the region to ride with the tide of change that is sweeping the global air transport scene in order to stay afloat with the other regions of the world.

Future Challenges: Economic Factors

Statistics released by the International Civil Aviation Organization show that, over the 1987–7 period, the aggregate South American and Caribbean economy (GDP) grew at an average annual rate of 2.4

per cent in real terms, whereas GDP per capita grew at 0.6 per cent.[9] The economy in this region was severely affected by recession in the late 1980s, but a robust recovery started in 1991.

After a record 5.3 per cent growth in GDP in 1997, the economy experienced a significant slowdown, resulting in an estimated growth of 2.5 per cent in 1998. In the latter part of 1998, financial market setbacks led Brazil to introduce severe austerity measures and a sharp slowdown in the country's economic performance. Some countries in the region such as Peru, Ecuador and El Salvador were adversely affected by El Niño earlier in the year which resulted in lowered growth and exports. Hurricane Mitch in November 1998 also had devastating effects in some Central American countries (especially Honduras and Nicaragua), especially on their agriculture sectors and industrial infrastructures. At the time of writing, the economic performance of the region was expected to slow down further in 1999, to 0.9 per cent. The economy is expected to recover to growth rates of 3.9 and 4.2 per cent in 2000 and 2001, respectively.

Over the 1987–97 period, operating revenues of the scheduled airlines of the South American and Caribbean region increased at an average annual rate of 8.6 per cent (compared to the world annual average of 7.1 per cent). Operating expenses for the same period increased by 8.3 per cent per annum. The overall financial performance of the airlines of the region has been poor over the whole period, with five consecutive years (1989 to 1993) of serious operating losses. A concerted effort of drastic cost cutting, airline industry restructuring and demand recovery led to a significant turnaround and brought positive operating results for four consecutive years. Many airlines had returned to profitability by 1995 and were reporting healthy net results in 1996 and 1997. In 1998, the airlines of the region achieved an aggregate operating profit of about $200 million.[10]

Policy Issues

The integration of a vast area such as the South American region, which covers some 11 000 kilometres from the southern border of Texas to the southernmost tip of Cape Horn, with the rest of America will have policy implications. However, from an essentially practical point of view, the region, which has an enormous geographic expanse, will tend to remain regionalized for a while, notwithstanding the macro political changes envisioned. What this means for development of air transport is that competition will remain the main consideration.

From a long-term perspective, by using the 'open skies' relationship with the United States, South America could build globalization on the foundation of its unique competitive position. South American carriers should penetrate international markets with consistent positioning in the areas concerned. However, this strategy requires a patient, long-term campaign to enter the foreign market, particularly in the United States and Canada.

One of the most effective tools in the particular context of South American carriers is to gain market access, which would technically be unlimited under an 'open skies' philosophy, through alliances with local partners. The presence of South American carriers in the United States would inevitably be linked to their ability to tap advanced skills and technologies in locations they are not accustomed to. To sound a note of caution, South American carriers should be selective in their alliances. They should be focused on particular activities and aim at obtaining a particular advantage. For example, particular national markets which may sustain end-to-end traffic established through markets by South American carriers need not be compromised by striking alliances with American carriers on such markets.

South American carriers would also be at an advantage in the American market if they upgraded their home bases by adding new dimensions supporting specialized training programmes and promoting research and development. If the vigour and vitality of a home base, however developed, deteriorates, a carrier should consider relocating the home base, particularly if the carrier has a strategic alliance with a more expansive carrier from the North.

The South American carriers could be positively influenced by the model of what is arguably the most spectacular strategic airline alliance so far, the 'Star' Alliance launched in 1997 by Lufthansa, SAS, United Airlines, Thai Airways International and Air Canada. Brazilian carrier Varig joined later, and it was expected that Ansett Australia and Air New Zealand would join the alliance in 1999. Recently, Singapore Airlines signed a commercial agreement with SAS – one of the 'Star' Alliance members – which will bring Singapore Airlines inextricably close to the alliance itself.[11] It is evident that the carriers of North America, Europe and the Asia–Pacific regions which form the 'Star' Alliance have skilfully manoeuvred their dominance of the regions they represent. The role of Varig as a South American carrier would be a good start for increased involvement in such alliances by carriers of South America.

The underlying philosophy of the airline alliances, typified by the 'Star' Alliance, is not so much an emphasis on the more effective use of resources such as labour, capital and national resources (which are inevitably important factors) but rather an overall reliance on the strategy of location, where the sharing of locations represented by the various airlines has enabled them to produce their goods and services in a consistent manner, thus achieving a status equivalent to a cartel, while still retaining their individual identities.

Airlines have developed both a corporate strategy and a competition strategy to cope with competition. Both these strategies are becoming increasingly complementary rather than being mutually exclusive, which they were at the inception of airline competition 50 years ago. As airlines began to compete with each other across the borders, they acquired the ability to locate themselves overseas, creating a compelling need for commercial airlines to be fully acquainted with locational strategy and competitive advantages of various locations. Very early in the game, giants such as PANAM and TWA began to realize that even the strongest company with an established position in the airline industry, unthreatened by competition from new entrants or smaller airlines, would start losing business if they faced a better or lower-cost product. The threat of new entrants, the bargaining power of supplies and customers and the superior quality or low cost of substitute products were arguably the underlying reasons for established airlines to begin experiencing a downturn in the 1960s, which was exacerbated through the 1970s and 1980s. These threats could not be effectively circumvented or overcome by the established carriers, partly because of the sustained circumscription of market entry imposed by Article 6 of the Chicago Convention.

The genesis of airline alliances therefore was a contrived symbiosis or coexistence between the new entrants or new competitors – who had the clout of resources but not the dimensions of a larger carrier – and the larger carrier itself who had an established product to offer. Together, these two types of carriers could eradicate such obstacles as product differentiation (which was a distinct disadvantage to carriers which did not have an established brand), capital requirements (again a disadvantage faced by a smaller carrier), economies of scale (which forced a smaller carrier to compete on a large scale) and government policy (which affected both types of carriers, particularly the larger carrier which had the resources to operate air services but not the market access to a given region).

Another type of commercial alliance which might be of interest to the larger carriers is the 'mega' alliance referred to earlier, typified by the 'Star' Alliance. The precursor to this type of alliance could have been the modest 'pool agreement' between two carriers operating third and fourth freedom traffic: that is, traffic purely originating and ending in each other's territories. The pool agreement was written into a bilateral air services agreement between two states in order to ensure equal enjoyment of market share between their carriers in the route between their states' territories. This notion gave rise to an extension of the principle of pooling, which was to share locational traffic on a fifth freedom, that is traffic which is picked up at intermediate points or points beyond on services between two states and, more importantly, a sixth freedom, traffic to which a carrier had no right but which could operate under the air traffic rights of another carrier, through a commercial arrangement such as a code share agreement signed by and between the carriers.

Another joint venture which would be of commercial interest for the expansion of South American carriers is code sharing. Code sharing between two airlines is essentially two different airlines posing as one, sharing or rotating aircraft crew and responsibility.[12] This has been called little more than a glorified inter-line agreement which occurs when one airline operates a flight but both its and another carrier's codes are used.[13] Thus, for example, a passenger who contracts with airline A to travel from Canada to Australia may find himself in the same aircraft with a passenger who contracted with airline B for the same journey.

The United States Department of Transportation (DoT) uses a somewhat technical definition for code sharing, which it calls 'a common airline industry marketing practice where, by mutual agreement between cooperating carriers, at least one of the airline designator codes used on a flight is different from that of the airline operating the flight'.[14] The DoT then classifies code sharing under this definitive structure into two types, the first being the typical international airline operation where two or more airlines each use their own designator codes on the same aircraft operation, and the second enunciating the domestic code shared flight where the code on the passenger's ticket is not that of the operator of the flight, but where the operator does not offer the service in his own name. DoT goes on to bifurcate international code sharing, where, in the first category, only one segment of the journey (which usually involves a connection) operates under two different codes, one used by an airline for its local traffic and the other used by its partner for the entire journey, and, in the second, the entire journey is advertised and displayed under the codes of the two airlines which share the flight concerned.[15]

The marketing benefits of code sharing have been identified as the ability of airlines to: coordinate schedules, transfer baggage easily, maintain common marketing activity by the sharing air carriers, use through fares, use single check-ins, share airport lounges, share frequent flyer programmes, and agree upon exactly which airline is legally responsible for the passenger's whole journey by air. American Airlines, one of the early proponents and participants in the code-sharing concept, adds the safeguarding of traffic rights to this list, where it is claimed that a stronger carrier in the market could be forced to code share with a weaker national carrier, thus spreading commercial benefits on a given route among two carriers equitably.

One of the most scathing attacks on code sharing is that it seeks to create the illusion that inter-line connections between code-sharing partners are the equivalent of on-line connections, which is not so. It is claimed that this alleged illusion is successfully carried out because passengers prefer on-line to inter-line connections by a ratio of approximately four to one, fooling them into believing that a code share is an on-line service. Robert Crandall, chairman of American Airlines, is of the view that allowing foreign carriers to deceive consumers into believing that a domestic code-shared service is really an extension of an international service of a foreign carrier effectively precludes genuine carriers from building strong, dependable on-line services.[16] Crandall also believes that code sharing is an anti-consumer marketing activity in that it causes multiple listings of the same flights in computer reservations systems and printed multi-airline schedules, thus debasing the quality of the information available to consumers.[17]

Code sharing really gathered momentum with the introduction of computer reservations systems (CRS). Major United States airlines found it attractive to engage in code sharing in relation to CRS as it provided them with better exposure on the CRS screen. Although a code-shared flight may not yet appear on a computer screen in its pristine form to be identified as such, code shared flights now appear in CRS as on-line connections and are thus given priority over inter-line connections, giving them an overall higher profile in the CRS and making them more likely prospects for booking by a travel agent.[18] These code-shared flights which appear as 'connections with aircraft change' on the screen, would enable such flights to appear at least four times on the same screen. Some countries therefore view code-shared agreements as efficacious marketing tools and dissociate the concept entirely from the issue of traffic rights.

In January 1995, United States Secretary of State for Transportation Fedrico Pena announced the International Aviation Policy Statement of the United States which primarily endorsed code sharing as a cost-efficient way for carriers to enter new markets and expand their systems.[19] Earlier, in December 1994, the US Department of Transport had released its report on international code sharing which it had commissioned from Gellman Research Associates (GRA).[20] Secretary of State Pena referred to the study as follows: 'This study fully supports the department's international aviation policy statement. It demonstrates that the movement towards globalization and transnational alliances through code sharing and liberalized bilateral arrangements delivers benefits not only for United States consumers but for the United States airline industry as well.'[21]

One of the issues that emerged from the study was that the critical factor in code sharing is not whether it is good or bad but whether it has certain undesirable effects that need to be addressed by policy makers. Based on an econometric consumer choice model that was applied to certain code-sharing agreements, as against non-code-shared flights, the study concludes that the negative impact on consumers as a result of potential deception is inconsequential, as any impact of such misleading practices would be cushioned by existing DoT safety nets. The GRA study's findings were also consistent with the overall DoT perception that all international traffic will ultimately be restructured into long-haul services linking intercontinental hubs, with intraregional spokes feeding traffic, leading to the proliferation of airlines and the expansion of code sharing.[22]

The study concluded that benefits to consumers, estimated at $37.4 million, were minuscule compared to approximately $10 billion that passengers spend each year on transatlantic tickets. Even if one were to assume, as the study suggests, that the number should be doubled, a gain of around $75 million was comparatively inconsequential. Another conclusion was that consumer benefits of code sharing were quantifiable not so much in fiscal terms but rather in terms of higher convenience, higher quality of airline service, and time savings generated through the shorter elapsed time offered by code-shared flights.

Yet another compelling commercial tool which would benefit carriers of Latin America is airline computer reservation systems, coming from one of the most rapidly developing industries today. This development is being driven in part by the enormous strides made by industrial technology. Traditionally, airlines have been at the helm of computer usage and their sustained use goes back 30 years. In the 1960s, the airlines inaugurated high-speed real-time reservations systems; today, these systems use some of the most sophisticated computer software in the world. CRS, which began as a simple means of placing an order for a seat on a plane, has now gone on to add various new dimensions to the carriage of persons and goods from one point to another by air, such as hotel reservations, car rentals, authorization of credit facilities to customers and theatre reservations, all of which cumulatively make CRS an effective marketing tool.

Inevitably, from progress and development emerges the immutable fact that, while some may benefit from the whole process of development, others may feel left behind, even to the extent of being run out of business. One of the corollaries to the phenomenal growth and development of the CRS process is the plight of airlines and travel agents who do not have the ability to participate actively in sophisticated and widespread CRS programmes. A travel agent usually gains access to a CRS through a terminal consisting of a keyboard and a visual display unit. The first step is usually to enter the key data – such as the departure and arrival points relating to an air journey. The system then responds by reflecting on the screen various flight options called up by the system according to the requested data and time of travel, and adjusted according to the priority criteria used in the reservations system concerned. Although CRS have the capacity to list all possible flight options between city pairs concerned, they usually display merely a small number of options, necessitating a 'search' for others. In view of pressures brought upon time and other resource constraints, the tendency is usually to settle for what is displayed on the screen. Needless to say, this process effectively precludes those options offered by airlines enjoying less priority than others from being made known to the prospective airline customer.[23]

The importance of code sharing in this process becomes all the more significant since a flight jointly served by two airlines who share each other's codes would have the leverage of both those airlines in the CRS to be displayed more prominently than a flight which is served by a single carrier. In other words, it is claimed that code sharing by airlines may ipso facto aggravate any imbalance that may already exist in the CRS in favour of those airlines which are prioritized in the systems for other commercial reasons. Barry Humphreys observes:

> The exclusion of an airline's services or the failure to show its correct fares or seat availability status can have a disastrous effect on its ability to compete effectively, and numerous cases have been documented to show that these are not merely hypothetical examples of anti-competitive behaviour.[24]

Brand culture, which essentially involves a particular flavour of a commercial product, could be used effectively by carriers in the Latin American states. In this respect, gaining market access to areas which are not available to these carriers, through franchising agreements, would be another positive consideration for development of air transport in the region. In its contemporary business garb, franchising has permeated a wide spectrum of businesses, introducing a sophisticated business relationship between two parties, thereby creating a contractual relationship. The franchiser, who develops a unique and individual way of conducting business, permits the franchisee to make use of the franchiser's business name and to use his business methods in the franchisee's business, subject to controls imposed by the franchiser.

The application of the principles of franchising fits in well with the modern exigencies of airline business, where the personality developed and projected by a highly successful airline has become of increasing importance to passengers, thus making an airline's image a marketable quantity. Some major airlines have indeed capitalized on this commercial possibility by developing much vaunted and attractive consumer-based brand personalities and using them as key marketing tools for attracting potential franchisees from whom they derive independent income by selling their names and business methods.

A fundamental advantage offered by franchising is its attractiveness to airlines as it allow them to protect and extend their brand to routes (which are otherwise commercially unviable) without actually operating air services to such routes. This is done by getting a franchisee to operate on such routes while using the name and livery of the franchiser, whereby the latter skilfully avoids the risk of capital investment but still derives income in the shelter of a franchise agreement. A notable example of franchising in the airline business can be seen in Europe in British Airways, which had six franchising agreements in the year ending March 1996.[25] The six franchisees, most of whom operated under the name British Airways Express (the exceptions being two who operated under the name British Airways) carried in 1996 a combined capacity of 3.4 million passengers to 80 destinations. The franchisees paid British Airways a fixed fee for the use of services they were obliged to use – such as reservations systems – and a fixed royalty for the use of the brand of the airline.[26] The franchisees could also offer their passengers air miles on British Airways in the latter's frequent flyer scheme.

It would also be of interest to South American carriers that, in extending its franchising agreements to international operations outside Europe, British Airways has also signed an agreement with Comair of South Africa, which has been obliged under the franchise provisions in the agreement to repaint its livery in British Airways livery, and outfit its cabin and customer service staff in British Airways uniforms to offer a typical British Airways in-flight service on Comair's franchised flights. In addition, Comair agreed to transfer its reservations systems to British Airways systems and offer its passengers membership in the British Airways frequent flyer programme.[27]

The other large British carrier, Virgin Atlantic, has also been reported as considering the extension of its short-haul franchise operations to longer routes. In 1994, Virgin Atlantic was operating two extremely profitable franchised flights between London and Athens and between London and Dublin, where the two routes were operated by independent carriers which used the Virgin brand name and livery on their aircraft.[28]

Another significant example of franchising agreements in the airline business is the one signed by Air France and BritAir – when

BritAir placed its entire staff and 23 aircraft under the brand name of Air France[29] – in exchange for Air France granting a dozen of its routes to BritAir, which operated 150 daily flights on these routes. Encouraged by the commercial efficacy and profitability of this agreement, Air France has been seeking additional franchising accords with smaller airlines in order to maximize the passenger flow into its hub at Roissy Charles de Gaulle Airport in Paris.[30] In October 1996, Lufthansa entered into a unique franchising agreement with Augsburg Airways, forming a partnership named 'Team Lufthansa' whereby Augsburg Airways operated, at its own cost, three German domestic routes with Lufthansa flight numbers and under quality control by Lufthansa.[31]

One of the compelling reasons for franchising to emerge as a marketing tool in the airline industry, particularly in Europe, is the European air travel market's polarization between scheduled and unscheduled (charter carriers). European charter carriers have grown prolifically in the last two decades as a backlash to increasingly high scheduled fares. In 1996, it was reported that, in the United Kingdom alone, 14 million passengers used charter flights on their vacation.[32] The growing disparity between the fares of scheduled carriers and the low package fares offered by charter carriers has launched in Europe the franchisee, the hybrid carrier in the form of a compromise between scheduled and unscheduled carriage enabling a small airline to offer competitive fares under the ever-important brand name of a large, prestigious carrier. The 'franchised' flight therefore offers the travelling public a *via media* – a comparatively low fare for a customized flight under the brand name of a large carrier.

The major concern caused by franchising is that major airlines use the services of smaller airlines to carry out franchise services by using a mix of franchise–code share agreements in order to obviate the necessity of operating on revenue-losing routes themselves, while retaining their presence on these routes through the franchisees' operations. The European Union has claimed that, by using franchising agreements in the above manner, major airlines have retained their unprofitable routes and also the valuable slots that go with such operations.[33]

Franchising, which has frequently been described as 'one of the greatest inventions of western capitalism'[34] and the 'dominating force in the distribution of goods and services',[35] is perhaps best described as the only form of business organization which, by its very nature, creates business units providing new entrepreneurs, new jobs, new services and new export opportunities.[36] The symbiotic relationship forged between the franchiser and the franchisee blends harmoniously to form a mutually convenient commercial arrangement between the parties: 'Franchising has provided the means for merging the seemingly conflicting interests of existing businesses with those of aspiring entrepreneurs in a single process that promotes business expansion, entrepreneurial opportunity and shared cost and risk.'[37] Be that as it may, one of the most serious shortcomings of the commercial relationship established by the franchise contract is the oft-experienced imbalance in the power between the franchiser and the franchisee in favour of the former, and the lack of information exchange between the parties to the contract. These factors have given rise to the suggestion that the traditional freedom of contract principles which obtain at common law should be modified to accommodate the franchise phenomenon. This call for modification of contract law principles to accord with the synergic relationship created by a franchise agreement is primarily based on the concern that the time and money invested by a franchisee in the promotion of the franchiser's trade name and trade marks can be jeopardized, and even forfeited, by the arbitrary action of the franchiser.[38]

In the context of franchise agreements between airlines, the personality of the franchiser, who lends his goodwill to the franchisee, plays a key role. The traditional view that goodwill is retained by, and belongs to, the franchiser also applies in the commercial aviation context, where the franchisee simply acquires a right to participate in a business system for a term and in a manner prescribed by the franchise agreement. The franchisee usually does not retain a right to assign the franchise to a third party, have the agreement reviewed on termination, or demand compensation upon non-renewal of the contract. However, there have been instances, particularly in the United States, where courts have been favourable towards protecting a franchisee's investment from forfeiture through the arbitrary and capricious action of a franchiser.[39]

Conclusion

The incontrovertible conclusion to any discussion on developing air transport in a particular region of the world is that the pre-eminent concern of the aviation industry should be to ensure safety in aviation. One regional civil aviation organization which has recognized the compelling need for the implementation of safety oversight in its region is LACAC. At LACAC's 11th Assembly (Manaus, 7–10 November 1994) some LACAC member states adopted the 'Manaus Declaration', which expressed its support of the role of the ICAO Council to establish a safety oversight programme and requested ICAO to implement the programme as quickly as possible.[40]

At the 12th LACAC Assembly, held in Panama on 5–8 November 1996, the Assembly adopted Resolution A12-4, which made reference to the Manaus Declaration as being the basis of aviation safety policy in the region and resolved to support ICAO efforts at safety oversight. The resolution also urged all member states to take the necessary measures to achieve technical perfection, to the extent possible in the implementation of aviation safety measures in their territories.[41]

These initiatives of LACAC are doubtless prompted by the overall thrust of the safety initiatives of the International Civil Aviation Organization, which has culminated in the ICAO Safety Oversight Programme. On 2 October 1998, ICAO concluded its 32nd Session of the Assembly, which commenced in Montreal on 22 September. The Assembly endorsed the establishment of a universal Safety Oversight Programme, which would comprise regular, mandatory, systematic and harmonized safety audits. These audits would be carried out by ICAO in all its 185 contracting states from 1 January 1999, with their consent and at their request, under a Memorandum of Understanding signed by and between the state concerned and ICAO.

The ICAO Safety Audit is aimed at determining whether individual states have the capacity to provide safe air navigation services to aircraft which traverse their airspace. This comes at a critical time in aviation history, with international civil aviation at the beginning of a new millennium, which, in its first 15 years, portends a virtual doubling of current air traffic both in the upper and the lower airspace.

At its 32nd Session, the ICAO Assembly recognized that the ICAO Safety Oversight Programme had reached a saturation point in terms of policy and sought to address policy in developing the programme further. It was considered at this session that there were regional deficiencies and shortcomings in the field of air navigation and that contracting states had to correct such problems. In its deliberations, the Assembly found useful the development of the United States safety programme in April 1998 through its Federal Aviation Administration (FAA) called 'Safer Skies' which was designed to achieve a fivefold reduction in fatal accidents. Through this programme, the FAA intends to address, among other things the CFIT issue, matters pertaining to engine failures, and weather and loss of control.

Taking the above into consideration in the context of its own Global Aviation Safety Plan, the ICAO Assembly adopted Resolution A32-15 which recognized that the primary objective of the organization is to continue promoting the safety of international civil aviation and noted that the expected increase in the volume of international civil aviation would result in an increasing number of aircraft accidents unless the accident rate was reduced. The resolution endorses the ICAO Plan while urging, inter alia, contracting states to examine and revise their laws if necessary to achieve a proper balance among the various elements of accident prevention efforts and to encourage increased voluntary reporting of events that could affect aviation safety. ICAO is instructed by this resolution to develop appropriate policies and guidelines in this regard. Therefore, in its regulatory role, ICAO provides a delicate but well sustained balance between providing guidance on the management of commercial development of air transport and the implementation of safety measures in civil aviation.

It is very clear that, in view of the political overtones moving towards liberalization, the air transport industry in Latin America should concentrate on available commercial tools, as discussed above, while staying on course with the main focus on safety, as the region has admirably sustained in the past.

Notes

1 Robert Booth (2000), 'South America – The Sleeping Giant', *Aviation Daily*, 14 January, p.7.
2 Ibid.
3 Latin American Civil Aviation Commission (Santiago, Chile, 21 to 24 July 1998), Summary of Decisions, p.21.
4 The amendment would come into force when two thirds of the total LACAC member states have deposited their documents of approval with the foreign affairs secretariat of the United States of Mexico.
5 Cartagena Agreement, 26 July 1988 (adopted in 1989) contained in *International Legal Materials*, XXVIII(5), Document Highlights, 1165.
6 Bolivia, Colombia, Ecuador, Peru and Venezuela.
7 Argentina, Brazil, Paraguay, Uruguay Treaty on Common Markets, 19 June, *International Legal Materials* (1991) XXX(4), 1034.
8 Also known as the Andean Pact or Andean Group.
9 'The World of Civil Aviation, 1997–2000', ICAO Circular 273-AT/113, Montreal: ICAO, pp.119–23.
10 Ibid.
11 ITA Press, 16–31 October 1998, p.4.
12 'Code Sharing: If It's Tuesday, This Must be Aeroflot', *Airways*, January/February 1995, 19. See also, 'Is Airline's Gain, Consumer's Loss?', *The Avmark Aviation Economist* (1994), II(8), October, 13.
13 'Coded Warnings', *Airline Business*, January 1995, 26.
14 *The Avmark Aviation Economist*, October 1994, 16.
15 Ibid.
16 See Robert Crandall, 'Chicago's Legacy, Barriers to Multilateral Liberalization', *Viewpoint*, 2(1), 12. Crandall cites the example of the British Airways–US Air code-sharing agreement which allegedly allows British Airways access to nearly six times as many world city-pair markets as are available to American Airlines. He further claims that, since British Airways now has the ability to gather passengers from almost anywhere in the United States and fly them across the Atlantic, and since it has created pseudo-hubs in the United States to connect with its real hub at London Heathrow, neither the British government not British Airways would have any incentive to let American Airlines or any other US carrier compete with British Airways for any substantial portion of

the traffic flowing across Heathrow from countries around the world to and from the United States.

17 Ibid.

18 See Jan Ernest C. de Groot (1994), 'Code Sharing – U.S. Policies and Lessons for Europe', *Air and Space Law*, XIX(2), April 64.

19 'Coded Warnings', *Airline Business*, January 1995, 26.

20 The objectives of the study were to develop a methodology to assess the effects of code sharing on the level and distribution of traffic among carriers with the capability to measure the effect of future code sharing agreements; to examine the effects of code sharing on the costs and profitability of airlines; to assess the effects of code sharing on consumers of airline services; and to project the future use and impact of code sharing over the next 20 years.

21 'GRA Report Sanctifies DoT Policy', *The Avmark Aviation Economist*, December 1994, 2.

22 Ibid.

23 For a more detailed analysis of this problem, see Chris Lyle (1988), 'Computer Age Vulnerability in the International Airline Industry', *Journal of Air Law and Commerce*, 54, 161–78. See also Vladimir D. Zubkov (1987), 'The Development of Computer Reservation Systems: The ICAO Viewpoint', *ITA Magazine*, 42, March/April, 3–7.

24 Barry Humphreys (1989), 'Different Approaches to a Common Problem', *ITA Magazine*, 53, January/February, 9.

25 These agreements were with City Flyer Express, Maersk Air, Brymon Airways, Loganair, Manx Airlines Europe and GB Airways. See 'Keeping Up Appearances', *Airline Business*, October 1996, p.38.

26 Ibid.

27 'British Airways signs up Comair of South Africa as Franchise Partner', *Aviation Daily*, 13 June 1996, p.434.

28 'Virgin long-haul franchise talks', *Travel Weekly*, 2 March 1994, p.4.

29 'Air France takes over regional Airline under Franchise Deal', *Aviation Daily*, 29 April 1997, p.179.

30 See 'Air France Chairman seeks more Franchises', *Air Letter*, Friday 17 January 1997, no. 13, 661, p.2

31 'Lufthansa Announces first Franchise Partner', *Air Letter*, Thursday 3 October 1996, no. 13, 591, p.1. See also 'Lufthansa Signs Augsburg Airways as Franchisee', *Aviation Daily*, 3 October 1996, p.19.

32 'Never the Twain', *Air Transport World*, 10/96, p.67.

33 'EC Concerned that Franchising is Blocking New Entrants', *World Airline News*, 17 April 1995, p.6.

34 U.S. House of Representatives Committee on Small Business (1990), *Franchising in the U.S. Economy: Prospects and Problems*, Washington, D.C.: U.S. Government Printing Office, p.1.

35 Ibid.

36 See *Franchising in the Economy, 1983–1985*, Washington, DC: U.S. Department of Commerce, 1985, p.vi.

37 U.S. House of Representatives Committee on Small Business (*supra*, n.34), p.12.

38 See B. Rau, 'Implied Obligations in Franchising: Beyond Terminations' (1992), *The Business Lawyer*, 47, 1053.

39 See *Shell Oil Co.* v. *Merinello*, 63 N.J. 402; also 307 A. 2d 598(1973). See also E. Pitegoff (1989), 'Franchise Relationship Laws: A Minefield for Franchising', *The Business Lawyer*, 45, 289.

40 ICAO Doc. 9637, *Annual Report of the Council 1994*, Montreal: ICAO, ch. III, pp.45–6.

41 Comision Latinoamericana de Aviacion Civil, XII Asamblea Ordinaria (Ciudad de Panama, 5 al 8 de Noviembre de 1996), CLAC/12, Sumario de Decisones, (30/12/96) p.14.

PART IV
CONCLUSION

25 Conclusion

Strategic alliances of the airline industry are but a natural corollary to the exponential growth of international air transport as an industry. The concept itself is based on the theory that, with rapidly increasing demand for air transport, requiring a doubling of the 16 000 world aircraft fleet by the year 2015, there would be a compelling need for new connections between points and more frequencies to serve these connections. There is no stopping this trend, which has already swept the aviation industry. There is, however, one point of caution. The fundamental postulate of air transport has been, and remains to be, safety of passengers. The proliferation of aircraft in the skies may challenge airline safety, if parallel measures are not set in motion to ensure the safe passage of the thousands of aircraft in the sky.

In 1997, the total scheduled international flights operated by the 705 carriers of the 185 contracting states of ICAO carried a total of approximately 1448 million passengers and 26 million tonnes of freight. In the same year, there were an estimated 16 993 operational aircraft (each carrying more than a weight of 9000 kg), which was a 59 per cent increase from 10 712 aircraft operating a decade ago. Also in 1997, 1309 jet aircraft were ordered (as against 1003 in 1996) and 674 were delivered in the same year.

If this were not sufficient to reflect the gigantic proportions to which international air transport has grown, more daunting figures loom ahead. For instance, it is estimated that the worldwide jet transport fleet will double by 2015. With the current aircraft accident rate at 1.76 accidents per million departures – which is the safest statistical record of accident rates in all modes of transport – there are aggressive calls to reduce this rate by half, to 0.88 accidents per million departures, by the year 2015. Moreover, the Gore Commission of the United States has bettered this figure by calling for an 80 per cent reduction in fatal aircraft accidents.

In 1995, 19 Western built jet aircraft were totally destroyed in air crashes, which killed 383 passengers and 39 crew members.[1]

Although this rate of loss has been steady for the past 10 years, there were three major losses in 1996: the Valujet and TWA aircraft in the United States and the world's worst mid-air collision in history New Delhi, where a Saudia Boeing 747 with 312 persons aboard collided with a Kazak aircraft carrying 37 passengers and crew. All on board were killed. More recently, in early 1998, the loss of a Swissair MD11 aircraft off the coast of Nova Scotia in Canada to be followed in 1999 by the loss of Egypt Air Boeing 767 off the coast of New York and the disasters of the Concorde in France and a Kenya Airways Airbus A-310 in Africa in 2000, reiterated yet again the enormity of the problem posed to aviation safety and brought to bear the compelling need for the international community to continue to take energetic and vigilant measures to curb the problem, if not totally eradicate it. International dimensions of aviation safety are all-encompassing, and are not limited to attacks on aircraft but include the management of airspace in order to prevent accidents caused by inadequate air navigation systems or human error. It is therefore prudent to address aviation safety within all its parameters, particularly in the context of the crowding of airspace brought about by the proliferation of aircraft movements.

In order to address the issue of aviation safety, the Council of the International Civil Aviation Organization (ICAO) convened in Montreal, from 10 to 12 November 1997, an international conference for Directors General of Civil Aviation to review the ICAO Safety Oversight Programme and to consider its expansion.[2] Almost simultaneously with this event, ICAO released its preliminary accident and security statistics for 1996, which show that scheduled air carriers from the 185 ICAO contracting states reported 23 fatal aircraft accidents in 1996, compared with 26 in the previous year.[3] Although the incident rate declined in 1996, the number of passenger deaths reported rose dramatically to 1135, compared with 710 in 1995.

The Conference concluded inter alia that ICAO should continue to fulfil its leading role with a view to making the Safety Oversight Programme more assertive and effective; that there should be a harmonized approach in conducting safety audits; and that the ICAO safety oversight programme should be expanded to other technical fields at the appropriate time, initially to include air traffic services, aerodromes, support facilities and services.[4]

Although the above figures portend a certain perceived gloom, the silver lining comes with the awareness of the enormity of the problem and identification of contributory factors to the aircraft accident rate. These factors include underdeveloped aviation infrastructure, poor airline operating practices, inadequate national aviation oversight of varying degrees, poor air traffic control capability, lack of navigational aids and radar coverage, and substandard airport equipment. Unsatisfactory meteorological facilities have also been identified as possible causes of aircraft accidents.

For its part ICAO, through its Air Navigation Commission, completed within the period 1995–8 the development of a framework which encapsulates the seminal ICAO activities in pursuit of aviation safety. The Commission created a comprehensive document which encompassed a Global Aviation Safety Plan (GASP) which aims at giving ICAO leadership to gain a commitment from states and the industry to enhance aviation safety worldwide.

On 2 October 1998, ICAO concluded its 32nd Session of the Assembly, which commenced in Montreal on 22 September. The Assembly endorsed the establishment of a universal Safety Oversight Programme which would comprise regular, mandatory, systematic and harmonized safety audits. These audits will be carried out by ICAO in all its 185 contracting states from 1 January 1999, with their consent and at their request, under a Memorandum of Understanding signed by and between the state concerned and ICAO. The ICAO Safety Audit is aimed at determining whether individual states have the capacity to provide safe air navigation services for aircraft which traverse their airspace. It comes at a critical time in aviation history where international civil aviation enters a new millennium, which, in its first 15 years, threatens a virtual doubling of the air traffic from the current situation both in the upper and lower airspace.

At its 32nd Session, the ICAO Assembly recognized that the ICAO Safety Oversight Programme has reached a saturation point in terms of policy and sought to address policy in developing further the oversight programme. It was considered at this session that there were regional deficiencies and shortcomings in the field of air navigation and that contracting states had to correct such problems. In its deliberations, the Assembly found useful the developments of the US safety programme developed in April 1998 through its Federal Aviation Administration (FAA), called 'Safer Skies', which was designed to achieve a fivefold reduction in fatal accidents. Through this programme, the FAA intends to address the CFIT issue, matters pertaining to engine failures, and weather and loss of control, inter alia.

Taking the above into consideration in the context of its own Global Aviation Safety Plan, the ICAO Assembly adopted Resolution A32-15 which recognized that the primary objective of the Organization is to continue promoting the safety of international civil aviation and noted, inter alia, that the expected increase in the volume of international civil aviation would result in an increasing number of aircraft accidents unless the accident rate was reduced. The resolution endorses the ICAO Plan while urging, inter alia, contracting states to examine and revise their laws if necessary to achieve a proper balance among the various elements of accident prevention efforts and to encourage increased voluntary reporting of events that could affect aviation safety. ICAO is instructed by this resolution to develop appropriate policies and guidelines in this regard. Therefore, in its regulatory role, ICAO provides a delicate but well sustained balance between providing guidance on the management of commercial development of air transport and the implementation of safety measures in civil aviation.

With regard to the subject of leasing, it could be said that the popularity of a lease contract lies essentially in the fact that both the lessor and the lessee gain optimum ownership and possession benefits, respectively, from a lease, which may not accrue from a straightforward sale. For instance, the lessor retains ownership of the property, which is still considered by most financiers to be the most substantial security for the purpose of transacting. Another great benefit of a lease is that it may provide and attract substantial fixed funding over a sustained period of time. From the lessee's perspective, his taxes would decrease in comparable terms from the lessor's rates through the benefits of manufacturing and processing credits, and also through delivery and installation costs, insurance premia and professional fees.

Another benefit of a lease is that it could be structured to be as flexible as the parties wish it to be. While leasing companies have more pliant policies in constructing lease contracts, they may also be willing, in most instances, to vary lease payments. Above all, a lease may allow the lessee a much needed 'stop gap' measure to fill in its airline operations with a few more aircraft, while not tying him down to committing himself to the purchase of a new or second-hand aircraft. A lessee airline could use a lease to run its operations at an optimum level, while retaining the option to update its airline fleet from time to time. This remains the most fundamental benefit of the lease agreement and makes it the most flexible tool in airline fleet management.

On the negative side, parties to an aircraft lease have to exercise extreme caution with regard to the safety consequences which a lease may entail. It is prudent to determine and arrive at a legally binding understanding between parties as to the specific states which will be responsible for regulatory aspects of safety in a lease and which airline operators are responsible for complying with safety standards, be it the lessor or the lessee. Other key areas for consideration are the measures necessary for safe operation of the leased aircraft (for example, crew familiarization and licence validation), the factors necessary for compliance with Article 83*bis* for the provision to be effective and efficiently implemented, the specific states involved, the safety functions to be transferred and the aircraft to be included.

States concerned should establish the types of leases which can be approved or need not be regulated, such as financial and operating leases of non-airline entities; leases of aircraft owned by air carriers of parties to relevant bilateral agreements if any are applicable; and wet leases in short-term, unforeseen situations, using a list of potential lessor airlines as approved sources.

Another need is to establish criteria for the approval of wet leases of aircraft from airlines of third countries, taking into consideration such factors as the right to use air traffic rights involved, the aspect of reciprocity of enjoyment of air traffic rights and the attendant benefit with regard to the traffic carried or in the use of particular routes.

Aircraft leasing is now a common practice in the airline industry and a rigid approach to leasing would indeed be counter-productive. At the same time, it would be distinctly detrimental to the future of the airline industry if one were to make the leasing agreement and arrangements between carriers pertaining to leases overtly flexible, resulting in the threatening of safety. The two aspects have to be addressed harmoniously so that a cautious balance of the elements of freedom and compulsion is maintained.

The issue of slot allocation and the need for more capacity to accommodate new slots for the increasing volumes of air traffic cannot be addressed in isolation. The issue, in its totality, has to mesh with the need to infuse more airport capacity according to opportunities of market access afforded to airlines, and with minimum loss of environmental and ecological equilibrium. A suitable individual case study in this regard is provided by the preparations undertaken by Kingsford Smith Airport in Sydney for traffic envisaged during the 2000 Olympic Games.

With Sydney's election as the venue for the 2000 Summer Olympic Games, the environmental impact of airport capacity and activity offered by Sydney, an aviation issue that has evoked some debate in the past, becomes once again worthy of attention. Kingsford Smith Airport has been in use since 1919, and is now the subject of Australian governmental policy which calls for the development of a third runway and the offer of adequate capacity until the runway is built.

All global environmental indicators show that the balance of nature is profoundly disturbed by the industrial practices of developed nations. The concept of 'sustainable development' has gained acceptability in recent years to obviate any concern that one might have about industry and other development eroding nature's balance. Sustainable development has been summed up by one commentator as development which requires land to be protected, the water recycled and the air kept clean so that future generations will inherit an environment which must not be worse than the environment of our own generation and, if possible, which is even better.[5]

The United Nations Conference on Environment and Development (UNCED) held in Rio de Janeiro on 3–14 June 1992 (more popularly called the Earth Summit) adopted the Rio Declaration on Environment and Development which broadly recognizes that the right to development must be fulfilled so as to meet equitably developmental and environmental needs of present and future generations.[6] The declaration also provides that, in order to attain sustainable development, environmental protection shall constitute an integral part of the development process and cannot be considered in isolation from it.[7] States are called upon by the declaration to cooperate in a spirit of global partnership to conserve, protect and restore the health and integrity of the Earth's ecosystem. In view of the different contributions to global environmental degradation, states are recognized as having common but differentiated responsibilities. The developed countries acknowledge, in the declaration, the responsibility that they bear in the international pursuit of sustainable development in view of the pressure their societies place on the global environment and of the technologies and financial resources they command.[8] States are called upon to cooperate to promote a supportive and open economic system that will lead to economic growth and sustainable development in all countries in order that the problems of environmental degradation are better addressed. It is emphasized in the declaration that trade policy measures for environmental purposes should not constitute a means of arbitrary or unjustifiable discrimination or a disguised restriction on international trade. States are called upon to avoid unilateral actions that deal with environmental challenges outside the jurisdiction of the importing country and are required to base environmental measures which address trans-boundary or global environmental problems on an international consensus as far as possible.[9]

The declaration recognizes that environmental issues are best handled with the participation of all concerned citizens, at the relevant level. At the national level, each individual has the right to have appropriate access to information concerning the environment that is held by public authorities, including information concerning hazardous materials and activities in their communities, and the opportunity to participate in decision-making processes. Public awareness should be facilitated by states which are required to make information readily available to any citizen who requests it. States are also required to provide effective access to judicial and administrative proceedings, including redress and remedy, as relevant.[10]

There is also provision in the declaration for states to enact effective environmental legislation. Environmental standards, management objectives and priorities are required to reflect the environmental and developmental context to which they apply. The declaration envisages that standards applied by some countries may be inappropriate, and of unwarranted economic and social cost, to other countries, particularly to developing countries.[11] Finally, the significance of environmental impact assessment, as a national instrument, is recognized where the declaration requires states to undertake assessment for proposed activities that are likely to have a significant adverse impact on the environment and are subject to a decision of a competent national authority.[12]

Consequently, the Rio Conference adopted Agenda 21, a wide ranging plan, which called for the establishment of the Commission on Sustainable Development to ensure effective follow-up to the Rio Conference, enhance international cooperation and rationalize intergovernmental decision making for the integration of environment and development issues. In a public statement, United Nations Secretary-General Dr Boutros Boutros-Ghali said:

> The challenge after Rio is to maintain the momentum of commitment to sustainable development, to transform it into policies and practice and to give it effective and coordinated support ... The United Nations must put its development objectives on par with its political and security commitments.[13]

The 53-member Commission, which was established by United Nations General Assembly Resolution 47/191, began its work in May 1993 and monitors, inter alia, programmes aimed at the United Nations target of providing 0.7 per cent of gross national product of industrialized countries for official development assistance, and actively interacts with other United Nations intergovernmental bodies, regional commissions and development and financial institutions, including the Global Environment Facility, a fund established in 1990 by the United Nations Environment Programme (UNEP), the United Nations Development Programme (UNDP) and the World Bank. The Commission was also mandated by United Nations General Assembly Resolution 47/191 to promote the incorporation of the principles of the Rio Declaration in the implementation of Agenda 21.

The non-governmental organizations (NGOs) which participated in the Rio Conference adopted the Earth Charter, which was a list of declarations and principles concerning environmental protection. The Earth Charter runs parallel to the Rio Declaration insofar as NGOs are concerned. One of the declarations of the Earth Charter is the Alternative Treaty on Trade and Sustainable Development which declares that international trade should be part of sustainable development. The treaty also requires that compensation, working conditions, land use and the exploitation of natural resources must be directed towards sustaining socially and ecologically balanced communities.[14]

The sustained interest in environmental protection shown by the world has made industries, including aviation, realize that they must take into account the adverse impact that their activities would have on the environment. Avi Gil makes a valid point when he observes that, in the near future, industries and governments will be compelled to take environmental issues seriously or lose their competitive edge.[15] Gil attributes this need for caution to customers' increasing demands for cleaner products and services, and the willingness of financial institutions to support environmentally conscious industries above others who are not so environmentally conscious.[16] Sustainable growth in airport development is therefore a necessity for survival of airports, and airport managements have to be guided by the legislature and planners alike to ensure sustainable development in the implementation of airport projects.

Airport expansion is a natural corollary to increased demand for air transport, and therefore the issue of environmental protection must essentially be viewed against the increasing demand for airport space. While it is incontrovertible that airport construction and expansion may have inevitable beneficial effects on a local community or national economy, the attendant environmental problems that may arise from such projects cannot be dismissed lightly. Prudent land use and waste disposal are important elements of the need for caution in airport development, and airport developers often have to take into consideration the land use policies of other jurisdictions. The broad objective is to facilitate allocation of land to the uses that provide the greatest sustainable benefits and to promote the transition by a sustainable and integrated management of land resources. In doing so, environmental, social and economic issues should be taken into consideration. Protected areas, private property rights and the rights of indigenous persons and their communities, among other considerations, have also to be taken into account.

In Europe, an Airbus Industrie study on politicoeconomic trends as they affect the airline industry has predicted that current and future events will render 24 European Airports frequency-limited and unable to take any more aircraft movements.[17] To counter this problem, Munich is building a new airport and Stanstead has been expanded as London's third major international airport, while Frankfurt, Manchester, Charles de Gaulle (Paris), Schipol (Amsterdam) and Fumicino (Rome) airports are all expanding rapidly. A study undertaken by the Stanford Research Institute (SRI) reveals that air traffic in Europe alone is expected to increase by 100 per cent, to about 500 million passenger movements, by the end of this decade and even triple to 740 million during the first decade of the next century.[18] The report claims that, by the year 2020, half the airports in Europe will be straining for capacity, even with potential extensions to the airports.[19] Airport congestion is expected to stultify the growth of the tourism industry, the airline industry and the entire communication system in general.[20] In the airline industry alone in Europe, 390 000 people had found employment in 1989, while the entire airline, airport and other governmental enterprises in Europe employed 540 000 personnel in the same year.[21]

The SRI Report, claimed to be a conservative one,[22] has recommended eight measures for implementation by IATA,[23] two of which are the development of an airport capacity monitoring programme and an airport support programme in Europe.[24] The SRI Report further states that the $1.5 billion expended by the European governments on upgrading airport facilities is inadequate to support even the existing infrastructure.[25] In response, IATA has set up an Infrastructure Action Group (IAG) to take anti-congestion action in Europe.[26] The main task of this group is to work closely with the already existing IATA Task Force on Airport Congestion, where the former would implement the findings and recommendations of the latter. The situation in Europe with regard to the increasing demand for airport capacity is thus identified as critical and is underscored by the fact that, in Frankfurt Airport alone, the 1985 traffic forecast for the year 2002 of 27 million passengers had been reached by 1989 – more than a decade ahead.

Airport congestion in Europe has grown so acute that in 1990 the International Civil Airports Association (ICAA) called for all governments concerned to legislate in order that more facilities in airports may be installed once more financial freedom is achieved by the airports through such legislation.[27] This concern runs parallel to the SRI Report's finding that severe capacity constraints over Europe have caused airlines such as Lufthansa as many as 5200 hours in holding patterns over Frankfurt, Munich and Düsseldorf in 1987, owing to acute congestion at airports.[28] This is approximately a 100 per cent increase on the previous year. The most recent statistics available at the time of writing show that the percentage of people travelling by air in Europe is increasing steadily by 15 per cent and that the trend will continue, owing to the steady increase in business traffic.[29] One of the most significant responses from the aviation community of Europe aimed at combating airport congestion in Europe was the meeting of the transport ministers of the European Civil Aviation Conference (ECAC) in Paris in April 1990. The ministers at this meeting initiated a programme with a view to improving airport infrastructures.[30]

In the United States, the problem of airport capacity is as acute and the big hubs, Chicago, Atlanta, Denver and Dallas/Fort Worth, are already experiencing inordinate delayed departures. A survey conducted in 1990 concluded that, of the 30 airports in the United States which have developed as hubs, at least two-thirds suffer more than 20 000 delay hours annually.[31] One of the measures that have been taken to counter airport congestion brought about by the influx of traffic is the support by the administration, the Department of Transport (DoT) and the Federal Aviation Administration of the levy of a passenger facility charge (PFC) that is now being imposed.[32] This charge is imposed by airports in the United States which, after application to the Department of Transport, obtain permission to charge a *head tax* of one to three dollars from each departing passenger. Revenue from the proposed fee is expected to contribute $623 million to the coffers of the Airport and Airways Trust Fund,[33] and it is claimed that this money will be utilized to improve the nation's transport system.[34]

At the 8th ICAO Air Navigation Conference in 1974, delegates adopted a recommendation

> that States not already doing so should, to the extent practicable, take action to develop programmes for compatible land use administration and planning around aerodromes, in order to avoid incompatible development in critical noise areas, both around new aerodromes and in respect of still undeveloped areas in the vicinity of existing aerodromes.[35]

The conference also noted that planning had been enforced in many states with encouraging results and recognized that the benefits which could be derived from proper land use planning could contribute materially to the solution of the problem of noise in the vicinity of aerodromes.

One expert view is that, since each airport has its own social, economic and political situation as well as a unique history and physical geography, allowance must be made for these factors, while special note must be taken of the future impact of noise caused by the proliferation of aircraft which will inevitably happen in the future.[36] The ICAO Council's Committee on Aviation Environmental Protection (CAEP) also holds the strong view that, while steps taken to replace noisy aircraft with quieter ones would cause the problem of aircraft noise at airports to decline in general terms in the next decade, the proliferation of air traffic in the future would eventually bring the problem back in its full force.[37]

It is also worthy of note that the 28th ICAO Assembly which held its sessions in Montreal from 22 to 26 October 1990 adopted Resolution A28-3 which inter alia urged the ICAO Council to promote, and states to develop, an integrated approach to the problem of aircraft noise, including land use planning procedures around international airports, so that any residential, industrial or other land use that might be adversely affected by aircraft noise is minimal.[38]

The Australian response to the deliberations of the world community and expert opinion seems to have been to amend the Federal

Airports Corporation and Civil Aviation Acts in January 1991 to extend the functions of the Federal Airports Corporation (FAC) and the Civil Aviation Authority (CAA) to include carrying on their activities to protect the environment from the effects of aircraft operations. In addition to these legislative measures that stemmed from the recommendation of the House of Representatives Select Committee on Aircraft Noise, the Minister for Transport and Communications also issued formal directives under the Acts in August 1991 to allocate appropriate responsibilities to the FAC and CAA.[39]

When any major improvement or change occurs at an aerodrome or airport, such as the building of the third runway at Sydney's Kingsford Smith Airport, planning strategies for the entire complex structure of aviation have to be revised. It is not only the effect on the people residing, working or schooling in the area that matters. There are also such factors as congestion caused in the terminal building through the injection of additional traffic, security implications and long-term planning for adaptation to the changing commercial and social environment brought about by the additional construction at the aerodrome that have to be taken into consideration. A well rounded revision of airport planning therefore becomes a necessity.

The vision of some American professors on the subject of computer reservation systems is the starting-point for the introduction and implementation of a suitable legal regime concerning the use of CRS on a global basis, such as the Internet. It is only logical to agree that definitions and delineation of legal principles with regard to such practices as computer fraud and abuse must be set in place. Firstly, measures must be taken at national level, where states could follow the broad principles of the ICAO CRS Code. This could be done on the basis that ICAO is the acknowledged world regulator of international civil aviation and has a mandate under Articles 44(*a*), (*d*) and (*e*) of the Chicago Convention. The first provision gives ICAO a mandate to ensure the safe and orderly growth of international civil aviation throughout the world; the second calls upon ICAO to meet the needs of the peoples of the world for safe, regular, efficient and economical air transport; and the third provision requires ICAO to ensure the prevention of economic waste caused by unreasonable competition.

Taking a cue from ICAO's overall mandate, therefore, it is not difficult to conclude that the ICAO CRS Code is the fundamental postulate for states to draft and implement their own laws in order to prevent and punish computer fraud, abuse, negligence and breach of contract in instances such as those emerging from the use of CRS on the Internet. For instance, states could give teeth to Article 11 of the ICAO Code which calls for appropriate measures by states to ensure that all parties involved in CRS operations safeguard the privacy of personal data by exercising their authority over air carriers, systems vendors and subscribers to make sure that data on CRS are protected.

Undoubtedly, the single most important consideration that states have to address when drafting local legislation on the Internet is the nature of the elements involved. The first important issue is that the Internet is not a single tangible element but a 'giant network which interconnects innumerable smaller groups of linked computer networks'.[40] This principle must be linked with the very notion of intellectual property which, as discussed in Chapter 8, relates to an original work of authorship which can be perceived, reproduced or otherwise communicated either directly or with the aid of a machine or device. Therefore intellectual property rights stem from the originality of a document and its position in cyberspace. Legislators should also bear in mind that, long before the computer was introduced on a commercial scale such as through the Internet, intellectual property law evolved through the common law of torts and legislation. Therefore it follows that, once a plaintiff successfully establishes a prima facie case of intellectual property rights infringement, he will be entitled to actual damages and lost income and profits. Also, when one attempts to infringe or actually infringes copyright, the property taken need not necessarily have been protected by a copyright notice. The infringement must be calculated to obtain commercial advantage or financial gain for the person who perpetrates the act.

Perhaps the greatest challenge for both international and national legislators on the complex issues of the effect of cyberspace on intellectual property and the application of principles of the laws of contract to activities in cyberspace (for purposes of establishing jurisdiction) is that cyberspace has no boundaries and therefore is impervious to national legislation. For instance, would state A be able to legislate, or would the court in that state be able to decide on the contractual rights of a person who makes an airline computer reservation in state A on a CRS which originated in state B? If such a consideration was to be addressed within the same country, matters would be much more simple, as for instance in the case of *U.S.* v. *Thomas*.[41] In this case, a Tennessee court convicted the plaintiffs who had operated a bulletin board of lewd images from California. Although the plaintiffs' activity was not an offence under the laws of California, it was an offence under Tennessee law. One could conclude from this decision that, while this common law principle may be workable on an inter-state basis, it remains to be seen whether, on an international basis, punishment for a computer offence would be enforceable in a jurisdiction in which the origin of the offence (such as the input of stolen CRS material) was elsewhere.

The *Thomas* decision of the United States does not conclusively establish that jurisdictional questions may be resolved only within states of the same country. It is highly possible, since the subject of offences committed on cyberspace or civil liability incurred in activities therein is fundamentally grounded on the laws of tort and contract at common law, for states to introduce national legislation demarcating jurisdiction to be applicable in such instances.

The above discussion also shows that the fundamental approach towards a common law legislative structure which would regulate cross-border cyberspace activity is, encouragingly, capable of being a modification of existing legal principles relating to non-cyberspace activity with regard to both the principles of contract law and the law relating to intellectual property. Therefore it would not be difficult for states of common law jurisdictions to enact appropriate legislation, should they prefer to do so.

Operators of web sites have to exercise caution in order to avoid being hauled into any jurisdiction in the event of adjudication. The airline which auctions its seats over the Internet is no exception. The first thing airlines must address is the need to establish with their possible clients over the Internet an explicit agreement prescribing applicable or governing law with regard to the agreement and an agreed jurisdiction in case of dispute. The airlines must also set out, as a condition, the types of persons it will not enter into contract with (such as persons whose geographic location may not offer the airline benefit from the contract). The bottom line is that airlines which advertise their seats for auction on the Internet should have well-thought-out, well-drafted conditions of contract which the offeror would have to read carefully, clicking his mouse to indicate that he agrees with them, before he makes his offer.

Initially, automated screening of passengers by the use of a 'smart card' – a piece of plastic with a magnetic strip on it – will probably be carried out by states on a regional basis (for example, to be used in Europe only by citizens of the European Community). With the further development of technology and evolution of air transport throughout the world, it is possible to envisage a stage at which this process of passenger clearance would be used on a wider scale. Sooner or later, therefore, the users and service providers of this technology would have to address the legal consequences of this process which may arise in certain circumstances.

One of the inherent dangers of the use of biometric identification and automated passenger screening lies in the aftermath of the discovery of an inadmissible passenger. If the travel document used is a 'smart card', the authorities may not have the support of documentation to explain to the passenger why he is found to be inadmissible. Authorities would have to address in particular the manner in which a person may be held under such circumstances until he is handed over to the carrier who brought him, for onward transportation.

The restraint of a person, without sufficient explanation, may be tantamount to the common law notion of false imprisonment, of which arrest is a species. False imprisonment is committed where a person unlawfully, intentionally or recklessly restrains another's freedom of movement from a particular place.[42] Physical detention is an essential ingredient for grounding an action in false imprisonment. Thus, if a person agrees to go to a police station voluntarily, he has not been arrested even though the person taking him would have arrested him on refusal to go.[43]

The law provides that, where an officer of a state authority, such as a police or customs officer, has reasonable grounds for suspecting that an arrestable offence has been committed, he may arrest without a warrant anyone whom he has reasonable grounds for suspecting to be guilty of that offence.[44] The offence of false imprisonment is one of 'basic intent' and, despite the paucity of authority as to whether the element of *mens rea* or intention is necessary to constitute the offence of false imprisonment,[45] at least one decision[46] has recognized the requirement. In the early case of *Christy* v. *Leachinsky*,[47] Lord Simonds, while observing that it was the right of every citizen to be free from arrest and that he should be entitled to resist arrest unless that arrest is lawful, concluded that a person cannot be arrested unless he knows why he is being arrested.[48] However, this principle has since been replaced in the United Kingdom by Section 28 of the Police and Criminal Evidence Act 1984 which provides, that where a person is arrested, otherwise than being informed that he is under arrest, he must be so informed as soon as practicable afterwards. While this provision holds incontrovertible the fact that a person who is arrested has to be informed of the grounds for his arrest, it dispenses with the exclusive need to inform the person at the time of arrest.[49]

In the more recent case of *Murray* v. *Ministry of Defence*,[50] the plaintiff sued the Crown for false imprisonment on the ground that she had been detained and questioned by members of the armed forces for 30 minutes before they indicated to her that she was under arrest. She claimed that her arrest took place only when she was informed that she was under arrest and that the preceding detention was therefore unlawful. The House of Lords at appeal held that, where a person was detained or restrained by a police officer and knew that he was being detained or restrained, such detention amounted to an arrest even though no formal words of arrest were spoken by the officer. Since the plaintiff had been under restraint from the moment she was identified, and must have realized that she was under restraint, she was deemed to have been under arrest from that moment, notwithstanding that the arrest took place formally a half-hour later.

Lord Griffiths, quoting an earlier decision,[51] endorsed the principle that arrest did not depend merely on the legality of the act but on the fact whether the person arrested had been deprived of his liberty. His Lordship went on to address the decision in *Christy* v. *Leachinsky*[52] and noted:

> There can be no doubt that, in ordinary circumstances, police should tell a person the reason for his arrest at the time they make the arrest. If a person's liberty is being restrained he is entitled to know the reason. If the police fail to inform him, the arrest will be unlawful, with the consequence that, if police are assaulted as the suspect resists arrest, he commits no offence. Therefore, if he is taken to custody, he will have action for wrongful imprisonment. However, *Christy* v. *Leachinsky* made it clear that there are exceptions to this rule.[53]

The exceptions that Lord Griffiths referred to were those expressed by Viscount Simon where, when circumstances were such that the person detained knew the general nature of the alleged offence, the requirement for informing him of the fact and grounds for his arrest did not arise. Viscount Simon held that technical or precise language need not be used and, since any person is entitled to his freedom, if restraint was used and he knew the reason for such restraint, that was enough.[54]

In the light of the above *cursus curiae*, it becomes evident that immigration authorities may have to address the potential danger of restraining seemingly inadmissible passengers who are rejected by the automatic screening process at the point of entry into their country. Therefore, at least initially, when the automatic screening process has not yet been widely used and tested, immigration authorities will indeed have to tread with an abundance of caution. One way to circumvent this potential problem may be to incorporate the biometric information in a machine-readable passport,[55] which has already been developed by ICAO and is in wide use. Here the passenger can 'swipe' the document as he places his hand for the biometric scan. If the turnstile fails to open, the state authorities will have a much more substantial document to examine. Forgery may be easier to prove on a document than on a mere plastic card.

With regard to trade secrets in the airline industry, in the aviation industry, the most critical business tools at the present time are information and technology. These tools become more important in the context of the acute competition seen both in the aircraft manufacturing industry and in the air transport industry. Protection of trade secrets, whether they are client lists or manufacturing designs, becomes of critical importance to the aviation industry. In order to establish that given material is a trade secret, the owner must have shown that he took the necessary precautions of keeping such material away from his competitors. Some reasonable measures that have been taken by aircraft manufacturers and airlines are the installation of alarm systems, card access readers, surveillance cameras and electrified fences. 'Firewalls' on computers, such as access codes, have also proved to be significant deterrents.

Courts may look at numerous factors to determine whether or not a given piece of information could be regarded as a trade secret. For example, if the information was already known outside the owner's business, he cannot reasonably expect a court of common law jurisdiction to consider his information as a trade secret. The courts would also obviously examine the protective measures used by the owner to keep his information from being released to the world. Another compelling factor would be the actual value of the information to the competitor.

Curiously, it is generally recognized at law that a trade secret should not be an absolute secret which is kept hidden by the owner. If such were the case, it could not be used or exploited to its full potential. Any information, to be useful, has to be shared with some who could contribute to its proper use. Therefore a trade secret can be released with controlled access. Controlled access of trade information can best be illustrated by the subject of the use of the airline product and its distribution over the Internet.[56] While airline reservation systems and related material should not be readily available to the world on the WorldWide Web, they should nonetheless be made available to interested parties through an access code.

One must also be mindful of the proliferation of economic intelligence gathering going on in the commercial world today. Economic intelligence gathering, as against industrial espionage or the blatant theft of trade secrets, is the lawful practice of seeking, researching and collecting useful information without violating existing laws. It is based on the recovery of legally available data. This practice paves the way for the information gatherer to gain commercial power and therefore all reasonably effective measures have to be taken by the owner of information if he is to protect information which he considers as trade secrets. The aviation industry is no exception.

On the important subject of trademarks, it is noteworthy that the airline industry is fast becoming one of the largest global commercial undertakings, and it is not uncommon to see within it particular characteristics recognized as being distinctive to particular airlines. In this context, those airlines which have established a name of repute would have to guard their trademarks zealously. Although, as discussed earlier, common law courts have set up stringent standards of conduct, and international regulation in this regard is fast moving to provide a comprehensive system of adjudication, airlines have resorted to their own tools of commercial management to obviate the inconvenience of trademark infringement by offering attractive franchising agreements to those who wish to use the names of reputed carriers. The franchise agreement in the airline industry has proved so far to be an ethical and expeditious implement of commercial management[57] and can indeed be considered a viable alternative to the tedious process of adjudication on trademark infringement.

With regard to refugees and inadmissible persons, when two states sign a bilateral air services agreement and both states designate carriers who would give effect to the agreement by carrying passengers, crew, mail and cargo between their territories, the designated carriers are expected to conform to the laws of the state to and from which they operate air services. By this fundamental fact, airlines become vulnerable to punitive sanctions if they are found to have contravened a local law by carrying an inadmissible passenger into the territory of a state. However, it is also an incontrovertible fact that all treaties are signed by and between states, be it the Chicago Convention or a bilateral air services agreement, and, to that extent, states should bear a degree of responsibility for persons who leave their territories for other states. An air services agreement confers upon one state the right to have its designated carrier operate air services to another country. The carrier acts as the conduit towards effecting the agreement. The right remains with the state.

Although airlines have to bear some responsibility of exercising prudence and an abundance of caution in accepting passengers on their flights, states have more responsibility in adhering to the treaties such as the Chicago Convention and the Refugee Convention which impose a responsibility upon them not to charge or fine airlines for bringing in undocumented or inadequately documented passengers, unless the airlines are shown to be prima facie negligent. A fortiori, it is time that states seriously considered the eminent sense in the recommendation of the Facilitation Panel of ICAO, that states should work together with airlines in alleviating the problem. It would also greatly help if the state from which an inadmissible person or refugee departs ascertained that he has the required documentation to be accepted by the State to which he is travelling. This is an implied obligation which a state has *erga omnes*.

The difficulties faced when considering market-based options on emissions trading with regard to aircraft engine emissions are multifarious. It is, for one, extremely difficult to develop scenarios for a workable mechanism in view of the imponderable trends of future air traffic and the technological breakthroughs in aeronautical science that may surprise us. The use of Global Navigation Satellite Systems (GNSS) as a part of the Communications, Navigation, Surveillance/Air Traffic Management (CNS/ATM) systems, in full force from the turn of the new millennium, will indeed make it difficult for totally accurate forecasts of traffic projections to be made.

There is also no practical modality suggested so far as to the criteria and monetary value of a workable environmental levy on aircraft engine emissions. In addition, the possible subsidies that may emerge with regard to fuel consumption in the face of the growing liberalization regime in global regulatory policy is another factor which would preclude accurate and sensitive data analysis with regard to an environmental levy or emissions trading. All these factors pose a daunting challenge to one of the most intriguing corollaries to modern day aviation. It is hoped that, as in other difficult circumstances, the world aviation community is able to overcome the many obstacles in this regard.

On the issue addressed in Chapter 11 – air carrier liability for injury or death caused by turbulence – it is clear that, for air carrier liability to be established in the case of death or injury to a passenger caused by turbulence, a clear link between the incident and the damage should exist. Although, in the past, some courts have given a wide interpretation to the word 'accident' at air law, such as in the *Seguritan* case, where failure to render medical assistance by the carrier was construed as grounds for liability, it is reasonable to assume that courts would view a carrier's conduct with regard to severe turbulence on the circumstances of each case. It has been pronounced scientifically that the intensity of turbulence cannot be precisely predetermined, nor can it be visually assessed. Under such circumstances, it may well be that a common law court would still anchor itself on the 1963 principle of the *Chisholm* case: that the carrier has only to take reasonable precaution. The courts would also be influenced by the more recent *Goldman* decision at appellate level, that the pilot should have effective knowledge that damage would probably result from his act.

While there is no doubt that prudent aeroplane operators are presumed to take every precaution against adverse weather conditions in-flight, it is a perennial judicial principle, as was decided in 1950, that a cautious operator should take whatever precautions are necessary or available to guard against dangerous conditions.[58] A fortiori, there is no doubt that any common law court would endorse the 1973 decision in *Fleming* v. *Delta Airlines*[59] that a pilot and, through him, his airline have a duty to warn contemplating passengers prior to departure of any foreseen rough turbulence, in order that the prospective passenger could decide whether or not to board the flight. The court held:

> Although an airline must bear the ultimate responsibility for deciding whether conditions permit a safe flight, it need not and, we think, must not arrogate to itself a decision which rightly belongs to each passenger, namely whether to fly under conditions which, although

> not hazardous, might prove to be emotionally or physically traumatizing.[60]

Prior notice obtained by the carrier of rough turbulence would, if undisclosed to the passengers prior to boarding, clearly obviate the Warsaw system limitations of liability.

Admittedly, it would be extremely difficult for an airline to determine latent illnesses, such as tuberculosis, of its passengers. Therefore instances of negligence pertaining to an airline accepting for travel a person infected with the TB bacterium may be rare. However, it would not be uncommon to evaluate critically the conduct of an airline after the fact: that is, by an assessment of the quality of air in the cabin and assistance offered to those infected in flight. Airlines have to follow carefully the guidelines issued by the World Health Organization, as discussed in Part II, and take initiatives on their own, such as those discussed in this chapter, so that they can convince a court that they acted like prudent, caring business enterprises in the face of a calamity.

It must be emphasized that, in selling an ticket for travel by air, an airline offers a composite service, not only to carry a passenger from A to B, but also to ensure that transportation is accomplished in a safe and sanitary manner. Therefore the services offered by the airline in the area of clean air in the cabin become extremely relevant and critical to the issue.

As for issues of liability under the Warsaw Convention, although the *Tseng* case[61] widened the scope of the word 'accident', the case itself addressed a personal security check on a passenger and it remains to be seen whether courts would interpret infection as an accident per se under the Warsaw Convention. It certainly could be argued that, in the light of the varied interpretations emerging from the *cursus curiae*, an accident under the Convention, although not explicitly defined in any past instance, could be considered as 'any incident unexpected and external to the passenger which is avoidable by the airline and which causes death, wounding or injury to a passenger'. Of course, the words 'death, wounding or injury' have still not emerged as clear concepts, despite the inclusion of the words 'bodily injury' in Article 16 of the new Montreal Convention.

With regard to negligence of the aircraft commander, it is not the intention of this chapter to offer a solution as to a most suitable manner of compensation under the Warsaw System.[62] Rather, the purpose of this chapter is to assess the role of tort law under the system of liability at private air law as a means of shaping the conduct of social elements. In the ultimate analysis, what matters is that the law in this area of commercial aviation must ensure that its role of administering fair and equitable justice encompasses safety and protection of the public it serves. If liability laws in commercial aviation were to accomplish that objective, it would be prudent to consider carefully the role played by the element of aviation safety in the wider context.

On behalf of the proponents of unlimited strict liability as a replacement for fault liability under the Warsaw System, one commentator recommends either a substantial increase in voluntary limits of liability or total abandonment of limiting air carrier liability, implying that either would benefit both the plaintiff and the defendant.[63] In 1979, Peter Martin suggested that the best future for the Warsaw system would be the abandonment of limitations.[64] He stated:

> There are very good reasons for imposing on carriers at least a very high standard of care, and even strict liability. Strict liability without limitations already applies in many States to third party liability to persons other than passengers and that is generally believed to be right … why should a passenger, therefore, be in a worse position than a person or owners of property on the ground?[65]

The insurance lawyers obviously need higher liability limits and specificity in this area. The steady disintegration of the Warsaw System, which is mainly attributable to its incompetence in providing for satisfactory compensatory limits, has been proved by figures released some years ago by the Rand Corporation showing that, in a cross-section of cases studied, Warsaw–Montreal tickets obtained a per capita compensation of US$184 000, while non-Warsaw–Montreal tickets had received double this amount. This amount has increased further over the years, demonstrating that the Warsaw limits are being left behind rapidly.[66] It is clear, therefore, that, if the Warsaw limits are to be retained, they must be extended, and the first step towards this goal is the ratification by states of the Montreal Protocols. It is also imperative that the scope of the Convention be extended to third parties such as air traffic controllers and manufacturers of component parts of aircraft to seek consistency and to give the insurance market a clear picture and more accurate assessment. It these parties were brought under the Warsaw umbrella, both the plaintiff and the defendant would be well served, in that the plaintiff would be assured of quick settlement and the defendant would be comfortable with the thought that his liability is limited. This could also preclude contingency fee appearances by lawyers.

One must, of course, consider that wilful misconduct as an exception to the limitation of liability rule appears in all three air law conventions that admit of liability limitations.[67] As discussed in Chapter 11, the original French text of the Warsaw Convention states that, if the carrier causes the damage intentionally or wrongfully or by such fault as, in accordance with the court seised of the case, is equivalent thereto, he shall not be entitled to claim the limitation of liability.[68] Drion[69] maintains that the English translation inaccurately states that the liability limitations of a carrier will be obviated if the damage is caused by his wilful misconduct or by such default.[70] The contentious issue in this question is, what kind of misconduct is required? Drion is of the opinion that, by approaching the issue in terms of conflicting concepts, the question whether 'faute lourde' as proposed originally in the French text and for which there was an English equivalent of 'gross negligence' was in fact more appropriate than the word 'dol', which now occupies the document and for which no accurate English translation exists, has emerged as to what standards may be used in extrapolating the words 'dol' or 'wilful misconduct'.[71] Miller[72] takes a similar view when she states that the evils of conceptualistic thinking that had pervaded the drafting of Article 25 and rendered it destitute of coherence have now been rectified by the Hague Protocol, which has introduced the words 'done with intent to cause damage or recklessly and with knowledge that the damage would probably result'.[73]

This confusion was really the precursor to diverse interpretations and approaches to the concept of wilful misconduct under Article 25 of the Warsaw Convention. The French government took steps by its Air Carrier Act of 1957 to rectify ambiguities in this area by interpreting 'dol' in the Convention as 'faute inexcusable', or deliberate fault which implies knowledge of the probability of damage and its reckless acceptance without valid reason,[74] making a strong analogy with the Hague Protocol's contents. This interpretation, needless to say, brought out the question whether such reckless acceptance would be viewed subjectively or objectively.

Rationales for the limitation of liability in private air law – which bring to bear the need to retain the notion of wilful misconduct in juxtaposition to limited liability – had been discussed by Drion in 1954,[75] when he adduced eight reasons: maritime principles carry a limitation policy; the protection of the financially weak aviation industry; the risks should be borne by aviation alone; the existence of back-up insurance; the possibility of the claimants obtaining insurance; limitation of liability being imposed on a *quid pro quo* basis on both the carrier and operator; the possibility of quick settlement under a liability limitation regime; and the ability to unify the law regarding damages.[76] The most pressing consideration at the present time relates to inquiring whether private air law needs the concept of limited liability or whether another system – such as unlimited strict liability as has been discussed in recent times – should be recommended.

The most compelling arguments for the limitation of liability in private air law are that it protects the financially weak aviation industry, unifies private air law against draconian domestic laws and expedites the payment of compensation. It is interesting to analyse these concepts in today's aviation context. We live in a world where complex litigation issues emerge, carefully thought out by contingency fee lawyers who have an inexplicable capacity to produce a variety of defendants out of a hat. For instance, now, there is a conscious awareness that there are co-liable parties: manufacturers of component parts, air traffic controllers and even government agencies such as airports authorities. Would it be fair to limit the liability of the carrier and expose these three categories of defendants to unlimited liability? There may also be the instance where the deceased or injured may have had enormous capacity to earn during his working life, which would be interrupted or terminated by an air accident. Does this mean that such a defendant settles for a limited sum of money as compensation and bears his losses? Professor Bin Cheng claims that the SDR 100 000 of the Montreal System is woefully inadequate and implies that a higher limit should be considered or the possibility of breakability of the limits should be endorsed, on the lines of the Warsaw Convention.[77]

Although it is prudent to approach this question with due regard to the economic ramifications of this strictly legal consideration, it is an incontrovertible fact that the primary objective of air transport is safe transportation of passengers, baggage and cargo. While it is conceivable that financial interests of the parties concerned would form a core issue in the aftermath of an accident, where it is not principles of legal rectitude, or issues of justice which would be prima facie considered, nevertheless the principal driving force – aviation safety – should take precedence over any other consideration. Therefore, although it is inevitable to consider the effect of limitation of liability as against unlimited strict liability, one must not lose sight of emerging trends which add to the thrust of aviation safety as the primary consideration.

On the issue of negligence of the aircraft commander, it is clear that both written provisions of aviation law and decided cases have unanimously imposed a presumption of absolute responsibility on the pilot for the safety of his aircraft. This responsibility directly grounds an action in negligence against the pilot in instances of seemingly unprofessional conduct. Unfortunately, this basic premise seems not to have been expanded or qualified in any way, either by written law or by the courts, leaving no general principles of law but the singular presumption of liability.

There are three questions which inevitably stem from the objective treatment given to this question:

1 Is the presumption of prima facie liability of the pilot for his

seemingly unprofessional conduct necessary and acceptable as a fundamental postulate?
2 Should this postulate be expanded to cover, on a general basis, exigencies of modern aviation?
3 If so, should the general basis applicable to all instances of seemingly unprofessional conduct of the pilot be viewed as applicable to special circumstances giving rise to special rules?

It is the view of the author that the answer to all three questions is in the affirmative. The presumption of responsibility and consequent liability for negligence should indeed remain as the starting point of determining bad airmanship of the pilot. The necessity for the insistence on this presumption is naturally based upon the fact that safety is the paramount consideration in aviation. In addition, the high-risk element of the operation of an aircraft by the pilot, the special training, expertise and skill required to perform the functions of a pilot and, above all, the fact that the pilot undertakes to carry out his functions assuring his employer of his capability to do so are compelling factors for retaining the presumption.

There are certain conditions which apply in exigencies of present-day aviation which should at least be taken into consideration in favour of the pilot, provided of course he does not, at any cost, show disregard for the safety of his aircraft and passengers. Such factors as congestion at airports, schedule planning where an aircraft, if delayed, would not connect passengers in transit and adverse weather conditions which would preclude an aircraft from being utilized in time by an employer who operates with only a few aircraft are some of the mitigating factors which should be taken into account. The pilot could, in such instances, prove that a decision was necessary to deviate from accepted practice if he did not envisage a risk to his aircraft and passengers.

Perhaps the most compelling factor which would apply to mitigate the harshness of treating the pilot's conduct as negligent is the human factor. At least 80 per cent of aircraft accidents have so far been attributed to human error of the pilot and a significant proportion of human error has been attributed to physical and mental ill-health.[78] Contributory factors to ill-health have been identified as limitations of human sensor functions, single channel of attention, false expectancies, ergonomics (poor designing of aircraft operational machinery) and stress.[79] It has been said that there is always some stress in the human body and the only way to be totally stress-free is to be dead.[80] In determining negligence of the pilot, the court should at least not discount the possibility of these medical factors in assessing his liability. With stronger reason, therefore, airline pilots should be vigilant regarding the ill-effects of drugs and alcohol in the workplace.

In applying the presumption of responsibility on the pilot, the courts should therefore require of the pilot to prove in mitigation the following:

1 He had adhered to accepted norms of regulatory practice pertaining to substance use at the workplace.
2 He had shown absolute dedication to ensuring the safety of his aircraft and the passengers at all cost.
3 It was impossible in a given instance to adhere to accepted professional practice and his conduct did not in any way prejudice the safety of the aircraft and the passengers.
4 His judgement was that of the reasonable professional man taking into consideration the special knowledge and expertise he possessed.
5 His conduct in deviating from accepted professional norms was justifiable as there was no risk involved at all, and such deviation would have precluded loss to his employer and inconvenience to passengers; or he was subjected to physical or mental debility at the time of such decision.

These general rules should, in all special circumstances, be applied with regularity. Then special rules, applicable to special circumstances, would naturally emerge through the common law.

On unruly passengers, the international community must take cognizance of the fact that the Tokyo and Montreal Conventions are ineffective if states do not make provisions in their own laws to give legal effect to the concerted action that is required at international law to combat offences on board aircraft, be they terrorist acts or acts of unruly passengers which may cause damage to persons and property on board an aircraft. They must be persuaded to ensure, for example, that their laws of custody are such as to permit the immediate inquiry prescribed by the Conventions to be properly conducted, an essential requirement if the evidence required for a successful prosecution is to be gathered. For this reason there should also be a requirement that an inquiry should follow any disembarkation.

States must also ensure that their laws in respect of extradition are framed in such a manner as to facilitate the state of registration in taking action against the perpetrators of crime or 'jeopardizing' acts on board its aircraft. These laws should also be at least receptive to the idea of the state of the operator exercising a jurisdiction in respect of events on board aircraft controlled by its nationals. States must also be persuaded of the need to exercise the criminal jurisdiction they have in respect of their own aircraft in such a manner as to deter potential offenders. Finally, states might embark upon a process of education to make their airport immigration and police authorities aware of the existence of both the Tokyo and Montreal Conventions and of their provisions for disembarkation and delivery.

The airlines must also embark on a programme of education within their own ranks. In general, there is great uncertainty on the part of captains as to the extent and limits of their authority and they are often in total ignorance of the two Conventions. All airlines should use guidance material on the relevant sections of the Conventions together with a current list of the contracting states. This material can prove invaluable when a commander is confronted by officials whose first reaction is often to refuse to permit a requested disembarkation or delivery.

Airlines do need to inform their pilots on the contents of the Conventions and to brief them on how to collect evidence, how to request an investigation and how to file a complete report of any incident. They also need to liaise with their own local authorities to ensure that they are aware of the extent and seriousness of the problem and of the measures which the international community has devised for dealing with it. There is much work to be accomplished by the security, legal and operations departments of the individual airlines. A further incentive is that such a programme of benign propaganda may have the collateral effect of persuading immigration authorities of the folly of insisting on putting potentially violent deportees on board our aircraft.

Finally, the airlines themselves can and must do more to deal with the problem themselves. Alcohol is the underlying cause of the majority of incidents, yet too often obviously drunk and unruly passengers are boarded – regardless of laws which make it an offence to enter any aircraft when drunk or to be drunk in an aircraft, as in the United Kingdom,[81] or for a pilot to allow a person obviously under the influence of drink or drugs to be carried in his aircraft, as in the United States. The airlines should be careful to include in their contract with their passengers a condition which permits them to refuse carriage for reasons of safety or if, in the exercise of its reasonable discretion, the carrier determines that 'the conduct, age or mental or physical state of the passenger is such as to … (ii) cause discomfort or make himself or herself objectionable to other passengers or (iii) involve any hazard or risk to himself or herself or to other persons or property'.[82]

Too often airlines fail to exercise reasonable discretion to avoid potential offences being committed. It is all too common an occurrence, once airborne, for cabin crew members, in the absence of clear instructions from their employer, to continue to supply alcohol to passengers, even when the signs of impending trouble are obvious.

Airlines are often strangely reluctant to impose the very effective sanction available to them of refusing to carry on the return leg a passenger who has been troublesome on the outbound leg of his journey. This is a powerful deterrent and each airline should explore the possibility of using it with their own legal adviser.

If potential troublemakers were aware that their disruptive behaviour was likely not only to be followed by effective action by the state authorities but also to result in their being blacklisted by airlines, it is probable that the aviation community would advance a considerable distance towards at least preventing the problem of crime and unruliness on our aircraft from spiralling out of control. Therefore the airline industry must embark on a programme of education and persuasion. It would indeed be interesting to see the outcome of the ICAO Study Group's findings and recommendations. The Group has before it several alternatives:

- to consider the relevance of the Tokyo and Montreal Conventions and develop further the applicable provisions therein to constitute text for a new Convention on the conduct of unruly passengers; or
- to consider developing an appropriate new Standard or Recommended Practice in Annex 17 to the Chicago Convention;[83] or
- to consider developing appropriate guidance material for states in handling offenders who injure persons or damage property on board aircraft or jeopardize the safety of aircraft by their unruly behaviour; and
- to consider the relevance of the Tokyo and Montreal Conventions and develop model legislation for the guidance of states in promulgating their own national laws to address the issue.

Usually, an international convention, as the Tokyo and Montreal Conventions have amply demonstrated, can only map out the nature of offences and charter jurisdictional and punitive guidelines. It is thereafter largely left to individual states to enact their own legislation, as indeed some states have already done. One of the ways in which the issue may be handled is for the ICAO Study Group to consider recommending the introduction of a new Standard (or Recommended Practice) in Annex 17 to the effect that states shall (or may) enact legislation to prevent offences committed by unruly passengers or to punish them after the fact of the commission of an offence. The next step would be to provide guidance to states on how such legislation may be drafted in terms of the various jurisdictional issues involved. It would not be unreasonable to expect such a group of experts to draught model legislation as its final task.

On the subject of abduction of children, although, as the discussion in this volume reflects, the liability of an airline for carrying an abducted child would have to be established taking into consideration the exigencies of each case and applying thereto the standard of reasonable and prudent airline practice, it must be recognized that the airline faces two jurisdictions, the state of departure and the state of arrival, in the carriage of an abducted child. In the first instance, the consideration would be whether the airline aided and abetted the offence of abduction, and in the second instance the consideration would be whether the airline brought in an inadmissible passenger without necessary documentation that would justify the recipient state in granting the passenger permission to enter the country. In both instances, airlines have to take the precaution of not appearing to be wilfully blind to the possibility of an abducted child being transported on their services and of not being criminally negligent in omitting to act on substantial warning given by an interested party beforehand. This is yet another issue on which states' authorities should work closely with airlines, in order that the burden does not fall squarely on the airlines' shoulders.

Canadian responses to child abduction bring to bear an ideal balance between the state and the industry. The Canadian government, in 1998, established the Missing Children's Registry, which is an internationally recognized law enforcement programme made up of four governmental departments under the government's 'Our Missing Children' Programme. The programme, which involves the Royal Canadian Mounted Police (RCMP), Revenue Canada, the Department of Citizenship and Immigration and the Department of Foreign Affairs and International Trade, is devoted to the search for and recovery of missing children and executes its official mandate by (a) intercepting and recovering missing and abducted children crossing international borders; (b) providing the issuance of border look-outs (if it is suspected that a child or child abductor is crossing international borders, look-outs will be issued with that country); (c) displaying posters of missing children at all border points in Canada, and (d) training law enforcement agencies and other agencies such as airline personnel in developing techniques in the detection of child abductors or abducted children.[84]

The Missing Children's Registry liaises and works in close relationship with both national and international law enforcement authorities such as the International Criminal Police Organization (INTERPOL). The Registry also works with active non-governmental and non-profit agencies within Canada. The Registry is mandated to assist all Canadian police forces in the investigation of missing children's cases, if such assistance is requested; to monitor the Canadian Police Information Centre (CPIC), which is the central database and computer system common to all police systems in Canada, with a view to following the missing persons file and taking necessary follow-up action; to prepare statistical bulletins, annual reports and articles on missing children; to coordinate and exchange information on prevention programmes within the Canadian police community and groups searching for missing children; to promote networking with organizations such as INTERPOL and other accredited agencies; to coordinate the travel/reunification programme designed to offer financial assistance to parents for the return of children abducted by a parent to Canada; and to participate in the Customs' Canada Project Return and International Project Return programmes that post border alerts.

The Sub-Committee on Human Rights and International Development, established under the Standing Committee on Foreign Affairs and International Trade, recommended in December 1998 that the Minister of Transport, in consultation with the provinces and territories, officials from the 'Our Missing Children' Programme and the airline industry, review the feasibility of creating a process for verifying documentary proof that both parents have agreed to international travel of children under 16 years of age before airline tickets are issued. It was further recommended by the Sub-Committee that the consultation should lead to the development of a specialized programme for training security and airline staff to identify and respond to possible child abductions.[85]

Measures taken by Canada towards the prevention of child abduction by air are excellent examples for international application. They certainly merit more careful consideration by states which are yet to implement a cohesive programme in this area, before this problem becomes more acute.

Notes

1 *1997 Britannica Book of the Year*, Chicago: Encyclopaedia Britannica, 1997, pp.58 and 372.
2 ICAO Doc. P10 16/97, p.1.
3 ITA Press, 284, 1–5 April 1997, p.10.
4 See Directors General of Civil Aviation Conference on a Global Strategy for Safety Oversight, Montreal, 10–12 November 1997, *DGCA/97*, Conclusions and Recommendations.
5 George Papagiorcopulo (1994), 'Airports and the Environment', *Airport Technology International*, pp.9–10.
6 Rio Declaration on Environment and Development, Principle 3. See Nicholas A. Robinson (ed.), *Agenda 21 and the UNCED Proceedings*, Vol. VI, New York: Oceana Publications, p.8; also U.N. Doc. *A/CONF.151/26* (Vol. 1) 12 August 1992, Annex 1.
7 Rio Declaration, Principle 4.
8 Ibid., Principle 7.
9 Ibid., Principle 12.
10 Ibid., Principle 10.

11 Ibid., Principle 11.
12 Ibid., Principle 17.
13 See UN A/RES/47/191, 29 January 1993. See also *U.N. Chronicle*, XXX(I), March 1993, 80.
14 See Adam Rogers (1993), *The Earth Summit, A Planetary Reckoning*, Los Angeles: Global News Press, p.263.
15 Avi Gil (1994), 'World's Airports Concerned About Handling of Several Crucial Environmental Problems', *ICAO Journal*, January/February, 10.
16 Ibid.
17 *Interavia Aerospace Review*, 4/1990, 301.
18 *Interavia Aerospace Review*, 5/1990, 381. See also *Airline Executive International*, May 1990, 16.
19 *A European Planning Strategy for Air Traffic to the Year 2010 Prepared by SRI for IATA*, Geneva and Montreal, ES-5. See also ITA Press, 118, 1–5 May 1990, p.16.
20 Ibid., ES-7. See also *Interavia Aerospace Review*, 4/1990, 301.
21 Ibid.
22 *Airline Executive International*, (*supra*, n.18), 16.
23 International Air Transport Association. IATA is an association of airlines and has over 200 members.
24 SRI Report, n.7, 1.3 and 1–7.
25 *Interavia Aerospace Review* (*supra*, n.18).
26 See, generally, *Flight International*, 30 May–5 June 1990, p.9.
27 *Airport Support*, May 1990, 5. See also, generally, page 7 for an account of the London airports' congestion problem.
28 See SRI Report, n.7 at 1-1-1.
29 Eurocontrol Operations Directorate, 'Summary of Air Traffic Statistics and Forecasts', June 1992, OPS/181/5, 4.
30 See ITA Press, 119, 16–31 May 1990, p.3.
31 *Airline Executive International* (*supra*, n.18), 18.
32 Ibid.
33 *Aviation Week and Space Technology*, 12 February 1990, p.133.
34 Ibid.
35 Doc. 9101, AN-CONF/8, Montreal, 17 April–11 May 1974, Recommendation 11/2.
36 Ray Walder (1993), 'Control of Land Use Near Airports is Best Means of Reducing Impact of Aircraft Noise', *ICAO Journal*, 48(1), January/February, 9–11.
37 John Crayston (1992), 'ICAO Group Identifies Environmental Problems Associated with Civil Aviation', *ICAO Journal*, August, 4.
38 Doc. 9563, Assembly 28th (Extraordinary) Session, Plenary Meetings, Resolutions and Minutes, 22–6 October 1990.
39 See Department of Transport and Communications (1992), *Annual Report 1991–92*, Canberra: Australian Government Publishing Service, p.22.
40 See *American Civil Liberties Union* v. *Reno*, 929 F. Supp. 824, 830 (E.D. Pa 1996).
41 839 F. Supp. 1552.
42 Smith and Hogan, *Criminal Law*, London: Butterworths, 1992, 7th edn, p.431. See also *Rahman* v. *Queen* (1985) 81 Cr App Rep 349 at 353.
43 *Campbell* v. *Tormey* (1969) 1 All ER 961, cited in Smith and Hogan, *Criminal Law* (*supra*, n.42), p.432.
44 Police and Criminal Evidence Act 1984, Section 24(6).
45 False imprisonment is generally considered under civil actions where the element of *mens rea* is not relevant.
46 *Re Hutchins* (1988) Crim LR 379.
47 (1947) 1 All ER 567.
48 Ibid., 575.

49 Smith and Hogan, *Criminal Law* (*supra*, n.42), p.438.
50 (1988) 2 All ER 521.
51 *Spicer* v. *Holt* (1976) 3 All ER 71, at 79.
52 *Supra*, n.47.
53 Ibid., 526.
54 *Christy* v. *Leachinsky* (*supra*, n.47), 572–3.
55 For a detailed account of the machine-readable passport see R.I.R. Abeyratne (1992), 'The Development of the Machine Readable Passport and Visa and the Legal Rights of the Data Subject', *Annals of Air and Space Law*, XVII, Part II, pp.1–31.
56 See Ruwantissa I.R. Abeyratne (1998), 'Infringement of Copyright in Airline Product Distribution Over the Internet', *The Journal of World Intellectual Property*, 1(1), January, 139–52.
57 For a detailed discussion of franchising in the airline business, see R.I.R. Abeyratne (1997), 'Franchising in the Airline Industry, Some Implications at Common Law', *Air and Space Law*, XXII(6), December, 284–90.
58 *Small* v. *Transcontinental and Western Air Inc.* (1950) 96 Cal App. 2d 408, 216 P. 2d 36.
59 (1973, SDNY) 359 F. Supp. 339.
60 Ibid.
61 *Tseng* v. *ELAL Israeli Airlines Ltd*, F. Supp. 155 (S.D.N.Y. 1996).
62 For a detailed discussion and analysis of the various initiatives taken recently by Japan, the International Air Transport Association (IATA) and the International Civil Aviation Organization (ICAO) in seeking a new regulatory system of private air carrier liability, see R.I.R. Abeyratne (1997), 'Regulatory Management of the Warsaw System of Air Carrier Liability', *Journal of Air Transport Management*, 3(1), 37–45.
63 Bin Cheng (1989), 'What is Wrong with the Montreal Additional Protocol No. 3?', *Air Law*, XIV(6), 232.
64 Peter Martin (1979), '50 Years of the Warsaw Convention: A Practical Man's Guide', *Annals of Air and Space Law*, IV, 248.
65 Ibid.
66 Werner Guldimann (1991), 'A Future System of Liability in Air Carriage', *Annals of Air and Space Law*, XVI, 96.
67 The Convention for the Unification of Certain Rules Relating to the Assistance and Salvage of Aircraft at Sea, Brussels, 1938, The Rome Convention, 1933, and the Warsaw Convention, 1929.
68 Article 25.
69 Drion, *Limitation of Liabilities in International Air Law* (*supra*), 195.
70 Ibid.
71 Ibid., 200.
72 Georgette Miller (1956), *Air Carrier's Liability Under the Warsaw System*, Amsterdam: Kluwer. p.200.
73 Hague Protocol, 1955, Article XIII.
74 Miller, (*supra*, n.72), p.202.
75 Drion (*supra*), 12.
76 Ibid., 12–13.
77 Bin Cheng (*supra*, n.63).
78 See C.A. Berry (1984), 'The Human Factor in Aircraft Accidents', collected papers of the 19th JALC Air Law Symposium.
79 Ibid., H - 9.
80 Ibid.
81 Air Navigation Order 1989, S.I. 1989 No. 2004, Article 52.

82 IATA General Conditions of Carriage (passenger and baggage) March 1988, Article VIII.
83 Annex 17 to the Convention on International Civil Aviation (Safeguarding International Civil Aviation Against Acts of Unlawful Interference), 6th edn, March 1997.
84 See *International Child Abduction: Issues for Reform*, p.17.
85 Ibid., Recommendation 12, p.25.

Index

Table of Cases